DEMOCRATIZING DEMOCRACY

Reinventing Social Emancipation: Toward New Manifestos

VOLUME 1

DEMOCRATIZING DEMOCRACY

Beyond the Liberal Democratic Canon

———————◆———————

Edited by
BOAVENTURA DE SOUSA SANTOS

VERSO
London • New York

First published by Verso 2005
Copyright in the collection © Verso 2007
© in the collection Verso 2007
© in the contributions the individual contributors
All rights reserved

1 3 5 7 9 10 8 6 4 2

Verso
UK: 6 Meard Street, London W1F 0EG
USA: 180 Varick Street, New York, NY 10014–4606
www.versobooks.com

Verso is the imprint of New Left Books

ISBN-13: 978-1-84467-147-2

British Library Cataloguing in Publication Data
A catalogue record for this book is available from the British Library

Library of Congress Cataloging-in-Publication Data
A catalog record for this book is available from the Library of Congress

Printed in the USA by Quebecor World

Contents

PREFACE

Ours is a paradoxical time. On the one hand, it is a time of great advances and amazing changes, dramatically brought about by the information and communication revolutions and the revolutions in electronics, genetics, and biotechnology. On the other hand, however, it is a time of disquieting regressions, a return of the social evils that appeared to have been or about to be overcome. The return of slavery and slavish work; the return of high vulnerability to old sicknesses that seemed to have been eradicated and appear now linked to new pandemics like HIV/AIDS; the return of the revolting social inequalities that gave their name to the social question at the end of the nineteenth century; in sum, the return of the specter of war, perhaps now more than ever a world war, although whether cold or not is as yet undecidable. The paradox resides in the following. On the one hand, the technical conditions to fulfill the promises of Western modernity appear today to be finally in place; on the other hand, it has become increasingly obvious that such promises were never farther from being fulfilled than today. The promises of liberty, equality, solidarity, and peace, heralded by Western modernity, constituted the major legacy of what came to be designated as social emancipation. Modern political struggles focused on the conception of such promises and on the ways to fulfill them or, on the contrary, on the ways to prevent their fulfillment. Thereby occurred the division between capitalists and socialists, liberals and Marxists, reformists and revolutionaries, nationalists and internationalists. For different reasons (at least apparently), such divisions today seem anachronistic or incapable of accounting for the cleavages that traverse the world. The difference between capitalists and socialists appears to have been totally and irretrievably resolved in favor of the capitalists. Moreover, if one considers that neoliberalism, contrary to what is commonly maintained, is not a new form of liberalism but rather a new form of conservatism, both liberalism and Marxism seem to be undergoing today a deep crisis as well. The same could be said of the cleavage between reformism and revolution. On the one hand, the idea of social revolution seems to have been erased from the political agenda, even the agenda of those who still consider themselves revolutionaries; on the other hand, reformism, that is to say, the idea of a gradual and legal improvement of the patterns of sociability, has been replaced by the concepts of governability and governance. Finally, the opposition between nationalists and internationalists seems to have lost its meaning in a time that designates itself as a time of globalization.

These changes are, or appear to be, so deep that the idea of a paradigmatic shift seems the only adequate one to characterize our time. It may be formulated in two different ways: ours is too late a time to be post-revolutionary and too premature to be pre-revolutionary; or, alternatively, ours is a time of modern problems (the unfulfilled promises of modernity) for which there are no modern solutions (those based on the above-mentioned dichotomies now in disarray). The first formulation owes more to the old paradigm than the second one. I prefer the latter because it captures more incisively the idea that, to my mind, should inform progressive thinking and action in our time: what is at stake is the reinvention of social emancipation itself.

This book is the first in a series of five that present the main results of an international research project that I conducted under the title *Reinventing Social Emancipation: Toward New Manifestos*. The project's core idea is that the action and thought that sustained and gave credibility to the modern ideals of social emancipation are being profoundly questioned by a phenomenon that, although not new, has reached in the past decades such an intensity that it has ended up redefining the contexts, objectives, means, and subjectivities of the social and political struggles. I mean what is commonly designated as globalization. As a matter of fact, what we usually call globalization is just one of the forms of globalization, namely neoliberal globalization, undoubtedly the dominant and hegemonic form of globalization. Neoliberal globalization corresponds to a new system of capital accumulation, a more intensely globalized system than the previous ones. It aims, on the one hand, to desocialize capital, freeing it from the social and political bonds that in the past guaranteed some social distribution; on the other hand, it works to subject society as a whole to the market law of value, under the presupposition that all social activity is better organized when organized under the aegis of the market. The main consequence of this double change is the extremely unequal distribution of the costs and opportunities brought about by neoliberal globalization inside the world system. Herein resides the reason for the exponential increase of the social inequalities between rich and poor countries, and between the rich and the poor inside the same country.

The project's assumption is that this form of globalization, though hegemonic, is not the only one and, in fact, has been increasingly confronted by another form of globalization. This other form, an alternative, counter-hegemonic form of globalization, is constituted by a series of initiatives, movements and organizations that fight against neoliberal globalization through local/global linkages, networks, and alliances. Their motivation is the aspiration to a better, fairer and more peaceful world that they deem possible, and to which they believe they are entitled. This form of globalization is still emerging. Its most dramatic manifestation occurs in the World Social Forum of Porto Alegre, of which three editions have already taken place (2001, 2002, 2003).

To my mind, this alternative globalization, in its confrontation with neoliberal globalization, is what is paving a new way toward social emancipation. Such a confrontation, which may be metaphorically characterized as a confrontation between the North and the South, tends to be particularly intense in countries of intermediate development, or semi-peripheral countries. It is, therefore, in these countries that the potentialities and limits of the reinvention of social emancipation manifest themselves more clearly. This is the reason why four of the five countries in which the project was conducted are countries of intermediate development in different continents. The five countries in question are: Brazil, Colombia, India, Mozambique, and South Africa.

The new conflicts between the North and the South occur in the most diverse domains of social, economic, political, and cultural activity. In some of these domains, however, the alternatives created by counter-hegemonic globalization are more visible and consistent, not only because there the conflicts are more intense, but also because the initiatives, movements and progressive organizations have reached higher levels of consolidation and organizational density. I selected the following five domains or themes to be analyzed in each of the five countries included in the project: participatory democracy; alternative production systems; emancipatory multiculturalism, cultural justice and citizenship; protection of biodiversity and the recognition of rival knowledges against neoliberal intellectual property rights; and new labor internationalism. To learn about the choice of countries and themes, as well as the assumptions underlying this project and the challenges it aims to face, the reader should go to the general introduction of this volume.

The series comprises five volumes.[1] The first three volumes deal with the above-mentioned five themes. To be sure, the themes are not watertight; there is intertextuality, now implicit, now explicit, among the different books. This first volume is concerned with participatory democracy. The main thesis of this book is that the hegemonic model of democracy (liberal, representative democracy), while prevailing on a global scale, guarantees no more than low-intensity democracy, based on the privatization of public welfare by more or less restricted elites, on the increasing distance between representatives and the represented, and on an abstract political inclusion made of concrete social exclusion. Parallel to this hegemonic model of democracy, other models have always existed, however marginalized or discredited, such as participatory democracy or popular democracy. Recently, participatory democracy has been gaining a new dynamics. It engages mainly subaltern communities and social groups that fight against social exclusion and the trivialization of citizenship and are propelled by the aspiration to more inclusive social contracts and high-intensity democracy. I mean local initiatives in urban or rural contexts that gradually develop bonds of inter-recognition and interaction with parallel initiatives, thus giving rise to the formation, as yet embryonic, of transnational networks of participatory democracy. To my mind, one of the major conflicts between the North and the South results from the confrontation between representative and participatory democracy. Such a confrontation, which derives from the fact that representative democracy has systematically denied the legitimacy of participatory democracy, will be resolved only to the extent to which such denial is replaced by the development of forms of complementarity between the two forms of democracy that may contribute to deepen one another. Such complementarity paves one of the ways to the reinvention of social emancipation.

This volume opens with a general introduction in which I succinctly present some of the general questions for which the project seeks answers. These questions are treated in detail in the last volume of the series. An introduction to the theme of participatory democracy, written by Leonardo Avritzer and myself, follows. There we try to identify the major problems of contemporary democratic theory, focusing in particular on the contribution of participatory democracy and having in mind the studies and analyses conducted in the project and presented in the next chapters.

The book is divided into four parts. In the first part, entitled *Social Movements and Democratic Aspiration*, the potentialities of participatory democracy and the obstacles to its development are dealt with in the light of concrete social experiences of the last two decades.

In chapter one, D. L. Sheth contrasts, on the one hand, the discourse and practices of India's social movements fighting for forms of local participatory democracy, capable of "returning democracy to the people," with, on the other, the discourse and practices of urban elites that consider such popular forms to be a threat to the politics of the national state and the market economy. The cultural embeddedness of India's social movements in the Ghandian conceptions of self-government (*swaraj*) illustrates the expansive and multicultural potential for democratic innovation in our time.

In chapter two, Sakhela Buhlungu shows the decisive contribution of the social movements and the structures of participatory democracy that shaped them toward the struggle against *apartheid* in South Africa in the 1980s. The author analyzes critically the way in which participatory democracy gradually declined as the transition to a post-*apartheid* society went on becoming consolidated. Such decline was in part due to the fact that the new demo-cratic state gave total priority to representative democracy while discouraging participatory democracy, even though the latter was inscribed in the Constitution.

In chapter three, Rodrigo Uprimny and Maurício García Villegas explain how a state institution that is basically very far from the citizens' democratic aspirations, such as courts, may, under specific given circumstances, be artic-ulated positively with regards to progressive social movements and provide positive answers to their claims. The court in question is a special one, the Constitutional Court of Colombia, created in 1992 in an equally special social and political context dominated by the political changes that led to the 1991 Constitution. The authors analyze the progressive judicial responses to the social claims of the indigenous and gay movements, unions, and mortgage debtors.

In the second part, entitled *Women's Struggle for Democracy*, the analysis focuses in particular on women's struggles for the recognition of their rights of democratic participation in the public space.

In chapter four, Shamim Meer studies the changes that affected the dif-ferent social movements during the period of struggle against apartheid and in the post-apartheid era, focusing, in particular, on women's movements, especially women workers' movements. Given the extremity of apartheid capitalist repression, women activists engaged in liberation organizations at the same time as they organized separately as women. The emergence of a black elite in the post-apartheid period, however, did not significantly change the situation of the majority of the population, let alone that of women workers. The answer to this situation has materialized in recent years through new social movements and the initiatives of citizens with roots in the most poor and marginalized sectors of society, and through their struggle for survival and dignity.

In chapter five, Conceição Osório analyzes the theme of the participa-tion of women in the Mozambican political arena, in particular in political parties. In an approach that converges with that of Shamim Meer, Osório shows that, in the context of the sexual discrimination that traverses the various domains of Mozambican society, the struggle by women for "occu-pation" of the political field and for full participation as a collective actor is an internally diversified struggle. While some "occupation" strategies con-tribute to challenge and weaken male dominance in the political arena, others end up reinforcing that same dominance.

In chapter six, focusing on the relation between union leadership and the Woman's Committees, Maria José Arthur analyzes the tension between class identity and sexual difference in the union movement in Mozambique. Tracing the various trajectories of several women union activists, the author shows how, as a consequence of the reorganization of unions in the 1990s, the identity of the "woman worker" was redefined in a new framework affected by the privatization process and the deterioration of the living conditions of the majority of the population. This is the context in which the author describes both the discourses that justify the discrimination against women on the part of union leadership and the women's strategies and practices that aim at the recognition of new articulations of the identities of woman and worker.

The third part, entitled *Struggling for Democracy in a Scenario of Civil War and Fragmented Despotisms: The Case of Colombia*, reveals how an aspiration to a substantive, high-density democracy can arise in the most difficult of circumstances, as is so well illustrated in the case of Colombia. In a situation that can be characterized as the degree-zero of social emancipation, the struggle for democracy, aside from its extreme difficulty, assumes surprising profiles and intriguing meanings.

In chapter seven, Francisco Gutiérrez Sanín and Ana María Jaramillo concentrate on the "pactist" experience in Colombia. Through the detailed study of two local situations, in Medellín and Boyacá Occidental, the authors show how pacts between the national government and certain local forces allow for handling the tension between macro-institutional forms and multiple, diffuse armed conflicts. In the cases under analysis, however, the consequence of such pacts is that the state acknowledges the power of armed groups and the sacrifice of the democratic rights of citizens in the name of peace and the preservation of the community. In such conditions, the "pactist" solutions, even though desirable at the national scale, may have perverse consequences at the local scale, compromising the possibility of emancipatory dynamics and maintaining the power of the armed groups and those sectors of the society that resort to violence.

In chapter eight, María Clemencia Ramírez analyzes the movement of the Putumayo *cocaleros* (peasants who grow and gather coca) in Colombian Amazonia. This is a civil movement fighting for citizenship rights *vis-à-vis* the state and especially the armed forces. The latter insist in doubly excluding the peasants—as drug dealers and as complicit with the guerrillas. Taking advantage of the participatory democratic spaces granted by the Constitution, the *cocaleros'* aim is to impose an alternative identity, that of a group of Putumayo citizens who are independent both of drug dealing and of the guerrillas.

In chapter nine, Mauricio Romero studies the mobilization of the banana workers in the Urabá region (Colombia), reporting the struggle waged by the union of workers in the agribusiness industry (Sintrainagro) to raise the sector's workers from the condition of subjects to the condition of citizens. Romero describes the form in which the Urabá banana workers, used to playing the role of victims, managed to reach protection, security and political participation in exchange for loyalty to a "political-economic order" controlled by the army and paramilitary forces. In their struggle for better living conditions, the Urabá banana workers had the international solidarity of Danish, Finnish, and Spanish unions, as well as that of the International Union of Foodstuffs Workers.

Part four, entitled *Participatory Democracy in Action*, is devoted to experiments in participatory democracy that were successful and reached a certain level of consolidation, but also to lesser-known instances of democratic participation and deliberation emerging in the most unlikely contexts.

In chapter ten María Teresa Uribe de H presents one such instance, the dramatic experience of a small village named San José de Apartadó, located in the region of Urabá. This village, confronted with the armed conflict in its territory—a conflict involving the army, the guerrillas, and the paramilitary groups—decided by democratic deliberation to establish itself as a "community of peace." It organized itself accordingly, underwriting a public pact, indeed a local constitution, by whose terms its members agreed not to get involved with any of the armed actors operating in the region, to demand rather their respect, and to produce their own autonomous social organization. This initiative, which gave rise to transnational solidarity, illustrates the possibilities of resistance in the most adverse circumstances, though also its high costs.

In chapter eleven, I present a detailed analysis of the participatory budget of the city of Porto Alegre, Brazil, perhaps the instance of participatory democracy that has earned the greatest recognition worldwide. I pay particular attention to the impact of the participatory budget on the distribution of public resources in favor of the neediest social groups, to the mechanisms of participation, and to the complex interactions between citizens, autonomous social movements, instances of participatory budgeting, the Municipal Executive, and the Municipal Legislative Assembly.

In chapter twelve, Leonardo Avritzer compares the participatory budget of Porto Alegre with the budget of Belo Horizonte in order to show that the elitist theories of democracy, so influential in the North, particularly in North America, are indeed negated by the experiences of participatory democracy. The latter have proved to be capable of handling administrative complexity at the same time that they renovate the political agenda by introducing new principles of justice in the distribution of public resources.

Chapter thirteen, by Patrick Heller and Thomas Isaac, introduces another significant experiment in participatory democracy, the decentralized planning of the state of Kerala, in India. This experiment, undertaken under the auspices of the Communist Party of India—Marxist (CPM), consisted in transferring investment decisions to local communities by means of mobilizing participation. The engagement of "civil society," formerly viewed with some suspicion, contributed to having actors and social groups, usually marginalized *vis-à-vis* the political process, effectively included. The articulation between democracy and social justice was thereby deepened.

Chapter fourteen, written by Emir Sader, is a general commentary on the chapters included in this book. The author interpellates the texts from the standpoint of a broad political horizon in order to highlight themes and problems that may escape analyses centered on case studies.

As I have already mentioned, this volume is the first in a series of five volumes. A brief reference to the remaining volumes is therefore in order.

Volume two, entitled *Another Production is Possible: Beyond the Capitalist Canon*, deals, on the one hand, with non-capitalist production alternatives that for the past two decades have been gaining new life in their resistance to the social exclusion and wild exploitation brought about by neoliberal globalization; on the other hand, it deals with workers' new struggles against such exploitation, pointing to a new labor internationalism. Alternative models to capitalist development, generally known as solidary economy, are analyzed, and case studies of popular economic organizations, cooperatives, communitarian or collective management of the land, and associations of local development are presented. Also analyzed are the new forms of the conflict between capital and labor, derived, on the one hand, from the end of the Cold War and, on the other, from the fact that in the last two decades labor has become a global resource, yet without the emergence of a global market. From this disjunction resulted the weakening of the union movement as we know it. Meanwhile, it is clear today that labor solidarity is reconstituting itself under new forms, both on a local and national level, as well as on a global level. The book deals in detail with some of these new forms.

Volume three, entitled *Another Knowledge Is Possible: Beyond Northern Epistemologies*, tackles the struggles and politics of recognition of difference that in the past two decades have been confronting imperial identities, false universalisms, the coloniality of power, and imperial epistemology, which are as germane to historical capitalism as the exploitation of wage labor. The confrontation among rival knowledges and the more and more unequal access to information and knowledge as a consequence of the latter's global mercantilization acquire special relevance. Such confrontation derives from the latest advances in biology, biotechnology and micro-electronics, which have transformed the wealth of biodiversity into one of the most precious and sought after "natural resources." Since most of this biodiversity is located in countries of the South and sustained by popular, peasant or indigenous knowledges, the issue (and the conflict) consists in deciding how to protect such biodiversity and such knowledges from the voracity with which the scientific, technological, and industrial knowledge transforms them into patentable objects and knowledges. The struggles and movements for self-determination and multicultural human rights are another object of study, as are the movements for the recognition of popular knowledges concerning biodiversity, medicine, environmental impact, and natural calamities.

Volume four, entitled *Voices of the World*, is a different book from the previous ones. Rather than focusing on the scientific and social analysis of alternatives, it focuses on the discourse and practical knowledge of the protagonists of such alternatives. One of the core concerns of the project *Reinventing Social Emancipation* is to contribute to renovating the social sciences (see the Introduction). One of the paths of renovation resides in confronting the knowledge the social sciences produce with other knowledges—practical, plebeian, common, tacit knowledges—which, although being an integral part of of the social practices analyzed by the social sciences, are always ignored by the latter. In this book, voice is given to activist leaders of social movements, initiatives and organizations, many of which are studied in the previous volumes. To this effect, long interviews were conducted and transcribed.

Finally, volume five, entitled *Reinventing Social Emancipation*, presents my theoretical, analytical, and epistemological reflection upon the major themes of this project and its main results. In addition, it reflects on the project itself as the construction of a scientific community under conditions and according to rules largely outside the conventional models.

Sixty-one researchers participated in this project; more than fifty-three initiatives were analyzed. A project of such proportions was possible only thanks to a demanding series of conditions. In the first place, adequate funding was available; I am most grateful to the MacArthur Foundation for financial support. Secondly, the project was made possible by a number of coordinators, one in each country, who helped me to select the themes and researchers, and finally to bring the various strands of the research to conclusion. I was fortunate enough to have the collaboration of Sakhela Buhlungu in South Africa, Maria Célia Paoli in Brazil, Mauricio García Villegas in Colombia, Shalini Randeria and Achyut Yagnik in India, and Teresa Cruz e Silva in Mozambique. My most heartfelt gratitude to all of them.

This project would not have been possible without the support of a dedicated and highly competent Secretariat. Sílvia Ferreira, Paula Meneses and Ana Cristina Santos shared administrative, scientific, and editorial tasks, but they all did a little bit of everything. In the course of three years, they accomplished a remarkable amount of work, creating the best conditions to make my meetings with the country coordinators and the researchers productive, to meet all of the researchers' needs and requests, and to facilitate the production of all the texts. Theirs was a Herculean task, and I am only too happy to mention this here in order to keep it from lying buried in the many pages of this series of books.

This project was based at the Center for Social Studies of the School of Economics of the University of Coimbra and greatly benefited from the support of the Executive Committee and its administrative staff. As usual, a very special word of thanks must go to Lassalete Simões, my closest collaborator and dear friend of more than ten years. She is the recipient of my most deeply felt gratitude.

The solidarity shown throughout by the governing bodies of the School of Economics of the University of Coimbra was always encouraging, as was the sympathy and support of my colleagues in the Department of Sociology, a gift all the more appreciated for being increasingly so rare in academic institutions. My sincere thanks to all of them.

Several translators collaborated with me in this volume, and I would like to thank all of them: Martin Earl, David Hedges, Andy Klatt, Jenny Newton, Lina Oliveira. Very special thanks to Mark Streeter, on whose generous time and competence I counted during the last phases of the preparation of the manuscript, and whose outstanding job as a copy-editor was invaluable.

Maria Irene Ramalho was ever an unobtrusive presence during the execution of this project. Thanking her, no matter how emphatically, would always be less than adequate. She alone knows why.

Boaventura de Sousa Santos

Note

1 Besides this English edition, this series is also being published in Brazil (Civilização Brasileira), Mexico (Fondo de Cultura Económica), Italy (Cittá Aperta Edizioni), and Portugal (Afrontamento).

GENERAL INTRODUCTION
Reinventing Social Emancipation: Toward New Manifestos

Boaventura de Sousa Santos

Although neoliberal globalization—the current version of global capitalism—is by far the dominant form of globalization, it is not the only one. Parallel to it and, to a great extent, as a reaction to it, another globalization is emerging. It consists of transnational networks and alliances among social movements, social struggles, and non-governmental organizations. From the four corners of the globe, all these initiatives have mobilized to fight against the social exclusion, destruction of the environment and biodiversity, unemployment, human rights violations, pandemics, and inter-ethnic hatreds, directly or indirectly caused by neoliberal globalization.

Thus, there is an alternative, counter-hegemonic globalization, organized from the bottom up. Among its most salient manifestations one could mention the protests in Seattle, in November 1999, against the meeting of the WTO; several protests in the following years against the meetings of the Multilateral Financial Institutions, the G-8, the European Union summits and the World Economic Forum in Davos (January 2000), Washington (April 2000), Melbourne (September 2000), Prague (September 2000), Nice (December 2000), Quebec (April 2001), Gothenburg (June 2001) and Genoa (July 2001); and the three editions of the World Social Forum, in Porto Alegre, in 2001, 2002 and 2003. Alternative globalization is, however, a wider phenomenon with deeper implications. It involves a great many initiatives, struggles, and local organizations occurring in many different parts of the world, but often ignored by the corporate media. They are more or less tightly connected through local–global alliances of different kinds.

The movement for an alternative globalization is a new political fact focused on the idea that the current phase of global capitalism requires new forms of resistance and new directions for social emancipation. From within this movement, made up of a large number of social movements and NGOs, new social agents and practices are emerging. They operate in an equally new framework, networking local, national, and global struggles. The problem with these new social movements is that in order to do them justice a new social theory and new analytical concepts are called for. Since neither the one nor the others emerge easily from the inertia of the disciplines, the risk that they may be undertheorized and undervalued is considerable. This risk is all the more serious as the counter-hegemonic globalization, given its scope and internal diversity, not only challenges the various disciplines of the conventional social sciences, but challenges as well scientific knowledge as the sole producer of social and political rationality. To put it another way, the alternative globalization raises not only analytical and theoretical questions, but also epistemological questions. This much is expressed in the idea, widely shared by activists, that there will be no global social justice without global cognitive justice. But the challenge posed by the alternative globalization has one more dimension still. Beyond the theoretical, analytical and epistemological questions, it raises a new political issue: it aims to fulfill utopia ("another world is possible") in a world apparently devoid of utopias (TINA: "there is no alternative"). The theme of this collection of books is alternative globalization.

PREMISES AND CHALLENGES

There are two fundamental premises underlying this project, one epistemological and one socio-political. The epistemological premise is that science in general, and the social sciences in particular, are currently undergoing a profound crisis of epistemological confidence. The promises that have given legitimacy to the privileged epistemological position of scientific knowledge since the nineteenth century—promises of peace, rationality, freedom, equality, progress, and the sharing of progress—have not only failed to materialize even at the center of the world system, but have also been transformed in the countries on the periphery and semiperiphery into an ideology that legitimizes subordination to Western imperialism. In the name of modern science, many alternative knowledges and sciences have been destroyed, and the social groups that used these systems to support their own autonomous paths of development have been humiliated. In short, in the name of science, epistemicide has been committed, and the imperial powers have resorted to it to disarm any resistance of the conquered peoples and social groups.

This imperial epistemology began to be consolidated in the middle of the nineteenth century and dominated the whole of the twentieth century. What is new today? In the first place, it is now clearer than ever that the universalism of modern science is a Western particularism, which has the power to define all rival forms of knowledge as particular, local, contextual and situational. Thus, there have been and there still are other, non-Western sciences and forms of modernity, as well as many other forms of knowledge, that are validated by criteria other than those of modern Western science. The epistemological diversity of the world is thus potentially infinite. All forms of knowledge are contextual, and the more they claim not to be so, the more they are. There is no pure or complete knowledge, only constellations of knowledges. Within these constellations, there are hybridizations, which, however, rather than contributing to the elimination of unequal power relations, frequently lead to their entrenchment. Unequal relations can be defined as the capacity of one form of knowledge to convert another into a resource or raw material. The constellations of knowledges in the field of biodiversity are only the most dramatic manifestation of an epistemological inequality that permeates all the thematic areas covered by this research project.

The recognition of other rival knowledges, even if distorted, is one manifestation of the crisis of epistemological confidence. But there are others. For instance, ecological disasters have shown that modern science has expanded the capacity of human action much more efficiently than the capacity to predict the consequences of that action. For this reason, the consequences of scientific action tend to be less scientific than the actions that caused them. As the nexus of causality becomes volatile, the world is paradoxically becoming overwhelmed with the undesired consequences of desired actions.

What is now new, therefore, is the recognition that there are rival knowledges providing an alternative to modern science, and that, even within this science, there are alternatives to the dominant paradigms. With this, the prospect of a multicultural science, or rather, multicultural sciences, is today more likely than ever. However, this possibility is not distributed equally among different scientific communities. Its credibility decreases in inverse proportion to the hegemonic dominance of the scientific paradigm, with its strict and narrow divisions amongst disciplines, its positivist methodologies that do not distinguish objectivity from neutrality, its bureaucratic and discriminatory organization of knowledge into departments, laboratories and faculties that reduce the adventure of knowledge to a matter of corporatist privilege. This is why it is precisely in the center of the world system, in the core countries and hegemonic centers of scientific production, that the capacity for true scientific innovation is today severely limited. New ideas, especially those that seek to bind science once again to its original promises, rarely get past the gatekeepers and the demands of the market.

This means that, although the loss of epistemological confidence is opening up spaces for innovation, the critique of epistemology will be for a long time much more advanced than the epistemology of criticism. In other words, it seems to me that, however lucid and radical our critique of the dominant scientific epistemology may be, our concrete work as social scientists will remain chained to the dominant paradigm, in terms of conceptual and analytical methodologies as well as in terms of organizational and infrastructural conditions, to a much greater extent than we would be willing to admit. This will be particularly the case of scientific practices certified by the hegemonic centers of scientific production. For this reason, in order to maximize innovation, it is necessary to start from non-hegemonic scientific communities.

This is the context that gave rise to the first challenge of this project. It was conceived and executed outside the hegemonic centers of scientific production by scientific communities from the semiperiphery and periphery of the world system. Of course, this fact is not enough in itself to guarantee the project's aim of scientific renovation. After all, social scientists are by and large heirs to the hegemonic scientific paradigm (although some more reluctantly than others). If this is the case, how can scientists working outside the hegemonic centers convert their ex-centricity and relative marginality into energy for innovation? And should this innovation be limited to the construction of new counter-hegemonic epistemologies or does it also have the potential to become a new hegemony itself? And, if so, will the new hegemony be better than the present one? From what point of view? And for whom?

Before discussing how it is possible to respond to this challenge, I will linger a little on the second premise of this project, which, as I have said, is of a socio-political nature. The successes of modern science are increasingly being measured by its capacity to subject ever more social relations in ever more parts of the world to the logic of global capitalism. This is the result of a long historical process that, since the fifteenth century, has had many facets and assumed many names: discoveries, colonialism, evangelization, slavery, imperialism, development and underdevelopment, modernization and, finally, globalization. This project starts from the idea that neoliberal globalization is not radically new: it is simply an exponential expansion of transnational relations, leading to a transformation of the scales of the units of analysis and of the measures of social change that until now have prevailed in the economy, society, politics and culture. As has always been the case throughout the history of modern capitalism and in all previous forms of globalization centered upon Asia, the Indian Ocean or the so-called Middle East, what we mean by globalization refers in fact to clusters of unequal social relations, and thus it would be more correct to speak of globalizations rather than globalization.

Since its beginnings, modern capitalism has been a project with a global vocation, and has always evolved through an intensification of global relations. Furthermore, there has always been resistance to this dynamic and predatory project, from the slave revolts to the struggles for national liberation, from workers' struggles to socialist projects, from new social movements to the Movement of Non-Aligned Countries. So, what is new about the situation in which we find ourselves today is, first, the unprecedented

intensification of transnational relations that, together with the new communication and information technologies, have produced profound changes
on the spatial and temporal scales of social action. The protracted historical
duration of secular trends seems anachronistic in the face of the instanta-
neous time of financial markets. But, on the other hand, the past, supposedly
left behind, has made a comeback in the form of religious fundamentalism,
unilateral pre-emptive aggressions and ethnic cleansing. Moreover, the cycles
of political action have become short-circuited by the erosion of the national
unit of decision-making.

Turbulence on the temporal scales has its counterpart in turbulence on
the spatial scales. The local is increasingly the other side of the global, and
vice versa; also, the national space is being transformed into an instrument
of mediation between the local and the global. Most importantly, this explosion of scales has brought about both interdependence and disjunction. The
feeling of disconnection and exclusion in relation to the transformations
occurring in space and time has never been so profound. In other words,
never have so many social groups been so connected with the rest of the
world by virtue of the intensification of their isolation; never have so many
been integrated by virtue of the way in which their exclusion is deepened.

A second new factor is the voracious way in which hegemonic globalization has come to devour not only its promises of progress, liberty, equality,
non-discrimination and rationality, but also the very idea of struggle for these
objectives. Hegemonic social regulation is no longer undertaken in the name
of some future project. As such, it has delegitimized all alternative future
projects previously designated as projects of social emancipation. The auto-
matic disorder of the financial markets is a metaphor for a form of social
regulation that does not require the idea of social emancipation to sustain
and legitimize itself. But, paradoxically, it is from within this void of regulation and emancipation that initiatives, movements, and organizations have
arisen all over the world, struggling simultaneously against forms of regulation that do not regulate and against forms of emancipation that do not
emancipate.

This leads to the second set of challenges that this project faced. Is it
possible to bring together what has been set asunder by hegemonic globalization and set asunder what has been brought together by it? Is this all that
counter-hegemonic globalization entails? Is it possible to contest the forms
of dominant social regulation and from there reinvent social emancipation?
Is not this reinvention just another trap that Western modernity has set for
us at the moment when we thought it was entering its final stage? What
contribution do researchers make to meet these challenges?

I am convinced that it was fatal for modern science and for the social
sciences in particular to have abandoned their aim of struggling toward a
fairer society. Barriers were set up between science and progressive politics,

knowledge and transformative action, rationality and the will to solidarity, truth and virtue, which permitted scientists to become, in good conscience, mercenaries of the ruling powers. Is it possible to reconnect that which has been so firmly separated? Is it possible to construct forms of knowledge that are more committed to the human condition? Is it possible to do this in a non-Northcentric and non-disciplinary way?

From such premises and such enormous challenges, only ambitious objectives could result. This project has two major objectives: first, to contribute to the renovation of the social sciences and, second, to contribute to the reinvention of social emancipation. These two objectives are in fact one: the renovation of science that we seek has no other aim than the reinvention of social emancipation.

RENOVATING THE SOCIAL SCIENCES

Considering the objectives above, the social sciences in which many of us have been trained are more a part of the problem than of the solution. Nevertheless, as I have already indicated, there are today some conditions that allow us to think of the possibility of renovating the social sciences. Such conditions, in fact, made possible this project and rendered it consistent.

The first condition is a general one. We are in a phase of paradigmatic transition. There is a crisis of epistemological confidence and the confrontation between rival knowledges is increasing. Dissidence within the scientific field is strong: forms of science-action, citizen science, popular science have been proposed; the multicultural character of science is being investigated; new connections between science and rival forms of knowledge have been suggested. In other words, there is an environment conducive to innovation, which means that innovation will not be prematurely voted a failure.

The second condition is more specific. This project brings together social science researchers in the South that have begun to question (frequently all by themselves) the limits of their analytical tools and the possible uselessness of their work. Often they have agonized over selling their knowledge to hegemonic interests, or committing themselves (for survival) to positions that betray their ideals of autonomy and political solidarity with the social struggles of the oppressed. This is the case when they are proletarianized as native informants at the service of the global consultancy industry.

The social scientists involved in this project mostly are from and work in semiperipheral countries. This was not a random choice. I am convinced that the so-called new interdependencies created by information and communication capital, rather than eliminating the hierarchies in the world, have actually deepened them. The names we use to define this hierarchy are important (developed and developing countries; First World and Third World; North and South; rich countries and poor countries) but they are less important than the recognition that this hierarchy exists and that it is becoming more marked. The hierarchy today is not only between countries; it is between economic sectors, social groups, regions, knowledges, forms of social organization, cultures, and identities. This hierarchy is the accumulated effect of unequal relations between the dominant and dominated forms in each of these social fields.

This hierarchy is today expressed in two ways: in the global–local dichotomy, in which the local is the subordinated counterpart of a reality or entity that has the capacity to designate itself as global; and in the trichotomy of core, semiperiphery and periphery that is applied especially, though not exclusively, to countries. The project was mainly focused on semiperipheral countries, or, in other words, countries of intermediate development that are also intermediaries in the regional–global linkages within the world system: two in Latin America (Brazil and Colombia); one in Asia (India); and one in Africa (South Africa). The working hypothesis behind this choice was, on the one hand, that it is in these countries that the forces of hegemonic and counter-hegemonic globalization collide most intensely; and, on the other, that, although these countries are outside the hegemonic centers of scientific production, over the years they have constructed strong and frequently numerous scientific communities.

These scientific communities, more than any others, have operated under a double disjunction. First, the theories and analytical frameworks developed within core or hegemonic science have shown themselves to be inadequate for the analysis of the realities of their countries. Second, hegemonic science has shown either a passive inability or an active hostility to recognizing scientific work autonomously produced in these countries, if and when it flouts the methodological and theoretical canons and terms of reference developed by the hegemonic centers of scientific production and exported (or imposed) by them at the global level.

The words of the Cuban literary critic Roberto Fernández Retamar in *Caliban and Other Essays* about the colonial reader apply to the social scientists of the semiperiphery better than to anyone else: "There is no one that knows the literature of the core countries better than the colonial reader." Indeed, the social scientists of the semiperiphery tend to know hegemonic science very well, even better than the scientists of core countries, because they know its limitations and frequently seek ways of overcoming them. This situation becomes more complex when it is compared to the situations of social scientists of the core countries or to that of those in the peripheral countries. The former, in their overwhelming majority, do not know (and if they do know, do not value) the scientific knowledge produced in the semiperiphery or the periphery. It is considered inferior in everything that is different or alternative. Therefore, it is easily cannibalized and converted into a resource or raw material by core science. In organizational terms, the result is the proletarianization of peripheral and semiperipheral scientists. The social scientists from peripheral countries, in their turn, in addition to working under more precarious conditions and being subject to all kinds of persecutions, feel isolated, unaware of the work that is done in the semiperiphery; and when they manage to overcome their isolation, seek to compensate for it with an uncritical allegiance to core science. Mozambique was included in this project in order to illustrate the possibility of alternative relations between the periphery and semiperiphery.

The epistemological objective of this project was, therefore, to bring together a significant number (or critical mass) of researchers mostly from the semiperiphery and to have them work together in different countries and continents without the control of core science, in order to reclaim the possibility of another kind of science, one that is less imperial and more multicultural and that accepts a more egalitarian relationship among scientists and among alternative forms of knowledge. Above all, this project aims to assert the possibility of putting this constellation of knowledges at the service of the struggle against different forms of oppression and discrimination—in short, of putting it at the service of social emancipation.

In this sense, the project is self-reflective about its innovative character. Like all projects of this type, however, it may run the risks of failure for unfeasibility or facile success for hegemonic co-optation. Aware of these risks, we have taken some precautions, which, from the perspective of hegemonic science, will be seen as reckless violations of the methodological canon.

First, this project did not have a structured theoretical framework. Its concerns are anchored in my previous work, mainly in my book *Toward a New Common Sense: Law, Science and Politics in the Paradigmatic Transition*.[1] I argue there that we are entering a period of paradigmatic transition in law, science, and politics, and that in such a context it is imperative to open up the theoretical, analytical and methodological canons as a condition for renovation and transformation. Thus, instead of a theoretical framework, the project had a set of broad analytical orientations that constituted a horizon within which various theoretical frameworks could fall. These orientations were expected to provide only a very loose guidance, having in mind that this project brought together not only different scientific communities but also different cultures. Just as an example, social emancipation is bound to mean very different things in different social, political and cultural contexts. Second, this project did not impose a single method or a single set of research methods; it was open to different methodologies chosen by the researchers themselves. Third, it did not make use of a series of working hypotheses, and even less of terms of reference. Very deliberately, the project assumed that the concerns and analytical horizons presented above were what was strictly necessary to motivate social scientists to join forces in the pursuit of objectives that are sufficiently important to be actively shared. The theory of this project was thus to be collectively constructed, from the bottom up, and the basic concepts to be worked out together. These violations of the methodological canon were not committed lightly. The risk of chaos and cacophony was there. I think, nonetheless, that, in the current conditions, running that risk was and is the only alternative to the proletarianization or "mercenarization" of science.

Still, against the grain of epistemological orthodoxy, this project explicitly assumed the plurality of rival and alternative knowledges, and sought to give voice to them, particularly through the sub-project *Voices of the World*. The idea was to bring scientific knowledge face-to-face with non-scientific, explicitly local knowledges, knowledges grounded in the experience of the leaders and activists of the social movements studied by the social scientists. The protagonists of *Voices of the World* are activists and leaders of popular movements and organizations who have learned in the struggle of resistance against hegemonic powers the practical knowledge that in the end moves the world and, more than anything else, gives meaning to the world.

Finally, and also in deliberate disrespect of the canon, this project privileged the definition of a vast analytical field, minimally burdened with theoretical or empirical concepts, and defined on general lines. It involved the identification of social fields in which the conflict between hegemonic and counter-hegemonic globalization is expected to be or to become more intense, and which are also fields of conflict between rival knowledges. It also involved, in each social field, giving an analytical priority to the struggles that resist hegemonic globalization and propose alternatives to it.

In giving priority to counter-hegemonic globalization, the objective was to contribute to the reinvention of social emancipation. In other words, science in this project involved the exercise of citizenship and solidarity, and its quality was gauged ultimately by the quality of citizenship and solidarity that it accounted for and promoted. Here lies the second objective of this project: the reinvention of social emancipation.

REINVENTING SOCIAL EMANCIPATION

There are three main difficulties raised by this objective, which correspond to as many challenges. The first concerns the notion of counter-hegemonic globalization itself. How can a cluster of initiatives or movements be considered a form of globalization? Many initiatives and movements that are analyzed here are local and occur in very circumscribed time-spaces. In many of these cases, it is clearly possible to identify connections and alliances with other foreign or transnational initiatives or organizations, and thus it would seem legitimate to speak of globalization. But, supposing that different initiatives with features in common, such as occur in the area of participatory democracy, arise in the same period in different parts of the world, but without any mutual contact or knowledge, should we speak of globalization in such a case?

The dominant conception of counter-hegemonic globalization tends to be restricted to the activities and protests of transnational NGOs and social movements. Undoubtedly, this transnational democratic movement of activism without borders is a form of counter-hegemonic globalization. But we should not forget that this movement developed out of local initiatives designed to mobilize local struggles to resist translocal, national or global powers. Focusing too much upon dramatic actions of a global nature (actions that usually occur in cities of core countries and that thus attract the attention of the global media) might make us forget that resistance to oppression is a daily task, undertaken by anonymous people away from the gaze of the media; indeed, without this resistance, the transnational democratic movement could not and would not be sustained. In my view, we are entering an era in which the dialectics of the local and the global replaces the dichotomy between the local and the global. Accordingly, in our time, social emancipation involves a dual movement of de-globalization of the local (*vis-à-vis* hegemonic globalization) and its re-globalization (as part of counter-hegemonic globalization).

If it is difficult to define the contours of what is considered local or global, then it is even more difficult to define what is considered hegemonic or counter-hegemonic. It is all too easy to define as counter-hegemonic all initiatives that resist the logic of global capitalism and create alternatives to it. We know that oppression and domination have many faces and that not all of them are the direct or exclusive result of global capitalism (think of sexual discrimination, ethnic discrimination or xenophobia, or even epistemological arrogance). It is, indeed, possible that some initiatives that present themselves as alternatives to global capitalism are themselves a form of oppression. In addition, an initiative that is perceived as counter-hegemonic in a particular country or community at a particular moment may be seen in another country or at another moment as hegemonic. Finally, counter-hegemonic initiatives and movements may be co-opted by hegemonic globalization, without this being noticed by activists, or without them perceiving it as a failure; indeed, it may even be seen as a victory.

The second great difficulty (and challenge, therefore) is the connection that we wish to make between counter-hegemonic globalization and social emancipation. What, after all, is social emancipation? Is it possible or legitimate to define it in the abstract? If it is true that there is not one but various globalizations, is it not equally true that there is not one but many forms of social emancipation? Just like science, is not social emancipation multicultural, definable and valid only in certain contexts, places and circumstances (since what is social emancipation for one social group or at a particular historical moment may be considered regulation or even social oppression for another social group or at a different moment in time)? Are all struggles against oppression, whatever their means and objectives, struggles for social emancipation? Are there degrees of social emancipation? Is it possible to have social emancipation without individual emancipation? For whom, for what, against whom, against what is social emancipation? Who are the agents of social emancipation? Is there any one privileged agent? Can hegemonic social and institutional forces such as the State ever be partners or active collaborators in actions of social emancipation? If they can, for what types of actions and under what conditions?

If we speak of the reinvention of social emancipation, does this mean that there have been other forms of emancipation before the one for which we are now fighting? How should those previous forms be defined? Why did they cease to be credible? How should their failure be defined? Are we struggling for new contents of social emancipation or for the old contents, presented through new discourses or pursued through new processes? More radically, in speaking of social emancipation, are we not speaking the hegemonic language that made unpronounceable the aspirations of so many peoples and social groups subjugated by North-centric science and political economy? Are we running the risk of promoting social oppression while using the language of social emancipation? As an alternative, could we reach our scientific and political goals without using the concept of social emancipation at all? Many of these issues were discussed in seminars conducted within the ambit of the project in the different countries in question. Many of them are approached again in chapters of the first three volumes of this series. In the fifth and last volume, I shall offer some of my answers.

The third difficulty and the third challenge to my mind are the most dilemmatic but also the most interesting of all. They concern the choice of themes proposed with the intention both of trying out new ways of producing knowledge and of examining their possibilities for social emancipation. The five themes proposed were: participatory democracy; alternative production systems; new labor internationalism; emancipatory multiculturalism, cultural justice and citizenship; and biodiversity and recognition of rival knowledges. Why were these themes chosen and not others? Why were they analyzed in the chosen countries and not in others? If it is true that globalization produces localization, and that it produces homogenization as much as differentiation, is it possible that these themes have the same relevance in different countries? Indeed, is it possible that they have the same meaning at all? If it is possible to detect any coherence between them, could this coherence be established without recourse to a general theory? Is there an alternative to the general theory, for example, a work of intercultural translation capable of creating intelligibility among the different themes, struggles, movements, and practices, without canceling out their autonomy and diversity?

The themes were proposed by me as those in which, in my opinion, epistemological, socio-economic, cultural and political conflicts between North and South, center and periphery, are today most intense and will continue to be so in the next decades. This is the result of an empirical observation that has not yet been adequately theorized. This observation did not in any way impose the specific choice of countries that was made. The focus on semiperipheral countries was theoretically informed as explained above. In addition to this, I wanted to include a semiperipheral country from each of the following three geo-regional blocks: the Americas, Asia and Africa, the latter being an extreme example of integration by exclusion. This choice resulted from previous studies of mine in which I sought to show that the semiperipheral countries assume the roles of intermediaries and have very distinct socio-political characteristics according to the regional bloc in which they are found. These differences are essentially the result of the accumulated effects of previous globalizations in each country and the twists and turns of the specific historical trajectory by means of which these countries have come into contact (usually by force) with Western modernity. According to this criterion, it would have been possible to select various other countries. My choices were made for basically pragmatic reasons. Some were countries in which I had already done research (Brazil and Colombia), and others were not at all familiar to me but, for some reason, attracted me powerfully (as was the case of India and South Africa). Mozambique, a peripheral country where I had also done research, was included in the project to illustrate, as I mentioned above, the counter-hegemonic potential of initiatives and movements in peripheral countries and to signal the strategic importance of local–global linkages between semiperipheral and peripheral countries, that is, the importance of South-South cooperation.

CONCLUSION

By way of conclusion, I shall state here succinctly the set of analytical orientations presented by me to the project researchers, as well as a brief description of the five themes that originated the case studies.

Analytical orientations

1. Although neoliberal globalization is by far the dominant form of globalization, it is not the only one. Parallel to it and, to a great extent, as a reaction to it, another globalization is emerging that consists of transnational networks and alliances among social movements, social struggles, and non-governmental organizations, which have been mobilizing themselves in the past two decades to fight against social exclusion, the destruction of the envi-

ronment and biodiversity, unemployment, human rights violations, pandemics, and inter-ethnic hatreds directly or indirectly caused by neoliberal
globalization. Thus, there is an alternative, counter-hegemonic globalization,
emerging from the bottom up. The central theme of this research project is
alternative globalization. Hence its title: *Reinventing Social Emancipation*.

2. In the coming decades, the conflicts between these two kinds of globalization are going to set the political agenda at the international, national and
even local levels. These conflicts will tend to be most acute in the semiperipheral countries, those countries of intermediate development, between
the core and the periphery of the world system. Particularly in semiperipheral countries with large populations, the exclusionary effect of the
prescriptions of neoliberal globalization may have a worldwide impact.

3. The conflicts between globalizations, in short, between North and South,
are going to be focused on certain issues. Some have evolved from older
conflicts that go back to the colonial period, while others are relatively recent.
In all of these issues the conflicts reflect unequal power relations. These conflicting issues are addressed in this project through the emancipatory
alternatives that have been put forward by subaltern social groups. The
thematic areas of the project are as follows: participatory democracy; alternative production systems; new labor internationalism; emancipatory
multiculturalism, cultural justice and citizenship; protection of biodiversity
and the recognition of rival knowledges (more on this below).

4. Being produced in the core countries and in the hegemonic centers of
scientific production, the social sciences tend to be North-centered and as
such are very inadequate to the task of giving a reliable account of social
transformations occurring in the South. In contrast, the social-scientific production of countries of intermediate development is at present extremely
valuable, although it is little known and rarely acknowledged by the hegemonic centers of scientific production. This science produced in the South
is not only valuable in itself. Once duly noted and credited, it can bring considerable contributions to the scientific community in general. Resorting to
it may amount to creating a new critical mass generating new research topics
and new analytical perspectives, thereby enriching the social sciences as a
whole the world over.

5. Aside from being North-centric and part and parcel of an imperial epistemology, the social sciences have also been too concerned with quasi-sterile
theoretical discussions, such as the relation between structure and agency or
between macro- and microanalysis. In my view, the central focus should
rather be on the distinction between conformist action and rebellious action.

This distinction is sustained in practice by behavior and attitudes *vis-à-vis* the forms and dynamics of power circulating in society. These forms of power—be they patriarchy, exploitation, commodity fetishism, unequal differentiation of identity, domination, and unequal exchange[2]—are confirmed and reinforced by conformist actions and contested and undermined by rebellious actions. The struggles and initiatives in each of the five social fields confront one or another of these forms of power in different ways. The focus on rebellious action in this project entails a radical proposition: namely, that there is social emancipation only if there is resistance to all forms of power. A strategy that is overly centered upon the struggles against one single form of power, neglecting all the others, however noble the intentions of activists, may contribute to increasing instead of relieving the global burden of oppression that subaltern social groups have to bear in their daily lives.

6. Throughout the world, social practices are ruled by ordinary, traditional, commonsensical knowledges outside the ambit of what is accepted as scientific knowledge. In most countries of the South, scientific knowledge has had very little impact on the lives of ordinary people and, even when it does, it fails to account for the needs and aspirations of local populations. These are often better served by local knowledges. Without discarding the value of scientific knowledge, it is imperative to bring it face to face with lay and local knowledges, knowledges grounded in the experience of the leaders and activists of the social movements, knowledges and wisdoms of individuals and groups that continue to embody the alternative globalization.

Main themes

1. *Participatory democracy.* Along with the hegemonic model of democracy (liberal, representative democracy), other, subaltern models of democracy have always coexisted, however marginalized or discredited. We live in paradoxical times: at the very moment of its most convincing triumphs across the globe, liberal democracy becomes less and less credible and convincing not only in the "new frontier" countries but also in the countries where it has its deepest roots. The twin crises of representation and participation are the most visible symptoms of such a deficit of credibility, as well as, in the last instance, of legitimacy. Furthermore, local, regional and national communities in different parts of the world are undertaking democratic experiments and initiatives, based on alternative models of democracy, in which the tension between capitalism and democracy is reborn as a positive energy behind new, more inclusive and more just social contracts, no matter how locally bounded they may be. In some countries, traditional forms of authority and government are being re-evaluated in terms of their potential for transformation from within, and for being articulated with other forms

of democratic rule. The tension between counter-hegemonic forms of high-intensity democracy and hegemonic forms of low-intensity democracy lies at the core of alternative globalization.

2. *Alternative production systems.* Debates about counter-hegemonic global-ization tend to focus mainly on social, political, or cultural initiatives. Only rarely do they focus on economic initiatives. By economic initiatives is meant local/global initiatives that consist in non-capitalist production and distribu-tion of goods and services, both in rural and urban contexts: cooperatives, mutualities, credit systems, cultivation of lands occupied by landless peasants, systems of water distribution, fishing communities, ecological exploration of the forests, etc. These are the initiatives in which the linkages between the local and the global are harder to establish, if for nothing else because they face more frontally the logic of global capitalism behind hegemonic global-ization, not only at the level of production but also at the level of distribution. Another important facet of alternative modes of production is that they are never exclusively economic in nature. They mobilize social and cultural recourses that render the inter-thematic linkages a necessary condition of their success. A market economy is indeed possible and even, within limits, desirable. On the contrary, a market society, as heralded by hegemonic glob-alization, is morally repugnant and most probably ungovernable. It entails a situation that I have designated as social fascism (Santos, 2002: 447).

3. *New labor internationalism.* Labor internationalism was one of most patently unfulfilled previsions of the Communist Manifesto. Capital globalized itself, not the labor movement. On the contrary, the labor movement organized itself at the national level and, at least in the core countries, became increas-ingly dependent on the welfare state. To be sure, in the twentieth century the international organizations and liaisons kept the idea of international labor struggles alive, yet they became hostage to the Cold War, and their fate was that of the Cold War. After the end of the Cold War, and in response to the most aggressive thrusts of hegemonic globalization, new forms of inter-national labor struggle have emerged, but they are still extremely precarious: a new and socially more inclusive debate on labor standards; international cooperation among unions concerning codes of conduct and the living wage; agreements on institutional cooperation among unions of different coun-tries within the same regional economic block (NAFTA, European Union, Mercosul); articulation among the struggles, claims and demands of the various unions that represent the workers of the same multinational corpo-ration in different countries; new forms of a more plural and inclusive labor activism that is more focused on issues of citizenship and encompassing the most severely marginalized sectors, such as the unemployed, immigrants, women and those working for the growing informal sector. In a more frontal

way than the alternative systems of production, the new forms of labor struggle face the logic of global capitalism in the latter's privileged turf, the economy, but their success depends more and more on the "extra-economic" bonds that they manage to construct along with the struggles in the other social fields included in this project.

4. *Emancipatory multiculturalism, cultural citizenship and justice.* The crisis of Western modernity shows that the failure of the progressive projects toward the improvement of the opportunities and living conditions of subordinate groups, inside and outside the Western world, was in part due to a lack of cultural legitimacy. This is true even of human rights movements. The universality of human rights must not be taken for granted, for the idea of human dignity may be formulated in different "languages." Rather than being suppressed in the name of postulated universalisms, differences must become mutually intelligible through translation work. Since the construction of modern nations was mainly accomplished by crushing the cultural and national identities of minorities (and often even majorities), recognizing multiculturalism and multinationality carries with itself an aspiration toward self-determination. The case of indigenous peoples is in this regard extremely significant. Even though cultures are relative, relativism is wrong, both as a philosophical and a political stance. In this regard, the potential for a counter-hegemonic globalization resides in developing criteria to distinguish emancipatory from reactionary forms of multiculturalism and self-determination. Aspiring to multiculturalism and self-determination often takes on the social form of a struggle for justice and citizenship, implying calling for alternative forms of law and justice, and new systems of citizenship. The plurality of juridical orders, made visible by the crisis of the nation-state, carries in itself, whether explicitly or implicitly, the idea of multiple citizenships coexisting in the same geopolitical field. In conditions to be made explicit, non-state juridical orders may be the embryo of non-state public spheres, as well as the institutional basis of self-determination, as is the case of indigenous justice. This will be so, however, only if the forms of informal, local and popular communitarian justice are an integral part of the struggles or initiatives occurring in the remaining social fields. For instance, popular or communitarian justice as part of initiatives of participatory democracy, and indigenous justice as a component of self-determination or the conservation of biodiversity.

5. *The defense of biodiversity and the struggle for the recognition of rival knowledges.* Thanks to the progress observed in the last decades in the life sciences, biotechnology, and micro-electronics, biodiversity is one of the most precious and sought-after "natural resources." For pharmaceutical and biotechnological firms, biodiversity increasingly appears at the center of the most

spectacular and lucrative product developments of the next decades. As a rule, biodiversity occurs in the South and mainly in lands historically owned by indigenous peoples. While technologically advanced countries try to broaden intellectual property rights and the right to patent biodiversity, some peripheral countries, indigenous movements, and solidary NGOs try to guarantee the preservation and reproduction of biodiversity by protecting the land, ways of life, and traditional knowledges of the indigenous and peasant communities. The most recent cleavages between the North and the South concern largely the issue of access to biodiversity on a global scale. Although all the topics included in this project raise epistemological problems to the extent that they state the validity of knowledges that have been rejected by hegemonic scientific knowledge, biodiversity is probably the topic in which the clash among rival knowledges is more obvious, and probably more unequal. It is also the topic in which the confrontation between hegemonic globalization and counter-hegemonic globalization is more violent, as witness the current designations of bio-imperialism and bio-piracy.

Topic one, concerning participatory democracy, is treated in volume one of this series. Topics two, on alternative production systems, and three, on new labor internationalism, are dealt with in volume two, while topics four, on emancipation and citizenship, and five, on biodiversity and rival knowledges, are discussed in volume three.

Notes

1 A highly revised edition, titled *Toward a New Legal Common Sense: Law, Globalization and Emancipation*, was published by Butterworths (London, 2002).
2 On these forms of power see Santos, 1995: 403–455 and Santos, 2002: 353–416.

References

Retamar, Roberto Fernández (1989). *Caliban and Other Essays.* Trans. Edward Baker. Minneapolis: U of Minnesota P.

Santos, Boaventura de Sousa (1995). *Toward a New Common Sense: Law, Science and Politics in the Paradigmatic Transition.* New York: Routledge.

— (2002). *Toward a New Legal Common Sense: Law, Globalization and Emancipation.* London: Butterworths.

INTRODUCTION
Opening Up the Canon
of Democracy

Boaventura de Sousa Santos and Leonardo Avritzer

When recently asked what had been the most important event of the twentieth century, Amartya Sen immediately replied: the emergence of democracy (1999: 3). With a more pessimistic view of the twentieth century, Immanuel Wallerstein also recently questioned how it was possible that democracy had changed from a revolutionary aspiration in the nineteenth century to a universally adopted, though empty, slogan in the twentieth century (2001: 1). What these two positions have in common, despite significant differences, is the assumption that democracy has played a central role in politics during the twentieth century. Whether it continues to do so in the century we have now entered remains to be seen.

The twentieth century was, in fact, one of intense dispute about the question of democracy. This dispute, which took place at the end of both world wars and throughout the period of the Cold War, involved two main debates. In the first half of the century, the debate was centered on whether democracy was desirable (Weber, 1919; Schmitt, 1926; Kelsen, 1929; Michels, 1949; Schumpeter, 1942).[1] If, on the one hand, this debate was resolved in favor of the desirability of democracy as a form of government, on the other, the proposal that became hegemonic at the end of the Second World War implied a restriction of broad forms of participation and sovereignty in favor of a consensus on electoral processes to form governments (Schumpeter, 1942). This was the hegemonic form of democratic practice in the post–war period, particularly in countries that became democratic after the second wave of democratization.

A second debate permeated the discussion on democracy in the post–Second World War period. This debate was about the structural conditions of democracy (Moore, 1966; O'Donnell, 1973; Przeworski, 1984) and also about the compatibility of democracy and capitalism (Wood, 1966).[2] Barrington Moore generated this debate in the 1960s by presenting a typology according to which countries with or without democratic leanings could be identified. For Moore, there was a set of structural characteristics that explained the low democratic density in the second half of the twentieth century: the role of the state in the process of modernization and its relation with the agrarian classes; the relation between the agrarian and urban sectors and the level of rupture provoked by the peasants in the course of the modernization process (Moore, 1966). Moore's objective was to explain why most countries were not, and could not become, democratic without a change in existing conditions.

Meanwhile, a second issue was linked with the debate about the structural requirements of democracy—the issue of the redistributive potentialities of democracy. The debate about this issue stemmed from the assumption that as certain countries won the battle for democracy they, along with the form of government, began to enjoy a certain distributive propensity characterized by the arrival of social democracy to power (Przeworski, 1984). There would be, therefore, a tension between capitalism and democracy, which, once resolved in favor of democracy, would place limits on property and imply distributive gains for underprivileged social sectors. Marxists, in their turn, understood that this solution demanded a total reformulation of democracy, given that in capitalist societies it was not possible to democratize the fundamental relation between capital and labor on which material production was based. As a result of this, in the scope of this debate, alternative models to liberal democracy were discussed: participatory democracy, popular democracy in the countries of Eastern Europe, developmental democracy in countries that had recently gained independence.

The discussion on democracy in the last decade of the twentieth century changed the terms of the post-war debate. The extension of the hegemonic liberal model to the south of Europe, still in the 1970s, and later to Latin America and Eastern Europe (O'Donnell, Schmitter et al., 1986) made Moore's analysis outdated. The perspectives on democracy in the second half of the twentieth century, with their discussions of the structural impediments of democracy, seem somewhat irrelevant, given that dozens of countries have begun the process of democratization. There are enormous differences both in the role played by the rural classes and in the processes of urbanization in these countries. Amartya Sen is among those who celebrate the loss of credibility of the idea of structural conditions when he states that the question is not whether a given country is prepared for democracy, but rather that one should begin from the assumption that any country prepares itself *through* democracy (1999: 4). Furthermore, with the dismantling of the welfare state and with the reduction of social policies in the 1980s, the analyses of the irreversible distributive effects of democracy by authors such as Przeworski or Lipset seemed to be unconfirmed. Thus, the discussion about the structural meaning of democracy was reopened, particularly for the so-called developing countries or countries of the South.

As the debate on the structural meaning of democracy changed its terms, a second question also surfaced: the problem of the form of democracy and its variations. This question received its most influential answer in the elitist solution proposed by Joseph Schumpeter, according to whom the general question of constructing democracy should be seen from the perspective of the problems faced in the construction of democracy in Europe during the period between the wars. What might be referred to as the hegemonic conception of democracy is based on this response. The main elements of this conception of democracy are the much emphasized contradiction between mobilization and institutionalization (Huntington, 1968; Germani, 1971); the valorization of political apathy (Downs, 1956), an idea stressed by Schumpeter, for whom common citizens possessed neither ability nor interest in politics, other than to choose leaders to make decisions for them (1942: 269); the concentration of the debate on democracy on the electoral designs of democracies (Lijphart, 1984); the treatment of pluralism as a form of sectarian incorporation and dispute between elites (Dahl, 1956; 1971); and the minimalist solution to the problem of participation via the discussion of scales and complexity (Bobbio, 1986; Dahl, 1991). None of these elements, which can be seen as constituting elements of the hegemonic conception of democracy, can adequately address the problem of the quality of democracy that resurfaced with the so-called "third wave of democratization." The more the classic formula of low-intensity democracy is insisted upon, the less the paradox of the extension of democracy having brought with it an enormous degradation of democratic practices can be explained. Moreover, the global expansion of liberal democracy coincided with a serious crisis in the core countries where it had been most consolidated, a crisis that became known as the crisis of double pathology: the pathology of participation, especially in view of the dramatic increase in levels of abstention; and the pathology of representation—the fact that citizens feel themselves less and less represented by those they have elected. At the same time, the end of the Cold War and the intensification of the processes of globalization implied a re-evaluation of the problem of the homogeneity of democratic practice.

The variation in democratic practice is viewed with great interest in the current debate on democracy, changing the very adjectives used in the political debate of the Cold War period—popular democracies versus liberal democracies. At the same time, and, paradoxically, the process of globalization (Santos, 2002) has given rise to a new emphasis on local democracy and on the variations of the democratic form within the national state, allowing the recovery of participatory traditions in countries such as Brazil, India, Mozambique, South Africa, and even Colombia, just to mention the countries studied in this project. We may, therefore, point to a triple crisis of traditional democratic explanation. There is, first, a crisis of the structural framework of the explanation of democratic possibility (Moore, 1966); second, there is a crisis in the homogenizing explanation of the form of democracy that emerged as a result of the debates during the period between the wars (Schumpeter, 1942); and, third, there is a new tendency to examine local democracy and the possibility of variation within national states based on the recuperation of participatory traditions that had been suppressed in the process of constructing homogenous national identities (Anderson, 1991).

In this introduction, we intend to move one step beyond and show that the democratic debate throughout the twentieth century got stuck on two complementary forms of hegemony:[3] a first form of hegemony based on the assumption that the solution of the European debate of the period between the wars would have meant the abandonment of the role of social mobilization and collective action in the construction of democracy (Huntington, 1969); and a second form of hegemony that assumed that an elitist solution to the debate on democracy, with the consequent over-valorization of the role of the mechanisms of representation, could have become hegemonic without linking these mechanisms to societal mechanisms of participation (Manin, 1997). In both cases, the hegemonic form of democracy (the elitist representative democracy) proposes to extend to the rest of the world the model of liberal representative democracy that prevails in the societies of the northern hemisphere, ignoring the experiments and discussions coming from the countries of the southern hemisphere in the debate on democracy. Starting from a reconstruction of the debate on democracy in the second half of the twentieth century, we aim to propose a counter-hegemonic course for the debate on democracy, redeeming what was implied in the debate of that period.

THE HEGEMONIC CONCEPTION OF DEMOCRACY IN THE SECOND HALF OF THE TWENTIETH CENTURY

The debate on democracy in the first half of the twentieth century was marked by the confrontation between two conceptions of the world and their relation with the process of western modernization: on the one hand, the conception that C. B. Macpherson baptized as "liberal democracy" (Macpherson, 1966), and on the other a Marxist conception of democracy that took self-determination in the world of labor as the center of the process of the exercise of sovereignty on the part of citizens understood as individual producers (Pateman, 1970). From this confrontation stemmed the hegemonic conceptions within democratic theory that came to prevail in the second half of the twentieth century. These conceptions are related to the answer given to three questions: that of the relation between procedure and form; that of the role of bureaucracy in democratic life; and that of the inevitability of representation in large-scale democracies. Let us examine each of the answers to these questions in detail.

The question of democracy as form and not content was the response given by the hegemonic democratic theory to the critique made by Marxist theory (Marx, 1871; Lenin, 1917). Hans Kelsen formulated this question in neo-Kantian terms, still in the first half of the twentieth century. According to him, the main point was to criticize the idea that democracy could correspond to a precise set of values and a single form of political organization:

> Whoever considers absolute truth and absolute values inaccessible to human knowledge must consider possible not only their own opinion but also the opinion of others. Thus, relativism is the conception of the world assumed by the idea of democracy [...]. Democracy offers each political conviction the same possibility to express itself and to seek the will of men through free competition. Thus, the dialectic procedure adopted by the popular assembly or parliament in the creation of norms, a procedure which develops through speeches and replies, came to be known as democratic. (Kelsen, 1929: 105–6)

In its initial formulation, Kelsian proceduralism sought to articulate moral relativism with methods for the solution of disagreements, methods that included parliament, as well as more direct forms of expression (Kelsen, 1929: 142). This moral relativism implied the reduction of the problem of legitimacy to the problem of legality, a reduction that Kelsen took from an incorrect reading of Weber. In the period between the wars and immediately after, Joseph Schumpeter and Norberto Bobbio transformed the proceduralist element of the Kelsian doctrine of democracy into a form of democratic elitism.

Schumpeter begins his reflection with the same element that would generate Bobbio's political reflection: the questioning of the idea of a strong popular sovereignty associated with a content of society proposed by Marxist doctrine. In his classic book *Capitalism, Socialism and Democracy*, Schumpeter criticizes this element by posing the question of whether it is possible for the people to govern. His reply is clear and involves a development of the procedural argument. According to him, we cannot think of popular sovereignty as a rational positioning on a given question by the population as a whole or by each individual. Therefore, the procedural element of democracy is no longer the way in which the process of decision-making refers to popular sovereignty, but precisely the opposite: "a political method, that is, a certain type of institutional arrangement to arrive at political and administrative decisions" (Schumpeter, 1942: 242). In this way, Schumpeter turns the procedural concern with the rules of decision-making into a method for the constitution of governments. The motive for excluding participation from this process is a part not of the procedural argument but rather of a theory of mass society that Schumpeter smuggles into the procedural discussion.[4]

Norberto Bobbio takes the next step in transforming proceduralism into rules for the formation of the representative government. For him, democracy is constituted by a set of rules for the constitution of majorities, among which it is worth emphasizing the principle of one person one vote and the absence of economic, social, religious and ethnic distinctions among the electorate (Bobbio, 1979). Thus, it is important to recognize that the first route of affirmation of the hegemonic conception of democracy in the post-war period leads from the valorization of pluralism to the reduction of sovereignty, and then from a broad discussion of the rules of the democratic game to the identification of democracy with the rules of the electoral process. At no time in the route that goes from Kelsen to Schumpeter to Bobbio is it clear why proceduralism does not admit enlarged forms of democracy.[5] On the contrary, the reduction of proceduralism to a process of elections of elites appears to be an *ad hoc* postulate of the hegemonic theory of democracy. This postulate cannot provide a convincing answer to two major questions: the question of knowing whether elections exhaust the procedures of authorization on the part of citizens and the question of knowing whether the procedures of representation exhaust the question of the representation of difference. We will return to these two issues later when we discuss the new forms of participatory proceduralism that have emerged in the countries of the South.

A second discussion was central in the consolidation of the hegemonic conception of democracy: the way in which bureaucracy and its indispensability were brought to the center of democratic theory. This discussion also refers to the period between the wars and to the debate between liberalism and Marxist theory. Max Weber began this line of questioning of the classical theory of democracy by positing, within the debate on democracy at the beginning of the century, the inevitability of the loss of control over the process of political and economic decision-making by citizens and its growing control by forms of bureaucratic organization. The main reason why Rousseau's conception of participatory management did not prevail was the emergence of complex forms of state administration, which led to the consolidation of specialized bureaucracies in most of the arenas managed by the modern state. For Weber, "the separation of the worker from the material means of production, destruction, administration, academic research and finance in general is the common base of the modern State, in its political, cultural and military spheres" (Weber, 1919, II: 1394). Weber's position, which is in direct dialogue with the formulations of Marx in *The Civil War in France*, is an attempt to show that the rise of bureaucracy does not derive from the class organization of capitalist society, nor is it a phenomenon restricted to the sphere of material production. For Weber, bureaucracy is linked to the rise and development of the modern state, and the separation of workers and the means of production constitutes a general and wide-ranging phenomenon that involves not only workers, but also the military, scientific researchers and all individuals engaged in complex activities in the economy and the state. Weber, however, did not intend to associate socio-logical realism with political desirability. On the contrary, for him the phenomenon of complexity posed problems to the functioning of demo-cracy insofar as it created a tension between growing sovereignty (the control of governments by the governed) and decreasing sovereignty (the control of the governed by bureaucracy). It is from this that Weber's pessimism in the face of the double emergence of the "iron cage" of the "administered world" and of the danger of emotional actions that might instigate new charismatic powers stems.

Throughout the second half of the twentieth century, the discussion about complexity and the inevitability of bureaucracy became more intense as the functions of the state also increased with the institution of the welfare state in European countries (Esping-Anderson, 1990; Shonfield and Shonfield, 1984). With the growth of state functions linked to social welfare, the dis-cussion about the desirability of the growth of bureaucracy changed in tone and acquired a positive connotation (the exception being the work of Michel Foucault). In the field of democratic theory, Norberto Bobbio was, once again, the author who synthesized the change of perspective in relation to the Weberian mistrust of the increase of the capacity of control of bureau-cracy over the modern individual. For Bobbio,

> As societies moved from a household economy to a market economy, from a market economy to a protected, regulated and planned economy, political problems which require technical skills increased. Technical problems demand, in turn, experts, specialists [...]. Technocracy and democracy are antithetical: if the protagonist of industrial society is the specialist, it is impos-sible that it could be the common citizen. (Bobbio, 1986: 33–4)

In other words, Bobbio radicalizes the Weberian argument by stating that the citizen, by opting for mass consumer society and the welfare state, knows that he is giving up control over political and economic activities in favor of private and public bureaucracies. However, one question does not seem to be resolved by the theorists who defend the substitution of the mecha-nisms of the exercise of sovereignty by citizens for the increase of bureaucratic control over politics: the skepticism about the capability of bureaucratic forms of management to deal with creativity and to absorb the information involved in public management (Domingues, 1997; Fung and Wright, 2003). The bureaucratic forms described by Weber and Bobbio are monocratic in the way they manage administrative personnel and in the way they advocate a homogenizing solution for each problem confronted in each jurisdiction. That is to say, the traditional conception of bureaucratic management advocates a homogeneous solution for each problem, at each level of administrative management within an administrative jurisdiction. However, administrative problems require increasingly plural solutions, in which the coordination of distinct groups and different solutions occur within the same jurisdiction (Sabel, 1997). Thus, the knowledge held by social actors becomes a central element not appropriable by bureaucracies for the solution of management problems. At the same time, it becomes increasingly clear that centralized bureaucracies are not able to aggregate or deal with all the information required for the carrying out of complex policies in social, environmental and cultural areas (Sabel *et al.*, 1999). This is the reason for the reinsertion of the so-called "participatory arrangements" in the debate on democracy.

The third element of the hegemonic conception of democracy is the idea that representation constitutes the only possible solution to the problem of authorization in large-scale democracies. Among the authors of the post-war period, it was Robert Dahl who defended this position most emphatically:

> the smaller the democratic unit, the greater the potential for citizen participation, and the lesser the need for citizens to delegate government decisions to their representatives. The larger the unit, the greater is the capacity to deal with problems that are relevant for citizens, and the greater the need for citizens to delegate decisions to their representatives. (Dahl, 1998: 110)

The justification for representation by the hegemonic theory of democracy rests on the question of authorization. Two main pillars support the argument of authorization: the first is related to the problem of the consensus of the representatives and came up, within classical democratic theory, in opposition to the forms of rotation in the decision-making process that characterizes direct democracy (Manin, 1997). According to this conception, the direct administration of the ancient city-states or Italian republics involved a lack of authorization, which was replaced by the idea of equal rights to occupy political decision-making posts. As the idea of consensus emerged within the debates on a rational theory of politics, the apportioning peculiar to the republican forms of decision-making no longer made sense and was replaced by the idea of consensus,[6] that is, by some rational mechanism of authorization.

The second form of justification of the question of representation leads to John Stuart Mill and the question of the ability of the forms of representation to express the distribution of opinions at the level of society. For Mill, the assembly constitutes a miniature of the electorate, and every representative assembly is capable of expressing the dominant tendencies of the electorate. Such an approach led the hegemonic conception of democracy to focus on the role of electoral systems in the representation of the electorate (Lijphart, 1984). By linking the problem of representation exclusively to the problem of scales, the hegemonic conception of democracy ignores the fact that representation involves at least three dimensions: authorization, identity, and accountability (the last of these was introduced into the debate on democracy very recently). If it is true that authorization via representation facilitates the exercise of democracy on a large scale, as Dahl argues, it is also true that representation makes the solution of the other two questions difficult: that of accountability and that of the representation of multiple identities. Representation through the method of decision-making by the majority does not guarantee that minority identities will be adequately represented in parliament. By diluting accountability in a process of re-presentation of the representative within a block of questions, representation also complicates the disaggregation of the process of accountability (Arato, 2000; Przeworski, Stokes *et al.*, 1999: 32). Thus, we arrive at a third limit of the hegemonic theory of democracy: the difficulty of representing specific agendas and identities. We will return to this point in the final part of this introduction.

We can see, therefore, that the hegemonic theory of democracy, at the moment at which the debate on democracy is reopened with the end of the Cold War and the widening of the process of globalization, finds itself facing a set of unresolved questions that lead to the debate between representative democracy and participatory democracy. These are particularly pointed questions in those countries in which a greater ethnic diversity exists, especially among those groups that find it more difficult to have their rights recognized (Benhabib, 1996; Young, 2000), and in countries in which the question of the diversity of interests collides with the particularism of economic elites (Bóron, 1994). In the following section, we will seek to recover what we refer to as a "non-hegemonic conception of democracy," and attempt to show how the problems mentioned in this section can be articulated from a different point of view.

NON-HEGEMONIC CONCEPTIONS OF DEMOCRACY IN THE SECOND HALF OF THE TWENTIETH CENTURY

The post-war period witnessed not only the formation and consolidation of democratic elitism, but also the emergence of a set of alternative conceptions that might be referred to as counter-hegemonic. The majority of these conceptions did not break with Kelsian proceduralism. They maintained the procedural response to the problem of democracy, linking procedure with a way of life and perceiving democracy as a way of perfecting human relations. According to this conception, which can be found in the work of authors such as Lefort, Castoriadis and Habermas, in the North (Lefort, 1986; Castoriadis, 1986; Habermas, 1984; Habermas, 1995) and Lechner, Nun and Bóron in the South (Lechner, 1988; Bóron, 1994; Nun, 2000), democracy is an organizing grammar of society and of the relation between the state and society:

> democracy reveals itself to be, in this way, historic society par excellence, the society that by its form gathers and preserves indetermination, in marked contrast to totalitarianism which, constructing itself under the sign of the creation of the new man, in reality acts against this indetermination. (Lefort, 1986: 31)

We can see, therefore, that the concern at the origin of non-hegemonic conceptions of democracy is the same that is at the origin of the hegemonic conception, but that it receives a different response. It has to do with the negation of substantive conceptions of reason and the homogenizing forms of the organization of society, and with the recognition of human plurality. Nevertheless, the recognition of human plurality comes about not only from the suspension of the idea of the common good, as Schumpeter, Downs, and Bobbio propose, but also from two distinct criteria: the emphasis on the creation of a new social and cultural grammar and the understanding of social innovation articulated with institutional innovation, that is, with the search for a new democratic institutionality. We will go on to develop both these aspects next.

The problem of democracy in non-hegemonic conceptions is closely linked to the recognition that democracy does not constitute a mere accident or a simple work of institutional engineering. Democracy is a new historic grammar. Thus, the issue is not, as in Barrington Moore, that of thinking through the structural determinations for the constitution of this new grammar. Rather, it is that of understanding that democracy is a socio-historical form, and that such forms are not determined by any kind of natural laws. Exploring this vein, Castoriadis provides us with elements to think through the critique of the hegemonic conception of democracy: "Some think today that democracy or rational investigation are self-evident, thus naively projecting the exceptional situation of their own society onto the whole of history" (Castoriadis, 1986: 274). Democracy, in this sense, always implies a break with established traditions, and, therefore, the attempt to institute new determinations, new norms and new laws. This is the indetermination produced by the democratic grammar, rather than only the indetermination of not knowing who will be the new holder of a position of power.[7]

Thinking about democracy as a positive rupture in the trajectory of a society implies approaching the cultural elements of this society. Once again, a space is opened to discuss proceduralism and its societal dimensions.

Within counter-hegemonic theories, Jürgen Habermas was the author who opened the discussion on proceduralism as a societal practice and not as a method of constituting governments. Habermas expanded proceduralism, reintroducing the societal dimension originally emphasized by Kelsen, by proposing the condition of publicness as capable of generating a new societal grammar. For Habermas, the public sphere constitutes a place in which individuals—women, blacks, workers, racial minorities—can problematize in public[8] a condition of inequality in the private sphere. The public actions of individuals allow them to question their exclusion from political arrangements through a principle of societal deliberation that Habermas refers to as principle D: "Only those action-norms are valid which count on the assent of all the individuals that participate in a rational discourse" (Habermas, 1995). Postulating a principle of wide deliberation, Habermas reintroduces societal and participatory proceduralism into the discussion on democracy, introducing a new element in the route that leads from Kelsen to Schumpeter and Bobbio. According to this conception, proceduralism has its origin in the plurality of the ways of life in contemporary societies. Politics, in order to be plural, must count on the assent of these actors in rational processes of discussion and deliberation. Therefore, democratic proceduralism cannot be, as Bobbio supposes, a method of authorizing governments. It must be a form of collective exercise of political power based on a free process of presentation of reasons among equals (Cohen, 1997: 412). In this way, the recuperation of an argumentative discourse (Santos, 2000), associated with the basic fact of pluralism and the different experiences, is part of the reconnection of proceduralism and participation. Thus, the procedures of aggregation that characterize representative democracy are seen to be patently insufficient, and the experiments of participatory proceduralism of the Southern countries appear in evidence, such as participatory budgeting in Brazil or the experiment of the Panchayats in India.

There is still an extremely important issue to be discussed, which is the role of social movements in the institutionalization of cultural diversity. This issue, which was already anticipated in the critique of hegemonic theory by Lefort and Castoriadis, appeared more clearly in the debate on democracy from the theory of social movements. Starting with Williams (1981), for whom culture constitutes a dimension of all institutions—economic, social and political—various authors within the field of the theory of social movements began to bring up the fact that politics involves a dispute about a complex of cultural significations. This discussion led to a widening of the field of politics in which there occurred a dispute on the re-signification of practices (Alvarez, Dagnino and Escobar, 1998). Social movements would be inserted into movements for the widening of politics, for the transformation of dominant practices, for the expansion of citizenship, and for the insertion of social actors excluded from politics. The literature on the re-signification of democratic practices had a particularly strong impact on democratic discussion in Latin America, where it was associated with the transformation of societal grammar. Lechner states, in relation to the current processes of democratization, that

> [i]n Latin America, the current revalorization of the formal procedures and institutions of democracy cannot be supported by established habits and recognized norms. It is not a question of restoring regulative norms, but of creating norms which constitute political activity: the transition demands the elaboration of a new grammar. (Lechner, 1988: 32)

Thus, in the case of various countries of the South, redemocratization did not involve facing the challenge of the structural limits of democracy, as the discussion on democracy in the 1960s supposed. By inserting new actors into the political stage, what democratization did was to instigate a dispute on the meaning of democracy and on the constitution of a new social grammar. Giving rise to this type of dispute, the extension of democracy that began in southern Europe in the 1970s and in Latin America in the 1980s brought up again, in the agenda of the discussion on democracy, the three questions discussed above.

In the first place, it posed again the question of the relation between procedure and societal participation. Due to the strong participation of social movements in the processes of democratization in the countries of the South, especially in Latin America (Escobar and Alvarez, 1992; Alvarez, Dagnino, and Escobar, 1998; Doimo, 1995; Jelin and Herschberg, 1996; Avritzer, 2002), the problem of the constitution of a social grammar capable of changing gender, race and ethnic relations, as well as the private appropriation of public resources, placed in the order of the day the problem of the need for a new social grammar and a new form of relation between the state and society. This grammar implied the introduction of experimentalism in the very sphere of the state transforming the state into an absolutely new social movement (Santos, 1998: 59–74).

In the second place, the accent on social participation also led to a redefinition of the appropriateness of the non-participatory and bureaucratic solution at the local level, posing once again the problem of scale within the debate on democracy. The success of most of the participatory experiments in the recently democratized countries of the South is related to the ability of the social actors to transfer practices and information from the social level to the administrative level. At the same time, the institutional innovations that appear to be successful in countries of the South are related to what Castoriadis calls the establishment of a new *eidos*, i.e., a new political order based on the creativity of social actors.

In the third place, there is the problem of the relation between representation and cultural and social diversity. As the number of actors involved in
politics grows, and the ethnic and cultural diversity of social actors and the
interests involved in political arrangements increase, John Stuart Mill's
argument on representation becomes less convincing. The most socially vulnerable groups, the less favored social sectors, and ethnic minorities are not
able to have their interests represented in the political system with the same
ease as the majority or more economically prosperous sectors. Forms of rel-
ativizing representation (Young, 2000) or of articulating representative
democracy and participatory democracy (Santos, 1998) seem to offer more
hope for the defense of subaltern interests and identities. For these reasons,
participatory democracy is considered in this research project to be one of
the five great social and political fields where, at the beginning of the new
century, social emancipation is being reinvented. In the next section we will
present a synthesis of the case studies of this project.

PARTICIPATORY DEMOCRACY IN THE SOUTH IN
THE TWENTY-FIRST CENTURY

The reinvention of participatory democracy in the countries of the South is
intimately related to the recent processes of democratization that those countries underwent. We are dealing, therefore, with countries that, according to
the hegemonic logic of the post-Second World War period, were not part of
the so-called democratic field. Until 1975, Mozambique lived under the
colonial yoke, and South Africa, until the end of the 1980s, lived under an
apartheid regime. For most of the twentieth century Brazil alternated between
authoritarian and democratic periods and Colombia lived in a severely
restricted democracy truncated by successive states of emergency and civil
war. The exception is India, the only one of the countries studied that
remained democratic throughout the whole period, interrupted only by the
declaration of a state of emergency in 1977. Even so, it was only with the so-
called "third wave of democratization" that participatory experiments such
as that of Kerala became possible.

All the countries included in this project have undergone processes of
transition or democratic expansion from the 1970s. Brazil and South Africa
were reached by the " third wave" in the 1980s and 1990s, the same happening in Mozambique, after having gone through a revolutionary and
socialist stage in the first decade after independence. Colombia took a different route. It did not have an authoritarian military regime, unlike most
Latin American countries, and it made, at the beginning of the 1990s, a great
effort at social negotiation, which resulted in a new Constitution and a law
of citizen participation. Among the countries of the South, India may be
considered the one with the greatest democratic continuity, although some

of the important processes of participatory democracy in the country are linked to decentralization and differentiated traditions of participation at a local level, which have been recently recuperated.

In all cases, along with the expansion of democracy or its restoration, there was also a process of redefining its cultural meaning or established social grammar. This process occurs in every trajectory of democratization. The inclusion of the case studies of Colombia is intended to show its presence, even in the most adverse conditions. Thus, all the cases of participatory democracy studied began with an attempt to dispute the meaning of certain political practices, with an attempt to expand the social grammar and incorporate new actors and new issues into politics. During the Brazilian process of democratization and the constitution of community actors, Arendt's idea of "the right to have rights" became part of the redefinition of new social actors (Sader, 1988; Dagnino, 1994). The same redefinition is detectable in many of the cases referred to in this volume: in the case of the march of the *cocaleros* (coca farmers and pickers) in Colombia, Ramírez shows that the struggle against the fumigation of the coca crops expresses an attempt on the part of the peasants in the Amazon region to demand, in a context of external violence, the recognition of an alternative identity to the one constructed by the state. Considered as drug traffickers and guerrilla sympathizers by the state, these peasants demand to be recognized as independent social actors and citizens of the country and of Putumayo, identifying their condition of citizens with a voluntary policy of coca eradication being negotiated with the Colombian government. Ramírez shows how this movement implied associating citizenship with a definition of belonging. By demanding this recognition, the movement sought to achieve representation *vis-à-vis* the state as a differentiated group with its own voice able to decide jointly on policies concerning the welfare of the inhabitants of Putumayo.

Also relating to Colombia, Uribe's study shows how the inhabitants of San José de Apartadó, by creating the status of a "community of peace," demand the legitimacy of a self-representation alternative to that conferred on them by both the state and violent actors (guerrilla and paramilitary). The same concept of identity can be seen in the cases of India and South Africa. D. L. Sheth shows how the hegemony of the model of liberal democracy in India did not prevent the emergence of social movements energized by participatory ideals and principles of social solidarity interpreted in the light of a Gandhian concept of self-government (*swaraj*). Buhlungu shows the strength of the new forms of solidarity and identity that emerged at the end of the 1980s and beginning of the 1990s stemming from the anti-apartheid struggle in South Africa, in which two strong collective actors played important parts: the civic movement and the labor union movement.

The questioning of representation on the basis of the struggle for identity redefinitions, which, by their greater inclusiveness and openness to difference, render possible the emergence of new political actors, is particularly visible in the case of the women's struggle for the appropriation of the public space. The complexity of these struggles resides in the fact that in them the articulations among sexual, class, and ethnic identities are particularly tense. The relationship between the "old" collective identities linked to trade union and liberation movements or to the political parties of the "old" left, and the emergence of differentiations within them, based on specific claims associated with race, gender or sexual orientation, has given rise to tensions and conflicts that may compromise alliances and coalitions essential to a "politics of equivalence" that is capable of simultaneously recognizing, respecting and negotiating difference.

Conceição Osório shows the different negotiation strategies of Mozambican women with a view to their insertion into the male-dominated political game. In the context of a post-colonial state that seeks to define externally an identity of the "modern" woman, there emerges the social construction of a female identity leading to "a differentiated appropriation of the ends of political action," even when men and women are part of the same political organizations. In her turn, Shamim Meer investigates the relationships between social and civic movements in the sectors of South African society that were oppressed under apartheid, and the transformations in the South African state in the post-apartheid era. The fate of those who played an active role in these movements has been very diverse. In the case of women, their situation, after decades of involvement in struggles against apartheid, appears to have improved, but this is particularly true for white women, who were the main beneficiaries of empowerment measures aimed at increasing women's participation in public institutions and in the private sector. Black women and poor women from rural areas remain outside this process. For the author, the combination of these two elements indicates that the major rifts and inequalities, which for many decades had characterized South African society, have been preserved in the post-apartheid era, and for this reason the democratization process is far from being complete. The emergence of a black elite linked to the state and the new political institutions has not meant that the situation of the majority of the population, especially the poor in rural and urban districts, has changed. What roles are the social movements that fought against apartheid now playing? What is the tension between representation and participation? How to renegotiate the identities of the disadvantaged in the new public spaces and institutions?

The focus on opposition to racism in the democratic struggle against apartheid does not seem to have given adequate expression to the interests of the majority of the black population. The passage of the ANC from liberation movement to majority party in the post-apartheid era has meant that many of the demands of social movements are now up for legislation, including those relating to the rights of women. The presence of movement activists in positions of responsibility within the state has facilitated this process. Yet it is also true that the positioning of issues relating to women and to the poor within a neoliberal framework and within liberal democracy has led to their being defined as problems requiring legislative solutions, thereby depoliticizing them and eradicating from the debate any reference to the forms of power that lie at their roots. This tension between "depoliticized" and "politicized" views affects the women's movements themselves. While the former invoke the liberal concept of the "common good" in order to justify their position, the latter invoke power relations in society and the structural inequalities that they create. The former run the risk of being co-opted, whilst the latter open up areas of debate that can unleash critical responses to the dominant liberal discourse, and in particular to the ways in which class, race and gender subordination is reproduced and maintained within state institutions.

In this regard, the chapter by Maria José Arthur is particularly revealing because it expands the questions of renegotiation of identities into new social domains and public spaces. She picks up the theme of the relationship between gender identity and class identity in a study of women in the Mozambican trade union movement, and focuses, in particular, on the relationship between the leadership of the unions and the Comités da Mulher (Women's Committees). These were created in 1993, within trade unions and confederations, as a result of the convergence of the process of internal democratization and the pressures of regional and international union confederations and organizations, and also as a response to economic and political liberalization. During the 1990s, the unions underwent a process of internal debate, repositioning and reorganization, with various unions breaking away from the Organização dos Trabalhadores Moçambicanos (Organization of Mozambican Workers)—the only existing confederation—in 1992, and establishing a second union confederation in 1997. From 1994 onwards, a system of tripartite negotiation was instituted, involving companies, unions, and the government, which enabled claims to be formulated on issues such as the minimum wage, income tax and problems with public transport and health. "Women's issues" re-emerged in this context, due to their increased visibility as a result of the privatization process. The identity of working women in a union context is strictly linked to the roles of mother, wife, and educator, within a tradition rooted in the liberation struggle itself, which allows the union leadership to restrict women's intervention in the unions to what is defined as "issues specifically relating to working women."

Starting from her position as a feminist militant and her close understanding of the demands of working women (this term is restricted to salaried workers and excludes domestic and rural workers and therefore covers a small proportion of women), the author focuses her analysis on the discourse of union leaders pertaining to the Women's Committees and on the openings for women's intervention that this discourse provides as well as on the constraints that it creates. These discourses continue to establish and justify discriminatory practices based on sexual difference. The mobilization, by women, of a wide range of strategies and practices to contest these discourses and the constraints that accompany them points to specific forms of articulation of the identities of woman and worker and the recognition of both.

Thus, in conclusion to this section it is possible to demonstrate that, apart from many differences between the various political processes analyzed, there is something that unites them, a common trait that is related to the counter-hegemonic theory of democracy: the actors who established new experiments in participatory democracy or who struggled for autonomous inclusion in pre-constituted institutions and public spaces put in question an identity that had been externally attributed to them by the colonial state, by an authoritarian and discriminatory state or by other social institutions. Claiming rights to locally distributed public goods (Brazil), and rights to participate and demand the recognition of difference (Colombia, India, South Africa, and Mozambique), implies questioning a social and state grammar of exclusion and proposing a more inclusive alternative.

What is at stake in these processes is the constitution of a participatory and inclusive ideal as part of projects of liberation from colonialism and social oppression (in India, South Africa, and Mozambique) or of democratization (Brazil and Colombia). India had an independence movement that was highly influenced by the philosophy and practice of Gandhi, which included the affirmation of an autonomous project for the country. As Sheth states, such a liberation movement, in its Gandhian dimensions, as well as its socialist and communist dimensions, implied a broad project of incorporation of the Indian masses—a movement that came together in a Constitution that was understood not only as a document of political organization, but also as an agenda for the social and political transformation of an independent India. This agenda emphatically included the idea of the participation and political inclusion of poor and marginalized tribal castes. Buhlungu shows us a similar agenda in the case of South Africa, given that the struggle against apartheid was inspired by a participatory ideal that simultaneously postulated the equality of citizens and the recognition of difference. For Buhlungu, every struggle, as well as the vision of freedom or liberation that inspires it, always contains a promise of a decentralized or participatory kind of democracy that is inclusive rather than exclusive. In the case of Mozambique, the institutionalization of liberal democracy occurred in the aftermath of a revolutionary experiment dominated by the ideals of participation, although, in practice, often curtailed by revolutionary authoritarianism and sexist domination. Thus, a common trait in post-colonial movements is the importance of participatory democracy. It is important because, as Castoriadis states, it creates an imaginary post-colonial normativity in which democracy, as a project of social inclusion and cultural innovation, is put forward as an attempt to institute a new democratic sovereignty.

Likewise, the recent processes of democratization also incorporate the element of the institution of participation. In the case of Brazil, during the process of democratization, community movements in various regions of the country, and particularly in the city of Porto Alegre, claimed the right to participate in decision-making at the local level:

> Participating means directly influencing and controlling decisions [...]. If the country is at a new stage, it is possible and necessary that the community movement advances and has a direct influence, presenting proposals discussed and defined by the movement on the [public] budget. (UAMPA, 1986; Silva, 2001: 122)

Among other benefits, this participatory drive came to bear fruit in the participatory budgeting experiments analyzed by Santos and by Avritzer. In the case of Colombia, the negotiation that led to the Constitution of 1991 generated a broad process of participation that led to greater political involvement and visibility of certain social actors. Among them, the indigenous movement that had been fighting for its recognition for some time must be emphasized. Uprimny and Villegas analyze the way this recognition was achieved at the level of the Constitutional Court, and in the third volume of this collection the indigenous issue will be dealt with in more detail.

THE VULNERABILITIES AND AMBIGUITIES OF PARTICIPATION

In the previous section we sought to show that the processes of liberation and the processes of democratization seem to share a common element: the perception of the possibility of innovation understood as the wide participation of different types of social actors in decision-making. In general, these processes imply the inclusion of issues until then ignored by the political system, the redefinition of identities and affiliations and the increase in participation, namely at the local level.

These processes tend to be the object of intense political debate. As we have seen, capitalist societies, especially in the core countries, consolidated a hegemonic conception of democracy (that of liberal democracy) with which they sought to stabilize and contain the tension between democracy and capitalism. This stabilization occurred in two ways: by giving priority to the accumulation of capital over social redistribution,[9] and by restricting participation by citizens, as much individual as collective, with the aim of not "overloading" the democratic regime with social demands that could put in danger the priority of accumulation over redistribution. The fear of "democratic overload" presided over the transformations that, from the beginning of the 1980s, occurred in hegemonic democratic theory and practice in the core countries, being then exported to the semiperiphery and periphery of the world system. The idea of "democratic overload" had been formulated in 1975 in a report of the Trilateral Commission prepared by Crozier, Huntington, and Watanuki (1975). They argued that the overload was caused by the political inclusion of social groups excluded in the past and by the "excessive" demands made by these groups on democracy. Thus, we can understand why at the moment when, via decolonization or democratization, the problem of the extension of democracy to the countries of the South was raised for the first time, the hegemonic conception of democracy theorized the question of the new grammar of social inclusion as an excess of demands. In the light of this, it is easy to conclude that the processes of democratic intensification that we have been discussing tend to be strongly contested by exclusionary elites, or "metropolitan elites" as Sheth refers to them. Because they go against hegemonic interests and conceptions, these processes are often fought head on or adulterated by co-optation or integration. In this resides the vulnerability and ambiguity of participation, present in a number of the cases analyzed in this volume.

In the case of South Africa, Buhlungu shows how, as the democratic, post-apartheid regime was institutionalized, the state, the political system and the ANC itself, which had activated the whole social movement in the 1980s, came to discourage and even demobilize popular participation, which had been so important in the toppling of apartheid, under the pretext that representative democracy, now established, guaranteed the adequate representation of the various social interests.

The vulnerability of participation to adulteration, whether by power imbalances, by co-optation by over-included social groups, or by integration in institutional contexts that erase its democratic potential, as well as its potential for transforming power relations, is well illustrated in several cases analyzed here.[10] The Colombian cases presented here are particularly illustrative of the vulnerability and ambiguity of participation. Uprimny and Villegas show how the 1991 Constitution incorporated excluded and oppressed forces such as representatives of demobilized guerrilla groups, indigenous peoples, and religious minorities, thus diminishing the influence of the liberal and conservative parties, which, up until then, had dominated the political stage in Colombia. According to them, in this pluralistic framework, the diagnosis of many of the delegates to the Constituent Assembly was that exclusion, the lack of participation, and weakness in protecting human rights were the basic causes of the Colombian crisis. This explains some of the ideological orientations of the 1991 Constitution: the broadening of participation mechanisms, the imposition of the duties of promoting social justice and equality upon the state, and the incorporation of a meaningful bill of rights, as well as new judicial mechanisms for their protection.

However, the authors show how a contradiction pervaded, from the beginning, the attempt to create a new institutional order, as both the government and the opposition assumed positions that worked against the pacification of the political arena and the expansion of participation and rights. The study Uprimny and Villegas concentrates specifically on the Constitutional Court created in 1992. For the authors, the case of the Colombian Constitutional Court shows how, in a situation of the demobilization of citizens, the demand for equality and justice can shift from the political field to the judicial field. Colombians' disenchantment with politics has led certain sectors to demand answers from the judiciary to problems that, in principle, should be debated and resolved by means of citizens' participation in the political sphere. This phenomenon is not exclusive to Colombia (Santos *et al.*, 1995), but in this country the weakness of the mechanisms for political representation runs deep, a fact that has enabled the Court to assume a more prominent role. Thus, in the case of Colombia, we have a double dimension. On the one hand, as the authors point out, Colombia has a tradition of weak social movements. On the other hand, many of the actors that dominated the Constituent Assembly became weak in the following years. Thus, Colombia appears as a special case of the vulnerability of participation, revealing the ambiguous impact of a strong judiciary on social movements.

From different perspectives the chapters by Francisco Gutiérrez Sanín and Ana María Jaramillo and by Mauricio Romero address the vulnerability of participation by showing different ways in which participation may turn into submission, and inclusion into exclusion. Gutierrez Sanín and Jaramillo lead us on a journey through Colombian society and what they call its "pactist" tradition. This has been at the center of attempts to resolve the tension between two elements of this society: the stability of the macro-institutional, democratic forms and a long tradition of diffuse, chronic armed conflicts. The solution to this tension has involved pacts that have maintained an unstable dynamic of wars that have led to pacts, and pacts that have led to new wars, all within an institutional context in which power, including armed power, is "subject to multiple restrictions." In this way, the "pendulum pact-war" has become the "attractor" of the dynamics of the conflicts in Colombian society. In the interplay between necessity and liberty, this social world, "governed" by an "attractor," wavers between the articulation of resistance and social protest expressed in a pendular language and the possibility of a grammar of its own, defining a different space for participation, citizenship and democracy. However, taking into account the experiences of the last 20 years, if on a national scale the pacts are indispensable, on a local scale they appear undesirable. In fact, the pacts result in one of three possible situations: the physical destruction of their protagonists, the breaking of the pact or the anti-democratic concentration of power in the hands of one or more of the protagonists, with particular combinations of these situations being also possible. This dynamic brings with it the perverse consequence that these options define "the mental and moral horizon of the alternative options," based on the articulation of "emancipatory languages and non-emancipatory materials."

Two cases, that of the Medellín militias and that of Western Boyacá, dominated by entrepreneurs linked to the emerald trade, illustrate this situation. The pacts led to the realization of effective agreements, but with obvious costs: the armed groups can continue to do what they have always done, but now under the aura of a legality conferred upon them by the state, while the democratic rights of citizens can be sacrificed in the name of preserving the community and the peace. This makes it difficult for any emancipatory solutions, given that these "territorial dictatorships" are not compatible with the rule of law at a national level. The tension between stable macro-institutional forms and the dynamics of violence could become a common characteristic of those countries, especially in the South, in which the importation of formal democracy is merely one of the means of becoming incorporated into globalization. The authors suggest that perhaps Colombia is more indicative of the future of global capitalism than of the legacy of a pre-modern past.

The dilemmas of participation and the struggle for democratic rights within a weak state in which fragmentary forms of tyranny proliferate is equally well illustrated by Mauricio Romero, this time in a social domain with strong traditions regarding democratic struggle, namely the union movement. Romero positions us in a unique context with regard to the violation of human and union rights, if for nothing else because Colombia heads the world statistics in the number of murdered union leaders. Taking as its topic one of the most important mobilizations for social rights of the last three decades—the mobilization of banana workers in the Urabá region (next to the Panamanian border) conducted by the workers' union of the agribusiness industry (Sintrainagro), the author analyzes the way in which this unique experience appears to be upgrading the workers in the banana sector from the condition of "subjects" to that of "citizens." Romero describes the way in which the banana workers of Urabá, accustomed to performing the role of victims, managed to get protection, security, and political participation in exchange for "loyalty to a political and economical order" enforced in the region by a non-state political and military actor, namely the paramilitary groups of struggle against the guerrillas. According to Romero, the rivalry among insurrectional political and military projects carrying a lot of weight in the region forced them to vie for the workers' support, the paramilitary sector having won. Besides having improved their life conditions by becoming citizens, the banana workers of Urabá also earned international solidarity from Danish, Finnish, and Spanish unions, as well as from the International Union of Workers of Foodstuffs. To Romero's mind, international activism was good both to counteract the relative isolation of Sintrainagro at the national scale, by creating allies and supporters *vis-à-vis* eventual changes in the national political dynamics, and to confer to this very union "autonomy and independence *vis-à-vis* the dominant local powers."

The same complexity of participation can be detected in Mozambique in the case study analyzed by Osório. Thus, according to the author, women's occupation of political space can be as much a contribution to the challenge of male domination as a consolidation of it. The case of Mozambique demonstrates that, in situations in which democracy does not involve a renegotiation of a more pluralist grammar, expressed by the increase in female participation, the social grammar itself comes into conflict with the working mechanisms of the political model. The author identifies three strategies adopted by women in relation to political participation: the adaptation to existing hierarchies and, therefore, to male superiority; the adoption of the masculine model as universal, using the weapon of formal equality to further women's power; and the vindication of an alternative model capable of subverting the dichotomies on which male power is based. Osório's analysis leads to a reflection on the vulnerabilities of democracy. For her, the exercise of democracy, in the context of globally legitimated systems, fails to satisfy the demands of new groups, as is the case of women. This case illustrates the need for a more plural and transversal action in the different spaces of production of the political. Thus, the author shows that, even in situations where the increase in participation exists, this increase, to become emancipatory, needs to be adjusted to the attempt to recreate political forms.

We can now systematize some of the characteristics of the cases in which participation does not manage to come into being at the end of a process of decolonization or democratization. There are at least three different cases we can think of. In the first place is that of Colombia, in which the forms of participation did not lose their legitimacy, but could not be established as an alternative model due to the reaction of conservative sectors and non-state armed actors. In Mozambique the practices of participation did not lose their legitimacy either, yet there is a need for a pluralization of the political grammar itself so that the plurality of society may be assimilated by democracy. And finally, we have the case of Brazil, in which the forms of participation can be part of a process of co-optation but can also represent a fundamental innovation capable of generating counter-hegemonic models of democracy, as we will go on to show in the next section.

THE POTENTIALITIES OF PARTICIPATION

In light of the research carried out, Brazil and India are the cases in which the potentialities of participatory democracy are most clearly manifested. We would like to stress, however, that this project's endeavor to broaden the democratic canon concerns not only the hegemonic model of representative democracy but also models of participatory democracy prevalent in the specialized bibliography, especially in the last decade. The practices of participation and democratic deliberation occur in the most disparate contexts and answer to very concrete needs and demands. Because of this utter contextuality and the novelty of the social grammar into which they often translate themselves, such practices are not easily recognized by the conventional models of participatory democracy. To broaden our views on contemporary democracy we need, therefore, to take the social grammars and contexts as starting points, rather than the models. The strength of the democratic aspiration of peoples is more tenaciously asserted in difficult contexts.

In this project, the most salient example of a difficult context is unquestionably the situation of civil war and the state of generalized violence in Colombia. It is in this context that a remarkable experience of participatory democracy has emerged since 1997: the communities of peace. The communities of peace are communities of peasants caught in the crossfire of war. Victims of recurrent massacres, the peasants of these communities are often expelled from their villages and lands. These communities then organize themselves to force both the paramilitary, the guerrillas and the national army to abide by the norms of humanitarian international law, which distinguish between civil populations and combatants. Their self-organization amounts to the elaboration, by democratic deliberation, of a social and political pact, a kind of local Constitution or internal law, in the terms of which the members of the community commit themselves to severing all the ties, whether direct or indirect, with the armed actors, be they paramilitary, guerrilla or the Colombian army. The internal regulations of the community are quite detailed, women and the youth playing a significant role in them. The commitment of a given community is presented to the armed actors and often there is negotiation to try to get from them the mutual commitment of allowing the peasants to return to their villages and there live in peace. Thus, a social grammar and a culture of peace, dialogue, and solidarity are created in the midst of the most anarchic violence. The objective is to let the peasants restore their communitarian bonds, retrieve their land, and resume agricultural production. This objective is synthesized in the projects of "life and hope" adopted by the communities of peace. Surrounded by violence and the culture of violence, the communities of peace are a fragile institution, but they do give strength to the populations that reject an armed solution for the conflicts.

The community of peace analyzed in this project is that of San José de Apartadó. In an eloquent and dramatic essay, María Teresa Uribe de H demonstrates the contradiction between participation, the pacification of political space, and civil war. Situated in a banana-growing area of Colombia, a sanctuary for guerrillas in the country, San José de Apartadó has a strategic geographical position in the Colombian conflict. The pact, called *Comunidad de Paz*, was announced in May 1997 with the help of the local diocese, the Intercongregational Commission for Justice and Peace and various NGOs. The strong international support for the declaration of the *Comunidad de Paz* obliged the paramilitaries to respect its neutrality.[11] The fragility of the pact is, however, quite noticeable in the asymmetrical fact that it was wholly respected by the community and later violated by the armed actors. After the first incursion of paramilitaries in April 1999, there followed various incursions of the guerrilla forces. As of 2000, 83 people had been killed in San José de Apartadó. The case of San José de Apartadó clearly reveals the interdependence of the deepening of democracy and the need for the constitution of a new social grammar based on pacification, which implies political negotiations beyond a local scale.

In his text on participatory budgeting, Leonardo Avritzer shows the way in which the Brazilian Constituent Assembly increased the influence of various social actors in political institutions as a result of new participatory arrangements. Article 14 of the 1988 Constitution guaranteed "popular initiative" in legislative processes. Article 29, on the organization of cities, required the participation of popular association representatives in the process of city planning. Other articles establish the participation of civic associations in the implementation of health and social welfare policies. Thus, the Constitution was able to incorporate new cultural elements, which had emerged at the level of society, into the emerging institutionality, opening up space for the practice of participatory democracy.

Santos and Avritzer show how, among the various forms of participation that emerged in post-authoritarian Brazil, participatory budgeting acquired particular pre-eminence. In the case of Brazil, the authors argue, the motivation for participation is part of a common inheritance of the process of democratization that led democratic social actors, especially those from the community movement, to debate the meaning of the term participation. In the case of the city of Porto Alegre, this debate was linked to the opening of actual areas of participation by the political society, in particular by the Workers' Party. This led to the emergence of effective forms of combination of elements of participatory and representative democracy, through the initiative of the administrations of the Workers' Party to articulate the representative mandate with effective forms of deliberation at the local level.

Participatory budgeting emerges from this intention, which, according to Santos, is manifested in three of its main characteristics: (1) participation is open to all citizens without any special status whatsoever being attributed to any organization, including community organizations; (2) the combination of direct and representative democracy creates an institutional dynamic that attributes to the participants themselves the definition of the internal rules; and (3) the allocation of the resources for investments is based on a combination of general and technical criteria, that is, the decisions and rules established by the participants are made compatible with the technical and legal demands of governmental action, also respecting financial limits.

According to Avritzer, these general principles are translated into three forms of participatory institutionality. In the first place, there are regional assemblies in which the participation is individual and open to all members of the community, and the rules of deliberation and decision-making are defined by the participants themselves. In the second place, there is a distributive principle capable of rectifying pre-existent inequalities in relation to the distribution of public goods. In the case of participatory budgeting in Porto Alegre and also in Belo Horizonte, this distributive principle is manifested in the so-called "tables of needs," whose elaboration precedes the process of deliberation itself. In the third place, there is a mechanism for dovetailing the process of participation and deliberation with the public administration, a process that involves, in the case of Porto Alegre, the functioning of a council that can deliberate on the budget and negotiate priorities with the local mayoralty.

We have, therefore, in the case of Brazil, a successful first form of combination of elements of representative democracy and participatory democracy. This combination occurs on distinct levels: on the local level, citizens participate in a process of negotiation and deliberation on priorities concerning the distribution of public goods. This process expresses an aspect that has already been emphasized in this text—the need for democracy to be articulated with a new social grammar. In the case of participatory budgeting, this grammar has two elements: the fair distribution of public goods and the democratic negotiation of the access to these goods among the social actors themselves. The regional assemblies, the lists of prior access to public goods and the Participatory Budgeting Council express this dimension that we designate above as participatory proceduralism, a process of expanded participation involving a broad public debate on the rules of participation, deliberation and distribution.

Participatory budgeting shows some of the potential of the expansion of participatory democracy. In the case of Porto Alegre, the participation of the population has increased practically every year, while in Belo Horizonte, apart from a little more variation, there has also been an increase. It is equally important to underline that participatory budgeting in Brazil has grown significantly. Between 1997 and 2000 there were 140 municipal administrations that adopted participatory budgeting, the vast majority (127) in cities of up to 500,000 inhabitants. In about half of the cases (71), these administrations were linked to the Workers' Party (Grazia, 2001). The extension of participatory budgeting to all the regions of Brazil, in addition to other political proposals, shows the potential of the extension of successful experiments in participatory democracy.

In the case of India, the potential of participatory democracy is equally visible. Sheth discusses how the political and participatory actions that were organized from the beginning of the 1960s existed as fragments of the earlier political and social movements—movements that had their origins in the Freedom movement. They worked in small and marginal spaces available to them on the periphery of electoral and party politics. But within three decades of Independence new social and political spaces opened up for them. Nevertheless, Sheth equally emphasizes that these forms of participatory democracy, because they do not follow the model of liberal democracy, are considered by metropolitan elites and the middle classes to be suspect and vehicles of negative anti-development and anti-national values. It is because of this that the combination of initiatives in participatory democracy with representative democracy only occurs in specific political contexts, as, for example, in Kerala—the case studied by Heller and Isaac.

The democratic challenge in India is extremely complex because, in addition to differences of class, sex, ethnicity, religion and region, differences of caste must also be taken into consideration. This is then a challenge in the field of the so-called democratization of democracy. The caste system was reproduced within the Indian political system, and inserted hierarchical relationships and profound material inequalities into it (Heller, 2000). Sheth shows how the very project of constructing a shared democracy for all castes and all social groups, establishing a symbolic reference common to the whole population of the country, became gradually subordinated to the particularist agenda of political society.

Two main forms of democratization of the Indian political system can be pointed to at present. The first is a form of local democracy based on the rupture with a grammar of exclusion at the level of society itself. This is the form that democratization has assumed in the province of Kerala. Here, in contrast to other parts of India, the associational infrastructure does not reproduce the dominant pattern of religious organizations and castes that reproduce a culture of inequality. Kerala has the highest levels of trade union membership in the country, and, in contrast with the national pattern, the unions also reach workers in the informal sector. Kerala also possesses a wide range of women's, student and youth organizations, sponsored by all the parties. Just the mass associations linked to the Communist Party of India have more than 4.7 million members.

We have here, therefore, a first case of a rupture with the restricted forms of democracy at the local level, a rupture that, in the case of Kerala, occurs first at the level of civil society, through the constitution of an associational grammar, and is extended to political society through the system of the Panchayats. This system was introduced by the Left Democratic Front in 1996 through the launching of the so-called "People's Campaign for Decentralized Planning." This campaign achieved a high degree of devolution of decision-making powers to the Panchayats. All 1,214 local governments in Kerala—municipalities and the three rural tiers of district, block and *grama panchayats* (the all-India term for village councils)—were given new functions and powers of decision-making, and have been granted discretionary budgeting authority over 40 percent of the state's developmental expenditures. The transfer of decision-making to the local level implied a process of qualitative change in participation and deliberation, involving assemblies in rural areas (*grama sabha*) in which more than 2 million people took part and development seminars (for the assessment of the resources and problems of the area and the formulation of a local development strategy) attended by more than 300,000 delegates, in addition to task forces involving 100,000 volunteers. We can, therefore, perceive an enormous process of participation unleashed by the transfer of the process of deliberation on the budget to the local level.

A second form of expansion of Indian democracy that is also related to the mobilization of the population at a local level is discussed by Sheth. It involves local movements that organize public hearings and popular courts with the aim of creating political and social constraints for local governments and thus force them to act in a more honest and efficient way. Sheth describes one of the most significant moments of these movements when, in December of 1994-95, several public hearings (*Jan Sunvai*) were held in various states and were attended by journalists. These hearings culminated in a 40-day sit-in (*dharna*) that compelled the government to make its accounts public through the Panchayat Raj.

As much in India as in Brazil, the most significant experiments in change in the form of democracy have originated in social movements that question practices of exclusion through actions that generate new norms and new forms of control of the government by the citizens.

We can point to some similarities and differences between the two cases. As to similarities, both experiments, in Porto Alegre and Kerala, emerged from a process of social renovation. In the case of Porto Alegre, as Avritzer points out, the experiment derived from a proposal of budgetary participation formulated in the 1980s by UAMPA (the Union of Neighborhood Associations of Porto Alegre), and in the case of Kerala, as Heller and Isaac point out, from experiments in participation at the local level conducted by civil society organizations, in particular by Kerala Sastra Sahitya Parishad. In the second place, in both cases, a political party had to take the political decision of giving up decision-making prerogatives in favor of forms of participation. In Porto Alegre, the Workers' Party fulfilled this role, and in Kerala it was the Communist Party of India. In both cases, the state plays a crucial role in legitimating participation and rendering it efficacious. Participation is in turn conceived of as part of a vaster political process of the state's democratic reform. In the third place, the proposal of participation involved the elaboration of complex rules of participation in both cases, as Santos shows in the case of Porto Alegre, and Heller and Isaac in the case of Kerala. It is important to underline that these rules—which, in the case of Porto Alegre, predetermine the distributive character of the participatory budget and establish incentives to participation for the poor population and, in the case of Kerala, make public the criteria for beneficiary eligibility and prioritization—will be fundamental to the success of the form of participation. The two cases that we can deem successful present two extremely important characteristics: first, they stem from changes in societal practices introduced by the social actors themselves; second, they recover local democratic traditions at first ignored by the hegemonic forms of representative democracy in these countries. Porto Alegre and Kerala express an attempt to extend democracy based on potentials of the local culture itself.

We can also point out some important contrasts between the two cases. In the first place, despite the importance of the Workers' Party in the experiment in participatory budgeting, the party has limited control of the process, and only a small percentage of participants in the participatory budgeting are affiliated with it. The control of the Communist Party of India over the process seems to be greater, which makes it dependent on an unstable political coalition in a state with a strong Islamic minority. In the second place, there is an important difference in the form of transference of prerogatives on the budget: the participatory budgeting in Porto Alegre and in Belo Horizonte decentralizes and democratizes only the process of deliberation, and leaves in the hands of the mayoralty the process of the administrative implementation of the decisions. In this case, the control of the public administration is made by the Participatory Budget Council in Porto Alegre and by COMFORÇAS in Belo Horizonte, thus creating a mechanism of administrative control that is relatively invulnerable to processes of corruption, given the excess of public mechanisms and forms of control. In the case of India, the resources are transferred to the committees themselves, which leads to accusations of corruption, as Heller and Isaac point out. Finally, everything seems to indicate that, in the case of Brazil, the participatory budgeting provides electoral advantages to those who practice it, such that other parties want to implement it, while the continuity of the Indian experiment was put in question by the electoral defeat of the Left Front in 2001.

Thus, the cases referred to here present contemporary democratic practice with not only the inconclusiveness of the debate between representation and participation, but also the need for a new formulation concerning the combination of these different forms of democracy.

CONCLUSION: THESES ON WIDENING
THE DEMOCRATIC CANON

There are more questions raised than answers given in the studies included in this volume. In this, they remain faithful to the central objective of the project "Reinventing Social Emancipation" in the context of which they were carried out. This project sought to draw new horizons for social emancipation, starting from practices that occur in specific contexts to provide answers to concrete problems. Therefore, it is not possible to draw from them universal solutions that would be valid in every context. At best, such practices are driven by wide aspirations of emancipation that they seek to realize in a partial and limited way.

Between the realization and the aspiration lies the imagination of the possible beyond what exists. This embedded imagination generates questions that constitute and shape the emancipatory horizons. These are not, then, just *any* questions, but questions that result from the excess of aspirations in relation to the realization of concrete practices. In the specific case of the theme of the project discussed in this volume—participatory democracy—the horizons are questions that address the possibility of widening the democratic canon. Through this widening, the hegemonic canon of liberal democracy is contested in its pretension to universality and exclusivity, thus giving credibility to counter-hegemonic democratic concepts and practices. In what follows, we will pose some questions and provide answers, in the form of theses, to some of the questions.

1. *The struggle for democracy is today above all a struggle for the democratization of democracy.* Substantively, democracy concerns the quality of human experience and the social relations that it makes possible. It can be defined as the entire process through which unequal power relations are replaced by relations of shared authority. Liberal democracy confined democracy to the political realm, strictly conceived of as the field that concerns the state's areas of intervention. This rendered the democratic process susceptible to constituting an island of democracy in a wide ocean of social despotisms. Santos has been arguing (1995: 403–55; 2002: 353–416) that in capitalist societies there are six large forms of power, hence of unequal relations of power: patriarchy, exploitation, unequal differentiation of identity, fetishism of commodities, domination and unequal exchange. These correspond to six main structure-agency time-spaces: household-place, workplace, community-place, marketplace, citizen-place, and world-place. As a substantive ideal and practice, democracy has to be struggled for in all these time-spaces involving different social and political processes. The more democratic these time-spaces are, the more democratic human experience as a whole will be. In each one of these time-spaces there is a tension between what is public

and what is private. The public space must therefore not be taken as a given, for that would mean to accept and legitimate the distributions of power presently in existence and the political actors already constituted.

The fact that the arena of democratic struggle has been confined so far to the time-space of the citizen-place calls for a sociological explanation, even though it has no political grounding. As amply demonstrated by the feminist movements, the ambit and constitution of the public space is open to dispute. From this substantive point of view, there is no true democracy, there is only democratization, a process without end. The fact that the following theses concentrate mainly on the conventional scope of democracy does not mean that we are not aware that the democratic range and aspiration is much vaster and deeper.

2. *As is the case of biodiversity, demo-diversity must be preserved and, whenever possible, expanded and enriched.* Democracy's modern history shows that there is not only one but rather many forms of democracy. The comparison between the studies and debates on democracy in the 1960s and in the last decade leads us easily to the conclusion that, on the global level, demo-diversity has been reduced in the last 30 years. By demo-diversity we mean the peaceful or conflictive coexistence in a given social field of different models and practices of democracy. In the 1960s, if, on the one hand, the hegemonic model of democracy—liberal democracy—seemed destined to be confined, as democratic practice, to a small corner of the world, on the other hand, outside Western Europe and North America, there existed other political practices that claimed democratic status and did so in the light of autonomous criteria, distinct from those that sustained liberal democracy. In the meantime, as these alternative political practices lost strength and credibility, liberal democracy gradually established itself as the sole and universal model. Its consecration was consummated by the Washington Consensus, the World Bank and the International Monetary Fund, when it was transformed into a political conditionality for the granting of loans and financial aid.

What this implies, from our point of view, is a loss of demo-diversity. The negativity of this loss resides in two factors. The first has to do with the justification of democracy. If, as we believe, democracy has an intrinsic value and not a mere instrumental utility, this value can in no way be assumed as universal. It is inscribed in a specific cultural context, that of western modernity. This context, because it coexists with others in a world that now is recognized as multicultural, can in no way claim the universality of its values. We know today that if this claim refuses to give the reasons that sustain it and to dialogue with others that eventually contest it, it will only be imposed by force as such; it will be nothing more than an imperial claim. And this imperial temptation is all the more noticeable as the overwhelming power of neoliberal globalization and of the institutions that, in its name, impose the adoption of liberal democracy on a global level becomes more pronounced. It makes no sense to postulate the universality of the values that sustain democracy on the basis that there is nothing in other cultures that opposes them, as Amartya Sen does (1999). Such a convergence cannot be postulated as a starting point. It has to be, if anything at all, the point of arrival of an intercultural dialogue in which other cultures can present that which they propose autonomously.

We support such a cultural dialogue and believe it enriches all who participate in it. The convergences that result almost always in forms of cultural hybridization have to be achieved in the practice of argumentation and in the argumentation of practice. Regarding the practices analyzed in this volume, we can see this hybridization surfacing especially in the case studies on India, but it is present in one way or another in the case studies on Mozambique, Brazil, South Africa and Colombia.

The loss of demo-diversity is negative because of a second factor, which, although autonomous in relation to the first, is related to it. It has to do with the distinction between democracy as an ideal and democracy as a practice. This distinction is central to the hegemonic model of democracy and was introduced into the debate to justify the low democratic intensity of established political regimes when compared with the revolutionary democratic ideals of the late eighteenth century and mid-nineteenth century. The universal imposition of the liberal model exacerbated this distinction to such an extent that actually existing democracy is frequently so far from the democratic ideal that it does not seem to be more than a caricature of it. Indeed, this distance is sometimes greater in core countries than in peripheral countries, although the opposite might appear to be the case. It is this distance that leads Wallerstein to respond to the question of what to think of democracy as it has been fulfilled with the reply that Gandhi gave when asked about what he thought of Western civilization: "it would be a good idea" (2001: 10).

This volume describes and analyzes democratic practices and aspirations that, in the different countries integrated in this project, seek to have democratic aspiration taken seriously, refusing to accept as democratic practices those that are a caricature of democracy, and above all refusing to accept as a fatality the low democratic intensity to which the hegemonic model has subjected the participation of citizens in political life. In a very distinct manner, these practices seek to intensify and deepen democracy, whether by asserting the legitimacy of participatory democracy, or by exerting pressure on institutions of representative democracy in order to make them more inclusive, or even by seeking denser forms of complementarity between participatory democracy and representative democracy.

3. *Representative democracy tends to be low-intensity democracy, a tendency that has deepened in recent times.* The reason for this tendency is that democracy confines itself to the citizen-space, of which it has a rather narrow conception, mainly centered on top-down relations between the state and the individual citizen. For the past 20 years, the intensity of representative democracy has decreased considerably for three main reasons. From the nineteenth century a certain tension between democracy and capitalism was generated. It resided in the capacity of representative democracy to bring about some social redistribution as social groups earlier excluded from the social contract managed to be included as a result of their struggles. This inclusion had the political form of economic and social rights and called for an increasingly stronger intervention by the state. A new political form emerged, known as the welfare state in core countries and as the developmental state in peripheral countries. In very distinct ways, these new forms of state consisted in turning the state into an active source of non-mercantile interactions (in the domain of health, education, welfare, and so on). For the past 20 years, these new political forms have been attacked and dismantled. Today, in the neoliberal world in which we live, the state is an active agent of mercantilization of social relations, which earlier had not been subjected to the law of value. The tension between democracy and capitalism has thereby disappeared and democracy has in fact become a conditionality of neoliberal globalization. With the increase of social inequalities came the increase of social despotisms. The latter lowered the intensity of a form of democracy that not only cohabits with them but also legitimates them.

The second reason for the loss of intensity of representative democracy resides in the increasing promiscuity between the two markets whose separation grounds the legitimacy of representative democracy: the political market and the economic market. The economic market is the outside border of representative democracy; it consists of the set of values that have a price and are exchanged as goods and services. The political market is its inside border; it is constituted of values and ideas that are discussed, combined, and articulated, but which have no price. During the last 20 years, the deregulation, privatization of public services, media-ization of politics and the financing of parties and political campaigns contributed to the contamination of the political market by the economic market. As a consequence, the political market ended up being subjected as well to the law of value. Extremely powerful economic agents ended up assuming public prerogatives (such as controlling the political agenda, obtaining monopolies over the provision of public services) by state delegation, thus bringing about new forms of indirect rule, typical of the colonial state.

The third reason for the loss of intensity of representative democracy resides in the rupture of the relationship between authorization and accountability. Elections have been the mechanism *par excellence* of authorization. Elections are indeed the means by which citizens give up the right to take decisions directly by delegating it to their representatives. Accountability has to do with transparency in the exercise of the representatives' mandate and with the political content of the relations between the representatives and the represented. Originally, accountability was exerted through several mechanisms (consultation, recall, suspension of the mandate, and so on), elections being the last resort (the failure of representatives to be reelected as punishment for their unaccountability). For the past few decades, partly due to the above-mentioned factors, not only did the few mechanisms of accountability disappear but the elections themselves stopped performing this function. Thereby emerged the two pathologies of contemporary representative democracy: the pathology of representation (citizens do not feel represented by their representatives) and the pathology of participation (citizens stop participating in elections because they are convinced that their vote is irrelevant). With the loss of intensity of representative democracy we run the risk of entering a period in which many societies are politically democratic and socially fascist.[12]

4. *Deepening democracy will increasingly depend on new complementarities between participatory democracy and representative democracy.* This is perhaps the question to which the studies collected in this volume provide the most answers. The solution given by the hegemonic theory of democracy to the problem of the relation between representative democracy and participatory democracy—the solution of scales—is not adequate because it leaves untouched the problem of social grammars, and offers a simplistic answer, which is exclusively geographic (the local as the only adequate scale for relatively non-complex citizen participation), to the problem of the combination of participation and representation.

The experiments studied in this project offer an alternative answer to the democratic problem. They show that the ability to deal with cultural and administrative complexity is not increased with an increase in scale. They also show, above all, that there is a process of cultural pluralization and recognition of new identities[13] that leads, as a consequence, to profound redefinitions of democratic practice, and these redefinitions are beyond the aggregative process specific to representative democracy.

In our opinion, there are two possible forms to combine participatory democracy and representative democracy: coexistence and complementarity. The first implies the coexistence, on various levels, of the different forms of proceduralism, administrative organization and variation in institutional design. Representative democracy at the national level (exclusive power as regards the constitution of governments; the acceptance of a vertical bureaucratic form as the sole form of public administration) coexists with participatory democracy at the local level, accentuating certain participatory characteristics that already exist in some democracies in core countries (Mansbridge, 1990).

The second form of combination, which we refer to as complementarity, implies a more profound articulation between representative democracy and participatory democracy. It presupposes the recognition by the government that participatory proceduralism, the public forms of monitoring governments and the processes of public deliberation can substitute part of the process of representation and deliberation as conceived of in the hegemonic model of democracy. Contrary to what this model seeks to achieve, the objective is to associate with the process of strengthening local democracy forms of cultural renovation related to a new political institutionality that reintroduces the questions of cultural plurality and the necessity of social inclusion into the democratic agenda. As much in the case of Brazil as in the case of India, the participatory arrangements enable the articulation between argumentation and distributive justice and the transfer of prerogatives from the national level to the local level, and from political society to the participatory arrangements themselves. Representative democracy is summoned to integrate proposals of cultural recognition and social inclusion into the political-electoral debate.

The concept of complementarity is different from that of coexistence because, as we have seen in the cases of Brazil and India, it implies a decision by political society to expand participation at the local level through the transfer and/or devolution of decision-making prerogatives at first held by governments. Thus, in the case of both participatory budgeting in Brazil and the Panchayats in India, regional assemblies or the decisions by councilors stem from the option taken by political society to articulate participation and representation. What is at stake is the democratic transformation of the state.

It seems obvious that the first form of articulation between participatory democracy and representative democracy (coexistence) prevails in the core countries, while the second (complementarity) begins to emerge in semi-peripheral and peripheral countries. If such is the case, it is possible to conclude that the deepening of democracy does not necessarily occur as a result of the same characteristics present in the core countries where democracy was first introduced and consolidated. The characteristics that enabled democratic originality may not be necessarily the same characteristics that enable its expanded and deepened reproduction. For this reason, the problem of cultural innovation and institutional experimentalism becomes even more urgent. If such a perspective is correct, the new democracies must change themselves into absolutely new social movements, in the sense that the state must change itself into a space of distributive and cultural experimentation. It is in the originality of the new forms of institutional experimentation that the emancipatory potentials still present in contemporary societies may be found. In order to be realized, these potentials need to be embedded in a society that invests democratic imagination in the process of renegotiating participatory rules of sociability.

5. *The strengthening of counter-hegemonic democracy must rely on articulations between the local and the global.* New democratic experiments need the support of transnational democratic actors, especially in the cases in which democracy is of particularly low intensity, as became clear in the case of Colombia. At the same time, alternative, successful experiments such as that of Porto Alegre and the Panchayats in India need to be expanded in order to offer alternatives to the hegemonic model. Therefore, the counter-hegemonic shift from the local to the global level is fundamental for the strengthening of participatory democracy. On the other hand, the construction of dense complementarities between participatory democracy and representative democracy lies in the development of mediations between local scales and national scales.

We have emphasized the idea that the hegemonic model of democracy has been hostile to the active participation of citizens in political life and, when it has accepted it, has confined it to a local level. The counter-hegemonic alternative answer lies in the transnational articulations between different local experiments in participatory democracy or between those local experiments and transnational movements and organizations interested in promoting participatory democracy. Counter-hegemonic globalization is based on these articulations, which allow the creation of the counter-hegemonic local, the local that is the building block of the counter-hegemonic global. These articulations give credibility to and strengthen local practices by the simple fact of transforming them into links of wider networks and movements with a greater power for transformation. In addition, such articulations make possible reciprocal and continuous learning, which we believe is essential for the success of democratic practices that are energized by the possibility of high-intensity democracy. Because we chose in this project to analyze local experiments in deepening democracy, the articulation between the local and the global emerges as a question to which we cannot give an immediate answer, but which we deem fundamental to answer in the future. Even so, some of the cases suggest this articulation. In the case of the community of peace of San José de Apartadó, this articulation is explicit. Uribe shows the importance of the network of transnational solidarity in making visible, on a national and international level, the struggle for peace in this Colombian community. In the case of participatory budgeting, we know that similar experiments have been appearing in a number of Brazilian cities and in other countries of Latin America, that the most recent experiments have benefited from previous ones, and that there are even networks of cities, namely in the context of Mercosur, whose aim is to discuss the different experiments and models of participatory democracy, their limits, and their potentialities. The strength of counter-hegemonic globalization as regards the widening and deepening of democracy largely depends on the widening and deepening of national, regional, continental, or global networks of local practices.

6. *The dangers of perversion and co-optation are imminent and can only be averted by constant democratic vigilance energized by the idea of democratizing democracy.* We have seen how the nineteenth-century revolutionary aspirations of democratic participation were gradually reduced to forms of low-intensity democracy in the course of the twentieth century. In this process, the objectives of social inclusion and the recognition of differences became perverted and were converted into their opposite. The practices of participatory democracy are in no way immune to the danger of perversion and adulteration. These practices, which seek to expand the political canon and, by doing so, expand the public space and the social debates and demands that constitute it, may also be co-opted by hegemonic interests and actors with the aim of legitimizing social exclusion and the repression of difference.

Perversion can occur in many different ways: bureaucratization of participation, by the rigidification of the participatory institutions and by the emergence of professionalized active citizens; reintroduction of clientelism in new guises through the co-optation of participation by conventional top-down politics; sectarian instrumentalization by powerful actors able to reduce the scope of deliberative participation; exclusion of subordinate interests through the silencing or manipulation of participatory institutions; delegitimation of lay and popular knowledge by the techno-managerial colonization of argumentative and deliberative contexts; manipulative use of devolution by the state so that the latter withdraws from its responsibility as guarantor of economic and social rights, thus transforming participatory democracy into a sham. These dangers can only be prevented by constant learning and self-reflection, from which incentives to new ways of deepening democracy can be drawn. In the field of participatory democracy, more than any other, democracy is an unlimited principle, and the tasks of democratization can only be sustained when they themselves are defined by increasingly demanding democratic processes.

Notes

1 This debate began in the nineteenth century. Up until then, it was generally assumed that democracy was dangerous, and, thus, undesirable. Its danger lay in attributing power of government to those most ill-equipped to exercise it: the great mass of the population, who were illiterate, ignorant, and socially and politically inferior (Williams, 1981: 82; Macpherson, 1966).

2 Like almost every debate about democracy, this one was anticipated by Rousseau: see his statement in *The Social Contract* that a society could be

democratic only when there was no one so poor as to be compelled to sell himself, and no one so rich as to be able to buy someone.

3 We understand the concept of "hegemony" to be the economic, political, moral, and intellectual ability to establish a dominant direction in the form of approaching a given question, in this case the question of democracy. We also understand that every hegemonic process produces a counter-hegemonic process in which economic, political, and moral alternatives are developed. In the case of the current debate on democracy, this implies a hegemonic and counter-hegemonic conception of democracy. For the concept of hegemony, see Gramsci (1973).

4 The Schumpeterian doctrine of democracy adopts wholesale the argument of the manipulation of individuals in mass societies. For Schumpeter, individuals in politics yield to irrational and extra-rational impulses and behave in an almost infantile manner when making decisions (Schumpeter, 1942: 257). He never sought to differentiate between large-scale mass mobilizations and forms of collective action, which makes his argument about the manipulation of the masses in politics extremely fragile. For a critique, see Melucci (1996) and Avritzer (1996). The vulnerability of the Schumpeterian argument did not stop it from being widely used by the hegemonic conceptions of democracy.

5 Bobbio analyzes, in a different way from Schumpeter, the reasons why the participation of individuals in politics became undesirable. For him, the central element that discourages participation is the increase in the social complexity of contemporary democracies (Bobbio, 1986). The argument of complexity as well as its limitations will be discussed later.

6 It is possible, none the less, to see that the explanation of the question of consensus by the hegemonic theory of democracy leaves much to be desired (Manin, 1997). For hegemonic theory, the problem of consensus becomes relevant only in the act of constituting governments. However, the act of constituting governments is an act of aggregating majorities, and rarely leads to consensus in relation to the identity and accountability of the governing body. Thus, if the explanation for abandoning the system of rotation of administrative positions seems to be correct, it by no means leads to the recognition of the superiority of the forms of representation in relation to the forms of participation. It only points to the necessity of a different basis for participation— in this case, consensus in relation to the rules of participation.

7 Among the authors of the hegemonic field, Adam Przeworski was the one who most emphasized the problem of the indetermination of results in democracy. For him, "democracy is a process of submitting all interests to the competition of institutionalized uncertainty" (Przeworski, 1984: 37). However, for Przeworski, "institutionalized uncertainty" is the uncertainty of whoever occupies positions of power in a situation of democratization and whether this result can be turned around or not. The concept of democracy with which we are working here implies a higher level of indetermination insofar as it involves the possibility of inventing a new democratic grammar.

8 The position of Habermas, however, tends to focus on a proposal of democracy for certain social groups and countries of the North. Criticized for the
limitations of his concept of the public sphere (Fraser, 1995; Santos, 1995;
Avritzer, 2002), Habermas seems to have only made an effort to integrate social
actors from northern countries (see Habermas, 1992).

9 For some authors, this priority is inscribed in the very matrix of the paradigm
of Western modernity, with its emphasis on the idea of progress based on
infinite economic growth. It is because of this that it occurred, although in
distinct ways, as much in capitalist societies as in the socialist societies of Eastern
Europe (Marramao, 1995).

10 Fung and Wright (2003: 33) identify the following problems confronting what
they call empowered participatory governance: power imbalances, limitations on
the scope of deliberative decision by external actors, rent-seeking, the balkaniza-
tion of politics, unrealistically high levels of commitment, and unsustainability.

11 On this question, see also Sader, in this volume.

12 On the notion of social fascism, see Santos, 2002: 447.

13 The theme of identities and the principle of the recognition of difference are
treated in detail in the third volume of this collection.

Bibliography

Alvarez, S., E. Dagnino, and A. Escobar (1998). *Cultures of Politics, Politics of Cultures:
Re-visioning Latin American Social Movements.* Boulder, CO: Westview.

Anderson, B. (1991). *Imagined Communities: Reflections on the Origin and Spread of
Nationalism.* London: Verso.

Arato, Andrew (2000). "Accountability and Civil Society," in Peruzzotti and
Smulovitz (eds.), *Societal Accountability.* Buenos Aires: Temas.

Avritzer, L. (1996). *A Moralidade da Democracia.* São Paulo: Perspectiva.

—— (2002). *Democracy and the Public Space in Latin America.* Princeton, NJ:
Princeton UP.

Benhabib, S. (1996). "Toward a Deliberative Model of Democratic Legitimacy,"
in S. Benhabib (ed.), *Democracy and Difference.* Princeton, NJ: Princeton UP,
pp. 67–94.

Bobbio, N. (1979). *Marxismo e Estado.* Rio de Janeiro: Graal.

—— (1986). *O Futuro da Democracia.* São Paulo: Paz e Terra.

Bóron, A. (1994). *Estado, capitalismo e democracia na América Latina.* São Paulo: Paz
e Terra.

Castoriadis, C. (1986). *As Encruzilhadas do Labirinto.* São Paulo: Paz e Terra.

Cohen, J. (1997). "Procedure and Substance in Deliberative Democracy," in
Deliberative Democracy. Cambridge, MA: MIT Press.

Crozier, M.; S. Huntington, and J. Watanuki, (1975). *The Crisis of Democracy: Report
on the Governability of Democracies to the Trilateral Commission.* New York: New
York UP.

Dagnino, E. (1994). *Os movimentos sociais e a emergência de uma nova noção de cidadania. Os anos 90: política e sociedade no Brasil.* São Paulo: Brasiliense.

Dahl, R. A. (1956). *A Preface to Democratic Theory.* Chicago: Chicago.

— (1971). *Polyarchy: Participation and Opposition.* New Haven, CT: Yale UP.

— (1991). *Democracy and its Critics.* New Haven, CT: Yale UP.

— (1998). *On Democracy.* New Haven: Yale UP.

Doimo, A. M. (1995). *A Vez e a Voz do Popular.* Rio de Janeiro: Relume Dumara.

Domingues, J. M. (1997). *Criatividade Social, Subjetividade Coletiva e a Modernidade Brasileira Contemporânea.* Rio de Janeiro: Contra-capa.

Downs, A. (1956). *An Economic Theory of Democracy.* New York: Harper.

Escobar, A., and S. Alvarez (1992). *The Making of Social Movements in Latin America: Identity, Strategy, and Democracy.* Boulder, CO: Westview Press.

Esping-Anderson, C. (1990). *The Three Worlds of Welfare Capitalism.* Princeton, NJ: Princeton UP.

Fung, A., and E. Wright (eds) (2003). *Deepening Democracy.* London: Verso.

Fraser, N. (1995). *Justice Interruptus.* London: Routledge.

Germani, G. (1971). *Política y sociedad en una época de transición; de la sociedad tradicional a la sociedad de masas.* Buenos Aires: Paidós.

Gramsci, A. (1973). *Letters from Prison.* New York: Harper & Row.

Grazia de Grazia (2001). *Experiências de Orçamento Participativo no Brasil, gestão municipal 1997/2000.* Rio de Janeiro.

Habermas, J. (1984). *The Theory of Communicative Action.* Boston, MD: Beacon Press.

— (1992). *Further Reflections on the Public Sphere. Habermas and the Public Sphere.* Cambridge, MA: MIT Press.

— (1995). *Between Facts and Norms.* Cambridge, MA: MIT Press.

Heller, P. (2000). "Degrees of Democracy: Some Comparative Lessons from India," *World Politics*, 52(4).

Huntington, S. P., Harvard University. Center for International Affairs (1968). *Political Order in Changing Societies.* New Haven, CT: Yale UP.

Jelin, E. and E. Hershberg (1996). *Constructing Democracy: Human Rights, Citizenship, and Society in Latin America.* Boulder, CO: Westview Press.

Kelsen, H. (1929). "Essência e Valor da Democracia," in H. Kelsen, *A Democracia.* São Paulo: Martins Fontes.

Lechner, N. (1988). *Los Patios Interiores de la Democracia.* Mexico: Fondo de Cultura Economica.

Lefort, C. (1986). *Pensando o Político.* São Paulo: Paz e Terra.

Lenin, V. [1917] (1987). *O Estado e a Revolução.* São Paulo: Hucitec.

Lijphart, A. (1984). *Democracies. Patterns of Majoritarian and Consensus Government in Twenty-One Countries.* New Haven, CT: Yale UP.

MacPherson, C. B. and Canadian Broadcasting Corporation (1966). *The Real World of Democracy.* New York, Oxford: Oxford UP.

Manin, B. (1997). *The Principles of Representative Government.* Cambridge: Cambridge UP.

Mansbridge, J. J. (1990). *Beyond Self-Interest.* Chicago: Chicago UP.

Marramao, Giacomo (1995). *Poder e Secularização: as Categorias do Tempo.* São Paulo: Unesp.

Marx, Karl [1871] (1976). *Preface and Introduction to a Contribution to The Critique of Political Economy.* Pekin: Foreign Language Press.

Melucci, A. (1996). *Challenging Codes: Collective Action in the Information Age.* Cambridge: Cambridge UP.

Michels, R. (1949). *Political Parties.* Glencoe: Free Press.

Moore, B. (1966). *Social Origins of Dictatorship and Democracy: Lord and Peasant in the Making of the Modern World.* Boston, MD: Beacon Press.

Nun, J. (2000). *Democracia: gobierno del pueblo o gobierno de los politicos?* Buenos Aires: Fondo de Cultura.

O'Donnell, G. A. (1973). *Modernization and Bureaucratic-Authoritarianism: Studies in South American Politics.* Berkeley: Institute of International Studies, University of California.

O'Donnell, G., Schmitter, *et al.* (1986). *Transitions from Authoritarian Rule: Prospects for Democracy.* Baltimore, MD: Johns Hopkins UP.

Pateman, C. (1970). *Participation and Democratic Theory.* Cambridge: Cambridge UP.

Przeworski, A. (1984). "Amas a Incerteza e Serás Democrático," *Novos Estudos Cebrap*, 9: 36–46.

— (1985). *Capitalism and Social Democracy.* Cambridge: Cambridge UP.

Przeworski, A., S. Stokes, *et al.* (1999). *Democracy, Accountability and Representation.* Cambridge: Cambridge UP.

Sabel, C. *et al.* (1999). "After Backyard Environmentalism," *The New Democracy Forum.* www.polisci-mit.edu.

Sabel, C., J. Zeitlin, *et al.* (1997). *World of Possibilities: Flexibility and Mass Production in Western Industrialization.* Paris; Cambridge; New York: Maison des sciences de l'homme; Cambridge UP.

Sader, E. (1988). *Quando Novos Personagens Entraram em Cena.* São Paulo: Paz e Terra.

Santos, Boaventura de Sousa (1990). *Estado e Sociedade em Portugal (1974–1988),* Porto: Afrontamento.

— (1995). *Toward a New Common Sense: Law, Science and Politics in the Paradigmatic Transition.* New York: Routledge.

— (1998). *Reinventar a Democracia.* Lisbon: Gravida.

— (2000). *Crítica da Razão Indolente.* São Paulo: Cortez.

— (2002). *Toward a New Legal Common Sense: Law, Globalization and Emancipation.* London: Butterworths.

Schmitt, C. (1926). *The Crisis of Parliamentary Democracy.* Cambridge: MIT Press.

Schumpeter, J. A. (1942). *Capitalism, Socialism, and Democracy.* New York: Harper & Brothers.

Sen, Amartya (1999). "Democracy as a Universal Value," *Journal of Democracy*, 10(3): 3–17.

Shonfield, A. (1969). *Modern Capitalism: The Changing Balance of Public and Private*

Power. London and New York: Oxford UP.

Shonfield, A., and Z. Shonfield (1984). *In Defence of the Mixed Economy.* Oxford: Oxford UP.

Silva, M. K. (2001). *Construção da Participação Popular.* Departamento de Sociologia. Porto Alegre: UFRGS.

Thomas Isaac, T. M. and P. Heller (2002). "Decentralisation, Democracy and Development: People's Campaign for Decentralized Planning in Kerala," in A. Fung and E. Wright (eds), *Deepening Democracy.* London: Verso.

UAMPA (1986). *A participação popular na administração municipal.* Porto Alegre: UAMPA.

Wallerstein, Immanuel (2001). "Democracy, Capitalism and Transformation," Lecture presented at *Documenta 11.* Vienna, March 16.

Weber, Max [1919] (1978). *Economy and Society.* Berkeley: California UP.

Williams, R. (1981). *Culture.* Glasgow: Fontana.

Wood, E. M. (1996). *Democracy Against Capitalism.* Cambridge: Cambridge UP.

Young, I. M. (2000). *Inclusion and Democracy.* Oxford: Oxford UP.

Part I

SOCIAL MOVEMENTS
AND DEMOCRATIC ASPIRATIONS

Micro-Movements in India:
Toward a new Politics of
Participatory Democracy

D. L. Sheth

Just when the global discourse on democracy has become one-dimensional, purveying the neoliberal model of market democracy as the only universally desirable model, and when the Indian state has linked itself to the vertical hierarchy of global economic and political power, significant countervailing processes have emerged in the form of political and social movements at the grassroots, making new, provincial and national-level alliances aimed at countering the state's policies of globalization. Led by small groups of social activists, these movements have been active in different parts of India for over three decades, working on disparate issues, albeit all concerning the struggles of the economically marginalized and the socially excluded, poorer populations. In the 1990s, many of them came together and joined larger, worldwide alliances and forums protesting against the hegemonic policies of the institutions and organizations representing global economic and political power.

In this process of opposition to globalization, the micro-movements have begun to raise a new discourse on democracy and to invent political practices, expanding the arena of politics beyond the representational institutions of elections and political parties. Thus, although the micro-movements had been fighting politically on several issues concerning the poor long before they joined the debate on globalization, it is the challenge of globalization that has brought many of them together on common political platforms at the provincial and national levels, making issues of participatory democracy a part of their ongoing struggles. It is in this emergent context of globalization that this chapter analyzes the discourse and politics of micro-movements and their role in reinventing participatory democracy as a form of social action and political practice, creating new spaces and infusing deeper meaning into democracy in the globalizing world.

MOVEMENTS AND GLOBALIZATION

The micro-movements

The micro-movements in India represent a varied and complex phenomenon. They are variously referred to as "grassroots movements," social movements, non-party political formations, social-action groups, and movement-groups. In this chapter I shall use these terms interchangeably but the reference is specifically to a particular genre of social movements that became visible and acquired political salience in the mid-1970s and that have since been active on a variety of issues which, in their own perception, are—directly or indirectly—related to what they see as their long-term goal of democratizing development and transforming society (Kothari, 1984; Sethi, 1984; Sheth, 1984). These movement organizations differentiate themselves self-consciously and sharply from the welfare, philanthropic and such other non-political NGOs. Although there is no systematic survey, compilations made from different sources by researchers and guesstimates provided by observers in the field suggest a figure in the range of twenty to thirty thousand such movement groups in the country (Kapoor, 2000).

In order to understand the terms by which the movement groups conceive and articulate the idea of participatory democracy, it is important to know the context in which they emerged and the challenges they confronted in the initial phase of their formation. A large number of them existed as fragments of the earlier political and social movements that had their origins in the freedom movement but were subdued and dispersed soon after independence when the liberal, modernist, English-educated ruling elite began to dominate public discourse in India. These were the groups that had their lineage in the Gandhian, socialist, communist and social reform movements but, by and large, had stuck out as groups of party-independent social and political activists (Sheth and Sethi, 1991). They worked in small, stagnant spaces available to them at the periphery of electoral party politics. But within three decades of independence, new social and political spaces opened up for them as well as for several new groups of social activists. This became possible, ironically, with the decline of institutional politics, which began in the late 1960s, giving rise to several mass-based movements of protests (Kothari, Rajni, 1988b). The issues of these protests varied from rising prices to corruption. The protest movements, however, acquired increased momentum in the mid-1970s, the largest and, politically, highest-intensity movement among them being the one led by Jayaprakash Narayan (popularly known as the J.P. movement). Seen in this context, what we recognize today as movement groups emerged and were consolidated in spaces made available to them by the decline of mainstream institutions of representative democracy: the legislatures, elections, political parties, and trade unions. Although the decline had begun in the late 1960s, it became visible when the Emergency was imposed (1975–1977) by Mrs. Indira Gandhi (Rajni Kothari 1989).[1]

The role of political parties in inducting new groups into politics by waging struggles for their legal and political rights was considerably reduced. Their ability to politically process issues arising in the economy, society, and culture greatly declined. They also ceased to attract young, idealist youth to mainstream politics. The parties, having failed to convert the economic demands of the poor and the deprived into effective political demands, often tended to take recourse to ethnicizing and communalizing economic issues for electoral gains. The result was that the political process, which in the 1950s and 1960s had worked for the inclusion of an increasing number of new groups in electoral and party politics, was halted in the mid-1970s, keeping large sections of ex-untouchables, tribal peoples, the occupationally marginalized and economically extremely poor groups from among the ritually low-ranking Hindu castes, as well as the other poor and landless among the minorities, on the periphery of the mainstream of Indian politics. Of course, this did not affect their electoral participation, but it did reduce their political sense of citizenship, since their struggle did not find articulation in the representational arena of politics. The populations involved in this process of political alienation, however, were dispersed and fragmented in many dimensions besides that of class. For that reason their struggles did not find a political language, even in the discourse of the left parties. They were seen simply as unorganizable masses with unaggregable votes. In sum, the political parties—having prematurely given up the "movement" aspect of their activities soon after independence—increasingly became electoral machines operating with makeshift arrangements at the grassroots level at election time. The consequence was, among other things, the emergence of a mobilizational politics by popular movements outside the institutional politics of representation, often having recourse to direct-action politics in order to register their demands with the government (Kothari, Rajni 1988b).

The trade unions, which to begin with were like labor wings of the political parties, with little autonomy of their own, became virtual bargaining counters between people of the same class, supposedly representing different interests. The unions showed a complete incapacity to expand their activities in the growing informal and unorganized sector of the economy. Workers in the unorganized sector had little to offer, either electorally or in membership fees. Tired after long years of struggle, the union leadership had got used to a cushy lifestyle and to a mentally non-taxing bureaucratic mode of functioning (Pansay, 1981). The result was the formation of many new activist groups championing the cause of workers in the informal sector of the economy. They addressed not only the issue of wages but also problems of health, education and childcare for workers' families, their larger objective being to raise in them the awareness of their rights and build organizational capabilities to fight for their realization.

The legislatures, too, reflected the decline in wider politics. Gone were the days when a socialist leader such as Ram Manohar Lohia could raise and sustain a protracted debate on poverty in the Indian Parliament. The political discourse in the legislatures began to be increasingly dominated by narrow legalistic positions held by the executive, and often endorsed by the law courts, rather than being informed by issues emerging from democratic politics. The Indian Constitution, which was conceived not only as an instrument of governance but also as an agenda for independent India's social and political transformation, was now treated as a document sanitized of the flesh and blood of movement politics, which represented the democratic aspirations of the people. It is in this context that, in the decade following the emergency, several movement groups began to take recourse to public-interest litigation and to provide free legal-aid services to citizens whose rights were being violated both by law and order and development administration—in the process, infusing activism even into the law courts.

One important, if unanticipated, consequence of the decline of institutional politics was the revitalization of the old social movements, with some of them aiming their politics directly against the Emergency regime. The anti-emergency movements gave rise, especially in the period between the mid-1970s and 1980s, to thousands of *new* micro-movements in the country. These movements were led by young men and women, quite a few of whom left their professional careers to join. They took up issues and constituencies abandoned by political parties and trade unions, and those ill served by the bureaucracy. The organizational form they evolved for themselves was not of a political party or a pressure group. It was that of a civil-associational group, leading political struggles on issues articulated to them by the people themselves. The key concept they worked with was democratizing development through the empowerment of the people (Sethi, 1984).

The discourse of globalization

In the early 1990s, the grassroots movements confronted an entirely new set of terms justifying the hegemony of the newly established post-Cold War global order. Earlier, until the end of the Cold War, a significant section of grassroots movements in India were active in protesting against the exclusionary, elite-oriented development model that was conceived and sought to be made uniformly and universally applicable the world over, by the post-Second World War Bretton Woods institutions and their sponsor countries. These protests, however, were articulated largely in the context of the discourse developed by new social movements in the West where the nuclear and environmental threats produced by the Cold War, were more poignantly felt. It was through this process that the idea and the campaign for "alternative development" grew in the West. Although this idea had been propagated and practiced in India for a long time by Gandhian activists, after independence it was marginalized within the development discourse dominated by India's modernist ruling elite.

The whole discourse on development suddenly changed, globally and in India, when the notion of alternative development was analytically formulated and propagated by the various global groups, clubs, and commissions. Some concepts developed by these proponents of alternative development became buzzwords for activists in the new social movements: appropriate technology, small is beautiful (à la Schumacher), pedagogy of the oppressed (à la Paulo Freire), eco-friendly lifestyles, limits to growth (à la the Club of Rome) were but a few among them. This discourse of the new social movements in the West found a great deal of resonance among the social activists in India—particularly for the *a*-political, Westernized ones, for whom it had almost an emancipatory effect. It gave cultural meaning to their activism and even helped them rediscover their own alternativist, M. K. Gandhi.

The idea of alternative development found new votaries even in the consumerist core of Western societies during the Cold War, when the threat of nuclear holocaust loomed large and access to the world's fossil-oil resources was threatened by what was then described as the "oil crisis." Concerns were expressed in world policy forums about "Third World poverty." Strange though it may seem today, deep anxieties were felt and expressed about the growing consumption habits of the middle classes in these countries. For it was feared that they, combined with the hunger and poverty of their masses, might lead to state policies resulting in rapid depletion of the world's natural resources. The conventional argument for development was now made with several caveats, sourced from the theory of alternative development. Thus, *sustainability* became a key word and consumerism a "challenge" to cope with. Saving energy and finding alternative energy sources became an important consideration for policy-makers of development.

All this changed as the Cold War ended, effecting a large rupture in the (global) politics of discourse. And this, just when the idea of alternative development was about to acquire wider acceptability and had even begun to inform policy processes at the national and global levels. A new discourse descended on the scene, engulfing the political spaces that the new social movements in the West and the grassroots movements in India had created for themselves through working for decades on such issues as peace, and pro-poor, eco-friendly development. The new discourse made its entry rather dramatically as a triumphalist grand-narrative that, among other things, subsumed within it the old idea of Development (Wallgren, 1998). Its immediate, if temporary, effect was to make protests of the grassroots movements against the hegemonic Cold War model of Development and their assertions for alternative development sound shrill and cantankerous, if not vacuous.

This was the discourse of globalization. Conceived and led by the victors of the Cold War, it claimed to establish a new global order that would put an end to the old one that had kept the world "divided"—economically, culturally, and politically. In its place it not just promised but communicated a virtual experience (as if that world was upon us!) of the world becoming *one* economy, (possibly) *one* culture and (eventually) *one* polity! Such a world could do, globally, without the messy institutions of representational demo-cracy, even as such institutions were to be made mandatory internally for every individual country. It assured that this new global order would be managed by a set of global institutions (served by experts and freed from the cumbersome procedures of representational accountability), which, being set-up and controlled by the world's few "self-responsible" and "advanced" democracies, would guarantee peace and order to the whole world. Moreover, since the monopoly of violence (including its technology) would be withdrawn from a large number of individual and often "irresponsible" nation-states (whose *natural* location is in the South) and be placed collec-tively in the hands of a few nation-states, which also are "responsible" and "civilized" democracies (whose *natural* location is of course in the North), it not only will eliminate international wars but alleviate poverty wherever it exists. These outlandish ideological claims of globalization, made and prop-agated globally by the world's most powerful (G-8) countries, have been lapped up by large sections of the Indian middle class and by the media, as if they represented a policy package offered by some really existing and dem-ocratically legitimate World Government!

The counter-discourse of movements

The grassroots movements took quite some time to recover from the ideo-logical onslaught of globalism and to devise their own terms of discourse to counter it. This was mainly because, by the end of the Cold War and two decades after the emergency, the movement-groups were by and large frag-mented into an almost isomorphic existence, with each group fighting its own little battle independently. Quite a few had lost the élan of social trans-formation, having acquired for themselves a fairly stable and comfortable financial base. Much larger quantities of funds were now made available to them by the international donor agencies that had their own agenda for influencing the politics of discourse in peripheral countries. Most movement-groups had thus become routinized in their activities and func-tioned as NGO bureaucracies. In short, in the early 1990s, the scene of grassroots movements in India was marked by a widespread feeling of pes-simism among the observers and participants of the movements (Kothari,

1993). There were indeed some groups, largely of Gandhian, left and social-democratic lineage, who stuck it out and kept fighting their battles for rights and socio-economic reconstruction at the grassroots, thus tenaciously retaining their character as *movements*. They, however, did not function at their earlier high levels of energy and remained starved for funds.

All this changed, almost suddenly, in the mid-1990s, when protests against globalization led by the few movement groups that had kept the tradition of struggles alive during the period of drift acquired momentum, as different sections of the poor in India began to acutely feel globalization's adverse impact. It got a big fillip as many more groups responding to the pressures at the grassroots returned from their NGO existence to the fold of movements. This produced a high degree of convergence among different types of groups and movements on a wide range of issues concerning globalization. It revitalized the entire spectrum of grassroots movements in the country, giving rise to a new discourse *and* politics aimed at countering the forces of hegemonic globalization (Sheth, 1999; Kothari Smitu, 2001). What follows is an account of the terms in which the movements view and resist globalization.[2]

First, activists of grassroots movements see globalization as an incarnation of the old idea of Development (with a capital D), but as politically representing the institutions of global hegemonic power more explicitly and creating new forms of exclusion socially. Globalization thus has intensified and expanded the destructive forces of Development—forces that disrupt communities, cultures and livelihoods of the poor without offering them any viable and dignified alternative. Similarly, globalization, like the Development Establishment during the Cold War, works for the constituent elements of its power structure—the techno-scientific, bureaucratic, military, managerial and business elites and a small consumerist class.

Second, a section of social activists, particularly those who were relatively *a*-political but active in the alternative development movements earlier, have become acutely aware of the role that the *politics of discourse* plays globally and nationally, in influencing policy choices of governments and international organizations. Consequently, some of them now are participating actively in shaping the terms of discourse globally on such issues as biodiversity, global warming, the construction of big dams, regulations concerning international trade and intellectual property rights and so on. In this process, they have become active in a variety of global "conventions," forums, and campaigns opposing the policies of the global power structure as well as in building more durable transnational alliances with similar movements in other countries, both in the South and in the North. In performing this "global role" they often explicitly articulate their long-term objective in terms of building and sustaining institutional processes for global solidarity. Put differently, their aim is to create global politics of popular (civil

society) movements with a view to building an alternative institutional structure of global governance, based on democratic principles of political equality,
social justice, cultural diversity and non-violence, and ecological principles
of sustainability and maintaining biodiversity (Sheth *et al.*, 2002). Leading
this discourse globally, a group of Indian activists interpret global solidarity
in terms of the ancient Indian principle of Vasudhaiva Kutumbakam (Earth
is one family) and link it to Gandhi's vision of *swaraj* (self-governance) and
swadeshi (politics of establishing people's own control over their environment—economic, social and cultural) (Pratap, 2001). It is in this context that
the movements differentiate between the two types of politics they engage
in: politics of establishing global solidarity and of opposing contemporary
globalization, a distinction that conceptually has been aptly captured by
Boaventura de Sousa Santos as hegemonic vs. counter-hegemonic globalization (Santos, 1997).

Third, another type of movement, representing largely the left and social
democratic strands referred to earlier, see globalization as intensifying further
the already existing economic and social inequalities in the country (Sainath,
2000). Thus, while the votaries of globalization celebrate the growth of the
middle class, the social activists see this phenomenon quite differently. In their
view, the programs of economic reform being implemented as a part of the
globalization package have consolidated and enriched the old middle class.
The "growth" of this class, in their view, largely represents the rise in the purchasing power of the small middle class that emerged during colonial rule
and expanded during the initial four decades after Independence, covering
largely the upper and middle strata of the traditional social structure. The
Structural Adjustment Programs (SAP), implemented in the name of
economic reforms—the recipe dispensed by the global financial institutions
across the world—far from improving the living standards of the poor, have
pushed them further down the social and economic ladder, and below the
poverty line (Kumar, 2000). Indeed, some fragments of the traditional lower
social strata have entered the "middle class," but this has been due to long-
existing social policies of the State—like affirmative action. In fact, with the
state shrinking in the process of globalization, there has been a reversal of this
process.

The few avenues of upward mobility that the policies of the Indian state
had opened up for the disadvantageously located populations in the traditional social structure are now narrowing. The market is increasingly
becoming the only avenue for upward mobility, and that too is monopolized
by the upper strata of caste society, using their traditional status resources.
Thus, economic globalization offers ever increasing standards of living to
those entering the market with some entitlements usually available to
members of upper castes, given their resources: land, wealth, social privilege,
and education. For large segments of the population outside the charmed

circle of the market, and disadvantageously located in the traditional structure, it means malnutrition, semi-starvation, disease, and destitution. This
relationship of the traditional social structure and globalization is emphasized
by the movements but is, strangely, ignored in the academic debates on
globalization.

The movement activists thus find it astounding that the colonial-type
exploitation of primary producers (the vast populations of tribals, artisans,
small and marginal farmers and landless labor) by a small urban-industrial
elite, and their cognate groups of upper-caste rural elite persists, even thrives,
in the so-called open economy of the market. In brief, in India the market
economy, instead of making a dent in the iniquitous social structure, is being
absorbed by it.

Fourth, the movements reject the claim of the Indian state that, in the
process of globalization, it has been playing a positive role for the poor, giving
a "human face" to economic reforms. Far from enabling the poor to enter
and find places in the market, the state undermines their rights to hold on
to whatever sources of livelihood that are still available to them. In the view
of leaders of some urban movements for citizen rights, the Indian state, in
fact, systematically and blatantly discriminates between the rich and the poor
in the implementation of economic reforms (Kishwar, 2001a). The result is
that a vast population affected adversely by the market-led model of
economic globalization is today unable to make a forceful enough demand
in mainstream politics for their survival, let alone "development." As the
market moves from the fringes of the polity to its center, democratically conceived political authority is giving way to new notions of economic and
political "order" that are being derived from principles of corporate organization, which by their very nature are not in accord with the democratic
principle of representative accountability.

Fifth, the combined impact of the retreat of the state and of the globalizing economy is that the poorest among the poor are neither able to become
full wage-earners in the economy nor even full-fledged citizens in the polity.
For them there is no transitional pathway in sight that can lead them into
the market. Nor can they return to the old security of the subjugated, which
they arguably had in the traditional social order. They have even lost the
claims on the state that the bureaucratic-socialist state at least theoretically
conceded. In short, the social-systemic nature of their exclusion continues
under globalization as it did under Development. State policies that, until
recently, aimed at removing the structural barriers facing the poor and
bringing them in the mainstream of political economy are now being discarded as "market-unfriendly."

Finally, the new ideology of globalization has, in the view of the movements, made issues of poverty and social deprivation in the peripheral
countries of the world ever more unintelligible in the global discourse. Even

more, it has blunted the transformative edge of the new social movements, which were once (when they really were *new*) in the forefront of the alternative development movement in the West as well as globally. In effect, the agencies of hegemonic globalization have been able to produce *new* terms of justification for the old Development project, i.e., of retaining the political and economic hegemony of the few rich and militarily powerful countries globally and of a small metropolitan elite within the country. The result is, today, unlike during the Cold War, development is seen and measured in terms of the extent to which a country can "integrate" (read subjugate) its economy to the world economic (capitalist) system.

The global discourse of protests

A significant shift has also occurred in the way the movements in India relate to the global discourse of protests. The increasing focus on issues of "governance" in the current global discourse has, in their view, reduced the importance of issues pertaining to social and political transformation. This has resulted in the agencies of hegemonic globalization seeking, simultaneously, to depoliticize development and undermine democratic movements by co-opting, financially and politically, some protest movements in the developing countries and in the global arena. In the process, such issues as environment, gender, human rights and even democracy are being redefined in terms radically different from those that were developed by the grassroots movements in the earlier paradigm of alternative development. For example, the issue of the environment is no longer seen as the one involving a political process (and movements) for re-organizing the economy and social-cultural life locally and globally on the basis of *primary* ecological principles. Instead, ecological issues are being recast in constantly shifting terms of "tolerable limits" and "admissible costs" of environmental damage that is expected to occur in increasingly higher proportions with escalating rates of economic growth—which also are expected and considered desirable. If any "politics" is involved in this redefinition, it is about transferring environmental costs from one sector of the economy to the other or, even worse, from one region of the world to the other.

The issue of human rights is being viewed in terms of economic and foreign policy considerations of the rich and powerful countries. These considerations pertain not only to establishing their oligopolistic rule over the world, but also to guaranteeing the "smooth" functioning of the multinational corporations in the peripheral countries. This is to be achieved by compelling governments of the peripheral countries to yield to conditions and terms that the MNCs dictate and think are necessary for such functioning. In the process, the multinationals have emerged as powerful global actors, often more powerful and wealthy than many nation-states, that often undermine the fundamental human rights (the rights to livelihood, habitat and culture) of the poor in peripheral countries, but remain unaccountable to any agency of global governance or a nation-state.

Even some "international" human rights groups today seem to act as political pressure groups on behalf of the hegemonic global forces, seeking to prevent the peripheral countries from making certain policy choices in areas such as land-use, labor legislation, exports and so on. Although this is done in the name of universalizing human rights, the selectivity of issues and the targeting of particular countries often betray their particularistic nationalist (Western) bias. The result is that in this new hegemonic discourse the thinking on human rights has been dissociated from concerns like removing poverty, fulfilling basic human needs and social justice. Poverty is increasingly seen as the failure of poor people to create wealth, not as an issue of the rights of the poor. It is no longer seen as a moral issue. In other words, the global discourse on human rights has ceased to be a discourse regarding social and political transformations; it has, instead, become a discourse about possible conditions that the powerful, "developed" countries can impose over other countries, ostensibly for bringing about a global-legal regime of rights.

In this discourse on rights, it is conveniently assumed that the institutions of *global civil society* endowing global citizenship (political equality) to all, and the mechanisms of global governance ensuring accountability of transnational organizations and the rule of law in international behavior, have already evolved and are *in situ*. Such an assumption has made it easy for the global hegemonic powers to target some poor, peripheral countries "not playing ball" with them for human rights violations, even as they ignore similar violations by governments of the countries pliable to their hegemonic designs. It is a measure of their dominance over the global culture of protests that, despite practicing such double standards, the global hegemonic powers are able to claim "commitment" to universalization of human rights and, at the same time, keep transnational corporations outside the pale of the global human rights regime.

In the discourse on democracy, the idea of global governance is gaining ground but, paradoxically, democracy still continues to be viewed as the framework suitable for internal governance of nation-states and *not* for global governance. Hence it is not difficult for an organization like the WTO to function without reference to any principle of transparency or of representational accountability, as well as autonomously of the United Nations institutions, even when it sits in judgment on issues that fall under the purview of international law and representative bodies such as the ILO. The institutions of global governance thus are supposed to be *self*-responsible, not accountable outside their own ambit. They are "accountable" only to their sponsors who are often the few militarily and economically powerful nation-states.

In global feminist discourse, sensitivity about the social-structural, economic and cultural complexities faced by women in poor countries in securing their rights has vastly receded; in its place the legalist and metropolitan concerns about women's rights in a consumerist society have acquired prominence. Thus, grassroots activists have come to believe that hegemonic globalization is bent upon monopolizing the global discourse of protests, with a view to legitimizing the hegemonic global order and undermining the processes of social and political transformations.

In this globally homogenized culture of protests, some movement groups in India find it increasingly difficult to join international campaigns, even though they may share many of their concerns. To them, such campaigns often seek to undermine the country's national sovereignty and, in their global articulation of issues show insensitivity to the historical and cultural contexts in which the issues are embedded. As a result, these groups often even refrain from articulating their opposition to the Indian state in terms and forms that, in their view, may delegitimize the role of the state in society. This is done not so much for "nationalist" considerations as for the fear that it would undermine the by now established democratic political authority of the state in protecting the secular and democratic institutions in the country.

In short, movement activists in India view globalization as a new, post-Cold War *ideology* justifying the rule of a hegemonic *structure of global power* seeking to establish the monopoly of a few powerful countries over resources of the whole world. As such, they find globalization to be inimical to basic democratic and ecological values: liberty, equality, diversity and sustainability. To them, its impact on poorer countries has been to produce new and more dehumanized forms of exclusion and inequality—worse than those created by the Cold War Development model, or even by colonial rule. They are particularly concerned about its adverse impact on democracy in India. For, while the poorer classes have found a long-term stake in democracy and have begun to acquire their due share in governance, the power of the state (elected governments) itself is being denuded and undermined by the global power structure in collaboration with the country's metropolitan elites. In other words, they see globalization as undermining and delegitimizing institutions of democratic governance. They see it as a force that seeks to undo India's democratic revolution.

THE NEW POLITICS OF MOVEMENTS

Based on such an assessment of globalization's adverse impact both for development and democracy, the grassroots movements conceive their politics in the direction of achieving two interrelated goals: (a) re-politicizing development and (b) reinventing participatory democracy.

Re-politicizing development

The main effort of the movements today is to keep the debate on development alive but also to recast it in terms that can effectively counter global and national structures of power. They are thus formulating old issues of development in new political terms, although their objective remains the same as before, namely, those at the bottom of the pile find their rightful place as producers in the economy and citizens in the polity. Accordingly, they now view development as a *political* struggle for the people's participation in defining development goals and devising means to achieve them. Their view of development is thus a non-hegemonic, pluralistic process, in articulating which they use insights inductively arrived at and criteria that have evolved through their own struggles. In this process they increasingly relate the globally debated issues such as feminism, ecology and human rights to the economic, social and cultural specificities of India in which these issues are embedded. Consequently, their politics is about making development a bottom-upward process, directly relevant to and an edifying experience for the poor and the oppressed. Thus, rather than altogether "opting out" of development they now seek to change the *power relations* on which the conventional model of development is premised. In the process some *new elements,* essentially political in nature, have entered in the grassroots movements' thinking and practice of development.

First, the old post-colonial critique of development, which invoked premodern nostalgia, has ceased to appeal to a large section of these movements. Although that kind of critique still remains a hobbyhorse of some esoteric activist groups and academic clubs, it finds little resonance in the changed aspirations of India's poor. Thus, at one level, movement groups see the power elements of the old Development model being encoded in the hegemonic structure of globalization that they oppose. But at the level of national politics they see the idea of development as representing the political and economic rights of the people who have been denied access to it because of their disadvantageous locations in the power structure. Hence they problematize development, seeking to create a politics for changing power relations in society. This change in perspective was effectively articulated by a well-known social activist, Aruna Roy, when she left a development NGO in the mid-1980s to found a movement group. According to her, the need of the time was to "redefine the paradigm of development—to see the whole process of development from a different perspective." And such a change in perspective would, she held, enable social activists to see development for what it really is, i.e., a political process. In her words: "Development is politics and there can be no development without political will [...]. In fact all acts of social and economic living are determined by the nature of politics" (Roy, Aruna, 1996a).

Second, the change in perspective was also a response to the change in the post–Cold War global politics of development. Movement groups in India now have a better understanding of the global politics of development. With the global development establishment having openly and officially given up its old promise of universalizing development for *all,* they are now able to see the real face of global hegemonic power. They are, therefore, not surprised that it has dismantled the Cold War structures of aid and assistance, and in their place a new global economic regime of trade and fiscal control has been set up. The movements see this change as representing a new political agenda on the part of the global power structure that aims at the dispersal of state control over the economies of the peripheral countries on the one hand, and the centralization of global political and military power in the hands of the world's already rich and powerful countries on the other. They see this as forming the basis for global hegemony today, through which these countries seek to maintain international economic and political stability under the continuing, and rather intensifying, conditions of inequality among and within nations.

This awareness has led some movement groups to form transnational alliances aimed at democratizing the global power structure. For example, quite a few movement groups in India have been actively associated with such counter-hegemonic global initiatives as the Convention on Biodiversity, Agenda 21, World Commission on Dams, Alliance for Comprehensive Democracy and so on. These initiatives are not just confined to the transcendental global space. They are concretely embodied in their activities at the national and local levels in the form of disseminating awareness and activating organizations at the grassroots level to identify and oppose specific policies, programs, and legislations meant to expand hegemonic global power.[3]

Third, all types of grassroots groups today, including even some conventional development NGOs, articulate basic issues of development in the framework of rights. For example, they no longer view poverty purely as an economic problem. They see it as a function of social-structural locations of the poor, because of which they are excluded from development (which is guarded by the legal, political, and economic immunities it provides to its insiders) and are imprisoned in poverty (the world constituted of vulnerabilities and exposures to exploitation for its politically unorganized and economically marginalized inhabitants). They do not, however, perceive the division between the two worlds in the one-dimensional terms of polarization between two economic classes. Their mobilizational strategies, therefore, focus on the new social-political formations that combine the categories of class, caste, ethnicity, and gender.

Let me illustrate this point briefly with reference to the human rights, the ecology, and the women's movements. The issue of human rights as viewed by the activists of several human rights groups is not limited to the conventional legal notion of civil liberties; it extends to situations in which individuals and groups are denied satisfaction of their basic needs. It is in this context that they articulate the issue of poverty in terms of rights and entitlements (e.g., the right to work) that the poor must have as citizens and as human beings. The politics of micro-movements, therefore, lies not merely in fighting particular infringements on the legal rights of citizens but in creating and expanding new political and civic spaces for them by converting the survival and development needs of the poor and the deprived into struggles for their economic, political, and cultural rights, and these not only of individuals *qua* individuals but of groups and communities surviving on the margins of the civil society. In the process, these movement activists link rights of access to and benefits from the development process with the issues of ethnic identity and human dignity, and view the satisfaction of material needs as a pursuit not detached from the spiritual and cultural aspects of human existence. This is why several social-action groups whose self-image is not of being human rights groups almost routinely take up issues of rights and cooperate with larger human rights movements.

Similarly, the ecology movements at the grassroots do not view ecology as merely a cost factor in development, as some development specialists do. Nor are they interested in specifying the tolerable levels of ecological destruction necessary for achieving higher levels of economic development, as do the policies of hegemonic globalization. Instead, they view ecology as a basic principle of human existence, which, if reactivated, can yield higher level principles for reorganizing the economy in a humane way and refocus development in terms of well being, in which, to use Gandhi's well-known phrase, "everyone shall have enough to satisfy one's need, but not greed."

The activists of the women's movements lately have been defining their problem not merely in terms of achieving equal benefits and access for women in the present system. They self-consciously take up such issues mainly for finding entry points to the submerged world of Indian womanhood; but their long-term goal, as they put it, is to change the working of the gender principle itself in the economy and society, such that both society and the economy become more just and humane. They find the ecological worldview of the movements more aligned with the feminine principle. The fusion of the ecological and gender principles, they argue, is conducive for a more humane economic and political organization of the society than that of Development, which, in their view, is founded on the principle of male domination over all aspects of human life and nature (Shiva, 1988). Their project, often working in tandem with the human rights and ecology movements, is thus to change the forms of organization and consciousness in society.

Guided by this broad perspective, movements are often able to forge links with each other in fighting for issues at the grassroots. It is not accidental

that ecology movements such as the Chipko movement have a large participation of women, and that in the Bodhgaya movement for the rights of the
landless in Bihar, women play significant leadership roles. Women are in the
forefront of the movements fighting for the rights of the population displaced by development projects, especially in Madhya Pradesh and
Maharashtra. Similarly, human rights organizations often team up with
women's organizations on issues of dowry, *sati*, rape, and equal wages.
Similarly, activists in women's groups play an active role in mobilizing and
assisting the victims of the Bhopal chemical disaster. At no time in independent India, in the movements led by the parties and trade unions, was
there ever such a high degree and such a sustained level of participation by
women as one witnesses today in the non-party political movements at the
grassroots.[4]

Fourth, the movements now see more clearly that the roots of rural poverty
lie in the pattern of urban growth in India. This has, among other things,
led to greater interaction and building of new organizational linkages
between the city-based and village-based social-action groups. Further, the
movements now realize the inconsequentiality of the established wisdom of
"inputs" serving as a major factor in rural development. This, in their view,
only represents a partial and lopsided understanding of the problem of rural
development. For making "inputs" available to poor farmers is more of a
political than an economic problem. The experience thus far is that it has
not helped a large majority of the poor who lack the economic and organizational capacity to receive and use inputs such as credit, seeds, fertilizers,
irrigation, and so on. These inputs are simply swallowed up by the upper
stratum of the rural society. So, the focus of their activity is now on creating
capabilities of self-development among the rural poor, even as they fight for
their rights to create and secure resources for collective development.

Thus, by redefining issues of development in *political* terms, the groups
working separately on different issues such as gender, ecology, and human
rights, or in the areas of health and education, are now conceiving their activities in more generic terms, as a form of social and political action aimed at
countering hegemonic power structures at all levels—locally, nationally, and
globally. An important consequence of this change in perspective was that
the grassroots movements, which were in a state of fragmentation and low
morale at the end of 1980s, began to regroup and arrive at common platforms on the issue of globalization. In the mid-1990s this led to the launching
of several new nationwide campaigns and to the formation of organization-
ally more durable coalitions and alliances. Among many such initiatives the
most effective and widespread in recent years has been the campaign for the
right to information—a series of local-level struggles for securing correct wages
for laborers working in public construction works for drought relief, culmi-
nating in a successful nationwide campaign for the right to information. The

older, ongoing movement of the 1980s, the Narmada Bachao Andolan, got a new boost and gave birth to a broad-based alliance of a number of social movements and organizations active at different levels and in different parts of the country. This alliance, known as the National Alliance for People's Movements (NAPM) has been launching, supporting and coordinating several campaigns on a more or less regular basis, protesting against programs and projects of the government and the MNCs representing the policies of hegemonic globalization. There have been many more such initiatives, but more recent ones among them include: A Campaign for People's Control over Natural Resources comprising several organizations active in rural and tribal areas covering about thirteen Indian states; the movement called There Is An Alternative, led by, among others, two previous prime ministers of India; The Living Democracy Movement for linking local-democracy decision-making to maintaining biodiversity; the movement for nuclear disarmament called the Coalition for Nuclear Disarmament and Peace, and so on. Although some of the above movements will be described in some detail in the next section, the point of mentioning these here is to show how the challenge of globalization has politically revitalized the scene of social movements in India which, by the end of the 1980s, was losing both momentum and direction, and, more interestingly, how it became possible for these movements to sustain their politics at a higher level of intensity, in the process recovering the hope of initiating a long-term politics of non-cooperation and a withdrawal of legitimation from the dominant power structures.

To sum up, the politics of different groups and movements, which began to converge in the mid-1990s, have acquired a common direction and a fairly durable organizational base. The convergence has been attained on the point of resisting the ongoing efforts of the bureaucratic, technocratic and the metropolitan elites to support policies of globalization and to depoliticize development. For, in their view, it is only through the politicization of the poor that they can counter the negative impact of globalization and make development a just and equitable process and a collectively edifying experience. Thus, by establishing, both conceptually and in practice, linkages between the issues of development and democracy the grassroots movements have begun to articulate their politics in terms of participatory democracy.

Reinventing participatory democracy

In theoretical discussions and in the practice of representational politics, participatory democracy has been treated, respectively, as a para-political idea and a peripheral political activity—a desirable but not an essential characteristic of a modern democracy. It is in the politics of grassroots movements, where the scope of democracy is being actively searched and expanded through their everyday political struggles, that participatory democracy is conceived as not just desirable but a necessary organizational form and political practice. Under the conditions of globalization, where the national-level institutions of representation are being subordinated to hegemonic global power with the structures of political and economic decision-making becoming more remote—even alienated—from people, the movements' continuing politics of participatory democracy has acquired a new relevance.

Participatory democracy and political theory

In contemporary democratic theory the notion of political participation is articulated in terms of political obligations and the legal-constitutional rights of citizens with respect to electing representative governments and ensuring their democratic functioning (Almond and Verba, 1963; Milbrath, 1965). By conceiving participation in the passive terms of limiting citizens' roles and activities to the institutional arena of elections, parties and pressure groups, the theory secures (or at least seeks to provide justifications for securing) the decision-making procedures of representative governments from the high-intensity politics of mass mobilization and direct action, which the occasionally surfacing popular movements generate in a representative democracy.

This indeed has succeeded to a large extent in lending institutional stability and political legitimacy to liberal representative democracy, making it appear as if it is the only natural form that democracy can have. But it has, at the same time, bogged down the theory's political imagination to pragmatic concerns of the old, "actually existing" democracies of the West. In the process, it has pre-empted options of the new and growing democracies to evolve and experiment with institutional alternatives for deepening democracy and choosing forms appropriate to their own respective cultural and historical contexts. Even more, the theory, by persistently treating liberal representative democracy as the ultimate form of democracy, has encouraged the view that in it, humankind has achieved the highest state of political development beyond and outside of which no democratic possibility exists. This even emboldened a North American political thinker to see the arrival and universalization of liberal democracy as heralding the end of history (Fukuyama, 1992).

This high-intensity discourse sustained throughout the Cold War has, ironically, produced an array of theoretical arguments that has succeeded in keeping representative democracy at the level of what Boaventura de Sousa Santos aptly describes as low-intensity democracy—which probably also suits the contemporary politics of hegemonic globalization (Santos, 1999). This, however, has resulted in a major theoretical casualty: that of pushing—if not altogether discarding—the concept of participatory democracy on to the margins of democratic theory.

Keeping democracy a low-intensity national-level operation may be conducive to the integration of the world (capitalist) economy, for it helps the
national governments of peripheral countries to disperse and dispel popular
democratic movements opposing the implementation of structural adjustments and other policies handed down to them by the global power structure.
But it is precisely for this reason that peripheral countries of the world undergoing globalization need to create a strong infrastructure of democracy at the
grassroots, without which their democracies cannot survive at the nation-state
level; worse, it may even endanger the very survival of their poor citizens.

Two moves made by the theorists of representative democracy have made
it possible, on the one side, to incorporate the concept of participation within
the theory's structural-functional paradigm (i.e., participation conceived as
a particular form of political behavior of citizens through which they elect
governments and are expected to keep their functioning on a democratic
track by working through their representatives), and, on the other, to treat
participatory democracy either as an archaic form of governance or an
impractical ideal that, if actually practiced—or even experimented with—is
fraught with dangerous consequences for democracy itself.

The first argument is elaborated through historicizing democracy in linear,
evolutionary terms. It traces the history of democracy from its origin in the
Athenian city-state, where it functioned as a direct, participatory democracy,
through the successive forms it assumed, until it acquired a complexly evolved
form of representative democracy—making it possible to function at a much
larger scale, such as that of a nation-state (sometimes the state of a continental size). This transmutation has in its view equipped representative-liberal
democracy to function even at a global scale and to carry out a plethora of
programs and policies pertaining to every aspect of lives of its citizens (Dahl,
1989: 1–24).

The point of this exercise, it seems, is to show that the beliefs and practices historically associated with the participatory democracy of a city-state
have no relevance today for a democracy located in the nation-state and even
less for tomorrow, when it is likely to encompass the whole globe as its territorial domain. Participatory democracy, the theory concedes, is indeed a
noble idea and some of its elements ought to be functionally incorporated
in representative democracy. But it is a regression to think of citizens directly
controlling and participating in governmental decision-making and may even
turn out to be a recipe for disaster in today's world. In the derivative theoretical discourse of Indian democracy, this fixing of participatory democracy
to the dead and gone past of the West has delegitimized any historical-
theoretical exploration premised on its existence in India's past. Hence the
idea of democracy as symbolized in the concept of the village republic is
treated by the Indian political theorists as an atavistic idea, not deserving any
serious theoretical discussion.

The other argument—unlike the previous one, which views democracy's history in structural-functional terms—is made in normative-analytical terms. It seems to be based on the fear of romantic appeal (utopian images) that the idea of participatory democracy evokes. In the view of those advancing this argument, propagating the ideal of participatory democracy often promotes simple, populist ideas about democracy. They further argue that the proponents of participatory democracy fail to recognize the fact that modern governments have to routinely depend in their decision-making on specialists and professional experts; the issues involved are so complex and technical in nature that they are beyond the grasp even of elected representatives, let alone ordinary citizens. Concepts such as direct or participatory democracy only serve as a distraction to the theorization of democracy for the globalizing world (Schmitter, 1999). A section of Indian elites, who believe that meritocracy provides a better form of democracy and good governance, has always sought political support for their position in this argument. They vociferously argue that for preserving institutional norms of representative democracy it is necessary to strictly limit, procedurally and structurally, the powers of elected representatives through the legal-rational institutions of bureaucracy and the judiciary. In their view, giving legitimacy to the idea of participatory democracy would only further expose representative institutions to majoritarian and populist pressures, often making for bad and irrational decisions that are not usually in the public interest. It was the dominance of this discourse in India during the initial decades after independence that allowed the consolidation of the hegemonic rule, albeit democratically consented, of a small social-political minority consisting of urban and English-educated members of the upper castes. They occupied a large number of positions in different sectors and institutions of the state, especially higher in the bureaucracy and judiciary, for over forty years after Independence. What had become an established, common sense view of governing India, however, began to be challenged by the end of the 1970s, when the movements of subaltern classes gained strength both in electoral politics and in civil society (Sheth, 1995).

The movements' politics of participatory democracy

The idea of participatory democracy was central to Gandhi's political thinking and practice, and inspired many activists of the freedom movement. He articulated this idea through the concepts of *swaraj* (self-governance) and *swadeshi* (community's control over resources) and by invoking the imagery of the "village republic" (*gram swaraj*) as representing India's democratic tradition.[5] These formulations were, however, stoutly rejected and virtually banished from mainstream political discourse after independence as representing Gandhi's impractical idealism. The idea of participatory democracy has, however, not only been kept alive but has developed conceptually and in practice by a section of grassroots activists who draw liberally on Gandhi's economic and political thinking—although many of them may not want to wear the Gandhian badge (Bakshi, 1998). In a different political and ideological context, M. N. Roy had critiqued representative form of democracy and pleaded for participative democracy. Based on his vision of participative democracy, Roy had prepared a detailed proposal for Constitution of Free India (Roy, M. N., 1960). These proposals, which did not receive any serious response in the then prevailing nationalist politics, have now been revived and reformulated by some activist groups in the changed context of globalization (Tarkunde, 2003).

The first comprehensive and politically effective proposal on participatory democracy for Independent India, however, came from Jayaprakash Narayan (J.P.). A popular socialist leader of the independence movement, J.P. joined the Gandhian movement about five years after independence. He raised the political profile of the movement high when, in 1954, he made a public pronouncement of dedicating his whole life to the movement, in his words, to "the Gandhian way." The issue of deepening democracy was central to his agenda for the movement, without which, he believed, only elite rule will perpetuate in the name of democracy.[6] This concern found a lasting expression in his treatise on non-party democracy in 1959 (Narayan, 1959). He critiqued the idea of representation by political parties and argued for a more participative and comprehensive form of democracy constituting a broad democratic base from which the power will flow upward to units using power allocated to them by the units below, on conditions of accountability and transparency. The amount and kind of power to be allocated to a higher unit will be as per the requirement of the unit. J.P.'s thesis, however, made little impact beyond Gandhian circles. It in fact drew sharp criticism from the liberal democratic theorists as well as the party politicians who saw it as a naïve exercise of an idealist, unaware of its dangerous consequences for democracy itself (Kothari, 1960). The document was virtually "withdrawn" from public discourse, but within two years J.P. came up with a politically more potent and comprehensive statement on the issue of participatory democracy (Narayan, 1961). Here J.P. rebutted the arguments of his critics and elaborated his basic thesis by theoretically and historically establishing the need for a comprehensive democracy, where both economic and political power is primarily held *and* exercised directly by the people from the base of the polity. It did not take very long for his vision of democracy to find a powerful political expression. He launched a massive movement in the early 1970s with the aim of, in his own coinage, restoring people's power (*lokshakti*) in democracy (Narayan, 1975). This idea of people's power fired the imagination of many young women and men, which, besides upstaging the government in Delhi, gave rise to a new genre of micro-movements, celebrated and characterized by theorists as the "non-party political process" (Kothari, 1984). This genre of movement groups that emerged from what became known as the "J.P. movement" has since been working at the grass-roots. They articulate participatory democracy in terms of the empowerment of people through everyday struggles for their rights as well as through harnessing their collective efforts to developing local resources for collective well being.

The most remarkable in this genre was the movement launched by Chhatra-Yuva Sangarsh Vahini in 1978, known as the Bodh Gaya Movement. It has since served as a source of inspiration nationally for many movement groups. This movement succeeded in seizing about ten thousand acres of land from the religious establishment in Bodhgaya, a district in Bihar, through non-violent direct action. The land was legally redistributed among families of tillers who were attached to the land for generations. In the course of redistribution, legal entitlements to land were given equally to women and men. More important than its outcome in the form of land redistribution was the process of change through which the movement's larger objectives and values of political and social transformation were kept alive, communicated, and partially institutionalized, affecting the lives of about three thousand participant households in the area. In fact the movement group ensured that the *dalits* (ex-untouchables), for whose land rights the movement was launched, remained in the forefront and among them the women performed crucial leadership roles. The movement created a new hope among social-action groups all over the country about the efficacy of using non-violent militancy as a means for social and economic transformation.[7]

Another, and equally significant, movement of the same genre in recent years has been the one led by Tarun Bharat Sangh. It is known to the outside world through its Magsaysay award-winning leader, Rajendra Singh. He joined and has revitalized the organization through his work since 1985 in the villages of Rajasthan. He and members of his group started work with a deep conviction that the people have the knowledge and the capacity to develop and manage their affairs collectively for their own well-being (that is how he saw J.P.'s message of "power to the people"), provided they stop looking to the government for help and become motivated to work on their own. In Singh's own words: "our fight [is] against the state for communities to have a say in their development. [...] Administrative system [...] tries to foist its own vision of development on communities, without bothering to find out what people need. In fact, it is a myth that development is for people, it is actually anti-people [...]. Schooled in the ideals of Jayaprakash Narayan and Acharya Vinoba Bhave working for social change was an obvious choice [for us]" (Singh, 2001).

Beginning their work in the mid-1980s, this group of social activists was able to establish, in the course of a decade and a half, a self-governing system of land and water management in about seven hundred villages in the perpetually drought-affected and poverty-ridden villages of Rajasthan. This was achieved through reviving the recessive knowledge and skills of the people themselves of building water-harvesting structures known locally as Johads. In this process the villagers not only went ahead and built a network of check-dams and small reservoirs without government help but took decisions, bypassing the government, on land use in the area, built boundary walls around common lands and afforested a huge, barren landmass. This became possible due to the social confidence that the people could recover with the water becoming available to them by their own efforts. The old forms of economic interdependence and social cooperation were now recovered and imbued with new economic and democratic political meanings. In Singh's eyes, this is a small, perhaps a short-lived, achievement. He sees a long political battle ahead for achieving real democracy for the people. In his words: "Unfortunately, the state in India does not appreciate communities trying to help themselves. If people start participating in development and questioning the money that ostensibly is being spent on them, it makes it difficult for those who run the system. For a bureaucracy schooled in the colonial tradition of ruling rather than working with people, grassroots democracy is an alien concept. So instead of development being a collaborative effort between people and the state, it is actually people versus the state" (Singh, 2001).

But the government saw all this quite differently, as an encroachment on its territory and a usurpation of its functions. The administration slapped hundreds of legal cases on the movement group and the villagers and threatened them with demolition of the dams, since they were built without the government's permission and the guidance of experts ("civil engineers"). Here is where the grassroot group's politics of mass mobilization and joining larger alliances helped: it became possible for the group, along with the villagers, to withstand the pressure and ultimately get the government to endorse the mode of self-governance they had evolved through their political struggles on the ground. Again, Rajendra Singh sees this as a temporary reprieve obtained by the winning of a battle, not a war. In his words: "Unless the communities are empowered and encouraged to develop stakes in development, winning the war is going to be difficult" (Singh, 2001).[8]

In the process of countering hegemonic globalization, the movements have added another dimension to their politics. This is about making law an important site of social and political action/struggle. In the course of implementing the structural adjustment programs and other globalization-related policies, the state has been actively assisting the Indian and multinational corporations to acquire land and other resources of the villages at a nominal cost. This involves withdrawing constitutional guarantees given to tribals regarding the alienation of their land and, in effect, extending such guarantees to MNCs as making land, water, and forest resources available to them cheaply, but at a great cost to the livelihood of the people and the ecology of the area. The enactment or implementation of such legislation and government orders are now challenged by the movement groups not just in the law courts but in the larger arena of civil society. The proceedings of public interest litigations, which earlier had remained by and large confined to the courtrooms as contentions between the state and social-legal activists, have now become matters of direct concern and involvement for the people themselves, constituting everyday politics of the movement groups.

In the process, new participatory forums have been evolved, such as documenting the effects of specific government policies and legislation on the people through participatory surveys and studies carried out jointly by social activists (including some professionals among them) and the people themselves, and disseminating results to the wider public, including the media. The most effective and innovative mode of consciousness-raising and of political mobilization developed in this process, and which has now become a common practice for movement groups all over the country, is organizing big walkathons *(Pad yatras)*. The *Pad yatras* are usually organized by activists representing organizations from different parts of the country that share a common perspective on and concern for a particular issue that they together wish to highlight for mobilizing public opinion. They walk long distances along with the people drawn from different locales who face a similar problem in a specific area—for example, a threat posed to their livelihood by a project of the government or an MNC. In the course of the walk they stop in villages and interact with people, show films, and stage plays that highlight the issues.

One among many such cases is the movement against bauxite mining in tribal areas of Vishaka in Andhra Pradesh. In 1991 a walkathon known as the *manya prante chaitanya yatra*, a consciousness-raising walk for an area facing ecological destruction, was organized by a couple of movement groups active in the area, SAMTA and SAKTI. Over fifty other social-action groups joined the march and prepared a report on the ecological destruction that they saw and experienced during the march. The report described how the region had come under a severe threat to its ecology and to the livelihood of people inhabiting it and how if the damage was not controlled it could cause ecological disaster for the entire peninsula of south India. The report also spoke of the displacement of 50,000 tribals, the massive deforestation and the problem of flash floods and silting that resulted.[9]

This *Chaitanya yatra* has since served as a basis for a decade-long and continuing movement for legal and social action in the state of Andhra Pradesh. During the last five years it has expanded widely, covering many other similar issues and movement groups working on them from different parts of the country. What is of interest here is the kind of politics the movement has developed for expanding its activities and sustaining itself for so long. At one level, through taking the issue of a threat to people's livelihoods to the law courts, it has created a nationwide alliance of similar movements, thus garnering a wider support base for its activities. Working through the alliance it has been able to project its work in the national media and contribute to building solidarity among movement groups. At another more crucial level the movement, through its mobilizational and consciousness-raising marches and myriad other activities, has been able to motivate people of the area to build their own community-based organizations, which now assert self-governance as a right and as the preferred way to protect and develop the means of their livelihood and culture.

The participative methodology of preparing and disseminating reports, which involved self-reporting by members of the affected communities as well as technical and financial input from well-known NGOs, movement leaders and reputed activist-professionals, succeeded in drawing nationwide attention to the usurpation, ostensibly by legal means, of tribal lands by corporations, which deprived the people of their livelihoods, identity, and culture.[10]

It was in the background of the sustained struggles, which the groups in the area carried on for about a decade, that it became possible for one of them, SAMTA, to go to the Supreme Court of India with a plea to close the calcite mines in the area because they threatened to uproot the local population and endangered the ecology of the area. Because the tribals were protected by Schedule Five of the Constitution against the alienation of their lands, and the mine threatened to destroy their livelihoods and, even more, violated their fundamental right to life given by the Indian Constitution to all citizens, SAMTA pleaded that the mine should be closed. Largely accepting the SAMTA plea, the Supreme Court of India gave a 400-page judgment in 1997, outlining the steps that needed to be taken to make the tribals *partners in the development* of scheduled areas (i.e., constitutionally protected areas populated by tribals). The court ruled that all private and public sector organizations functioning in these areas should give not less than 20 per cent of their jobs to local people and an equal amount of seats to their children in educational institutions. The court also stipulated that each industrial unit in the area part with 20 per cent of its profit and make it available for the kind of development that would be in the interest of the local people.

In essence the court recognized the local people as legal stakeholders in the development of the area in which they live. It made the people's participation in development necessary, and their claim to a share in the benefits of development legitimate. This landmark judgment, known in India as the SAMTA judgment, has since become a rallying point around which many struggles are now waged jointly by action groups in the country: first, to secure implementation of the court's mandatory rulings as well as its recommendatory provisions; second, to test and expand legal and juridical meanings of the judgment for wider application; third, to use it politically for creating a bulwark of resistance to prevent implementation of the government policy that, as a part of the globalization package and under pressure from multi-nationals, seeks to withdraw guarantees given by the Constitution to the people under its Fifth Schedule.

In the course of the six years since the Supreme Court's judgment on this, a number of marches, demonstrations and conventions have been held in different parts of the country, on a more or less regular basis by social movement groups. One remarkable example of how the SAMTA judgment energized the micro-movements, which had struggled for a long time without making much headway in securing the ecological rights of the local (tribal) communities, is the case of the Adivasi movement in the Rayagada district of Orissa. The movement, aided and assisted by the National Committee for Protection of Natural Resources (NCPNR), itself a network of over forty social-action groups, succeeded in highlighting the plight of the Rayagada tribals and the injustice done to them by forcibly acquiring their lands for bauxite mining. The movement effectively used the SAMTA judgment in making the government officials aware of their obligation to implement the Supreme Court judgment in Orissa (Hiremath, S. R., *et al.*, 2001).

Different from the above campaign for preventing the government from enacting certain kinds of legislation, another movement seeks to compel the government to implement its own rules and regulations honestly and effi-ciently. Its politics center around holding public hearings and people's courts with a view to creating political and social sanctions for the local govern-ment administration to compel it to observe and make public the rules and regulations by which it is governed in its implementation of development programs. It began as a struggle launched by a mass-based organization in a village in Rajasthan founded by Aruna Roy, who gave up her job in the Indian Administrative Services (IAS) "to work with the people." The organ-ization, named Mazdoor Kisan Shakti Sangathan (MKSS [Union for Empowerment of Peasants and Workers]), addressed the problem most acutely felt by the people themselves—government officials were cheating laborers working on government construction sites by not paying them minimum wages fixed by the government.[11] Besides being underpaid, the people in the area did not get enough work through the year, because sanc-tioned development programs often remained on paper with the allocated money being pocketed by government officials and elected leaders. Since all this was done with the knowledge of the "higher-ups," no amount of peti-tioning helped; only direct democratic action by the people was seen as a possible remedy. In December 1994, several public hearings, Jan Sunvai, were held by MKSS, where the workers were encouraged to speak out about their problems with the bureaucracy—especially narrating specific details about the underpayment of wages and unimplemented development schemes—in the presence of local journalists and people of surrounding villages from different walks of life. It took several public hearings to persuade some among the accused parties—the contractors, engineers and local elected leaders—to accept the MKSS invitation asking them to avail themselves of the opportunity of their self-defense by responding to people's charges of corruption. All this had little impact on the administration and for people outside the local area until a marathon 40 day sit-in, a *dharna*, was organized in the nearby town of Beawar in 1996, followed by another series of public hearings, demonstrations, and processions. This compelled the Rajasthan government to amend the Panchayati Raj Act, entitling citizens to get certified copies of bills and vouchers of payments made and the muster-rolls showing the names of laborers employed (payments were often made by forged bills and shown against fictitious names of people who never worked on the site). This grew into a state-level campaign demanding that the Rajasthan government pass comprehensive legislation granting citizens and organizations the right to information. This culminated in organizing a nationwide campaign—the National Campaign for People's Right to Information—which prepared model legislation for the Right to Information. By extensively canvassing a model bill, the campaign succeeded with about half a dozen state assemblies passing similar legislations. Eventually, the Parliament too was forced to pass such a bill, though in a vastly diluted and truncated form. As might be expected, about eight months after its passage, it still has not been publicly notified for implementation. But that is a different story.

In short, the innovative politics of the MKSS—as well as of many other such organizations not reported here—working explicitly on the principle of making democracy participatory and responsive, has initiated a larger and long-term political process by which people can effectively participate in making laws by compelling legislators at the local, state, and national levels to formulate legislation the people want—in some cases even making the legislatures adopt drafts of laws prepared by the grassroots movements based on the information and insights gained through their own struggles and through wider consultations on different civil-society forums.

There are numerous other cases of the movement groups articulating different elements of participatory democracy in the course of their struggles for democratizing development (Smitu Kothari, 2000b). For lack of space, only brief mention can be made of a few. For example, there are city-based movement groups such as SEWA (Self-Employed Women's Association) in Ahmedabad, with a long and formidable record of work among self-employed women for their economic and political empowerment and social emancipation (Rose, 1992). There are two other recently founded organizations in Delhi: the Manushi Forum for Citizen Rights and the Jan Parivahan Panchayat of Lokayan. These organizations have been running campaigns for protecting the economic rights and expanding the freedoms of the self-employed urban poor, such as street-hawkers and rickshaw-pullers (Kishwar, 2001b and c). As part of the campaign, film shows, photographic exhibitions, and marches are organized in different localities in the city. The media campaigns, on the whole, demonstrate how the implementation of economic reforms blatantly discriminate between the rich and the poor and how the rules are often used to prevent people from exercising their right to make a living (Kishwar, 2001a; Lokayan, 2002). Public hearings are held revealing the harassment of street-hawkers and rickshaw-pullers by government officials, which focus not so much on the implementation of rules as on collection of corruption money. Similar movement groups fighting for the rights of the urban poor have been active in Mumbai, Bangalore, Hyderabad, Calcutta, and other cities, whose work is equally, if not more, important. The short point is: a new civil-society politics—different from conventional trade union politics—has emerged in the cities, focusing on the rights of the urban poor in making livelihood choices and use of urban spaces.

Similar new movements addressing issues of livelihood and the use of common spaces have emerged in the rural and tribal areas. They aim at empowering the *gram sabhas* by making them self-governed and participative decision-making bodies managing the affairs of their own villages (Kothari, Smitu, 2000a). One such movement, for example, explicitly conceives of participatory democracy as an "antidote to globalization." Its politics is about giving organizational shape to Gandhi's ideas of *swaraj* and *swadeshi* at the grassroots level. Led by an activist trained in the J.P. movement, Mohan Hirabai Hiralal, the movement has motivated people to establish their own governance of, to begin with, forests in the area. Today, the villagers themselves maintain the forest ecology and make judicious use of forest produce. The self-governance movement is now being expanded to many more villages, covering other areas of collective life. The movement's credo is: *we* are the government in our village and there shall be *our* government in the region, the nation, and the world. Interestingly, this movement group has also theoretically worked out a "blueprint" for the organizational structures required for a participatory democracy from the village to the global level, specifying the long-term objectives and values by which they should be informed.

Conclusion

The distinctive feature of movement politics is, thus, to articulate a new discourse on democracy through sustained political practice. This is done at three levels: (a) at the grassroots level through building people's own power and capabilities, which inevitably involve political struggles for establishing rights as well as a degree of local autonomy for people to manage their own affairs collectively; (b) at the provincial and national levels through launching nationwide campaigns and building alliances and coalitions for mobilizing protests on larger issues (against "anti-people projects and policies") and creating organizational networks of mutual support and of solidarity among movements; (c) at the global level, by a small section of movement activists who in recent years have begun to actively participate in several transnational alliances and movements for creating a politics of counter-hegemonic globalization. In all this, the long-term goal of the movements is to bring the immediate environment (social, economic, cultural, and ecological) that the people live in within their own reach and control.

Such politics of movements, however, often brings them into confrontation with the state, the bureaucracy, the law and order machinery, the local power structures, and now increasingly with the multinationals penetrating the rural and tribal spaces in India. The micro-movements sometimes come into conflict also with political parties and established trade unions. The activists of movements, however, view such confrontations as an aspect of the larger, long-term struggle for political and social transformation, and not as means of competing with political parties in the arena of representative politics for acquisition of state power. They thus view their everyday struggles as a process of expanding political spaces trans-locally through raising people's consciousness and building their own organizations. In the process, in the areas they have been active, they contribute to creating a political culture of participative democracy.

The movement activists have developed their own critique of the prevalent macro-structures of political representation as well as a view of local politics. Their critique is not theoretically derived; it has emerged from the experience of day-to-day political struggles on the ground.[12] In their view, the representative institutions have imprisoned the process of democratization in the society. The way out from such an impasse is the spread of their kind of politics—the politics of micro-movements. Movements, they believe, by involving people deeply in politics will, in the long run, change the terms of justification for the state for holding and using power. This probably explains their epistemic preference in articulating their politics in terms of the "reconstruction of the state" rather than of the "acquisition of state power."

Although the movements usually work in local areas, they invariably define local issues in trans-local terms. Theirs is thus a new kind of local politics that, unlike the conventional politics of local governments, is not linked vertically to the macro-structures of power and ideology, either of a nation-state or of the global order; nor is this politics parochially local. It expands horizontally through several micro-movements of people living in different geographical areas and socio-cultural milieus, but who are experiencing the common situation of disempowerment caused by mal-development and contemporary forms of governance that are imperiously distant, yet close enough to feel their coercive edge.

Thus viewed, the long-term *politics* of movements is about the withdrawal of legitimation from the hegemonic and exclusionary structures of political power and horizontalizing the vertical structures of social hierarchy by strengthening the parallel politics of local, participatory democracy. In this process, the micro-movements address, on the one hand, the problem of making institutions of governance at all levels more accountable, transparent and participative and, on the other, create new political spaces outside the state structure, in which the people themselves are enabled to make decisions collectively on issues directly concerning their lives. Although I have no penchant for coining new terms, I think it will be more appropriate to characterize this new politics of movements as "societics."

All this, however, does not mean that grassroots actors and organizations define the politics of movements in direct opposition to the institutional framework of Indian democracy. In fact, they view institutional democracy as a necessary, though not sufficient, condition for pursuing their parallel politics of movements, through which they seek to raise the social consciousness of people and democratize the hegemonic structures of power in society. In that sense, their politics is about working around and transcending the prevalent institutional structures of liberal democracy—rather than confronting them directly with a view to capturing state power.

In a nutshell, the movements conceive of participatory democracy as a parallel politics of social action, creating and maintaining new spaces for decision-making (that is, for self-governance) by people on matters affecting their lives directly. As a form of practice, participatory democracy for them is thus a long-term political and social process aimed at creating a new system of multiple and overlapping governances, functioning through more direct participation and control of concerned populations (that is, of those comprising these governances). It is envisaged that through such politics the almost total monopoly of power held today by the contemporary (totalist) state would be dispersed into different self-governing entities but, at the same time, the macro-governance of the state, albeit confined to fewer nationally crucial sectors, would be carried through democratically elected representative bodies, at one level overseeing the system of micro-governances and, at another, being responsive and accountable to them.

Notes

1 In June 1975, a state of internal emergency was imposed on India by Mrs. Indira Gandhi as a stratagem to continue in power after she had been disqualified from her membership in the Indian Parliament after being found guilty of electoral malpractice by a High Court judgment delivered on 12 June.

During the emergency, which lasted for two years, the constitutional rights of citizens, including some fundamental rights, were suspended. The emergency regime was stiffly resisted by several political parties and social activists. For an account, written during the period, of how constitutional rights were undermined by the emergency regime, see Kothari, Rajni (1989).

2 The following account is based on my close and continuous association and interaction with activists of several movement groups throughout the country since 1980. I also have extensively used the materials they regularly produce and disseminate in the form of booklets, pamphlets, leaflets, and newsletters, which do not easily yield to the academic style of citations. As such, it incorporates parts of my earlier writings on grassroots movements, cited here. The activists and movements appearing in this chapter by their names suggest my greater, often accidental, familiarity with their work, inasmuch as the absences suggest my ignorance—and the lack of space—but in no case any lack of their salience in the field.

3 For example, witness the activities of a network of grassroots organizations founded by the leading activist of transnational ecological movements, Vandana Shiva; the network is known as Jaiv Panchayats—The Living Democracy Movement (Shiva, 2000).

4 It is significant to note in this context that major popular movements in India today, such as the campaign for Right to Information, the campaign for Saving the River Narmada (Narmada Bachao Andolan), the movement for the rights of self-employed women and of street-hawkers and rickshaw-pullers in cities, and the Campaign for Maintaining Biodiversity and against intellectual property rights are all led by women.

5 For a concise and pointed exposition of these concepts see M. K. Gandhi (1968a, b, c, d, e).

6 For a perceptive, cogent and authentic account of J.P.'s life and work, see, the introduction to his selected writings, edited by Bimal Prasad (1980).

7 For a detailed history and political account of the movement, see Prabhat (1999).

8 Report by P. Sirvaram Krishna of SAKTI (mimeo); also reported in *Newstime*, 13 March 1991.

9 All quotes are from the leader of the movement, Rajendra Singh (2001). For a comprehensive account of the contribution made by this movement, see Kishwar (2001b).

10 Surveys and studies carried through participatory-action research has, by now, become a common practice for the movement groups. There are special groups of activist-academics, such as the Alternative Survey Group, that regularly carry out studies and publish their findings. Such studies are devised, self-consciously, to counter the politics of positivist knowledge that privileges experts and excludes people from decision-making on matters of vital interest to them (Sheth, 1999).

11 The MKSS almost ideally fits the concept of "micro-movement" explicated in this chapter. The campaign it initiated for the right to information has

become a nationwide movement. It has built a large network of movement groups, human rights organizations, media leaders, intellectuals, and professionals. Unfortunately, I cannot do justice to some innovative political concepts and practices developed by this and other such movements in the space available here. For a detailed account of the MKSS movement and the vision of its founder see the following: Bakshi (1998); Aruna Roy (1996a and b); Aruna Roy and Nikhil De (1999); Roy Bunker (1999); and Dogra (2000).

12 In the course of the last five years, the issue of participatory democracy has received more serious and focused attention from the leaders of micro-movements. Several pamphlets, booklets, newsletters, and articles have been prepared and disseminated by them for wider discussion and, possibly, for future campaigns. The basic principles and concepts were, as we saw earlier, enunciated by Gandhi and Jayaprakash Narayan. Some activist-thinkers in recent years have incorporated these in their politics and have renewed the debate through their own writings. For example, see Aruna Roy (1996); articles in the special issue of *Samayik Varta: Loktantra Samiksha* (July-August 2000), especially those by Patnayak, Yadav, Bhatttacharya and Pratap; Pratap (2001); Kumar (2001); and Tarkunde (2003). My presentation here of the movements' conceptualization of participatory democracy is largely based on the above-mentioned materials.

Bibliography

Almond, Gabriel, and Verba, Sidney (1963). *Civic Culture*, Princeton, NJ: Princeton UP.

Bakshi, Rajni (1998). *Bapu Kuti: Journeys in Rediscovery of Gandhi*, Delhi: Penguin Books-India.

Bhattacharya, Dipankar (2000). "Janata ka Zameeni Sangharsh aur Loktantra," *Samayik Varta*, 23(10–11): 18–19.

Dahl, Robert (1989; Indian edition 1991). *Democracy and its Critics*, Hyderabad: Orient Longman, pp. 13–33.

Dogra, Madhu, and Bharat (2000). *MKSS: A Profile of a People's Organization*, Delhi: Bharat Dogra.

Fukuyama, Francis (1992). *The End of History and the Last Man*, London: Penguin.

Gandhi, M. K. (1968a). "Swadeshi," in Shriman Narayan (ed.), *Selected Works of Mahatma Gandhi*, Volume 4, Ahmedabad: Navajivan Publishing, pp. 256–60.

— (1968b). "Non-cooperation," *Selected Works*, Vol. 5, pp. 203–8.

— (1968c). "Civil Disobedience," *Selected Works*, Vol. 5, pp. 209–16.

— (1968d). "Swadeshi" *Selected Works*, Vol. 5., pp. 336–9.

— (1968e). "Village Communities," *Selected Works*, Vol. 5, pp. 344–7.

Hiremath, S. R., *et al.* (2001). "Report of the Study Team on Adivisi Movement in Rayagada District of Orissa Against Forcible Tribal Land Acquisition For Bauxite Mining (in violation of the Supreme Court order in the SAMTA

Judgement," *Samay Parivartana Samudaya*, Karnataka: Dharwad.

Kapoor, Rakesh (2002). "Civil Society in India: A Background Paper," prepared for the Centre for the Study of Developing Societies (CSDS) project on Civil Society Building in India, Delhi: CSDS. Mimeo.

Kishwar, Madhu (2001a). "Laws, Liberty and Livelihood," *Manushi*, No. 122: 8–15.

—— (2001b). "Villages in Rajasthan Overcome Sarkari Dependence," *Manushi*, No. 123: 4–16.

—— (2001c). "Bribes, Beatings and Blackmail: Loksunvayi of Delhi's Street Vendors," *Manushi*, No. 124.

Kothari, Rajni (1960). "Jayaprakash Narayan's Thesis: Report on a Discussion," *The Economic Weekly*, 12(15).

—— (1984). "Non-party Political Process," *Economic and Political Weekly*, 19(5): 216–24.

—— (1988a). "Decline of the Moderate State," *State Against Democracy: In Search of Humane Governance*, Delhi: Ajanta: 15–36.

—— (1988b). "Decline of Parties and Rise of Grassroots Movements," *State Against Democracy: In Search of Humane Governance*, Delhi: Ajanta: 33–54.

—— (1989). "End of an Era," *Politics and the People: In Search of Humane India*, Delhi: Ajanta: 235–50.

—— (1993). "The Yawning Vacuum: A World Without Alternatives," *Alternatives*, 18(2): 119–39.

Kothari, Smitu (2000a). "To be Governed or Self-govern," *Folio*, 18: 18–21.

—— (2000b). "A Million Mutinies now: Lesser-known Environmental Movements in India," *Humanscape*, October: 5–9.

—— (2001). "Globalisation, Global Alliances and the Narmada Movement," in Kathryn Sikkink, S. Khagram, and J. Riker, *Restructuring World Politics: Transnational Social Movements, Networks and Norms*, Minneapolis: U of Minnesota P. (forthcoming).

Kumar, Arun (2000). *Globalisation: A Consensus of only 3% Indians*, CSDS (mimeo), Delhi.

—— (2001). *Anchoring Indian State and Polity to Vernacular Wisdom: A Small Step Toward Swaraj*, Delhi: CSDS. Mimeo.

Lokayan (2002). "Report on Cycle Rickshaws in the National Capital Region" (also in Hindi), prepared by Rajendra Ravi and the Jan Parivahan team at Lokayan, Lokayan, Delhi.

Milbrath, Lister W. (1965). *Political Participation*, Chicago: Rand McNally.

Narayan, Jayaprakash (1959). *A Plea for Reconstruction of the Indian Polity*, Varanasi: Akhil Bharat Sarva Sangh.

—— (1961). *Swaraj for the People*, Varanasi: Akhil Bharat Sarva Sangh.

—— (1975). "Total Revolution: Why and How?" in Bimal Prasad (ed.), *A Revolutionary's Quest: Selected Writings of Jayaprakash Narayan*, Delhi: Oxford UP.

Pansay, Sandeep (1981). "The Datta Samant Phenomenon," *Economic and Political Weekly*, 16–17: 1–8.

Patnayak, Kishan (2000). "Vishwa Main Loktantra ka Bhavishya," *Samayik Varta*, 23(10–11): 11–17.

Pendse, Sandeep (1981). "The Datta Samant Phenomenon," *Economic and Political Weekly*, Vols 16–17: 1–8.

Prabhat (1999). *Zamin Kiski, Jote Uski: Bodhgaya Bhumi Andolan*, Patna: Kisan Vikas Trust.

Prasad, Bimal (1980). "Introduction," in J. Narayan, *A Revolutionary's Quest*, pp. ix–lxviii.

Pratap, Vijay (2000). "Yah Vimarsh kis liye," *Samayaik Varta*, 23(10–11): 3–7.

— (2001). "Vasudhaiva Kutumbakam: A New Alliance for Democracy in the Era of Globalisation," Delhi: CSDS. Mimeo.

Rose, Kalima (1992). *Where Women are Leaders: The SEWA Movement in India*, London: Zed Books.

Roy, Aruna (1996a). "From Bureaucracy to People's Movement," *Lokayan Bulletin*, 13(1): 51.

— (1996b). "*Survival and Right to Information: Third Gulam Rasool Memorial Lecture*," Hyderabad: Forum for Free Expression. Mimeo. Abridged version published in *Lokayan Bulletin* (1999), 16(1): 1–13.

Roy, Aruna, and Nikhil Dey (1999). "Footnotes to a Dharna," *Lokayan Bulletin*, 16(1): 45–51.

Roy, Bunker (1999). "The Politics of Waste and Corruption," *Lokayan Bulletin*, 16(1): 19–40.

Roy, M. N. (1960). *Politics, Power and Parties*, Dehradun: Indian Renaissance Institute.

Sainath, P. (2000). "The Age of Inequality," in Romila Thaper (ed.), *India: Another Millennium*, Delhi: Penguin-India, 152–68.

Santos, Boaventura de Sousa (1997). "Toward a Multicultural Conception of Human Rights," Zeitschrift fur Rechtssoziologie 18(1): 1–15.

— (1998). *Reinventar a Democracia*, Lisbon: Gravia.

Schmitter, Philippe C. (1999). "The Future of Democracy: Could it be a matter of Scale?" *Social Research*, 66(3): 933–58.

Sethi, Harsh (1984). "Groups in a New Politics of Transformation," *Economic and Political Weekly*, 19(7): 305–16.

Sheth, D. L. (1983). "Grass-Roots Stirrings And the Future of Politics," *Alternatives* 9(1): 1–24.

— (1984). "Grassroots Initiatives in India," *Economic and Political Weekly*, 19(6).

— (1991). "Crisis of Representation," *Seminar*, 385.

— (1995). "The Great Language Debate: Politics of Metropolitan versus Vernacular India," in Baxi and Parekh: 187–215.

— (1999a). "Globalisation and the Grassroots Movements" *Seminar*, 473: 77–82.

— (1999b). *Knowledge Power and Action: Challenges Facing the Grassroots Movements for Alternative Development: I. P. Desai Memorial Lecture*, Surat: Centre for Social Studies.

— and Harsh Sethi (1991). "The NGO Sector in India: Historical context and current discourse," *Voluntas*, 2(2): 49–68.

— Vijay Pratap, and Ritu Priya (2002). "Making Institutions Compatible with Southern Movement Aspirations for a Democratic Order: A Minimalist Perspective," Leena Rikkila and Katarina Sehm Patomaki (eds.), *From Global Market Place to Political Spaces*, Helsinki: Hakapaino, pp. 87–125.

Shiva, Vandana (1988). *Staying Alive. Women, Ecology and Survival in India*, New Delhi: Kali for Women.

— (2000). "Jaiva Panchayat: A Movement for Living Democracy," Pamphlet, *Navadaniya*, Delhi.

Singh, Rajendra (2001). "I was called a Dacoit, Terrorist and Fraud," *Hindustan Times*, 12 August.

Tarkunde, V. M. (2003). "Partyless Politics and People's (Humanist) State: A Picture for Public Discussion," *The Radical Humanist*, 66(10): 1–4.

Wallgren, Thomas (1998). "Political Semantics of Globalisation," *Development: SID Journal*, 41(2): 30–2.

Yadav, Yogendra (2000). "Bharat ko Loktantraka Ka Ek Naya Shastra Gadhana Hoga," *Samayik Varta*, 23(10–11): 27–32.

2

Reinventing Participatory Democracy in South Africa

Sakhela Buhlungu

INTRODUCTION

The People Shall Govern!

Every man and woman shall have the right to vote for and stand as a candidate for all bodies which make laws;
All the people shall be entitled to take part in the administration of the country;
The rights of the people shall be the same regardless of race, colour or sex;
All bodies of minority rule, advisory boards, councils and authorities shall be replaced by democratic organs of self-government.

(from the *Freedom Charter*, as adopted at the Congress of the People
on 26 June 1955 in Kliptown, near Johannesburg)

Every social struggle is an endeavor by a section of society to achieve emancipation from some social evil that those involved in such a struggle consider repugnant. Indeed, what inspires people in different societies to take part in such struggles is a vision of how social relations can (and should) be structured or restructured. Such a vision may be couched in different terms, depending on the context in which the struggles are being waged. For some, it is simply "freedom," while for others it may be "democracy," "socialism," etc. But every struggle, as well as the vision of freedom or liberation that inspires it, always contains a promise of a decentralized or participatory kind of democracy that is inclusive rather than exclusive. In some struggles this participatory democratic utopia is explicitly articulated, while in others it is generally assumed to be the end-goal. In small social groups participatory democracy conjures up images of an assembly where all members of the group have a right to attend and to participate on equal terms in debates and decision-making. For large groups, participation suggests a highly decentralized system where ordinary members of a social group or an entire society have rights to participate both directly and indirectly in decision-making. In a nutshell, the participatory democratic utopia is about the expansion of cit-izenship in a formal as well as substantive sense, and it is usually the working class and other marginalized sections of society who champion these ideas, as they stand to benefit the most in a participatory dispensation.

However, few struggles and revolutions in the history of humanity have resulted in lasting experiments in participatory democracy, and even the few that succeeded were short-lived. Thus, many revolutions have disappointed the vast majority of those who sacrifice the most and act as the shock troops of revolution. But the welfare state and the social regulation regime that accom-panied it went a long way in ameliorating the impact of the marginalization of the subordinate classes, and thus helped to maintain a degree of credibility for the capitalist economic system. The supersession of the social regulation regime of the welfare state by market regulation from the 1970s onwards has resulted in unprecedented social exclusion and marginalization of millions of people from subordinate classes.[1] Exclusion and marginalization are synony-mous with the current phase of globalization and its hegemonic ideological accompaniments such as free markets, minimal state intervention, fiscal disci-pline and cost recovery for all services provided by the state.

There are different, and competing, notions of democracy and all of them revolve around the model of citizenship that is envisaged. Parry and Moyser (1994) have suggested two broad categories or notions of democracy, namely, the "participatory or radical" conception and the "realist" conception. These authors argue that the participatory school seeks to expand citizen partici-pation beyond traditional forms such as voting and signing petitions by encouraging the population to "play an active part" in government (1994: 45–46). The genealogy of these ideas goes back to models of citizenship expounded by theorists such as Rousseau and J. S. Mill, but it should be added that their influence has permeated most modern currents of radical social science. The realist notion, on the other hand, advocates a much more conservative and limited notion of participation that does not extend too far beyond voting at regular intervals. Schumpeter's theory of democracy, which hinges on the view that "the electorate is incapable of action other than a stampede" (1987: 283), is an example of such a truncated and conservative notion of democracy. The model of citizenship that this notion of democ-racy implies is an exclusionary one that caters only to the elites in society.

South Africa has just emerged from a period of protracted conflict where the majority of the population fought heroic struggles against the injustice of apartheid minority rule. That struggle represented an attempt to achieve the expansion of social citizenship through the inclusion of all the country's people in its social, economic and political life. Indeed, the *Freedom Charter*, a social democratic document adopted by a multiracial "Congress of the People" in 1955, represented an attempt to include all citizens in the affairs of the country by calling for the following:

- the right of all to be guaranteed political rights;
- equal rights for different social groups;
- the nationalization of strategic sectors of the economy;
- a radical land reform program;
- the protection of human rights of all citizens;
- a guarantee of work and security for all;
- the provision of education and housing; and
- the respect of the rights and sovereignty of all nations.

In the context of apartheid South Africa, the charter represented a counter-hegemonic project that sought to address the inequalities and social exclusion of the system. At the heart of the document is the clarion call "The People Shall Govern!" which was inspired by notions of participation and "self-government" at the lowest levels of the social structure. The charter was used by many generations of activists in different spheres of life such as civics, education and health as a guide to action in struggling for the establishment of "organs of people's power." But the *Freedom Charter* was not the sole origin of notions of participatory forms of democracy. A vibrant progressive trade union movement had been in existence since the early 1920s, and by the 1950s this movement had relatively strong democratically elected structures of representation and leadership (Lambert, 1988). When the movement was crushed in the 1960s, it took a while to re-emerge, but when it finally did so in the early 1970s it consciously nurtured a tradition of democracy that combined elements of direct participation and representative democratic rule in its structures. This chapter reviews the emergence and development of the discourse of participatory democracy in South Africa during and after the struggle for liberation by drawing on examples from the civic and trade union arenas of that struggle. It also seeks to identify and highlight factors and social processes that have undermined participatory democracy since the early 1990s, particularly under the democratic political dispensation that was inaugurated in 1994.

THE PARTICIPATORY DEMOCRATIC TRADITION IN SOUTH AFRICA

Since the early 1900s the freedom struggle in South Africa went through several qualitatively different phases, all of which sought to expand the definition of the freedom envisaged. But two of these phases have had an enduring impact on the discourse of democracy that emerged at the height of the freedom struggle in the 1980s and early 1990s. The first period was in the 1950s, when mass agitation gave rise to radical notions of democracy. The *Freedom Charter*, discussed above, captured this new spirit of a radical democratic discourse with its phrase: "The People Shall Govern!"

At that time, this was a very radical notion, inspired as it was by the ideas of socialists, many of whom were active in the Communist Party of South Africa (later renamed the South African Communist Party [SACP]) and in the national liberation movement that was gaining prominence in the colonized territories throughout the world. However, state repression and the banning of liberation movements in the early 1960s frustrated progress toward the goal of ensuring that the "people" were the ones who governed South Africa.

In the late 1960s and 1970s, ideas of participatory democracy gained further popularity within the liberation movement and found expression in experiments of democratic participation in the liberated zones created by national liberation movements in other colonized territories. Basil Davidson's (1981) account of the establishment of participatory and representative forms of democracy in the liberated zones in Guinea-Bissau illustrates the centrality of institutions of political and social self-government in "transforming support or sympathy into active and voluntary participation by rural multitudes" (1981: 163). At the height of the mass mobilization phase of the South African liberation struggle, similar notions of liberated zones were influential among activists and movement leaders. For example, in 1986 the United Democratic Front's (UDF) journal, *Isizwe*, noted that the demand for the people to govern was being taken up by millions of ordinary South Africans:

> The building of people's power is something that is *already beginning to happen in the course of our struggle*. It is not for us to sit back and merely dream of the day that the people shall govern. It is our task to realize that goal now. We must start the process of liberating South Africa. We must begin to place power in the hands of the people, in all spheres—the economy, education, culture, crime control, health, in fact, wherever it is possible. (UDF, 1986: 2)

The journal went on to elaborate the shape that this form of government would take:

> We are struggling for a different system where power is no longer in the hands of the rich and powerful. We are struggling for a government that we all vote for. We are struggling for elected bodies in our schools, factories and communities. We want laws that are widely discussed throughout our country, street committee by street committee *before* they are even debated in parliament. We want courts where workers, peasants and teachers can be elected as magistrates. We want elected magistrates rooted in the communities in which they are serving. We want an army that belongs to all, in a country where all citizens are armed. (UDF, 1986: 4)

The township struggles of the 1980s were inspired by these ideas and, indeed, many activists sought to implement a participatory model of democracy in several arenas, including civic and residents' associations, schools, universities and workplaces. However, all these attempts and experiments were fraught with contradictions and tensions, all the more so because of the hostility of state agencies and other authorities. Mayekiso's (1996) book on township politics in the Alexandra township in Johannesburg is one of the best accounts of the extremely difficult task of establishing "organs of people's power" during South Africa's struggle for liberation.

The second phase of mobilization and struggle that had an impact on democratic discourse is the one that began in the early 1970s at about the same time when the new trade union movement emerged. Even though this phase owed its origins to the earlier period of mass mobilization and activism, the philosophical formulation and packaging of its ideas had a much stronger intellectual derivation than the earlier one. In this regard, the work of Richard Turner, a young philosopher who had studied in Cape Town and Paris, represents the most developed search for emancipation that moved beyond received traditions and notions of democracy. His seminal book, *The Eye of the Needle: Toward Participatory Democracy in South Africa*,[2] was inspired by what he termed "the necessity of utopian thinking." Turner argued that it was necessary and possible to move away from the notion that society and social institutions are "natural entities, part of the geography of the world in which we live" (1980: 2):

> In order to reflect on our values, then, we have to see which aspects of our society are the necessary result of the imperatives of human nature and of organizations, and which aspects of it are changeable. We then need to make explicit the value principles embodied in our actual behavior, and to criticize these principles in the light of other possible values. Until we realise what other values, and what other social forms, are possible, we cannot judge the morality or otherwise of existing society. (1980: 3)

Turner then proceeded to discuss his "ideal possible society," which revolved around the notion of participatory democracy. The two principal requirements of this type of social system would be that it "enables individuals to have maximum control over their social and material environment, and encourages them to interact creatively with other people" (1980: 34).

The two phases of the South African struggle can be conceptualized as overlapping and mutually reinforcing stages in the evolution of utopian thinking in the search for social emancipation in South Africa. During the first phase, emphasis was on defining participatory democracy as an ideal or a goal to be achieved at the point of liberation. The *Freedom Charter's* call for the establishment of "democratic organs of self-government" in a post-apartheid society was part of this discourse. During the second phase, not only was participatory democracy a goal for the future, it was also seen as practice within organizations of the pro-democracy movement. In a sense, this deepening of the discourse, which entailed translating the ideal into a "real utopia," could be observed most clearly in trade union and community/civic struggles from the 1970s onwards.

One of the traditions for which the post-1973 trade union movement has continued to pride itself is that of democracy and worker control of its internal structures and the decision-making within them. Freund argues that this was a "distinctive kind of grassroots democracy" because "decisions that concerned basic organizational issues were taken in a format that involved a high level of involvement and acceptance by ordinary members" (1999: 438). This tradition goes back to the formation of these unions in the early 1970s. In many of them the principle of worker control permeated every aspect of their organization and functioning, for example:

—the emphasis on shop floor structures led by democratically elected shop stewards;
—the creation of representative structures in which worker delegates were the majority;
—the practice of mandated decision-making and regular report-backs to members;
—factory-level bargaining, which allowed workers and shop stewards to maintain control of the bargaining agenda and the conclusion of agreements;
—the subordination of full-time officials to control by worker-dominated structures; and
—the involvement of workers, at all levels, in the employment of full-time officials.

The principle of worker control was built into the founding constitution of the Federation of South African Trade Unions (FOSATU) in 1979 as well as that of the Congress of South African Trade Unions (COSATU), which was established in 1985. According to Baskin, the rationale for this was "to prevent union officials from dominating COSATU structures" (1991: 57). But, more importantly, worker control was aimed at ensuring the durability of union structures by allowing workers to take full responsibility for the functioning of their unions. This was necessitated by the hostility of employers and the state, which resulted in the unrelenting harassment and detention of union leaders.[3]

The 1980s saw unprecedented levels of militancy and mass mobilization in many townships throughout the country. These processes were accompanied by the mushrooming of civic organizations, which sought to contest power in a context where puppet structures of the apartheid regime were in charge of civic administration. Mzwanele Mayekiso, then a civic activist in Alexandra township in Johannesburg, argues that 1986 represented the high point of mobilization and mass political involvement in the township:

> Our most heady period of township organizing was the few months in early 1986 when we could really claim that apartheid rule was being displaced, street by street, by our own form of self-government. It was a liberating experience, though it did not last for long. (1996: 67)

The form of self-government that Mayekiso discusses had a very strong participatory dimension which pivoted on the establishment of "organs of people's power" such as street and area committees, "people's courts," *amabutho* (self-defense units made up of volunteers), and student representative councils. The virtues of these forms of organization were manifold. Above all, they ensured participation by people at the lowest level of social organization, namely the street. The street committee was actually a general meeting of all residents in a street, which provided opportunities for building unity and political involvement by all in matters that affected them. Although there were often problems and tensions in these structures, such as that between the youth and older members of the communities, street committees were generally effective in encouraging mass participation at the neighborhood level of the township. Street committees would then elect representatives to area committees, which would, in turn, elect representatives to township-wide civic associations. The civic organization was a coordinating body of struggles and campaigns for the entire township.

A series of other overlapping structures, such as people's courts and self-defense units, were often established, particularly in those townships that had relatively well-functioning street and area committees. The most effective people's courts were those that had been established under the auspices of existing street and area committees to ensure some kind of political accountability. In the case of Alexandra township, Mayekiso also makes the point that the integrity of the courts always depended upon a "community mandate," and that once community structures became weak and leadership absent because of detention, the courts ran the risk of degenerating into kangaroo courts.[4] These courts were open to all members of the streets who wished to attend. The notion of a people's court emerged as an alternative to the unjust judicial system of apartheid and relied on members of the community reporting their cases there rather than taking them to the conventional courts. The system drew a lot from the African justice system where emphasis was on rehabilitation rather than punishment. An example of a successful people's court in Alexandra's 7th Avenue is described by Mayekiso (1996):

Initially it was run by the youth, but the elderly were later called in to preside. The courtroom itself was a tiny corrugated iron shack with benches to sit on and a table for the secretary to write minutes on. Both the accused and the complainant would sit among people respected in the community. The chairperson would open the discussion on the issue. The accused and the complainant would then give their sides of the story. The house would deliberate on the issue. One rule was that no one would be undermined or threatened. At the end, an amicable solution to the problem would typically be reached. Both parties would embrace each other. (1996: 82)

This discussion now turns to the invention of the democratic tradition within mass movements in South Africa. Hobsbawm (1983) has used the term "invented tradition" to refer to a set of practices that are usually regulated by certain rules to engender particular norms and values. He has also argued that the repetition that is implicit in this process implies continuity with the past. Of relevance for our purposes in this discussion is his assertion that "ancient materials" are often used to "construct invented traditions of a novel type for quite novel purposes" (1983: 6).

A large store of such materials is accumulated in the past of any society, and an elaborate language of symbolic practices and communication is always available. Sometimes new traditions could be readily grafted on old ones, sometimes they could be devised by borrowing from the well-supplied warehouses of official ritual, symbolism and moral exhortation—religion and princely pomp, folklore and freemasonry (itself an invented tradition of great symbolic force). (1983: 6)

In South Africa, democracy in general, and participatory democracy in particular, are dimensions of a tradition that was invented by the liberation movement as a whole, including the trade unions and civic organizations. The emergence of the democratic tradition in South Africa is often attributed solely to left intellectuals. For example, the tradition of democratic unionism is often understood solely as the contribution of the young generation of activists involved in the re-emergence of unions after 1973. Some, like Friedman (1987), have gone so far as to suggest that the white student activists and university intellectuals were the main source of the democratic ideas that were alien to the black workers who constituted the membership of these unions. However, a closer examination of the evidence suggests that the democratic tradition in the unions and in civic organizations owes its origins to a very wide range of influences and sources, among which were cultural, traditional, political, and intellectual influences. Thus the evidence shows that any attempt that seeks to examine and understand how the democratic culture and tradition were invented needs to go beyond the simplistic notion that only a select group of intellectuals brought the democratic culture into the mass movement.

An examination of how these traditions were invented is simultaneously an attempt to understand the social character of trade unions and civic organizations and how they bear the imprint of the cultural heritage and social experiences of their members and leading activists. It would appear that the democratic tradition in union and civic politics was a complex fusion of the lived experiences of egalitarianism and grassroots participation shared by working-class people and the intellectual contributions of activists from different social and political backgrounds. The next section of the chapter attempts to identify some of these contributions and experiences and to discuss the economic and political context in which a robust tradition of participatory democracy emerged in trade unions and the civic movement.

PARTICIPATORY DEMOCRACY AND THE LIVED EXPERIENCES OF THE WORKING CLASS

The making of a mass movement and the associational forms to which it gives rise involves a series of social processes of mobilization and construction of new forms of solidarity and new identities. It is in the construction of these forms of solidarity and new identities that the lived social experiences of the different groupings that come together become crucial. In other words, a social group does not enter into new associational forms as a *tabula rasa*. In his seminal study of the making of the English working class, E. P. Thompson (1963) refers to the formation in 1832 of a society of weavers in Ripponden, a weaving village in the Pennines, and the remarkably radical tone of its founding rules, which were based on notions of communal cooperation and egalitarianism. This was during the time when Robert Owen's intellectual influence among the working class was at its height. Thompson's comments on the significance of the society's rules have relevance for our argument here:

> This is not just a translation of Owen's doctrines to the context of a weaving village. The ideas have been shaped, laboriously, in terms of the weavers' experience; the emphases have shifted; in place of the messianic stridency, there is the simple question: Why not? One of the small cooperative journals was aptly entitled Common Sense: its emphasis was on the "Trading Associations." (1963: 794)

Thompson's account underlines the argument we make in this discussion that intellectual influences seldom take root in a vacuum. More often than not, they are received in a social and cultural milieu that has produced its own traditions, norms and values, which shape the lives of people in particular ways. Thus the adoption of new doctrines should rather be conceived of as a dialectical blending of intellectual influences and the experience of working-class people. In the case of the new unions in South Africa, the different groups of workers that were part of the new processes of mobilization brought with them a number of lived social and cultural experiences that coalesced into what became the democratic tradition of these unions. Some of these experiences were not necessarily democratic in themselves, but they promoted the search, by workers, for more egalitarian alternatives. The discussion below identifies and discusses some of these lived experiences.

Religious influences

Many of the workers who joined unions during and after 1973 had deep religious backgrounds, while many others had some distant affiliations with different religious formations in their communities. The dominant religion was the Christian faith, which was practiced through different denominations. Religion had a profound influence on the new unions in the 1970s, and in many cases this influence was still visible in the 1980s. First, it imbued many with a sense of justice and provided them with a rationale for challenging oppressive and exploitative relations in society. Thus Salie Manie, then Western Cape leader of the South African Municipal Workers' Union (SAMWU), could find no contradiction between his Islamic faith and his activism:

> My mother was a religious instructor at the mosque. Religion has always played a central role in my life. The concept of justice has been ingrained in our family. My mother brought us up not to compromise on what was right. I believe in God. I also believe in social justice. I see myself as a Muslim, but I also see myself as a socialist. (Gabriels, 1992: 77)

The new "black theology" that emerged during the early years of the Black Consciousness Movement (BCM) made an explicit link between the teachings of the Christian faith and the struggle for democracy in the country. Indeed, in the 1970s and 1980s many church organizations and centers began to make a statement about whose side they were on by making church centers available as venues for union meetings. This was at a time when many hotels and other venues in "white" towns were hostile to black unions and other liberation organizations. Emma Mashinini, the first general secretary of the Commercial, Catering and Allied Workers' Union of South Africa (CCAWUSA), recalls that when the union was established in 1975 she could not rent an office in its name because of the Group Areas Act and had to resort to asking the white National Union of Distributive Workers to use its name to rent the premises. Later, the landlord evicted the union because he did not like the regular stream of militant workers visiting the offices. At this point, Mashinini was offered offices at Khotso House, the building that housed the national office of the South African Council of Churches (Zikalala, 1993).

Second, there were cases where religion or religious rituals acted as a unifying force in the new unions. One of these rituals was the prayer at the start of union meetings, which acted not only to unite those in prayer but also to lend legitimacy and respectability to the struggle. The use of religious prayers at the start of union meetings was associated with the older generation of workers and it remained an important ritual until a younger and more militant generation of workers took the lead in the 1980s.

Third, one example of the influence of religion on the new unions is the way in which religious hymns were adapted to the context of struggle and how the unions learned to use the power of song to mobilize workers into action. The power of song was not only in the lyrics but also in the rhythm. In the same way that song and dance play an important part in African cultural life, it came to play the same role in the unions, only now with greater religious derivations.

Finally, many of those who came to occupy leading positions in the new unions had prior experience of leadership in religious organizations of various kinds. One example of these leaders is Sipho Kubheka, who rose to become the general secretary of the Paper, Printing, Wood and Allied Workers Union (PPWAWU). Before he joined the unions in the early 1970s, he was a lay preacher in one of the independent African churches, where he had gained experience in public speaking, negotiation and organizing skills. (Since leaving the union in 1996, Kubheka has become active again as a part-time minister in the church.) Philemon Bokaba, an ex-shop steward of NUMSA at African Telephone Cables (ATC) near Pretoria, who served as a national vice president for many years in the 1980s and 1990s, was an active official of his church for ten years before joining the union. He says that the skills that he gained as a church official were very useful in enabling him to perform his union duties.

In a nutshell then, although the Church is a hierarchical organization, it had a very influential role in the construction of the democratic traditions of the union movement. Indeed, in the context of apartheid South Africa, many church bodies had a relatively developed system of self-government and rank-and-file participation.

Traditional influences

The new unions also owed some aspects of their character to what remained of traditional African political culture, in particular, the tradition of debate and consensual decision-making by members of the community gathering at an *imbizo*[5] or *lekgotla*. Moses Mayekiso argues that the experiences gained in these traditional structures in rural settings were part of the mosaic of lived experiences that gave birth to the democratic tradition of unionism in the 1970s.[6] There are many examples that show that this could be adapted and transferred into proletarian and other non-traditional settings. These gatherings were used by many migrant workers to debate issues and to resolve disputes among "home-boy" groups in South Africa's urban areas and mining compounds. Indeed, part of the reason why many unions took root relatively quickly in urban and mining hostels or compounds is the fact that these traditional structures were used as mobilizing forums for union activities.

However, we must add that just like religious institutions, traditional structures tended to be hierarchical and were biased in favor of older men because maleness and age were associated with experience and wisdom. Suffice it to say that these experiences influenced the emergence of a more democratic culture of conducting union affairs, particularly the culture of debating issues until consensus emerges. In his book *Command or Consensus*, Hammond-Tooke (1975) describes the operation of local administrative councils (an *imbizo* and an *inkundla*[7]) in a traditional setting in South Africa's rural villages:

> The "chairman" of the council is of course the headman. In theory he guides the discussion, and the decisions are made in his name; in practice much depends on his personality and on the forces ranged for or against him in committee. We have seen how, in the traditional decision-making process, great emphasis was laid on consensus, so that decision-making was the product of an essentially "political" interaction between council members who were equal to one another. The official position of the headman in the bureaucratic structure has tended to skew this extreme democratic system, for he is now backed by the Administration. (1975: 141)

Hammond-Tooke referred to these structures as "tribal democracies" where there was "relatively little 'authority' attached to indigenous political officers. Political officers could command, but only after the order had been formulated by a process that involved consensus" (1975: 216). In many ways, the union workplace general meeting and the local shop stewards' council bear a lot of similarities to the *imbizo*, especially in the way in which debate is conducted and consensus achieved.

Experience in cultural and sports organizations

The suppression of political and union activity in the 1960s was not accompanied by an obliteration of other social and cultural forms of organization among black South Africans. Indeed, in many areas the absence of political activity led many to find solace in other "non-political" social and cultural activities such as sports and cultural bodies like dance clubs, choirs, and so on. Many of these bodies were run on strictly formal and relatively democratic lines, thus providing opportunities for those involved to gain basic organizational skills such as chairing meetings, operating bank accounts, keeping minutes, and participating in open debates and in the election of leadership. The skills gained from these experiences helped in the building of the democratic trade union movement and should not be underestimated.

Mutual help clubs or "societies"

Equally important in the building of the democratic union movement is the experience gained by working-class black South Africans in a variety of voluntary mutual help clubs. These take various forms, depending on the function they are supposed to serve. The *masingcwabane* or burial society is a voluntary association established by people who then pool money, collected on a monthly basis, to be used in the event of a death of a member or his or her relatives. What is relevant about this form of association is the way it manages its affairs. A well-developed *masingcwabane* will have a bank account, elected officials—chairperson, secretary, treasurer—and will keep a record of its meetings, which are held at regular intervals. In addition, it will have a democratic way of taking decisions and accounting for money spent. In the townships, the *stokvel* and its many variants, such as the *moholisano* and the "society," are formed as savings clubs where members take turns to receive all the funds collected every month. But in all these clubs, there are regular meetings and there is democratic debate about how much the contributions should be, who to admit to the club, and so on.

School struggles

Many of the workers who formed the new unions in the 1970s had come through a period of turbulence in the education system where they had been thrust into positions of leadership in struggles against the authoritarian education authorities. Although many of these experiences did not necessarily result in the formation of democratic structures, the experiences remain important nevertheless because it was in fighting these struggles that these activists came to embrace democracy as an ideal. For example, Nelson Ndinisa, a former shop steward and past president of the then South African Railways and Harbor Workers' Union (SARHWU) recalls a protracted struggle at his high school, Osborne High in Mount Frere, which led to his eventual expulsion before he could write his matric. He says that at a certain stage of that struggle he played a leading role because he could understand that things were not right. He attributes his political awareness to a history teacher at the school:

While he was doing history he would give us more ideas of what is happening. So he was actually the one, so that when these things happened in Soweto we had a better understanding of them. Now when the [Transkei] independence came he was able to articulate what it means. Generally in the rural areas people didn't understand. But we tried to form a student grouping on that side and we said that people must really understand that what we are getting is not really independence. So, that was the background as we started to know that something is wrong. I have always believed that that teacher actually played a critical role because he was able to explain and analyse the situation. Naturally, I was a good reader in black history and all those things, where we came from, why and all those things.[8]

Bobby Marie was also a student activist before he joined the unions. It was during this time that his political awareness developed and his student idealism propelled him toward involvement in democratic organizations in the community.[9]

Previous union experience

Many of the workers who joined unions in the 1970s had previous union experience, many of them having joined unions affiliated to the South African Congress of Trade Unions (SACTU). Many of these unions were run democratically and had elected shop-floor committees. Thus many of these older workers would have had some experience of belonging to a democratic organization. Indeed, a study conducted in 1974 revealed that many members of the new unions in the Durban-Pietermaritzburg area regarded Moses Mabhida, a SACTU leader, as one of the most influential leaders in the old Natal province (Lambert, 1988: 161–231). Many of these workers later became activists and leaders in the new unions.

Political and civic movements

Many of the members of the post-1973 unions had previous experience as members of political or liberation movements that had embraced democracy as their goal. Many of these members would have participated in movement activities in the 1950s and 1960s, and some of their experiences were brought into the new unions after 1973 and, according to Baskin (1991), many of them became frontline activists in the struggle to establish these unions.

In later years, movement activists from the civic associations, the United Democratic Front (UDF), and the Africanist and Black Consciousness Movement organizations joined the unions and brought with them considerable experience and skills in mass mobilization and organization. But it is equally true to say that many union leaders brought their experience into these liberation movements.

Liaison committees

After the passing of the Black Labour Relations Regulation Act in 1973, many employers orchestrated the formation of liaison committees as a strategy to bypass or avoid trade unions. Many workers who were to become union leaders in later years participated in these committees. These structures were not democratic but they alerted those involved in them to the problems of working in toy-telephone structures. But to dismiss the entire experience as a negative one would be mistaken. In these structures, some workers learned organizational skills that are essential for running a democratic organization, for example, chairing meetings, taking minutes, giving reports and basic negotiation skills.

Negative experiences of apartheid authoritarianism

Petrus Mashishi, the president of SAMWU, says that most black workers did not join trade unions because they liked them. "We joined the trade unions because of the way we were treated" (Ginsburg and Matlala, 1996: 88). Millions of black workers experienced, in one form or another, the authoritarian nature of apartheid rule and these negative experiences predisposed them to some form of democracy, both as practice within their unions and as an ideal form of government for the entire society. Indeed, for those in the liberation struggle broadly, belonging to a democratic organization and being involved in the fight for democracy placed them on some kind of moral high ground *vis-à-vis* their apartheid oppressors.

Fear of repression

Many activists who participated in the early years of union organization and mobilization argue that unions had no choice but to be democratic. Jeremy Baskin argues that the post-1973 unions "made a virtue out of necessity."[10] Democracy, he says, was made necessary by the hostile environment of employer resistance and state repression and to avoid the victimization of a few individuals. It also ensured that when leaders were victimized, the organization would continue to function since the members took responsibility for the survival of the union.

The contribution of lived experience highlighted above has been neglected by scholars of the South African trade union movement. Part of the reason for this omission could be that some of the experiences do not originate in organizational milieus that are known for being democratic. Indeed, many of the experiences originated in undemocratic environments. However, all these experiences highlight the importance of workers' lived experiences and the fact that transformative associational forms, modes of collective solidarity and identities are never constructed out of pure antecedents but emerge out of life as it is lived by those who participate in the construction of those new associational forms, solidarity, and identities. This approach helps us move away from elitist approaches that always ascribe new ideas to an "intelligent outsider."

Having said the above, we should also note that many of the organizations and arenas where these experiences were gained were often conservative and backward looking. The negative or conservative lived experiences were also capable of being mobilized for different reasons. For example, the traditional experiences could be mobilized by ethnic groupings whose purpose was to collaborate with the apartheid government. In a similar way, religious sentiments could be exploited by conservative groups to discourage political involvement or to encourage collaboration with the apartheid state. Thus, "lived experiences" is a weapon that cuts both ways in that some of these can be mobilized in a transformative way while others can be mobilized in a retrogressive direction. It is here that the role of leadership and intellectuals becomes important, for they play a role in packaging and mobilizing these lived experiences to fit in with the transformative project. This discussion now turns to the contribution of intellectuals in the emergence of the tradition of democratic unionism. Here "intellectuals" is used in its broadest possible sense to include organic intellectuals and others who perform a general leadership role in organizations.

The intellectual contribution to the emergence of democratic unionism

The contribution of intellectuals in the emergence of the democratic tradition of unionism in South Africa is not in dispute. What is at issue is the form that this contribution took as well as the composition of the intellectual group involved in union organizing and mobilization. With reference to the South African trade union movement, the term "intellectual" has been associated only with a particular group of activists who were white and university educated. Many of these activists were employed by the unions, but there were a few of them who were based at universities as researchers and lecturers. Among some black officials and leaders in the unions, the term was used to refer to white officials who had administrative skills and possessed analytical skills that enabled them to "theorize" about the suffering of black workers. Many of these black leaders and officials resented the power of these intellectuals, which derived from their privileged background in the middle class of white society, and thus the term "intellectual" had the connotation of "privileged fellow-traveler" for whom the struggle was not a life-and-death issue.[11]

In this discussion the term is used in a much wider sense, which could be construed to include Gramsci's two categories of traditional and organic intellectuals. Webster (1992) has also used the term in this way with reference to the unions, but he also took it further by disaggregating the category of intellectuals further into five sub-categories, namely, professionally trained intellectuals, party intellectuals, freelance research intellectuals, union-made intellectuals, and grassroots intellectuals. For the purpose of this discussion, the most important role for intellectuals in the trade union movement was the "packaging" of a set of ideas into an ideology and a coherent political program. For the intellectuals to do this, they needed to possess analytical and administrative skills as well as an understanding of the lived experiences of the workers they were organizing. Few of the groups of intellectuals identified here possessed both strengths. Indeed, the strength of the intellectual contribution to the development of post-1973 unions was the combination of different groups possessing different strengths. For example, the strength of a worker leader and official such as Moses Ndlovu in Pietermaritzburg was that he understood the lived experiences of the workers that he organized and could translate abstract terms into a language that the workers understood. By contrast, some of the white officials that he worked with could read many books on theories of trade unionism yet needed to combine this strength with Ndlovu's knowledge to ensure that new strategies were effective.

PARTICIPATORY DEMOCRACY AS EMANCIPATION

At this point we turn to the central theme of this discussion, namely, the emancipatory value of participatory democracy and why it is central to any project of social emancipation. In this regard, we should recall that, in his book *The Social Contract*, Rousseau identified two propositions regarding the importance of participatory democracy. First, participatory democracy is important because it provides every citizen with an opportunity to participate in political decision-making. The significance of this is that this form of democracy allows for the expansion of citizenship and the inclusion of those who would otherwise be excluded from the affairs of a community or the society as a whole.

Second, Rousseau appreciated the psychological effect of participatory democracy on the participants by "ensuring that there is a continuing inter-relationship between the working of institutions and the psychological qualities and attitudes of individuals interacting within them" (Pateman, 1970: 22). At the core of this proposition is the notion that the participation is free from coercion, is meaningful, and is an expression of the autonomy of the participants.

These propositions are germane to our discussion here, particularly insofar as they help us debunk conventional notions of freedom and democracy, which are based on two misleading dichotomies. The first dichotomy is that of "oppression versus democracy," which presents the issues in a zero-sum fashion. In other words, many would argue that either you have freedom or you have oppression, but you cannot have elements of both at the same time. This sort of reasoning then leads to an assumption that once you get rid of oppression, you get a democratic system that includes everyone in decision-making. However, existing evidence shows that most democratic transitions do not necessarily result in an inclusion of the majority in processes of decision-making nor do they lead to psychological emancipation as envisaged by Rousseau. All they result in is a formal kind of democracy where participation by the majority is limited to participation in periodic elections.

In the same way, under an oppressive regime there is always room for the oppressed to exercise some control and participation in deciding certain issues that affect their lives. This participation and control become more visible as the struggle intensifies and as ordinary people realize that they need to "build the future today." To some extent, the period from the mid-1980s to the early 1990s was such a period in South Africa, when alternative institutions and politics replaced, even if temporarily, the hegemonic institutions of the apartheid regime. Thus the people's courts, the street and area committees, the workers' industrial area committees, the local shop stewards' committees, and the workplace general meetings of this period represented a moment of emancipation for those involved. However, the problem with these enclaves of emancipation is that their scope is circumscribed and their influence confined to the small local communities that are constantly under threat of being disrupted and reincorporated under the orbit of the oppressive regime.

The second dichotomy that is often misleading is that of "reform versus revolutionary rupture" and how the former is associated with continued oppression (albeit in a modified form) and the latter with freedom and democracy. Many struggle activists and scholars tend to see a separation between the struggle itself and the ultimate goal of that struggle. In other words, there is often failure to conceive of struggle itself as an emancipatory moment when the oppressed consciously reject the constraints imposed on them by the oppressors and begin to work toward a new society based on new principles of social organization and governance. Thus the obsession with the moment of revolutionary rupture leads many to fail to appreciate the significance of embryonic moments of social emancipation as they unfold during the struggle itself. However, what history has shown us is that the moment of rupture, whether it is ushered in through a violent revolution or peaceful negotiations, seldom lives up to expectations in terms of its emancipatory possibilities. What it achieves, instead, is to disarm activists and demobilize all of those who, in their communities, workplaces, schools, and organizations, were involved in building real utopias that gave meaning to their lives.

The foregoing discussion serves to highlight the centrality of participatory democracy to the discourse of emancipation. It also suggests that participation can be a method of conducting a struggle as well as a goal of that struggle. This observation has implications for the way we conceive of freedom and democracy because it helps us avoid the dichotomous approach that limits our understanding of the dialectical nature of social change.

A related additional point is what Pateman refers to as the "educative" or "social training" function of participatory democracy, which leads her to characterize the participatory democratic model as

> one where maximum input (participation) is required and where output includes not just policies (decisions) but also the development of the social and political capacities of each individual, so that there is "feedback" from output to input. (1970: 43)

In South Africa this was more evident in the trade union movement in the 1980s and the early 1990s. The grassroots structures of the unions, in the form of workplace general meetings and local shop stewards' councils, served as a training ground for millions of organized workers as they deliberated on internal union policy matters as well as issues pertaining to their wages and conditions of employment and broader political issues of the time. For these workers, unions had become veritable "schools of democracy" and out of this experience many of them graduated into regional and national roles. Since the democratic political transition, thousands of these men and women have been called upon to perform leadership roles in other arenas, such as politicians in local, provincial and national government, civil servants, managers in the private sector, and leading figures in non-governmental organizations.

In their comparative study of democracy and capitalist development in the twentieth century, Rueschemeyer, Stephens and Stephens (1992) have argued that the working class is the "most consistently pro-democratic force" because it has an interest in achieving its political and social inclusion (1992: 8). In South Africa, this class also took the lead in experimenting with models of democracy, both participatory and representative in their mode of organization, and in fighting for democracy as an ideal for the whole society. Indeed, the mobilizing strength of the pro-democratic movement derived, to a large extent, from the democratic and participatory character of the movement's organized formations.

The section that follows reviews some of the strengths and weaknesses of these experiments and considers some of the factors that led to the decline of the participatory tradition during the transition to a post-apartheid society.

THE DECLINE OF PARTICIPATORY DEMOCRACY DURING
THE TRANSITION TO A POST-APARTHEID SOCIETY

According to Rueschemeyer, Stephens and Stephens (1992), a relatively weak working class enables the middle classes to take a leading role in struggles for democratization, with the consequence that democracy is often limited. But then they caution that in each historical case, one needs to examine the specific configuration of class coalitions and the relative strength of different classes in order to understand how the balance of power shapes the prospects for democratic change. An examination of the South African case shows that the working classes were not weak. Indeed, the working class was highly mobilized and well organized on a number of fronts, particularly in its trade unions and civic organizations. Prior to the 1994 elections, the main liberation movement, the African National Congress (ANC), which had to re-establish itself as a mass-based political party after 30 years of imprisonment, exile, and underground operation, found that it had no choice but to embrace radical notions of political democracy and economic redistribution as outlined in the union-initiated Reconstruction and Development Program (RDP). How did it come about, then, that the country ended up with a conventional model of democracy that leaves very little scope for mass participation? The answer lies in the configuration of class forces within the liberation movement, relations among the different networks in the liberation movement and the re-alignment of class forces since 1990.

Before the unbanning of the exiled ANC, the SACP and the Pan-Africanist Congress (PAC) in 1990, the political stage of mass-based opposition politics was occupied by the trade union movement, the UDF, civic organizations, and several other civil society organizations. But by far the most powerful and best-organized forces were the unions, particularly the Congress of South African Trade Unions (COSATU). In all these organizations, notions of establishing "democratic organs of self-government" were very influential, as spelt out in the *Freedom Charter*. It was envisaged that these structures would become the new institutional forms through which power would be exercised in a liberated South Africa. Thus in 1986 a prominent community leader gave a very optimistic assessment of the new structures of "people's power," asserting that in some townships people were taking over power by "starting to run those townships in different ways" (Sisulu, 1986: 104). He then went on to identify some of the developments in this regard:

> People exercised power by starting to take control in areas such as crime, the clearing of the townships and the creation of people's parks, the provision of first aid, and even in the schools. I want to emphasize here that these advances were only possible because of the development of democratic organs, or committees, of people's power. Our people set up bodies which

were controlled by, and accountable to, the masses of people in each area. In such areas, the distinction between the people and their organizations disappeared. All the people young and old participated in committees from street level upwards. The development of people's power has caught the imagination of our people, even where struggles are breaking out for the first time. There is a growing tendency for ungovernability to be transformed into elementary forms of people's power, as people take the lead from the semi-liberated zones. (1986: 104)

In a similar way, the trade unions had become organs of people's power and were posing fundamental questions about the economy and how it should be managed. Some were beginning to spell out the form of management that they envisaged, in the form of workers' councils that would be similar to those in place under the Yugoslavian system of worker self-management. Incidentally, Richard Turner (1980) had devoted a considerable amount of space in his book discussing participatory democracy, and he was also in favor of worker self-management through workers' councils.

However, from 1990 there was a marked decline of the participatory democratic discourse and several reasons can be advanced for this. First, the negotiated nature of the democratic transition had a demobilizing effect on ordinary citizens and thus undermined efforts toward self-organization at the grassroots level. During the negotiation phase of the transition, the future of the country seemed to depend more on the outcome of deal-making by a few leaders, and grassroots democratic structures, which had emerged in the course of struggles, did not seem to matter to these leaders. In 1991 a frustrated unionist expressed these sentiments about the ANC's approach to the political negotiations:

How can you mobilize your mass membership for action around demands, when at any moment someone will go off and negotiate with your opponent again—you don't know on what mandate, and what was agreed? It simply confuses people. They don't know what they are acting for, so they do nothing. (cited in Von Holdt, 1991: 19)

The effect of this was that power gradually slipped out of the hands of grassroots structures such as street committees, civic organizations, local union structures, women's organizations, and youth bodies and became centralized in the hands of those who were close to, or part of, the political negotiations process. Since 1994, this demobilization has translated into a kind of mass inertia and an expectation that the leadership and the democratic government should "deliver" services.

Second, the leadership of the unbanned ANC brought a different style of leadership into the mass democratic movement. Most of these leaders had just come back from prison or exile and were often out of touch with developments within the democratic movement. The negative aspects of the style that they brought into the democratic movement were secrecy, lack of consultation (of ANC members and members of the ANC's allied organizations), reliance on certain personalities such as Mandela and the fact that most of these leaders did not come from defined constituencies in the form of local and branch structures. All of this discouraged any form of direct or indirect participation by those operating in local structures of the mass movement.

Third, many of the exiled leaders who came back into the democratic movement had "an inadequate understanding of mass organization and action" (von Holdt, 1991), and dominated the leadership ranks of the ANC. In exile, almost all of these leaders had been hosted by authoritarian regimes and some had assimilated the negative practices of their host governments. Even though these leaders proclaimed that they wanted to establish a democratic system founded on the spirit of the *Freedom Charter* to let the people govern, many of them had embraced the Schumpeterian notion that the masses cannot participate or govern. However, these "exile" and "prison" leaders of the ANC remained extremely powerful within the movement because of the "revolutionary aura" that many ordinary people associated with being imprisoned or being exiled. Indeed, many of the so-called internal leaders also felt obliged to defer to the "leadership," who had earned that status by virtue of having made the sacrifice of going to jail or into exile. In the moment of excitement with important leaders and deal-making that promised to bring about what had seemed impossible even at the height of the mass struggles of the 1980s, many began to take the participatory democratic tradition for granted and to assume that a representative kind of democracy would lead to the same outcomes. In the minds of many, it seemed impossible that such a "tried and tested" leadership could deviate from the democratic course and act in a way that was at variance with the aspirations of the majority.

Fourth, the South African transition occurred at the same time as the collapse of state socialism that to many had come to symbolize a radical alternative to capitalism. What also disappeared with the collapse of the Eastern bloc were utopian notions of social transformation, and this left many activists and movement intellectuals content with limited or elite notions of democracy. Many of these activists and intellectuals were won over to the view that "there is no alternative" (TINA), and several of them have actually joined the ranks of the capitalist class by riding on the wave of so-called "black economic empowerment."

Fifth, processes of class formation or elite formation have accelerated, with many of the leading activists, who were part of the tradition of democratic participation, having become beneficiaries of new opportunities created by the deracialization of society. Thus the discourse of a collective participatory democratic culture has been overtaken by one of individualism and careerism where empowerment is seen to emanate from taking advantage of opportunities created by deracialization.

Sixth, the state-sponsored campaign of violent terror that was unleashed on the democratic movement soon after the unbanning of the ANC and the release of Nelson Mandela had a debilitating effect on the practice of democracy in organizations. The violence was clearly intended to demoralize communities, to terrorize activists, and to smash the innovative forms of resistance and organization that had developed over the years. Many local structures, such as street committees and local shop stewards' councils, ceased to meet, and many activists and members of organizations stopped attending meetings. In the circumstances, decision-making was left to a few individuals, thus engendering a new style of leadership that lacked accountability.

Finally, there were many other factors that led to a diminution of the democratic tradition in mass organizations in the early 1990s. Among these has been the generational change in the mass organizations that were part of the struggle. For example, many of the union activists from the 1970s to the early 1990s have moved on and have been replaced by a new generation of younger activists who were not part of the social experiences of the earlier period.

All the above have coalesced into a new culture of organization and leadership that stands in contrast with the nascent tradition of participatory democracy in South Africa. This elite culture of democracy coincided with the intensification of South Africa's insertion into the global economy. All of these processes have engendered a new political culture in organizations and state agencies that is beholden to national and global capitalist interests. This culture seeks to reinforce rather than challenge the hegemonic processes of globalization, and it is about the marginalization, rather than the empowerment, of subordinate classes, grassroots movements, and local communities. Indeed, this culture appropriates the language and discourse of democracy to oppress, marginalize, and atomize rather than emancipate. Thus, today, in the face of a growing challenge by grassroots movements and activists, the usual refrain by many government representatives is that "the government has a duty to govern." Gone are slogans about "organs of people's power" or such clarion calls of the heady days of the democratic struggle in the 1980s as "The People Shall Govern."

In 1991 the National Union of Mineworkers (NUM), the largest and most influential union that is an affiliate of COSATU, adopted a resolution on the political alliance between COSATU, the ANC, and the SACP in which they noted that "decades of illegality have imposed serious limitations on the ANC." The resolution then pointed out that the unions that had experience and leadership had a duty to build the ANC and that the "accumulated experience of participatory democracy, accountability and mandates of the trade union movement must permeate ANC structures at all levels" (cited in von Holdt, 1991: 27). However, these good intentions have failed to materialize. Not only did the unions and other mass organizations fail to infuse their participatory democratic culture into the ANC, but many unions and community organizations themselves have been losing that culture of participation, mandates and leadership accountability. One of the most effective excuses used by unaccountable leadership in organization today is that issues associated with global economic restructuring are complex and, under this pretext, small groups of individuals end up making all the decisions.

TOWARD A PARTICIPATORY DEMOCRATIC TRADITION

Despite the changed national and global conditions, there is scope for revitalizing the participatory democratic tradition in South Africa. Indeed, the national democratic dispensation does open up space for political contestation and mobilization without the threat of state repression. However, for such attempts at resuscitating the participatory democratic tradition to be successful, certain conditions need to exist. First, there must be a thorough-going critique of the current dispensation and a contestation of the notion of democracy itself. Such a critique and contestation would be aimed at re-appropriating the ideals of democracy and injecting an emancipatory content into the discourse and practice of democracy. Such a critique and contestation must seek to place participatory democracy at the center of the new discourse as a means to the end, namely social justice and emancipation.

In the context of South Africa and many other countries in the developing world, social emancipation should be understood in the context of the realities facing subordinate classes, namely, poverty, hunger, violence and crime, patriarchy, racism, social marginalization, and the legacy of colonialism as manifested by dependency on the developed countries. All these realities are obstacles to social inclusion and emancipation in that they exacerbate social marginalization and the exclusion of subordinate groups and classes. In this regard, participatory democracy is one of the ways in which the social and political inclusion of the marginalized and oppressed classes can be guaranteed in a reformed social system. This implies that, in addition to seeking to expand arenas of popular democratic participation, a project of social emancipation should also seek to identify and resuscitate past structures as well as preserve existing structures that enhance participation at grassroots levels of society. In this regard, the participatory elements of African traditional modes of government discussed earlier in this chapter could be adapted and combined with representative forms. The experience of the trade union movement and civic organizations shows that it is possible to do this without these forms losing their integrity. However, this resuscitation and preservation of certain forms of government and decision-making would have to be accompanied by an acknowledgement that participation is a crucial dimension of social emancipation that allows subordinate classes to articulate their interests and assert their power. Left-wing intellectuals and organic intellectuals from these classes would then have to contest the notion that representative democracy is the only way to make decisions and run government in modern societies. They would have to show that the popular refrain by the elites and their intellectuals that "participation in contemporary society is impossible" because of the complexity of the issues and the size of the population is nothing but a justification for the exclusion of the majority from shaping their future.

However, asserting the virtues of participatory democracy is not an easy task, particularly under the current hegemonic paradigm where decentralized decision-making is considered by many to be inefficient and primitive, while representation by elected representatives and consultants is considered efficient and modern. This cynicism and elitism can also be found among current and past community activists and unionists. A former unionist has argued that, in a context where union membership has grown by leaps and bounds and "as issues become more complex," the unions must accept that "substantial decision making will have to end up in the hands of a few individuals rather than structures of any kind" (Schreiner, 1994: 47). A project of social emancipation has to contend with this elitism and cynicism and make a convincing case showing why participatory democracy is a minimum requirement for the emancipation of subordinate classes.

Second, the above suggests a need to go beyond a critique and begin to explore "real utopias" that enable local communities and grassroots structures to shape the agenda of social emancipation. This would go a long way toward alleviating the alienation associated with what Rose (1967) termed "the mass society," where individuals are socially isolated from one another. But most importantly, it would achieve an objective that Turner identified as being of cardinal importance to the project of social emancipation:

> It is to give individuals the maximum possible amount of control over what happens to themselves and hence the maximum possible amount of freedom to decide what they want, and then to act to get it. Its object is to free the individual both from the direct power of others and from the power of hidden social forces. It is not a choice, but a framework within which choice becomes possible. (1980: 83)

Third, attempts to reinvent democracy and social emancipation must speak the language of real people grappling with real problems in all spheres of society. Successful cases of community and worker mobilization and organization in the South African struggle show that participatory democracy is most successful when subordinate classes are able to appropriate and translate intellectual discourses into action to better their conditions. This implies that such discourses have to be intelligible enough to lend themselves to practical and meaningful application and experimentation. Thus these discourses must also suggest realistic and winnable goals that build cumulatively toward more fundamental changes.

Fourth, there is a need to forge new local, regional, national and international networks to link local struggles and build overarching solidarities that allow for the sharing of experiences and the removal of atomization of subordinate classes and their struggles. In the main, these have got to aim at the free or voluntary exchange of experiences and knowledge rather than the creation of bureaucratic structures. This would have to entail creative uses of different forms of the mass media and new forms of communication to assert alternative or counter-hegemonic forms of globalization.

Finally, the above implies a need to reinvent the left itself so that it grasps the challenges of building counter-hegemonic global struggles and experiments in alternative forms of social organization. It also means that the left has got to rethink its role within the changing conditions of neoliberal globalization. In particular, the role of left intellectuals needs to be assessed since they stand in a very powerful position to shape and reshape discourses; however, there is always a danger that some may abuse the power and authority that derive from their intellectual role because they confuse it with political leadership. This is important because intellectuals have the power to lend legitimacy to certain discourses and to delegitimize others.

Thus, the reinvention of social emancipation and the revitalization of participation as its kernel is simultaneously a political and an intellectual project and, as such, requires contestation at both levels. In the era of global neoliberalism, such contestation needs to occur at all levels, including the global arena. Among other things, it has to contest the trivialization of everything local and counter the glorification of the so-called global village, whose essence is inscribed with the interests of capitalism.

Notes

1 For a detailed discussion of the difference between social and market regulation see the excellent piece by Standing (1997).

2 The book was first published in 1972. Turner was murdered by apartheid assassins on 8 January 1978.

3 Jeremy Baskin, personal interview, 24 February 2000.

4 A kangaroo court is an unprocedural or improperly constituted trial. It is deemed unprocedural and unfair because it does not follow fair and procedural norms. Kangaroo courts are therefore part of what some term "rough justice."

5 This is a traditional African village assembly, usually presided over by the chief or his/her representative. It is usually an open forum where members of the

village gather to discuss issues that affect them. These gatherings are still widely used in South Africa's rural villages as democratic forums.

6 Moses Mayekiso, personal interview, 11 August 1999.

7 This is a traditional African court where villagers gather to hear and adjudicate cases of a civil and criminal nature. Today this structure has been modified to suit modern circumstances. The people's courts in urban black townships in the 1980 were modelled on this structure.

8 Nelson Ndinisa, personal interview, 20 April 1999.

9 Bobby Marie, personal interview, 26 October 1999.

10 Jeremy Baskin, personal interview, 24 February 2000.

11 See, for example, comments by Andrew Zulu on intellectuals as cited in MacShane, Plaut and Ward (1984: 70). Petrus Tom also made a similar comment at the end of his book when he warned workers: "My message to the working class is that nobody will liberate you except yourselves. Don't give your struggle to intellectuals, academics and other organizations who do not have the workers' interests at heart, who want to further their aims at the expense of the workers" (1985: 68).

Bibliography

Baskin, J. (1991). *Striking Back: A History of COSATU*. Johannesburg: Ravan.

Davidson, B. (1981). *The People's Cause: A History of Guerrillas in Africa*. Essex: Longman.

Freund, B. (1999). "The Weight of History; The Prospects for Democratisation in South Africa," in J. Hyslop (ed.), *African Democracy in the Era of Globalization*. Johannesburg: Witwatersrand UP, pp. 431–41.

Friedman, S. (1987). *Building Tomorrow Today: African Workers in Trade Unions, 1970–1984*. Johannesburg: Ravan.

Gabriels, H. (1992). "The Leader of the Cape Town Municipal Strike in 1990—Interview with Salie Manie," *South African Labour Bulletin*, 16(4): 77–9.

Ginsburg, M., and W. Matlala (1996). "At Home in the Union—Interview with Petros Mashishi," *South African Labour Bulletin*, 20(6): 86–8.

Gramsci, A. (1971). "The Intellectuals," in Q. Hoare and G. Nowell-Smith (eds), *Selections From the Prison Notebooks of Antonia Gramsci*. London: Lawrence and Wishart.

Hammond-Tooke, W. D. (1975). *Command or Consensus: The Development of Transkeian Local Government*. Cape Town: David Philip.

Hobsbawm, E. (1983). "Introduction: Inventing Traditions," in E. Hobsbawm and T. Ranger (eds.), *The Invention of Tradition*. Cambridge: Cambridge UP, pp. 1–14.

Lambert, R. (1988). "Political Unionism in South Africa: An Analysis of the South African Congress of Trade Unions." Unpublished PhD thesis, University of the Witwatersrand, Johannesburg.

MacShane, D., M. Plaut, and D. Ward (1984). *Power!: Black Workers, Their Unions and the Struggle for Freedom in South Africa.* Nottingham: Spokesman.

Mayekiso, M. (1996). *Township Politics: Civic Struggles for a New South Africa.* New York: Monthly Review Press.

Parry, G., and G. Moyser (1994). "More Participation, More Democracy?" in D. Beetham (ed.), *Defining and Measuring Democracy.* London: Sage, pp. 44–62.

Pateman, C. (1970). *Participation and Democratic Theory.* Cambridge: Cambridge UP.

Rueschmeyer, D., E. H. Stephens, and J. D. Stephens (1992). *Capitalist Development and Democracy.* Chicago: U of Chicago P.

Rose, A. (1967). *The Power Structure: Political Process in American Society.* New York: Oxford UP.

Schreiner, G. (1994). "Restructuring the Labour Movement After Apartheid," *South African Labour Bulletin*, 18(3): 43–49.

Schumpeter, J. A. (1987). *Capitalism, Socialism and Democracy.* 6th ed. London: Unwin.

Sisulu, Z. (1986). "People's Education for People's Power," *Transformation*, 1: 96–117.

Standing, G. (1997). "Globalization, Labour Flexibility and Insecurity: The Era of Market Regulation," *European Journal of Industrial Relations*, 3(1): 7–37.

Thompson, E. P. (1963). *The Making of the English Working Class.* New York: Vintage Books.

Tom, P. (1985). *My Life Struggle.* Johannesburg: Ravan.

Turner, R. (1980). *The Eye of the Needle: Toward Participatory Democracy in South Africa.* Johannesburg: Ravan Press.

United Democratic Front (UDF) (1986). "Building People's Power," *Isizwe*, 1(2): 2–14.

Von Holdt, K. (1991). "The COSATU/ANC Alliance: What Does COSATU Think?," *South African Labour Bulletin*, 15(8): 17–29.

Webster, E. (1979). "A Profile of Unregistered Union Members in Durban," *South African Labour Bulletin*, 4(8): 43–74.

Webster, E. (1992). "The Impact of Intellectuals on the Labour Movement," *Transformation*, 18: 88–92.

Zikalala, S. (1993). "Interview with Veteran Unionist Emma Mashinini," *South African Labour Bulletin*, 17(4): 87–9.

3

The Constitutional Court and Social Emancipation in Colombia*

Rodrigo Uprimny and Mauricio García-Villegas

INTRODUCTION

The purpose of this chapter is to evaluate the emancipatory potential of some rulings of the Colombian Constitutional Court. During the past nine years, the court has had a leading role in Colombian political life. In general terms, it has been vigorous in its protection of the rights of individuals and minorities, as well as in its intention to control abuses of power. The court's labors have been considerable, not only because of the sheer number of rulings it has made and the variety of subjects it has addressed, but also because it has, to a certain degree, surprised Colombian society with its progressive orientation. This explains the fact that the court has won a certain amount of appreciation and prestige from social sectors and groups that are very critical of other state bodies but that perceive in the court's decisions some of the few real opportunities for truly protecting their rights.

The Colombian constitutional experience is atypical and it appears to be unrelated to counter-hegemonic issues: on the one hand, cases related to these issues appear in a contemporary liberal capitalist state institution and, on the other hand, they make use of the law, seen as the most essential instrument for domination in this state model. How has this been possible in Colombia? Is it not contrary to common sense to talk about counter-hegemonic emancipation coming from the state? Are we then dealing with a sort of "hegemonic emancipation"? Our objective in this chapter is to explain how, and with what limitations, these cases are significant in terms of emancipation,[1] as well as how they have acquired unusual importance not only in Colombia but also in other semiperipheral countries.

* We wish to thank the following students from the National University for their valuable contributions to the empirical research in this essay: Magda Ayala, Paola Jiménez, Úrsula Mendoza, Liliana Rincón, and Ernesto Mieles. We would also like to thank Professors Diego López, Rodolfo Arango, and Danilo Rojas for their comments.

The organization of this chapter largely follows from the methodology that we have employed. It was impossible to evaluate systematically the entire body of the court's work, but at the same time we felt it necessary to analyze, in empirical terms, the impact of its decisions. For this reason, we decided to combine theoretical reflection with some case studies that we thought were significant. We will start by presenting the most relevant positions in the theoretical debate regarding the potential to achieve social change through judicial decisions. We have tried to establish a "dialogue" between the arguments in this debate and the cases that we have studied in Colombian constitutional jurisprudence, taking also the social and institutional reality into account. In this exercise, we endeavor to take advantage of the analytical richness of the theoretical discussion in core countries in order to develop a new conceptual framework that can be used to understand the relationship between law and social emancipation in semiperipheral countries, and in Colombia in particular, as well as the possibilities and limitations of constitutional justice in this respect.

THE THEORETICAL DEBATE

The study of the emancipatory dimension of the rulings rendered by constitutional judges in Colombia is a topic that is less specific than it seems at first. Since the mid-1980s, judges have taken such a leading role in a significant number of democratic countries that some authors have spoken of a transfer of the burden of democratic legitimation from political bodies to judicial ones (Santos, 2001a). The judges in the limelight have been, on the one hand, criminal judges in their fight against political corruption and, on the other, constitutional judges in their defense of fundamental rights. The Constitutional Courts have assumed particular importance in the countries of Eastern Europe and in many others around the world that are in a process of democratic transition.[2] These courts have played a key political role, often contrary to the role foreseen for them by the reigning political system and even at times in opposition to the logic of the capitalist marketplace. This leads to a *judicialization* of political conflicts, which in its turn implies a politicization of judicial conflicts (Santos, 2001a). The Constitutional Courts of Hungary[3] and South Africa[4] are the best-known examples, but other equally important instances are the Supreme Courts of India,[5] Russia, Korea,[6] and Colombia, as we will show in this chapter.

However, the counter-hegemonic character of legal protagonism should be analyzed with great care since the main international development agencies—which do not exactly represent a symbol of counter-hegemonic struggle—have for over a decade been dedicating the core of their resources to promoting judicial authority.[7] This caution is above all necessary in the sphere of civil and criminal law, since this is the privileged context of the phenomenon of judicial globalization. In effect, a good part of these international resources are destined to increase the efficiency of those legal processes most necessary to the functioning of the capitalist market, and therefore a *prima facie* empathy can be posited between judicial efficiency and hegemonic interests.

The situation of constitutional judges appears to be different. In the first place, they have not been the privileged beneficiaries of the economic resources mentioned above, and, in the second place, their decisions usually affect essential hegemonic interests, as we will see below in the Colombian case. Thus it is important not to confuse the meaning of these parallel developments: on the one side, an increase in judicial efficacy intended primarily to protect globalized capitalist interests[8] and, on the other, the leading role of judges in the attack on corruption and violation of fundamental rights. In general terms, different and even contrary logics are involved, although in certain circumstances they can be mutually reinforcing.[9]

After these considerations, let us return to the theoretical debate. To what extent can progressive judicial rulings engender significant social change? Is the legal struggle in the courts a profitable strategy for social movements and for the political left? Is the law an effective instrument for social emancipation? These are some of the key questions of the debate on the judiciary and social change that took place during the 1980s in the United States. During the 1970s a good part of the political struggle was directed at achieving legal reform or obtaining judicial decisions that could counter discrimination. This strategy was known as the Civil Rights Movement. A decade later, academics debated the evaluation of this process (the civil rights experience). On one side were those authors who, from the sociology of law, supported the position that significant social changes could be won through judicial decisions (Rosenberg, 1991: 21–30). On the other side were the Critical Legal Studies scholars, who led and encouraged this debate, and who took a skeptical position concerning legal battles. In their opinion the struggle for civil rights did not bring the anticipated results.[10]

In the semiperipheral states the law/social change debate is posited in less instrumental terms than in the core countries. That is to say, the terms of the debate are less related to the logic that links legal aims, means, and results. This might have several explanations. The first grows out of the classic distinction between the state and civil society:[11] in the semiperiphery, this dichotomy—as well as its derivations: law/society, public/private, law/politics—is often even more problematic than it is in the core countries. As a consequence, the autonomy of legal discourse with respect to other social and institutional discourses tends to be more precarious. The law, and particularly public law, has less autonomy from the political system. The legal system takes on in good measure the dynamics of the political system so that a type of isomorphism occurs between, on the one hand, political discourses,

which relate less to the representation of social interests than to mere ideological debates, and, on the other hand, legal norms, which follow less the
technical requirements of social regulation than the political necessities of
institutional legitimization. The second reason is more specific and directly
linked to the first: in these countries, state law is a more precarious instrument of social influence than it usually is in the core countries. Two facts
may illustrate this precariousness: one is the marked difference that exists
between *law-in-books* and *law-in-action*. A good part of *law-in-books* either fails
in instrumental terms or is created to fulfill aims that are different from the
ones for which it was designed. The second fact is that of legal pluralism,
that is, the existence of a number of official and unofficial sources of regulation that are frequently interrelated in complex interactions.

Colombia follows this general tendency of the semiperipheral countries
in that the autonomy of the legal system is reduced, not only with respect
to the political system—as a result of the political instrumentalization of
law—but also with respect to the social system, as a result of the lack of legal
effectiveness and the prevalence of legal pluralism. However, this tendency
is accentuated in Colombia. Beyond the social anomie in politics that is characteristic of the entire subcontinent, there are three additional aggravating
elements that are intimately interrelated. They are the following: 1) the
relative failure of governments' efforts to strengthen social democracy both
through agrarian reform (Findley, 1972: 923; Gros, 1988; Pinto, 1971) and
through the extension of social rights; 2) the devaluation of the democratic
system as a result of its militarization through the existence of a state of
exception and its strongly exclusionist and clientelistic political character;
and 3) the close relationship that is found in Colombia between the anomie
of the political discourse and violence throughout the course of its political
history (Pécaut, 1978, 1997; Deas, 1995).

Three additional points of clarification attenuate this perhaps excessively
politicized image of Colombian law in favor of the state. In the first place,
the hyper-legality of Colombian institutional life is related not only to an
institutional strategy of legitimation but also to a civilian tradition that dates
back to independence and that has made possible a certain control of the
executive power through legal decisions and the electoral system. The
creation of the Constitutional Court, for example, would not have been
possible without the existence of a strong tradition of judicial review in
Colombia. In the second place and linked to the first point, it is important
to bear in mind that the use of law for institutional legitimization in
Colombia is effective only to the degree that at least a minimal level of
instrumental efficacy is achieved (Edelman, 1971; Bourdieu, 1986: 14). The
fact that a common strategy of political legitimization is making the law
live up to its claims and ambitions, that is, making law efficacious, cannot
be overlooked. Finally, and this is the point most germane to the subject of

this chapter, we have to take into account that, although the production of law with legitimizing intentions has been a more or less fruitful strategy of social domination, it is also a double-edged sword. The symbols of social change and protection of rights that it embodies may be appropriated by social movements, individuals, or even by state institutions, and particularly by judges, who take the law seriously and use it as an instrument of resistance or emancipation from hegemonic power. In this case, the legal strength of the state might be a useful element in articulating emancipatory social practices, or at least in stimulating practices of resistance to hegemonic power. The Constitutional Court moves, therefore, in this border zone between institutional weakness and emancipatory social practices.

REASONS FOR THE COURT'S PROGRESSIVE ACTIVISM

The Colombian Constitutional Court's progressive activism raises at least the following question: bearing in mind that the few comparative studies that exist on judicial institutions underline that the courts and the law tend to be conservative and to reflect and protect the existing dominant interests,[12] what elements could then explain the Colombian Constitutional Court's progressive tendencies and prominent role? There is no easy answer, but there are some elements that could explain this evolution.

The Constitutional Court was created under the new Constitution that the Constituent Assembly approved in 1991. However, Colombia already had a long tradition of judicial control over constitutionality. Going back to at least 1910, the Supreme Court of Justice was granted the binding authority to rule on a law's constitutionality. As a consequence, when the Constitutional Court began operating in 1992, the Colombian legal and political culture was already very familiar with the judicial review, to the point that few in the judicial community thought it strange that this court had the power to annul laws that had been approved by Congress.[13] The court could therefore act vigorously, without fear that the executive branch or the political forces would decide to shut it down, as has happened in other countries in which the first task that constitutional courts have faced has been to win legitimacy for its role.

Second, the procedural design makes the access to constitutional justice in Colombia very easy and inexpensive. Thus, since 1910, when public actions were instituted, any citizen may ask that any law be declared unconstitutional, without needing a lawyer or any other formalities. The 1991 Constitution also created the *tutela* action, by virtue of which any person, without any special requisites, may directly request that a judge intervene to protect his or her fundamental rights. It is relatively easy for citizens to transform a complaint into a legal issue that the constitutional justice system must decide upon and within a quite short period of time. As has been demonstrated in comparative legal studies, greater access to justice brings about greater political influence for the courts (Jacob *et al.*, 1996: 396 ff.).

Thirdly, the procedural design of constitutional justice also confers enormous legal powers on the court. In practice, due to its ability to annul, for constitutional reasons, other judges' decisions, the Constitutional Court has been growing in prominence as a super-court. And this also facilitates its activism, since there tends to be more judicial activism and leadership, as comparative sociology demonstrates, in countries where most of the authority is concentrated in a single supreme court, such as in the United States. This contrasts with countries such as France where this power is distributed among different courts and jurisdictions (Jacob *et al.*, 1996: 389).

Beyond these institutional legal elements, there are two structural political factors that have stimulated the court's activism: the crisis in representation and the weakness of the social movements and opposition parties. Colombians' disenchantment with politics has led certain sectors to demand answers from the judiciary to problems that, in principle, should be debated and resolved by means of citizens' participation in the political sphere. This phenomenon is not exclusive to Colombia (Santos *et al.*, 1995), but in this country the weakness of the mechanisms for political representation runs deep, a fact that has enabled the court to assume a more prominent role. On many occasions, what has taken place is not that the court takes on other powers, but rather that it has stepped in to fill the vacuum that they have left. This intervention appears legitimate to broad sectors of society that feel that at least one power exists that acts in a progressive and able manner.

On the other hand, Colombia has a historical tradition of weak social movements, compared to other peripheral or Latin American countries.[14] Furthermore, in recent years, violence has considerably raised the costs and risks of their actions—many leaders and activists have been murdered. These two factors—historical weakness and growing risks—tend to strengthen the judicial role, especially that of the Constitutional Court. In effect, since access to constitutional justice is cheap and easy, and constitutional judges tend to adopt progressive positions, it is natural that many social groups are tempted to make use of legal arguments rather than resorting to social and political mobilization, which has enormous risks and costs in Colombia.

All of the above may explain the court's activism, but an obvious question remains: why did this court take on a progressive role when it could have undertaken a different kind of activism?[15] To answer this question, the characteristics of the process of constitutional transition take on considerable relevance.

The 1991 Constitution was not the product of a triumphant revolution but rather grew out of complex historical context as an attempt to come to an agreement for broadening democracy in order to confront violence and political corruption. Under these circumstances, some political and social forces that had been traditionally excluded from running for office in Colombia played a very important role in the Constituent Assembly. These included representatives of demobilized guerrilla groups, indigenous groups, and religious minorities.[16] In this pluralistic framework, the diagnosis of many of the delegates was that exclusion, the lack of participation, and weakness in protecting human rights were the basic causes of the Colombian crisis. This explains some of the ideological orientations of the 1991 Constitution: the broadening of participation mechanisms, the imposition of the duties of promoting social justice and equality upon the state, and the incorporation of a meaningful bill of rights, as well as new judicial mechanisms for their protection. The 1991 Constitution is not, therefore, in Teitel's words, "backward looking" but rather "forward looking" (1997: 214) in that, more than attempting to codify the existing power relations, it projects a model of the society to be built.

All of the above explains the Constitution's generosity on the subject of rights, including not only the classic civil and political rights, but also conferring great legal force to social rights and what are known as collective or third-generation rights. This is conducive to a certain amount of judicial activism in favor of human rights, which had less legal grounding in the previous constitution.

However, the court's active intervention in developing the progressive components of the Constitution would not have been necessary if the political forces themselves had taken on this task. But what took place was that many of the social and political actors that dominated the 1991 Constituent Assembly were considerably and rapidly weakened in the following years. The forces that have dominated Congress and the electoral scene since 1992, although not declared enemies of the 1991 Constitution, have not been committed to cultivating it.

On the other hand, there is also a strong tension between the social content of many of the Constitution's clauses and the development strategies that the Colombian government has implemented since 1990. Thus, while the Constitution to some degree demanded more state presence and the authorities' intervention in redistribution, the government was implementing development plans that tended to cut back on the state's social presence and let the market forces assign resources. Perhaps the area most fraught with tension, although not the only one, was the field of labor law. While the 1991 Constitution enshrined important labor and union guarantees, and conferred domestic legal force to the International Labor Organization (ILO) conventions, the Gaviria government (1990–94) was pushing through a labor reform that affected job stability.

This tended over time to create a growing tension between the normative Constitution (the text, the values, and the rights set out in the charter) and the real Constitution (the relation between political forces) (Gómez, 1995).

The weakening of the political forces that wrote the Constitution in Congress, and the government's neoliberal strategies, meant that one of the few institutions that was capable of applying the 1991 Constitution's progressive content was the Constitutional Court. And the Constitutional Court, from its first rulings, decided to take on this function with vigor. Over the years, the court has therefore come to represent itself as the body that implements the values of freedom and social justice set out in the Constitution, thus gaining significant legitimacy among certain social sectors. But it continues to walk along the razor's edge since its progressivism also explains the energetic criticism coming from other sectors, particularly connected to business groups and the government, which have attacked the court's jurisprudence as populist and naive. These actors have not limited themselves to reproaches; they have also, so far unsuccessfully, attempted to pass numerous reforms to eliminate the court or at least to curtail its power considerably. Thus, on several occasions, while some sectors in Congress have tried to bring about constitutional reforms to limit the court's power, the representatives and leaders of some social movements have showered it with praise and support.

Our hypothesis to explain the court's progressive activism can thus be summarized as follows: the design of the Colombian Constitutional Justice and the legal culture make the court's significant activism institutionally possible. The crisis in representation and the weakness of the social movements are conducive to the use of legal mechanisms by certain social actors. The 1991 Constitution also stimulates a progressive vision by the court, which, because of the vacuum left by the weakening of the constituent forces, tends to see itself as the power that is responsible for implementing the values enshrined in the Constitution. The court's progressivism is made possible, in turn, by the weakness of the forces that oppose it and of the attempts at constitutional counter-reform.

There is no doubt that all of the above might never have taken place. The 1991 Constitution, and its broad bill of rights, might have had a purely rhetorical effect and served to legitimize the dominant order. This is what took place in the 1970s with the approval of human rights agreements that Colombian judges never enforced. But the court's judges decided to take advantage of the political context that we have described and to promote the Constitution's emancipatory content. And they have succeeded in doing so, at least at the legal level, although, as we have seen, with great effort and difficulty. Although things could have been different, some purely causal and contextual facts have had a decisive influence. In accordance with chaos theory, a slight variation in certain decisions could have had enormous consequences in the unfolding of constitutional jurisprudence. For example, some of the court's progressive and controversial decisions were made by a narrow margin of five to four. The slightest change in the court's composition would have led to the triumph of the opposing theses. Now, it is a known fact that some judges considered to be progressive were elected in the Senate by a narrow margin over other candidates with more conservative political and legal orientations. If only one of these progressive judges had not been elected, then very likely some of the court's jurisprudence would never have existed. Also, at other times, attempts to suppress the court's significant powers were on the verge of succeeding. But, to date, the court has managed to hold on to its power and progressive activism. And in this way, a sort of tactical counter-hegemonic alliance has been gradually established between the Constitutional Court—or at least between some justices on the Constitutional Court—and certain social sectors that have been excluded or hindered from developing the emancipatory values enshrined in the 1991 Constitution (Cepeda, 1998: 76).

CASES

The Colombian context discussed above could therefore explain a certain progressive activism on the part of the court. But what has been the actual impact of this jurisprudence? To evaluate this issue we have decided to analyze four cases. These not only have intrinsic importance because of the impact of the court's decisions and the social movements that are involved, but also because of the very diversity of the cases, which lends itself to a comparative and contextual reflection on the emancipatory potential of constitutional justice.[17]

The indigenous movement

No other social movement in Colombia over the last thirty years has equaled the indigenous movement in combativeness, strength, and achievements (Gros, 1993: 11).[18] Furthermore, among the Latin American indigenous peoples' movements, the Colombian movement is by far the one that has achieved the most legal and political gains (Gros, 1994: 118). This is surprising given that the share of the indigenous population of Colombia is quite small compared to other Latin American countries such as Bolivia, Mexico, and Ecuador. Moreover, the Colombian indigenous population is scattered throughout the country and is culturally very heterogeneous (Rappaport, 2000: 8).[19] How, then, do we explain its strength and its achievements? One explanation may lie precisely in the fact that the percentage of the Colombian population that is indigenous is quite low and that the concessions made by the government do not represent an unacceptable price to pay for the gains in political legitimation. This would explain the lack of opposition within the dominant elites to the process of recognition and protection of indigenous cultures that was initiated with the 1991 Constitution.[20]

The specificity of the Colombian situation, then, lies in the political will of the state, initially manifested in the support of the government for the indigenous cause in Congress, and later in the rulings of the Constitutional Court. We will highlight some of the important decisions the court has made in this matter. It has protected the right to cultural autonomy of the U'Wa people against the intended exploitation of oil by the multinational company OXI and the Colombian government in places considered by the U'Wa people as part of their territory. The decision was based on the conception held by this people that the land, including the subsoil, is sacred (Arenas, 2001). The court has limited the right to religious freedom of some indigenous people of Arauca who converted to Protestantism and tried to proselytize within indigenous territory against the regulations of traditional authorities. It has respected the decision of traditional authorities to impose physical punishment as a penalty for the commission of offenses, in opposition to the provisions of the Colombian penal code.

The most characteristic and fruitful elements of recent indigenous struggles are related to the decisions of the Constitutional Court. These elements include: an emphasis on cultural rights over economic considerations; an alliance, made possible by this emphasis, between "indigenous intellectuals"[21] and the Constitutional Court (Rappaport, 2000: 31); and the internationalization of the indigenous political struggle. In general terms, the indigenous leaders that we have interviewed agreed that the achievements of the last decade "could not have been obtained without the backing of the court," that no other state institution has been so favorable to the movement (LZ: 24; RB: 2), that most rulings on indigenous peoples have been received by the communities as "political triumphs" (EA: 26), that frequently the court has been more generous than expected (RB: 2), or that at least "it has acted in accordance with what was established in the 1991 Constitution" (RB: 3).[22] They also claim that its decisions have assisted indigenous people "to become aware of their rights" (RB: 3), have united indigenous peoples (C: 7), and have made "their struggles more visible" (LZ: 23).

However, the strengthening of the legal battle was not without controversy within the indigenous movement. There are two opposing tendencies at work: on one side are those leaders who, taking a pragmatic attitude, think that the interests of the movement are better served by adopting a strategy of negotiation with the government, without implying by this that anything fundamental is ceded.[23] Others, from a position that can be called fundamentalist, suspect any concession coming from institutions, and thus use the law only as another instrument of pressure, without any implication of accepting the law of the state.[24] This tension, although never reaching the point of a definitive rupture, has been creating communication problems among traditional leaders,[25] as well as difficulties concerning issues of representation,[26] strategy, and political behavior.[27]

The trade union movement

Similar to what took place with the indigenous movement, starting in the 1960s, the trade unions' political strategy in Colombia was essentially ideological, confrontational, and very much influenced by the Marxist concept of class struggle. The 1991 Constitution was enacted at a time when the social movements, and the left in general, were in crisis. This moment coincided with the appearance of new social struggles that were generally oriented toward the recognition of minorities. The trade union movement has had difficulties adapting to this new sort of political struggle, which is more centered on recognition than economics (Fraser, 1998), not only because its interests are essentially economic, but also because of the influence that the tradition of working-class struggle continues to have on Colombian trade unionists. However, the Constitutional Court's decisions on the subject of equality, more than anything else, have facilitated the unions' adaptation to the new political contingencies.[28] Prior to the 1991 Constitution, the trade unions' legal strategy was limited to defending workers' rights through the negotiation of collective labor agreements. As neoliberal hiring and firing policies increasingly undermined labor law, this strategy was reduced to its minimum expression.[29] In this context, legal defense gained importance, fundamentally through the use of *tutela* actions. This new strategy has led to a new culture of negotiation among the trade unions, more pragmatic and less centered on staunch ideological principles.[30]

The broadening of the legal concept of the Constitutional Court's decisions that protect workers' rights based on constitutional principles rather than labor law sparked this change of perspective in the trade unions' political action. In effect, by upholding *tutelas*, the court has ruled on certain discriminatory practices against unionized workers, practices that nevertheless did not break any labor laws. Thus, for example, the court ordered a company to rehire the unionized workers that it had laid off. Despite the fact that the layoff was carried out in accordance with all the legal requirements, the principle of equality was invoked because only unionized workers had been laid off.[31] In a similar case, the court ordered the rehiring of 209 unionized workers of Empresas Varias de Medellín, based on International Labor Organization principles (Ruling T-568 of 1999).[32]

Union leaders generally consider the workers' legal battles before the Constitutional Court as a sign of hope in a context in which workers' rights are being undermined as never before.[33] The economic crisis, state policies that encourage downsizing, and the situation of violence and insecurity that characterizes the defense of workers' rights[34] have seriously affected the trade unions' political strategy. In this context, the Constitutional Court's decisions have been called "a lifesaver" (AV: 2) and "an emergency resource" (AV: 4). Thus the labor activists view the court as the only legal body that can halt with some success the deterioration of labor conditions in recent years.[35] At the same time, the leaders are aware that the court cannot bring about structural changes; it can only partly halt the state's onslaught against their rights. The court is therefore seen as a symbol that the trade unions should embrace to articulate a defensive and effective battle (EG: 1; AV: 4). Furthermore, the labor leaders agree that this symbol's importance is circumstantial, i.e., that it is due to the fact that the trade unions find themselves defenseless nowadays; because of this very reason, in the medium and long term it is the political struggle and not the legal battle in court that will be fundamental and decisive for workers' rights (AV: 4).

Gay rights

Gay rights groups became more visible after the 1991 Constitution.[36] At the same time, since then, and especially in the wake of several Constitutional Court rulings, legal regulations concerning homosexuality began to change substantially. Several labor regimes, such as those concerning educators and civil servants, provided disciplinary sanctions for homosexual conduct. The court has been attacking gay discrimination on all these fronts. Although certain aspects of the court's jurisprudence have been criticized as timid and insufficient,[37] in general these decisions are considered very advanced, not only by many members of gay groups in Colombia, but also by experts in other countries (Morgan, 1999: 265). How, then, has the court's jurisprudence contributed toward a greater social and legal recognition of gays?

Our interviews suggest that some gay activists saw legal and political potential in the court's generally progressive orientation. They decided to bring cases before the court in order to have it rule on gay rights. The impact of their legal victories appears to have extended beyond the legal field in that they have strengthened gays' sense of identity and self-respect. The greater visibility that gays have achieved is due not solely to the legal content of the court's decisions, which forbid discrimination, but also to the language in which the sentences are couched, and to the fact that the court has openly studied these issues; all this has meant that the subject has ceased to be taboo. Through its great legal creativity, the court's doctrine has enabled gay groups to make progress in achieving their rights, even in fields where they were not able to succeed directly in terms of constitutional justice. Thus, although the court admitted that the law restricted marital union to heterosexual couples, it declared that the Constitution did not prohibit homosexual unions. Based on this bit of constitutional doctrine, a legal team designed a marriage contract for gay couples that is made before a notary. And the first gay "weddings" have already been celebrated in Colombia, something that would have been unthinkable before the court's decisions.[38] Finally, both the doctrine that the court has produced and the greater visibility of the gay movement have led some sectors in Congress to recently present a bill to fully recognize homosexual and bisexual rights.[39]

Thus gay activists' creative use of legal resources and the court's progressive decisions have improved the legal situation of gays and have provided them with greater social acceptance. This change has been so marked that some of them have become an active political minority. However, despite the above-mentioned progress, discrimination against gays in Colombia is far from over. In some aspects, it has become more subtle. This appears to be related to the fact that the population tends to accept gays in theory but continues to have difficulties coexisting with them. Constitutional action seems to be less effective in fighting this sort of discrimination. On the other hand, what is more serious is that in Colombia there are still atrocious manifestations of violence against gays. This is especially true of gays from low-income groups who are murdered in what are known as "social cleansing" operations. Finally, despite greater visibility and a certain degree of participation in politics, it would be tenuous to claim that a solid movement exists to defend gay rights. At the most, one can say that there are groups with various interests that periodically converge to hold marches or bring a case before the courts.

The court and UPAC debtors

Starting in 1997, Colombia went into a deep recession that, combined with certain economic policy decisions, aggravated the situation of about 800,000 people who had taken loans to buy their houses in the so-called UPAC system (unit of constant purchasing power). Two years later, there was talk of 200,000 families on the verge of losing their homes (Acosta, 2000: 19 and 160).[40]

These debtors were largely from the middle class, people who usually do not participate in social protests in Colombia. However, the situation grew to such proportions that the debtors began to establish associations to defend themselves from the financial institutions; they organized peaceful marches[41] and sent petitions to the government and Congress, asking for changes in this financing system and for some relief for the debtors. Some debtors began to propose strategies of civil disobedience, and refused to continue making payments on their mortgages or to hand over their homes to the financial institutions.

Very soon (due to the lack of response by the government and Congress, according to some), the debtors and their associations resorted to judicial strategies and brought lawsuits before the Constitutional Court, against the norms that regulate the UPAC system. Between 1998 and 1999, the court handed down several rulings on the UPAC system, which in general tended to protect debtors. Thus it tied the UPAC to inflation, forbade interest from being added to the capital debt, and ordered that mortgages be recalculated to relieve the debtors' situation. Furthermore, the court ordered that a new law be passed within seven months to regulate housing financing.

The public and the media gave considerable attention to these decisions. The court was placed in the eye of the storm because, although the debtors and some social movements lauded its decisions, business groups, some government sectors, and many analysts fiercely attacked it for overstepping its boundaries and for its ignorance of how the market economy operates. For these reasons, they proposed that the court should not rule on the constitutionality of economic legislation.[42]

In this context, in late 1999 Congress debated and passed a new law on housing financing that incorporated, among other things, 2,000 billion pesos ($1.2 billion dollars) in relief for debtors and once again tied the cost of mortgages to inflation. It is clear that without the Constitutional Court's rulings it would not have been possible to immediately modify the UPAC system, despite the social turmoil it was causing.[43]

As we can see, the mortgage debtors' organizations were spawned in reaction to a payment crisis that threatened them with the loss of housing, and above all they sought solutions that would allow them to keep their homes. Although the debtors held street protests and engaged in political action, it was the judicial strategy, especially the cases presented before the Constitutional Court, that was dominant and that defined the movement's profile as a kind of civil disobedience with legal foundations based on constitutional arguments. The transformation of individual complaints into Constitutional Court debates and the use of other judicial instruments gave these rapidly growing organizations a certain amount of success.

It is not easy to evaluate the emancipatory potential of the mortgage debtors' movement and the court's jurisprudence. There is no doubt that the court's rulings led to a certain amount of financial relief for a significant number of debtors, and perhaps because of this they did not lose their homes. It is also true that now debtors had *more resources* for fighting eviction. Finally, constitutional litigation led to a greater articulation between the debtors and their associations, creating a middle-class civil disobedience social movement against the financial sector and the state's housing policy. Obviously, the constitutional justice system did not create the movement, but it did contribute to its dynamism. The constitutional justice litigation not only gave these debtors and their organizations considerable political visibility, it also modified the sense of their interventions. The issue was no longer about the complaints of isolated debtors, but rather a collective questioning, upheld by the court, of the state's policy on housing and the behavior of the financial institutions.

But the risks and limitations of this strategy have also been made apparent. Thus it is not clear that the court's decisions will translate into greater access to housing for the low-income sectors since, on the one hand, some of its measures might depress the construction sector even further and, on the other hand, it appears that these measures have protected, above all, middle-class debtors, at a substantial budgetary cost for the state. Furthermore, the excessive weight of the legal strategy has limited the associations' potential, some of which have simply become centers for receiving specific complaints about problems in getting mortgages recalculated.

THE EMANCIPATORY POTENTIAL OF
CONSTITUTIONAL JUSTICE

In the second part of this chapter we showed the surprisingly progressive activism of the Constitutional Court as well as the causes that have made it possible. Then we presented four case studies and discussed the way in which different social actors, after having been the beneficiaries of court decisions, have been able to articulate emancipatory social practices. In this final section, we will address the issue of the relationship between progressive judicial decisions and emancipatory social practices.

The effectiveness of the court's progressive decisions

In Colombia, governments have always shown a strong propensity for using constitutional law as a weapon of legitimation. The difficulties of political maneuvering have transformed law into a discourse that is essential to responding to citizens' demands for security and social justice. However, since the promulgation of the 1991 Constitution, this political strategy has become ambivalent. If, on the one hand, the goals of institutional legitimation have been, at least partially, achieved, on the other hand, unprecedented social expectations have been created among social groups and movements that have adopted the legal struggle for rights as an essential component of their political struggle. Therefore, it is important to distinguish between these two aspects of progressive law.

In the first place, law can be used to reactivate collective hope. Hope for a better society, like most fundamental collective values, has different facets: one of them is related to the acceptance of and confidence in the present, another to the possibility of future change through action. The first operates as a remedy for rebellion, the second as a remedy for conformity. Progressive constitutions are both a concession of the state apparatus benefiting individuals, and thus a remedy for rebellion and an indication of a potential to better citizens' rights, and thus a vehicle for promoting change and a remedy for conformity. One possible government strategy is to establish different time schedules for these two effects: laws are passed with the aim of obtaining political advantage through popular approval in the short term; there then begins the struggle for interpretation and application of the laws within a specific set of political, economic, and social possibilities. In Colombia, governments have manipulated the phasing of these two effects, one of which is immediate, the other delayed.

But this is not the only possibility, and here the other facet of progressive law comes into play. The strategy of producing law with the aim of institutional legitimation can backfire and become a remedy for conformity rather than a remedy for rebellion. This effect originates in the profound rejection that citizens evince to any pronouncement that affects the most important *topoi* of social coexistence, such as justice or equality. Even less do they accept abuse when, in addition to being known, it is openly discussed; so a political power that, for its own gain, manipulates a situation in which injustice is seen and felt, and in addition is vocalized, finds its margin of maneuverability reduced. What has occurred with the creation of the Constitutional Court in Colombia is that, on one hand, the discourse on rights based on the Constitution has been particularly progressive and inclusive, and, on the other hand, the diffusion of this discourse in society has made its political appropriation by groups and social movements possible. Unlike what formerly occurred when rights were only on paper, during the last decade the social mobilization resulting from some of the court's decisions has been quite significant. As the cases analyzed in this chapter show, progressive jurisprudence has served more to spawn anti-conformist practices than to quench rebellion.

Accordingly, the emancipatory power of certain of the court's decisions lies in the fact that they contain a political message: they make concrete the expectations encoded in the Constitution and, to this extent, actors find in this message a pretext for political action. In other words, the court has an important role in shaping political practices because, on the one hand, it raises an emancipatory political consciousness among some excluded social groups and, on the other hand, provides possible strategies for political and legal action to remedy their situation.[44] The decisions of the court have an important constitutive dimension in that they create, help to create, or strengthen the identity of political subjects. This is especially clear in the case of the so-called new social movements that demand recognition of issues of gender, culture, or dissenting opinions. The court has contributed to forging the political identity of these actors and through this very process has forged its own identity.

To summarize, the Constitutional Court can favorably affect the social and political reality of social movements. As we have already said, this influence comes not only from the court's coercive capacity to order certain behaviors that favor the protection of individuals' rights, but also, and frequently more importantly, from its capacity to inculcate a spirit of nonconformity in the hearts and minds of the members of social movements and the people in general. This spirit of nonconformity is based on the authoritative assertion that injustice exists and should be remedied. It is obvious that the latter symbolic effect is also frequently achieved thanks to the former instrumental effect. Each case shows a specific combination of instrumental efficacy and symbolic effects of the court's decisions. So, for example, while the trade unions and the UPAC movement show the predominance of instrumental efficacy, in the case of the gay rights movement and the indigenous movement it is the symbolic effects that seem to have been more important.

Judicial activism with emancipatory potential

The relationship between progressive judicial decisions and emancipatory social practices is a complex phenomenon; we cannot talk of a direct causal relation, much less in a country such as Colombia, where the instrumental efficacy of law is very precarious, as we have seen. The social influence of judicial decisions does not seem to be sufficiently weighty in itself to produce direct and effective instances of social change, but neither is it irrelevant to the evaluation of these changes. What kind of relation or connection exists between progressive law and social emancipation? Since it is not a simple causal relationship, we need to examine the conditions or factors that permit judicial decisions to have an impact on social emancipation. It seems to us that these factors are the following: 1) the type of judicial decision; 2) the specific social context in which the ruling is made; 3) the kind of social actor that receives the ruling; 4) the predominant political strategies of this social actor; and 5) the international environment in which emancipatory practices are developed.

The court: types of decision

From the analysis of the Colombian case studies and comparative theoretical debates (Chemerinsky, 1998) the conclusion can be drawn that the impact of a judicial decision partly depends on the nature of the writ emitted by the judge. So, it is obvious that a decision that annuls an offense or a crime is practically self-executing because, once taken by a constitutional judge, the conduct is no longer punishable and, in principle, no person can be sentenced for that offence. In turn, if an individual is incarcerated for that reason, the person can petition the judges, and even the Constitutional Court, to order his or her release. This type of decision, then, has an immediate effect. However, when a judge orders other authorities to carry out specific actions—such as building a hospital or improving prison conditions—it is quite possible that greater resistance will be encountered, since the authorities that are responsible for compliance can obstruct the enactment of decisions through many different means if they are not in agreement with the court's criteria. They can, for instance, invoke budgetary restrictions, administrative difficulties, operational problems, and so on, and thus postpone compliance with a judge's order for a very long time. Judges cannot take action to enforce the order because the other authorities are not openly in contempt.

An important variable that affects the effectiveness of judicial decisions is, then, the type of decision. Following in part the terminology proposed by the American federal judge William Wayne (1997: 302 ff.), we can differentiate two forms of progressive judicial activism. In the first a judge can recognize rights that are disputed by political forces that consider that those rights are not clearly derived from the legal order. This activism, which Wayne calls jurisprudential activism, consists in legally decreeing certain values or conferring specific rights on certain social groups; for this reason we propose to call it value-based or ideological activism. The decisions of the Constitutional Court to decriminalize euthanasia and the consumption of drugs have this character. In other cases, the existence of a right may not be contested, but the decision that the judge makes to challenge a violation of that right may be criticized as activist by those who think that the legal solutions or remedies decreed invade the competencies of other state entities. This second form of activism is then "remedial," according to the classification proposed by Wayne, which we endorse here. In the Colombian case, a typical example of this activism is found in those court sentences that ordered the improvement of the subhuman conditions in prisons. In effect, few deny that prisoners have the right to minimal conditions of dignity, but they question whether the court, rather than the government, should be the entity that orders the authorities to carry out specific projects to achieve this objective.[45]

However, there is more to the story. Perhaps it would be useful to further refine the distinction. Thus, on the subject of legal remedies, it is usually easier for a judge to enforce a prohibition than a prescription (an order to carry out specific actions or behaviors). In the first case, it is more difficult for other authorities to excuse a violation of the legal order. Therefore, we should differentiate between positive remedies (prescriptions) and negative remedies (prohibitions). Likewise, in what concerns ideological activism, at times constitutional judges act against the majority in order to "create" a right that has never been recognized in the jurisprudence, while in other cases their action tends to "preserve" a guarantee that already existed but which is threatened with elimination by political forces. For this reason, it is perhaps useful to differentiate between "innovational" and "preservationist" ideological activism.

The following table summarizes and typifies the types of decisions that can be taken by a progressive court:

Table 3.1. Types of progressive activism.

Ideological activism		Remedial activism	
Innovational activism	*Preservationist activism*	*Positive remedies*	*Negative remedies or prohibitions*
Decriminalization of the consumption of drugs	Protection of job stability against the deregulation of labor contracts	Improvement of prison conditions	Putting a stop to the filling of the Urrá dam

The analysis of decision types is useful in the evaluation of the potential emancipatory impact of a decision. In general, it may be assumed that it is easier to execute negative remedial orders (prohibitions), while enormous controversy and opposition can be generated by an innovational ideological activism, especially when it is expressed in prescriptions. This explains the fact that in the case studies discussed a significant part of the emancipatory impulse of the court originated in "remedial" decisions that contained prohibitions.

The decision environment: the political costs

Progressive decisions usually bring with them high political costs for the court. These costs are difficult to evaluate in a context of institutional, social, and political fragmentation such as that of Colombia. For this reason, such costs should be carefully weighed in each case, in its particular relation to an institution or a sector of political opinion. The specificity of Colombia, once again, is the tremendous fragmentation of political forces, both those that oppose as well as those that support the work of the court. This leads the court to operate in a fashion relatively independent of the political system. In these circumstances, the court makes its decisions with the tranquillity coming from the sense of being supported by public opinion, on the one hand, and, on the other, knowing that up to the present the opposition has not been able to design a political strategy that can question its institutional stability. But, at the same time, in a country at the edge of civil war and in the midst of a crisis of legitimacy that affects the whole state, it faces the uncertainty and the disquiet that arise from the prospect of being the first victim of a conservative constitutional reform. In summary, beyond the specific dangers that originate in concrete decisions against specific social and institutional actors, the court is subjected to a general danger that functions as a sort of backdrop against which it acts. This danger, which is extremely difficult to evaluate, consists in the more or less latent possibility that the political forces unite to finish off the court through constitutional reform. This general danger acquires a similar, if less dramatic, connotation when the election of new judges takes place—as happened at the end of 2000. This posits the danger of the court's neutralization through the appointment of conservative judges.

What then is the relationship between the political costs that we have discussed and the social effect of progressive decisions? The social impact of the court's progressive decisions seem to be greater in social and political contexts in which there is a consensus on the values and principles defended by social actors and by the court. We call these contexts "consensual" to differentiate them from those in which differences predominate, which we will term "dissentious." Of course it is difficult for actual cases to conform exactly to an ideal type; what we find is that they are usually located along a spectrum of intermediary possibilities. So, for example, the case of the indigenous people, at least during the first five years of the court's functioning, is a good example of a consensual context. Since the time of the National Constituent Assembly, there has been a favorable opinion with respect to the cause of indigenous peoples. This opinion has disintegrated somewhat during recent years as a result of confrontations with the government originating in the economic costs of the indigenous movement's demands, especially those of the U'Wa people. Something similar happens with the UPAC movement, which seems to enjoy broad public support. The trade unions and the gays, however, seem to operate in a less favorable political climate in which support for their cause is relative and a significant opposition faces them.

The recipients of decisions: the vision of legal strategy

The emancipatory potential of a judicial decision is also linked to its reception by social actors. First of all, it is important to point out that there is a huge variety of social actors. Perhaps the most important factor for our model is the degree or type of internal cohesion among the decision's beneficiaries. Here we will distinguish three types. First we find the more detached actors who usually seek an individual interest and who only become engaged in collective practices when it works to the advantage of their own individual strategy. An example of this type of actor is found in the movement of those affected by UPAC. This is a very strong movement that took the court's decision as its banner, but that, at the same time, can easily disintegrate if the implementation of the court's decision presents difficulties. The second type refers to actors who are strongly united by community bonds; their priority is the general interest. The indigenous peoples are a good example of this type of social actor. They have created perhaps the most consolidated movement and the one that is least affected by political tides. Their strength lies in the fact that their reason for opposition is the defense of community values whose legal protection is founded upon the decision of the court. This decision is then a secondary, although important, component of the movement's strength. Finally, we have those actors who are linked to a social movement whose internal cohesion depends on shared political interests. This is the classic social movement (Touraine, 1988). The case of the trade unions that fight for the interests of their members based on decisions of the court is a good illustration of this type of social actor. Their internal cohesion does not depend exclusively on the court's decisions but these latter can bring new life and energy to their political struggle.

The relative weight of the legal strategy

What influence does the court's decision have on the strategy of the counter-hegemonic struggle of social actors? Two possibilities are of interest for our purposes. The first arises when the judicial decision explains, at least in a large part, not only the emancipatory struggles of social actors but also their existence, their combativeness, their achievements. This is the case, for example, of the UPAC debtors, who found their most important element of cohesion and struggle in the court decision. Something similar can be said of the gay movement, though to a lesser extent. The second possibility occurs in cases in which the legal strategy—not perceived as essential, or not even as an important element of political struggle in the past—suddenly acquires an unusual importance at a specific time. This often coincides with a moment of crisis in the political strategy or comes at a time when the movement faces the danger of disintegration. The amount of importance the legal strategy acquires originates in great part in the decision by the court. This is the situation of the trade unions studied in this essay, as well as that of NGOs and, perhaps to a lesser degree, the indigenous peoples. In the first case we can speak of a constitutive legal strategy and in the second case of a conjunctural legal strategy.

The international dimension

As a result of the growing influence of globalization, it is unquestionably relevant to take into account the international dimension, and in particular the existence of a certain legal globalization, in order to examine the potential progressive impact of legal decisions. The case of Pinochet is a good illustration because it is beyond doubt that the Chilean Supreme Court of Justice would not have been able to lift the ex-dictator's immunity had Pinochet not previously been detained in England as a result of the extradition request of the Spanish judge Garzón. These decisions, which reflect the existence of a certain internationalized legal space opposed to impunity, strengthened the Chilean judges in the domestic space, allowing them to take measures that would have seemed impossible just months before.

Likewise, in some of the case studies, the international context favored some of the directions of the Constitutional Court, as happened in the decisions related to labor issues where the court referred to ILO resolutions to protect trade union rights within the country. As Boaventura Santos has noted, "the democratic potential of justice will increasingly depend on the emergence of international forms of justice more suited to confront the systematic damage produced by structural conflicts at the level at which it is produced—the global one" (2001b). This does not mean, obviously, that this globalized legal or semi-legal space that is in the process of formation always works in favor of the emancipatory potential of constitutional courts. On occasion, it can be a formidable obstacle since agreements on economic integration can void many progressive judicial decisions. But it is unquestionable that the existence or deficit of international legal or political supports is a significant variable to explain the impact of the decisions of a constitutional court.

The Colombian Constitutional Court, like all constitutional courts around the world, deals with a permanent tension between the need to protect fundamental rights and the need to maintain the existing economic and institutional conditions. But this tension seems particularly strong in Colombia due to several reasons. First, there is a constitutional charter that is not only very progressive, but also very emphatic and normative in what concerns the judicial protection of fundamental rights. Second, the Constitutional Court maintains a strong political independence that derives from the weakness of the mechanisms of representative democracy, a phenomenon that, although visible in almost all the countries of Latin America, is exacerbated in Colombia as a consequence of violence. This explains both the absence of an organized political opposition to the rulings of the court and the existence of organized political support for those same rulings. The importance of the court as a political actor depends on its detachment from the traditional political system. Finally, there is a mixture in Colombia of authoritarian and democratic institutional practices that makes the work of the Constitutional Court more difficult. In fact, the country is still experiencing all the problems of state-building—in the Hobbesian sense—which explains certain very authoritarian components of the current reforms. One example is the so-called "faceless justice," through which the state seeks to obtain, practically at any cost, the monopoly over coercion, which illustrates the tendency to establish permanent exceptions to constitutional guarantees. But, on the other hand, the project of the construction of citizenship that has been developed since the 1991 Constitution is typical of more solid constitutional states. These conflicting logics—a state of exception and a project for citizenship—directly affect the functioning of the court and explain both its power and its weakness.

In these circumstances the court has to combine, on the one hand, a rhetoric of community and social solidarity that feeds citizens' hopes, and on the other, the institutional practices that permit the maintenance of an effective state in a context of war, economic precariousness, and neoliberal globalization.

CONCLUSIONS

The effectiveness of progressive judicial decisions is increased when the following factors are combined: remedial judicial decisions, preferably determining what must not be done (prohibitions); consensual contexts or audiences; political appropriation by movements that adopt the legal strategy as a constitutive part of their political struggle and of their identity as a movement; and international support. We believe that this is the ideal combination of factors or conditions that allows progressive judicial activism to have a greater potential for bringing about emancipatory practices. It should be stressed that this is not a categorical assertion, but rather a tendency. It is not even required that all these factors be present in order to bring about emancipatory practices. Nor does the fact that these take place necessarily guarantee emancipation. Since this is an explanation that only indicates tendencies, empirical research is always indispensable for corroborating the veracity of tendencies in concrete cases. However, this does not mean that this is a mere working hypothesis. It is a postulate that may be contrasted and disproved but this should be done by means of empirical research, as we have done to substantiate it.

The second caveat is the following: for the research that supports this chapter, we selected cases that we hypothetically considered to be emancipatory. After the empirical research was carried out, we concluded that emancipatory practices had in fact resulted from the court's progressive rulings on these cases. However, it is clear that not every progressive decision leads to social emancipation. An interesting complement to this research, which we hope to undertake in the near future, would be to expand the number of cases studied to include progressive decisions that have not led to emancipatory practices. This would make our explanations more conclusive and comprehensive.

Having made these clarifications, we should now draw some conclusions. Reviewing the emancipatory practices studied here, it is possible to see that not all conditions always hold true, and that in some cases they are fulfilled to a greater degree than in others. Let us look at the elements that are lacking or incomplete in each case. In the indigenous movement, a constitutive strategy appears to be lacking; in the gay movement, the consensual element is insufficient; in the UPAC movement, the international aspect is non-existent; the trade unions appear to lack at least three factors: the audience does not appear to be consensual, the movement is neither detached nor community-based, and the strategy is not constitutive. The trade union movement's distance from the notion of potentially emancipatory activism that we have proposed is surprising. What, then, is the explanation for the emancipatory character of the trade union practices that are connected to the court's decisions?

Perhaps the most notable difference between the case of the trade unions and the others can be made clear by referring to the distinction that is currently made between new and old social movements. While the old or classic social movements were characterized by their activism on political issues generally tied to class interests (Giddens, 1984; Touraine, 1977), the new social movements (NSMs) act on a broader range of issues, generally related to cultural concerns and to social and political recognition (Santos, 1998: 312; Fraser, 1998). The latter have mushroomed since the mid-1980s and are part of a new globalized culture of rights. They are generally led by minority groups that seek social and political recognition. The characteristics of the political struggle of these movements are consistent with the ideal factors that we have defined and, in particular, with the emancipatory struggle of the cases studied here. There are at least three elements that the NSMs and these case studies have in common. In the first place, these are new groups or movements for which the legal strategy is an essential element not only to their emancipatory struggle but also to their survival and their identity as a political group or movement. In the second place, the above is closely related to the fact that these movements are relatively dispersed and still in a period of consolidation. Finally, these movements or social groups generally seek the recognition of rights that, for the most part, can be fulfilled by rulings that contain prohibitions. The remaining elements, which appear to provide an important source of support for the NSMs (the international dimension and the consensual environment), are less important in our cases, which leads us to think that their contribution to emancipatory practices is relatively minor.

Having said this, how do we explain the fact that the trade union movement, and in particular the workers' union at the Empresas Varias de Medellín, appears to be far removed from the factors we have presented? What does it mean that most of these factors do not apply to this case? As has already been indicated, critical legal theory maintains that the legal strategy may have counterproductive effects on the global strategy of classic social movements. This is due to the fact that, in these cases, the political strategy, and not the legal one, is inherent to the movement's identity and, in consequence, the legal struggle makes sense only to the degree that it fits into the more fundamental and global political strategy. Much has been written, especially from a Marxist perspective (Tushnet, 1984), on the dangers of concentrating a political struggle on a legal strategy. As we saw in the first section of this chapter, political struggles conducted through law are accused of obscuring the true direction of the struggles, thus stripping social movements of their ideology and alienating their members. Based on these premises, the legal critics have deduced that the legal strategy should be avoided in favor of other actions. As Santos has explained, by using the legal strategy, social movements run the risk of trivializing, depoliticizing, and disintegrating their political fights, being therefore unable to transform such fights into structural changes (2001b: 196, 201). However, it is important to bear in mind that the critical opinion that maintains that these practices are not lasting and may be counterproductive in the long run, does not preclude the fact that emancipatory practices may be achieved through the law. These criticisms have been strongly refuted in contemporary sociology of law, and our study appears to confirm the validity of this refutation in semiperipheral contexts.

In any case, the emancipatory character of the legal strategy used by unions, and particularly by the union at the Empresas Varias de Medellín, seems incontrovertible. If this is the case, we ask once again, why do our factors seem so far removed from the conditions that gave rise to these practices? Let us recall the specific conditions that provided the context for the trade union struggle at the Empresas Varias de Medellín. According to the workers interviewed, the decision to rehire the laid-off unionized workers came at a time when the union was in crisis and those affected were without hope. The *tutela* action was launched in an atmosphere of general skepticism and as a last resort. The court's favorable decision changed this scenario to such an extent that the political struggle took on a national dimension through the assistance provided by this factory union to other trade unions in similar situations. In these conditions, it is not an exaggeration to say that, for the union at the Empresas Varias, the legal strategy revived its political strength and, as a consequence, in the past two years it has taken on a central role in the context of the movement's political struggle. The weakening of the traditional union battles and the enormous expectations generated by the *tutela* explain this situation, which is undoubtedly exceptional for trade unions, in which the legal strategy assumes such a primordial importance that it appears to be practically a type of constitutive strategy, at least for the period analyzed. As such, the relative weight and importance of the legal strategy for the Empresas Varias union approximates what takes place with either community-based or detached social movements. However, we should not forget the critical warning that the legal strategy involves greater risks for the long-term struggle of classic social movements.

Something similar happens in the case of indigenous people. Here also the legal strategy was conjunctural. We have showed how the movement's struggle before the Constitutional Court has produced important emancipatory effects. The explanation lies in the fact that over the last decade the legal strategy has become an essential element of the political fight so that the classical strategies of political confrontation have been somewhat overshadowed. But also in this case we should take into account the risks involved in using the legal strategy—the denaturalization or simply the weakening of the movement's community-based cohesion.

In summary, both classic social movements and the new social movements may achieve social emancipation by means of a legal strategy made possible by the court's progressive stance. In the case of classic social movements, for this to happen it appears to be necessary that they find themselves in a situation in which it is extremely difficult to make progress by traditional means of political struggle. Nevertheless, the risks of this strategy are clearly greater for these movements.

On this subject, it is important to bear in mind that the emancipatory purposes of the court also make it face risks. Colombia's social and institutional fragmentation is such that non-consensual contexts are increasingly prevailing over consensual ones. Under these circumstances there are two risks for the Constitutional Court. First, there is an increasing danger that the court's enemies might manage to consolidate a strategy to eliminate or curtail its powers, as has been attempted in the past. Second, there is the danger that the court, for its own protection, might adopt a conservative attitude in its decisions. These two risks affect the court's emancipatory potential. Last, but not least, the worsening of the armed conflict in recent years in Colombia might reduce the impact of the court's rulings, given the fact that many areas of the country are now controlled by illegal armed groups that obviously do not respect the legal order.

However, neither the risks nor the emancipatory potentialities are to be considered as immutable givens. Both elements should be contrasted and evaluated according to their concrete context. The case of Colombia and the theoretical discussion therefore demonstrate that it is necessary to abandon extreme positions when replying to the question of whether or not it is possible to achieve emancipatory transformation through judicial channels. The context and certain creative decisions by the actors involved have a decisive weight, and for this reason it is important to undertake comparative studies in order to reach a better contextual understanding of the possibilities and limitations of these strategies.

Our study confirms one simple but important idea. In some contexts, law in general and constitutional justice in particular can become an instrument of social emancipation. But it is not for this reason that law loses its dimension of social domination. Thus, the emancipatory possibilities of constitutional justice are limited and the predominance of judicial strategies has risks for the dynamism and creativity of social movements. In any case, these risks should be weighed against the progressive potentialities of con-stitutional justice, which we have tried to describe and systematize in the previous section. Two consequences follow from this conclusion. The first is academic: it is important to develop comparative studies in order to have a better understanding of the contextual possibilities and limitations of judicial strategies. The other is political: constitutional justice can become an impor-tant tool for democratic progress whenever it is seen as a component of broader social struggles. The fulfillment of the emancipatory promises of many constitutions is too serious a matter to be left only to constitutional justices.

Notes

1 This means that we immediately discard the notion that hegemony is some-thing pre-constituted, as a consolidated institutional fact. Instead, at least for the Colombian case, we will adopt an open, malleable, and constructed concept of hegemony (Laclau and Mouffe, 1985; McCann, 1994) not only in what concerns the state as an apparatus for domination, but also in what concerns social movements as victims of that domination.

2 On this point see Tietel (1997), Malloy (1977), Nino (1989, 1992), and Linz and Stepan (1996) as examples of an extensive bibliography.

3 On the Hungarian case see Zirzak (1996) and the periodic reports on and analyses of the Hungarian Court in the *Journal of Constitutional Law in Eastern and Central Europe*, in particular the following updates: 1993, Vol. II, 1; 1994, Vol. III, 3–4; 1995, Vol. IV, 3. See also *The Hungary Report*, 102 (9 April, 1995), 104 (22 April, 1995), 106 (7 May, 1995).

4 On the South African case see Klug (1996) and Burnham (1997).

5 On the Indian Supreme Court see Sripati (1998) and Crossman and Kapur (1997).

6 See Yang (1998).

7 This phenomenon is linked to what has been called "the rule of law project" promoted by international development agencies. During the last decade, rule of law reforms have been identified as a crucial mechanism for promoting development in Latin America, as well as other semiperipheral countries. Rather than a reflection of the prevailing forces in society, law is perceived as an effective instrument for promoting change. Upon this assumption several billions of dollars have been "invested" in law projects, particularly within the context of the judicial system. The major financial institutions involved are the World Bank, the United States Agency for International Development (USAID), and the Interamerican Bank for Development. See Santos (2001b).

8 A phenomenon of co-optation of civil justice by commercial and business interests has been noted and is well studied. See Santos *et al.* (1996) and Rodríguez (2001).

9 So, for example, in a country like Colombia, the increased efficiency of criminal judges, beginning with the strengthening of the Attorney General, seems to have served, at least in certain cases, to diminish impunity, which undoubtedly favors not only hegemonic interests but also the protection of fundamental rights. See Uprimny (2001).

10 Not everyone, however, agreed with this stance; two different positions can be identified: a radical and a moderate approach. The radicals argued that the legal strategy was an illusion (Tushnet, 1984; Balbus, 1977): on one hand it weakened the counter-hegemonic political struggle by diverting attention toward a legal reform process and, on the other, its efficacy for the collective ended up being minimal given the individualistic character of rights. The view of the moderate critics, however, was that despite the existence of a prevailing tendency toward domination, the law, at least at times, could favor social movements. Robert Gordon, for example, argued: "The categories, principles, and rhetoric of law and legal argument deliver real resources to get some leverage on social change" (1998a: 653). In his opinion the laws passed have not always benefited capitalists; they have also, although to a lesser extent, served workers, women, the poor, etc.; the marginalized can eventually turn the legal rhetoric to their advantage (1998: 646). This is then, according to Trubek, a matter that is open to investigation and cannot be decided in advance through theoretical generalization (1977: 554). Agreeing with this view, the new critics of the 1990s believe that legal reforms of a social character and against discrimination can be a useful mechanism of political struggle. This position is generally held by minority rights advocates (Minow, 1987; Crenshaw, 1988) and by scholars representing the Legal Consciousness Studies approach (Ewick and Silbey, 1998; McCann, 1985; 1994). In their opinion, the social impact of progressive judicial decisions is a complex phenomenon that has been simplified. Progressive judicial decisions cannot be categorized beforehand as mere ideological manipulation or as straightforward evidence of social change (McCann, 1994).

11 In the core countries, explains Santos (1998), state autonomy is an outcome of needs and interests that originate in the space of production. In Europe, industrialization preceded a parliamentary system, which followed the general interests of capitalist expansion. In the semiperiphery of the world system, however, the formation of the space of citizenship preceded social organization, and specifically the organization of production, and always maintained a great autonomy with respect to that space of power (Santos, 1998: 154).

12 This is due not only to the structural role of the law but also to the mechanisms for selecting judges, which favor only those who share the views of the dominant social and political forces, reserving the highest positions in the courts for them. See Jacob et al. (1996: 8 and 390). In a comparative study of five developed countries (USA, Germany, Japan, England, and France), the authors state that "although the details of judicial selection vary greatly, the

outcome is similar: the men and women selected to judgeships almost always hold safe, sound, middle-of-the-road opinions." It is true that this may have changed, since in recent years judges, for different reasons, have taken on more prominent roles in nearly all countries, both developed and developing ones (Santos *et al.*, 1995).

13 On the legal evolution of constitutional control in Colombia, see Rozo (1997).

14 On this weakness, see Uprimny (1996).

15 This question obviously presupposes a non-identification between activism and progressiveness, since there may be a conservative activism, such as in the US Supreme Court in the early twentieth century. Furthermore "up until recently the best known instances of court activism were politically conservative, if not reactionary" (Santos, 2001a).

16 On the Constituent Assembly see Buenahora (1992). For an optimistic assessment of the democratic character of the Constituent Assembly, see Fals Borda (1991), who was one of its members.

17 The empirical research was carried out over a period of eight months, with the participation of four research assistants. We conducted 25 in-depth interviews, some of them in remote places such as the Sierra de Santa Marta, where some indigenous communities live.

18 The indigenous movement in Colombia has been especially strong since 1971, following the Third Assembly of the Regional Indigenous Council of Cauca (CRIC). For a history of these mobilizations see Findji (1992: 112 ff.).

19 It is estimated that 64 indigenous languages and as many different worldviews exist in Colombia (LZ: 22; these symbols, here and from now on, refer to the names of the leaders who were interviewed during the research).

20 However, this is not a common explanation. The receptive attitude of the state tends to be explained by more obscure purposes, such as the need to assert its intervention in indigenous territories (Gros, 1993: 13) or the desire to co-opt and disarm indigenous leaders (Rappaport, 2000: 5). Although we do not deny the possible existence of these goals, we believe that the need for institutional legitimation through a representative process predominates (Santos and García Villegas, 2001). In recognizing indigenous populations, the dominant political elite seems to have found legitimizing symbolic dividends that are greater than the risks of the relative contractual inclusion of indigenous peoples (Gros, 1997).

21 Bilingual leaders who have studied in the universities of large urban centers and who perform ably in both indigenous and white environments. These intellectuals participate in elections for political offices, use the legal system, and speak out through the mass media.

22 For indigenous leaders, however, this does not constitute grounds for special commendation but is simply the court's commission (GM: 4; C: 7, FT: 16). In their opinion, nothing has been given to indigenous people; the court did nothing more than recognize a right that other institutions do not recognize.

23 These are usually indigenous people who, thanks to the system of decentralization that has been in effect since 1986, have been elected as mayors or town
councilors in municipalities located in indigenous territories.

24 These are leaders who defend tradition, usually advised politically by white
intellectuals and anthropologists, many of whom preach a certain indigenous
fundamentalism.

25 Some intransigent leaders argue, for example, that the indigenous question is
predicated on the impossibility of communication between two worldviews,
two mutually incomprehensible bodies of knowledge. According to Gabriel
Muyuy, for example, "not even the most progressive and consistent magistrates
can understand the essence, the thought, and the wisdom of the spiritual leaders
of our communities" (GM: 4). The constitutional idea of a multicultural nation
is a contradiction in terms and, therefore, indigenous people should struggle
for a sovereign nation (CH: 11). The pragmatists, however, believe that cultural
principles should not be an obstacle to getting benefits from the state in the
political arena and through the means that the state itself defends, such as the
law.

26 The so-called "indigenous intellectuals" spend most of their time in Bogotá
or other large urban centers and only communicate from time to time with
their traditional authorities, who usually understand little of the political
strategy that they are advocating.

27 Almost all the indigenous leaders interviewed recognize that one of the major
problems with the legal strategy is that those elected to public office from
within their ranks adopt the vices of the traditional political class, such as corruption, clientelism, demagoguery, and so on.

28 According to Eduardo Garzón, union leader and head of the United Front
political movement, the court has changed the trade union political culture
through the *tutela* action (EG: 4).

29 According to Luis Alfonso Velázquez, currently there are 840 enterprises in
receivership and during the past five years over 5,000 more companies have
been liquidated. The Chamber of Commerce has cancelled over 32,000 commercial registers over the past 10 years. Under these circumstances, the strategy
for collective negotiation has been profoundly affected (LAV: 1 and 2).

30 According to the union members at Empresas Varias de Medellín, starting in
1993 the role of the traditional union leader—whose sole effective strategy
was political confrontation: "We must take to the streets, participate in marches
[...] he who speaks to the bosses is a turncoat,"—weakened and in his place
arose a leader more inclined toward pragmatism and negotiation (EEVV: 10).

31 This case refers to ruling T-436 of 2000, which struck down the decision by
the Codensa electric company to lay off over 2,000 workers. From a legal
point of view (statutory law), the laid-off workers had no recourse since they
had received severance pay.

32 In this ruling the court ordered that laid-off workers be re-hired and receive

compensation. These workers had filed a *tutela* suit as a desperate last resort, after having attempted all other political strategies. The success of the lawsuit was such a triumph that union leaders began providing assistance to unions located in different cities around the country in order to help them prepare similar *tutela* cases.

33 "The court is an oasis in the middle of the desert," says Luis Eduardo Garzón (EG: 4).

34 According to data provided by Luis Eduardo Garzón and Luis Alfonso Velázquez, during the past ten years, 2,500 labor leaders have been killed throughout the country. Violence has affected practically all endeavors involving social or political mobilization. For more on this subject, see Pécaut, 1997.

35 Marcel Silva, professor of labor law and union consultant, maintains that "when there is no possibility for the right to association to prevail, when we are persecuted, when we are mistreated, when our leaders are murdered, in this very bleak picture, the court's rulings are the only thing that cheers us up" (MS: 5). Some radical labor leaders interpret this as a "carrot and stick" strategy on the part of the state. Along the same line, others feel that this is something like "granting concessions to a dying man," referring to the right to association (MS: 5).

36 For more about these facts and changes, see Guzmán Duque (2000). Newspaper articles also reflect the greater social and political visibility of gays. See, for example, the articles from *El Tiempo* (13 November 1994, p. 7B), entitled "Los gays de Bogotá salen a la luz" ("Gays in Bogotá come out of the closet"), from *El Espectador* (28 June 1999), "Comunidad gay da la cara" ("Gay community stands up"), or the article on lesbians in *Semana* (April 1996), "Juego de damas" ("Game of checkers").

37 On the subject see Motta (1998) and Guzmán (2000).

38 See, for example, *El Tiempo*, 13 December 1998.

39 See Bill No.97/99, presented by Senator Margarita Londoño (*Gaceta del Congreso* No. 305, 10 September 1999).

40 See also *El Espectador*, 29 April 1997 and 1 June 1999. For an economic analysis of the debtors' financial crisis, see Echeverry *et al.* (1999), and Castellanos and Suárez (1999).

41 In February 1999, for instance, about 2,000 people participated in a demonstration at Cali that debtors called "stations of the cross" (see *El Espectador*, February 1999). In December 1998, debtors had organized a "march of pots and pans" to complain about the fact that they were practically starving because of their mortgage payments.

42 The president of the Colombian Banking Association said that the court was politicized, which was "inflicting enormous economic damage to the country." For this reason, it was necessary to limit this "super power that the magistrates have today, which threatens the normal course of the national economy" (see *El Espectador*, 6 June 1999). Salomón Kalmanovitz, co-director of the Central Bank, claimed that the court had overstepped its functions, that

"Court hearings are replacing Congress," and that its rulings were an obstacle to economic development (*El Espectador*, 24 March 2000).

43 See *Gaceta del Congreso*, 24 December 1999, Year VIII, No. 603, pp. 5 ff and 26 ff.

44 This discussion does not differ greatly from the analyses of the subject in core countries (McCann, 1994; Sheingold, 1989). However, the way in which this symbolic effect operates and its specific implications are quite different in the context under examination here.

45 It is obvious that a sentence may often have both attributes, since it may recognize a contested right and formulate bold orders to remedy violations. Some rulings on health care have been of this kind, because the court, going beyond existing legal regulations, not only recognized that a person had the right to medical treatment (ideological activism), but also prescribed precise behaviors to the authorities (remedial activism). However, the distinction between these two types of activism, which is connected to the classical differentiation between rights and remedies, is relevant since they have different impacts and give rise to different kinds of resistance.

Bibliography

Acosta, Amylkar (2000). *El viacrucis del UPAC. Los inquilinos de la ira*. Bogotá: IDEAS.

Arenas, Luis Carlos (2001). "Poscriptum: Sobre el Caso U'wa," Boaventura de Sousa Santos and Mauricio García Villegas (eds), *El Caleidoscopio de las Justicias en Colombia*. Bogotá: Uniandes, pp. 143–56.

Balbus, Isaac (1977). "Commodity Form and Legal Form: An Essay on the 'Relative Autonomy' of the Law," *Law and Society Review*, 11: 571–88.

Bourdieu, Pierre (1986). "La force du Droit, elements pour une sociologie du champ juridique," *Actes de la Recherche en Sciences Sociales*, 64, Paris: 3–16.

Buenahora, Jaime (1992). *El Proceso Constituyente*. Bogotá: Tercer Mundo.

Castellanos, Jorge, and Felipe Suárez (1999). "Financiación de vivienda: retos y soluciones," *Debates de Coyuntura Económica*. Bogotá, Fedesarrollo, 49: 7–18.

Cepeda, Manuel José (1998). "Democracy, State and Society in the 1991 Constitution: The Role of the Constitutional Court, in Eduardo Posada Carbó," *Colombia: The Politics of Reforming the State*.

Chemerinsky, Erwin (1998). "Can Courts Make a Difference?", Neal Devins and Davison M. Douglas (eds.), *Redefining Equality*. Oxford: Oxford UP, pp. 191–204.

Crenshaw, Kimberle (1988). "Race, Reform and Retrenchment: Transformation and Legitimation in Antidiscrimination Law," *Harvard Law Review*, 101: 1332–1387.

Crossman, Brenda, and Ratna Kapur (1997). "Secularism's Last Sigh? The Hindu Right, the Courts, and India's Struggle for Democracy," *Harvard International Law Journal*, 113: 113–70.

Deas, Malcom (1995). "Canjes violentos: Reflexiones sobre la violencia política en Colombia," in Deas and G. Daza, *Dos Ensayos Especulativos sobre la Violencia en Colombia*. Bogota: Fonade, pp. 1–86.

Echeverry, Juan Carlos, *et al.* (1999). *UPAC: evolución y crisis de un modelo de desarrollo*. Bogotá: Planeación Nacional (mimeo).

Edelman, Murray (1971). *Politics as Symbolic Action: Mass Arousal and Quiescence*. Chicago: Markham.

Ewick, Patricia and Silbey (1998). *The Common Place of Law; Stories from Everyday Life*. Chicago: Chicago UP.

Fals Borda, Orlando (1991). "La accidentada marcha hacia la democracia participativa en Colombia," *Análisis Político*, 14: 46–58.

Findji, Maria Teresa (1992). "From Resistance to Social Movement: The Indigenous Authorities Movement in Colombia," Arturo Escobar and Sonia Alvarez (eds.), *The Making of Social Movements in Latin America: Identity, Strategy and Democracy*. Boulder, CO: Westview, pp. 113–33.

Findley, Roger (1972). "Ten Years of Land Reform in Colombia," *Wisconsin Law Review*, 3: 880–923.

Fraser, Nancy (1998). "Social Justice and the Age of Identity Politics: Redistribution, Recognition, and Participation," Grethe B. Paterson (ed.), *The Tanner Lectures On Human Values*. Vol. 19. Utah: Utah UP, pp. 3–67.

Giddens, Anthony (1984). *The Constitution of Society*. Berkeley: California UP.

Gómez, Juan Gabriel (1995). "Fueros y desafueros. justicia y contrarreforma en Colombia," *Análisis Político*, 25: 71–9.

Gordon, Robert (1998). "New Developments in Legal Theory," David Kaiyrs (ed.), *The Politics of Law. A Progressive Critique*. New York: Basic Books, pp. 281–93.
— (1998a). "Some Critical Theories on Law and Their Critics," David Kaiyrs (ed.) *The Politics of Law. A Progressive Critique*. New York: Basic Books, pp. 641–61.

Gros, Christian (1988). "Reforma agraria y Proceso de paz en Colombia," *Revista Mexicana de Sociologia*, 50(1), January–March, 287–302.
— (1993). "Derechos Indígenas y Nueva Constitución," *Análisis Político*, 19, May–August: 8–24.
— (1997). "Antropología en la Modernidad," *Indigenismo y Etnicidad: el desafío neoliberal*. Bogotá: Instituto Colombiano de Antropología (ICAN), pp. 15–59.
— (1994). "Colombia indígena. Identidad cultural y cambio social," *Análisis Político*, 22, May–August: 118–20.

Guzmán Duque, Federico (2000). *Apropiaciones: homosexuales y derecho en Colombia*. Graduate thesis. Bogotá: Departamento de Antropología de la Universidad de los Andes.

Jacob, Herbert, *et al.* (1996). *Courts, Law and Politics in Comparative Perspective*. New Haven, CT: Yale UP.

Klug, Heinz (1996). *Constitutionalism, Democratization and Constitution-Making for a New South Africa*. Madison: University of Wisconsin Law School.

Laclau, E., and Chantal Mouffe (1985). *Hegemony and Socialist Strategy: Toward a Radical Democratic Politics*. London: Verso.

Linz, Juan, and Alfred Stepan (1996). *Problems of Democratic Transition and Consolidation; Southern Europe, South America, Post-Communist Europe*. Baltimore, MD: Johns Hopkins University Press.

Malloy, James (ed.) (1977). *Authoritarianism and Corporatism in Latin America*. Pittsburgh: U of Pittsburgh P.

McCann, Michael (1985). "Resistance, Reconstruction, and Romance in Legal Scholarship," *Law & Society Review*, 26(4): 733–49.

McCann, Michael W. (1994). *Rights at Work, Pay Equity Reform and Politics of Legal Mobilization*. Chicago: U of Chicago P.

Minow, Martha (1987). "Interpreting Rights: An Essay for Robert Cover," *Yale Law Journal*, 96, 1860–1915.

Morgan, Martha (1999). "Taking Machismo to Court: The Gender Jurisprudence of the Colombian Constitutional Court," *Interamerican Law Review*, 30(2): 255–342.

Motta, Cristina (1998). "La Corte Constitucional y los derechos de los homosexuales," *Observatorio de Justicia Constitucional*. Bogotá: Siglo del Hombre, Universidad de los Andes, 290–99.

Nino, Carlos S. (1989). "Transition to Democracy, Corporatism and Constitutional Reform in Latin America," *University of Miami Law Review*, 44(1), 129.

— (1992). "The Debate Over Constitutional Reform in Latin America," *Fordham International Law Journal*, 16(3): 635.

Pécaut, Daniel (1978). *Orden y Violencia en Colombia 1930–1954*. Bogotá: Siglo XXI.

— (1997). "Presente, pasado y futuro de la Violencia," *Análisis Político*, 30, IEPRI, Universidad Nacional de Colombia, Bogotá, 3–36.

Pinto, Anibal (1971). *Tres Ensayos sobre Chile y América Latina*. Buenos Aires: Solar.

Rappaport, Joanne (2000). "Redrawing The Nation: Indigenous Intellectuals and Ethnic Pluralism in Colombia." Bogotá (mimeo).

Rodríguez, Cesar (2001). "La justicia civil y de familia," in Boaventura de Sousa Santos and Mauricio García Villegas (eds), *El Caleidoscopio de las Justicias en Colombia*. Bogotá: Uniandes, 547–614.

Rosenberg, Gerald N. (1991). *The Hollow Hope*. Chicago: U of Chicago P.

Rozo, Luz Zoraida (1997). "Origen y evolución del régimen de control constitucional en Colombia," *Derecho del Estado*, 3, 45–62.

Santos, Boaventura de Sousa (1995). "Los tribunales en las sociedades contemporáneas," *Pensamiento Jurídico*, 4. Bogotá, Facultad de Derecho, Universidad Nacional, 5–38.

— (1998). *De la Mano de Alicia; lo social y lo político en la post-modernidad*. Bogotá: Siglo del Hombre, Uniandes.

— (2001a). "Los paisajes de la justicia en las sociedades contemporáneas," in Boaventura de Sousa Santos and Mauricio García Villegas (eds), *El Caleidoscopio de las Justicias en Colombia*. Bogotá: Uniandes, 85–150.

— (2001b). "Derecho y democracia: la reforma global de la justicia," in Boaventura de Sousa Santos and Mauricio García Villegas (eds), *El Caleidoscopio de las Justicias en Colombia*. Bogotá: Uniandes, 151–207.

Santos, Boaventura de Sousa, Maria Manuel Leitão Marques, João Pedroso, and Pedro Lopes (1996). *Os Tribunais nas Sociedades Contemporâneas. O Caso Português*. Porto: Afrontamento.

Santos, Boaventura de Sousa, and Mauricio García Villegas (eds) (2001). *El Caleidoscopio de las Justicias en Colombia*. Bogotá: Uniandes.

Scheingold, S. (1974). *The Politics of Rights, Lawyers, Public Policy, and Political Change*. New Haven, CT: Yale UP.

Sripati, Vijayashri (1998). "Toward Fifty Years of Constitutionalism and Fundamental Rights in India: Looking Back to See Ahead," *American University International Review*, 14, 415–95.

Teitel (1997). "Transitional Jurisprudence, The Role of Law in Political Transformation," *Yale Law Journal*, 106, 2009–80.

Touraine, Alain (1988). *La Parole et le Sang*. Paris: Odile Jacob.

— (1977). *The Self Production of Society*. Chicago, IL: Chicago UP.

Tushnet, Mark (1984). "An Essay on Rights," *Texas Law Review*, 62(4), 1363–402.

Uprimny, Rodrigo (1996). "Violencia y acción colectiva: una comparación entre Bolivia y Colombia," in AAVV, *Gobernabilidad, constitución y democracia en Colombia*. Bogotá: Universidad Nacional, 213–27.

— (2001). "Las transformaciones de la administracion de justicia en Colombia," Boaventura de Sousa Santos and Mauricio García Villegas (eds.), *El Caleidoscopio de las Justicias en Colombia*. Bogotá: Uniandes, 261–315.

Urrutia Montoya, Miguel (1976). *Historia del sindicalismo en Colombia*. Bogotá: Uniandes.

Wayne, William (1997). "The two faces of judicial activism," David O'Brien (ed.), *Judges on Judging. Views from the Bench*. Chatham: Chatham House.

Yang, Kung (1998). "The Constitutional Court in the Context of Democratization: the Case of South Corea," *Verfassung und Recht in Ubersee*, 31, 160–70.

Zirzak, Spencer (1996). "Hungary's Remarkable, Radical, Constitutional Court," *Journal of Constitutional Law in Eastern and Central Europe*, 3(1), 1–56.

Part II

WOMEN'S STRUGGLE FOR DEMOCRACY

4

Which Workers, Which Women, What Interests? Race, Class, and Gender in Post-Apartheid South Africa[1]

Shamim Meer

INTRODUCTION

The title of this chapter comes from two main points that I made in a previous paper.[2] There I attempted to assess the challenges for NGOs and social movements five years after the first democratic government in South Africa. I noted that many of the workers who had founded the militant unions of the 1970s and 1980s, which came to form the Congress of South African Trade Unions (COSATU), are no longer members of trade unions today.[3] Large numbers of these workers have been retrenched in the past decades and are mostly back in the rural areas. As they are predominantly unskilled, their labor is no longer required in industry, which requires both skilled labor and less labor. Hence, while the numbers of workers who make up COSATU membership remains relatively the same today, the numbers are kept constant by new entrants to the unions, largely white-collar workers, who come from areas such as the public sector and banking. The significance of this point is that it indicates that the militant workers who built the strong union movement have been casualties of the capitalist system. The question this raises is how their interests might be advanced, if at all, in the new South Africa today.

The second point I made in that paper was about women. I noted that the one group within South African society that has made gains in post-apartheid South Africa seems to be women. Yet if we look at which women have made gains it becomes clear that it is not black working-class or poor rural women who have made gains but rather mainly white women, as a result of empowerment strategies that aimed at making proportional the numbers of women workers in public and private sector institutions.

The significance of these two points, taken together with an assessment of how poor black rural dwellers are faring in the post-apartheid South Africa, indicates that the fault lines of the old South Africa are more or less intact. Some black folk and some women have entered the ranks of the elite. But by and large the interests of the majority of South Africa's citizens, unskilled women and men, and those among the rural and urban poor, remain inadequately addressed.

This situation raises questions about the role of the post-apartheid state in redressing the imbalances created by apartheid capitalism and colonialism. It raises the question of why, despite the African National Congress's (ANC) stated commitment to addressing the needs of the majority, it appears to be failing to do so.

This situation also raises questions about the social movements that fought to bring an end to apartheid—questions of what has happened to these movements and to the individuals who helped to build and take them forward.

While the national democratic struggle privileged race, this has not translated into the interests of the majority of black people being met. An effective women's lobby succeeded in bringing gender under the spotlight within the transition and in the period of democratization, yet the benefits for women so far are shaped by the privileged race and class positions they bring with them from apartheid. The struggles of organized workers did not enable them to keep their jobs in the face of retrenchments and the growth of temporary jobs. This is because of the ways in which race, class, and gender systems of exploitation and oppression interact with and support the status quo.

The ways in which race, class, and gender dynamics simultaneously affect citizenship and democratization need to be considered. Most analyses of South Africa focus on either race and class dynamics, or both, and ignore gender. This results in flawed discussions of transitions, democracy, and citizenship as they fail to consider women's and men's differential experiences of race, class, and citizenship.

The overarching framework of the new government does not place the poor, or the eradication of the massive inequality within South African society, at the center of its agenda. Despite a rhetoric of concern for the poor, and a stated desire to end the injustices caused by apartheid, seven years into democratic rule the government's policies by and large continue to favor the historically privileged. Nor does the overarching framework particularly provide gains for the majority of South Africa's women. The ANC's shift to neoliberalism and the embracing of the Washington Consensus leads to favorable outcomes for a few and for lives of continued hardship for the majority. The former homelands continue to be the most poverty-stricken parts of the country, and together with urban shack settlements continue to re-create apartheid along the lines of race. Commissions are set up by the state to address poverty and issues such as moral regeneration, but these operate within the flawed neoliberal capitalist logic and can take us no closer to redressing the inequalities of our country.

There is little empirical evidence that South Africa is moving away from its position as one of the most unequal societies in the world. Poverty and inequality take a racial, gendered, and spatial form. Are the same interests being served today as under apartheid, more or less? Are the same prior notions of citizenship in place?

The ANC, ostensibly a party driven by the dreams of the Freedom Charter and, in the run-up to the 1994 elections, by the promises of the Reconstruction and Development Program, has apparently given up these dreams and promises for austerity under its macro-economic GEAR (Growth Employment and Redistribution) policy—referred to as South Africa's homegrown structural adjustment policy.

The promise for the future lies in social movements/groupings in society emerging to make claims and hold the state accountable. Yet this seems to be slow in coming. The social movements of the 1980s and early 1990s are today non-existent or in disarray.

Critical questions for the present include: What has happened to the once strong civil society? What are the gaps and opportunities to shift state agendas? What are some of the actions that carry promise for change in the interests of poor rural and working women?

This chapter looks at some of the explanations offered for understanding the present context—explanations that highlight the transition as an elite pact that dealt with political questions but evaded key economic questions. It argues that movement organizations were able to make and win claims within the transition, particularly as a result of their position in the Tripartite Alliance of the ANC, COSATU, and SACP (South African Communist Party). These gains included the Reconstruction and Development Program (RDP), the stated policy of the ANC on the eve of elections; institutions such as the Commission on Gender Equality (CGE) and the Office on the Status of Women (OSW) to advance women's rights; and significant numbers of COSATU leaders, SACP members, and women on the ANC list of parliamentarians. However, despite these gains, women's organizations and workers' movements[4] have not been able to sustain their influence, and this has resulted in the government's dropping of the RDP and in economic policies that favor the interests of the rich and powerful.

A critical question for the present is how organizations and groupings representing the interests of the majority who continue to be economically marginalized should position themselves in relation to the state. This question is all the more vexing when the individuals who work the state apparatus today come from those very organizations and who were in many cases their founders. In other words, many in the state are the same people who built the movement organizations.

The crucial issue of maintaining links between the movement organizations and the institutions within the post-apartheid state has been neglected, as has the question of how these organizations may be sustained.

This chapter argues that engagement with state institutions and the state as a vehicle for redressing social inequalities was not sufficiently problematized by these organizations and movements. It was rather assumed that the ANC party would automatically deliver on the basis of its historical record as a national liberation movement. This chapter points to conceptual and political shortcomings on the part of academics, left theorists, policy-makers and movement organizations, arising from inadequate considerations of the ways in which systems of race, class, and gender combine to perpetuate the economic exclusion of the vast majority of South Africans and points out the significance of these shortcomings given the links between theory and practice.

THE CRISIS OF POVERTY AND INEQUALITY

Apartheid capitalism was responsible for alarming rates of poverty and inequality in South Africa. As Jay Naidoo, minister without portfolio in charge of the RDP, told the *Star* newspaper in March 1996, the black 75 per cent of South Africa's population was living in Third World conditions with a standard of living slightly better than that of Congo, while the white 12 per cent of South Africa's population enjoyed a standard of living equal to that of Canadians. In terms of income distribution, land distribution, and water distribution, South Africa was one of the most unequal societies in the world (Lipton *et al.*, 1996).

A report on Key Indicators of Poverty in South Africa prepared for the RDP office (RDP, 1995) highlighted the extent of poverty (as measured by income) in South Africa, as well as the racial, spatial, and gendered nature of poverty. Overall the report found that 53 per cent of South Africa's population were classified poor, experiencing high unemployment, hunger and malnutrition, inability to pay for, or lack of access to, health care and basic services, and the risk of homelessness.

By race, 65 per cent of all Africans were poor and nearly 95 per cent of South Africa's poor are African. Five per cent of South Africa's poor were colored and less than 1 per cent were Indian or white. Thirty-three per cent of all coloreds, 2.5 per cent of all Indians, and 0.7 per cent of all whites were poor.

Poverty was more extreme in rural areas, and within rural areas more extreme in the former bantustans. Hence nearly two-thirds of the country's poor lived in the Eastern Cape, Kwa Zulu Natal, and the Northern Province.

The study did not look at differential access to income between women and men within households, and it is therefore unable to deduce women's differential experience of poverty. The study did, however, make note of household headship by gender and noted that households headed by females were found to have a 50 per cent higher poverty rate than male-headed households.

The study found that less than one-third of Africans had internal taps, flush toilets, electricity, and refuse removal. The greatest concerns of the poor were jobs, piped water, housing, food aid, electricity, and schools, in that order. Among the rural poor, clinics and roads were additional high priority issues.

Five years after the advent of the post-apartheid government there was little indication that poverty and inequality were being alleviated or reduced or that significant moves were being made for their eradication. Instead, as Hemson (1999) points out, there was evidence of increasing gaps between rich and poor, with rural incomes declining, and with the poor not able to afford the services that are provided. For example, large numbers of rural water projects stopped functioning months after they were completed, and many poor households had their newly installed electricity and telephone services disconnected. State spending on health had been drastically reduced, making it difficult to implement new health policies aimed at benefiting the poor. Child support grants intended for the poorest 30 per cent of children reached only 0.8 per cent of them, and only 0.06 per cent of agricultural land had been transferred to black communities (Hemson, 1999).

Today, poor community and school water supplies are constantly under threat of being cut off, or are actually cut off as increasing unemployment and poverty make it impossible for communities to afford payments for water. Such communities call out in protest "end the new apartheid—the rich against the poor" (Chant at a mass meeting in Hammersdale, Kwa Zulu Natal—29 April, 2001).

Rather than addressing poverty and inequality as a central concern, South Africa today bends under global pressures. As Sitas (1999: 6) reflects, "instead of placing the urban and rural poor at the centre of our agenda and encouraging pro-people and pro-poor development, we drifted into the logic of global power—downsize, casualise, subcontract and marginalise" (Sitas, 1999: 6).

Hence South Africa has not achieved even the very narrow notion of emancipation explored by Klug (2000)—i.e., simple freedom from the oppression of structural poverty. The situation today is one where the so-called two nations of First World and Third World continue, where spiraling crime rates create First World walled cities and paramilitary security companies; where South Africa wins a world first in the biggest bird airlift in the recent Cape penguin saga; where a wealthy Cape businessman brings over opera divas to spot opera talent on the Cape Flats, including Kayelitsha, while the taxi and bus war continues to claim lives.

UNDERSTANDING THE TRANSITION—ELITE PACTS AND MOVEMENT ORGANIZATIONS

The situation in South Africa today needs to be understood against the background of the nature of the transition and of the political and economic choices made by government. At the same time, the role of movement organizations needs to be understood within the transition and within the present.

Like most negotiated settlements, the South African settlement took the form of a pact between elites on each side. Like transitions in Latin America and Eastern Europe (Jaquette and Wolchik, 1998), social movements played active parts, but crucial decisions resulted from the negotiations among elites. The settlement required that consensus be reached by the various political parties and most notably by the ANC and the National Party, as well as by capital. Elites had to make a special effort

> to learn each other's basic objectives, philosophies and discourses, and they had to begin to make concessions—mainly rhetorical, but to some degree concrete—to build trust between negotiating parties with once vigorously opposed interests. Gradually, across many sectors of society, a kind of "coerced harmony" was imposed. (Bond, 2000: 56)

The consensus reached reflected a middle ground, with extreme elements on each side marginalized. The parties concerned had to shift significantly from previously held positions in order to achieve this middle-ground consensus.

The negotiated settlement was based on restructuring the political sphere while leaving the economic power structures relatively intact. Marais (1998) points out that this was in keeping with the ANC's position of emphasizing the political over the economic.

In addition it is a tendency that negotiated settlements usually frame the broader crisis within society in political terms. As Carlos Villas (quoted by Nzimande in Marais, 1998: 90) points out, transitions do not "project into the economic sphere, nor do they provide the framework for any substantial change in the level of access of subordinate groups to socio-economic resources—by income distribution, creating employment, improving living conditions etc."

The ANC thus negotiated a settlement without a clear program of dismantling the "two nations" society—one a nation impoverished with living conditions and life chances equal to the poorest countries of the world, the other a nation equivalent to a western nation.

Movements were able to push and win gains, particularly since the ANC was in alliance with COSATU and the SACP. COSATU and the civic organizations under the umbrella of the South African National Civics Organization (SANCO) initiated and developed the RDP to address the gap in ANC economic policy. This became the strategic program and election manifesto of the ANC just before the 1994 election.

Women's organizations came together during the negotiations in the Women's National Coalition (WNC), and made inroads in bringing attention to women-specific demands. The ANC Women's League spearheaded the formation of the WNC, which brought together women's wings of the parties engaged in the negotiations, with a range of other women's organizations, such as the YWCA, church women, Afrikaans women, and Jewish women. The influence of the women's lobby from within the Tripartite Alliance (of ANC, COSATU, and SACP), as well as through the WNC, can be seen, for example, in the RDP's stated concern for women, especially among the rural and very poor groupings of South African society, as well as in the lobby's ability to prevent the adoption of a clause in the country's Constitution that threatened to exempt traditional leaders from the equality clause in the Constitution, a clause that safeguards gender equality (Meintjes, 1996).

However, perhaps more powerful than the pressure of working-class and poor people's social movements in constitution- and law-making was pressure from more traditional power centers of capital, powerfully organized white agricultural farmers and traditional chiefs.

With regard to traditional leaders, the South African Constitution recognizes the role of traditional leadership and customary law, although these are subordinate to the fundamental rights in the Constitution and to gender equality (Klug, 2000: 29). However, the role of traditional leaders remains a gray area and has not been adequately dealt with within the Constitution or in the arena of the local state, resulting in continued battles between chiefs and the state. During the local government elections in 2000, for instance, chiefs protested the new local authority demarcations and stalled the election process as they saw this as an attempt to erode their powers.

The reality for most rural dwellers who continue to be trapped in the former homelands (and among whom the larger proportion are rural women in a context of continued male emigration to the cities) is a reality under traditional systems within which women's access to land and authority continues to be through men. Democratic rights thus evade these citizens of South Africa. Mamdani (1998) makes the point that democratization in African contexts cannot be a simple reform of civil society, but rather has to include a dismantling of the mode of rule that is legitimized in customary law. He notes that preoccupation in African and South African studies with the mode of production has ignored the mode of rule and the specific form colonial power took in Africa and that there has been a failure to address the mode of power containing rural populations. The focus has been on rights from which the colonized were excluded on the basis of race and this view excluded consideration of the regime of custom through which rural populations were ruled. The focus of movements has thus been urban-biased. Mamdani (1998: 288) notes that "infatuation with the notion civil society conceals the actual forms of power through which rural populations are ruled" and that "without reform of the local state democratization will be superficial, but also explosive."

THE RECONSTRUCTION AND DEVELOPMENT PROGRAM (RDP)

The Reconstruction and Development Program (RDP) had a central commitment to meeting the basic needs of housing, electrification, jobs, the redistribution of agricultural land, clean water and sanitation, a cleaner environment, full reproductive rights for women, universal primary health care, social welfare, and education. The RDP attempted to link the provision of basic needs with economic growth. The RDP document noted that a key catalyst in achieving RDP objectives was an active state, biased in favor of the interests of the disadvantaged majority and a strong civil society.

However, alongside the watering down that had taken place in the negotiated political settlement the RDP too was to be watered down. As Marais (1998: 177) notes, "the paradigm of the transition (inclusion, conciliation, consensus, stability) applied also to the RDP, a non-surprising development." By the time it became a program of government it had lost its transformative thrust.

In April 1996, the RDP office was downgraded. Its offices were closed down and its functions were transferred to the offices of the deputy president and the finance minister on the grounds that the RDP had been integrated successfully into line-function departments.

ADOPTING GEAR

A further shift away from any notion of redistribution was seen in June 1996 when the government released its macro-economic plan GEAR. Instead of placing the fight against poverty and the needs of the majority of black South Africans in the center, this policy focused on consolidating business confidence, enhancing the environment for private sector expansion, and liberalizing the economy. GEAR represents a trickle-down approach. It does not promise an easing of poverty or inequality and hence is not in the interests of poor women or poor men.

The point needs to be made that while economic growth is necessary, growth does not in itself reduce poverty or address inequality. Bond (2000) notes that market-oriented policies have never anywhere in the world made for strides in development areas. GEAR has clearly failed to meet its own targets. Economic growth in 1996 was more than 10 per cent lower than GEAR had predicted, 71,000 jobs were lost—a far cry from the predicted 126,000 new jobs predicted for June that year.

In mid-1994, the government began to implement the General Ageement on Tariffs and Trade (GATT). The effect of GATT, as Adelzadeh and Padayachee (in Marais, 1998) point out, would be to erode regulatory domestic laws and government regulation at all levels, to promote programs for privatization and deregulation, and to weaken worker rights and unions.

Neither Bond (2000) nor Marais (1998) looks at the differential impacts of GEAR or GATT on women and men. Feminist scholarship on structural adjustment programs elsewhere has highlighted, for example, how women's reproductive burdens increase as a result of less social spending on the part of states. In South Africa, one of the effects of deregulation has been the closure of clothing and textile firms, and this has affected women's employment since women make up the majority of the workforce in these sectors.

Marais (1998) makes the charge that government policy since 1994 had been consistent, since even the Reconstruction and Development Program was based on liberalization, free markets, and the cultivation of business and investor confidence. In his view, the basic-needs concept and civil society role remained as rhetoric.

Soon after the new government came in it became clear what class interests were to be privileged in the new order. The mass-based organizations no longer seemed to be heard. Mandela, on May Day 1994, as reported in the *Sunday Times*, assured investors that "not a single reference to things like nationalism" remained in ANC economic policies and that these has been "cleansed of anything that will connect us with any Marxist ideology."

Jeremy Cronin of the South African Communist Party, another of the ANC's alliance partners (quoted in Marais, 1998) remarked that the arguments of capital were "more attractive and more persuasive to a wide range of ANC leadership than the counter arguments which are less confident, less coherent."

MOVEMENT ORGANIZATIONS UNDER APARTHEID

In attempting to understand the question of social movements it is important to understand state–society relations and the ways in which movement organizations are shaped by the state at the same time as they impact on the state.

As Alvarez (1990) notes, the political strategies and discourses of movements are responses to state policies. At the same time, movements impact state discourses and public policies. The relationship between states and movements are thus dynamic and dialectical.

In the South African context movement responses were shaped by the repression unleashed by the colonial and apartheid capitalist states, and these movements were able to pressure the state at various points. The history of resistance in South Africa has been characterized by periods of open political resistance as well as by periods of apparent quiescence during which movement organizations operated underground.

Resistance, and accounts of resistance, are also shaped by prevailing ideologies of gender. So, while historical accounts of resistance against apartheid note the class and racial character of the movements and struggles, most analyses have been silent on issues of gender subordination and treat the social actors within resistance organizations as undifferentiated. Yet it is clear that state repression affected women and men differently. Women engaged in political resistance against the colonial and apartheid states, even though much of this resistance took place within male-dominated political organizations that recognized the women's question (as propounded within Marxist and national liberation discourse[5]) but did not consider gender disparity as a fundamental contradiction that needed to be addressed in order to attain a more egalitarian society.

Hence women were active in the ANC and SACP from their very formation. Individual women made significant contributions within these organizations. And at various points specific groups of women rose up in protest and action, as in the case of protests against beer brewing and pass laws.[6]

With the revival of open political activity in the 1970s and 1980s, dispersed organizational efforts in various parts of the country came together in a strong national trade union federation—the largest the country had ever seen, in the Black Consciousness Movement, and in the establishment of the United Democratic Front (which brought together mainly urban based community organizations from all over the country). This period saw the coming together of student, community, and worker struggles. University students and intellectuals played a significant role in facilitating and supporting the emerging trade union movement through organizations such as the Wages Commission and the Institute for Industrial Education. Political activity was sparse or non-existent during this period in the rural areas, including the white-owned agricultural farms and the homelands.

Black workers resisted the onslaught of racial capitalism that prevented them forming or joining trade unions. In the 1980s trade unions became stronger. There were divisions among the newly formed unions in this period, with some aligned to the ANC/SACP, others under the federation FOSATU (Federation of South African Trade Unions) taking a position that emphasized worker control, and some under the federation NACTU (National Council of Trade Unions) aligned to black consciousness organizations.

In the mid-1980s, the ANC-aligned and FOSATU-affiliated unions came together with several independent unions to form the federation COSATU. In the 1990s COSATU continued to function as an independent organization at the same time as it joined the Tripartite Alliance.

WOMEN ORGANIZE UNDER APARTHEID

What has been referred to as the women's movement in South Africa emerged essentially out of national and worker struggles. The key actors of the women's movement have been UDF women's organizations, ANC women, and trade union women. Their organization was shaped by the pre-vailing political and economic repression and to a lesser extent by the gender dynamics within the UDF, ANC and trade union movement.

Women in communities and trade unions became increasingly more vocal and active during the 1980s. Ideas of liberation were framed within notions of nationalism and socialism, with these two isms sometimes coming together and sometimes coming into conflict.

Women active in trade unions and community organizations as well as women students engaged in discussion on women's role in the liberation struggle and within trade unions at the same time as they engaged in strug-gles alongside men in these organizations. Women's concerns were shaped by socialist and nationalist ideas, and, as they faced these challenges, many women activists were inspired by second-wave feminism and by black and Third World national feminism.

Women in trade unions made links between struggles in the factory, the community, the country, and at home. Given their position in society, in relation to the state and capital their struggles brought together race, class, and gender.

There was much debate about the place of feminism within the national liberation movement. For some, taking up women's struggles was seen as diverting the struggle from the major contradiction that might be cast as either national liberation or socialist revolution, depending on who was doing the casting. However, these debates took place in a context where the more pressing and more critical debates were between socialists and nationalists, debates that intensified as the UDF was formed and as FOSATU became COSATU. At times, in deference to what were perceived as more pressing issues, women's activism took the form of supporting the general movement without raising specific gender issues.

Yet the very agreement that women should be active and involved in organ-izations, even if this was framed in terms of male-dominated movements needing more numbers (to fight the state or individual capitalists), highlighted key issues of gender oppression—issues of reproductive responsibilities, for example, which prevented many women from active participation in organizations.

Some of the discussion on the need for shared reproductive responsibili-ties between women and men in the household was thus framed within the context of strengthening women's role in the struggle. The discourse was therefore couched largely as one of instrumentalism—women's membership in trade unions, for example, as a means to signed recognition agreements with individual factory managements, since in order to be recognized unions had to show a membership comprising 51 per cent of the total workforce.

However, things did not stop there. Once they were union members women raised issues such as maternity leave, sexual harassment, and the sharing of reproductive work with men. Women also raised the issue of violence from male partners. The challenge to bosses was extended to challenges at home as well as to male comrades in the union. Trade union women began to form separate structures—women's forums—as safe spaces where they could voice their concerns, strategize around how to get the male leadership to take up their concerns, and discuss how to get women into the trade union leadership structures that were all male.

As women's involvement in trade unions grew so did their involvement in the emerging community organizations and in women's organizations such as the United Women's Organization (based in the Western Cape), the Natal Organization of Women, and the Federation of Transvaal Women. Attempts were made to bring the various provincially based women's organizations together into a Federation of South African Women and later into the UDF Women's Congress. These attempts at a national formation did not sustain themselves.

During the mid-1980s, tension erupted between UDF organizations and women in COSATU. UDF women questioned the existence of the COSATU women's forums, which they saw as parallel structures that prevented women from joining the UDF aligned women's organizations. Women's forums also came under fire from another quarter, for different reasons—from men in trade unions who saw women's forums as a waste of time.

Women in COSATU have not had an easy time getting their interests met. For example, in the late 1980s and early 1990s they lost on their demands for unions to take on the issue of sexual harassment in the union, and they lost battles for a quota in COSATU's leadership. However, their framing of these demands led to much discussion within COSATU Congresses on these issues. Trade union leader Maggie Magubane makes the point that many of the gains made have been paper gains, since COSATU membership and leadership continue to carry patriarchal attitudes. "We have to listen to male comrades saying there is no way they can be led by a woman. We have to listen to certain shop stewards insisting women can't be elected as office bearers—it is against tradition" (Magubane, in Meer, 1998: 74). Women trade unionists found themselves having to defend the need for the women's forums they had won in earlier years since male leaders were of the view that "gender was about women and men"—a view that depoliticizes by removing the notion of male power as well as the notion of women's subordination. Sexism and sexual harassment continue as features of women's experience in COSATU and its affiliates today.[7]

When the ANC was unbanned the question of the future of the UDF affiliates was a key strategic issue. The ANC was about to embark on setting up branches in every corner of the country and the UDF organizations including the civics were seen as competing structures. Discussion ensued on whether civics should continue to exist and, if so, what their relation would be to ANC branches (Marais, 1998). Some UDF affiliates collapsed into the ANC branches, but some civics under SANCO withstood pressure to disband, and even extended into new areas such as the former homelands where they had not previously had a presence. The UDF women's organizations all disbanded and collapsed into the ANC Women's League. This meant that organizations set up and sustained over five to ten years, which had developed memberships, infrastructure, and projects, were suddenly no more.

Cronin (1992, in Marais, 1998) notes that the disbanding of the UDF organizations was evidence of thinking that the UDF was the B team that was not required once the A team (the ANC) was back. This also contains evidence of the notion that movement organizations serve the role of transmission belts for the party. The disbanding of the UDF organizations was a tragedy and it has been difficult to remobilize in more recent times.

In the period preceding the negotiations, when negotiations were already on the cards, ANC women strategized to get women's concerns on the agenda of ANC policy discussions. Notable among these initiatives were the November 2 statement committing the ANC to gender equity, the commission on the emancipation of women, the inclusion of the demand for safe abortions within health debates, and an ANC policy department conference on unpaid labor.

ANC women pushed for a quota on the ANC executive in 1991 in order to ensure that women made up at least one-third of the party's leadership, but lost this demand. In the intervening years ANC women campaigned on this issue, and picked it up again in the run-up to the country's first democratic elections, this time winning a one-third quota for women on the ANC list for parliament. This won for women 101 of the 400 seats in the first democratic parliament. Two points need to be noted in relation to this gain. First, it was facilitated by the electoral system of proportional representation, a system that has the shortcoming of not facilitating direct accountability to constituencies. Second, it needs to be borne in mind that the quota is party policy rather than state law (as is the case in Uganda) and that a continued quota is therefore at the whim of the party.

Alongside the resistance organizations of the 1980s and 1990s there were a range of supportive NGOs and a vibrant independent press. On questions of women and gender, two publications—*SPEAK,* a magazine for grassroots women, and *Agenda,* a journal—contributed to the airing of debates among community, trade union and political activists, students, and academics.

MOVEMENTS AND THE STATE IN THE TRANSITION AND IN THE NEW DEMOCRACY

As the ANC took part in negotiations, the relationship between movement organizations and the apartheid state shifted away from direct confrontation.

Movement organizations came out in protest from time to time as the negotiations faltered.

Southall and Wood point out that COSATU's membership in the Tripartite Alliance (of ANC, SACP, and COSATU) was a means to ensuring that "working class bias prevailed in the politics and programmes adopted by the ANC once in government." That is, even though as a governing party the ANC would have to be committed to pursuing the national interest, "the Tripartite Alliance was forged to ensure that, henceforth, the newly democratic government in South Africa would be labour friendly" (Southall and Wood, 1999: 68).

In the post-1994 era, however, relations between the state and unions have been tense, particularly around GEAR, and certain labor laws. An issue that has been raised in discussion and debate is on whether workers' interests would be better met if COSATU left the Alliance. COSATU itself has raised criticism around its role in the Alliance. Bhulungi (1997: 72) cites a COSATU discussion document, 'A Draft Program for the Alliance', which notes: "The Alliance never sat down to systematically look at the challenges of the transition and formulate a strategy, and what role our various formations should play in that strategy." In this document COSATU laments that policymaking has become the domain of consultants, conservative economists, bureaucrats from the old order, and international financial institutions such as the World Bank and IMF. It notes that the RDP has been undermined by a range of forces and that organizations of the people have been demobilized and "most activists are no more sure of what the strategic objectives are" (Bhulungu, 1997: 72).

The dominant COSATU position is however for continued involvement in the Alliance while challenging government when workers' interests are threatened.

Southall and Wood point out that COSATU was critical of the substance as well as the lack of consultation around GEAR. Yet COSATU gave its full backing to the ANC in the 1999 election, "pronouncing it in favour of workers and the poor." COSATU has engaged in mass demonstrations at the same time as it engaged in negotiations with business in NEDLAC (National Economic Development and Labor Council) and opened a parliamentary office to pressure parliament.

Continued retrenchments have meant the loss of large numbers of union members, for example, from the male mining and female garment and textile sectors. COSATU's attempts to organize unemployed workers in the 1980s have been abandoned. With the demise of the South African Domestic Workers Union, for instance, COSATU has not seen it as a matter of priority to address the needs of domestic workers. Nor does COSATU see it as a matter of priority to address the needs of the survivalist end of the informal sector (largely a women's sector). Given its change in membership—from predominantly blue-collar to increasingly white-collar and its increasingly narrow bent to addressing member interests, COSATU seems to be drifting away from the strong political unionism that linked national liberation and class interests.

Neither COSATU nor the Tripartite Alliance has considered systemic gender discrimination or the position of women as a priority. These organizations are themselves both male-dominated and imbued with patriarchal ideologies.

Women in trade unions were on the defensive in the 1990s—having made gains in the mid-1980s, they had to struggle to defend these. While ANC women won a one-third quota in the ANC party, COSATU women have to date not won this, and talk of the glass ceiling within trade unions remaining intact.

THE WOMEN'S NATIONAL COALITION

In 1991 the ANC Women's League spearheaded the formation of the Women's National Coalition (WNC). The WNC brought together some 60 organizations, including women from the major political parties for the single purpose of developing a charter of women's rights.

By strategically taking up the opportunities opened up by the transition and the unfolding process of democratization, the WNC was able to get gender higher up on the agenda. It played a key role in ensuring that women's equality took precedence over customary law in the South African Constitution. It campaigned for and won the national gender machinery (the OSW, CGE, and gender focal points in almost all line-function departments) intended to advance women's interests. It also played a role in sensitizing all political parties to women's votes and therefore to the advisability of increasing the numbers of women in leadership.

The WNC came close to being a movement. Criticism leveled against the WNC, however, notes its domination by political parties; that it seldom arrived at consensus because of the diversity of its members (Abrams 2000); that it never resolved the issue of abortion, for example; that it raised more middle-class issues rather than those of women who were working, unemployed or not organized; and that ultimately it failed to form a women's movement, although it tried (Duarte, quoted in Meer, 1998)

Members of the WNC executive and steering committee were involved in the national negotiations as advisors and lobbyists. They devised this strategy to counter the problem of a male-dominated negotiation process during the first round of national negotiations (CODESA). Women from various political parties were concerned that women were excluded from the various delegations, and to address this concern they came together to set up a Gender Advisory Committee (GAC) within the first round of negotiations (CODESA). But political violence within the country led to the breakdown of the CODESA talks just as the GAC was getting off the ground. When the second round of talks—the Multi-Party Talks—took off in March 1993, the WNC had set up a national office, a campaign strategy and a monitoring process through a Negotiations Monitoring Team. This enabled the WNC to make its significant contribution when traditional leaders objected to the equality provisions in the bill of rights.

The WNC-inspired Women's Charter was released in June 1994. However, the hope that the charter would become the focus for the mobilization and organization of a strong and effective women's movement in South Africa has not been realized. Meintjes attributes this in part to the diversity of interests represented within the organization with no unifying issue to sustain it, and to leadership problems since its leaders were "sucked into parliament where energies have been dispersed in national politics and the tasks of the moment, rather than in fighting the gender struggle" (1996: 61).

Accounts of the WNC highlight the success in bringing together a diverse group of women but in emphasizing this tend to obscure a more textured understanding of the WNC itself as well as of the period with its opportunities and constraints (Meintjes, 1996; Hassim, 2000).

A number of points need to be noted.

First, the WNC needs to be seen in relation to the pre-1991 struggles within and between women's organizations, as these tensions shaped outcomes within the coalition. These include tensions between "workerists" (socialists) and populists (nationalists), which took the form among women of tensions between COSATU and UDF women, and tensions between exiles and non-exiles. One outcome of these tensions was the tentative engagement of the trade union women in the WNC, and this influenced the class bent of the organization.

Second, it needs to be noted that the demobilization of the UDF women's organizations resulted in the absence of a strong core of resistance organizations that the WNC could draw on.

Third, because of the key strategic role played by the ANC Women's League in the WNC, tensions within the ANC Women's League had an impact on the WNC. The split in the ANC Women's League after the 1994 election, when two competing groups fought for control of the organization, resulted in the ousting from leadership of the more feminist and strategically directed group, which had spearheaded the WNC and the challenges to the negotiations. Even before this defeat tensions in the ANC had made participation of the ANC in the WNC more erratic. The loss of these strategists, together with the exodus of WNC executive members into parliament and the decision that parliamentarians could no longer be WNC members, was a blow to the organization and it has to date not recovered a strategic role in gender politics in South Africa.

Fourth, the charter and the strategies of the WNC seem to reflect a middle ground in much the same way as the negotiations among the major parties did. It would seem fair to say that this was translated into something close to a liberal feminism with liberal strategies that did not challenge class or race privilege in any significant way.

Fifth, that women from diverse backgrounds were able to come together when they did is not surprising since the men from these organizations were already talking to each other in CODESA and later in the final round of negotiations. In the first instance, what these women had in common was their exclusion from the process of talks.

Sixth, it needs to be noted that while in effect the WNC functioned as an independent organization, key players within the organization were women's wings of political parties. These organizations were themselves not independent but rather bound by party policy and discipline.

What is significant is the way the WNC was able to use the space opened up by the transition to set up a Gender Advisory Committee, and a Monitoring Committee to monitor and shape the outcome of the negotiations. Most significantly, the WNC (together with its affiliate the Rural Women's Movement) was able to intervene in the process of developing the constitution and able to overturn a clause proposed by traditional leaders to exempt traditional authority from the equality clause of the constitution, which enshrines gender equality (Meintjes, 1996).

At the same time, a climate conducive to getting gender and women's issues heard had been developed from the early days of the struggle: women's involvement in the struggles in significant numbers and with significant impact including the pass campaigns of the early 1900s and the major protest of 1956; women's active raising of their concerns and their active involvement in COSATU and UDF; the discussions and debates about women's liberation and national liberation; gender as an international human rights issue; the UN decade for women; and the increasing pressure from international donor organizations had all contributed to a climate where no self-respecting revolutionary or aspirant to state office could ignore gender.

Overall, the WNC was not able however to sustain its organizational impetus beyond the development of the charter. Alongside the changing political context, the difficulties in keeping its diverse member organizations together after the charter had been completed, the conflicts within the ANC Women's League, the exodus of large numbers of WNC members into parliament all contributed to the weakening of the organization. This exodus affected other movements such as trade unions, civic organizations, and NGOs as well.

FACING NEW CHALLENGES

The ANC in South Africa had to make the shift from a liberation movement to a majority party in the state. Having come from movements did not translate into a positive relationship between movements and state. A glaring gap between RDP rhetoric about movements and the actual approach to movement organizations soon appeared.

The ANC government's attitude toward organization in civil society has been ambivalent. The RDP had noted that the existence of a strong NGO sector was an important contribution to ensuring a strong vibrant civil society, which in turn was vital to ensuring the delivery of basic needs.

Contrary to the strong call made in the RDP document for partnerships between the state with civil society government, attitudes to civil society have in reality been ambiguous. During the period of negotiations, movements were turned on when a show of mass support was needed by the leadership engaged in negotiations, and then turned off again when no longer needed, and at times elements in the ANC viewed civil society (and NGOs) as irritants (Marais, 1998; Cronin, 1992).

There has been an increasing push that NGOs and community-based organizations (CBOs), which had in the days of anti-apartheid activism supported mass-based movements, shift their attention from "struggle" to "development." And development activity increasingly came to be defined in relation to the mainstream international development agencies, such as UN agencies, the World Bank and IMF, that is, in purely technicist rather than political terms—as though power and struggles are not factors that determine whose interests will be met in the name of development in post-apartheid South Africa.[8]

THE PERVASIVENESS OF NEOLIBERALISM

The new context in which we find ourselves is framed by neoliberal economic policies and liberal notions of democratic rights. There is an over-reliance on markets and the law as though access to markets and the law are not shaped by race-, class- and gender-based advantage and disadvantage.

The goal of the national liberation struggle was to take over the state machinery and this resulted, despite the sunset clause that apartheid-era civil servants would remain in office, in large numbers of individuals from the ANC, its allies and the many struggle organizations going into the national parliament, the nine provincial parliaments, local government and the various tiers of the state and parastatal bureaucracy.

Many former activists are in the state machinery. Those in trade unions challenge the state in defensive action as gains won in the past come under threat. Some former activists located in NGOs attempt to make inroads for the most marginalized in various sectors, such as land reform, AIDS, and development; women activists are active in land reform, reproductive rights, health policy, in work against violence against women and rape, and in AIDS work. Initiatives such as the Women's Budget Project, the Gender Advocacy Project and the New Women's Movement represent new initiatives to bring women's concerns to current processes of democratization.

Much of this activity takes place in terms set by the government, and from a perspective that privileges law-making as a means of redress. Women in all of these organizations engage with state departments, state personnel, and the gender machinery (CGE and OSW). They use the space in the present to research, train, and lobby individuals and structures within the state. So, for example, magistrates and police are trained on issues of rape and gender-based violence in order to make these institutions more responsive to women's concerns.

They struggle in the new context with the challenges of entrenching the new democracy. As Jaquette and Wolchick (1998: 7) note in the context of Latin America and Eastern Europe, the return to democratic politics created unexpected problems for the women's movement and for social movements in general. Democracy meant that:

> brave new concepts had to be turned into workable legislation, that sustained organisational effort would be needed to ensure women's issues would be taken up by the political parties and that legislation would be implemented and monitored. [...] Heady enthusiasm of the transition with its sense of mass involvement and solidarity gave way to smaller and more focused efforts.

Alvarez (1990), writing on Brazil, notes that inroads made by feminists during the transition will not automatically be transformed into permanent paths to effective power and political influence. This is borne out by the situation in South Africa.

Gains made by women in South Africa include a range of legislation of specific concern to women as well as relatively more women-sensitive general legislation. Overall, however, gains made by legislative and political reforms won by activists remain mired in a framework that does not question neo-liberal economics or notions of liberal democratic rights. Ideas of socialism seem to have disappeared overnight and the dominant discourse for all parties (including most trade unionists and gender activists) is on neoliberal terms.

A central problematic is that many of the activists in trade unions, communities, or NGOs do not problematize sufficiently the outcome of their strategic decisions. Miller and Razavi (1999) point to the danger of feminists (and this applies to other movements as well) becoming locked in the dominant neoliberal trend. They note that with the growing influence of neoliberal philosophy, which is inherently opposed to policy interventions aimed at achieving social equity, feminist policy advocates tend today to link gender equity to more acceptable policy concerns such as growth and market efficiency. Feminists thus use the efficiency discourse of neoclassical economics. They talk of gender-based distortions instead of human rights. They frame domestic violence in terms of economic cost. They do this because they will be heard more readily by those concerned with promoting economic growth and removing market distortions. However, as Goetz and Mayoux (both in Miller and Razavi, 1999) argue, reframing gender-equity concerns in terms of social and economic efficiency gains has the effect of depoliticizing the issue. It also runs the risk of making women more exploitable, as the tendency to highlight investing in women can mean an intensification of women's workloads.

Fraser (in Miller and Razavi, 1999) notes that policy-making institutions tend to depoliticize certain issues by framing them as impersonal market imperatives, or private ownership prerogatives or technical problems. Struggles take place over the meaning of concepts.

Miller and Razavi note tensions between those feminists who advocate win–win scenarios and call for policies for "the common good," very often in the language of liberal individualism, and those using confrontational discourses that tend to be rooted in a more structural understanding of women's subordination. Approaches cast in neoliberal terms are open to co-optation and instrumentalism and to risks of neutralizing the transformative nature of the feminist agenda. On the other hand, contestation over concepts such as efficiency can be a way of subverting the dominant neoliberal discourse.

Within government departments, NGOs, and the private sector in South Africa, the notion of transformation takes the form of a number count of black and female bodies without addressing ways in which the state continues to reinforce existing race, class and gender disparities in society. At the same time assessments of how people are faring in these institutions seem to focus more on whether the new entrants (for example, women parliamentarians) are fitting into these institutions and less on whether they are able to make significant changes in the interests of the most marginalized (see for example the CGE study, 1999).

In addition, transforming state institutions tends to be treated as an end and the focus is on making them more representative of the demographics of South African society. There is little focus on the role of these institutions in entrenching democracy. Entry into these institutions thus becomes a means to embourgeoisement rather than as a means to improve living conditions within society (Sitas, 1998).

A state-centric perspective has become the dominant trend, so, for example, the CGE book *Redefining Politics* talks only of parliamentary politics, as though politics does not exist outside the formal state arena. An article by Tenjiwe Mtintso in the same publication calls for women outside parliament to organize in order to constitute a base and support for women in parliament, ignoring the possibility that women outside parliament should organize to hold parliamentarians accountable. It is as though the leaders of the liberation movement, having moved into the state, have also moved the spotlight on to the state and anything outside this arena is devalued and/or invisible.

Then there is the big question—one that many try to understand—of how it is that those who championed other causes in the past are now pursuing goals so contrary to what they stood for (or seemed to stand for in the past). And coupled with this is the question of why this has happened so soon—hardly two years into the new democratic order.

What of the hopes that trade unionists and women would make their mark in the interests of workers and the poor once in parliament? The track record on this score is not good. The South African minister of trade and industry, a former trade union and SACP leader, now serves as chair of the WTO and promotes GEAR and WTO policies. The current minister of land and agriculture, who was the secretary of the Women's National Coalition, today promotes policies geared at creating a black farming elite, offering very little for the likes of the women marchers in Mpumalanga.

Collins (1997) raises questions of accountability in relation to trade unionists on the ANC list of parliamentarians. She points out that COSATU did not consider questions of accountability when they took the decision to send 20 of its senior leaders to parliament as ANC candidates in the 1994 national election. She notes that there was a lack of a structured relationship between these leaders and the unions they came from, a lack of any labor caucus in parliament, and confusion over which organization these leaders represented (ANC, COSATU, or individual affiliate). Issues of accountability came into question also when some of these trade union leaders begin to leave parliament to join investment companies—it was not clear whether this had the support of the unions and COSATU.

For women in parliament questions of accountability are more difficult since there is no national organization representing women today. Yet accountability could be exercised in relation to community-based movements that exist and in relation to ensuring links between women inside parliament with women in trade unions and community-based groupings. However, this seems to be non-existent. And what is worrying is the state-centric perspective that suggests that links between women inside and outside parliament should focus on the needs of women inside parliament.

This is understandable, since ANC women and men who entered parliament for the first time in 1994 were overwhelmed by the rules of the game within this institution and have had to make huge adjustments. However, what this view ignores is the importance of continued organization in society to hold parliamentarians accountable.

Mtintso (1999) notes that new women MPs had to prove themselves, that women progressed from being completely overwhelmed to feeling empowered and able to function in the system, that women needed to learn the rules and how to change them. However, it would seem that the experience to date has been for most more about learning how to function in terms of the rules, with little change taking place.

Mtintso also refers to the gap between gender activists inside and outside parliament and notes that an active gender contingent is needed, at the core of which should be women in parliament. She asserts that gender activism from all sectors of civil society should be strong and work with those in parliament. Such activists, she notes, should be organized in a strong women's and feminist movement to act as a power base for activists in parliament. Miller and Razavi also refer to the link between women inside and outside in a way that tends to privilege the insiders, in noting the importance of "strong external women's constituencies to support internal gender policy advocacy."

While it is clear that a link between outsiders and insiders is crucial, the nature of this link, and on whose terms the link is made, seems a crucial question that needs to be explored. For example, what class interests are to be served by such an alliance?

Miller and Razavi (1999) summarize key issues raised by feminists in considering entryism as a strategy. They note that pushing transformative agendas from within while adapting to the techniques and practices of the bureaucracy is a complex business. Feminist engagement strategy, they point out, aims to promote change within existing bureaucratic structures even if it is recognized that change will be incremental.

The strategy of implementing change from within demands a wide variety of skills—an in-depth understanding of how the bureaucratic machinery works, astute political skills to identify where the strategic points of leverage in the policy establishment are, and how allies can be cultivated despite the distrust of traditional bureaucrats.

In addition to the problems of links and accountability is the question of embourgeoisement and a new morality that takes over alongside the transformation. As Buhlungu points out, "processes of class formation or elite formation have accelerated with many of the leading activists who were part of the tradition of democratic participation as beneficiaries of new opportunities created by the deracialized society." In this context, the "discourse of collective participatory democracy has been overtaken by one of individualism and careerism where empowerment is seen to emanate from taking advantage of opportunities created by deracialization" (Buhlungu, 2002: 163).

The transition opens up new opportunities and contradictions (Sitas, 1998). The version of nationalism that survives is about "empowerment and accumulation paths of a new power bloc of pragmatic populists who are heirs of global processes of empowerment. This reshaping of the political elite has been a further nudge toward a logic of disintegration of social movements."

Saul (1999) asks whether the ANC leadership has chosen market solutions to serve leadership's nascent class interests or because market solutions are developmental or inevitable under current global and local conditions. He suggests that in order to make their conservative economic choices palatable government dresses up policies in radical rhetoric and in "African Renaissance" speak.

It is clear that a range of forces shapes the present. Sitas (1998) notes that trends such as globalization, institutional transition, and the developing new circuits of power all shape the new. The capacity of the state to shape outcomes is reduced by South Africa's new entry into world markets. Change is also limited by struggles between power blocs with competing agendas—between old apartheid-era civil servants and the newer ANC-aligned entrants.

The transition "generates a logic of disintegration" (Sitas, 1998: 43) that shapes and affects social movements that have ushered in the transformation in the first place. Broader political arrangements shape the form and functioning of social movements that in their turn continue to shape the logic of the broader process in subtle ways. "Revolutionary vanguards and organizations can never shape transitions at will, rather they are shaped and the conditions they face are shaped by broader structural forces, not least of which are the international and political parameters" (Sitas, 1998: 43).

The former liberation movement transforms itself as processes of transformation, accompanied by class formation and realignment, and former goals are no longer shared (Bhulungu, 1997).

REINVENTING SOCIAL EMANCIPATION

Saul (1999: 64) asks

just how long the mass of South Africans—so used to mobilising historically to advance their interests—will themselves rest content with the kind of bleak perspectives granted them by 'magical market realism' before they are also moved to reactivate the struggle to realise more humane and genuinely developmental socio-economic strategies in their country is one of the key questions as we approach the millennium.

Over the past seven years, poor rural and urban communities and workers have mobilized around a number of issues. Their actions have taken the form of land invasions, protest marches, and demonstrations on a range of issues.

As Sitas (1998) notes, there has been a "shift from a militant social movement approach to a variety of initiatives, not necessarily connected, each with its own dynamics, compromises and innovations that spell both resistance and accommodation to central arrangements" of the post-apartheid government.

More recently there is more glaring evidence of desperation among the poor and marginalized. So, for example, in Mpumalanga, in November 1999, rural women marched naked in the streets to make their demands heard. Seventy-year-old Josephine Tsabedza and 27 other rural women spent a week in jail after being arrested for marching naked down the main road of Beffelspruit in Mpumalanga in protest against a local chief who refused to recognize their rights to land. Tsabedza said: "We marched all along the streets naked to show the chief we are angry and we wanted to show him our empty stomachs. My main worry is the children. That's why I ended up in jail. I did all this because of hunger" (Shongwe, 2000: 18). The women felt guilty about their week in jail because they had better meals in jail than their children and grandchildren at home. On average each woman has between five and nine children to feed and clothe. Often these women are the sole breadwinners. They need land so that they can grow food for their children.

In Isipingo, outside Durban, in February 2001, residents held protest meetings and marches against evictions by the local ANC-dominated council. One of the families facing evictions was 65-year-old Mrs. Munisamy, her 27-year-old daughter, Kantha, who has cancer, and her 6-year-old grandson. They live in an empty council flat. Their income used to be Mrs. Munisamy's pension of R540 a month, which was stopped for seemingly bureaucratic reasons. Their rent is R268 a month, rates R61 a month, and they must pay lights and water bills in addition. Mrs. Munisamy is asthmatic but cannot afford to go to the hospital. A speaker at the protest meeting of 800 people reminded residents that they beat apartheid and urged them to defeat this new enemy and to fight the evictions together. Legal action resulted in a stay of the evictions. The residents coming together resulted in action (Pithouse, 2001).

In Mpumalanga Township, outside Hammersdale, in Kwa Zulu Natal, residents attended a rally on 29 April 2001. The township is located in a semi-rural area as a result of apartheid's design that blacks should not live near white suburbs. Most residents had jobs in the nearby poultry industry, but are now unemployed as the industries have closed down. Residents cannot afford to pay for services and have been threatened with water cuts. The rally was to resist this.

Whether and how such actions will all come together is yet to be seen. However, what seems clear is that it is unlikely that the movements of the 1980s will play much of a role in bringing together the various individual protests.

The women's movement organizations of the 1980s—the Women's National Coalition, the Rural Women's Movement—are no more. The UDF women's organizations are no more because they disbanded to form the ANC Women's League, and the Women's League seems immobilized as a result of key executive members being in parliament and hence not available to build a movement.

The NGOs of the 1980s, which supported community and trade union struggles in the 1980s when the perpetrators were the agents of the apartheid state, are silent on these struggles today. Development NGOs pressure government but at same time try to do so within the neoliberal logic and within an agenda set by the state. In addition, NGOs are dogged by the lack of funds, a crisis that it was hoped government would address on recognizing the importance of a strong NGO sector.

The form and nature of the trade union movement has changed and its ability to shape the transition is wavering. Within trade unions today organization building is not a priority—leaders spend more time in policy-related efforts in a bid to influence state law and policy. Union activists and the rank and file have been demobilized. They neglect to build their independent power and confuse strategic direction with those of the ruling party (Bhulungu, 1997).

CONCLUSION

The role of a strong movement organization outside state structures is crucial in ensuring that representatives do in fact represent the interests of their constituencies. However, the continued existence of the South African trade union movement together with trade unionists in parliament has not resulted in worker interests being met by the new government. This is seen in the ongoing tensions between COSATU and government on issues of GEAR, the Labor Relations Act, and the Basic Conditions of Employment Act over the past few years, as well as in the increasing retrenchments that have meant a change in union membership from mainly blue-collar to increasingly more white-collar. In the present context, rather than promising to constitute a strong pressure on the state, the trade unions seem instead to be weakening.

Women's organizations today are represented by a range of smaller, more focused initiatives, rather than by an umbrella organization, and these attempt to work on advancing specific interests. The significant women's organizations of the 1980s were wings and sections of the male-led trade union and liberation movements. Given the extremity of apartheid capitalist repression, women activists engaged in the liberation organizations at the same time as they organized separately as women. The fate of women's organizations was thus tied to the broader movement.

The women who went into parliament, as was the case with the trade unionists and the SACP members, went in as ANC party representatives and their allegiance therefore has to be in the first instance to the party.

The question of interest representation is linked to broader processes including the ways in which the global and national systems of race, class, and gender systems articulate. Policies of government in South Africa today, as well as responses by activists, tend to be framed within an overwhelming neoliberal logic. The interests of women and men among the rural and urban poor are not being adequately addressed. The high rates of poverty and inequality, as highlighted in this chapter, continue along lines determined by apartheid legislation and policy.

Attempts to understand the transition and the present moment of entrenching democracy highlight that elites made decisions, although movements played a role; they also highlight the fragmenting effect of transitions. Thus, while transitions open up opportunities, they also seem to have a desta-bilizing effect on movements. And the weakening of movements allows the state to move ahead relatively unchecked. Hence policies such as GEAR, which do nothing to address the issues of poverty and inequality that continue from the days of apartheid.

In South Africa today, race, class, and gender continue to determine access to economic privilege. The transition led to a balancing act and a search for a middle ground. The nature of the democracy being entrenched is one based on liberal notions of rights, comparable with neoliberal economic doctrine.

This chapter has attempted to show how movements were shaped by state responses during apartheid, the period of the transition, and the period of emerging democracy. It also attempted to highlight the dialectical relation-ship between movements and the state.

The danger in the present is in the tendency for demands to be framed on neoliberal terms. The dangers of entryism lie in new entrants fitting into the system without challenging it, and in using entry as a means to embourgeoisement.

The seeds of challenges to neoliberalism lie perhaps in the dispersed movements that are developing in various parts of the country. Challenges need to be made to shift the rules of the game, rather than tinkering with capitalism. We may perhaps have to accept the idea of incrementalism but we need to be clear about the direction in which incremental shifts are taking us.

Notes

1 I would like to thank the African Gender Institute's Associate Program at the University of Cape Town for providing a base while I worked on this chapter. My thanks also to those who commented on earlier drafts: Boaventura de Sousa Santos, Sakhela Buhlungu, Jane Bennet, Amina Mama, Michelle Friedman, Sisonke Msimang, Ari Sitas, Fatima Meer, Anne Major, Roshilla Naicker, Shireen Hassim.

2 "The Demobilisation of Civil Society: Struggling with New Questions in Development," *Development Update* 3(1) (1999).

3 The workers who formed the militant trade unions were predominantly black workers.

4 In referring to these movements I do not mean to suggest that the category workers does not include women—rather I am referring to organizations that were set up to take up these specific interests. Women in trade unions have organized to make unions more responsive to their interests, with mixed results. While making gains in certain areas women in trade unions have to date not won the demand for a quota to ensure representation on the national executive committee of the trade unions.

5 See Hutchful, 1999.

6 See for example Kros (1980) and Wells (1980).

7 See Orr (1999).

8 See Escobar (1994) and Ferguson (1994) on critiques of the development industry and the depoliticization of what are essentially political issues.

Bibliography

Abrams, K. (2000). "Fighting for Women's Liberation during the Liberation of South Africa: The Women's National Coalition." Thesis submitted in partial fulfillment of the requirements for the M. Phil. degree in economic and social history, Faculty of Modern History, Wadham College, Oxford. May 2000.

Alvarez, S. (1990). *Engendering Democracy in Brazil: Women's Movements in Transition Politics.* Princeton, NJ: Princeton UP.

Bond, P. (2000). *Elite Transition: From Apartheid to Neoliberalism in South Africa.* Pietermaritzburg: U of Natal P.

Buhlungu, S. (1997). "Flogging a dying horse? COSTU and the alliance," *South African Labor Bulletin*, 21(1), 71–8.

— (2002). "O reinventar da democracia participativa na África do Sul," Boaventura de Sousa Santos (ed.), *Democratizar a Democracia: os caminhos da democracia participativa.* Vol. 1, Colecção *Reinventar a Emancipação Social: Para Novos Manifestos.* Rio de Janeiro: Record, 133–70.

Collins, D. (1997). "An open letter to Johnny Copelyn and Marcel Golding," *South African Labor Bulletin*, 21(1), 79–80.

Commission on Gender Equality (CGE) (1999). *Redefining Politics: South African Women and Democracy.* Johannesburg: CGE.

Cronin, J. (1992). "The boat, the tap and the Liepzig way," *The African Communist*, 130.

Escobar, A. (1994). *Encountering Development: The making and unmaking of the third world.* Princeton, NJ: Princeton UP.

Ferguson, J. (1994). *The Anti Politics Machine: 'Development', Depoliticization and Bureaucratic Power in Losotho.* Minneapolis: Minnesota UP.

Goetz, A. (1999). "Mainstreaming Gender Equity to National Development Planning," in C. Miller and S. Razavi (eds), *Missionaries and Mandarins: Feminist Engagement with Development Institutions*. Intermediate Technology Publications in association with the United Nations Research Institute for Social Development.

Hassim, S. (1991). "Gender Social Location and Feminist Politics in South Africa," *Transformation*, 15, 65–81.

— (2000). "Gender Politics in South Africa: Rights, Needs and Democratic Consolidation," in M. Smith (ed.), *Globalising Africa*. Africa Society.

Hemson, D. (1999). "A paralysis of will? Dealing with the apartheid debt". Paper presented at the launch of Jubilee 2000 (South Africa), University of Durban, Westville.

Hutchful, E. (1999). "Marxist Responses to The Challenge of Gender Relations," in A. Imam, A. Mama and F. Sow (eds), *Engendering African Social Sciences*. Dacca: Codesria.

Jaquette, J. S. and Wolchick, S. L. (1998). "A Comparative Introduction," in J. Jaquette and S. Wolchik (eds), *Women and Democracy: Latin American and Central and Eastern Europe*. Baltimore, MD: Johns Hopkins UP.

Klug, H. (2000). "Community, Property and Security in Rural South Africa: Emancipatory opportunities or marginalised survival strategies?" Paper presented to Symposium on Reinventing Social Emancipation, Coimbra, 23–26 November 2000.

Kros, C. (1980). "Urban African Women's Organisations and Protest Protest on the Rand," *Africa Perspective Dissertation* No. 3. Johannesburg: Africa Perspective.

Lipton, M., M. de Klerk, and M. Lipton (1996). 'Introduction', in *Land, Labor and Livelihoods in Rural South Africa*. Durban: Indicator Press.

Mayoux, L. (1999). "Gender Accountability and NGOs: Avoiding the Black Hole," in C. Miller and S. Razavi (eds), *Missionaries and Mandarins: Feminist Engagement with Development Institutions*. Intermediate Technology Publications in association with the United Nations Research Institute for Social Development.

Mamdani, M. (1998). *Citizen and Subject: Contemporary Africa and The Legacy of Late Colonialism*. London: James Currey.

Marais, H. (1998). *South Africa limits to change: the political economy of transformation*. Cape Town: U of Cape Town P.

Meer, S. (ed.) (1998). *Women Speak: Reflections on our struggles 1982–1997*. Cape Town: Kwela Books in association with *SPEAK*.

— (1999). "The Demobilisation of Civil Society: Struggling with New Questions," *Development Update*, 3(1).

Meintjes, S. (1996). "The Women's Struggle for Equality During South Africa's Transition to Democracy," *Transformation*, 30, 47–63.

Miller, C. and S. Razavi (eds) (1999). Introduction, in *Missionaries and Mandarins: Feminist Engagement with Development Insitutions*. Intermediate Technology

Publications in association with the United Nations Research Institute for Social Development.

Mtintso, T. (1999). "Women in Politics: A Conceptual Framework," in Commission on Gender Equality (CGE), *Redefining Politics: South African Women and Democracy*. Johannesburg: CGE.

Orr, L. (1999). "Assessing Gender Structures in COSATU," report for Naledi, Johannesburg.

Pithouse, R. (2001). "The Aunties' Revolt," *Sunday Tribune*, 4 February.

Saul, J. (1999). "Magic Market Realism," *Transformation*, 38, 49–67.

Reconstruction and Development Program (RDP) (1995). *Key Indicators of Poverty in South Africa*. Pretoria: RDP.

Shongwe, N. (2000). "Women strip naked to show hungry stomachs," *Land and Rural Digest*, 20, 18–20.

Sitas, A. (1998). "South Africa in the 1990s: The Logic of Fragmentation and Reconstruction," *Transformation*, 36, 37–50.

— (1999). "Scrap Nations: The prospects of the poor at the end of the second Christian millennium." Paper presented at the launch of Jubilee 2000 (South Africa), University of Durban, Westville.

Southall, R. and G. Wood (1999). "COSATU, the ANC and the Election: Whither the Alliance?", *Transformation*, 38, 68–81.

Wells, J. (1980). "Women's resistance to passes in Bloemfontein during the inter-war period," *Africa Perspective*, 15.

5

Political Power in Mozambique and Women's Activism[1]

Conceição Osório

INTRODUCTION

"I have been touched by taking the path from the sidelines to the state, and on this journey meeting different expressions of power. The power of the powerless and the power of those in power." (Virreira, 1999)

The welfare state, "embodying" in Mozambique a collectivist revolutionary ideology,[2] allowed women to become visible in the public sphere, changing their access to claims for equal rights in comparison with the colonial past.

This equality should be understood more as a formal expression of revolutionary political discourse than as a change in the social relations of power that surround gender relations.

As I shall seek to show in the first part of this chapter, the political strategies in the first 15 years of independence reinforced women's subordinate position in the framework of the political model, while at the same time revealing a "woman with rights." This means that women's access to rights in the context of the welfare state is delimited by norms and discourses that relocate women to roles enclosed in a logic of subordination; in other words, women's rights depend on conforming with the status conferred on them by the "androcrat" (Seidler, 1994). The evidence of discrimination against women in this period is found in the discourse and in the forms of occupation of power and the exercise of politics. The "essentiality" of female nature becomes the basis for legitimating domination, which has translated into multiple constraints on political action by women outside the normative framework that has defined their responsibilities as wives and mothers.

The struggle by women for access to political power in Mozambique in the 1970s and 1980s was configured by an ideology that did not permit mechanisms for individual political affirmation, the penalty for which was exclusion from the national revolutionary process. With the break away from revolutionary ideology and its replacement by a liberal ideology at the end of the 1980s, the regulatory and neutral character of the state led to the concealment of domination (Stetson and Mazur, 1995: 9). The result of the liberal policies in Mozambique in the field of women's human rights is the strengthening of the concept that stresses the need for women to have an institutional presence, while draining politically the struggle to change gender relations. Besides being insufficient, the legal changes we have witnessed seek to conceal the basic mechanisms of inequality. At the same time, the quantitative increase in the number of women in the civil service and in the political parties has in itself been used as a force for change, without questioning the structures, hierarchies, and value systems that surround and determine the status of women in institutions.

Thus the question of quotas could have the perverse effect of reducing change in gender relations to a female presence in the corridors of power, if we forget that the transformation of forms of domination includes incorporation (in discourse and in political activity) of the systems of differentiation that configure female identity (Pitanguy, 1999).

Since the mid-1980s, the feminist movement has focused some of its attention on the capacity to transform political organizations from within the dominant model. Faced with the growth in the number of nongovernmental organizations (NGOs) and their transformation into mere executors of government policy or of international agendas, women's organizations have sought to reflect on the usefulness of women's participation in institutions of power (Astelarra, 1999). The debate has centered on two positions: the first denies that existing institutions have any capacity for transformation, considering that maintaining them as a sphere of power is structurally justified by the "androcracy" that underlies the social model; from this point of view, and to the extent that power sharing "seeks" formal equality, the participation of women is aimed at concealing continuing inequality, and drains the feminist movement of its capacity for self-affirmation.

The second position (which defends women's occupation of political power) highlights the need to occupy spheres of political decision-making, seeking at the same time to influence and change not only the legal framework that supports the inferiority of women, but fundamentally the mechanisms that legitimate and recognize the political sphere as a male preserve, where women are accepted but not included.

The political praxis of women the world over has demonstrated abundantly that most women who reach leadership functions in the political machinery have taken on board the "masculinization" of power. Spin-doctor logic, the manipulation of information, and strategies for persuasion increase the effectiveness of institutions without changing the political modes of thought and action. While important legal victories are achieved, the movement is unable to revive feminist propositions through these women.

It was in this context that at the end of the 1990s the question of political participation by women was studied in order to link institutional presence to forms of action (for example, joint participation with other political movements) that might highlight, draw attention to and recognize the existing diversity and differences. From a theoretical point of view, this debate allows us to advance the production of knowledge, with a greater number of objects and conceptual constructs, without fear of upsetting the legitimacy of the universal framework of reference. As Virginia Guzmán has said:

> Feminism faces the challenge of weakening the barriers that hamper the spread of knowledge produced so as to influence cultural and academic output more systematically, without losing its creativity or becoming domesticated at the time of choosing its areas of interest, topics and approaches. (1999: 5)

If modern democracy, with its focus on the need for ideological pluralism, within which conflict exists, is an essential requirement for women's political participation, the modes and the "framework" that make such participation possible hamper the emergence of new ways of exercising power. As I shall try to illustrate through the words of the respondents, the political sphere in its present configuration does not encourage the inclusion of women as subjects. Since conflicts are socially constructed, the recognition of what constitutes conflict depends on the patriarchal model, that is, women's challenge to domination is perceived as a deviation from identity. The woman who does not conform to the ways in which political action is structured and ranked hierarchically is penalized by the members of the organization and by society.

With the introduction of a multi-party system in Mozambique in 1994,[3] women's access to and occupation of new places of power has followed a globalizing democratic logic that tries to obey the rules of dominant international agendas. Thus female empowerment appears basically as a way to legitimate the model of political activity, inasmuch as the ways of structuring places of power remain unchanged and the rules of the political game are consolidated—at least apparently. For example, 27 per cent of the members of parliament in Mozambique currently are women, and 40 per cent of the representatives of the majority party are women, although this number does not reveal, first, any difference in women's participation between the two parliamentary sides, and second, any change in perceptions or in parliamentary activity in relation to approaches, references, and proposals for new political strategies.

However, the continued presence of women in the sphere of power provides potential for redefining the political space. In the Mozambican case, while there is as yet no collective questioning of the criteria for access to power and of the positions occupied by women, individual speeches by leading women have begun to show a certain disquiet about the inequality in the status of women and displeasure/anxiety at the lack of incorporation of the female system of differentiation in the exercise of power. Thus, as cracks appear in the intimacy of the male political model, strategies appear, albeit fragmented, that question the legitimacy of the sources and modalities of the exercise of this power.

This chapter seeks to analyze, through the roles and functions of women in the leadership of political parties, how access to political power is achieved, the representation of power, and the forms of occupation of the political sphere, translated into differing expectations toward the exercise of power. In order to analyze these three dimensions, I highlight the need to link the following components: the impossibility of isolating women's participation in the political sphere from the socialization mechanisms in the family, which configure female identity around values that exclude them from the current models of political intervention; any analysis of women's political participation must take account of the relationship between the formal definition of women's human rights and the way in which they are socially appropriated and recognized; the occupation of political space by women must take account of particular facets of female behavior, such as greater readiness for collective work and for dialogue. Thus I use the concept of power from the perspective of Foucault of action upon action in a relationship of violence, which, acting against the other, provokes resistance and confrontation and unleashes the struggle against subjection of the subject (Foucault, 1990).

With regard to women's access to power, I consider two central questions: one relates directly to the mechanisms of socialization that hamper women's access to power, in other words, to how the "general conditions" cause the political sphere to be a discouraging one of "outsider" intervention. The other question concerns the influence that family networks might have on women's access to power, both from the point of view that choice may be determined by group interests and that a woman's presence in the field of political power may result from individual motivation separate from the influence of the family network.

I also intend to deal with the way(s) in which political power is represented by women who occupy important positions in political organizations, in other words, how leaders of the parties[4] "exercise" power, mainly in matters they regard as fundamental to their activity. Moreover, I shall seek to identify the mechanisms providing the framework for gender relations within the political parties, ascertaining the functions carried out by men and women, the "political value" attributed to them, and the different fields of intervention. I consider two main hypotheses. The first is that women's access to leadership in political parties is governed by an overall context that, while recognizing the need to make women visible, at the same time hampers the political participation of women as subject.

The second hypothesis is that, while women's occupation of political space conforms to strategies of male domination (that is, the presence of women in the leadership of political activity not only does not threaten the mechanisms of functioning and structuring political power, but rather reveals the mainte- nance of subordination through the existing power relationships), at the same time, the disparity in the criteria for access to a political career and to funding, as well as disillusion with the rules of the game, enable women to develop strategies conducive to the production of alternatives to the political model. The period analyzed in this chapter is 1992 to 1999, corresponding to changes in the political system. The units of study were: the two biggest parties in the national political spectrum, FRELIMO and RENAMO and the Front for Patriotic Action (Frente de Acção Patriótica—FAP), one of the parties created after the peace accords, fundamentally urban-based intellectuals.

While the choice of FRELIMO and RENAMO as units of study is due to their being the two largest parties (in terms of visibility and expectations of winning power) and their having been involved in armed conflict, the choice of the Front for Patriotic Action results from less immediate reasons. As a small party, visible only in very restricted circles (apparently without ambitions to win power), whose political discourse questions the function- ing of the democratic system in Mozambique, we think that testing the proposed hypotheses in the FAP could provide us with a new and interest- ing perspective on the problem.

From October 1998 to June 1999, 35 interviews were conducted, 28 with women and seven with men.[5] The interviews were semi-structured and sought to bring out and link, from a gender perspective, the construction of social relations within the family, access to leading places in the parties and how these were occupied. As regards our target group, we interviewed 14 women from FRELIMO, nine from RENAMO and five from FAP, with ages ranging from 25 to 70 years. The mean age of the female respondents was 40.4 years, while the FAP women were the youngest. The educational level of the female respondents ranged from higher education (four), through general secondary schooling (15) to upper primary (nine). The women members of FAP and FRELIMO had the higher levels of education. We interviewed four men from FRELIMO, one from FAP and two from RENAMO, with an average age of 40 years and educational levels ranging from higher education (two) through upper general secondary schooling (three) to lower general secondary schooling (two). Of the men, the RENAMO members had the lowest levels of education.

The women in general were more open, taking more frequently a critical position toward the functioning of the party, particularly with regard to dif- ferences in access for women to party resources and the party hierarchy. Their discourse often contradicted their own statements praising the party, which served to reveal the contradictions between the "politically correct" and practice in the party organizations. The men's discourse was more elaborate and reflected the positive positions of the parties on the inclusion of women, although highlighting the maleness of the political field through metaphor and allegory and the "acceptance and good will" of men in allowing women political visibility.

BUILDING UTOPIA: THE FIRST 15 YEARS ...

The changes to the political model introduced in 1994, effected with the holding of the first multi-party elections, created new spheres of public intervention, allowing the production of new forms of access to and occupation of political space. The recent history of the country was marked by a political and ideological orientation that simultaneously defined the breadth and the limits of political activity by citizens, "enclosing" it within a normative framework that governed access to public space in the first 15 years of independence.

The systems of political values were supported by a series of rituals, symbols that are essential to understanding the questions raised today by the introduction of a democratic system, since their function was the integration/exclusion of citizens in the project to build a socialist nation. Revolutionary equality as the legitimating factor in the social order was, as regards women, the basis of the struggle for emancipation (in its various dimensions). Opposition to colonial forms of organization, together with challenges to elements of traditional structures (which were able to manipulate/maintain/reproduce) carried out through a revolutionary and modern political project, brought about violent breaches in the social structure.

The occupation of power was guided by loyalties and solidarity built during the armed struggle, in a context where the participants wanted to replace kin relationships and the "natural" order, on which traditional authority rested, with "revolutionary political ideals."

These conditions apparently opened new opportunities for women to assert themselves: while freedom of rights was guaranteed, from a legal viewpoint, mainly in the Constitution,[6] the political discourse also highlighted the emancipation of women as an essential condition for the sustainability of the new society.

Thus, the public visibility of women appears in a context of liberating the country from colonial domination and imposing a system that aims to configure social practice on the basis of new political objectives. The Mozambican Women's Organization (Organização da Mulher Moçambicana —OMM)[7] emerged as the body that brought together women's aspirations for emancipation. The political discourse of the organization challenged what the new political power regarded as the object of opposition: colonial/

traditional society. This mixing of two forms of social structure in the same political battle created a double ambiguity in the discourse of the women activists in the OMM: on the one hand, the rejection of colonial modernity (including the Churches) and, on the other, the negative depiction of forms of traditional organization, such as bride-price[8] and polygamy.

At the same time, this discourse, which highlights the demand for equality between men and women in access to goods and resources, is based on the paternalism of the ruling party. The literacy campaigns for women, the struggle against violence, the involvement of women in tasks of national reconstruction co-exist, without any apparent contradiction, with the function of "cultural mobilizers" at rallies led by men. Critically examined in a socially progressive discourse, the struggle for women's emancipation is shaped by the language, the categories of analysis, and the priorities that orient the political field. While wishing to break from conservative positions, it does not in fact question the social model that determines the roles and functions of social actors through gender inequality. Seeking legitimacy by means of equality between men and women, those in power in fact conceal the maintenance of a subordinate status for women.

As women could conduct their struggle only within the framework of the party organization, the result was that their expectations for emancipation became affiliated with the system of ideas of a party dominated by men—in the composition of its leadership, in its totalitarian practices and in its exclusion of difference. The women's movement, therefore, was not constituted as a social movement with its own identity, but submitted to a political power that defined its objectives and strategies under pain of exclusion from the national project. This meant that forms of male domination were not called into question and that those in power relegated women to the role of "companion to the committed man" or "she who feeds the combatants."[9] The "androcratic" is thus legitimated.

The possibilities for challenging this model were restricted by the categories used to consider the situation of women: they should have access to public space, they should be able to exercise their rights, but their rights and public access should be guided by the interests that are constructed in the private sphere. This meant that women were given the roles primarily of mother, wife and companion ("comrade") and, on the basis of these, women's right to public respectability was or was not recognized. Women were judged, penalized, or rewarded for party loyalty and for moral behavior. It was not unusual during the 1977 party building campaign that the most frequent accusations against women focused on Judaeo-Christian morality.[10]

At the same time, women who did rise to the leadership of party organizations were mostly the wives or other relatives of political leaders, or women (a minority) who in some way or another constituted a political reserve from the national liberation struggle.[11]

The few women who performed leadership functions in the civil service were not outstanding for their struggle for women's rights, often taking extremely conservative positions on matters such as abortion, divorce, and common-law marriage. The inclusion of women in the political field was thus done through the reproduction of the patriarchal model and the maintenance of a social order that keeps politics a male domain. Gender relations, understood as relations of power, were thus built around a discourse on equality that made women's visibility rely on strategies of male domination.

However, political activity was not without its contradictions and ambiguities, visible mainly in the OMM, where party control, through former women militants, began to be challenged and led recently to an attempt to break away from the FRELIMO party.[12]

GLOBALIZATION QUOTAS AND THE LOCAL CONTEXTS OF WOMEN'S ACCESS TO POLITICAL POWER

With the changes to the system introduced in 1992, new political parties were created, allowing new problems to arise, as well as new questions and new and differing ways of finding solutions for political participation by women.

However, a study conducted in 1994 on women's participation in politics showed that the gender perspective in the composition of party leadership was expressed through "politically correct" discourse while maintaining a paternalist perspective among the party leadership regarding the role of women.[13]

In the context of the decentralization of state administration, the first municipal elections were held in 1998. By providing citizens with the opportunity to participate in the resolution of concrete problems in the municipality, local power allows questioning of the functioning of politics as an "ideological abstract" and a political competition, creating possibilities for direct involvement by the people.

While research into women's political behavior and their intervention in local power shows that access to decision-making positions is still oriented by kinship networks, it uncovers how the way these positions of power are occupied and raises the quality of female intervention (Osório et al., 1999).

If the special characteristics of municipal politics can open the route to new forms of exercising power—in the broadest sense of exercising citizenship—and therefore promote women's political participation, the occupation of positions that are organized, structured and ranked according to the male model of power (as is the case with the political parties) gives rise to various constraints, both in terms of access to power and in the forms of expressing this power.

Analysis of political party programs shows that all of them mention the importance of women's access to power, although only the FRELIMO party established a quota system. At the same time, while women's participation appears as a democratic imperative in the party principles, they are almost always relegated to female positions, that is to say, women are expected to bring their recognized skills in private life to the public domain. Women remain some sort of guarantee of family order and well-being, as much in official discourse as in incentives to political participation.[14]

Regardless of the political parties studied, women's access to power is essentially through either kinship/party networks or through kinship/ethnic networks, that is to say, women's entry into politics is almost always related to their family background, from which they derive recognition and worth. The "androcratic" model not only intervenes in women's access to places where they are strangers, it also orients and determines how women perceive and behave in politics. As I shall show in detail below, the majority of the women constituting the universe for this study,[15] regardless of their party, or ethnic or other characteristics, achieve power via men, whether this achievement is mediated by ethnic, religious, or social factors.[16] "My family is renowned in the party [...] my father was a fighter [...] I was called [...] they needed me [...]," a party leader told us.[17] Identification with a party is almost always through a male figure, and the party itself represents a paternal figure, obedience and loyalty. The exploitation/transfer of family mechanisms of socialization to the party, as an abstract entity, reflects women's need for social recognition to participate in a strongly male domain (where violence in power relations appears as a male virtue).

It is interesting to note that access to power by women who were soldiers in the national armed liberation struggle or the recent civil war also happens in a logic that puts the importance of acts of bravery or sacrifice in second place and highlights in some way or another belonging to the group. This means that affirmation attained at times of instability (war) is not translated into real occupation of power.

In general, the post-war place reserved for these women (and with the reorganization of political and military power) is either in the women's organizations or in subordinate positions in the parties. The "disorder" of war is followed by the ordered and "natural" sharing out of places and functions. Unlike the (younger) men with similar status, the age of women in the political leadership is between 35 and 40 years, and they are widows, divorcees, or single. A relatively important number of the women interviewed have intermediate schooling and have shown proof of party loyalty.

There is a clear tendency to use differing criteria in the recruitment of men and women, expressed for example in the greater circulation and distribution of power among men, with "new faces" frequently appearing to occupy important positions in the party hierarchies.[18] The rigidity of party machines, despite renewal of the power arena, is related to the impermeableness (impossibility?) of institutions to change or to the incorporation of new ways of doing politics; in other words, continuity of and resistance to change, as a condition for survival, reveals the ambiguity/conflict of a discourse on equity and equality in relation to the way organizations express them (Gaspard, 1995).

At the same time, the greater presence of women in the field of political power has caused some discomfort, which is reflected in the use of arguments related to respect for party cohesion[19] and in attempts to limit participation or involvement by women party leaders whenever the issue is to advance with proposed legislation in favor of women's rights. As I shall seek to analyze, if the disquiet produced by the political presence of women has not yet been translated into change in the model for exercising power, there are signs of conflict with the model of participation—both at the level of discourse and in strategies—visible, for example, in the circulation of information and in harmonizing positions among women leaders, beyond party interests.

The explanation for the need for women to participate in politics, regardless of their political affiliation, varies between recognition that others make use of their capacity and need their presence (which leads the women to accept, or rather, obey the decision), response to individual or collective injustice and the fact that they are subject to electoral scrutiny. As one woman leader in the FRELIMO party told us: "before we used to be appointed [...] there were no elections. [...] Also, women were there almost always just to applaud [...], fill out the numbers. [...] Now they must listen, we argue."[20]

Since the political field is thoroughly foreign to the forms of socialization and construction of the female identity, the individual will of a woman to participate in decision-making processes is regarded as social deviation. Thus the few women who struggle for power are seen in the public mind as "men" or as "bad women." This negative representation is confirmed when only women fight for the same position. As several respondents from different political parties told us, "power struggles among women are considered the result of jealousy that always exists between women, of the hatred they have for other women [...] and because they always prefer a man in charge [...]."[21] The main constraints on women's access to political power thus lie in the conflict between the different processes of socialization and between these and the model of political organization that, by restricting women's participation in politics, causes conflict between their desires and expectations and the responses that politics offers them.

THE REPRESENTATION OF POWER: THE COLLECTIVE MIND AND THE SOCIAL CONSTRUCTION OF DIFFERENCE[22]

The perceptions that men and women have of power should be analyzed in accordance with the social experience of each group, which may or may not be in line with the dominant system of values. At the same time, since the representations are components of the cohesion of one group as opposed to another and thus express the system of differentiation, they are also open to instability and change. This means that conflict between representations within the same group and sphere or between different groups and spheres illustrate not only strategies for adaptation to particular historical contexts, but also collective forms of response to domination; otherwise, they constitute a means of maintaining domination.

With regard to the representation of power by women in Mozambique who play leadership roles, the discourse of the great majority (regardless of their form of access or political motivation) resorts to the normative foundations that guided their socialization. Two variables are present in this discourse: one linked to the social construction of inequality—"men are born with power"—and the other that arises from political activity and appears as the product of the exercise of power by women.

The "characteristics" inscribed in the "habitus" of women and men that lead them to appropriate the objectives of political activity differently results in the exclusion of women from power, be it in the private sphere (although the function of maintaining the family is guaranteed mainly by women) or the public, where the characteristics of a "habitus" are reproduced that are not recognized as central to the order of things, or rather, whose social recognition derives precisely from its submission to the "androcratic" model. This means that women either harmonize the private with the public in a logic of submission produced within the family, or break away from it, adopting mechanisms of political activity that confer on them apparent equality. Various FRELIMO and RENAMO women leaders said: "Women have to win power. [...] Men not. [...] We have to demonstrate hard work [...], we can't fall asleep. [...] When we make mistakes everyone points the finger because we are women."[23]

Similarly, the male leaders of the different parties interviewed (with differences only in detail) agreed on the "value" of political work by women, without, however, calling into question the functional mechanisms of party organization or the traditional roles of women. As one party leader told us:

> She is a boss and I respect her. I also respect her at home, but she is a mother and wife and I am the head of the family. There are two different spouses. [...] Women are always fighting amongst themselves [...]. They [women] must never forget that behind every woman there is always a man [...].[24]

Political practice has allowed these differences/conflicts among various perceptions of power and its use to be uncovered, and at the same time it permits the production of innovative elements in the representation of power by women.

Power is doing things to help other people. It is collective work. It is asking opinions then acting. It is authority and it is action. It is access to knowledge. It is to have awareness. [...] We work on the basis of passivity. We don't like aggressiveness [...]. We don't want to exclude men. We want them to accept the difference. [...] We have our own way of behaving in power. We can't forget that we are mothers [...]. I like being a mother.[25]

While the majority of the women view power as a mission, as serving others, some women in the opposition parties have more conflicting images of their political participation: "I want to make my voice heard [...]. A child that doesn't cry doesn't suckle. [...] Power for me is not being afraid of going for re-education," some women leaders in RENAMO said.[26] All of the women regard the democratic system as an opportunity for affirmation: "now the electors want you and it's because something clicks in you and the person is more calm, more comfortable," women leaders of FRELIMO, RENAMO, and FAP told us.[27]

The differences in the perception of power are also shown in the way both sexes describe their political activities. While the objectives of exercising political power are almost always linked to the objectives of the organization for women and for men, the women leaders highlight—although often in fragmented statements—concrete activities of mobilization of people to participate in social development programs, with education at the top of their list of political concerns. Statements by men, often more detailed, show the focus of the male leaders on the plans of their party as the guardian of the "just idea" that serves to legitimate the vision of centralized and absolute power.

Moreover, women and men perceive the characteristics of political activity differently, although there is no great difference among the parties. The women say that the men are egocentric and when they appear it is because they want to take advantage of something. They also claim that the women are more honest and that it is men who are involved in corruption. They accuse them of being convinced that they are able to do everything, and that by the fact of being the head at home, they think they have the right always to be in charge. They round off, saying that for the men to be the head is a right.[28] The men say that power is linked to the general objectives and that it is the exercise of authority. They agree that women should participate, but claim they are very emotional and that they then have other priorities, such as the home and their children.[29]

The differing representations are thus the result of conflicts that pose women against the dominant cultural model, conflicts that simultaneously contain proposals for cultural innovation and awareness of a social relationship of domination.

ALTERNATIVES IN POLITICAL ACTIVITY OR HEGEMONIC CONSOLIDATION OF THE POLITICAL MODEL?

The risks of reductionism in explaining the ways women occupy the political field prompt extra care in dealing with the problem. Among women of such different groups, ethnic origin, religions and ideology, how can one identify the norms that can lead to the global without losing sight of the individual? Is it possible to find common threads among the multiplicity of female views on politics experienced and politics appropriated? In the last analysis, will there be a link between the multiple inequalities and the differences that allow us to talk in specific ways to women about the occupation of political space?

Some of my respondents from the three parties noted that women like to listen, to think a lot and that they do not like war, pointing to the need to adapt what they think to what others want.[30] These words on the purpose of primary socialization show, on the one hand, how inequality in gender relations is a permanent feature in the social relations between men and women, and, on the other, that this inequality underlying the social model is one of the foundations of conservation and reproduction.

Elements such as competition, hierarchies, and "violence as a male virtue," essential to the functioning of the model of political activity, are absent from female discourse on power (Colflesh, 2000: 7).

The production of an innovative discourse (in the realms of power) of inclusion, emotionally and profoundly communicative, reflects the need to transpose the roles learned within the family to politics. In this regard, a female FRELIMO leader told us: "what I really like is to talk with people […], to resolve concrete problems […]."[31]

The systems of normative values of family relations that continue to buttress political activity by women are in conflict with the mechanisms for the functioning of the political model. In the light of this conflict, the occupation of the political sphere is done in different ways. First, there is a group of women who adapt or try to adapt to the rules, to the hierarchies and to the party structure, accepting male superiority and inferior positions. They say: "what is to be done […] power is to have strength […] and who has strength is the man […]."[32]

For these women party leaders (many coming from the OMM), gender inequality in the distribution of resources is not perceived as such or it is taken as natural. Their political priorities highlight the grand objectives of the father-party, from a perspective of accepting inferiority. They are conservative and when confronted with possible alternatives for politics, namely with regard to the exercise of rights, these women shelter behind the protection of wisdom and of male action.

Adoption of the rules of the political game characterizes a second group of women leaders. Also characteristic is their profoundly male discourse that is at the same time professional and contentious. This group regards competence for the exercise of power as the main criterion, while gender relations and discrimination against women are problems they think are solved, inasmuch as the law guarantees or may come to guarantee human rights. Women's rights are regarded as part of a general framework that is neutral and regulates behavior. The inequality and difference between men and women are understood only from the formal point of view. They do not, within the parties, question the construction and social reproduction of inequality, remaining aloof from the struggle of the women's movement. A statement from one of these women leaders is illustrative: "when I go to the Women's Forum they say 'you women MPs do nothing for women,' but that's not true, because in the party we have to be united in one voice, otherwise there is a complete collapse at the base level."[33]

Competence is a fetish for these women. It makes them adapt to the full the rules imposed by male domination (Muraro, 1999). Regarded and described as cerebral, cold and aggressive by their peers, these "adopted" women borrow male traits that function simultaneously as factors for inclusion (in the party organizations) and for exclusion (from the female condition). They do not subvert the institutional order, but, as with the first group, they are a guarantee of the reproduction of the mechanisms of domination, and at the same time they remain on the sidelines of the social reproduction process. Rewarded and punished for the appropriation of a sphere that is socially recognized as being exclusively one of male values and practices, these women make an "offering" of their female condition, adjusting it to party needs (Bourdieu, 1998).

In power relations, these women in the end always have positions of inferiority, either because their "characteristics" were bought off against the "habitus," leading them to violent splits (personal and social), or because they are subject to continuous and systematic control from the "adoption." On the other hand, it is not by chance that the "adopted" women, much more than their male colleagues, develop attitudes of empathy with the organization and with its hierarchy, eliminating points of divergence and conflict.

Joining a party or a political project should be understood (for this type of leadership) as "consenting" orthodoxy (Ansart, 1977), in which the effectiveness of politics is greater inasmuch as they are the focal point for the interests of everyone as a whole and remain above the intra-party struggle, in absolute conformity with the power imposed/consented. In this way of thinking, the democratic system does not represent for these women a necessary imperative for female participation.

A third form of exercising power corresponds to subversion of power from within. By this I mean that, while we are not dealing with a proposal to break away from the current political model, the strategies for occupying political space developed (by another group of women) contain elements of resistance to the functional mechanisms of political organizations (Hackney and Hogard, 1999). In terms of political or personal biography, this position does not apply to only one of the categories identified above. These are the former freedom fighters, members of women's organizations or career politicians. What do these women have in common?

Many of our respondents[34] made such statements as: "we must work together. [...] We are women [...], we suffer [...] I want to be master in my own home. [...] I want to be happy. [...] I see no contradiction with RENAMO women [...]."

The women in this group represent themselves above all as women, in other words with many and varied objects of attention, with the multiple capacity to be and to live in different places and projects (Facio, 1999). Demanding the right to harmonize the private with the public, breaking away from the rigidity and classification of roles and structures, they build and rebuild the path between the family and the party; donning the mantle of difference, they bring emotion and dialogue to politics. These women invent a pioneering discourse full of allegory and utopia, rejecting male patterns and their categories of analysis. They subvert the instruments of domination by circulating information and knowledge, encouraging participation and integration and rejecting the creation of hierarchies in the family and the party. The leadership of these women gives priority to the sense of mission, responsibility toward others, honesty, the humanization of power, and ethical behavior.

Faced with strategies of domination entrenched in the maintenance of political power, these women adopt a line of action that seeks to question the fundamental mechanisms of the political model through the exercise of citizenship. They do not identify themselves as victims, but seek out space for affirmation that turns them into political subjects. "I like football [...] and it has happened that I have led football delegations, but people abroad did not even shake my hand. They thought I was a masseuse or the wife of a leader [...]."[35]

The cohesion expressed by strong words (honesty, participation, mission) and by the symbolic paraphernalia is often ambiguous and contradictory. "I'm tired [...] I want to stay at home [...]. Women are their own worst enemy [...]. I work for women but it seems they don't understand," are statements illustrative of an emancipating and unified discourse.[36]

While there is no individual or collective awareness in this group of a proposed alternative to the dominant political model (translated into an ideological system recognized by its producers and by its recipients), the praxis and the discourse (although fragmented) represent, on the one hand, the incapacity of the current organizations to adapt/adopt new experiences and new conflicts, and on the other, they show the existence of tension, not only produced and reproduced within the parties (and which are in the end the reason for their effectiveness), but which are innovative in relation to the structure, hierarchy and functional mechanisms of the political parties. These tensions, touching the nature of the dominant political model, in fact constitute a new path for political action. It is not by chance that "honesty," "dialogue," and "participation in the selection of political options" are words used not just as elements of a new political identity, but also as opposition to what they think identifies maleness. Thus the great majority of our women respondents, even those belonging to the "adapted" group, make such statements as: "women don't drink [...], they are more honest [...]. When they say they will do something, it's because they will do it [...]. Women are more serious [...]. Women think of others, they are less egocentric [...]."[37]

In the power relations established in the intra-party context, these women are constrained in political activity by less access to resources, by the occupation of positions classified as female and by invisibility in the political sphere. Some women[38] said that, if there are cars, they go first to the men, that when they want to work in the districts they have no means to do it, that women always work a lot, but they are never paid attention, and that they could "give" more, but they are not allowed to. When they participate in activities of civil society for the defense of women's rights, their positions are rarely recognized or supported by their organization. Democratic pluralism allows the development of mechanisms for the acceptance of political activity by women, which leads these women to seek political unity within and between parties, even without a formal harmonization of interests.

The recognition of the difference demanded by these women is in fact a struggle against the culture of equality, whose main objective is to sap the feminist struggle, subjecting it to a legalistic conception of rights. Male ideological control within party organizations is expressed in the relations of power, through mechanisms that are at once instruments of exclusion and of ideological vigilance. This control can range from systematically calling meetings at night to surveillance of women's sexual behavior. Persuasion is an important means of domination, often reflected in appeals for "solidarity among comrades" and belonging to a "select group," creating unifying elements for the group from opposition to the "enemy." This categorization, which is effective for men and for women (in the sense that it eliminates internal contention), is of great symbolic violence whenever dealing with women (Ansart, 1977). What is at stake here is not just eliminating opposition or gaining more power, but the survival of the model of party organization. The question (although it may not be clearly understood) is not to win voters or defeat an internal adversary; what is at stake is the emergence of a new way of "being" and "doing" politics. The diffusive strategies of persuasion thus find a type of resistance not controllable by the system.

The exercise of democracy, in the context of globally legitimated systems, fails to "satisfy" the demands of new groups, as is the case with women, in which the need for more multiple and lateral activity in the different places of political production leads to the "invention" of political activity that integrates more political/social intervention. Insofar as the parties maintain existing integrating elements with the intention of strengthening them, at the symbolic and practical levels, they become successive challenges that allow the emergence of identifying elements that configure new means of belonging (Ansart, 1977). We are thus faced with a double movement of conservation/adaptation of the old institutional order (with a symbolic and normative universe of domination) and of infringement/re-creation of ways of thinking and living for politicians.

These "non-hegemonic" contexts lead to reflection not only about how a modern democratic system might be structured, but also about the compartmentalization that pluralist democracy causes in the different spaces and forms of exercising democracy. In other words, what the women who are in "formal" power are demanding is not egalitarian participation in political decision-making, but the inclusion of (multiple) difference in the way politics is organized and practiced. The need to have the private and the public interact in the exercise of female political power is present in many of the words of our respondents:

> Society does not accept seeing a woman with power. [...] They say the woman leaves her family disorganized [...], they say the husband should not allow her to remain out of the house [...]. The family, often for fear of the neighbors, does not support the woman. [...] She sometimes then has to leave politics [...].[39]

This discourse illustrates the need to think political power through the family, the place *par excellence* to build power relations based on the discrimination against women (Melkiori, 1997). The mechanisms for building identities that reveal how the family hierarchy is built and how the distribution of power is linked are central elements for analyzing how the private became female and how the public became male.

Considering the context of interaction between the modern and the traditional in Mozambique, with traditional family organization ceding only formally to the urban nuclear family—characteristic of the majority of the respondents—it is useful for the compression of the dialogue between the private and the public spheres to bear in mind some of the mechanisms for socializing boys and girls that give them different and unequal access to and control of resources. Girls are clearly socialized for domestic life and develop capacities in the family that will legitimate them as women in adulthood.

A consequence of the learning expressed in the division of labor and the distribution of authority in the family is the configuration of roles and functions that define a woman's fate. Her skills prepare her for acceptance/conformity to submission. Being a housewife, mother, and wife constitute the completion of a mission for a woman, the essence of the female nature. This female vocation to care for the other is expressed, from the point of view of value systems, by a symbolic universe whose effectiveness extends beyond family relationships[40] and from the point of view of norms, by concrete impediments to sharing authority.[41] The constraints on access to resources, be they economic, legal, or political, are supported by the sex-gender system, which guarantees the reproduction of inequality in the various social spaces.[42]

These elements are present in the identity of the three groups of female leadership. "Adopted," "adapted," or "different," the women party leaders reveal conformity (which may or may not be accepted either by the "adapted" or by the "adopted") with primary socialization and on social categorization. If in the two extreme cases of classification of the female leadership, agreement between the party and the family is resolved through appropriation ("adopted") and by rejection/concealment of the political model ("adapted"), in the third case ("different") the mechanisms of subordination, although expressed differently, are clearly perceived in the intra-party relations of power. A negative and demeaning representation of female political activity is not the only factor present, as these women clearly understand. The female politician seeks to reconstruct the public space for intervention on a basis of equality in difference, by transferring the acquiescent roles learned in the family to the political field, not repudiating socialization for "the other," and at the same time developing strategies for adapting the family model.

> My husband is not into politics [...], so I try to discuss with him [...], I try to integrate him into the life of the party [...], I ask his opinion. [...] The woman has responsibilities in the party, but not at home [...]. At home I mustn't forget that I'm a mother [...]. I don't like anyone else tidying my husband's clothes. I must do it. [...] Before I had a domestic worker, I used to cook all night because next day I had work.[43]

Unable to face the conflict with domestic inferiority, women seek to expand their sphere of intervention in party organizations, incorporating their difference in the ways of exercising power.

On the one hand, questioning the essentialism that roots gender relations in biology, and, on the other, rejecting the essentialist accusations of the post-modernists, the feminist theorists of difference reaffirm gender as "the collection of values and characteristics that determine masculinity and femininity and in each culture and at in each historical moment" (Facio, 1999). It is this integrating, multiple and innovative practice of some women leaders in Mozambique that, if continued, may produce liberating effects on the political model.[44]

CONCLUSIONS: DOUBTS

The introduction of a multi-party system in Mozambique after a period of socialist orientation took place in a context of strong domination by a democratic model. In a country without a democratic tradition (at least that recognized in modern Western practice), having emerged from colonialism and a civil war that destroyed people and institutions, the state had the responsibility of organizing and defining the rules of the new political game, structured around the two sides in the armed conflict.

With the end of the war and an increase in economic dependence, the formalization of democracy exposed the extreme fragility of the political field on the one hand, divided as it was between two forces without any political program, and, on the other hand, revealed the incapacity of the social forces to take action or innovate (Touraine, 1994). The fragility of civil society (in the broadest sense), economic dependence, and social instability have led to an emptiness in political debate, with political discussion focused on petty economic solutions. At the same time, the political party parties, ever more enveloped in a logic of power, are becoming incapable of sparking any democratic activity. For its part, the state, which established the model of political organization with regard to norms, hierarchies, and values, has been unable to recreate mechanisms that allow social inclusion of citizens.

With regard to the struggle of women for their rights, the political parties either ignore it or turn it into capital in their relations with international agencies or urban elites (in election periods). Thus the political participation of women is apparently taking place in a weak context from the point of view of democratic culture. Women's access to power is still hampered by primary socialization that discriminates against them in relation to resources, such as schooling, health care and employment, which keeps them in a situation where new mechanisms of inequality are produced. An example of this is the strong appearance of women in the informal markets, which, by causing a split from the identifying "core," makes old conflicts become visible and at the same time causes new conflicts to appear. But it is these splits that contain the potential for liberating factors to appear: conflicts in the private domain become worse in so far as the hierarchies and positions established there are interrupted by the logic of the market, of a labor market that makes insistent appeals to capacities to convince, to deceive, and to struggle for survival. It is this struggle for economic survival that tends to unleash a series of acts of resistance and defiance that result immediately in attracting violence (mainly domestic violence) and at the same time create conditions for collective action by women.[45]

The weakness of political debate in the parties, their internal stratification in non-democratic patterns and particularly the absence of a political/ideo-logical identity have two apparently contradictory results. If on the one hand the conception of the political field as a totalitarian one (in which networks of loyalty/commitment determine the circulation of power) produces a kind of ossification in party life and its detachment from social expectations (and a consequent decline in its capacity to mobilize), at the same time groups emerge within the parties (without a system of thought expressed in common practices) whose ideas have force enough to mobilize to a point where pressure for reform is produced. Although the political praxis of many women leaders is not founded on a conscious strategy for emancipation, the political weakness of party organizations permits the configuration within the party of space where women can begin to produce ideas on self-recognition.

Throughout this study, mainly as the data were being collated, it was possible to identify three forms in which political space is occupied that correspond to the differing methods of appropriation, adaptation to and resistance to the dominant political model. The analysis did not permit conclusions about possible groupings by age, life history, social origin, educational level, or polit-ical ideology. It became clear that regardless of the political profile, or participation in war (of liberation and civil), the women include themselves in one of the three categories identified: "adopted," "adapted," and "different."

However, these different ways of thinking about and experiencing politics do not serve to make a firm classification of the occupation of political space. As I shall seek to demonstrate, the classification is the result of an attempt to find (on the basis of making the Foucault concept of power operational) common trends toward the model of political organization. Thus women with higher or intermediate education may be found both in the group that adopt the male model of the exercise of power and in the group that tries to subvert and contest the very same model. In the same way, the political parties and the possible differences in their constitution and activities do not determine the position of women toward the male patterns of exercising power.[46] I think that from the research carried out, one should basically seek the mechanisms that differentiate women's political behavior in the inter-action between social exclusion/inclusion and politics happening both in the restricted sphere of the party organizations and within the family, or even in other circles, such as women's organizations or the trade unions.

In the case of Mozambique, it is interesting to note that, returning to an earlier idea, while the situation of democratic institutions opens them to diversity, the specific characteristics of the country allow new prospects to open, not for women's rights, but notably in the possible appearance of alter-natives for democratic practices brought about by women.

This work shows that, in the specific case of Mozambique, the ambigu-ity between the democratic system (hardly consistent or regulated) and the instability of political and social life, create potential for the establishment of space for freedom and innovation. Only in this way can it be understood that under a pure and clearly androcratic model (often to the point of absurdity, if we consider the historical times), there is a group of women leaders who, by resisting male domination in the political parties and through their own actions, seek recognition of their difference and the establishment of new values. While preserving their emotional selves, these women inscribe their actions on the collective mind, seeking to sustain the difference and increase inclusion (Facio, 1999).

However, the possibility for an alternative and its formalization as the re-creation of democratic life depend on numerous factors, not least of which is the capacity of the system to include diversity, a diversity that does not become opposition, but rather a combination of private life with public life, of professional success, of relations of affection, of family ties, and also seek to ensure that men find other ways of combining the different aspects of their existence (Touraine, 1994: 156).

Notes

1 Information was collected during a research seminar on Women and Political Power in Mozambique. I should like to thank Katia Taela, Ernesto Macuácua, Norinho Ernesto, Mário Jorge, Sónia Cintura, Ana Paula Jambosse, Guilherme Mussane, Samito Nuvunga, João Carlos, Quitério Langa, Godwin Mata, Manuel Pacacheque, and the students who demonstrated persistence in gathering the data; I share this work with them. I am grateful for the critical support and solidarity of my friends Maria José Arthur and Luís de Brito. Many thanks go to Carlos Serra for his comments. My profound appreciation goes to the women and men who went beyond reluctance and diffidence to open their hearts to us.

2 At independence in 1975, the country came to be governed by a people's democratic political system, modeled on that of Eastern European socialist countries.

3 The Republic's Constitution, revised in 1990, provides for the creation of a multi-party system. The Rome Accords were signed in 1992, ending the civil war, and the first parties emerged in the new political climate. Legislative elections were held in 1994.

4 In this work I use the concepts of party, institution, and organization in a broad sense: they all possess a structure, hierarchy, norms, and strategies for political activity.

5 The interviews were coded according to sex and political party. The names of women in FRELIMO have the letter "m" in front; RENAMO women the letter "b" and FAP women the letter "c." The names of men in FRELIMO have the letter "r" in front, RENAMO men the letter "s" and FAP men the letter "t."

6 However, it should be remembered that the country's first Constitution discriminated against women in that a Mozambican woman who married a foreigner lost her citizenship.

7 The Mozambican Women's Organization was created in 1973.

8 Bride-price is a means of formalizing ties between two families through marriage. It transfers the subordination of the woman from her own family to that of her husband (who is the mediator of domination), expressing and socially legitimating gender inequality.

9 Anthem of Mozambican women.

10 Sexual "liberalism" was the accusation, mainly against women, often used in the process to build the FRELIMO party, and was a way of keeping "spirited" women out of politics.

11 In the latter case, these women were appointed according to their loyalty to the leader and in order to neutralize internal arguments.

12 In 1994, the OMM decided to split from the FRELIMO party, but joined it again two years later.

13 For further information see Brito and Weimer, 1994.

14 It was not unusual in the last elections to hear party leaders extol the beauty of Mozambican women and their spirit of sacrifice, regarding them as praiseworthy attributes in politics.

15 Although I specifically mention Mozambique, we found in many studies conducted in Africa (see for example MacFadden, 1995) and Latin America (Astelarra, 1992) that the model of public political activity discriminates against women, both in the way it is organized and in the basic norms around which it is structured.

16 Given that the concept of class has not been studied in the light of the new circumstances and theoretical frameworks, I prefer to use social group: even though it is much more ambiguous, it is more workable. As we shall see below, access to power is effected within a logic that is foreign to female skills, but the occupation of power by women, while allowing the emergence of compromise, will also permit the model of domination to be challenged.

17 Interview with Maria Bernardo.

18 It may be noted, for example, that contrary to what happens with male "promotion" in the political parties, the inclusion of women in the leadership is subject to a logic of containing one or other dominant force. For example, in the case of men, their classification into groups that represent forces in conflict is clear, but women "promoted" do not support ideological or other opposition.

19 Speeches in parliament by women in favor of women's rights are always governed by a party logic.

20 Interview with Maria Gomes.

21 Such statements were made by Marta Alberto, Mónica Francisco, Maura Cortês of FRELIMO; Belmira Raúl and Benedita António of RENAMO; Rui Moita and Raúl Francisco of FRELIMO; and Samuel David of RENAMO.

22 The concept of social representation as it is used here assumes a collection of images, stereotypes, and values that characterize the way in which groups or quasi groups see themselves as opposed to the other group. Thus I include in this analytical category both the values of belonging to a given group and the different ways of illustrating power.

23 Maria Gomes, Maria Leonardo, Benvinda Leão, Bela Cassimo, and Belarmina Alves made statements along these lines.

24 Interview with Sérgio Santos.

25 This view of power is reflected in interviews with Maria André, Marta Silva, Margarida Tavares Maria Costa, Maria Campos, Bela Cassimo, Bernardete Cossa, and Belarmina Alves.

26 Statements of this sort are found in the interviews with Benvinda Leão and Brigida Sousa.

27 Statements from Maria Gomes, Bernardete Cossa, Carmo Chaves, and Conceição Issufo.

28 Statements along these lines were made by the respondents Margarida Tavares, Maria Leonardo, Benvinda Leão, and Bernadete Cossa.

29 Statements on these lines were made by the respondents Rui Moita, Raul Francisco Romulo Bento, Rui Pelembe, Sergio Santos, Samuel David.

30 Statements of this type were made by Marta Silva, Margarida Tavares, Bela Cassimi, Belarmina Alves, Carmo Chaves, and Conceição Issufo.

31 Interview with Margarida Tavares.

32 Statements of this sort were made by the respondents Marta Alberto, Monica Francisco, Maura Cortes, Belarmina Alves and Benvinda Carimo.

33 Interview with Monica Francisco.

34 Interviews with Maria Gomes, Margarida Tavares, Maria Costa, Marcela Candido, and Maria Leonardo.

35 Interview with Manuela Orta.

36   Interview with Maria Costa.

37 Statements of this type appear in the interviews with Maria Gomes, Margarida Tavares, Maria Leonardo, and Benvinda Leão.

38 Statements of this type appear in the interviews with Maria Campos, Mercedes Temba, Maria Leonardo, Benvinda Leão, Belarmina Alves.

39 Statements of this type were made by Manuela Orta, Marta Silva, Maria Leonardo, Benvinda Carimo, Bernarda Ahgee.

40 The husband's bath must be ritually prepared by the wife, as well as the husband's food (who must always be served first).

41 One of the most contentious issues in the debate around the passage of the family law is the article that mentions the possibility that a woman may also be the head of the household. Groups supported by the Churches and by the traditional authorities have conducted a real witch-hunt, dubbing the proponents "ill-loved foreign women, trouser-clad women." The political parties, including FRELIMO, with its history of "emancipatory" speech-making, have

not taken a position, arguing that "We are listening to the people."

42 The adoption of the concept of the sex-gender system toward the end of the 1980s aimed at highlighting women's control over their bodies and their sexuality as a basis of inequality. This perspective arose in opposition to the progressive sapping of the concept of gender and to the advance of conservative forces, who tried to reduce the struggle of the feminist movement to the public arena.

43 Maria Bernardo, Marta Alberto, Monica Francisco, Maria Campos, and Benvinda Carimo made statements of this type.

44 This topic is developed by Alda Facio in relation to women's political practice in some countries of Latin America.

45 Action by women neighbors is becoming more frequent in Maputo, where they prevent women being thrown out of their homes by their husbands; also, in the informal markets, women band together to fight against inspectors or being moved to other selling places.

46 The analysis I make tends toward what the feminist movement "of difference" has argued: rejecting the "essentialism" in the construction of identity, both male and female, does not deny the approach that seeks the underlying reasons for sexual discrimination in the construction and normative elements of the social model (including those that govern reproduction and sexuality). The aim of the essentialist accusation against feminist claims is often to negate the special characteristics of the women's liberation movement that make it a sphere of social emancipation, regardless of the nature of its location or linkages.

Bibliography

Ansart, Pierre (1977). *Idéologies, Conflicts et Pouvoir*. Paris: PUF.

Astelarra, Judith (1992). "Recuperar la Voz: el Silencio de la Ciudadanía," *Feminismos Fin De Siglo, Género y Cambio Civilizatorio*. Ediciones de las Mujeres. Isis International, 47–57.

— (1999). "Autonomia y Espacios de Actuacion Conjunta," *Feminismos Fin de Siglo*, especial *FEMPRESS*, http://www.fempress.cl/ base/ne_feminismo.htm.

Bourdieu, Pierre (1998). *La Domination Masculine*. Paris: Seuil.

Brito, Luis, and Berhard Weimer (eds) (1994). *O Espaço da Mulher no Processo Multipartidário. Seminário (Maputo, 6–7 de Outubro de 1993). Relatório final*. Maputo: UEM; Friedrich Ebert Foundation.

Colflesh, Nancy Anne (2000). "Women as Leaders: Piecing Together their Reflections on Life and the Principalship," *Advancing Women Leadership Journal*, 3(1). http://advancingwomen.com/awl/winter2000/colflesh.html.

Facio, Alda (1999). "Comunion en la Diversidad," *Feminismos Fin de Siglo*, especial *FEMPRESS*, http://www.fempress.cl/base/ne_feminismo.htm.

Foucault, M. (1990). *Deux Essais Sur le Sujet et le Pouvoir*. (Mimeo).

Gaspard, F. (1995). "Des Partis et des Femmes," *Démocratie et Représentation*. Paris: Kimé, 28–60.

Guzmán, V. (1999). "Posibilidades y Riesgos de la Institucionalida," *Feminismos Fin de Siglo*, especial *FEMPRESS*, http://www.fempress.cl/base/ne_feminismo.htm.

Hackney, Catherine E., and Elaine M. Hogard (1999). "Women in Transition: a Mission of Service," *Advancing Women Leadership Journal*, 2(1). http://advancingwomen.com/awl/winter99/hackney.html.

MacFadden, P. (1995). "Challenges and Prospects for the African Women's Movement into the 21st century." Harare: Feminist Studies Center, Zimbabwe, 10–21.

Melkiori, Paola (1997). "Messages from Huairou. Notes for a Redifinition of the Space of Politics," *Canadian Women Studies*, 17(2), 8–17.

Muraro, Luisa (1999). "Un Language que lo Vuelva Memorable," *Feminismos Fin de Siglo*, especial *FEMPRESS*, http://www.fempress.cl/base/ne_feminismo.htm.

Osório, Conceição, *et al.* (1999). *Mulher e Autarquia. Relatório de Investigação.* Maputo: UEM, CEA, NORAD.

Pintanguy, J. (1999). "Caminamos y Tropezamos … Pero Caminamos," *Feminismos Fin de Siglo*, especial *FEMPRESS*, http://www.fempress.cl/base/ne_feminismo.htm.

Seidler, Victor J. (1994). *Unreasonable Men – Masculinity and Social Theory*. London: Routledge.

Stetson, Dorothy McBride, and Amy Mazur (orgs.) (1995). *Comparative State Feminism.* Thousand Oaks, CA: Sage.

Touraine, A. (1994). *Qu'est-ce que la Démocracie?* Paris: Fayard.

Virreira, Sonia (1999). "Del Poder De los Sin Poder Al Poder De no Poder," *Feminismos Fin de Siglo*, especial *FEMPRESS*, http://www.fempress.cl/base/ne_feminismo.htm.

6

Ghosts Haunting Unions: Women Trade Unionists and the Struggle for their Rights, Mozambique, 1993–2000

Maria José Arthur

INTRODUCTION

To be a woman and a trade unionist is still a challenge today, even if the present conjuncture—a Constitution guaranteeing equality of rights and the numerous international conventions of the UN and the ILO—seems favorable to women's full participation in civil and government structures. Unions, like other organizations, including political parties, show little transformation in their functioning, whether in response to the new demands of globalization or to incorporate women's claims (Bouchardeau, 1993; Osório, 2001). If the external pressure of regional and international union federations, along with the climate of so-called "democracy" in the country, leads to the creation of women's committees in unions and their central organizations, women now grouped in such new organs continue to have to struggle for recognition and acceptance.

This chapter aims to analyze the discourse of the union leadership in the women's committees and the possibilities and constraints delimiting action for women. It is important to understand how the discourses (re)establish gender difference, justifying discriminatory practices still in operation in the unions. On the other hand, what consciousness do women have about the constraints surrounding them and what are their points of reference for action? What are the individual and/or collective strategies used to get around the constraints imposed on them? Are today's demands based on the limits of a hegemonic women's identity, or do they in fact struggle against these limits? These questions will be studied on the basis of a multiplicity and diversity of practices, which is the only way to unveil the specificity of women struggling for their rights. What practices reveal contestation in spheres of action and in "représentations de soi"?[1]

When I began to work on the topic of women unionists,[2] what most interested and motivated me was the discovery of a feeling of strong combativeness that they conveyed, while defending the need for unity and solidarity among all union leaders. Clearly, in the course of the work, I became aware of how idealized this image that they constructed for my benefit was, and this aspect itself took on great significance for the interpretation of the data. However, whether in solidarity or competition, whether courageous or "timid," in their own way, individually or collectively, these women struggled for affirmation and recognition.

I also worked with men union leaders who, without exception, recalled the history of the unions, today's "democratic challenges" and the long history of concern of their organization in relation to women. It was only at the end that I could ask the more penetrating questions on my list.[3] None of the secretaries or the secretariat members referred to conflicts with the committees, despite their obvious existence and their occupying much attention on the part of the direction. Only among the union members was I informed of such conflicts.[4]

The whole experience of seeing myself confronted as a researcher and as an actor—in a context full of tension and manipulation—led me to question the pertinence of my work, and the possibility of perceiving the complexity present in the internal logic of the committees' functioning and the modes of their integration in the unions. As a militant feminist, I was conscious of the power relations that can be established between researcher and object of the inquiry, given the realities and conditions of inequality affecting and surrounding all such work. It was necessary to respect the voices heard and attempt to construct a reciprocal relationship. I could not also prevent myself from feeling a certain empathy founded in common interests for, in the end, the struggle of unionists for equality is also my struggle as a woman and citizen. I attempted to turn this proximity into an asset enriching the perception and interpretation of what was said.

On the other hand, I have been told on various occasions that studying women unionists is of little relevance in a country such as Mozambique, where the number of workers is about a million in a total of about 17 million.[5] Moreover, when speaking of women unionists, the percentage among all wage earners is relatively even lower. According to data from one of the union federations, in 1999, in the various branches of activity covered by its member unions, there was a total of 175,293 workers, 103,957 (59.3 per cent) of whom were unionized.[6] The number of workers and their level of unionization, according to the direction of the committees of the same federation is the following: in a total of 174,866 workers, 43,953 are women, and there is an average level of unionization of 62.46 per cent.[7]

Clearly such telling information can leave no one untouched, but it has perhaps the value of helping us reflect on the purpose of the research being undertaken: we might say that such questioning has the merit of functioning as an antidote to self-indulgence, thus forcing reconsideration of the objective of what we do.

First of all, notwithstanding the low level of expression of the union movement in Mozambique, its internal struggles should be understood as a further manifestation of the multiple and complex forms of citizens' resistance before the state and against the growing and authoritarian liberalization of the economy. On the other hand, as a militant of women's human rights, I sought always to give my research an emancipating character, and I believe that this perspective can increase understanding of distorted, or at least not entirely visible, daily contradictions. It is thus that possibilities for social transformation are created (Lather, 1991: 52, cited by Humphries, 1997).

Although not subscribing uncritically to "women's ways of knowing," "women's experiences," or simply "women's knowledge" (Alcoff and Potter, 1993: 1), I take the view that research with emancipating objectives can be determinant for the integration of forms of knowledge and the experiences of the most excluded social groups. Thus conceived, it implies an active, interpretative and responsible position (Ardovini-Brooker, 2000; Williams, 1999).

In this chapter I begin by presenting the context in which the committees of women are formed in the unions, the "official" view of them given by the male union leadership and the perceptions of the union members who serve and work in them. I then briefly trace the career of three of these leaders, whose expectations and strategies are particularly illustrative of this specific period in the history of the union movement in Mozambique and of women's struggle for the achievement of their rights. In effect, individual perspectives are converted into biographical structures in the sense that "human beings cross frontiers between different groups, and in various situations and through time, accumulate diverse groups of experiences, orientations, competencies and likes" (Hannerz, 1997). It is a matter of taking individual social experiences as revealing culture as it is lived (Michelat, 1987: 199).

CONTEXTS FOR THE CREATION OF COMMITTEES OF WOMEN WORKERS IN THE UNIONS

The committees of women workers[8] were created in 1993, in a context of great transformations for the union movement, confronted as it was then with economic and political liberalization. The Mozambican government formally joined the IMF and World Bank in 1984 and the first readjustment program (PRE—Program of Economic Rehabilitation) was introduced in 1987. The objectives of PRE were to stop the decline of production, reduce financial imbalances, promote economic "efficiency," eliminate the informal market, and re-establish healthy relations with commercial and financial partners. The principal measures were the liberalization of prices—supposed to constitute an incentive for producers—the adjustment of the internal and external terms of trade, the reduction of public spending, and the privatization of state enterprises.

The raising of wages by 50 per cent was not sufficient to maintain the standard of living in the face of the immediate rise in prices. The overall result of PRE in the period 1987–89 shows that the chosen development strategy excluded the most marginalized strata, whose situation worsened (Cliff, 1991). The reaction of the government was to include an emergency program within PRE so as to reduce poverty. From 1990, a social component was introduced with the Program of Economic and Social Rehabilitation (PRES). In 1989, the government promulgated decree 21/89 concerning the alienation of state property. Two years later, law 15/91 established the rules for restructuring state companies through privatization.

These policies above all affected workers: in 1987 alone, 35,000 workers were dismissed. With the continued application of PRE measures, intensified by the privatization of companies, the number of dismissals increased, mainly of women workers.[9] The first alarm signals were given by national and international NGOs that maintained relations with the unions, and were at times the supporters of union programs (Bonni, 1995, Assis, 1997). Thereafter, the exclusion of women resulting from privatization became an unavoidable problem in public debate, which the unions could no longer ignore.

The accelerated degradation of living conditions led workers to react. In 1990 there was a series of strikes in Maputo city and province. Faced with the inertia of the unions, the strikes were directed by committees created *ad hoc* by workers. Union organizations were surprised by this unexpected development and were divided. Workers on strike did not get support from their union leaders.[10] The unions were then confronted with a situation that they had no means of controlling and that they now attempted to understand.[11] According to an evaluation of the Mozambican Workers Organization (OTM)[12] in 1996,[13] more than five hundred firms had been privatized since 1987. Meanwhile, privatization neither reduced poverty nor contributed to improving employment or economic growth. On the other hand, the OTM denounced the numerous infractions of the labor law, particularly dismissals without notice, delay in payment of wages, and the non-recognition of unions by the management of firms with private or mixed capital holdings. This last aspect interfered directly in the search for solutions on the part of the union movement. In general, the government was criticized for not having created an effective system for controlling privatization.

As a result of the context of economic liberalization, the unions were obliged to alter their character and their functions.[14] Workers demanded intervention of a different nature and more democratic functioning. The unions then attempted to prove to their members that they were capable of acting on their behalf and of negotiating with the government and the owners,[15] and of abandoning the old practices now thought to be very authoritarian.[16]

At the end of 1991,[17] legislation on the freedom of union activity (Law 23/91) was passed, allowing union associations to acquire juridical sanction without being associated with a central congress. This law sparked off claims of functional autonomy among some union leaders. In 1992, three unions declared themselves independent of the OTM and constituted a provisional association called Free and Independent Unions of Mozambique (Sindicatos Livres e Independentes de Moçambique—SLIM).[18] In 1997, SLIM was constituted as a central congress under the designation National Council of the Free Trade Unions of Mozambique (Conselho Nacional dos Sindicatos Livres de Moçambique—CONSILMO). This schism produced internal change within the OTM and a change of leadership capable of dealing with the new situation.[19]

Under pressure from the union movement, in 1994 the government created a "Tripartite Labor Commission" (also called the "Tripartite Forum on Social Conciliation").[20] In the same year, there were for the first time face-to-face negotiations between the government, the employers and the unions (OTM and SLIM). Matters brought to the negotiating table by the unions were the increase of the minimum wage, the reduction of taxes on wages and the insufficiency in public transport as well as deficiencies in the area of health services.[21]

It was in this context that there arose in the debate the need to act on the "problems of women," which privatization had made more visible. On the other hand, Mozambican unions are members of the Southern Africa Trade Union Co-ordination Council (SATUCC), which, in 1991, approved a Workers' Social Charter, reformulated in 1996 on the basis of observations made by member countries. In the later version, one of the most important aspects emphasized is "the equality of treatment for men and women" in relation to employment, remuneration and careers, and its application was encouraged.[22] In 1993, Mozambique was the only country in SATUCC not yet to have created women's structures within unions and which showed low levels of women's representation in their leadership organs. Even in 2000, in the OTM-CS, women's representation in leadership was the following:

Presidium: 0%
Coordinating Council: 15%
Executive Secretariat: 25%
General Secretaries of National Unions: of 13, only one woman
Members of the Secretariat of the National Unions: of 52, only seven are women
National Councils of the Unions: between 10 and 15%.[23]

As can be appreciated, women union functionaries occupy lower-rank posts in the staffing structure.

It was in this context that committees were created to represent women workers in all the central union organizations of the OTM and SLIM. In the case of SLIM, a "National Committee of Women Workers" (CONMUT) was constituted in 1994, and the "Committee of Women Workers" of the OTM in 1996.[24] These organs are exclusively for women, and their leaders are elected by assemblies of unionized women. In the two national organizations, the processes were different, but the debates and meetings that preceded these were partially effected in common.[25]

DISCOURSES AND PRACTICES IN RELATION TO COMMITTEES OF WOMEN WORKERS

It is unquestionable that the creation of the committees occurred above all through pressures external to the union movement in Mozambique and that this aspect was decisive in their integration and functioning. The already existing tensions, in large part the result of dismissals owing to privatization, were not in themselves sufficient to originate a movement of women unionists demanding more equality and serving as a means of developing pressure to respect the founding spirit of the committees. If, later on, the women unionists who directed the immediate process of constituting the new organs and others who subsequently adhered to the project took over the initiative, it is clear that they had no role in the initial conception and definition of its sphere of action. The limits and frontiers were delineated, at the level of discourse and of practice, by the top union leadership.

Once the national union leaders had decided to create the committees, the first priority was to ensure the support of provincial and workshop union leaders, and also that of women members, groupings until then excluded from the discussions. In each of the two union federations, "Commissions for the Creation of Committees" composed of women were established in order to mobilize women workers to support the project. National union leaders took on the responsibility for the mobilization of officials at the various other leadership levels.

As the creation of the committees was a project common to both federations, the unionist discourse appeared in public to have a certain uniformity. It was explained what the committees were, their objectives and the place of women in the union movement. The press was regularly invited to participate in seminars for women union members or to the founding meetings of committees. Each national meeting for the creation of committees was presided over by a national secretary or his representative. Training seminars for women unionists also took place in the presence of leaders, who gave opening or closing speeches or even conducted their operations.[26]

One of the more salient aspects of the discourses on the committees was their clear demarcation from the Mozambican Women's Organization

(Organização da Mulher Moçambicana—OMM),[27] which from 1976 to the end of the 1980s had created groups in all companies. The main criticisms were that this organization had overstepped its competencies in the work-place by interfering in questions that were not strictly to do with "labor," such as the domestic violence to which some women workers were subject and the control of "morality." This refusal to consider the OMM in the workplace as the predecessor of the Women's Committees can perhaps be seen as the clearest indication of how their action—despite strong party over-sight—was considered subversive of existing male powers. In a seminar organized by the Committees of the OTM-CS at the end of 2000, a provin-cial union leader declared: "Before, one heard: women are equal to men at work and at home, but that has all changed. We no longer speak of eman-cipation but of gender. That is acceptable."[28] But this position is never explicit in the official discourse, which makes it understood that, as the unions are establishing themselves as independent of the political party in power, the OMM cannot serve as a model because it is a party organization.

Thus, in their speeches, union leaders underline above all that the Committees are the result of the democratization of union organization and insist on the priority given to the problems and interests of women:

> We feel deeply the need for the participation of women alongside their male companions and for the struggle for the equality of rights in our sphere. Only in this way will it be possible to find the most secure way for coordi-nated and united action, enabling Mozambican unionism greater strength to defend union and labor rights, accompanied by women—the inseparable companions of men.[29]

No union dared to contradict this position, which represented the new image union organizations give themselves. Indeed, union leaders insist on the antecedents of this project of "the emancipation of women," giving the impression that they were always involved in it and that unions have fought for a long time on behalf of women's interests. During a seminar entitled "Possible strategies to encourage women to accept positions of leadership and sensibilization on gender,"[30] one leader emphasized: "After national independence, women, as mothers, wives and workers, were engaged in widely different sectors of production, in socio-professional training, accord-ing to the orientations of the new Constitution and Labor Law." He went on to say that equality is not constructed only through laws, for "the social, economic and political foundations of discrimination against the woman worker are very deep"; however, "women *also form part* of Mozambican society."[31]

On no occasion is there contestation of the concept of "women's eman-cipation," borrowed from FRELIMO social theory. The discourses state that women are oppressed by "traditional" society, which considers them as inferior to men; that the emancipation of women must be effected through their integration at work; that women must be supported and oriented in overcoming the beliefs and attitudes of the system of domination in which they were educated.[32] This last aspect is essential to understand the status of the committees in the union structure. At the opening of one seminar for women workers, one general secretary said in his speech that, in co-ordination with the union leadership, the committee "will guide and justify the destinies, objectives and socio-economic and professional interests of the women worker, so that women can confront their problems without complexes."[33] This reference goes back to what is designated "women's inferiority complex," which FRELIMO described as "the alienation of women."

Finding the origin and justification of this position requires an incursion into FRELIMO social theory on "women's emancipation." If it is clear that the equality of women is established as a universal right in the stated principles and written texts of the law, difference is (re)established from FRELIMO social theory referring to "the alienation of women." Long oppressed and humiliated—say the discourses—women assume the position of being dominated and reproduce it. Emphasis is therefore required on the need to combat this female passivity and resignation so as to recruit women to the cause of struggle. Although it is admitted that men also have "prejudices" as regards women, the "alienation of men" is never mentioned. Difference thus constituted justified an emancipation different in time and under male orientation,[34] rather than giving them autonomy to decide and act in function of their own interests. Difference is thus continuously redefined in the production of discourse, always magnified to legitimate renewed exclusion (Riot-Sarcey, 1993b). This ambivalence, already visible during the armed struggle (Arthur, 1998a), reproduces itself in each new context (Kruks, n.d.).

Thus the discourses of the unions, elaborated in new contexts, reproduce ambivalence concerning "women's emancipation," contain contradictory representations of women, and articulate the idea of a "tradition of passivity" for women, which both support and legitimate male power. As another general secretary stated, "women are very timid and slow in everything. They bring with them the domestic ideal. They are vulnerable to many temptations: for this reason we seek to integrate them."[35]

Union discourses should be read in terms of two main registers. The first, public, addressed both internally and externally, present what the committees are and their importance for the union organization. At a second level, the less official, exclusively internal discourse relates above all to the ways in which the committees function. It is here that representations operate about women in the workplace, where they have a real as well as a legitimating function. Common social representations about women in the labor sphere are real discourses in the sense of fixing the limits of women unionists' action, reinforcing the systems of control on the activity of the committees. The partial character of women's citizenship is thus reproduced in the unions. The tension between the stated principles and the execution in practice of the project is permanent. The articulation of the two discourses rests on the implicit connection between them: the ideal situation it is necessary to reach and the real situation that needs to be considered in order to reach the defined goals. Thus is justified the supervision to which the committees are subjected: the need to create conditions for women "to develop the knowledge and strategies to uphold and struggle for their rights in the world of work."[36] Full participation will only be possible "if women shake off traditional prejudices, which limit them to maternity, obedience to spouses and to domestic labor, etc., contrary to the Mozambican Constitution."[37]

The identity of working women is held to be indissoluble from their functions as mother, wife, and educator, materialized and made worthy as female contributions to society and the country.[38] This position conjoins with that of FRELIMO on female roles and constitutes the basis on which the first Labor Law (8/85) was elaborated.[39] If unions defined as a high priority the full application of laws protecting women, at the same time they limited the struggle of the committees simply to that of upholding "the specific rights of women." Thus, the committees are constituted as "the specific structures of women, so that they can participate in the taking of decisions on specifically women's questions,"[40] which limits not only their sphere of intervention but also the competencies they are attributed. Based on this logic, many more or less open means are put in place by the union leadership to control the committees' activities. The general tendency taking shape is that of maintaining the exclusion of women in the centers of union decision-making.

Until 1998, one of the central debates was conducted around the status that should be accorded to the committees at the national level: should they constitute an "area" or a "department"? The secretaries of "areas" are part of the national executive secretariat and fall under the general secretary. On the other hand, the heads of "departments" are subordinated to an "area," and thus have more limited autonomy, with no independent budget.[41] In the unions affiliated to SATUCC, the committees are considered as "areas" and the first proposals of the OTM and SLIM were similar. However, this position was much contested, mainly at the provincial and company level, where union leaders were kept somewhat apart from the debates that preceded the creation of the new organs.[42] Moreover, at the time of the founding of the committees, the unions had already held their national conferences, which take place every five years, and which are the only meetings with the legal competence to alter statutes. Thus the committees began their working on the basis of provisional regulations and the decision on the type of statute they would have in the union structure was postponed until 1997.

At the end of 1997, 15 of the 17 unions had already held their national conferences and the results were as follows: twelve maintained the status of "area" for the committees, while three changed their position and integrated the committees as "departments." Despite this result, the committees are still not considered "areas" similar to others. This is apparent from the National Council of the union for the textile industries: "The representatives of the Women Workers Committee only participate in meetings of the Secretariat when necessary."[43] Or, as explained by a provincial secretary of the same union, the women leaders would only be called to intervene "if the problems relate to women."[44] This position is shared by other unions, which justify it by referring to the definition of the committees as having to treat only the specific interests of women.[45] This problem has yet to be resolved and the situation of the committees in the union organization remains imprecise. Thus the recognition of the existence of problems specific to women workers, considered by everyone to be an achievement for women, is used to distance them from discussion and intervention in other levels of union functioning. Through a kind of conjuring, women find themselves set apart exclusively with the "female problems" that are the competence of the committees, and for this reason, distant from "real" union problems. Even if the discourses seem to favor full participation of women in the unions, in reality they exclude them and sustain discriminatory practices. One of the first acts of interference by the union leadership occurred during the elections of the secretaries of the committees, with the aim of keeping out those thought to be too independent. This critique was never formulated publicly, even in the seminars for the membership. These cases were mentioned in interviews[46] or in informal conversation.

Another form of control is through avoiding the committees' financial autonomy: most of them cannot have independent bank accounts, even when dealing with donations given specifically for committee programs. These are controlled by the union leadership, which frequently use them for their own needs. In most of the criticisms made on this question, what is at issue is not the principle of sharing the means at disposal with other sectors of the unions, but the fact that they are excluded from control of the resources. This matter was discussed in a seminar attended by 23 members of the committees.[47] In some cases, it was revealed, there was even the diversion of union funds for the personal use of the union secretary.[48]

Most of the union leaders control the visits abroad of the members of the committees. Invitations for meetings and seminars are never given directly to the secretaries of the committees, and the union leadership decides who should participate.[49] In the case of Esmeralda M., each time conflicts arose with her superiors, the latter prevented her from going abroad, such visits being considered as rewards.[50] Indeed, such forms of control are also employed with other intentions.

In the process of constitution of the committees, there is always a common underlying fear—of the "autonomy" of these organs. Various union leaders have spoken of women's organizations that they know about in other union federations that, according to them, have such a large field of responsibility that they seem to constitute unions independent of those that created them. We can say then that one of the specters that haunts them is the possibility that the committees, by means of foreign support, will come to distance themselves from the unions and acquire an autonomous logic and dynamic. Hence the hierarchical dependence, the limitation of the sphere of action and above all the control on visits abroad. With the exception of a few militants, well known or of confidence, union leaderships ensure that participation in outside events is done by rotation. They justify this on the grounds of promoting equality of opportunities among members of the union, from top to bottom, and between the various regions of the country. Thus it is not uncommon that a woman unionist is in Maputo only to catch the plane and on her return has no time to share and discuss the results of the meeting or conference.

Women among the union leadership attempt to counter this policy so that there can be continuity in contacts with the other federations to which they are affiliated, which would enable a more consistent relationship as well as participation by the country in debates important in the making of the respective policies and programs. On the other hand, they also want permanence of representation in groups that participate in thematic seminars (such as the informal sector, collective bargaining, globalization), in order to keep up with the development of the discussion and contribute actively to it.[51] However, the populist character of the leadership's position meets support among the militants on the ground and those who, residing outside the capital, consider themselves discriminated against in relation to such opportunities.

The fear of autonomy of women's committees in reality hides fear of the growth of an independent dynamic of struggle for women's rights, which would threaten the existing hierarchies. The demonization of feminism is a process initiated with the creation of the OMM in 1973, still during the liberation struggle: "The ideological offensive which, disguised as the struggle for the liberation of women, seeks [...] to divide men and women. [...] This ideological offensive is an offensive of capitalist society to confuse women and divert their attention from the real objective" (Machel, 1974: 83). Feminism is thus seen as a foreign, bourgeois project, driven by women who do not share revolutionary ideology (ibid.: 82).

This same mechanism for disqualifying certain forms of struggle by imputing to them designs that are strange, foreign or non-indigenous has also been directed at the union movement itself quite recently by the government. From May to July 2000, during negotiations in the Council for Labor Conciliation, there was a dispute over the adjustment of the minimum wage. Faced with the combined resistance of government and employers to the unions' proposal of a 30 per cent increase, the unions called a general strike for 26, 27 and 28 July. Although doubtful of the organizational capacity of the unions to mobilize, as a result of public adherence to the proposal the government gave way and the strike was avoided.[52]

The government reacted as if feeling discredited: on 29 July, at a meeting in Xai-Xai, Joaquim Chissano, president of the republic, revealed that during the negotiations of social conciliation "there were foreign specialists in strike organization in the country, but they had been discovered before they could act in conjunction with the unions." Out of "prudence"—in his words— names were not divulged, but he warned that interference in internal matters from the outside would not be tolerated and that this was not the first time that such events had occurred.[53] In a note directed to the government, the union leadership denied any involvement by foreign unionists and assumed full responsibility for their conduct of the process.[54]

Thus, in the era of globalization, it is clear that only the circulation of capital is acceptable and that international solidarity between workers is something "strange" and dangerous. This same mechanism is used in relation to the committees: there is always present the accusation of "foreign manip- ulation" each time more autonomy and expansion of the limits of action are demanded.

UNIONIST REPRESENTATIONS OF THE COMMITTEES OF WOMEN WORKERS

Some of the union leaders have begun to have a greater presence in the public arena. They are interviewed by the press, speak in seminars and meetings of the committees and give presentations in regional colloquia on labor and unionism. It is important to see how the committees are presented and whether the women share the conception of the union leaders. On the other hand, in what way do they explain the subordination of women and what ways do they propose to guarantee equality of rights? How do these leaders interpret the difficulties that the committees confront in union organ- izations?

The meetings preceding the creation of the committees afforded women unionists space for the exchange of ideas and experiences at different levels, which, in part, enabled the building of a platform of understanding, consid- ering that formerly there was no organized movement. The debates were organized around "problems of women in the world of work" and solutions were proposed. The conclusions were compiled into a training manual,[55] the objective of which was to make known to women unionists the state of analysis and the proposals. This practice had the result of creating a common, official language, used in the public arena, even where the militants have divergent conceptions and experiences, and also served to motivate activism of the unionists. Indeed, consciousness that the qualities of a group form the basis of its discrimination justifies the struggle in defense of its rights (Burn, Aboud, Moyles, 2000).

In the manual, the committee is defined as "a structure created in the union federations at all levels, from the national unions to the base, to pursue the problems specific to women in the labor market" (OTM *et al.*, 1995: 26). The Committees must "serve as a forum for the creation of support and assistance strategies among working women" (ibid.: 61). These two aspects, the existence of "specific problems" and the need to develop solidarity among workers are also emphasized in the paragraphs dealing with the objectives:

> To organize working women in the common struggle for the attainment of equal rights and opportunities for all; guarantee that the union takes responsibility for the specific problems of women; mobilize women so that they engage in the union movement; uphold the specific rights and interests of working women; promote respect of laws protecting working women; train and educate working women in matters relating to labor and union legislation (ibid.: 26–7).

The obligations of women unionists are presented as: participate in the union movement, "assume the effective execution of their work," "actively show their capacities and interests," uphold their interests, "make the best use of their personality, dignity, labor and capacities" (ibid.: 36–7).

These proposals reaffirm in part the discourses of the union leadership, namely the question of "specific women's questions" and the protective measures that must be undertaken. But they go further in certain aspects, such as the emphasis given to the solidarity necessary between workers, the denunciation of double work shifts and the principle of cooperation with other women's organizations that struggle for women's rights. It can be noted that this type of cooperation is based on the recognition that the constraints workers confront are not restricted to relations in the workplace. Although, in other ways the committees are widening their action, as formerly occurred with the OMM.

However, the emergence of new positions occurs in a tense climate, as witness the numerous contradictions in the discourses of the committee leaders. The starting tableau may be defined by the union leadership, but it is then upset by the words of the women. Thus the affirmation of the idea that "the working woman is naturally given to the caring of children, the elderly and the husband,"[56] is followed by a denunciation of the double work shift.[57] Or, reference to the full realization of the "mission" as mother and wife is frequently accompanied by an exhortation to women's combative spirit.[58]

Other discourses constitute true cleavages, perhaps not immediately rec-
ognizable because care is taken to moderate the language. Thus, when power
is demanded, this is justified by the preoccupation of imposing more justice
and of making the best use of female qualities. This was the argument
defended during one of the seminars for women unionists:

> Why power? We, women, we like power very much. We want it because
> we know that with it we can influence society so that there can be
> more justice and fewer conflicts. We want power, but also the division
> of labor in the union, in the workplace, at home [...]. We want to con-
> tribute with our knowledge, our experience as women, as mothers, as
> professionals. Our experiences as women are different from those of
> men. Thus we can create a more complete union. We wish that what
> we are and represent be fully valued. We do not want to imitate male
> attitudes. We want to be female also in power.[59]

In the analysis of "women's problems," the basis of all the programs of the
new organs, while apparently adopting the viewpoints of the leadership of
the unions, the militants of the committees develop their own position,
revealing a "viewpoint from within." These problems are considered the
result of "sexual discrimination": here are included the dismissals *en masse*
as a result of PRE and privatization, discrimination in evaluation and promotion, exclusion from leadership positions, discrimination in access to
professional training, low status given to certain jobs and categories considered to be women's, lack of respect for laws protecting women, particularly
during pregnancy, wage discrimination, sexual harassment, and "women's
inferiority complex and other negative behavior."

While "sexual harassment"[60] is minimized by the union leadership,
women unionists consider it revealing of power relations and place it among
the priorities for action. With respect to the "women's problem" called the
"women's inferiority complex," all the union leaders see this as one of the
main obstacles to equality between men and women in the sphere of labor.[61]
Members of the committees characterize it thus:

> Women have inferiority complexes; they are not at ease in speaking in
> meetings and do not defend themselves amongst their colleagues. For this
> reason, we must develop courses giving them confidence in themselves and
> the instruments required to assert themselves as women workers and even
> union leaders.[62]

Yet, "women's inferiority complex" is at times presented as a "natural trait,"
which means that women are individuals it is necessary to control and watch
over:

At the same time, women contribute to the worsening of their problematic situation. They fight among themselves, they waste their time in malicious gossip, real psychological terrorism. Thus, the project cannot go forward and women cannot demand a just wage owing to poor labor relations and poor behavior.[63]

This interpretation, which is similar to the viewpoint of union leaders and justifies the measures the latter design to prevent greater autonomy of the committees in the union structures, has effects in the practice of the committees and their militants consequences (Arthur, 1998b).

In the committees' programs, training is defined as a priority, the "means to improve the quality of all activists and to stimulate participation of women workers."[64] Training courses are organized through the Union Training Scheme common to all unions. Their declared objectives are the training of union leaders and of women workers in the companies (the "ground level"). Here, the intention is to improve knowledge on what constitutes a union movement so as to widen the base of adherence to the unions. Training directed toward women unionists contains four main modules: the place of working women in the union movement, their problems, the legislation that protects them, and the tasks of the committees. Great attention is paid to study of the legal texts guaranteeing equality between the sexes (the Constitution) and protection of women workers (in the Labor Law).[65]

The training also seeks to prepare militants of the committees to participate in collective bargaining through study of the law defining these (33/90), discussion of the importance of this type of instrument so as to enforce women's rights, and the presentation of ways of elaborating an inventory of the main problems to bring to collective bargaining. Demands already identified are the creation of crèches, social centers, and transport,[66] all showing a concern to harmonize family responsibilities with working life.

If the militants apparently share the conceptions basic to the creation of the committees as well as the priorities established in the plans for action, divergences are visible in the practices and positions in relation to the control exercised by the union leadership. There are open criticisms about the mechanisms operated by the latter. The militants are divided around these criticisms, depending on the type of relations that they maintain with the respective leadership. Some are accused of being "informers" in the service of the secretaries of the committees. This subject has never been openly discussed and the accusations are vague, with no names given and no proof of such "collaboration."[67] What is important to note is the climate of suspicion that has gradually emerged.

Women unionists do not all have the same positions, although there is a common perception of the need to deal with the problems of working women and recognition and that until now the unions have marginalized this aspect. In the meantime, if solidarity exists, there are also conflicts and rivalries dividing the militants. These disputes, frequently called "intrigues" by the women themselves or by the union leadership, are thus bereft of all political content even when in reality they are about struggles for power. Considered incapable of playing the political "game," women are thought to bring "small" domestic quarrels with them to the unions. In this way, importance is taken away from the struggles of women unionists between themselves and with the union hierarchy, while justifying at the same time the intervention of the union leadership so as to conduct the committees in the "right direction" (Arthur, 1998b).

The common platform of action, based on the identities "woman" and "unionist," is weak because of the constraints of meaning of these terms. The category "woman" is linked to images of mother, wife and sister, while "unionist" is identified with images of worker and combatant. On both sides, militants have as point of reference practices of subordination in relation to men and the leadership. In this context, daring to think any differently is not without risk. The dilemma equality/difference is very present in collective and individual strategies, even if it is not conscious.

As soon as a woman engages in the struggle for women workers' rights, she speaks in the name of "women," although what is similar to women does not stem from a common identity but from discourses available in societies (Charles, 1996: 9–13). Rarely are the constructions about what "woman" means contested. On the contrary, there is always a tendency to accompany each claim with justifications, so as to make clear that the demands are made on the basis of the category "woman"—the matrix for action, never questioned. There is always present the fear of exceeding the limits of what is considered convenient. There are tensions between the norm to respect and the need to live according to one's wishes, "between what should be and what is, with the risk of being nothing" (Riot-Sarcey, 1988: 36). Imprisoned in this logic, women have difficulty in harmonizing their activities and their conformity to female types considered "normal." To what point can confrontations go without the risk of being trapped in a stigmatized image?[68] We are faced with a relation of forces that does not directly imply coercion, but rather a kind of "existential violence," exerted through the authoritarian attribution to each person of an individuality whose principles are external to it. These are procedures inspired by morals and reason, which impede a human being from constituting the self as a subject according to its own inclinations (Foucault, 1992; Riot-Sarcey, 1993a).

Faced with a limited choice of possibilities of action, women unionists have few alternatives: accept these conditions, challenge them openly, or seek to change them. Women's strategies and options are diverse. An apparent acceptance of the "rules of the game" established by the union leadership may hide a strategy to achieve personal objectives and to reach a seat of power. On the other hand, examples of direct confrontation show how difficult it is to succeed that way.

Through the experiences of three women unionists presented below it is possible to perceive the diversity of motivations and interests of the women in the committees.

THREE WOMEN, THREE EXPERIENCES

The three women whose careers we trace below all occupy or occupied positions of leadership in the committees. The challenge is to identify what constitutes the specificity of these individual life stories and comprehend the ways in which wider social forces act on the individual, profoundly shaping subjective experiences (Bozzoli, 1985).

Luisa M. is one of the leaders of the committees of the OTM-CS. Like many others, she began work in the unions as a staff member, before becoming known after independence for her political activity in the neighborhood-dynamizing groups. She is well known as a senior activist in the unions and for having fulfilled various leadership roles before the formation of the committees, having participated at crucial moments in the history of the movement—for example, taking a position in favor of the conservative wing during the internal struggles of 1992.[69]

As a committee leader, Luisa M. has a highly centralized and authoritarian managerial style, observable in seminars and in day-to-day relations: union members stand up when she enters the room, as is the practice with general secretaries of the unions. This imposition, however, may also be motivated by the search for recognition by the union hierarchy, considering that these are the unwritten norms guiding interactions and relations within the group—as has been observed in other situations when women are nominated for positions of authority (Hackney and Hogard, 1999).

Apart from this, the members address her using the term "mama," which denotes distance and great respect. In the meetings in which I happened to be present, once Luisa M. had given her opinion, the discussion was closed, which showed the authority she has over the other important members of the committee. I asked myself on what this was based.

Luisa M. maintains close relations with the union leadership consistent with her seniority and long experience, which make her trustworthy, and perhaps because of this she is accused of exercising vigilance in its favor.[70] The members of the committee complain that all their opinions about the functioning of the unions expressed during the internal meetings are transmitted to the union leadership. Although there is no proof, it is suspected that Luisa M. is the informant,[71] which may be justified by the affirmation that her relations with the leadership constitute a special means of getting them to accept the committees and to remind them constantly that they are also part of the union organization and as such they must be taken into account by the movement.

One of the aspects characterizing the leadership of Luisa M. is the rigorous control in the management of funds, including the definition of strategies for their use. By these means the possibility of acting in conformity with the policies of the leadership of the committee are conditioned. Thus criticisms made of her are discreet.

Luisa M. upholds a strategy of unity between the unions and refuses on principle a division between committees of the two federations. She justifies her position affirming that at the level of women workers the commonality of interests should lead to the overcoming of all differences. Although attractive, because it appeals to solidarity in struggle, in reality this discourse retraces very real power strategies: being part of the OTM-CS and close to the central leadership of the committees, the subordination of those affiliated to CONSILMO is a means of widening her area of influence.

Luisa M. cultivates the appearance of modesty, which hides her determination, for she is a woman of power. Through the work of the committees, she seeks to impose herself and assert her authority through her knowledge of formal and informal networks in the union organization. Having no particular competencies, she chose these means to affirm herself.

Ana A.[72] was the coordinator of a Committee in a national union and executive secretary of the committee in the OTM-CS. She is 39, is married and has four children. Ana A. finished secondary school (including training in accountancy) after starting work. Later she also did professional training in laboratory techniques and informatics. At the age of 16 Ana A. began her working life as a clerk in a company that had been nationalized. her union activities began in 1982 and in 1990 she was elected deputy secretary of the OMM in the company. As a result of this activity, through having become known by the women in the company and the union, Ana A. was chosen in 1993 to preside over the commission to set up the committee in her union, and was elected secretary of it in 1996. From 1994 she was a member of the National Council of her union and in 1995 was elected president of the Control Committee at the provincial level. Ana A. is also active politically at the local level: she was elected to be part of the political and decision-making organs, respectively, in 1988 and 1986. Her position in these posts was confirmed in elections in 1997.

It was Ana A. who took the initiative to contact me, because she was at the center of a conflict that put her against the leadership of her union. According to her version, problems began when she was directing the preparations for the creation of the committee: her attitude was considered very independent. The secretary-general of the union accused her of being disrespectful, aggressive and "confusionist."[73] The leadership of the union tried without success to prevent her being elected to the committee. Almost at the same time, Ana A. was also elected to the secretariat of the committee of the OTM-CS. Some months later Ana A. was informed of the withdrawal by her firm of the authorization enabling her to be away from work to attend meetings of the committee in the OTM-CS. She then learned from the company management that the decision stemmed from an unfavorable report given by her superiors in the union.

In this situation, Ana A. perceived that she was facing organized hostility and sought to obtain justice in the higher structure of her union organization and with the leaders of other committees. Although there was the verbal promise of support, there was also a certain hostility from some of her more influential women colleagues, who commented that she had made some mistakes, that she had "spoken too loudly." These attempts did not produce any result and the case was never resolved. Ana A. recounts:

> I was desperate. During the whole process of the creation of the committees in the OTM, there was much insistence on the need of women to struggle to achieve their total emancipation so as to enjoy liberty and equality of rights in relation to men. There was also emphasis that all the strategies had to be based on solidarity among women. Even more, one of the functions of the committees was to serve as the base for the development of solidarity. If I was suffering harassment in my union as a result of my positions in defense of women, the other committees should help defend me, above all the committee of the OTM-CS! So where is this solidarity? What is happening is that union leaders officially accept the creation of the committees, but at heart are fearful of allowing women to take positions of greater importance in the unions. In most cases it is clear that they think that women cannot have the same rights as men, perhaps because they consider them inferior.

Ana A. had other, more open, conflicts concerning the management of funds of the committee of her union. The secretary general had diverted part of the donations given for training seminars. Ana A., deprived of resources to develop the planned activities, brought up the situation inside the union and also with the donors, for which she succeeded in organizing proof.[74]

The end of the process was the dismissal of Ana A. and her husband, who was also an employee of the company. According to her, the decision was suggested to the firm by the leadership of the union, so as to exclude her definitively from the committee. In fact, having lost her waged position in the company, her affiliation in the union lapsed. What seems to confirm

Ana's version is that the dismissals related to the readjustment of privatized companies are mainly of unqualified workers, which is not the case of Ana and her husband.[75] Ana A. sought to defend herself by directing letters to the higher structures of the union and of the federation, and to the "Women's Forum," the NGO that coordinates the activities of women's organizations. Here she produces proof of the bad faith of the union leadership: approval of her discharge by the company union committee was made before the company itself was aware of the matter. As the secretary-general of the union is the cousin of a manager of the company, Ana A. suspects that her discharge was effected through him. She also denounces the absence of transparency in the taking of decisions. The secretary-general is the only one with the right to an opinion and intimidates other members of the secretariat.

Ana A. has never received replies to her letters and, still very shocked, accuses her superiors—and in some cases produces evidence—of compromises with the male leadership of the unions, using as a pretext for non-intervention the autonomy of the national unions.[76]

Ana A. struggled and did not keep quiet. One of her strategies was personally to inform most of the committee secretaries of her situation, which resulted in their raising the problem in a seminar and demanding the adoption of a position. This reserved protest was immediately silenced and did not go forward.

On the other hand, Ana A. obtained funds and traveled more than 800 kilometers to meet with the president of the National Control Council of her union and to demand that the irregularities in the process be investigated. He agreed with her, but confessed to not having sufficient courage to challenge the executive of the union. Once again, there was no result.

This example seriously poses the question of the application of a policy of equality between men and women in the unions. Ana A. emphasized with a certain fatalism that the difference between the reality and what is written is enormous: "The unions struggle against the committees of women in various ways. They seek to manipulate and intimidate women unionists who say no. Notwithstanding all the democracy that is proclaimed, the unions operate in an autocratic, authoritarian and anti-democratic manner."

Between 1997 and 1999, with the help of international aid agencies, Ana A. conceived and directed a continuous training project—not affiliated to any union—for women unionists, which involved all the militants of the committees, and organized temporary paid work for the participants. This project closed in 2000 as a result of lack of financing, and at the moment Ana A. is unemployed.

Esmeralda M. was the secretary of the committees of CONSILMO. She is 42 and is a widow with two children. Her family invested much in the education of their children; she was able to attend secondary school in the Swiss Mission and trained as a primary school teacher.

Esmeralda M. was one of the first women unionists I interviewed; she was very reserved and opened up only after the fourth meeting. When we became closer, she made an enormous contribution to the work. Esmeralda M. knows the case of Ana A., but could not intervene because she does not belong to the OTM-CS.

Esmeralda M. began her professional career in 1974 as a primary school teacher in a district in Maputo province. Interested in the great political changes of the period, she returned to the capital city, Maputo, even before independence. She began work in 1975 as a wage earner in a corporatist union surviving from colonial times. With the dissolution of the union, she kept the same job in the recently created production councils and later, when unions were created according to sector, she was employed in one of the three that subsequently formed CONSILMO.

In the union, Esmeralda M. began as a cashier and progressively advanced in her career. She finished secondary school and attended night courses in accounting. When I came to know her, she was the highest-qualified wage earner in the accounting section. She trained other staff members, including her boss, the secretary for administration and finance of the national union. Esmeralda's professional capacities have never been recognized and she complains: "I am the most senior of the women workers in my union, even in relation to those in office. The only sign of recognition is reference to this seniority during meetings, as if I were the historical archive of the union."[77]

Esmeralda M. describes herself as "honest" and states that this has not helped her in the organization. In 1997 they demoted her by two points in her category. This decision originated with the leadership, which justified it by saying that she was overworked and needed to rest. Esmeralda believes this attitude was motivated by vengeance and with foresight. In practice she controlled almost all the finances of the union and did not allow fraud in the operations for which she was responsible: "They called me the 'block' because I only paid properly accounted expenses."

She was appointed to direct the commission to create committees when SLIM was formed, which later converted into CONSILMO. At that time Esmeralda M. was very close to the person who came to be secretary-general of the union. She knew of the existing corruption and thought that the new candidate would improve the situation of the organization. She therefore gave her support and as she was better educated than the others, participated actively in the elaboration of the new statutes of SLIM. But as soon as "her" candidate took over the direction of the union, she was sidelined. Apart from this, after being elected secretary of the committees, she encountered new struggles, which did not contribute to the improvement of her relations with the leadership.

Esmeralda complains that she received numerous amorous suggestions from the secretary-general and other members of the secretariat. During visits abroad for conferences, when there were mixed groups, it was quite usual "in the middle of the night for your colleague or chief to knock on the door." At that time they were usually drunk, she adds. Esmeralda says she never acceded and this resulted in a surprised reaction, her colleagues accepting with difficulty that a woman alone as she was could refuse their proposals. Indeed, for this reason, she began to be called "woman–man," and other epithets. She states she attaches no importance to such attitudes.

An important problem for Esmeralda M. continues to be corruption, which she considers to be the use of means and goods of the organization for personal ends, without respect for the fundamental objectives of the union. This corruption takes diverse forms: diversion of funds, improper use of the budget, and favoritism. Authoritarian methods are the result of this situation, as they are necessary to silence critics and dissidents. The male opponents to the present direction of the union—also called the "silent opposition"—(Roserat, 1991: 64) tried to recruit Esmeralda M. to their ranks, but she remained on the sidelines, although she shared some of their positions. She thinks that beyond the critique is the ambition of supplanting the present leadership "so as to be able to do the same thing," as had happened before. She does not want to be instrumentalized again.

In respect of the relations between the leadership and the committees, Esmeralda is conscious of the control that is exercised over their activities and the militants:

> Internally, the committee is ignored, except when delegations come. Women are then invited, just for show. On these occasions, the least word is minutely analyzed, so they will know who to marginalize. For example, when there was a training course organized by a Brazilian union federation, for the first time the women were invited. The teachers said to us: "We do not have a program. You must raise the questions to be debated and then attempt to reach solutions." One of the women present indicated the absence of democracy in the union and the weak participation of workers from the firms. She also mentioned that there were only three people who took decisions, contrary to statutory principles. As a result of this contribution, she was called to a closed meeting to analyze her behavior. She received much criticism and her name was put on the blacklist. [...] A curious fact is that no one dares to do anything to change the situation.

The committee has no budget of its own, and does not even have the simplest equipment, such as paper or a typewriter (not to speak of a computer). Esmeralda M. regrets that much money is spent uselessly, such as in the exaggerated quantities of food and drink each time there is a reception.

Consumption is always high and what is left (whisky and beer) is divided among the members of the leadership and their cronies.

Esmeralda does not believe in female solidarity. Although she has good relations with women militants of the unions, she has no particular friends. She judges women harshly who, she says, are fearful and dread repression and at the same time are proud of their reputation as "rebels." Esmeralda M. is a little cynical about the situation of the union, which she thinks is "hopeless." She thinks that if she were a man her career would have been different, but that she would certainly not have been on the side of the leadership, because the cause of her exclusion does not reside solely on the fact of being a woman, but also on her attitude: "The leaders like to have their boots licked, but this I cannot do."

In 1997, Esmeralda M. wished to begin studying again and later leave the union. This was in agreement with her family's opinion, which had pressed her for some time to look for another better paid job with fewer problems. However, at the end of the year she was dismissed from her functions as secretary of the committees in the union head office, by decision of the secretary-general, without consulting the assembly of women unionists that had elected her. Nominated in her place was a unionist who does not live in the capital, which leaves the committee totally inoperative.

In 2000, Esmeralda M. resigned and, with help of Ana A., competed for a post in a women's NGO, where she presently works.

CONCLUSIONS

The inability of the unions to react to the new problems posed by liberalization since 1987 revealed their dependence on political power. It was internal struggle and workers' protest movements that led to the process of democratization of the organizations. However, in the OTM as well as in CONSILMO, the discourses and practices that define and guide the action of the committees show much homogeneity and at the same time insulation from the debate on the need for internal democracy. Leaders of the two union federations agreed to limit the actions of the new organs to "women's problems" and to maintain them in strict dependence on the existing structure of the union. Discourses on the participation of women and on the rights of women workers are similarly conservative and, although they do not contest the abstract principle of equality, they (re)create difference between genders that legitimates discriminatory practices.

The history of women's participation in the unions gained visibility with the creation of the committees, above all because prior to this period women's contestation was disqualified—because it was developed around the OMM— or because they did come to constitute themselves into organized pressure movements. However, the adherence of women to the project of creating committees reveals a consciousness of inequality, and the process of their creation, centered on the general debate of "women's problems," contributed to the formation of a common platform between women unionists.

Women union militants recognize themselves as different, although this recognition does not always imply making the best use of characteristics considered female. The three women whose careers were recounted above reflect diverse discourses and strategies, all based on a presumed female identity. There is at least the appearance of a posture of acceptance of male protection, and of the application of dominant models of organization and management by the unions of the committees. It is an authoritarian model, which severely restricts participation of women unionists, but which can also be seen from other viewpoints. On the one hand, if the male leadership instrumentalizes a woman leader, it is equally, to a degree, instrumentalized in a markedly individual struggle for power. On the other hand, despite everything, the committees are increasingly "accepted" in a dynamic of acceptance/imposition that results from a negotiation of power spaces: they are seen to be centrally important for the union organization as a symbol or as the appearance of democracy but, at the same time, their potentially subversive character is removed and mechanisms are activated to make them inoffensive to the established order. The very imposition of authoritarian models of leadership contributes to this to the extent that the committees do not introduce new, more democratic, forms of participation that might come to empower protest movements within the unions.

In this search for power, the strategy of the first leader is necessarily through the reinforcing of the committees in the union structure, thus to create spaces that can come to enable new contestation. Clearly, the control exercised over women militants seeks to impede this possibility, but their existence is important for the emergence of other voices. The risk is that these spaces for discussion will themselves become subject to hierarchy.

We next have a discourse that argues for the solidarity that should be promoted and materialized in the practice of the committees. The strategies of this militant are based on the demand for the values implicit at the time of the founding of the Committees, and she does nothing more than require their full implementation in the name of the "true" nature of these organizations—which is echoed among other women militants. Unable to help their colleague, they nevertheless recognize that such would be the course most in keeping with the objectives that are said to orient the committees.

Finally, the third militant does not accept being different through being a woman and reacts when she is attributed women's characteristics and behavior, in which she does not recognize herself at all. Although struggling for greater transparency and participation, she thinks this should be developed within the union, failing which the committees would not have the possibility of acting. If she does not believe in women's solidarity, it is because in the final analysis she does not recognize the difference.

In the struggle to effect their rights, various paths are followed by women unionists. Accepting or refusing the models that are imposed, contesting male domination in the union takes the form of demands for citizenship. In practice, the abstraction of the individual "before the law," bereft of social characteristics, which constitutes the legal basis of citizenship, is refused. This equality before the law is not a principle of social equality, but rather of neutrality and impartiality between the parts that appear before the law as equals—which omits the social causes of inequality, whether wealth, class, or sex, and treating individuals without the social characteristics of inequality (Cohn and White, 1997). However, while investing in "gender training" of women unionists and women union leaders, the strategies of the committees follow the line of "promotion of women" and rarely contest the power relations that form the basis of gender inequality. But to what extent does the isolation of the women's organizations, their financial weakness and the difficulty in obtaining help at the local and international level permit other options?

Five years after their creation, in assessing the functioning of the committees we can highlight the increasingly wide involvement of women unionists in their activities, at the national level and in the workplace, as well as their slow but progressive insertion in the national unions and federations. Although the dominant strategy is to avoid direct confrontation, in practice conditions are being created such that when women unionists decide to struggle in a more frontal and open manner for their rights they will have a forum and appropriate organs to make their voices heard.

But, to the present, the fairy-tale solidarity between women, a trap into which it is easy to fall—perhaps because we need to believe in it—only exists when conditions so permit and strategies coincide. Conflicts and tensions indicate the diversity of interests and spheres of action, but discontent exists and the union leadership shows knowledge of it. After all, ghosts have the power to terrify because at times they do interfere in the world of the living.

Notes

1 The expression of M. Foucault.
2 The research forming the basis of this chapter took place in 1997 in Maputo; some of the information was updated in 1999 and 2000. Twenty-four women's committee leaders and 15 leaders of national and provincial unions and workplace committees were interviewed. Observation was possible through participation in seminars and workshops organized by the committees and national union organizations. Informants are referred to in the text by

pseudonyms. Most of the existing statements used in this chapter are unpublished, and were consulted in the archives of the OTM-Mozambican Labor Organization and the documentation center of the Friedrich Ebert Foundation in Maputo.

3 That this preoccupation was common to general and provincial secretaries prompted me to reflect on its significance, which is more than it appears at first sight. In fact, by giving me at the outset a key to understanding the creation and the place of the committees, my informants were establishing the structure within which the interview would be circumscribed. Speaking of women unionists, they referred to them as "others," as if I myself were not female. Implicitly, I was seen as an equal, as if I did not have the same femaleness as the militants of the committees. This attitude was important to understand the nature of the relations that they maintain with women unionists, whom they think they should guide and help, while at the same time limiting the action of the committees.

4 With these members, relations were always much more cordial, based on mutual recognition. Although an "outsider," I was still seen first as a "woman." From the first interviews, my informants showed great openness and, despite knowing that I had regular meetings with the union secretaries, none thought it necessary to ask me to make sure that nothing of our conversation "escaped." However, they did warn me against doing so with other women I might still interview. It was as if it were thought in some way impossible that I might denounce them to the men while, through an excess of confidence, I might make known the subject of our talks to other militants. This attitude of confidence had a tendency to grow with some and diminish with others. As my contacts broadened and I began to see the conflicts between unionists, they became more prudent. There was always doubt as to what I might have been told and concern to give me their version of the facts. This situation was difficult to manage, the more so as some attempted to show they were closer to me than others. At the end of a certain period, I became aware that my presence was being used in the power games in play in the committees.

5 According to the 1997 Census, 1,049,906 individuals are wage-workers. Of this number 233,641 are women. Agriculture, forestry, and fishing are not included in these statistics.

6 OTM–CS, Departamento de Organização, 1999. There is no information on the sex proportions. It was not possible to obtain data relating to the three unions affiliated to CONSILMO.

7 Comutra, OTM-CS, 1998.

8 The expression "woman worker" means waged women, who represent the exception. Domestic workers or peasants are not included in this category. The expression "man worker" does not exist.

9 Information from the "Seminar on privatization in the democratic process—political and social effects," Maputo, 1996.

10 Today, however, some admit that these *ad hoc* committees arose because the union committees did not represent the workers and not only were divorced from their members but also did not defend them (PADEP, 1996, "Entrevista colectiva," Maputo).

11 From 1992, the unions included in their training programs a module on PRE, its social and economic effects, and privatization.

12 The single union created in 1983 and converted into a union federation in 1990.

13 See "Seminário sobre as privatizações no processo democrático—efeitos políticos e sociais," organized by SLIM, Maputo, 4–5/11/1996.

14 In their initial formulation, the Production Councils, afterwards transformed into the OTM, controlled by the Frelimo Party, had the function of mobilizing workers for the "battle of production"(Machel, 1976).

15 The unions, supported by international union federations and NGOs, began analyzing unionism in Mozambique. Various seminars with this aim were held between 1992 and 1996. One union leader, asked to evaluate this transition, stated: "It was only then, with multi-partyism, that we began to see that we affirmed 'Viva Frelimo! Viva Samora!' instead of 'Viva *Us!*' We could not hold strikes, we could not make direct criticism of the government, even when we saw great wrongs being done, because the government was ours and our co-operation was only with socialist countries" (PADEP, 1996, "Entrevista colectiva," Maputo).

16 On the analysis that the union members make of this period, see SIN-TIQUIGRA, 1997a.

17 Frelimo officially abandoned Marxism–Leninism in 1990, at the time of the V Congress. However, from 1987, the OTM had not received state financial support.

18 The OTM continues with 14 unions, while SLIM represents only three.

19 According to one union leader: "This law gave new impetus to the union movement in Mozambique. However, there were different viewpoints about its application, content and perspectives for union action" (Simbine, 1995).

20 Decreto 7/94.

21 According to an evaluation made in 1997, there was still no real "Tripartite Forum" that might resolve rapidly and effectively the problems arising during the transformation process (SINTIQUIGRA, 1997a).

22 SINTIQUIGRA, 1997b.

23 Information disclosed at "Seminário do Comutra para Política de Género," OTM-CS, Matola, 11–13 November 2000.

24 Given the similarity of these OTM and SLIM/CONSILMO bodies, to facilitate exposition we will use "Committees" to mean both COMUTRA and CONMUT.

25 This cooperation is maintained today, through training and education programs.

26 For example, the training seminar for the metalworkers-union, SINTIME, in 1996, the title of which was "The role of women in union activities." No

woman unionist was asked to preside at the sessions, and of the six addresses given, only one was delivered by a woman.

27 Created by Frelimo in 1973, it had the juridical status of "mass democratic organization" (Organização Democrática de Massas—ODM).

28 "Seminário do Comutra para Política de Género," OTM-CS, Matola, 11–13 November 2000.

29 Mula, 1996; the borrowing from the OMM song of the expression "inseparable companion" should be noted.

30 Tembe, 1996.

31 My emphasis.

32 See the following references: Cossa (1996), Manjaze (1996a, 1996b, 1997), Matusse (1996), Mula (1996), Nhaca (1995), Simbine (1995), Tembe (1996), Zunguza (1996).

33 Cossa, 1996.

34 "The party as the conscience of women" (Gadant, 1989: 211).

35 João T., personal interview, 1997.

36 Cossa, 1996.

37 Tembe, 1996.

38 See the intervention of D. Tembe (1996) above, and Júlio A., personal interview, 1997.

39 Lei de Trabalho, 8/85, Preamble: "All rights must be guaranteed to women workers, in complete equality with men, while adequate conditions must be created for their integration at work, enabling the simultaneous development of their creative capacity and the upholding of their superior function as mothers and educators."

40 Tembe, 1996.

41 See "Estatutos da OTM-CS" and those of unions affiliated to SLIM.

42 Collective interview with the executive secretariat of SINTIME, 1997; Júlio A., personal interview, 1997; Alvaro M., personal interview, 1997.

43 SINTEVEC, 1997.

44 Luís B., personal interview, 1997.

45 Collective interview with the executive secretariat of SINTIME, 1997; Jaboco M., personal interview, 1997; Horácio E., personal interview, 1997; Santos M., personal interview, 1997.

46 Ana A., personal interview, 1997; Rita F., personal interview, 1997; Esmeralda M., personal interview, 1997.

47 Fundação Friedrich Ebert//Comités de Mulheres de Sindicatos Nacionais, 1997.

48 Ana A., personal interview, 1997.

49 Conclusions from the seminar "Estratégias futuras para os Comités de Mulheres Trabalhadoras" (Fundação Friedrich Ebert/Comités de Mulheres de Sindicatos Nacionais, 1997).

50 Esmeralda M., personal interview, 1997.

51 Alda B., personal interview, 2000.

52 For one sector of public opinion, the government's position was suspect, and indirectly accused it of being on the side of the employers, seeing that one sector of its membership are also entrepreneurs (*Savana*, 28 July 2000, "Com o governo no meio do barulho, empregadores e sindicatos arrastaram-se"). Leaders of various political parties argued that the strike would have been justified and even inevitable, accusing the government of being unwilling to resolve labor problems at a juncture in which social differentiation was increasing and the gap between rich and poor wider than ever (*Notícias*, 26 July 2000, "Oposição acusa o Governo de faltar à vontade política"; *Savana*, 28 July 2000, "Apesar da aparente cedência do Governo, trabalhadores continuam desiludidos com salário mínimo"). There was also general praise for the union leadership—until then suspected of close connection with the party politics of FRELIMO—for having conducted the negotiations with firmness.

53 "Estrangeiros tentaram apoiar na organização da greve—disse Chissano em Xai-Xai," *Domingo*, 30 July 2000.

54 Artur M., personal interview, 2000.

55 OTM-CS/Comité Nacional de Educação e Formação Sindical, 1995.

56 Taju, 1996.

57 Chemane, 1995.

58 Timana, 1996.

59 Almeida, 1996.

60 Also called "sexual persecution" in the manual.

61 The committee of the transport union defines as one of its objectives: "To combat superiority or inferiority complexes, which constitute the insuperable basis of discrimination against women" (SINTRAT, 1996).

62 Rita F., personal interview, 1997; see also, Esmeralda M., personal interview, 1997; Dora T, personal interview, 1997.

63 OTM-CS/Comité Nacional de Educação e Formação Sindical, 1995: 42.

64 OTM-CS/Comité Nacional de Educação e Formação Sindical, 1995: 5.

65 Articles 154, 155 and 156, of the first Labor Law (8/85) after independence.

66 OTM-CS/Comité Nacional de Educação e Formação Sindical, 1995: 85–86.

67 Marta M., personal interview, 1997; Ana A., personal interview, 1997; Dora T., personal interview, 1997.

68 This is a current debate for the feminist struggle. If the deconstruction of identity has a fundamental importance for the conduct of a policy of resistance, it can also provoke a certain instability: who are we and why are we struggling? If it is necessary to be critical about the concept "woman" they wish to impose, how do we discover what we are? Snitow puts this question in the following manner: "It may be a pleasure to be *we,* and it may be strategically imperative to struggle as *we,* but who, they ask, are *we?*" (1990: 10; author's emphasis).

69 The former leadership was opposed for its authoritarianism, but persisted in blocking change. This crisis of the OTM led to the schism resulting in the founding of SLIM (see Moyana, 1995).

70 As was noted by Rita F., personal interview, 1997.

71 Rita F., personal interview, 1997; Aida B., personal interview, 1997.

72 Five interviews in 1997.

73 "Confusionist": neologism in national political parlance, used to stigmatize individuals who do not follow a politically convenient line and for this reason represent a malign influence on others.

74 The diversion of funds was confirmed by the agency that financed the committee's activities.

75 The latter had secondary level training in Cuba.

76 Other union members have confirmed to us Ana A.'s version (Marta M., personal interview, 1997; Esmeralda M., personal interview, 1997).

77 Quotation from the document Esmeralda M. wrote at my request, in which she presents her situation and her feelings in relation to the functioning of the committee and the unions.

Bibliography

Alcoff, L., and E. Potter (1993). *Feminist epistemologies*. New York: Routledge.

Almeida, M. A. de (1996). "Estratégias de liderança," *Seminário Nacional de preparação do ASATUW III*. Maputo (mimeo).

Ardovini-Brooker, J. (2000). "Feminist Epistemology: A Reconstruction and Integration of Women's Knowledge and Experiences" (http://www.advancingwomen.com), accessed 17 January 2001.

Arthur, M. J. (1998a). "Mozambique: women in the armed struggle," in P. McFadden (ed.), *Southern Africa in Transition: a gendered perspective*. Harare: SAPES, 67–82.

— (1998b). "Percepções sobre a mulher no mundo do trabalho," in A. Loforte and M. J. Arthur (eds), *Relações de género em Moçambique: educação, trabalho e saúde*. Maputo: DAA/UEM.

Assis, A. (1997). *Estudo sobre o movimento sindical em Moçambique*. Maputo: Fundação Friedrich Ebert.

Bonni, M. H. (1995). *The Trade Unions movement in Mozambique: challenges and new tasks for the future. A preliminary study*. Maputo: Fundação Friedrich Ebert.

Bouchardeau, H. (1993). "Un parcours politique," in M. Riot-Sarcey (ed.), *Femmes pouvoirs*. Paris: Kimé, 51–8.

Bozzoli, B. (1985). "Migrant women and South African social change: biographical approaches to social analysis," *African Studies*, 44(1), 87–96.

Burn, S. M., R. Aboud, and C. Moyles (2000). "The Relationship Between Gender Social Identity and Support for Feminism" (http://www.findarticles.com/m2294/2000_June/66012099/p1/article.jhtml), accessed 15 January 2001.

Charles, N. (1996). "Feminist practices: identity, difference, power," in N. Charles and F. Hughes-Freeland (eds), *Practising Feminism: Identity, Difference, Power.* London: Routledge, 1–37.

Chemane, C. (1995). "A participação da mulher nas actividades sindicais," *Seminário dos líderes sindicais.* Maputo (mimeo).

Cliff, J. (1991). "Destabilization, economic adjustment, and the impact on women." Paper presented at *Workshop on Economic Policy, Equity and Health,* Harare, 18–21 February.

Cohn, E. S., and Susan O. White (1997). "Efectos de la socializacion de los valores legales sobre la democratizacion" (http://www.unesco.org/issj/rics153), accessed 8 November 1999.

Cossa, R. (1996). *Discurso de abertura do Seminário do SINTIME Sobre o papel da Mulher na Actividade Sindical.* Maputo (mimeo).

Foucault, M. (1992). "Deux essais sur le sujet et le pouvoir," in H. Dreyfus and M. Rabinow, *Michel Foucault: un parcours philosophique.* Paris: Gallimard, 297–321.

Fundação Friedrich Ebert (FFE)/Comités de Mulheres de Sindicatos Nacionais (1997). *Estratégias futuras para os Comités de Mulheres Trabalhadoras.* Maputo (mimeo).

Gadant, M. (1989). "Les comunistes algériens et l'émancipation des femmes," *Peuples Meditérranées*, 48–9, 199–228.

Hackney, Catherine E., and Elaine M. Hogard (1999). "Women in Transition: A Mission of Service", *AWL Journal*, 2(2), Winter.

Hannerz, U. (1997). "Fronteras" (http://www.unesco.org/issj/rics154), accessed 8 November 1999.

Humphries, B. (1997). "From Critical Thought to Emancipatory Action: Contradictory Research Goals?" *Sociological Research Online*, 2(1) (http://www.socresonline.org.uk/socresonline/2/1/3.html), accessed 8 November 1999.

Kruks, S. (n.d.). "Mozambique: some reflections on the struggle for women's emancipation." (mimeo).

Lather, P. (1991). *Getting Smart: Feminist Research and Pedagogy with/in the Postmodern.* London: Routledge.

Machel, S. (1974). *A libertação da mulher é uma necessidade da revolução, garantia da sua continuidade, condição do seu triunfo.* Maputo: Edições da Frelimo.

— (1976). "Discurso à classe operária," in Comissão de Implementação dos Conselhos de Produção, *Organização dos Conselhos de Produção.* Maputo: Edições do Partido Frelimo.

Manjaze, P. J. (1996a). *Discurso de abertura do Seminário Nacional do Comité da Mulher Trabalhadora do SINTEVEC.* Maputo (mimeo).

— (1996b). *Discurso de encerramento do Seminário Nacional do Comité Da Mulher Trabalhadora do SINTEVEC.* Maputo (mimeo).

— (1997). *Discurso de abertura do Seminário Nacional do Comité da Mulher*

Trabalhadora do SINTEVEC. Maputo (mimeo).

Matusse, H. (1996). "Papel da mulher trabalhadora no desenvolvimento da economia nacional," in *Conferência Constitutiva do Comité da Mulher Trabalhadora na Província e Cidade de Maputo.* Maputo (mimeo).

Michelat, G. (1987). "Sociologia da ideologia e entrevista não-directiva," in M. Thiolent (ed.), *Crítica metodológica, investigação social e ênquete operária.* São Paulo: Pólis, 191–212.

Moyana, S. (1995). "Problemas do sindicalismo em Moçambique," in *Relatório e Documentos do Seminário sobre o "Sindicalismo em Moçambique—Experiências e Desafios"* Maputo: Fundação Friedrich Ebert, 25–40.

Mula, A. (1996). *Discurso de abertura da Conferência Constitutiva do Comité da Mulher Trabalhadora na Província e Cidade de Maputo.* Maputo (mimeo).

Nhaca, S. (1995). "Os líderes e o respeito da democracia sindical a partir do comité sindical até ao topo," in *Seminário dos líderes sindicais,* SINTRAT. Maputo (mimeo).

Osório, C. (2001). "Poder político e protagonismo feminino," *Projecto a Reinvenção da Emancipação Social.* The electronic edition can be consulted at http://www.ces.fe.uc.pt/emancipa. The text is published in volume 1 of the collection.

OTM-CS/Comité Nacional de Educação e Formação Sindical (1995). *Manual do Curso da Mulher. Nível Básico.* Maputo.

Rex, J. (1996). "National Identity in the Democratic Multi-Cultural State?" *Sociological Research Online,* 1(2) (http://www.socresonline.org.uk/socresonline/1/2/1.html), accessed 7 November 1999.

Riot-Sarcey, M. (1988). "Les sources du pouvoir: l'évenement en question," *Les Cahiers du GRIF (Le genre de l'histoire),* 37/38, 25–41.

— (1993a). "Femmes, pouvoirs," in M. Riot-Sarcey (ed.), *Femmes pouvoirs.* Paris: Kimé, 9–25.

— (1993b). "De l'histoire politique et des pouvoirs. Du positivisme à Michel Foucault," *Futur Antérieur,* supplement "Féminismes au présent," 9–36.

Roserat, C. (1991). "Le syndicalisme et les femmes," *Cahiers du GEDISST,* 2, 63–73.

SINTEVEC (1997). *Síntese da II Sessão do Conselho Nacional do SINTEVEC.* Beira (mimeo).

SINTIQUIGRA (1997a). "Experiências sobre o balanço do desempenho na Comissão Consultiva do Trabalho," in *Seminário Regional de capacitação dos quadros e dirigentes sindicais da zona sul.* Maputo. (mimeo).

— (1997b). "Carta Social dos Trabalhadores da África Austral," in *Seminário Regional de capacitação de quadros e dirigentes sindicais da zona centro.* Beira (mimeo).

SINTRAT (1996). "Proposta de Regulamento Interno do Comité," in *Conferência Constitutiva do Comité da Mulher Trabalhadora na Província e Cidade de Maputo.* Maputo. (mimeo).

Snitow, A. (1990). "A gender diary," in M. Hirsch and E. F. Keller (eds), *Conflicts in feminism*. New York: Routledge, 9–43.

Simbine, N. (1995). "Como o movimento sindical deve agir na defesa dos direitos e interesses dos trabalhadores de forma mais coesa," in *Seminário dos líderes sindicais*, SINTRAT. Maputo (mimeo).

Taju, D. (1996). "O papel da mulher na actividade sindical," in *Seminário do SINTIME sobre o Papel da Mulher na Actividade Sindical*. Maputo. (mimeo).

Tembe, D. (1996). "Estratégia a adoptar para encorajar a mulher na liderança e breve sensibilização sobre o género," in *Seminário do SINTIME Sobre o papel da Mulher na Actividade Sindical*. Maputo. (mimeo).

Timana, A. S. (1996). *Discurso de abertura do Seminário Provincial da OTM para Formação Sobre Gestão e Desenvolvimento da Mulher Trabalhadora*. Maputo. (mimeo).

Williams, S. H. (1999). "Truth, Speech, and Ethics. A Feminist Revision of Free Speech Theory," 30 (http://www.Genders.org/g30/g30_williams.html), accessed 1 February 2000.

Zunguza, J. T. (1996). "Negociação colectiva ramal e empresarial" in *Seminário Provincial da OTM para Formação Sobre Gestão e Desenvolvimento da Mulher Trabalhadora*. Maputo (mimeo).

Part III

STRUGGLING FOR DEMOCRACY IN A
SCENARIO OF CIVIL WAR AND
FRAGMENTED DESPOTISMS:
THE CASE OF COLOMBIA

7

Paradoxical Pacts

Francisco Gutiérrez Sanín and Ana María Jaramillo

CHAOS AND THE PACT TRADITION

Colombia combines two features that have generated experiences, convictions, practices, and skills shared by wide sectors of the population: stability of macro-institutional forms and a long tradition of diffuse, chronic and scathing armed conflicts. But we should be wary of easy conclusions. These traditions are not necessarily "violent" or "intolerant" in an explicit or direct manner. In fact, the need to govern and to make decisions in an institutional environment in which power—including the power of weapons—is subject to multiple restrictions has fostered a strong *pactist* tradition in which every war generates agreements and each agreement generates wars (see Uribe, 1997; Gutiérrez, 1997; but of course the best reference for understanding the phenomenon is still the prodigious *A Hundred Years of Solitude*). This pendular movement is part and parcel of our constitutional practice and thought. The result is that the pendulum pact war constitutes the attractor of the dynamics of our conflicts.

In this context, "attractor" has two possible interpretations: 1) the social conflict converges toward a certain configuration, or 2) it is essentially described by this configuration. Here, we will assume that both meanings are more or less equivalent, although this is a little inexact. What we want to highlight is that this notion leads directly to the classical tension between necessity and freedom. If our description of the pendular movement that characterizes Colombian society is acceptable, a question immediately arises: is it possible to imagine "exits" or even "new cycles" in a social world governed by an attractor? In other words, can statements of resistance and social protest be articulated only in a pendular language or can they generate their own grammar? Throughout this text, we will maintain that this question is both extremely crucial and ambiguous.

The ambiguity lies in the fact that the strong *pactist* tradition of Colombia in recent years has given way to a series of "high-level blockage" traps, to use Elster's terms (1992: 105): a form of very sophisticated adaptation, which, however, given its own convoluted elaboration, blocks the transit toward new social forms. A brief review of the peace pacts in the last 20 years allows us to assert that they are indispensable at the national level, but undesirable at the local level.[1] They generate one of the following three outcomes: the physical destruction of the protagonists of the pact[2] (as in the case of the *politicides* of the Unión Patriótica and of Esperanza, Paz y Libertad); the rupture of the pact (as has happened many times in the negotiations between FARC and the state); or the antidemocratic concentration of power in the hands of one or several of the protagonists of the pact—or even a combination of some of the previous outcomes (see Romero, 2001, on unionized workers in Urabá). They also constitute, somewhat perversely, the mental and moral horizon of the alternative options: the strategy for emancipation is based on processes of peace in which the interlocutors and protagonists, as well as their opponents, are warlords.

This may be unavoidable, but it gives origin to a series of paradoxical dynamics in so far as it forces an articulation between emancipatory languages and non-emancipatory materials. The common denominator of these outcomes is both a substantial loss of density of participatory life and an equally remarkable narrowing of the cultural and intellectual horizon on which society and its possibilities of transformation are conceived. This is the other side of the very real effect of the decrease of violence (again, see the experience described in Romero, 2001). In this case, emancipation cannot name itself because it is caught in the pendular dynamics, and it can only aspire to be recognized as an alternative through a counter-factual exercise (what would happen if we stayed in one extreme of the pendular movement?).[3] But the counter-factual discourse has a problem of scale (the impossibility of translating the national into the local and vice versa), and also a problem of perspective (as soon as you approach *extreme B* of the pendular movement the costs of *extreme A* diminish and those of *extreme B* increase). The national experience has demonstrated that, as it advances, the costs of the negotiation are felt to be excessive by wide sectors of the population.

On the other hand, this *pactist* tradition that we are talking about is recursive in time and space. Experiences produce historical memories that concentrate on a group of visible precedents and shared conventions that bridge different languages, experiences and aspirations. However, this generates long chains of social arrangements that, at the same time, express and disturb hierarchies. This is clearly shown in the very practice of war, in which, for example, the urban militias developed policies of cleansing in their territory, attacking, harassing, and even physically eliminating drug consumers, but dramatically changing, in this process, the power relations in the areas under their influence.[4] We will see a similar, although clearly differentiated,

effect in another aspect of the process of the militias: a syncopated tradition-
alism that defends the image of a community past with guns, motorcycles,
and wild *salsa* music, and which indirectly destroys all of the conditions on
which the notion of a traditional community is based.[5]

Now then, the very idea of recursion leads to the following question:
Pacts among whom? To answer this question we will have to go "beyond
fragmentation." Contrary to what one would assume from liberal criticisms
of violence (such as intolerance or fear of diversity), in Colombia the destruction of the other is founded—actually and discursively—on fear of the similar
(and of oneself).[6] Instead of the social explosion so obsessively blocked by
the national elites, we have experienced a social implosion, in which poor,
Catholic, *mestizo* young people shoot poor, Catholic, *mestizo* young people.
The armed groups—and also their correlate, the peace pacts—are conceived
as pedagogic projects with the mission to discipline and mold a mass that is
simultaneously represented as a source of legitimacy and of incivility. This
forces us to carefully study how limits are defined. What resources are needed
to trace limits? It is evident that to just state them is not enough. The subtle
plot that supports the specific "us," in opposition to the generic and discursive "us" ("us" the poor, "us" the watchmen of morals, or "us" who are
outside the law), is made of long chains of people, territories, and artifacts,
inseparable from the *local* exercise of differentiation that is one of the keys
to the Colombian war. Thus tracing limits is not a simple academic game:
to know who we are and who they are is a military matter, literally a matter
of life and death. But inasmuch as the contours of differentiation are only
supported by local experiences, we again meet with the simplification and
erasure of the identity marks when we move from "small scales" to larger
scales. The negotiators of the process of the militias in Medellín had great
difficulty in understanding the multiple segments of the "reinserted" groups.
This underscores the fact that, at different scales, different languages and
mental maps operate (Santos, 1997a). Simply, there is no discursive device
to name the local conflicts from a national and macro stance or a way to
conceive new possible worlds from micro-territorial wars.

In sum, in Colombia there is an armed resistance based on an ethos, a
practice, and some protest discourses (opposing and/or bitterly criticizing
the state or the current social order). At the same time, they are governed
by the attractor *pactism*/violence. Thus, it is difficult to see in them a new
social and cultural horizon. This phenomenon can be envisioned from three
different perspectives:

a) The "hegemony effect." "The words, images, symbols, forms, organizations, institutions and movements used by the subordinate populations to
name, understand, confront, adjust to, or resist domination have been molded
by the very process of domination" (Roseberry, quoted in Binford, 2000).

For example, the power of the cult of the Virgin Mary in social sectors involved in protest is carefully documented (Salazar and Jaramillo, 1992). The militias[7] made an effort "to cleanse" their areas of bums, "undesirable" people and gangsters in an exercise of effective security transcending the restrictions of the state of law that evokes the demands of a hysterical right. It is also possible to see how the pedagogic agenda of armed sectors reflects the expressions, rituals, books, and procedures of school life just as it was lived directly by their leaders and militants, who use them as instruments of control of their social base: there are "manuals of coexistence" (FARC), "catechisms of coexistence" (Western Boyacá), and, in Medellín, if somebody were sentenced to death or murdered, they would say that s/he had "failed" [the year].

b) The "percolation effect."[8] But at the same time, hegemony is a relationship that is always evolving. As the subordinate sectors appropriate the discourses and practices of the dominant sectors, they transform them and introduce innovations that are passed on to the elites who, in turn, give them an "official form." This, again, irrigates the society, producing changes, and so forth. We find many examples of this in the Colombian case: from the many ways of killing to military tactics, everything is in a constant process of appropriation and imitation. *Parlache*, a social dialect that was developed among lower-class young people and that had to do with the use of drugs and the unemployment crisis, transcended the borders of the place where it originated and became a dialectal form shared by many social sectors in the city. The *pactist* experience is also exposed to this effect.

The elites, it is true, wanted to handle the country through "conversations between gentlemen" (according to the accurate expression of Wilde), but today the barrio life in Medellín or the town life in Western Boyacá is a derivation of the "friendly" chats and agreements among different armed actors of very dissimilar origins: they decide to put an end to the "fratricidal" fights and to impose rules for the games that operate as frameworks for daily life, creating scenarios to settle disagreements. This experience, in turn, is picked up by the elites, who imitate the plebeian disturbance of the original practices. Thus, contestation sometimes gives birth to extensive two-way cultural circuits (global and regional ones—a phenomenon that emerged quite early, as in the case of the influence of the Tupamaros on the iconography and conception of revolutionary justice among certain sectors of the Colombian guerrillas[9]) that imply learning, innovation, and appropriation, and that are often related to the creation and establishment of counter-cultural tastes within the market economy.[10] We underscore that the percolation effect can be vertical (between elites and subordinate sectors), horizontal (between two different moments of society, though not hierarchically related, as in the connections between politics and crime that we will discuss later on), and diagonal (a combination of these two).

c) The "uncertainty effect." As we have suggested, since the exercise of differentiation is based on chains that are only interpretable in local environments, beyond them the frontiers are blurred and any motivation can be used to justify an act. Local differentiation produces national non-differentiation. Anyone can be a victim; anyone can be the victimizer. Alliances are made and unmade in a matter of days (Jaramillo, Ceballos, and Villa, 1998: 56). This situation of extreme fluidity—"turbulence" (Gutiérrez, 1997)—generates an impression of sameness, and therefore everything is solved with collective self-deprecation. The most hated person in the Colombian national discourse is the first person plural: an "us" imagined from "a community of guilt" (Cubides, 1999). If this is used to cope with uncertainty—offering specific objects for the distribution of responsibilities—it also has the immediate result of undermining the idea of democratic control and distributive justice.[11] Moreover, it reduces the politics of protest to a half-tone between rebellion and self-help ("learn to be better"[12]), underlining, very eloquently, the relationships between diverse modalities of contestation and mercantile circuits.[13]

The uncertainty effect can be examined from another point of view, that of the state. In the cases that we examine here, we cannot speak exactly of an absent state: Medellín is one of the most important cities in the country, with around two million inhabitants, the most efficient institutions (as a matter of fact, efficiency is a grounding part of its sense of identity) and an important presence of security organs. Western Boyacá, hardly a couple of hours away from the capital, Bogotá, is the center for the production of a very important natural resource (emeralds) controlled by the state until the 1960s. As we will see throughout the text, more than with a weak state, here we meet with an excluding, inequitable[14] and porous state that generates extreme forms of uncertainty at the regional and local levels, at the same time that it strengthens diverse advanced modalities of guarantees at the national level (see Uprimny and Villegas, 2003).

The rest of this chapter is organized as follows: first, we introduce an explanation of the ideology of war that makes explicit how the environment of the discourse of protest and contestation was established. This, in turn, offers an interesting viewpoint to see, though obliquely, what this kind of contestation is in our context. Second, we introduce two cases: the militia experience in Medellín, and that of the emerald miners in Western Boyacá. On the one hand, we have protest groups of impoverished youths strongly influenced by the armed left, and on the other we have plebeian entrepreneurs involved in organized crime and interested in keeping the central government away. In spite of the enormous distance separating them (see Table 7.1), they share at least the following features: a) they are eminently local/regional, but they also have a clear global component (in the case of the militiamen, this is absorbed through ideologies and cultural consumption. In the case of Boyacá, one of the central motivations for peace was to be inserted successfully into the world market—one of the more visible results is an international emerald stock market that takes place in Bogotá every year); b) they are *pasadistas* (Mariátegui), that is, religious, nostalgic moralists and defenders of tradition (the most eloquent illustration of this is maybe the great relevance of Catholic imagery); c) however, they think of themselves as pedagogic and liberal, and appropriate important parts of the modernizing intellectual discourses that fed the constitutional change of 1991, with explicit accusations against intolerance and impunity. Once again, we are not entitled to conflate the two cases into a single category, since each shows a different way of assuming the territory in connection with rights; d) they have a conflicting, but at the same time cooperative, relationship with the national state. Finally, we sketch a comparison between the two experiences and draw some conclusions.

Table 7.1. COMPARISON OF THE TWO EXPERIENCES

Issue	Medellín	Boyacá
Hierarchies	Weak and diffuse	Strong
Territorial control	Unstable	More stable
Economic resources	Minimal	Very important
Globalization	Ideological-political	Economic
Counterbalances (exogenous or endogenous)	Many	Very few
Main social sector	Youth from the popular sectors	"Capitalist pariahs 15"
Still existent	No	Yes

IDEOLOGIES AND DISCOURSES OF THE ARMED PROTEST

The raw material on which this section is built is simple: from the 1980s onwards, a specific group of "marginal" intellectuals grew in Colombia. It was divorced not only from the institutionalized academy but also from the legal actors who have a certain degree of visibility in the Colombian public record (Scott, 1985). Furthermore, it was organically linked to diverse armed groups, many of which were volatile and diffuse.[16] In other words, the justification of the armed struggle gradually ceased to be intellectually respectable,[17] but did not disappear. On the contrary, it found new niches, expressions, and languages. It is still quite important because, contrary to what one might suppose, argumentative ability is a matter of life and death for the more or less peripheral armed organizations that have emerged in Colombia in the last 20 years. Urban militias, large peasant guerrilla groups, guardians of the drug traffic, paramilitary groups, sometimes even gangs, appeared either as intellectualized projects or, with time, discovered that without a layer of intellectuals they would not reach that national, regional or municipal relevance to which they aspired. In some cases, it was clear that they simply could not survive without ideas and rationalizations—an ironic but fully consistent expression of Descartes in the tropics: "I think, therefore I am," "I am justified, therefore I survive" (see also Gutiérrez, 2001). These intellectuals would endow the projects with a vision of the future, with the ability to create an "imagined community," in Benedict Anderson's expression, and with the construction of an interface to present and represent themselves before the "larger society." A crucial aspect of such an interface was that it combined rhetorical and iconic aspects; it produced reasons, but also believable images capable of capturing the imagination of wide sectors and of proposing positive stereotypes for emulation. Think of the effects achieved, at the end of the 1980s and the beginning of the 1990s, by the image of hooded men surrounded by microphones, explaining their *modus vivendi*, dictating their reasons, in short, building new forms of visibility. To meditate about our war also implies to recover that iconic and argumentative fabric, as well as the rhetoric, practices, skills, and social techniques that simultaneously constituted the armed groups' historical condition of possibility and specific identity "signature."

However, at a certain level of abstraction that discourse is generally quite simple. Precisely because of its condition of (relative) marginality, it grants little space for mediation between instrumental objective and explanation. The latter has to follow the former rigorously. On top of the thought, one places the coif of immediate utility, thus following a strong national tradition.[18] But inevitably it becomes refined, inasmuch as it is addressed to heterogeneous audiences and, therefore, must be stripped of its most simple and brutal coercive and justifying dimensions. The refinement, certainly, is developed in a specific direction: above all, it will be stylized and standardized, dwelling in a continuous re-enunciation of some few central motives that are considered untouchable. In other words, an "armed violentology" appeared and developed, managed by a specific layer of intellectuals, and dedicated, among other things, to explaining, documenting and legitimating before heterogeneous audiences their practices and procedures. "Armed violentology" is not at all ineffective, and neither is it a particularly spectacular feature worthy of being mentioned only because of its extravagancy.

Although we do not yet have the ability to fully interpret the common senses—the "rhetorical *topoi*" (Santos, 1997b) or the "winning strategies" (Hinttikka, 1973)—of "armed violentology,"[19] we can suggest some basic intuitions in this direction.[20] Let us begin by highlighting the fact that in these cases the desired future involves a combination of peace and vigilance (Huggins, 1991), which, in turn, implies a brutal tension between the impulse toward collective incorporation (of a more regional character in the example of Boyacá, more social in that of Medellín) and a radical ignorance of individual rights through a gregarious reconstruction of society. If there is an obsession in the two experiences that we are reviewing, it is a rejection of all forms of individualism and selfishness: it is necessary to keep up with the rhythm of a common project. Since society is a project, and rights are means and not ends, any expectation of guarantees is subordinated to a notion of discipline and organization. In other words, the armed group extrapolates its disciplinary experiences and expectations, some of them completely idiosyncratic, to the territory in which it has established its domain. A resident from Medellín recapitulates with approval: "Today we are a threatened community and that is good for me: there can't be thieves, robbers. There can't be drug addicts, and those who are will have to hide [...] we all know that we have to behave." The obsession of the militias for making people behave well and for educating them had a thousand faces: "A drunk rude husband who arrived home and wanted to [beat] his wife, no, he was not killed, but he was sensitized: you have to be an example for your family and if you are not, you have to leave this place, because here we do not need antisocial people" (both testimonies quoted in Jaramillo, Ceballos, and Villa, 1998: 88). In Boyacá, the *guaquero* organizations (artisan emerald miners), once the peace pact was formalized, decided to get rid of those who misbehaved. "Some delinquent fugitive *guaqueros* settled at Quípama River, but they were received with the demand that they respect the already accepted forms of coexistence" (Ocampo, Rangel, and Díaz, 1993: 13). There, they did not need antisocial people either, because they endangered the delicate balances conquered with so much effort. "Recently, around April 1993, facing the imminent recapturing of the control of the Coscuez mine by the partners of Esmeracol with Carranza, the *guaqueros* were forced to leave the mine of their own will. If this order was not obeyed, the bosses would be forced to 'clean' the area in order to guarantee the exploration by the legitimate state contractors" (Ocampo, Rangel, and Díaz, 1993: 32). Notice how the "cleaning" metaphor is used to invoke a gregarious image in which transgression is equivalent to illness and, therefore, must be eliminated.[21] Thus violence and intolerance are not actually linked here. The problem has to do with disciplining and homogenizing the social base that operates as a source of legitimacy and over which you also shoot. The "small intellectuals," to use Gramscian terminology, express this disciplinary enthusiasm through codes, manuals, catechisms, poems, and hymns that together with the direct speeches in public squares constitute the most powerful weapon in their rhetorical repertoire. For example, the organized *guaqueros* of Quípama, led by a powerful don of the precious stone traffic, elaborated a "code of coexistence" in which "disposing of garbage in the streets is prohibited, the handling of contaminated water is demanded, and robbery and dishonesty in business are settled before the police inspector" (ibid., 12).

The vision of the future associated with this gregarious reconstruction shows a movement from the epic to the pastoral and from the eponymic to the local landscape: no more founding heroism like that of the leftist projects that gave a first impulse to the militias at the beginning of the 1980s (see the following section), no more references to the mythology of hero-ideologists but a mentality of survival at the service of an inclusive restoration. A militiaman says: "The Ché bled to death, the rest is history." He, on the other hand, wanted to live. Where? Another militiaman gives the answer: in a self-managed and integrative community. "Since I began working with the organization, I like festivals a lot, brother, for example when there was a wonderful cultural weekend, there, with music bands, the whole day there were bicycle and sack competitions among children, there was a game here with a greasy pole and the children, all of them happy, everything was, brother, very nice, there, one saw everybody smiling, for example, old men playing dominoes and poker over there, drinking *guarito* [spirits], over there, the old women joking and making *sancocho*. If you understand me, brother, that is all great for me" (quoted in Gutiérrez, 1998). A revolution to establish the tranquility of the barrio and to recover the local color? If one remembers the extreme conditions of insecurity in the barrios in Medellín at the peak moment of the militias, one will immediately discover that this program was not trivial at all. It constituted indeed an "inclusive restoration": claiming rights and entitlements for groups, but denying them to the individuals of those groups on behalf of a community with nostalgic values.[22] Hence their disturbing mixture of conservatism and protest, of solidarity and cynicism.

We can see this contrast more clearly in the relationship between transgression and resistance. In Colombia, social protest has gone through several cycles. In the period in which the narratives of both cases begin (around 1980), the country was at the same time in a very intense moment of a crime cycle and at a turning point for the entrance of drug trafficking into several forms of making politics and war. To turn protestors into criminals was, and still is, a key tool in the repertoire of answers to social protest. It was approximately at that time that the epithet "narco-guerrilla" was discovered. At the same time, a whole set of institutional designs and conflict dynamics were producing a percolation effect between the political and the criminal worlds across the ideological spectrum. The unwanted side-effects of that mixture of texts (discourses) and contexts (the mixing processes) were huge. In a surprising result that shows all the links of the chain hegemony–percolation–uncertainty, the 1980s witnessed the conscious attempt of organized criminals to become political actors, and of the protest groups to justify their bonds with criminality. When the intellectuals of different armed projects defined the "official society" as a territory to be entered and exited—an image they shared with wide sectors of the elite and with several "formal"[23] discourses—they produced a sophisticated "topology of exclusion and incorporation": there were two escape routes, delinquency and rebellion, that generated two isomorphic pairs, irruption/stigma and rebellion/prosecution. The purpose of establishing differentiations in order to produce a unique identity signature, together with the justification of the existence of all the "outsiders" or excluded, would lead not only to discursive contortions but to volatile alliances between bandits and police forces (which are deeply involved in this game of trying to be inside and outside at the same time), between them and militiamen, between militiamen and the drug dealers, and so forth, in a frantic carrousel that is extremely difficult to follow but that is NOT incoherent, inasmuch as it responds to a unique mental map. To kill bandits/to empower them, to differentiate between bandits and revolutionaries/to make them identical, become powerful cognitive games marking our peace and war processes and are tied to a long tradition (regarding this point, see the work of Sánchez and Meertens, 1984).

THE URBAN MILITIAS IN MEDELLÍN

The emergence of the militias has a recent antecedent in the period of strong violence that began in the mid-1970s with paid killers (*sicarios*). In the 1980s, with the boom of the drug traffic, favorable conditions were created for the interconnection of diverse processes already under way: the appearance of gangs in the barrios, the consolidation of gangs of delinquents and problems related to the corruption of the police and other security organisms. The drug traffic did not create anything new, but it did introduce important changes in the forms of organization and operation of delinquency with the formation of gangs specialized in paid killing, the use of the most modern armament and the capacity of developing joint activities and criminal business (the so-called "*cruces*") with the police, the army, the judges, and the inspectors.

To this, one can add the guerrillas' presence, with the formation of some commands or groups dedicated to obtaining financial resources or performing terrorist actions. In their negotiation process in the 1980s, the M19 created some "peace camps" with a strong component of military training. Many of these "camps" gave birth to bands of delinquents. The experiment of the M19 also had an important influence on the crisis of the traditional model of the guerrillas' presence in the city, which was based on the creation of commands for the performance of attacks, hold-ups, and blackmailing to support the guerrilla fronts in the rural area. This *modus operandi* was questioned by militants and sympathizers of the National Liberation Front and of the Marxist-Leninist Communist Party, which favored a strategy of military political work in the barrios to put an end to the excess of criminals and to establish a moral and communal order.

The militias themselves originated in the Barrio Popular no. 1, in northeast Medellín. This barrio is a heterogeneous conglomerate of low middle-class and lower-class sectors and of recently occupied neighborhoods. One of the main goals of the project was to defeat powerful gangs that had completely taken over these territories, many times with the complicity of the authorities. The success obtained in a first phase with the "cleansing" work was the key to its acceptance by the population and the neighborhood associations (Juntas de Acción Comunal). The militias defined themselves by the control of territories temporarily abandoned by the gangs, and by the appropriation of a function that the state should fulfill—security. "We are a state within the state," stated Pablo García, the leader of this project.

The military and political training of the founders of the militias was later retaken by some urban guerrilla nuclei and by the gangs, which shows the interconnection between political delinquency and common delinquency, additionally favored by drug traffic. This turns the militias into openly ambiguous actors in their discourses and practices. Although in their official statements and in their declarations to the media a leftist language was used, their activities were concentrated on eliminating the gangs to protect the community against the disorder caused by *chichipatos* (criminals who steal and rob in their own neighborhood), drug addicts, and rapists.

The experience of the People's Militias (Milicias del Pueblo) worked as a role model for other leftist organizations that established their own groups. They sought to copy a successful organizational model in a growing market of demand for security. However, this process of growth was offset by a weakening of the political dimension, with the massive recruitment of youngsters with no political training but with military experience, and the selective entrance of delinquents to the militias. This mechanism served the double purpose of re-socializing and co-opting individuals with the best military technique and the highest morale for fighting, but increasingly muddled the nature of the territorial control of the militias. Furthermore, the internal control—the ability of a personalized leadership, ideologized but weak, to model the behavior of the cadres—also became precarious. The abyss between the disciplinary mentality—which also inspired a war against bad behavior—and daily praxis became deeper and deeper. If in the beginning it was clear "who was who"—at least for those in the barrio who had called upon the militias to "cleanse" their territory—the task of identification became increasingly difficult, even for the protagonists of the military action.

In so far as the territory to be overseen also expanded, the different militias started to compete with each other, and this increased the so-called "settlings of accounts" among them.

More than because of the vicissitudes of war or because of political reasons, peace agreements began to be considered due to the coincidence between the burnt-out feeling of a generation of survivors and the atmosphere of optimism caused by the convocation of a Constituent National Assembly in 1991, which was expected to help design "a new country." The struggle with the gangs stagnated, and it was not clear who was actually fighting whom. The barrios that had been enthusiastic about the militias because they had expelled the criminals and established a certain moral order began to get tired and to rebel against their arbitrary power. The older militiamen began to evaluate their own trajectories from an ideological stand different from the one they held at the time of their involvement in the armed struggle.

From 1991 on, the first encounters between the founding nucleus of the militias and the local authorities took place, but the national government assented to a formal process of negotiation only in 1994. Time in this case was on the state's side, but both parties had high stakes in the negotiations. The militias expected to obtain political recognition and some advantages in order to consolidate their areas of influence. They risked being accused of treason by those forces that did not want to participate in the process. For the government, it was an opportunity to demonstrate its willingness to establish peace, in the face of the failure of negotiations with FARC. It feared, however, that the militias were not proper political actors, and that they were so divided that in fact there was nobody with whom to establish a dialogue. The local government, in turn, acted as a third party with its own interests, and it promoted the process as a unique event in Latin America (which in fact it was).

Between February and May 1994, a negotiation process with the participation of the Milicias del Pueblo, the Milicias del Valle de Aburrá (under the National Liberation Army), and a dissident sector of the latter, the Milicias Independientes del Valle de Aburrá, took place in Santa Helena, near Medellín. Other militia groups rejected any possibility of negotiation.

The process soon took an unexpected turn: the almost central role of the government's negotiators consisted in trying to prevent different factions of the militias from entering into a war of extermination, amid crossed accusations of complicity with the delinquency, with the authorities or with both. The urban war had served somehow to "freeze" the militia leaders into a conspiracy mentality (applied to their internal opponents), fed with popularizing literature and a visual military culture, but unable to come to the technical level required by a negotiation with the state. Even worse, the negotiation process weakened the social bases of the militiamen. The increment of homicides of militiamen in the barrios produced uncertainty among the inhabitants of the north-eastern area, who had not been consulted about the convenience of a negotiation with the government and an eventual demobilization of the militias.

After six months of struggles, an agreement was reached and publicly signed on May 26, 1994 in the northeastern area. The central points of this agreement were:

—Social investment in the communes for the improvement of the community infrastructure and the increase in the coverage of basic health, education and recreation, as well as the creation of "nuclei of civic life."

—Creation of a cooperative of surveillance (Coosercom). The government signed a contract committing itself to paying a monthly amount of 150,000 to 500,000 pesos to 358 members of the cooperative, and to lend them up to 1,750,000 pesos. The cooperative would have five headquarters and surveillance coverage of 32 barrios in the north-eastern and north-western communes. The operation of Coosercom would be assessed by the Government's Office (Secretaría de Gobierno), and it was based on an explicit commitment of its members to respect the fundamental rights and freedoms of the community and to work jointly with the security services of the state in the prevention of crime, abstaining from assuming behaviors reserved to the police.

—Political privileges. The agreement did not include the concession of political privileges (for example, a minimum number of seats in the Municipal Council). Everything depended on the initiative of the militias to promote the establishment of a political force or to make agreements with other opposition groups. The only possibility validated was that of being invited to discussion forums per zone and organs of the administration on the mayor's initiative.

—Judicial benefits. This was the most discussed point due to the difficulties of adapting the points established in Law 104, 1993, to the situation of the militiamen. Many of them were being prosecuted not for political crimes but for common delinquency. For these militia members, what could be achieved was the concession of pardons and the suspension of criminal prosecution for collaborating with justice.

The agreement was plagued with difficulties. First of all, the creation of the cooperative placed the militiamen, reinstated in civil life, in a false position.[24] Their two missions should be to control the population and to offer information to the police. This turned them automatically into "traitors" in the eyes of their former partners, and favored the degradation of an atmosphere already poisoned by mistrust and mutual accusation. The work of surveillance of the barrios, exercised no longer by the militiamen but by the members of the cooperative paid by the state itself, generated a discomfort that increased with the violations perpetrated by the members of the cooperative and their complicity with criminal acts. In the aftermath of the negotiation, numerous accusations of homicides, threats, blackmailing, and banishment on the part of the members of Coosercom were presented before the Ombudsman's Office (Defensoría del Pueblo), the Public Prosecutor's Office (Fiscalía) and the Social Pastoral. How could an organization whose main feature had been its expeditious character and its accusation of the slowness and complicity of the authorities become an appendix of the police?

Only 47 days after the signature of the agreements, an event that compromised the development of the whole process took place: Pablo García, the main leader of the Milicias del Pueblo, was murdered. The possibility of guaranteeing the cohesion of a direction team totally disappeared in the midst of the new actions of crossed revenge that unfolded soon after this event. The investigations of the public prosecutor to find the people responsible for Pablo García's murder culminated with the detention of the boss of the Milicias Independientes del Valle de Aburrá, who was accused of being the intellectual author of the crime. After Pablo's death, there was endless killing of militiamen of different factions.

In the electoral terrain, the militias also suffered a serious setback with the few votes obtained by their candidate to the town council of Medellín. As has happened in Colombia to many other actors, they had great difficulties in translating civil recognition into political recognition. For the militias, this was even harder since they were not prepared to cohabit with independent civil society organizations. For example, the social investment in the areas agreed upon with the government, instead of contributing to the legitimation of the militias, became a factor of discord among leaders and social organizations that accused the militias of unduly appropriating the achievements that were the result of community work. The voters in areas controlled by the militias chose to support the candidates of the traditional parties. The militiamen did not perceive that there was a huge gap between the elaborate and complex political culture of a generation of manual workers and their own proposals, with opaque literate references for the initiate and full of idiosyncratic experiences. Once again, the cohesive "us" of a local war ("us" of this street, "us" of this block, against those of the next one) did not have any possible translation into the scale of political life in a modern metropolis.

The relationships between Coosercom and the government became increasingly conflicted in the face of the difficulties related to the implementation of certain judicial privileges. A Supreme Court verdict struck down the benefits obtained by the militiamen, establishing that they should comply with the provisions contained in Law 1194 of 1989. Furthermore, the local authorities were uninterested in the follow-up of a process for which the national government was responsible, and there were tensions among the Coosercom, security organisms and the 4th Army Brigade regarding the delivery of ammunition in view of the disappearance of weapons and their permits.

Although around 1995 the failure of the process was evident, the government tried to introduce some correctives to revert its dynamics, but to no avail. The liquidation of the cooperative in 1996 put an end to this experience, but not to the existence of groups of militias, which continued to operate in other areas, although under difficult conditions due to the strengthening of gangs that, in turn, have used the same methods as the militia for the "protection" of people living in its areas of influence. Coexistence pacts in the barrios also continued to be made, but with the mediation of local authorities through the officials in charge of peace and coexistence.

THE EXPERIENCE OF WESTERN BOYACÁ

Perhaps the first economically meaningful enclave taken over by organized crime in Colombia was the emerald business. Given in concession by the state to private companies, the emerald mines became a space where paternalistic practices, mafia protection, and violence comfortably cohabited. The network of complex relationships between the state and illegality illustrates the differences between a "porous state" and an "absent state." From the establishment of the republic (1819), legislation was passed according to which the resources of the subsoil were the exclusive property of the nation. Until 1946, the "nation's reserves" were administered through a system of concessions, with the presence of foreign companies and of illegal occupants. In 1946, the administration of the emerald mines passed to the central bank, the Banco de la República, whose status was also ambiguous (it operated as a central bank, but it was in the hands of a board of directors from the private sector. It would only become a real public entity about twenty years later). Through complex regional, ethnic, and political networks, the bank's administration encouraged the illegal economy, sometimes in conflict and sometimes in connivance with the central government. There were several attempts to correct such an anomalous situation, but they were always unsuccessful. The state has indeed been present, but it has unsettled pre-existing social relationships instead of regulating them (this brief summary is based on Guerrero, 2001, and Guerrero, 1986).

The above-mentioned pre-existing social relationships must have been, from very early on, a complex combination of verticality and social mobility. We are talking about a simultaneously hierarchical and dynamic society, in which not only violence but also primary allegiance supplanted the legal establishment as a guarantor of contracts. The *guaqueros*, workers who went to the mines to try their luck, could enter the business if they got a *plantero* (a mediator who provided the tools and other indispensable conditions to begin the work). But they owed loyalty and respect mainly to the "leaders," entrepreneurs with their own armed forces who, in most cases, had also begun as *guaqueros*. The combination of intimidation, conspicuous expenditure, and vertiginous social upward mobility gave the leaders an enormous influence on the *guaqueros*.

> They perform multiple functions, because they act as judges when they punish offenders and reward their more faithful servants: they are referees in family quarrels or employers that give work in the mines to their relatives or friends [...] the leaders are characterized by a combination of benevolence with the poor and an implacable coldness with those whom they consider their enemies. They have performed the role of both judge and party in dealing with all sorts of conflicts, watching that everybody gets what they consider fair, and even end up defining actions concerning public order and security in the municipalities and in the whole region. (Uribe, 1992: 100)

The stability of such a paternalistic domination was occasionally disturbed by killings involving territorially defined gangs. These "wars" involved not only different armed groups but also wide sectors of the population, in so far as the restrictions and prohibitions established by the conflicting parties implied, for example, the closing off of certain roads or areas, not to mention the possibility of vendettas that might affect the relatives of combatants. Moreover, the authorities also took sides in the conflict, because the enormous wealth generated by the emerald business was used to buy their connivance and even their direct participation. "The police force is not well regarded by the population in general," says an interesting government report.

> During the last war, members of the police and of the army rented their uniforms, and agreed to perform official actions that exacerbated the rivalries even more. For example, a death that re-ignited the last war, that of Torcutato López, was executed by a soldier following the orders of the Vargas: the police arrested people that were wanted by the rival gang in order to facilitate their elimination. Some people were even killed in jail, since the paid gunmen hired to execute them had direct access to these prison facilities. (Ocampo, Rangel and Díaz, 1993: 26; see also Guerrero, 2001)

In the 1980s, the most virulent wave in the chronic confrontation among *esmeralderos* started. This time the conflict had to do with the control of the Coscuez mine. It is difficult to establish an exact date, since different oral sources, authors, and testimonies offer slightly different versions. More important than to locate the day, month, and year of the beginning of this new phase is to highlight that two large national wars were taking place at the time. On the one hand, the dispute over the control of coca crops and the mutual accusations of having denounced to the authorities the existence of such crops set Molina, an *esmeraldero* leader, against Rodríguez Gacha, a don of the drug traffic. On the other hand, the *esmeralderos* soon became involved in a territorial dispute with FARC, and created armed groups to fight them. This led them into an alliance with the paramilitary, whose headquarters were close by at that time. "In January 1987, the mayor of Otanche denounced to the press the existence of an 'alliance between common criminals and the 12th Front of the FARC' whose objective was to control the resources of the emerald mines in Boyacá. This alliance made people from the emerald area look for protection among the inhabitants of Puerto Boyacá" (Peñate, 1991). But it is not clear that these groups were able to develop a collective action, and, in fact, at the moment in which Rodríguez Gacha was in the paroxysm of his dirty war against all that smelled of the left, he was also fighting against opposing *esmeralderos*. In 1989, Rodríguez Gacha died in a police operation. In 1990, Víctor Carranza, in the name of peace and of good business, was able to begin conversations with other leaders, and was recognized as a *primus inter pares* for his long-term vision.[25] Once again, the local rhythms coincided with the global ones, and the constitutional ethos of 1991 seemed like a big river in which all the pacifist slopes converged. The arguments in favor of pacts were enunciated nationally but were then appropriated in different ways by different actors. The conversations quickly produced results, and in September 1990 all the *esmeraldero* factions signed the first peace agreement, which ensured the joint exploration of Coscuez. Later, a more institutional option was chosen with the establishment of a Committee of Development and Normalization presided by the bishop of Chiquinquirá, and including the most prominent *esmeralderos*, the governor of Boyacá, the police departmental commandant, the commandant of the Sucre battalion based in Chiquinquirá, and the manager of the company Mineralco (Ocampo, Rangel, and Díaz, 1993: 27).

How does this bizarre peace pact work? Several features should be highlighted. First, "internal peace" did exist, if by that we understand a formal end to the hostilities among the *esmeraldero* factions, and the consequent decrease in diverse kinds of homicides (Ocampo, Rangel and Díaz, 1993; see also Table 7.2).[26]

But the connections with the national war continued. Víctor Carranza, for example, did not stop in his fight against drug dealer Leonidas Vargas, following the tradition of conflict between *esmeralderos* and drug dealers (*El Espectador*, 1998; Guerrero, 2001). He also continued with his activity on the other flank: Carranza was arrested and imprisoned when the Prosecutor's

Table 7.2. COMMON HOMICIDES IN THE MUNICIPALITIES OF WESTERN BOYACÁ BETWEEN 1984 AND 1998

Municipality/ year	1984	1985	1986	1987	1988	1989	1990	1991	1992	1993	1994	1995	1996	1997	1998	TOTAL
CHIQUINQUIRÁ	18	18	28	27	30	34	26	14	52	45	34	28	31	24	25	434
BRICEÑO	10	6	9	2	8	16	9	7	10	1	1	3	3	0	4	89
BUENAVISTA	12	0	6	11	11	21	16	14	11	8	1	3	3	2	2	121
CALDAS	4	3	4	4	6	10	8	2	8	2	1	4	4	3	2	65
COPER	4	10	3	6	9	8	9	7	6	10	1	0	5	4	0	82
LA VICTORIA	3	11	4	3	8	4	11	8	1	3	0	1	0	2	1	60
MARIPI	17	23	37	45	19	41	23	11	14	12	4	7	7	3	6	269
MUZO	54	25	78	42	68	109	84	23	24	17	6	14	3	7	5	558
OTANCHE	18	24	31	32	25	13	17	32	34	27	10	9	8	19	9	308
PAUNA	24	32	17	28	31	39	19	27	43	46	12	14	12	9	13	366
QUIPAMA	0	0	0	30	63	95	37	17	11	6	3	8	7	2	2	281
SABOYA	5	8	6	8	8	20	8	7	5	13	8	7	9	7	4	123
SAN MIGUEL DE SEMA	1	1	2	0	5	2	2	3	2	6	4	3	6	1	1	39
SAN PABLO DE BORBUR	41	32	54	82	41	46	22	27	64	74	25	45	47	16	27	643
TUNUNGUA	2	4	0	1	2	3	3	5	3	2	0	0	0	0	0	25
TOTAL	212	197	279	321	334	461	294	204	288	272	110	146	145	99	101	3,463

Source: Boyacá Police Department

Office found serious indications that he was involved in paramilitary activities (*El Tiempo*, 1998). This generated multiple protests in Western Boyacá. It was believed that the prosecution of Carranza was only the first step in an attempt by the central government to dismantle the *esmeralderos'* power. Miguel Espitia, mayor of Quípama, expressed the following unconsciously Brechtian admonition: "The government should look at us in another way and understand that the leaders of this country are apostles of peace and that Don Víctor deserves respect, solidarity for his cause. This is a case that affects us all, and if we remain indifferent, tomorrow they will take us all. Because of this, we should remain united" (Records of the Verification and Normalization Committee, Coscuez, 1 April 1998).

Second, the Church has played a central role. Even the vocabulary ("apostles," "catechism," "faith") used in the basic discursive routines is colored by Catholicism. In the peace agreement that put an end to the hostilities between the parties in dispute there is a meaningful combination of the typical motives that fed the Constitution of 1991 and basic Catholic categories: "Solidarity of the same race, as Christians, brothers in the same faith," we defend "mutual harmony, […] community organization for progress, respect for all human rights, for legal norms." In sum, "we have decided to opt for the civilized and Christian way of dialogue, coexistence, concord, harmony, respect for individuality and understanding."

Furthermore, the Church has been the only party with credibility in the mediation processes. Since in these "conversations between gentlemen" there is a permanent temptation to not behave as gentlemen (the mutual post-pact accusations include murders, turning the authorities against a leader, slanders and rumors), the Church is the last instance to which one can appeal, and in spite of all the difficulties that this role implies,[27] it has learned to keep it without losing face. In addition, it has offered to the process a network of intellectuals and mediators, the priests in every town, able to formulate the terms of civic coexistence through sermons and the use of the "catechism," as well as the participation in specific disputes. "Some parish priests in Muzo and Quípama act as mediators in conflicts among the clienteles of the different leaders. These clienteles are made up of all the people in the leader's retinue, especially ordinary people without any position or rank. In this sense, the parish priests have represented a support and a channel for airing the disputes among families in favor of contrary parties in times of war" (Ocampo, Rangel, and Díaz, 1993: 22).[28] The line that separates mediation and justification is indeed a thin one. "The bishop of Chiquinquirá is an ally of the leaders, his intervention has been a bridge and mediation in quarrels and confrontations to death" (Ocampo, Rangel, and Díaz, 1993: 13). The intervention of the priests "does not exclude the exaltation of the influence of the bosses as authority figures." This is corroborated many times not only in the field but also in interviews with the protagonists of the pact.

What the leaders are proposing is in fact the reconstruction—invention would be a better word because there is no precedent—of a traditional community under their leadership. To the Church, a double civilizing role is attributed: on the one hand, to educate the social bases in civic skills and to disarm them, in a literal and figurative sense, and, on the other hand, to accompany the leaders in their maturation process, so that they are able to solve their dilemmas of collective action. For this reason, the social structure that serves as a correlate to the pact is a pyramid: "The departmental authorities describe as a pyramid the structure of the peace agreements in western Boyacá. At the base, we have the *guaqueros*, in the middle the merchants, and at the top the leaders" (Ocampo, Rangel, and Díaz, 1993: 45). Going back to the anti-political and civic slogans predominant among public opinion in the 1990s, they have also subordinated the traditional political class, making theirs the role of mediation of the politicians or using it to their own benefit. The leaders launch mayors and councilmen and support them. They are paid off with loyalty and deference. If there are not many cases of direct intimidation against the municipal authorities on the part of the leaders, this is perhaps due to the fact that disobedience is quite uncommon (although this does not mean that it is non-existent). But the range of the leaders' influence, and their capacity to subordinate the political middlemen, is not confined to the municipal field: "In the course of one of our visits we met a deputy and a municipal council representative that were inside the facilities of the Quípama mine, presumably working as *guaqueros*; their dependence on the leaders is evident" (Ocampo, Rangel, and Díaz, 1993: 28). However, as the pact developed, political competition started and some leaders had to face resounding, and unexpected, electoral defeats. The political middlemen find that peace has produced democracy. For an interviewee, "When we were at war, there were restrictions and several times the first mayors were the only candidates. The town's first two mayors chosen by popular election were the only candidates. In those elections there were no more candidates; they were of course imposed candidates, but since then there has been more democracy and more candidates in the elections."

But obviously it is a strange democracy, even taking into consideration that the opening seems to have been real, and this highlights the ambiguous role of the state. Since peace has led to real results—a decrease in homicides—the state would not want to destabilize the pact. Therefore, it does not intervene and in effect turns a blind eye,[29] but at the same time it allows the participation of the governor, and commandants of the army and the police in the Committee of Normalization. This is curious enough, since the official policy of the armed forces during the last ten years has been to refuse to participate in negotiations with guerrillas, arguing that they did not have anything to talk about with outlaw groups.[30] However, the armed forces in Boyacá have fluctuated between acceptance of the pact and alarm at the *esmeralderos'* armed power and illegal activities, keeping complete silence on the latter's connections with paramilitary activities.[31] The *esmeralderos*, in turn, see themselves as defenders of legality, and continue to see the central government as their adversary, at least while their two basic demands are not met: demands of a regional character (which the government would be willing to accept to a certain extent) and judicial immunity for the leaders (impossible to grant, among other reasons because of the international repercussions that it would have). Meanwhile, following Carranza's lead, the emerald activity has been successfully internationalized. This highlights the fact that traditionalist restoration and globalization not only can cohabit, but that there are even situations in which one is a prerequisite for the other, as Ocampo, Rangel, and Díaz have already pointed out (1993).

This situation can be maintained only if there is a politicization of war and peace among the *esmeralderos*. Some typical motives in the most openly political peace pacts—"forgive and forget," "a fresh start," regional and social demands, strict respect for the law in the post-pact period, guarantees—were imported directly from other processes, and the imitation has sometimes been truly meticulous. Nevertheless, the most important legitimating role corresponds once again to traditionalist civic conduct: to appease, to make behave, and to teach and lead a social base that has violent customs and is indifferent to the common good. The promise of a new, much better, life is associated with good behavior. Thus it is understandable that the pact has been celebrated in every locality as a true civic festival—usually paid for by the dominant leader—with speeches that proclaim the beginning of a new form of social regulation. But one cannot forget that, on behalf of the common good, petty thieves, transgressors, personal and political opponents are stigmatized, exiled, and even eliminated—they are all enemies of order.

If the machinery seems perfectly oiled, this is an erroneous impression. There are people who can look critically at and denounce this pyramidal order. With simple and direct words, they make the victim's voice, not that of the victimizers, be heard:

> Mr. Archbishop of the Diocese of Chiquinquirá, I greet you with all respect. I, Pedro Pérez, [write to you] with the purpose of making you aware of the following anomalies that have been afflicting the region of Muzo. The self-defense group, or whatever they call it, because the authorities are aware of all these crimes that are silenced because they are not announced on the radio, catch the people and take them at night to the Minero river [...] there they shoot them dead, they steal their documents so that no name appears. It is not possible that there is no justice, because to my understanding a person that kills another and takes all he has is unsociable, it is not as [they believe], that the unsociable one is the dead person. (Letter, personal file)[32]

Conclusions

The two cases that we have presented are, in many ways, deeply different, but they have something in common: an "inverted Lamarckianism." Necessity hinders, rather than facilitates, the appearance of an organized whole. The more cycles of the pendular movement there are, the more difficult it is to think outside this movement. This is not by chance, and it points to the possible importance of the Colombian case. Inasmuch as the export of formal democracy to Third World countries is one of the most important characteristics of political globalization, the tension between stable institutional macro-forms and violent dynamics, with the resulting pendular "attractor," could become widespread. For the analysts who have denounced the wrongs of the country as the result of the weight of pre-modernity, the irony may consist in the fact that the Colombian experience points more to the future of global capitalism, at least in the less-developed territories, than to its past.[33]

It is important to stress the fact that the pacts described here were not simple legitimating instruments or purely strategic maneuvers. All the parties involved made concessions, and the result was that the agreements in fact saved many lives. But the costs are also evident. The armed actors in both cases saw the opportunity to continue doing the same thing, although under new forms and with the aura of legality that the symbols and guarantees of the state confer.

As for the options for democratic development, both cases—and especially the militias—have an integrative component, but at the cost of sacrificing the individual rights of each member of the *communities* they want to incorporate. Taking this into account, the possibilities of formulating ideas on democratic emancipation are reduced. In the first place, there is no adequate language for formulating national proposals, in so far as certain demands are unacceptable under the rule of law (for example, the judicial immunity of armed actors for crimes such as homicide). In other words, the possibilities of success for these territorial dictatorships are inversely proportional to those of the establishment of a viable national framework in the world order. The socio-technical correlate of this is the inability of the armed discourses to propose policies in universalistic terms. Their speeches, admonitions, manuals, and catechisms say something—much, in fact—to their social bases, but they do not make sense when the scale of enunciation is amplified. Second, their synchronization with globalization is merely opportunistic, in the sense that they use the resources offered by it to produce a territorial enclosure based on tradition. Third, the mixtures in all the dimensions—via imitation, alliance, co-optation, representation (in the theatrical sense, as in the case of criminal actors who adopt political roles and vice versa)—are so dense that it is difficult to know "who is who" and "what is what." As we said in the beginning, the more sophisticated the exercise of local differentiation, the more complicated it is at the national level.

We highlight the fact that this experience is and has been criticized with great clarity by all kinds of voices. "Inverted Lamarckianism" refers only to the ability to make proposals. The criticism, which is certainly not restricted to the academic sphere, has centered on denouncing a certain "Colombian model," a complex system of interdependent conflicts with very visible (and unpleasant) emerging features: a terrorist state by delegation (a political form that has quickly achieved prominence), with constant regional shifts between territorial dictatorship and war, all of this amidst "a savage model of development that denies rights" (García, 1995). In many parts of the world, this may sound increasingly familiar.

Notes

1 Several actors, including terrorist groups of the extreme right, have taken advantage of this fact to mobilize broad social sectors against the peace policies. For example, in 2000, a group of peasants of Magdalena Medio, Asocipaz, supported by Carlos Castaño's vigilante group, led a powerful mobilization to prevent the government from granting a clearance area (*zona de despeje*) to the National Liberation Army. The immediate referent of this successful demand was the experience of the clearance area of FARC (Revolutionary Armed Forces of Colombia).

2 This could be, at least partially, a result of self-destruction, as we will see below. In actual cases, the three outcomes can be combined, in different processes and periods.

3 Threats of a civil war.

4 This could be true even in the case of the paramilitary groups. This explains their difficulty in leading a block of the extreme right. The paramilitary groups, staunch defenders of the old order, have turned to social practices that irreparably weaken the old order (plunder, alliance with the drug traffic, military use of resources such as gasoline and information). Something similar happens in the case of Boyacá which we will discuss later.

5 For example, changing gender roles for good. See Salazar, 1993.

6 A novel by the Antioquian writer Manuel Mejía Vallejo, *Aire de Tango*, develops this topic marvelously. A lower-class young man murders his teacher and role model precisely because he wants to imitate him.

7 Rural armed groups also developed similar practices.

8 We understand percolation as an iterated mix.

9 According to the periods established by Mario Aguilera.

10 The canonical example is surely the icon of Ché Guevara.

11 Of course, this is often consciously taken advantage of—and designed—by the elites: "We are all guilty" is a foundational statement of Colombian Republicanism (see Gutiérrez, 1998). Here there is a combination of hegemony and uncertainty, with mutual feedback.

12 Many militiamen changed the readings of the Marxist manuals for those of Deepak Chopra. The cases of re-conversion from political militancy to religious illumination are not scarce. Less provoking, but more significant, is that the armed activity of the militias—and the pacifying one of the *esmeralderos* in Western Boyacá—has been guided by a powerful pedagogic agenda whose center is the idea of self-reform and personal growth.

13 As in many other countries, self-help literature is invariably that which has sold best in recent years. The ratio of books sold to books read is perhaps also very high.

14 That is, unable to build "the material basis for consensus," to use Przeworski's expression (1995).

15 According to Marco Palacios's expression.

16 A common matrix of critical thought led to the modernization and re-founding of Colombian social science in the 1960s and 1970s. Later developments led to the institutionalization of the activity of planning within the state, and to the creation of autonomous academic communities in the universities. Some of the sectors that remained at the margins of this process—either because they considered it a betrayal or because they were not incorporated into it—supported new phases of the armed struggle. Being in a different activity, they knew well the argumentative repertoire of "the other" intellectuals, as became evident in the many debates that occurred in the last decade between figures located at both sides of the barricade (Gutiérrez, forthcoming). Of course, as time goes by, the distance between the two languages has increased, and the possibilities of translation have diminished.

17 This was not evident until very late in the 1980s.

18 The permanent game between "negation" and "recovery" of traditions is, as we will see, one of the most remarkable aspects in armed argumentation.

19 Maybe it is not possible to find them, and so it is necessary to begin with a typology: on the one hand the protest forces, on the other the paramilitary groups, etc. Nevertheless, an important aspect that should be stressed is that the paramilitary groups develop, in the discursive field, a subordinate and clearly imitative role that sometimes has an evident tone of an inverted Leninism. See, for example, Quiñones Nova, 1990, the bible of the members of the self-defense groups in wide areas of the Magdalena Medio. This is a clear and tragic example of percolation. See also Cubides, 1997.

20 A still more ambitious, and perhaps necessary, proposal would be to decipher the "ideology" of the armed groups—in Van Dijk's sense (1999) of "fundamental coordinates of social groups"—and then to evaluate similarities and differences between such groups.

21 The militiamen from Medellín also responded to the explicit demand of "cleaning" their barrios. In fact, the notion of racial cleaning/purity/ superiority has a long tradition in the department of Antioquia, and must have been inherited, amid multiple mediations and discontinuities, by the militias.

22 This may not be confined to the cases we are discussing. In an extensive interview, Jaime Guaracas, one of the historical commandants of FARC, defended the revolution on behalf of a community existing before and not after capitalism. "Those regions were so healthy, that one really wants to go back to those times" (Aldana, 1999: 32). This spirit pervades the whole interview.

23 Notice that in this exercise only literate people, with the ability to study, understand, translate and read the press, the academic texts, and government declarations, could be involved.

24 But the perspective of the government negotiators and of the militiamen should not be taken lightly: the members of the organization only knew how to make war, and their "reinsertion" into non-qualified manual labor would be unacceptable to them.

25 The trajectory of Carranza, a first-generation multi-millionaire of rural origin, is an example of another version of the "literate revolution": self-taught, he quickly learned how to move in business and in politics. In association with professional teams and allied institutions, he managed to develop his own discourse for the region (*El Espectador*, 1998 A).

26 In fact, the decrease has been substantial but partial: there are less dead people than during the war, but more than before it began. Something similar happens with the militia process in Medellín that we have just described. Apparently, the pacts did "stabilize," but did not "normalize."

27 Every leader would want the Church to be an impartial guarantor of the agreement and at the same time to favor his interests.

28 In the barrios influenced by the militia in Medellín, the priests also constituted a network of enormous importance for mediation activities and for the consolidation of the vision of a "desirable environment."

29 This produces strangeness and bitterness among the *esmeralderos*. The president of the republic was not present at either the signature of the pact or the celebration of its tenth anniversary. He was represented by delegations, and sent uncompromising, anodyne greetings.

30 They also attended the conversations with the militiamen.

31 The denunciation of such connections has been exclusively entrusted to the Public Prosecutor.

32 Spelling and punctuation have been adjusted.

33 This idea is stated and developed in detail in Gutiérrez (1997).

Bibliography

Aguilera, Mario (2001). "Justicia guerrillera y población civil, 1964–1999," Boaventura de Sousa Santos and Mauricio García (eds.), *El caleidoscopio de las justicias en Colombia*. Bogotá: Colciencias, Icanh, Universidad de Coimbra-CES, Universidad de los Andes, Universidad Nacional de Colombia, Siglo del Hombre, 389–422.

Aldana, Luis Alberto Matta (1999). *Colombia y las Farc-EP: Origen de la lucha guer-rillera. Testimonio del comandante Jaime Guaraca*. Nafarroa: Txalaparta.

Anderson, Benedict (1991). *Imagined Communities: Reflections on the Origin and Spread of Nationalism*. London: Verso.

Binford, Leigh (2000). "Empowered speech: social fields and the limits of testi-monio" (mimeo), LASA.

Cubides, Fernando (1997). "Los paramilitares y su estrategia," *Documentos de trabajo/Paz Pública*. Bogotá: Universidad de los Andes.

— (1999). "La violencia en Colombia junio de 1962: Glosas de un lector de hoy," *Revista Colombiana de Sociología*, 4(1), 34–42.

El Espectador (1998a). "Campesino, guerrero y conciliador," 11 March 1998, 4.

— (1998b). "Fiscalía acorrala a Carranza," 11 March 1998, 4.

El Tiempo (1998). "Carranza-Vargas: sin tregua," 4 March 1998, 3.

Elster, Jon (1992). *El cambio tecnológico. Investigaciones sobre la racionalidad y la trans-formación social*. Barcelona: Gedisa.

García, César Antonio (1995). "Conflicto en Urabá," *Gaceta del Congreso*, 29 September 1995.

Guerrero, Javier (1986). "La economía esmeraldífera y la violencia: la microhisto-ria institucional y contra-institucional," *5th Conference on Colombian History*. Bogotá: ICFES, 227–48.

— (2001). "Las esmeraldas en Colombia: de la corrupción a la criminalidad organizada" (mimeo).

Gutiérrez, Francisco (1997). "Gestión del conflicto en entornos turbulentos," Adriana Barrios (ed.), *Conflicto y contexto: resolución alternativa de conflictos y contexto social*. Bogotá: Tercer Mundo; Colciencias; Instituto Ser; Programa de Reinserción, 79–118.

— (1998). *La ciudad representada. Política y conflicto en Bogotá.* Bogotá: IEPRI-Tercer Mundo.

— (2001). "The courtroom and the bivouac. Reflections on law and violence in Colombia," *Latin American Perspectives* 28(1), 56–72.

— (in progress). "Cursos discursos: apuntes sobre la violentología armada en Colombia (1980–2000)" (mimeo).

Hintikka, Jaakko (1973). *Language, games and information*. Oxford: Oxford UP.

Huggins, Martha (1991). *Vigilantism and the State in modern Latin America. Essays on extralegal violence*. London: Praeger.

Jaramillo, Ana María, Ramiro Ceballos, and Marta Inés Villa (1998). *En la encruci-jada. Conflicto y cultura política en el Medellín de los 90*. Medellín: Secretaría de Gobierno de la Alcaldía de Medellín; Programa para la Reinserción; Red de Solidaridad de la Presidencia de la República; Corporación Región.

Nova, Hernán Quiñones (1990). *Magdalena Medio en marcha por la paz. Capitalismo democrático: alternativa nacional*. Puerto Boyacá: Fucpader.

Ocampo, Myriam, Carlos Rangel, and Teresa Sánchez de Díaz (1993). *Oficina de orden público y convivencia ciudadana*. Santa Fé de Bogotá: Ministerio de Gobierno.

Palacios, Marco (1995). *Entre la legitimidad y la violencia*. Bogotá: Norma.

Peñate, Andrés (1991). "Finanzas guerrilleras. Informe preliminar 1 – Análisis de prensa" (mimeo), 23 April.

Przeworski, Adam (1985). *Capitalism and Social Democracy*. Paris: Editions de la Maison des Sciences de L'Homme; Cambridge UP.

Romero, Mauricio (2001). "Los trabajadores bananeros de Urabá: ¿de súbditos a ciudadanos?", *Project Reinventing Social Emancipation*. This text can be consulted online at http://www.ces.fe.uc.pt/emancipa.

Salazar, Alonso J. (1993). *Mujeres de fuego*. Medellín: Corporación Región.

Salazar, Alonso J., and Ana María Jaramillo (1992). *Medellín. Las subculturas del narcotráfico*. Bogotá: Cinep.

Sánchez, Gonzalo, and Donny Meertens (1984). *Bandoleros, gamonales y campesinos. El caso de la violencia en Colombia*. Bogotá: El Áncora.

Santos, Boaventura de Sousa (1997a). "Pluralismo jurídico, escalas y bifurcación," Adriana Barrios (ed.), *Conflicto y contexto: resolución alternativa de conflictos y contexto social*. Bogotá: Tercer Mundo; Colciencias; Instituto Ser; Programa de Reinserción, 63–76.

— (1997b). "Hacia una concepción multicultural de los derechos humanos," *Análisis Político*, 31, 3–16.

Scott, James C. (1985). *Weapons of the Weak. Everyday Forms of Peasant Resistance*. New Haven, CT and London: Yale UP.

Uprimny, Rodrigo, and Mauricio García (2002). "Corte Constitucional y Emancipación Social en Colombia," Boaventura de Sousa Santos (ed.), *Democratizar a Democracia: os caminhos da democracia participativa*. Col. Reinventar a Emancipação Social: Para Novos Manifestos. Vol. 1. Rio de Janeiro: Record. This text can be consulted online at http://www.ces.fe.uc.pt/emancipa.

Uribe, María Teresa (1997). "La negociación de los conflictos en el ámbito de viejas y nuevas sociabilidades," Adriana Barrios (ed.), *Conflicto y contexto: resolución alternativa de conflictos y contexto social*. Bogotá: Tercer Mundo; Colciencias; Instituto Ser; Programa de Reinserción, 165–182.

Uribe, María Victoria (1992). *Limpiar la tierra*. Santa Fé de Bogotá: Cinep.

Van Dijk (1999). *Ideología*. Barcelona: Gedisa.

Wilde, Alexander (1982). *Conversaciones de caballeros*. Bogotá: Tercer Mundo.

The Politics of Recognition and Citizenship in Putumayo and in the Baja Bota of Cauca: The Case of the 1996 *Cocalero* Movement[1]

María Clemencia Ramírez

> What surprises me is the bravery of some of the people there in such a complicated environment, negotiating in the presence of the drug traffickers, the guerrillas, the protest movement, the repression against the movement …
>
> (Interview with the advisor to the minister of the interior during the negotiations of 1999)

During the months of July, August, and September of 1996, more than 200,000 *cocaleros* (peasants who cultivate and harvest coca) marched to the cities and capitals of the Guaviare, Putumayo, and Caquetá Departments and to the Baja Bota[2] region of the Cauca Department in Colombia's western Amazonia to protest the Samper government's policy of coca crop fumigation.

The 1996 *cocalero* movement in Putumayo cannot be understood in isolation from previous civic movements. From a long-term perspective, these movements represent conjunctural manifestations of a social movement of the region's inhabitants centered on the demand for recognition by the Colombian nation-state of both their citizenship and their rights. These movements are manifestations of the politics of recognition (Taylor, 1995)[3] and of the politics of citizenship, through the demand for "the right to have rights" (Dagnino, 1998).[4]

This study of the 1996 events will demonstrate that civic strikes and movements followed by the initiation of negotiations must be seen as more than just demands for better living conditions by the inhabitants of this Amazonian region. The civic strikes reiterate to the ruling class the historical condition of Putumayo as home to a marginal population, a zone of "abandonment" to which the "development" of the central region does not extend. This may be due to a lack of political will at the center, the

conception of Putumayo as an "empty" region destined to receive populations displaced from the interior, local government corruption, or the
implementation of programs that do not take into account the realities of
Amazonia, among other reasons.

A regional political leader referred to the civic strikes in Putumayo since
the 1970s in the following words:

> These social phenomena are due to and stem from the vacuum of tradi-
> tional political leadership. If truth be told, this traditional leadership is
> oriented primarily toward benefiting individuals, interest groups, or parties,
> but with few exceptions there hasn't been representation at the congres-
> sional or provincial level that has taken the leadership to truly stimulate the
> development of the department. As a consequence, confronting this vacuum
> and the innumerable problems they face, the people have taken it upon
> themselves to organize themselves in social movements, in civic movements
> that have resulted in very long strikes. This may have been costly for the
> region in weakening the fragile economy, particularly commerce, in the dif-
> ferent municipalities of the department. It has also been costly in lives and
> costly because it has generated a conflictive environment; it deepens some
> conflicts that have sprung up here among the people. (Interview with local
> political leader in Mocoa, 1999)

The repeated civic strikes can be characterized as strategic actions by the
colonos, or settlers, to make themselves visible, to be heard, and to confront
the state's image of the region. In this context, by rejecting the fumigation
of their coca crops, the *colonos* are questioning their characterization as people
at the margins of the law, migrants looking only for easy wealth, not as people
seeking to improve their standard of living, as they describe themselves. They
assert their identity and reject the idea that they have no roots in the Amazon
region, and that they wish only to enrich themselves as individuals and return
to their places of origin. These representations ignore the *campesinos* and
make them invisible, even though they have inhabited the region for three
generations and consider themselves Putumayans, not criminals.[5]

At the center, the perception of the Amazon frontier, of the periphery, is
mediated by these identifying markers, as is evidenced by the repressive
measures taken in response to these civic mobilizations. Even when the
demonstrations have not been violent, they have been repeatedly characterized as "guerrilla instigated" since the 1980s. This has effectively denied the
region's inhabitants their agency, subsuming their demands, their needs, and
their construction of collective local and regional identities into the dynamics
of the armed conflict, and recently into the implementation of the international war on drugs and/or the war on insurgent groups.

Conditions for the beginning of the *cocalero* marches of 1996

As a result of Decree No. 1956 of 1995, entitled "Colombia's Commitment in View of the World Drug Problem," the Samper government instituted measures for a frontal assault on drugs that were immediately felt in Putumayo. In December 1995, another civic strike was announced, in view of the noncompliance of the government with the agreements signed as a result of an earlier civic strike, from 20 December 1994 to 11 January 1995. Thus, on 4 January 1996, *El Tiempo* featured the headline, "Another Strike Brewing in Putumayo," and went on to explain that "the *campesinos* are only waiting for the word to initiate the Putumayo strike." The article describes a letter sent to President Samper on 26 December 1995, in which the *campesinos* reject the National Plan for Alternative Development—PLANTE (Plan Nacional de Desarrollo Alternativo), saying that it offers no solution to the *campesino*, and informing him that they "are organizing and preparing the second strike, of course in solidarity with other departments as well" (*El Tiempo*, 4 January 1996: 1A).

For its part, the government took measures in the drug war that turned out to guarantee that the strike would break out and would have the active participation of the *campesinos*: first, the police and the army acted to control the sale of gasoline and cement, both necessary in the production of coca paste, in the departments of Guaviare, Caquetá, Putumayo, Vaupés, Vichada, and Meta, through the 13 May 1996 Resolution No. 0001 of the National Narcotics Council (Consejo Nacional de Estupefacientes). Second, by means of Decree No. 0871, also of 13 May 1996, all municipalities in the departments of Guaviare, Vaupés, Meta Vichada, and Caquetá were designated as special law enforcement zones.[6] Third, two military operations were to be carried out. Plan Condor was intended to destroy crops and laboratories, seize precursors, and interdict trade. Operation Conquest, in the words of President Samper, entailed "the destruction of more than 27,000 hectares of coca, which represents 70 per cent of the coca cultivated in Colombia and approximately 15 per cent of the world total. To this end, the Armed Forces and Police will carry out an anti-narcotics operation in an area of Guaviare Department where nearly 60 per cent of the illegal crops in Colombia can be found." The government asserted that together with operations Condor and Conquest, it had "continued to move forward in the consolidation of the PLANTE program (*La Nación*, 10 July 1996: 17).

The president's ignorance of the concerns expressed for a year and a half by the *campesinos* concerning both the PLANTE program and the fumigation of their crops was evident. A few days after Guaviare was designated as the target of a military anti-narcotics operation on 16 July 1996, Operation Conquest was begun and the *cocalero* marches ensued. The *campesinos* began to mobilize against the declaration of a special law enforcement zone, against the consequent army abuses, and against the widespread fumigation that was being carried out in the department.

In mid-1995, an International Seminar on Illegal Crops had been held in Bogotá, and an agreement had been reached to mount coordinated demonstrations if fumigation were initiated in any one of the three departments. Thus the events in Guaviare set off support marches in Putumayo on 25 and 26 July, heading for the cities of Orito, San Miguel (La Dorada), Valle del Guamués (La Hormiga), and Puerto Asís. Likewise, in Caquetá Department, where the Anti-Narcotics Police had begun fumigation in Remolino del Caguán on 22 July, marches set off on 29 July (*La Nación*, 27 July 1996: 11).

The Armed Forces and Operation Conquest

Concerning the demonstration in Putumayo, police authorities "said they were surprised by the arguments used by the demonstrators," since until that time "the Government [had not] been specific about implementing fumigations in this department," one of the reasons given by the police for their assertion that the movement was sponsored by narco-guerrillas. (*El Tiempo*, 28 July 1996: 15A).[7] Nor had the Putumayo Department been declared a special law enforcement zone, in contrast to Guaviare and Caquetá. However, the leaders of the movement expected it to be so declared at any moment, and were doing everything possible to avoid this outcome. Strongly identifying with the struggles in other departments, they were also supporting them in their declarations against the measure.[8]

The idea that the guerrillas were behind the strike was again put forward by the armed forces and the central government, as it had been in the previous civic strike. This had permitted and legitimated the use of force to repress the movement, and violent measures had been taken against it. On 7 August 1998, General Bedoya, then ex-commander of the armed forces, accused the government of not having supported "large operations against the Revolutionary Armed Forces of Colombia—FARC [Fuerzas Armadas Revolucionarias de Colombia]—like Operation Conquest," adding that "[w]e have a new tragedy, the result of bad government, of a lack of will to make the political decisions to liquidate the problem of drug-trafficking" (*El Espectador*, 7 August 1998: 5A). This statement makes it clear that to General Bedoya, who was directing military operations in the zone at the time of the marches, drug-trafficking and the FARC were equivalent. Thus, from his point of view, the priority of Operation Conquest was to oppose the insurgency, or narco-guerrillas, as the military call them, and to be directed only secondarily against illegal cultivation, the target as defined by President Samper. This logic explains the statements of General Bedoya after the initiation of the marches in Guaviare: "We're going to take back this territory that is flooded with illegal crops. The government and the armed forces are going to combat this scourge. This is a war and we're going to win it. We're beginning it; it's going to take a while, but we're going to win it completely" (Statements on *Noticiero AM-PM*, 7 July 1996).

The conquest of Amazonia becomes the narrative that dominates, directs, and legitimizes the actions of the armed forces. A group identity is imposed on the *cocaleros*, who are represented as "mafioso masses, sponsored by the FARC cartel" (Statements of General Bedoya in Padilla, *Cambio 16* #164, 5 August 1996: 18). They are assigned, that is, a negative collective identity as a social group outside the law. This view essentially recreates the historical period in which the Amazon region was represented by the Spanish conquistadors as being inhabited by "savages," today by migrants and criminals under the orders of the guerrillas. In each case an "indomitable" group of people must be brought under control, dominated, and "normalized." Thus is the public image of the *campesino* movement transformed.

What's more, General Bedoya emphasizes that the mafiosi lend money to these migrants to plant, harvest, and process the coca and that once they begin to collect on those loans, "these people from every part of the country have no way to respond and are trapped, kidnapped by the FARC, which forces them to promote strikes like these that we are seeing." He asserts that the repressive measures must be sustained and the special law-enforcement zones maintained, "to protect the people who are prisoners of the mafia. They are slaves, moved around like herds of animals by the FARC terrorists" (Statements of General Bedoya in Padilla, *Cambio 16* #164, 5 August 1996: 18-20). It is thus denied that the *campesinos* are independently motivated, that they take any initiative. They are even compared to animals, and in thus dehumanizing them their exclusion from "civilized society" and their "barbarism" are reaffirmed. The "cleansing" of the region of crops and laboratories and of migrants and adventurers at the margins of the law, and the incorporation of this border region into the nation-state and, even more importantly, into the rule of law and civilization, are what legitimize the military operation.

Amazonia is portrayed as an uncivil society[9] needing to be civilized in order to develop into a true civil society. This seems to be the underlying logic of the discourse used by the central state in its approach to popular mobilization or, in the words of the military, "the disturbances" in the zone. This perspective legitimizes the use of repressive measures and the exercise of state violence to pacify these *colonos*, be they victims or accomplices of the guerrillas.

General Mario Galán Rodríguez illustrates this point of view, saying that "the strike in Putumayo is unquestionably being led by Fronts 32 and 48 of the FARC, which have forced the *campesinos* to come out and protest against the government. The *campesinos* don't know why they are in these protests, and the terrifying thing is that they've been compelled to leave their farms to gather in the three municipalities. The only interests at stake here are those of the narco-guerrillas," and those interests are purely economic (*La Nación*, 2 August 1996: 9). This exemplifies what Gutiérrez and Jaramillo (2001) call the criminalization of social protest, "a key instrument in the repertoire of responses to contestation" in Colombia, and the paradoxical relationship between the political and the criminal that began to manifest itself during the 1980s, when "the conscious effort of organized crime to become a political actor and of opposition groups to explain their ties to criminality" were observed.

"We were obliged to march voluntarily": the FARC and the Civic Movement for the Comprehensive Development of Putumayo (Movimiento Cívico por el Desarrollo Integral del Putumayo) in the organization of the *cocalero* movement

The previous civic strike had taken place between 20 December 1994 and 5 January 1995, and had covered the municipalities of Orito, San Miguel (La Dorada), and Valle de Guamés (La Hormiga). During that period, the Regional Civic Movement of Putumayo[10] was formed. After a year and a half of existence, it expanded to cover other municipalities of Lower Putumayo, such as Puerto Asís and Puerto Guzmán. Local movements were also organized in a coordinated fashion in Orito, Puerto Guzmán, Puerto Asís, and Puerto Leguízamo, in an attempt to assert political and ideological hegemony throughout the region.

> We returned to Putumayo [after the International Seminar on Illegal Crops, 14 and 15 July 1995] and the leaders agreed to organize another strike. The problems to be addressed were on the one hand organizational and on the other operative: What will we do? In Orito the problem was tactical and in Puerto Guzmán and Puerto Asís it was organizational and political: What social and political characteristics will this movement assume? The decision was then made for all the leaders of Putumayo, Upper, Middle, and Lower, to meet together. At this meeting the leadership broke with the Civic Movement of Orito, Valle del Guamués, and San Miguel, and, with Campesino Unity (Unidad Campesina) of Puerto Guzmán, formed the Civic Movement for the Comprehensive Development of Putumayo. The movement was organized by *veredas*, or districts. Leaders were chosen for each *vereda* and financial contributions were pledged or made by all present. Orito, Valle de Guamués, and San Miguel were the most experienced. (Interview with advisor to the Base Group, 1999)

This Regional Civic Movement of Putumayo, which became the Civic Movement for the Comprehensive Development of Putumayo, set out to build a "unified struggle," meaning not only the unification of all kinds of movements in the department, that is, ethnic, political, and social, but also coordination with movements in other departments where illegal crops were cultivated, such as Caquetá, Guaviare, and Meta:

> We discussed a national mobilization so that the House of Representatives would meet in order to address this matter as a social problem affecting the country. And in a year and a half we have been able to prepare [...]. [W]e wrote a very ambitious document and we were aware that it was utopian; we were saying, we need to mobilize at least a million *campesinos* in Colombia to make the state understand that this is not a criminal problem, it's a social problem. (Interview with indigenous leader, the director of OZIP during the marches, 1999)

This national mobilization was also intended to put forward the necessity of agrarian reform, given the magnitude of the problem. In addition, the creation of a National Board of Negotiations (Mesa Nacional de Concertación) was proposed to analyze state policy with regard to crop substitution, seeking to upgrade the discussions previously conducted only at the regional level.

In Putumayo, the Civic Movement for the Comprehensive Development of Putumayo began the process of identifying leaders in the community such as members of the Communal Action Committees (Juntas de Acción Comunal), teachers, health workers, and so on, to begin preparations for the marches. The goal was to build a department-wide civic movement that would involve all 13 municipalities of Putumayo, and in which not only indigenous and *campesino* coca growers and harvesters but also leaders of other sectors would participate.

This movement was not exempt from the ambivalence that has characterized social and political practice in Putumayo. It was subject to tension over whether or not to maintain autonomy as a social and/or political movement with respect to both the traditional parties and the armed groups that operated in the region. During the 1996 *cocalero* movement, two things had become clear: the structural problem of the Western Amazon region (Putumayo, Caquetá, and Guaviare) in relation to the violence and conflicts engendered by the growing of coca and drug trafficking; and the strong and active connection between the *campesinos* and the guerrillas.[11]

The ambiguity of this alliance is made clear in the words of a *campesino*: "We were obliged to march voluntarily." The guerrillas not only supported the movement but promoted it in an authoritarian manner. Nevertheless, to claim that the *cocalero* movement was the result of fear and/or guerrilla terrorism is to gloss over the organizing processes characteristic of the local population, to legitimate the view from the center that could assert in the press, "Guerrillas Responsible for Strike in Putumayo," and to deny the *campesinos* and other inhabitants of Putumayo their agency in the organization of the movement, as well as their desire and ability to participate in the discussion over regional development plans and policies during negotiations.[12]

In addition, it is important to stress that the FARC have promoted the practice of decentralization and citizen participation in the Amazon region as a function of their general political line:

> Popular local governance is an alternative form of participation in civil society that affords people an opportunity to denounce the reigning clientelism and corruption, and to move toward the solution of their most deeply felt needs and problems. For this very reason citizens have the political obligation to exercise it, in order to be really free. [...] [L]ocal power should contribute to the stabilization and adaptation of localities seeking to construct a collective identity within the framework of their given local diversity. It should help prepare the people to come to terms with social change, always seeking the common good, the basis of all republican legitimacy. (FARC, *Revista Resistencia*, 1998)

From this perspective, the FARC promotes not only the demands made by the *campesinos* for state services and infrastructures, but also their demands for citizen participation in the planning and execution of other projects to benefit the region. It follows from this political line that the FARC does not seek to substitute itself for the state as a provider of public services and welfare. The state should serve the people and be answerable to them for its actions. This concept is reflected in the FARC approach to public administration at the municipal level. The mayor must produce an administrative plan, implement projects, and present reports to demonstrate that funds have been used to benefit the community and have not been squandered or mismanaged, that is, that the needs of the community are being served. In the same way, the FARC supports the civic strikes to demand that the state fulfill its functions. Thus it is not so clear that they oppose the state presence and investment in the Amazon region. FARC activities have been interwoven with state policies in the region. I therefore differ with Ferro and Uribe (2001) who, in their study of Caquetá, conclude that, for the FARC, the marches were "primarily seen as part of the development of a political-military project" whose strategic goal is the taking of power. Thus, they describe "alternate citizenship" as a "political project of the FARC, which intends to engage the population as citizens of a new state ruled by that organization."[13]

By lending logistical support to the *cocalero* movement, the FARC not only helps strengthen the negotiating position of the Civic Movement leadership in their demands upon the state but is also able to present itself as the defender of *campesino* interests. In the words of *Comandante* Joaquín of the FARC's Southern Block, "The FARC supports the civilian population in the demands they make of the corrupt elements, because we have nothing to defend but the interests of the population." And in reference to the 31 August 1996 takeover of the Las Delicias military base in Putumayo and the holding hostage of 60 soldiers, he says: "Ours was an act of solidarity against the inhuman, repressive, and punitive treatment being meted out to the *campesinos* in the south of the country, whose only crime was to demand that the state fulfill its obligations" (ANNCOL, 1998: 3).

Nevertheless, one must keep in mind that the relationship the FARC establishes with the *campesinos* is ambivalent. While on the one hand they promote participatory democracy, they simultaneously exercise authoritarianism over the population. This provides the basis for the FARC's double discourse; by proclaiming themselves the defenders of *campesino* interests, they legitimize both their military actions and their authoritarianism. This was made clear in the outcome of the movement.

The Communal Action Committees as an organizational network for the marches, and their relative autonomy from the FARC

The role played by the FARC in the organizational conception of the marches, at both the preparatory stage and at the time of their execution, has been acknowledged. However, "it was the communal action committees that took responsibility for what needed to be done in each *vereda*" (testimony of a *campesino* in Puerto Asís, 1999). It should be pointed out here that the Communal Action Committees were brought together in a network that facilitates social and political relations among the inhabitants of Amazonia at the *vereda*, municipal, and police inspectorate levels. Government, FARC, and political party representatives establish their working relationships in the *veredas* through their contacts with the leadership of the Committees. The leaders of the Civic Movement for the Comprehensive Development of Putumayo and of the Pacific Movement of Cauca (Movimiento Pacífico del Cauca), for the Case of the Baja Bota of Cauca,[14] organized the marches through the Communal Action Committees:

> At first we organized it through the police inspectorates. That was the first part, that the police inspectorate would call the *veredas* together. In the meeting of *veredas* we would just deal with the presidents of the Communal Action Committees. Then we went down as soon as this group was oriented, and there were three- or four-day workshops; we did workshops on the whole problem, on the whole situation that was coming. They went and they led their workshops as they understood things and then we would get the reports. The people gave their reports and among the most important

things that we saw was that they didn't respond to the *campesinos'* questions but rather that they would bring questionnaires with them to find out about the strengths and weaknesses of the people, because we were going to go *vereda* by *vereda* and at one point we spread out. Sometimes forty of us would go and sometimes one would go alone. They would tell us in such and such a place three *veredas* are meeting, so one guy would go here and one there. That's how we divided ourselves up. (Interview with an indigenous leader, director of OZIP during the marches, 1999)

Consciousness-raising was begun in these workshops about the imminence of fumigation as a central policy of the government at that time and about the importance of unifying the Civic Movement regionally and by depart-ment, incorporating municipalities not previously identified as coca-producing, such as Upper Putumayo, Sibundoy, Santiago, San Francisco, and Colón. Further, there were explanations of the national and international contexts relevant to illegal crops. In this way the leaders sought to stimulate volun-tary and informed participation by the inhabitants of the *veredas* involved in the mobilization. In addition to the workshops, there were forums on illegal crops and fumigation. The desire for the genuine participation of the community is a constant throughout each phase of the mobilization and afterwards, when the movement is evaluated and compliance with the accords is monitored. The leaders try not to reproduce the practices of the dominant political culture from which they want to distinguish themselves. In their own words, they do not want to "become a head without a body" (statement of a leader at a civic strike evaluation meeting, 24 September 1996).

It is clear that the actions promoted or supported by the FARC have not negated the capacity of the governed to react or to act as individual or col-lective subjects. The people of the region negotiate with the FARC as an institutional representation of authority, but while the FARC does exercise authority to maintain order, control, and discipline in the region, it is seen by the inhabitants of Amazonia not as a state within a state, as some have asserted, but as "a government within the government," as Manuel Marulanda Vélez has defined their practices (interview in *Semana*, 18 January 1999: 22). The authority of the FARC is at once accepted and resisted by the population. A leader of the Communal Action Committee in Piamonte comments:

It's the FARC that have empowered us and they are responsible for the orga-nization's progress. The guerrillas help the people organize and promote the coordination of the Communal Action Committees. The guerrillas establish order in the region and they are obeyed. And the community has become aware of the necessity to organize itself and give information when the census is taken. Before they didn't want to collaborate and they treated me like I was just being nosy. (Testimony of the leader of the Communal Action Committee of La Consolata, in Piamonte, 1988)

Although the FARC's orders are obeyed, they are often challenged and negotiated. This was the case in the Baja Bota of Cauca when the marches were about to begin. The FARC had determined that some of the *veredas* would head for Caquetá, and some for Putumayo. However, people from some of the *veredas* of the Baja Bota were opposed to leaving their zone, because their agenda included pressuring for the creation of a municipality and they saw this as their great opportunity:

We were never advised by the guerrillas; what we have done has been based on the convictions of our own leaders. As I was telling you, in the strike they opposed us, the guerrillas, because they wanted us to go to Putumayo and Caquetá. We didn't do that and they disagreed with us. Because we said that we had to struggle in Cauca. No, there was no confrontation. They just stopped helping us. They didn't help us. There wasn't any discussion about it, they just sent word that they weren't helping us and we would see what we could do. Because they thought we were a weak group. Both the guerrillas and the government thought that since it was such an isolated zone, our strike was going to fail. And it was one of the best strikes there was, because it had a national impact due to its being peaceful, because of the quality of the negotiators, and because of the things we gained in the negotiations. It was one of the best.

One complains louder when the pain is greater. If the pain isn't great, you hardly complain at all. But if the pain is great, then yes, there can be a dialogue. That's what happened to us, because since we felt the need, and saw the need, we motivated ourselves because we had to solve the problems. (Interview with a member of the Negotiating Commission of the Civic Strike in the Baja Bota of Cauca, 1998)

It is clear that the space to negotiate with the guerrillas is created by the population and stems from their own needs and earlier struggles. The establishment of a municipality in the Baja Bota of Cauca had been proposed by the community since the 1980s. This demand had been the focus of earlier civic movements and the people of the zone took it up again at this opportunity.[15] However, although some *veredas* of the Baja Bota did not head for Caquetá and Putumayo, others did. So the tension and ambivalence in the relationship with the FARC didn't go away, although it is maintained that they were not "advised" by the guerrillas. It is important to point out that the government and the guerrillas were seen in the same light. Both predicted that the strike would fail, and both were proved wrong;

the movement maintained its autonomy and won a victory in the establishment of the Municipality of Piamonte.

With respect to Putumayo, the women's representative in the Base Group[16]
also points to the relative autonomy of civil society in relation to the FARC:

> The guerrillas named some people and civil society named other people to
> lead the marches, so they opposed their orders [referring to orders from the
> FARC]. (Interview with the women's representative in the Base Group,
> February 1999)

With regard to the role of the FARC in organizing the movement, a
campesino woman from the Baja Bota of Cauca says:

> Let's say coordinators, not directly, but yes, they were working with us there.
> They took charge of forming the committees; they saw who would distrib-
> ute the supplies, and they also requested help from Popayán. Baby formula
> for the children was sent over from there, and they organized who would
> prepare it for the children. Every day the children got formula. If they hadn't
> been there maybe things wouldn't have been as organized as they always
> were, because you know sometimes when there are things like that, some
> people want more than others, and problems come up. Even the way it was
> there were fights sometimes. After three days when the people were set up
> with their shelters, then they arrived and got it organized how we were going
> to build the shelters. (Interview with Oliva Macías, 1999)

We can conclude that the FARC reserved for itself the responsibility for
the general organization of the march and for overseeing each of the tasks
and prohibited the production of coca and commercial activities during the
organizational period, but that the *campesinos*, through their leaders, brought
concrete proposals to the negotiating table on behalf of the movement and
that their leaders defended the interests of the population they represented.

The negotiations: a space to confront identities and demand the recognition of their history of violence and displacement

The central government's negotiating delegation was made up of a delegate
from the President's Office, an advisor from the Ministry of the Interior, the
vice-minister of agriculture, and representatives of the ministries and decentralized state institutes. This delegation traveled to Putumayo with orders not
to negotiate on any point concerning eradication or fumigation of illegal
crops, but to reach agreements on the provision of services and the construction of infrastructural projects already budgeted for (interview with the
delegate of the presidency at the negotiations, 1999).

For their part, the leaders of the Civic Movement, meeting with the leaders of the communal action committees in the different towns where they were active, elected their representatives to the negotiations and traveled to Orito to begin the process.

> The Orito negotiating team was selected by the Civic Movement for the Comprehensive Development of Putumayo. There were 600 people from Puerto Guzmán, and they joined with Puerto Limón and Santa Lucía to make a total of 4,000. They demanded the right to elect a delegate to the talks themselves. They didn't allow the car to set off from Mocoa without him and they threatened to turn back if the car didn't take him. They called the mayor to ask his permission and that's the way it got done. (Testimony of the women's representative in the Base Group, 1999)

As can be deduced from this testimony, the *campesino* participants in the marches were able to exert pressure to be allowed to participate in the negotiations, but the Civic Movement maintained its leadership. The goal was to have a representative of each municipality, representatives of the organized *campesino* groups, and of the Civic Movement leadership.

Among the government negotiators in Putumayo there was a consensus to recognize the Civic Movement as the representative of the *cocaleros*. In the words of the Interior Ministry advisor, comparing the negotiations in Orito with those in Caquetá, where different groups led the negotiations, "In Putumayo we always had the same interlocutors and always saw the same people." Another government representative also recognized "the long-standing civic tradition of combativeness and of struggle" in Putumayo (interview with a representative of the governmental Solidarity Network during negotiations, 1999). Ferro and Uribe (2001) do not ascribe autonomy to the *campesino* march leadership in the Caquetá negotiations, even though a FARC commander interviewed by them states that "Although the movement followed some very general orientations, its organization, from operational questions to the negotiations, was exclusively under *campesino* leadership." This account coincides with the situation that I have described in Putumayo.

The leaders of the Civic Movement began the negotiations with a presentation on the history of regional colonization in order to understand why coca is the most important local crop. They began by describing the Amazonian colonization as a result of Colombia's internal conflict during the period of political violence, as well as the continual expulsion of *campesinos* from the Andean region, the lack of land being among the principal causes. They also pointed out the lack of adequate policies for the Amazon region, and, most importantly, its virtual abandonment by the state. They explained their understanding of a regional identity within the Colombian nation state, a regional identity molded by the conflict and the consequent arrival of the displaced population, all of which defined the region as marginal in relation to the center of the country.[17] Consequently, they demanded state and government recognition of the social and economic problems of the region that result from these historical and structural factors. The same document continued: "For these reasons, the [social] problematic deserves a different approach from the state and the government than that taken toward the drug traffickers and the insurgency" (first draft of the initial proposal of the Civic Movement for a negotiated agreement, courtesy of Teófilo Vásquez, 1996).[18] This position challenged the identity that had been assigned to them, an oppressive stereotype that made them invisible and precluded the idea that they should be consulted on their own situation. A *campesino* expressed this idea:

> And if we actually continue growing coca, then how can they tell us that we have to submit to national and international public opinion, to say that it's we *campesinos* who grow coca, when it's part of the problems that you yourselves have recognized? We're shown as drug traffickers or narco-guerrillas all around the world, when we have a right to some honor as *campesinos*. We're demanding that it be recognized that we're forced to break the law, that's exactly what it is, and that's just as much of a right too. Do we have to put up with seeing ourselves portrayed to the public as criminals because we plant coca to support our families? Isn't that against the constitution too? (Oscar Reyes, spokesperson for the communities speaking at the negotiations. (Óscar Reyes, spokesman for the communities in the negotiations, Orito, 1996)

So the *campesinos* ask the state and the government to recognize them as social actors:

> The *campesino* who submits to voluntary eradication and substitution *should be a social actor and a valid interlocutor in the search for [these] solutions there*, and not a completely distant subject; because we consider that as part of the problem we are also part of the search for solutions. (A *campesino* leader speaking at the negotiations, August 1996. Emphasis added)

The government representatives, for their part, put the legal problem ahead of the social and economic problems of the region:

> In a country like Colombia there are certain laws that we must obey, let's be clear on that. A number of us have reiterated that, and have done so on several occasions. When the minister of the interior was asked about the scope of the commissions, he was very clear. The Colombian policy toward the drug problem, toward trafficking in narcotics, would not be negotiated.

One of the elements of that policy, specifically Law 30, tells us that the person who grows coca is committing a crime. That's what impedes us from considering gradualism. There are things here we can discuss and that surely, for example, the idea that the small grower is a valid interlocutor in the search for comprehensive solutions, but in what way? *Dr. Díaz told you a moment ago that that was completely acceptable, not as a social actor but as a valid interlocutor, because the recognition of a social actor can't be based on the fact that that social actor is committing a crime.* (PLANTE representative speaking at negotiating session. Emphasis added)

To be denied any role but that of valid interlocutor to implement programs is seen by the *campesinos* as depriving them of their agency, of their full and active participation in the definition of those programs, and of their recognition as a social group. It is a continuation of the state policy of setting policies and designing programs for the eradication of coca without consulting them, a way of doing things that has meant the failure of the production projects in the Amazon region.

In addition, the government representatives repeated the impossibility of negotiating issues like the gradual substitution of other crops for coca or the social recognition of illegal crops. They also blurred the position of the Civic Movement:

> The movement insists that they are not interested in a comprehensive agrarian policy, in electrification, in roads, in health, in education, in housing, in human rights, in telecommunications, or in territorial organization. Instead the movement begins with the premise that Colombian legislation on the control of narcotics must be changed. This commission regrets that position and understands that what this movement and its organizers are asking for is a legislative reform process that is the responsibility of the National Congress. (vice-minister of agriculture speaking at the negotiations in Orito, 1996)

The leaders of the movement responded to make it clear that they were not demanding the negotiation of the law but rather a formal recognition of a social problem that cannot be solved with the fumigation of the coca crops (*El Tiempo*, 7 August 1996: 10A).

What stands out in the position of the government representative is his wish to turn the discussion toward an agreement on basic needs and infrastructure. He rules out further discussion of the fundamental structural problem of the Amazonian economy, and beyond that, of the agricultural sector in the country. The Civic Movement leaders were prioritizing structural solutions over the negotiation of the series of needed services that the government representatives wanted the negotiations to concentrate on. To the *campesinos*, the problem was not just whether or not to eradicate coca, as the government commission asserted. The problem that they wanted considered was the history of violence and repression that they have been subject to, and their lack of alternatives. That is, they demanded the recognition by the state of their historical marginalization and exclusion. Faced with the unwillingness of the government to consider this, the Civic Movement leaders suspended the talks for one day.

The ambivalence of the state representatives toward the *cocalero* movement and the signing of the first agreement

The *cocalero* movement demonstrated the internal divisions of the state representatives. In the first place, the ambivalence of the local and regional authorities toward the national representatives was made clear. They could choose to act as public servants, identify with the state, and therefore support the central government, or they could identify with the social, economic, and political problematic of the region, and therefore support the *cocaleros* and/or the leaders of the Civic Movement.

The local officials identified themselves as Putumayans and sided with the *campesinos*. Some of them also acted as advisors to the Civic Movement leaders at the negotiations. The mayors, for their part, did not feel a commitment to the central government representatives, since in their opinion the process of decentralization brought them problems rather than solutions. From the beginning of the movement they had supported the demand of the *campesinos* to negotiate with central government officials, since it was they who had the authority to make decisions concerning national funds and subsidies. The governor vacillated, siding now with one side, now with the other, depending on the situation.

But there was an even sharper division among the representatives of the central government. On the one hand were the attorney-general, the director of PLANTE, and the commander in chief of the armed forces. This sector of the government considered coca-growing *campesinos* to be drug traffickers. Therefore the attorney-general exerted pressure on the minister of the interior to insure that his representatives at the negotiations not sign any agreement that would undermine the policy of fumigation and total eradication of coca, which he equated with signing negotiated agreements with criminals. This pressure was in part a response to the government's position at that moment, as it was being evaluated for its ties to drug trafficking. It had been decertified by the United States in January 1996, and was facing a second decertification in 1997, which in fact did come to pass.

The other sector of the government was primarily represented by the Solidarity Network (Red de Solidaridad), and by other officials at the table who had a history of work in the region. They wanted to be able to reach an agreement, despite the threat that they could be investigated for negotiating with drug traffickers. They wanted to avoid further loss of prestige by the government, but they also sought to forge closer ties with the *campesinos* in order to neutralize the support the guerrillas were providing them. For these reasons, this sector supported the idea of the Civic Movement to sign an initial agreement for an Emergency Plan for Comprehensive Development, to be called "For a Putumayo without Coca and Sustained in an Solidary Economy." They had insisted that the phrase "without Coca" be added to avoid conflict with the other sector of the government:

> So really around this idea of a Putumayo without coca, everyone had his own interpretation. For us it was a more basic thing. More than to achieve a political alliance among the *campesinos*, our strategy was to achieve an alliance between the *campesinos* of Putumayo and the authorities, at least the national ones or the ones we were representing. And we had a strong interest in allying ourselves with them, of demonstrating that with an alliance basically between the *campesinos* and the government, it was possible to construct a different Putumayo. […] To the guerrillas this alliance is a disaster, but that's our goal, to win over the campesinos. The guerrillas' goal is to maintain their military control over the area, their influence. (Interview with the representative of the president at the negotiations, 1999)

The government negotiators felt that the Civic Movement leaders were under pressure from the FARC:

> They were speaking in the name of a civic movement and yes, the Civic movement exists, but we all know that behind the Civic Movement there is a lot of pressure by the armed actors in that region. What we were seeing from our side's point of view, the state's, was that their positions were very closed, not very spontaneous. It was they, not we, who were representing the state, who were very cautious about what to write, what to sign, what commitments to make. We were really representing a tremendous political will to try to resolve the problem. (Interview with an official of the Solidarity Network, 1999)

Nevertheless, it wasn't clear that the Civic Movement negotiators were completely dependent on the FARC to make decisions for them. Another official indicates that the FARC wanted to put off the signing of the agreement, but, despite their position and that of the attorney-general, it was signed:

> And a version was drawn up that was broad and vague enough to avoid any danger of legal action by Attorney-General Valdivieso, who was monitoring absolutely every move and every decision. We couldn't even finish a draft

proposal in Orito before there was a public reaction to the attorney-general and the government having made or not made concessions in the negotiations. Everyone was watching and spying on everyone: the FARC, the government. (Interview with the advisor to the minister of the interior, Popayán, 1999)

The first agreement that was signed stated that the *campesino* representatives should produce this Emergency Plan for the Comprehensive Development of a Putumayo without Coca, thus securing a decision-making role for the *campesinos*. It was also agreed that voluntary eradication and substitution would require a joint effort on the part of the *campesinos,* the *colonos,* indigenous people, the government, and cooperating international parties. In this way the small coca producer achieved practical recognition as "a valid interlocutor in the definition and implementation of comprehensive solutions" (Agreement of 1996). In other words, their voice regarding policies and projects in the region was recognized.

General Bedoya immediately declared that the agreement had been signed behind the army's back, said that there should not have been negotiations with people at the margins of the law, and reiterated that the overriding need was to continue fumigating (*El Espectador*, 28 August 1996: 3A). Fumigation is another form of violence, as the *campesinos* made explicit on the signs that they carried in the marches: "Fumigation equals unemployment, violence, displacement, poverty, etc; Samper has declared war on us; No more abuses; No to fumigation, yes to peace; Support the strike!"

For his part, the minister of the interior declared that "the fumigation of illegal crops was not negotiated in the agreements signed on Sunday in Orito with the coca growers of Putumayo," adding that "[t]he government takes its responsibility very seriously. We intend to eradicate illegal crops in the country, a non-negotiable step toward our fundamental goal, which is to be a nation without coca" (*El Tiempo*, 13 August 1996: 3A).

A *campesino* representative at the negotiations, however, indicated that "in order to avoid fumigation or any other method of forcible eradication of illegal crops, we agreed with the government on a voluntary plan of crop substitution" (*El Tiempo*, 13 August 1996: 3A). The *campesinos* considered the Emergency Plan for Comprehensive Development to be a plan for the gradual substitution of legal crops for coca and the establishment of an alternative economy.

These two understandings of the initial agreement are completely opposite. While the government said that eradication had not been negotiated, the *campesinos* said that they had achieved agreement on a plan for voluntary eradication as opposed to forced eradication by means of fumigation, and that this was an implicit recognition of the small *campesino* producers. Each side had its own interpretation and each side claimed a victory.

SEEKING SOCIAL EMANCIPATION THROUGH
THE CONSTRUCTION OF CITIZENSHIP AND THE EXERCISE
OF PARTICIPATORY DEMOCRACY

Santos (1998) has described how the hegemonic global forces of exclusion that he calls social fascism are resisted. They are confronted by the initiatives of grassroots organizations, of local and popular movements that endeavor to counteract extreme forms of social exclusion and open new spaces for democratic participation. Such is the case of the *campesino cocaleros*, a stigmatized population, subjected to Law 30 of 1986, the Narcotics Statute, which criminalizes them. Their geographical space, Amazonia, has historically been constructed as a home to "savages" or criminals, a space of exclusion and marginalization. The *cocalero campesino* social movement demanded inclusion through negotiations (*concertación*) with government agencies, as described by Foweraker with reference to those Latin American social movements that had principally sought "local and immediate solutions to concrete problems" and "concentrate these demands in the state as provider of public services and guarantor of the conditions of collective consumption" (1995: 32). The demand for negotiations and signed agreements in Putumayo represents the demand for social, civic, and political citizenship rights, and for the recognition of local social and/or political movements. In the last analysis, it is a demand for inclusion in the nation-state, in the participatory democracy that it promotes, but to which Putumayans have not had access, and it is an assertion of new democratic forms and new manifestations of citizenship.[19]

Considering that "[a]utonomy, far from being incompatible with hegemony is a form of hegemonic construction" (Laclau and Mouffe, 1985:140), I argue that the *cocalero* movement sought an articulation with the hegemonic state discourse concerning democracy and citizen participation as a form of empowerment. It displays new processes of signification, which, although molded by hegemonic discourses, seek to contest them, redefine them, link up with them, or abandon them. This autonomy should be understood as both interconnected with and in opposition to the hegemonic state and other dominant groups in the region, such as the FARC. We must also keep in mind that the *cocalero* movement emerged as such in response to the state's stigmatization of *campesinos* for their growing of coca. The movement's power thus derives from the systematic abuses of the state, that is, the indiscriminate fumigation of coca crops, a repressive policy promoted by the United States without regard for the basic needs of the region's inhabitants, and without regard for their repeated demands for an alternative solution. As coca growers they are the first link in the chain of global drug trafficking, but they are the weakest link, and locally coca is simply a crop like other crops. While economically advantageous, it does not substantially change the living conditions of its growers. Molano (1994) has pointed out that coca-growing has not only brought military repression, but has also strengthened the position of the *campesino colonos*, to the extent that the government has considered it necessary to negotiate with them directly and to take their interests seriously, as we have seen in the analysis of the Putumayo negotiations.

In Putumayo, the sense of extreme exclusion is a defining trait, so the struggle to construct citizenship is a struggle for "the right to have rights." Arendt (1949: 30), who coined this phrase, noted that the existence of rights had been transformed from an *a priori* condition to a demand. She also emphasized the right of every human being to belong to some political community, because it is within such communities that rights materialize. Citizens themselves must defend their rights, but particularly the right not to be denied the rights that accrue to community members, and above all the right to citizenship. In a context of exclusion, the definition of a "new citizenship" becomes both a cultural and political act. With regard to exclusion, social movements, and citizenship, Foweraker (1995: 113–14) concludes:

> The question of exclusion is critical to an appreciation of the relationship between social movements and democracy in contemporary Latin America. [...] Indeed, in the present context of partial democracy, the best working definition of a social movement is a popular organization which can make plausible claims to exercise a perceptible impact on the extension and exercise of the rights of citizenship.

This questions the assignment of places of exclusion in society, a predetermined social order, and demonstrates the fundamental character of citizenship as a politics of culture (Dagnino, 1998). The political appropriation of constitutional rights and, above all, of the principles of citizen participation, was the only discernible legal strategy of advancing the *cocalero* movement for social emancipation in a conflictive and marginalized area.[20] Thus the Civic Movement for the Comprehensive Development of Putumayo called upon the national government to collaborate in the solution of Putumayo's problems, stating:

> In this situation we speak as Putumayan citizens first, without any kind of political preference, without sectarianism. *We are simply exercising our citizenship rights*, on a moral basis and in solidarity. We understand that it is the general population that is most negatively affected. We ask the national government to lend us a helping hand to surmount the complex set of problems that we experience. If that does not happen, this will soon become a breeding ground for illegal and disruptive acts, which may bring profoundly negative and undesirable consequences. (Main presentation of the Civic Movement at the regional forum "Peace and Human Rights," Puerto Asís, 7 May 1997. Emphasis added)

To identify oneself first as a citizen of Putumayo is of course an identification with one's birthplace or current place of residence; yet, above all, it is the re-establishment of one's contract or relationship with the state.[21] As Tilly (1996) says, the relationship with the state defines citizenship. This relationship may be weak or strong, depending on the transactions that take place between the state and the people under its jurisdiction.[22]

In identifying first as citizens and second as Putumayans, citizenship was being constructed, defined by membership and a sense of affiliation where none had existed before, or at least none that had ever been made explicit or recognized as such. The *campesinos* were implicitly claiming to belong in the region, contradicting their characterization as rootless migrants in search of easy money. This demand for "membership" was an exercise of "the politics of citizenship."[23] But, above all, they sought to be recognized by the state as an distinct group, with a voice to represent them, and the right to define together with the state the policies that would benefit them as residents of Putumayo. To this end they proposed citizen participation according to the guidelines laid out in the Constitution. Through this citizen participation, they sought to contest the illegality of their situation. As Putumayan citizens they wished to act within the law, and even more, to bring the law to life. This implied a form of empowerment for them because they sought recognition and participation as a differentiated social group with roots in this region, and, above all, with a voice to defend their rights as small growers of coca.[24]

They were struggling for the right to participate in defining policies and a specific plan for Amazonia in order to secure their inclusion in the nation-state. As Hall and Held point out (1989: 181), the state must intervene to assure an appropriate conception of citizenship. The leadership of the Civic Movement sought to secure this intervention, so much so that they warned the state that if a hand was not extended to them, "illegal and disruptive acts" would be committed. During the negotiations, they insisted that the government should guarantee economically feasible alternatives to coca. Even though they spoke of the need for popular participation in decision-making and in project- and program-design, they also insisted, both in the negotiations and in the implementation of the agreements, that the government was ultimately responsible for the success of any projects that would be effectuated. The government was also held responsible for the strike. One banner read, "The government is forcing us to strike." The *campesinos* believed that the Colombian state was responsible for the spreading cultivation of illegal crops, and the least it could do was give them time to consolidate an alternative economy, which is why they insisted on negotiating a gradual eradication of coca. They also brought to the table a long-standing complaint that weighed heavily on the popular memory—the government has never been able to provide needed services to the population. Given the popular conception of the state as an institution that should care and provide for the population, people have tended to maintain a passive attitude, waiting to receive services. Two banners thus read, "We are a peaceful people waiting for solutions," and "Our need for public services makes us strike."

Jelin (1996) has described how the relation between subordinate social sectors and the state in Latin America has generally been expressed in terms of clientelism or paternalism, rather than in terms of citizenship, rights, and obligations. Within this paradigm, the oppressed wait passively for the state to provide services, and their subordination comes to be seen as the natural order of things. Nevertheless, Jelin also recognizes that resistance and opposition to domination have increased among the oppressed, accompanied by a consciousness of their social rights and an increasing struggle for them. This is the situation today in the coca-growing areas of Putumayo. Self-affirmation as Putumayan citizens also means compelling the state to commit itself to addressing popular demands. They believe that for crop substitution to be viable and to succeed it is not enough for the grower to express his interest; a commitment on the part of the government is also called for, and the political will should originate with the state. Even with the tendency to wait for the state to solve problems, the stimulation of citizen participation represents the first step from a passive to an active and participatory attitude that demands not only social rights, like education, health care, roads, credit, and coca substitution projects, but also political and civil rights. This demand for commitments by the state accords with the assertion of Uprimny and Villegas (2001) that the 1991 Constitution provides for "active state intervention in the search for social justice," despite other provisions for privatization and neoliberal policies.

While the discourse of active citizen participation in the construction of projects and programs is prevalent among both public officials and *campesinos* in the region, so is the opposing discourse of state abandonment and its resulting impetus for the population to make demands upon the state, wait passively for its response, and blame state inaction for their situation. This tension between active collaboration and the making of demands, then waiting for basic needs to be satisfied, is at the heart of relations between local officials and the community. These contradictory discourses mediate Putumayans' perceptions and expectations of the state, as well as the strategies they have used in order to achieve recognition.

In addition, citizenship rights include protection from the arbitrary exercise of state power. This would preclude the kind of delegitimation of the *cocalero* movement and previous civic movements in Putumayo, as well as the persecution of movement leaders, all of which the armed forces have been responsible for. In this region, the rights to life and to peace have become rights which must be struggled for. The agreements established a Human Rights Commission in anticipation of the threats to which movement participants might be subjected, and the Presidential Office of Human Rights was requested to establish an open phone line for strike leaders and participants (1996 Agreement). In the midst of the armed conflict, in a zone dominated by the army, the paramilitaries, and the guerrillas, the construction of citizenship becomes a form of resistance.

Tilly (1996) has argued that citizenship and public identity should be seen as social relations that are continuously open to interpretation and negotiation. In this sense it is important to understand the significance of the phrase "Putumayan citizen" in the current context of the war against drugs and/or the counterinsurgency. Recognition as citizens means visibility as a differentiated group; it means an identity not defined as collaborators of the guerrillas or the drug traffickers; and it means beginning the construction and strengthening of a positive identity with the support of the state. In other areas of armed conflict, like Urabá (Romero, 2001) and San José de Apartadó (Uribe, 2001), the construction of citizenship also represents their inhabitants' search for autonomy, for emancipation from subordination to the dominant forces of the guerrillas and the paramilitaries.

The local construction of the state

If we examine the state's practices in Putumayo, we may gain some insight into its paradoxical construction in the popular imagination and the political culture there. On the one hand, the state is menacing; it is feared. On the other hand, it is a paternalist state that should provide for the people's needs, but is not fulfilling its parental responsibilities. It is a state that one simultaneously fears and desires. In the political culture of the region, a bipartite understanding of the state makes it comprehensible, but only to the extent that it can be both good and bad at the same time.

This view of the state in the region also reflects the political practices of public officials,[25] as was seen in the negotiations. As has been pointed out, various dimensions and faces are entailed as a result of the powers, discourses, and practices that cohabit within the concept of a single entity, the state.[26] In synthesis, the contradictions, ambivalences, ambiguities, and paradoxes observable in both the practice of public officials and the popular representation of the state all contribute to the formation of the state in Putumayo, as well as to the form of subjection and/or resistance to it. In the words of Sayer: "The polysemic, ambiguous, contradictory quality of these putative state forms, even as they oppress, they also empower. It is not a question of either/or but both/and" (1994: 389).

As I have been arguing, it was precisely the contradictory practices of the state that gave birth to the *cocalero* movement. Gupta describes the process in theoretical terms: "Seizing on the fissures and ruptures, the contradictions in the policies, programs, institutions and discourses of 'the state' allows people to create possibilities for political action and activism" (1995: 394). Through their demand for citizen participation, a constitutionally guaranteed civil right, the *cocalero* movement leaders acquired the power to contest the government's fumigation policy, which itself ran counter to this principle, and gained recognition as "legitimate and necessary interlocutors in the development and implementation of comprehensive solutions." The movement was able to appropriate the provisions of the Constitution, demonstrating the ability of social movements to strengthen their positions by making use of existing legal mechanisms.[27]

The discourse of state absence that permeates all social strata in the region is internalized as a disaffection, becoming a constituent of the subjects' identity and particularly of their subjection. In a context of the exclusion and distorted recognition of the inhabitants of Amazonia by the state (as migrants without roots, looking for easy money), a mirror image is established within which an "identification" takes place, as described by Lacan (1977). The inhabitants of Amazonia come to assume the very exclusion, abandonment, and invisibility imposed upon them, which then transforms them as subjects. Politicized collective identities emerge and give birth to social movements in response to the state that intervenes in the zone not to exercise its paternal responsibilities and compensate those who have suffered by its absence, but to represent them as criminals and to castigate them with violence, thus reiterating their condition of marginality. The *campesinos* and *colonos* cannot establish their citizenship rights if the state does not let them, if it does not recognize them as "social actors," or if it continues to assign them to a marginal status as "fifth class" or "bad" citizens.[28] This feeling of abandonment is also shared by local state representatives such as mayors, and those officials who blur the line between the state and civil society when they cease to identify themselves as agents of the former and become active members of the latter. The absentee state is blamed for the situation. But at the same time its presence is desired and demanded, this demand being the motor of the *cocalero* movement.

The two governing powers that exercise juridical functions in the zone— the local state and the FARC—do not necessarily supplant each other. This situation also applies to other regions. Uribe (2001) describes how, in San José de Apartadó, *campesinos* juxtapose the institutional presence of the state to the political-military power of the guerrillas. The tension that exists between the state and the guerrillas, on the one hand, and between the people of Putumayo and each of their two "governments," on the other, makes the definition of boundaries between the state and civil society even more complex. Foucault (1994/1976) emphasizes the generalization of discipline and power to the extent that social subjects appear to be condemned to subjection and that political or ideological opposition to the disciplinarian structures is nonexistent. But the *cocalero* movement challenged and contested *campesino* subjection by both the state and the guerrillas. Throughout this ethnography of the 1996 *cocalero* movement I have sought to emphasize the agency of its subjects. As Abrams (1988) has told us, the power of the state is not only external and objective but also internal and subjective, working through the subjugated people themselves.

The inhabitants of Putumayo still face the challenge of determining how to achieve the construction of a new state in the region, a state characterized by participation rather than paternalism, in which active citizenship is implicit. They continue to face the challenge of inclusion in a nation-state in the difficult context of armed conflict.

In search of political representation

By the end of the civic strike, the leaders of the Civic Movement had gained a lot of influence with the inhabitants of the region, and the possibility that they could form a political movement with the potential to gain representation at the national level became a threat to the traditional political parties:

> The truth is that afterwards the elections were coming. The *campesinos* and all the common people were practically begging Luis Emiro, who had been at the forefront of the marches and the negotiations, to run for the House [of Representatives]. There was a consensus in the department, not just in the rural parts but in the cities and everywhere, that it was a given that if Emiro ran for the House, he would win resoundingly. The surprise was that Emiro didn't run, specifically because the FARC wouldn't let him. That is a great contradiction. (1999 interview with the administrator of the Mocoa Hospital at the time of the marches)

The FARC did not support the consolidation of the Civic Movement as a social and political movement. In addition, it did not promote the elaboration of the Comprehensive Development Plan, contradicting its policy of supporting the inhabitants of the region in local governance. The FARC also labeled the *campesino* leaders "sellouts" because they were receiving salaries from the Solidarity Network for their work in elaborating the Plan.[29] The ambivalence of the FARC came through again; although it encouraged and assisted in the organization of the mobilization, it did not permit the Civic Movement to slip out of its control.

For its part, the state also failed to commit itself to the implementation of a broadly based crop substitution program,[30] the fundamental objective of the Comprehensive Development Plan:

> The government didn't have the political will to negotiate a new development model, and later the guerrillas also failed to show the will. The Plan

was very ambitious, it was very good, it had gone to the root of things. A lot of time was invested, more than a week, day and sometimes night, analyzing things deeply. There were some very good approaches but there wasn't the will to follow through, and then there was a lack of clarity, confusion on the part of the guerrillas in their attitude toward the process. (Interview with a local official, advisor to the Base Group, 1998)

Furthermore, the paramilitaries entered the region after the marches. They were determined to fight the FARC, which had demonstrated its ample presence and power in the south of the country. This determination was expressed in the conclusions of the third national summit of the paramilitaries, the Movement of Self-Defense Units of Colombia (Movimiento de Autodefensas de Colombia), held in November 1996. They expressed the urgent need to reconquer zones that the guerrillas had wrested from them, among them Putumayo: "The department of Putumayo is another priority. It is urgent to divert men and resources to this mission. The subversives have been able to establish a parallel government there, which is truly perilous for the nation" (*Semana*, No. 824, 16 February 1998: 30).

The leaders of the Civic Movement were threatened and did not participate in the elections because they felt that their lives were in danger. They returned to clandestine work or to what could be called the political culture of marginality. Before the elections of 1997, the Civic Movement addressed itself to the *campesinos* of Putumayo to explain the withdrawal of its candidates from the process. One of the Civic Movement leaders spoke at a public meeting in the Puerto Asís Park and recounted the history of political violence, the "dirty war" unleashed against the leaders of alternative political parties like the Liberal Revolutionary Movement (Movimiento Revolucionario Liberal), the Communist Party (Partido Comunista), and the Patriotic Union (Union Patriótica). He assailed the social inequality and the abandonment of the region:

Don't we carry a *cedula de ciudadanía* [national identity card] like they do? [referring to the ruling class] The difference is that they are thieves and we are humble. That's the big difference, but we're Colombians. We *are* Colombians, and we're the ones who work. Or is it that you have to leave the country to understand that the department of Putumayo is producing such wealth and doesn't have a single meter of paved road. Don't our taxes count? Our taxes should be used to invest here in town. So, since the leaders who are there in power running things are exactly the same ones who have plundered the people, who have robbed the people, we're proposing the necessity of postponing the elections so that we can sit down together, not just the guerrillas, but also the *campesinos* and the workers, to talk about resolving the problems that we have today, and you will see that if these problems are solved, nobody will see the need to fight, because if nobody is trampling on their rights ... (Address by Civic Movement leader in the Central Park of Puerto Asís, September 27, 1997)

The reference to citizenship in this discourse reveals that it is power relations that are at stake. The citizenship being demanded is a political identity, as described by Mouffe: "Citizenship [...] not as a legal status but as a form of identification, a type of political identity: something to be constructed, not empirically given" (1992: 231), and, above all, a status constructed in a diverse and conflictive environment. Van Gunsteren has indicated that citizenship should be seen as "an area of contestation and struggle" and that "[t]he ambiguities of citizenship are particularly indicative of conflicts over who will have what kind of say over the definition of common problems and how they will be tackled" (1978: 10). The *campesinos* and workers demand to be taken into account as differentiated sectors of the population who are not represented by the guerrillas in the discussion of national problems. By demanding the right to political participation, they are asserting their citizenship (Foweraker, 1995).

The dilemma for the Putumayans continued to be how to sustain their representation as a distinct social and/or political group and, even more, how to secure commitments from the state, how to get the state to provide a democratic space, all in a region dominated by several armed actors and where the government had not demonstrated the political will to support *campesino* initiatives and thus take on the problem of Amazonia and coca cultivation in a structural fashion.

To the *cocaleros,* their month-long "sacrifice" meant that they realized their organizational capacity and that together they could "put the state in a bind," in the words of a government representative at the negotiations (interview with the delegate of the presidency at the negotiations, 1999). The 1996 *cocalero* movement conferred recognition and power on the *campesinos* and gave them an opportunity to contest the identity that had been assigned to them as guerrillas and/or drug traffickers. Given this opportunity, they spoke openly of coca cultivation as a subsistence crop like other subsistence crops, and they made the small *campesino* producers in the marginal areas visible as a social group.

The mayor of Piamonte, in the Baja Bota of Cauca, a member of the Inga indigenous group, referred to the *cocalero* movement as a marker of identity for the *colonos* of the region when he said, "Before the marches, the *colonos* didn't have an identity but now they do, even though they don't have a long history in the territory like ours [referring to the indigenous communities]" (Conversation with the mayor of Piamonte, 1 March 1999).

The *cocalero* mobilization lives on in the memory of the inhabitants of Putumayo and of the Baja Bota of Cauca as a historical referent, culturally appropriated as a political symbol, both of their identity as *colonos* and *campesinos* of Amazonia, and of the power they can wield when they organize to demand their rights as citizens within the framework of participatory democracy highlighted in the Constitution of 1991. Their mobilization became an emancipatory struggle against abandonment, stigmatization, and marginalization.

Notes

1 This chapter forms a part of my doctoral dissertation in the Anthropology Department at Harvard University. The fieldwork was carried out in Putumayo and the Baja Bota of Cauca as part of a project, funded by Colciencias, that I directed for the Colombian Institute of Anthropology. The project also covered Guaviare and Caquetá. My fieldwork was also partially funded by the United States Institute of Peace and the Wenner-Gren Foundation for Anthropological Research.

2 The southern region of the department of Cauca, known as the *Bota Caucana*, or the "Caucan Boot," has an area of 4,479 square kilometers and is the largest municipality in Cauca. Until 1996 it had only one municipal seat, Santa Rosa, located in the upper, Andean part of the Bota. Due to the rugged terrain, it takes up to twelve hours to get to the lower, Amazonian part of the Bota (the *Baja Bota*). Because of this isolation, the people of the Baja Bota have more often looked to Caquetá or Putumayo than to their own department of Cauca for administrative services such as health and education.

3 Taylor (1995: 249) defines the politics of recognition in relation to the construction of identities:

> Our identity is partly shaped by recognition or its absence, often by the nonrecognition or misrecognition of others, and so a person or group of people can suffer real damage, real distortion, if the people or society around them mirror back to them a confining or demeaning or contemptible picture of themselves. Nonrecognition or misrecognition can inflict harm, can be a form of oppression, imprisoning someone in a false, distorted, and reduced mode of being.

4 Dagnino (1998: 50) says that the social movements in Brazil struggle for "the right to have rights," which means that their struggle is not only for previously defined rights, but also for "the invention and creation of new rights, which emerge from specific struggles and concrete practices."

5 The colonization, or settlement, of Putumayo began in the early twentieth century as a consequence of social, economic, and political conflicts in the center of the country. These conflicts created a refugee population that migrated in search of land to "improve their standard of living." On the other hand, this area has also been settled by missionaries, the military (defending border areas as a safeguard to national sovereignty), and the government (through regional development programs). On the different periods of immigration to the region and the origin of migrants, see Ariza, Ramírez, and Vega (1998).

6 The zones are defined as folows:

> These law enforcement zones are defined as those geographical areas in which, in order to re-establish public security and social harmony which have been affected by criminal or terrorist organizations, the application of one or more of the exceptional measures described in the articles below becomes necessary, without prejudice to other measures that may have been taken as a result of the previous disorder and that remain in effect. The rights of residence and movement are restricted [...]. Such restriction entails the limitation or prohibition of the exercise of these rights by such means as curfews, military checkpoints, the requirement of special authorization for travel and of safe conduct documents, citizen registration with municipal authorities, previous notification of municipal authorities of the intention to travel outside the municipal seat. (Decree 0717: 18 April 1996)

7 While Caquetá and Guaviare were then being subjected to intensive fumigation, the fumigation in Putumayo began two years after the marches, in June of 1998, in the municipality of Puerto Guzmán along the Caquetá River.

8 Nevertheless, every person I asked about Putumayo having been declared a special law enforcement zone answered affirmatively, since they were subject to military surveillance. The fact that they shared the same problems as the departments so designated, and their contiguity with them, established a metonymic relationship that led the inhabitants of Putumayo to declare that they were subject to this provision of law.

9 During the eighteenth century, when the question of a modern civil society began to be discussed, "incivility was the ghost that permanently haunted civil society [...] civilization therefore denoted an ongoing historical process, in which civility, a static term, was both the aim and the outcome of the transformation of uncivil into civil behavior" (Keane, 1998: 117). This civilizing process was in hands of the privileged classes of Europe, because it was assumed that it was among the unprivileged that violence was reproduced.

10 The Civic Movement developed out of several civic strikes that took place in Putumayo in the 1980s. After the 1982 strike, the Civic Movement was organized as an electoral vehicle. Several of its candidates were elected to municipal councils and in 1988 it entered into a coalition with the Liberal Party, hoping to achieve representation at the national level. This compromised its position as an alternative formation. Local political groups, wanting to maintain their independence from the traditional political parties, formed a new political movement called Campesino Unity (Unidad Campesina) (interview with a local political leader in Mocoa, 1998). This tension between maintaining or even creating an autonomous and independent political party to represent the interests of the regional population and to enter into coalitions with the traditional parties in order to maximize voting power became a structural political practice in Putumayo.

11 In studying the Amazon region we should take note of Uribe (2001), who refers to the heterogeneous population of San José de Apartadó, also a site of refuge and resistance, saying that "all that they have in common is their condition of victimization and exclusion." The relations that guerrilla groups have had with the population of San José de Apartadó since the late 1960s, she continues, are based not so much on a political or ideological identity as on "a kind of moral sensibility derived from the experience of exclusion and flight, on the psychic scars of physical violation, of inequality, of recognition denied, and perhaps because the people and the armed groups share a diffuse sense of justice, verging on vengeance, that legitimizes extra-institutional violence as a balancing of accounts thrown out of equilibrium by the violent repressions of recent history." Even though this initial identification has been modified by events, the relationship between guerrillas and *campesinos* in Amazonas must be seen in the light of this shared feeling of exclusion.

12 Romero (2001), referring to the persistent relations between social movements and armed groups in Urabá since the late 1970s, points out that "there has been a tendency to castigate social organizations without recognizing that the actions of armed groups have made it possible for the social movements to advance their agendas." I consider this point fundamental if we are to understand the relationship that the *cocalero* movement leaders established with the guerrillas and to fully appreciate the decision-making capacity of the *campesinos* in relation to the FARC.

13 Jaramillo (1988: 23–4) asserts that in zones where the state of law is practically nonexistent and cannot guarantee or demand "the basic rights and duties of the entire population," the guerrillas have organized "an atomized population lacking stable institutions to struggle for their needs and demands," a role that serves the guerrillas' desire for local legitimacy and consensus. He also points out the paradoxical nature of the guerrillas' acceptance of this role, "that their own struggle can take the form of exerting the necessary pressure so that these communities may be integrated in a stable fashion into the polity and institutionally recognized by the Colombian state, enjoying the benefits and guarantees to which many of their compatriots in more accessible or developed regions are entitled." Legrand (1994) comments on Jaramillo's argument by saying that "the FARC guerrilla movement seeks its own inclusion in society more than the overthrow of the government," a view that coincides with the available evidence from Putumayo.

14 In the Baja Bota of Cauca, the strike was organized by the Pacific Movement of Cauca (Movimiento Pacífico del Cauca), as had been that of 1994 against the Argossy oil company, which operated in the zone. As in Putumayo, the 1994 list of demands was taken up again in 1996. The strike began on 4 August and lasted a month and ten days. Negotiations took place in Popayán, and the government of Cauca financed the leaders' travel there. The leaders of the Civic Movement of Putumayo worked jointly with the Pacific Movement of Cauca in both the strike of 1994 and that of 1996.

15 Beginning in 1955, the inhabitants of the Baja Bota began to ask for annex-
    ation to either Caquetá or Putumayo. From 1980 until they succeeded in 1996,
    they sought the establishment of a new municipality to improve their access
    to state services.

16 The *campesino* representatives at the negotiations were called the Base Group.
    One representative was elected for each municipality in Putumayo.

17 As in the case of San José de Apartadó described by Uribe (2001), the migra-
    tion into Amazonia is characterized by a heterogeneous population identified
    by the stigma of exclusion and/or abandonment.

18 Uribe (2001) describes the emancipatory and autonomous actions of the
    inhabitants of the Peace Community at San José de Apartadó as directed not
    only at the state, but at the counter-state (the guerrillas), and the para-state
    (the paramilitaries). In Putumayo though, the *campesino cocaleros* also seek
    autonomy from drug traffickers.

19 Jaramillo (1988), Zamosc (1990), and Legrand (1994) agree that while *colonos*
    in the border areas may support the guerrillas, they also seek integration into
    the structures of the state, "which in an ambiguous way still provides them
    with some hope" (Legrand 1994: 25). Thus they question the idea that the
    colonos are primarily seeking autonomy. Instead they believe that the *colonos*
    seek incorporation into society more than they oppose the state. Other authors,
    such as Molano (1988) and de Rementería (1986), have expressed the contrary
    view.

20 In the case of the Peace Community that was established in San José de
    Apartadó in March 1997, social participation, autonomy, and transparency were
    its political and ethical foundations. Rather than "a strategy to evade the rigors
    of war, it is, as they themselves say, a political option" (Uribe, 2001).

21 Tilly proposes that we "confine the definition of citizenship to a certain kind
    of tie: a continuing series of transactions between persons and agents of a given
    state in which each has enforceable rights and obligations uniquely by virtue
    of (1) the person's membership in an exclusive category, the native-born plus
    the naturalized and (2) the agent's relation to the state rather than any other
    authority the agent may enjoy" (1996: 8).

22 In Urabá, according to Romero (2001), a leader of the political movement
    Hope, Peace, and Freedom (Esperanza, Paz y Libertad), an ex–guerrilla of the
    People's Liberation Army (EPL, Ejército Popular de Liberación), explains that
    the demobilization of that group opened a political space "for the struggle for
    democracy and social justice," which meant an acceptance of state institution-
    ality and above all the construction of democratic spaces for negotiation
    (*concertación*) with the state. He maintained that "We are constructing a differ-
    ent referent, one closer to citizenship." To this ex-guerrilla, the construction
    of citizenship is the real revolution in Urabá.

23 For Hall and Held, "a contemporary 'politics of citizenship'" must take into
    account not only the role that social movements have played in expanding the

claims to rights, but also questions of membership. They call attention to the complex interplay of identity and identification in modern society, and to the differentiated ways in which people now participate in social life. However, they point out that citizenship "has tended to absorb 'differences' into one common universal status—the citizen," and therefore recognize that "there is now an irreconcilable tension between the thrust to equality and universality entailed in the very idea of the 'citizen,' and the variety of particular and specific needs, of diverse sites and practices which constitute the modern political subject" (1989: 176–7). Young (1995) concurs, and moreover considers the idea of universal citizenship to be repressive, inasmuch as it denies group differences. She introduces the concept of "differentiated citizenship" to refer to the incorporation into the political community of differentiated social groups, with representation as such, whose rights are defined in relation to their membership in particular groups.

24 Talking about social justice, Young argues that social movements "have offered an emancipatory meaning of difference to replace the old exclusionary meaning" (1995: 207). She also argues that social equality, the goal of these movements, should be reconceptualized in order that group-specific rights and policies do not contradict general civic political rights of participation and inclusion of all in public life and in the democratic process. She also points out that the recognition of group-specific rights may lead to a restigmatization of oppressed groups, justifying new exclusions. According to Young, "group representation can help protect against such a consequence. If oppressed and disadvantaged groups can self-organize in public and have a specific voice to present their interpretation of the meaning of and reasons for group-differentiated policies, then such policies are more likely to work for than against them" (1995: 222).

25 I am drawing on Abrams, who defines the state system as "a palpable nexus of practice and institutional structure centered in government and more or less extensive, unified and dominant in any given society [...]. The state comes into being as a structuration within political practice" (1998: 82).

26 Abrams writes along the same lines:
> The state is, in every sense of the term, a triumph of concealment. It conceals the real history and relations of subjection behind an a-historical mask of legitimating illusion; contrives to deny the existence of connections and conflicts which would, if recognized, be incompatible with the claimed autonomy and integration of the state. (1988: 77)

27 Uprimny and Villegas (2001) explain the recourse to juridical mechanisms by social actors as a result of the crisis of political representation and the weakness of the social movements. But in Putumayo, the utilization of the Constitution is closely linked to the strengthening of the social movement.

28 A PLANTE official at the negotiations explained:
> Because if we look over time, the illegal crops in Putumayo have not produced

development. On the contrary, they have created tremendous social divisions and social decomposition, crime, bad elements. *Bad Colombian citizens* are thriving here in Putumayo around this false economy that is coca. (Remarks of PLANTE official at the 1996 Orito negotiations. Emphasis added)

29 In October 1997, it was reported that, in fulfillment of the agreements signed on August 19, 1996, a total of 72,000,000 pesos, provided by the Solidarity Network, was distributed among the thirteen leaders and representatives of the "Community Sector Base Group" (Grupo Base Sector Comunidad) (Advances to the compromises in the Department of Putumayo, 28 October 1997, Puert Asís, Putumayo).

30 There was the need for a broad inter-institutional program that would pledge the resources of different state institutions that were necessary to support voluntary eradication of coca by small growers, as well as to initiate crop substitution programs. During the *cocalero* movement, the Solidarity Network wanted to show that voluntary eradication and joint work with the *campesinos* were possible. On the other hand, PLANTE, as a program of the Presidency for the substitution of illegal crops, was part of a context of anti-drug policies. Thus, its goals and assessment indicators had to be defined by the war on drugs. It was this context that prevented PLANTE from defining autonomous programs for social development with an emphasis on a comprehensive rural development, which was exactly was was needed to support the execution of the Plan for the Comprehensive Development of Putumayo. This plan was expected to establish alternative proposals for the cultivation of coca by the *campesinos* in the region.

Bibliography

Abrams, Philip (1988). "Notes on the Difficulty of Studying the State," *Journal of Historical Sociology* 1(1): 58–89.

Agreement between the negotiating commission of the national government and the negotiating commission of the Civic Strike of the Department of Putumayo, "For a Putumayo without coca and sustained in an economy of solidarity." Emergency Plan for Comprehensive Development. Orito, 19 August 1996.

ANNCOL (1998). "Los soldados del Ejército sienten que esta guerra no es de ellos." Interview with guerrilla commandant Joaquín Gómez, Bloque FARC-EP of Colombia

Arendt, Hannah (1949). "The Rights of Man: What are they?" *Modern Review* 3(1): 24–37.

Ariza, Eduardo, María Clemencia Ramírez and Leonardo Vega (1998). *Atlas Cultural de la Amazonia Colombiana: la construcción del territorio en el siglo XX.* Bogotá, Ministerio de Cultura-Instituto Colombiano de Antropología, Corpes Orinoquia, Corpes Amazonia.

Civic Movement for the Comprehensive Development of Putumayo (1997). Main Presentation to the Regional Forum "Peace and Human Rights." 7 May Puerto Asis, Putumayo.

Civic Movement of Putumayo. Letter to President Ernesto Samper Pizano. 26 December 1995.

Dagnino, Evelina (1998). "The Cultural Politics of Citizenship, Democracy and the State," in *Cultures of Politics and Politics of Cultures. Revisioning Latin American Social Movements.* Sonia Alvarez, Arturo Escobar and Evelina Dagnino (eds). Boulder, CO: Westview, 33–63.

De Rementeria, Iban (1986). "Hipótesis sobre la violencia reciente en el Magdalena Medio" in *Pasado y Presente de la Violencia en Colombia.* Gonzalo Sánchez and Ricardo Peñaranda (eds). Bogotá: CEREC, 333–48.

First Draft of the Initial Proposal of the Civic Movement for an Agreement, 1996. Courtesy of Teófilo Vásquez.

FARC (1998). "El Poder Local," *Revista Resistance* 17. http//burn.ucsd.edu/ ~farc-ep/RevistaR/Resistencia17/podlocal.htm.

Ferro, Juan Guillermo and Graciela Uribe (2001). "Las Contradicciones Políticas Presentes en las Marchas de los Cocaleros del Departamento de Caquetá, Colombia (1996)," in Santos, *Reinventing Social Emancipation.*

Foucault, Michel [1976] (1994). "Two Lectures," in *Culture, Power and History,* Nicholas B. Dirks, Geoff Eley Sherry Ortner (eds). Princeton, NJ: Princeton UP, 200–221.

Foweraker, Joe (1995). *Theorizing Social Movements.* Boulder, CO: Pluto Press.

Gupta, Akhil (1995). "Blurred boundaries: the discourse of corruption, the culture of politics and the imagined state," *American Ethnologist* 22(2): 375–97.

Gutiérrez, Francisco and Ana María Jaramillo (2001). "Pactos Paradójicos," in Santos, *Reinventing Social Emancipation.*

Hall, Stuart and David Held (1989). "Citizens and Citizenship," in S. Hall and M. Jaques (eds), *New Times. The Changing Face of Politics in the 1990s.* London: Verso, 173–88.

Jaramillo, Eduardo (1988). *Estado, Sociedad y Campesinos.* Bogotá: Tercer Mundo Editores.

Jelin, Elizabeth (1996). "Citizenship Revisited: Solidarity, Responsibility, and Rights," in *Constructing Democracy. Human Rights, Citizenship and Society in Latin America,* Elizabeth Jelin and Eric Hershberg (eds). Boulder, CO: Westview, 101–19.

Keane, John (1998). *Civil Society. Old Images New Visions.* Stanford, CA: Stanford UP.

Lacan, Jacques (1977). *Ecrits. A Selection.* Trans. Alan Sheridan. New York: Norton.

Laclau, Ernesto and Chantal Mouffe (1985). *Hegemony and Socialist Strategy. Toward a Radical Democratic Politics.* London: Verso.

Legrand, Catherine (1994). "Colonización y Violencia en Colombia: Perspectivas y debate," in *El Agro y la Cuestión Social.* Absalón Machado Cartagena (eds). Bogotá, Banco Popular, Caja Agraria, Veco: Tercer Mundo Editores, 3–26.

Molano, Alfredo (1994). "Algunas consideraciones sobre colonización y violencia," in *El agro y la cuestión social.* Absalón Machado (eds). Bogotá, Banco Popular, Caja Agraria, Veco: Tercer Mundo Editores, 27–41.

— (1988). "Violencia y colonización," in *Revista Foro* 6: 25–37.

Mouffe, Chantal (1992). "Democratic Citizenship and the Political Community," in *Dimensions of Radical Democracy,* Chantal Mouffe (ed.). London: Verso, 225–39.

Padilla, Nelson Freddy (1996). "Estamos en la dolorosa," *Cambio 16,* No.164 August 5, 1996, Bogotá.

Romero, Mauricio (2001). "Los Trabajadores Bananeros de Urabá: de Súbditos a Ciudadanos?" in Boaventura de Sousa Santos, *Reinventing Social Emancipation.*

Santos, Boaventura de Sousa (1998). "Reinventing Social Emancipation. Exploring Possibilities of Counter-Hegemonic Globalization." Research Proposal Presented to the MacArthur Foundation. Centro de Estudos Sociais, School of Economics, University of Coimbra.

Semana No. 872. "Tirofijo se destapa."Por primera vez el jefe de las Farc habla sobre el canje y el proceso de paz. 18 January 1999, Bogotá.

Summary of the commitments reached between the national government and the negotiating commission of the Civic Strike of the Department of Putumayo. October 28, Puerto Asís, Putumayo.

Taylor, Charles (1995). "The Politics of Recognition," in *Campus Wars. Multiculturalism and the Politics of Difference,* John Arthur and Amy Shapiro (eds). Boulder, CO: Westview, 249–63.

Tilly, Charles (1996). "Citizenship, Identity and Social History," in C. Tilly (ed.). *Citizenship, Identity and Social History.* Cambridge: Cambridge UP, 1–17.

Uprimny, Rodrigo, and Mauricio García Villegas (2001). "Corte Constitucional y Emancipación Social en Colombia," in Santos, *Reinventing Social Emancipation.*

Uribe, Maria Teresa (2001). "San José de Apartado, una comunidad de paz o un nuevo pacto fundamental" in Santos, *Reinventing Social Emancipation.*

Van Gunsteren, Herman (1978). "Notes on a theory of citizenship," in *Democracy, Consensus and Social Contract.* Pierre Birnbaum, Jack Lively, and Geraint Parry (eds) London: Sage, 9–35.

Young, Iris Marion (1995). "Social Movements and the Politics of Difference," in J. Arthur and A. Shapiro (eds). *Campus Wars. Multiculturalism and the Politics of Difference.* Boulder, CO: Westview, 199–223.

Zamosc, Leon (1990). "El Campesino y las Perspectivas para la Democracia Rural," in *Al Filo del Caos. Crisis política en la Colombia de los años 80.* Francisco Leal Buitrago and Leon Zamosc (eds). Bogotá, Instituto de Estudios Políticos y Relaciones Internacionales: Tercer Mundo Editores, 311–79.

Decrees and press articles

Decree 0717: April 18, 1996. Presidencia de la República. Bogotá.

Decree 0871: May 13, 1996. Presidencia de la República.

Resolution 0001 of 1996. Consejo Nacional de Estupefacientes. 13 May Bogotá

El Espectador. "Bedoya Acusa al Gobierno." 7 August 1998: 5A.

— "Mi hora cero. Guerra en el Sur." Column by Jimena Duzán. 28 August 1996: 3A.

El Tiempo. "Se gesta otro paro en el Putumayo." 4 January 1996: 1A.

— "Paro indefinido en 12 pueblos del Putumayo" 28 July 1996: 15A.

— "La fumigación no tiene limitaciones." 13 August 1996: 3A.

La Nación. "Palabras del Presidente Ernesto Samper Pizano en la Presentación del Balance del Plan Córdoba y los resultados de la Operación Conquista." 10 July 1996: 17.

— "Afirma el general Mario Galán: hay intereses de la narcoguerrilla." 2 August 1996: 9.

— "Reinician Fumigación." 27 July 1996: 11.

9

The Banana Workers of Urabá: From "Subjects" to "Citizens"?

Mauricio Romero[1]

The banana workers of Urabá, a region close to the Panamanian border,[2] have mobilized one of the most significant campaigns for political, civil, and labor rights that Colombia has experienced in the last three decades. They have organized a trade union that includes all the workers of the banana industry, which is unique in the Colombian agricultural sector. Close to 15,000 members are affiliated to Sintrainagro,[3] including workers on plantations located in other regions of the country. This organization achieved a common framework for collective bargaining at the end of the 1980s, thus superseding the previous process, which involved nearly 310 contracts negotiated per company.

Following the decentralization policies that began at the end of the 1980s, Sintrainagro worked to increase workers' possibilities of accessing local political power. Likewise, it led an important drive to improve the workers' living conditions during the 1990s. Furthermore, this trade union is in the forefront of the organization of a Latin American federation of agricultural workers that already unites a large number of the wageworkers in the continent's banana industry. How have they achieved this in the midst of such a ferocious and ruthless armed conflict as the Colombian one, in which Urabá has been one of the most affected areas? Can this new situation, as the current leaders argue, be considered as the beginning of a movement toward citizenship?

The extension of citizenship rights to a specific group is no guarantee of a democratic regime—as the authoritarian governments of Mussolini, Hitler, Franco, and Salazar demonstrate. However, during the life of these regimes, bonds of citizenship were created with the population that, according to these leaders, made up their respective nations. Seen in this light, citizenship is a social relation that unites a specific human group with a state. This bond implies mutual obligations and a sense of individual dignity associated with a degree of social inclusion and a sense of belonging to a political community, usually a national one (Tilly, 1995; Pécaut, 2000). In the case of Urabá, this relationship has meant bartering for protection, security and a level of regional political participation for the workers and their allies unequalled in other parts of the country. This has been achieved in exchange for loyalty to a politico-economic order, even though this order required the elimination of one of the most important political forces of the region, the Patriotic Union or UP, and related movements (Cuartas, interview, 26 October 2000).

It is also important to underline the fact that this loyalty is not to the national state centered in the capital Bogotá, but rather to a regional order that arose out of the consolidation of a non-state military apparatus that defines itself as counterinsurgent. Although the outcome is still uncertain, if the pattern that has predominated over the last decade continues, the military and political control that AUC[4] has achieved in the banana-growing region could grow, and particularly that of ACCU,[5] the strongest organization within the alliance. Should this occur, the consolidation of anticommunist political identities can be predicted, although it is not easy to say what other features will define them. Nevertheless, while the possibility of a successful peace process between the central government and the Revolutionary Armed Forces of Colombia (FARC) exists, this particular order is threatened. Likewise, the outcome of a prolongation of the existing situation, with blockades on the highways that connect Urabá to the center of the country and the sabotage of electricity supplied to the zone causing interruptions of economic activity, is unpredictable.

In any event, questions about this regional order in Urabá continue to arise. As an anti-revolutionary force and renovator of regional security and order, AUC had usually established alliances with economic and political elites threatened by the insurgents and with sectors of the state security forces. This was the way they consolidated their advance in other areas of the country, to the detriment of the influence and control that guerrilla groups had maintained for decades. In Urabá, however, the coalitions included Sintrainagro, the most important and well-established workers' organization in the region. They also included Esperanza, Paz y Libertad (Hope, Peace and Liberty), a former guerrilla organization that began in the mid-1960s as a Maoist-influenced splinter group of the Communist Party and operated as the EPL (Popular Liberation Army) until they accepted the government's peace proposal in 1991 and disarmed. The banana workers have made significant gains within this regional political configuration—an outcome of the armed conflict in Colombia and of the regional political and military rivalry between the different insurgent forces. How should their social and political advances be viewed when they have been obtained in such circumstances, and especially if their advances came at a cost to other workers or urban dwellers, negating their political, civil, and labor rights?

Strategic interactions and unexpected alliances

The current conditions of banana workers in Colombia contrast with the situation of their counterparts elsewhere in Latin America, who are organized in company-based trade unions (when any union organization exists), have relatively low salaries and limited access to institutional political power. What road led to this unusual situation for the Colombian banana workers when only 20 years ago their meetings were clandestine, their living conditions miserable, and unionizing was, if not illegal, highly frowned upon by the authorities and businessmen? How did they get these prerogatives in the midst of the fierce armed conflict that has been waged in Urabá over the last two decades? It is even more difficult to understand how they achieved it when one of the sectors most affected by the political violence was precisely that of the banana workers.

To answer these questions is even more significant given the political changes that occurred in the region. The largest electoral force in the late 1980s and early 1990s—the Patriotic Union or UP, a coalition of leftist and social democratic groups, including the pro-Soviet Communist Party—was wiped from the political map as a result of violence against its militants and supporters. The UP was an attempt to create a legal political movement with the participation of the FARC. It was the outcome of the peace talks held between Belisario Betancur's Conservative government (1982-1986) and the guerrillas in 1983. The electoral field they had gained in the late 1980s was seized again by the Liberal Party, the UP's main political rival in Urabá (CINEP, 1995).

Two additional circumstances have further complicated this scenario. The first is the growing military and political influence that counterinsurgent paramilitary groups supported by banana producers, ranchers, drug lords and security forces organized under the United Self-Defense Groups of Colombia have gained in the zone. The second is the apparent alliance between these paramilitary groups and the political movement Esperanza, Paz y Libertad, previously mentioned, which operated under the name of Popular Liberation Army (EPL) until 1991. This organization had an important influence, from the late 1970s onwards, among the banana workers and landless peasants in Urabá, as did the FARC (Garcia, 1996). How did the EPL end up allied with their former enemies for the purpose of confronting the FARC instead of continuing to build the alliance that these two organizations had formed in 1987? How did the banana workers come to terms with this "pact with the devil" between the former EPL militants and the paramilitaries?

Any attempt to answer these questions reveals the "accommodation" strategies of vulnerable groups that are facing adverse situations or more powerful rivals. One interpretation, although tentative given the instability of the situation, would suggest that we examine how radical identities and projects were assimilated in the new order established by paramilitaries, banana producers and the Liberal Party, with the support of the armed forces, from the mid-1990s, and how it transformed their utopias and their projects. Likewise, an examination of recent union developments enables us to understand the international activism recently begun by this trade union and its responses to the changes in the world banana market.

I argue here that the "assimilation" of the workers and their allies in a regional political arrangement has come at a cost for the different sectors involved in the agreement operating today in Urabá. The workers and the political sector that finally prevailed have not been merely "victims" of this developing order, but have also achieved a position that offers them social, political and economic advantages in addition to the opportunity to sway the nature of this concurrence of forces. That is, these workers have acted in accordance with a memory, an idea of their own utopias and projects, modified by the circumstances they confronted, but they have done so as active agents and subjects of rights, capable of making decisions. This was facilitated by the strategic alliance with both legal and illegal business, sectors of the central state, such as the armed forces, and regional politicians linked to the Liberal Party.

Banana producers have had to accept the presence of a strong and self-reliant union; the liberal politicians a party-based organization linked to the union that competes for power at the local level; and the security forces a political organization made up of ex-guerrillas holding institutional power. In the same vein, by uniting with the former guerrilla members and workers, traditional politicians, banana producers, and the army blocked another possible direction the armed conflict could take in this region—an alliance between the insurgents still in arms, the FARC, and the banana workers and poor urban dwellers. This trajectory would have been still more risky to the interests and projects of traditional politicians, businessmen and the military. The fact that the central government of the day and the local politicians all belonged to the Liberal Party was critical to opening the coalition of regional power to a new associate, one previously considered "foreign to the Colombian nation" by the privileged sectors. The advocacy role of the Presidential Advisory Board for Peace and its advisers, who facilitated the agreements, was also important.

My argument relies on two main analytical tools. The first is the strategic interactions among social actors, their alliances, conflicts and transformations, and the second is the interactions between political identities and broader networks. The changes in the dynamic between identities and networks propitiate transformations in these identities. These two elements allow us to understand variations in actors' strategies as a result of political interaction, rather than as a result of behaviors attributed a priori. In fact, this work does not impute to individual or collective actors attributes or behaviors derived from the level of development (modern/industrial or traditional/pre-industrial) or from the social category to which they belong (artisans, peasants or workers' wives). Rather, it relies on a situated account of actors immersed in their relational setting (Somers, 1993).

Thus, a fierce competition was unleashed between guerrilla forces—EPL and FARC—in the banana belt in the context of the EPL's negotiations with the government in 1990–91. The decision of the EPL to disarm and to take advantage of the opportunity to enter the political arena legally, instead of continuing with their insurrection and conspiracy, led to contention between these two groups, each vying for the support of the workers. Each needed to defend and justify their chosen path—revolutionary or legal. This struggle degenerated to the point of armed attack on the social bases of the other group's followers, killing close to three hundred banana workers in 1995 alone (Sandoval, 1997). The clash between these two groups was also used to advantage by paramilitaries and security forces to eliminate those whom they considered "guerrilla collaborators," without differentiating between the groups.

The intensification of the struggle led to a rapprochement between the EPL, now the political movement Esperanza, Paz y Libertad, and their former antagonists—the army, banana producers, and paramilitaries—and converged into an alliance to confront the FARC and their armed and civilian supporters. For the private sector, regional politicians, and counter-insurgent forces, the coalition with the workers neutralized the possibility of a more serious loss of public order at the local level. This would result from an alliance of workers and the guerrilla group still in arms, or from a successful peace process that would mean the legalization and association in a single project of the different tendencies of the revolutionary left.

For this reason, this study emphasizes the changing character of the political identities of both the elites and the subaltern groups. From this perspective, identities are considered to be constructed in a process that is more the outcome of collective action than its cause and basis (Calhoun, 1991). That is, identity is not a static or pre-existing condition that exercises a causal influence on mobilization, but rather an outcome of political interaction (Tilly, 1998). This analysis also explores the role of collective mobilization, state intervention and the armed conflict in the struggle to give new meanings to the received notions about citizenship, representation, and participation (Dagnino, 1998; Warren, 1993). Therefore, public identities, including citizenship, are understood to be social relations that are always open to new interpretations and to negotiation (Tilly, 1996).

This text has four sections. The section that follows presents the historical background, centered on the decade of the 1980s, the competition between the militants of the EPL and the FARC, and the strengthening of the trade union movement during the peace talks of this period. The text

continues with an analysis of the regional political restructuring at the beginning of the 1990s and the repositioning of the banana workers in this new
field of political and military forces. Finally, it takes up the subject of the
new labor internationalism and the possible areas of agreement between
workers and entrepreneurs to confront the changing conditions of the world
market. In the conclusion the argument is recapitulated and three points are
emphasized: the unpredictability of the historical development of the armed
conflict in Urabá, the relative incorporation of the banana workers into the
new local order, and the role that alliances with more powerful groups play
in this incorporation.

Revolutionaries, workers, and peace talks in the 1980s

The living and working conditions of the banana workers in the 1970s and
the early 1980s were deplorable. "They gave you a cardboard box to sleep
in right in the packing plant. [...] [W]e slept like dogs, to be blunt, but that
is the way it was. The workday was up to 18 hours long. We had to work
from 6 a.m. to midnight at times, only to start again the next day at six"
(García, 1996: 105). The growth in production required the organization of
camps or "tambos" on the plantations, although the housing conditions were
precarious and the possibilities of family life slight. There was no electricity,
drinking water or toilets.

> That place was one big humiliation. I worked until 10 at night; the next day
> beginning at 5 in the morning I was up again, they rang a bell. You don't
> even see your family because you work up to two months without any rest,
> even on Sunday. [...] There was never a time when I said, "I'm going to stay
> home Sunday with my family." (García, 1996: 106)

The life in the camps was sad—"the men lived alone with their wives and
families far away and no source of distraction; this lasted well into the 1980s.
'Lonely males' [machosolos], they called them" (Sandoval, 1997: 180).

Banana production was the first labor relation for most of the workers
and for many owners, who initially arrived in the region as colonists. Two-
thirds of the workers were black and had been peasants, miners, or fisherfolk:

> In the first phase of the industry—the 1960s and 1970s—the workers worked
> up to 20 hours a day; they didn't know that they had to be paid for overtime.
> They didn't know that after two months they had the right to compensation
> for unfair dismissal, they didn't even know if they had been fired with cause
> or not. They didn't know that Sundays were paid differently from other days
> [...] people had no idea that they had the legal right to unionize. (García,
> 1996: 105)

This lack of knowledge of the law extended to a significant number of the investors and owners themselves, who either did not know the labor law or thought it contrary to their interests or ideologies. So, from the beginning labor relations were open to arbitrariness, to individual retaliation, and even to the use of force between workers and producers.

In this context, the right to organize reached the social and political agenda. However, it was not debated in public because of the political monopoly of the Liberal and Conservative parties—a legacy of the power-sharing agreement of 1958 between these two dominant parties, which over time developed a markedly anti-union stance. To social injustice and political exclusion, the proposals of the different Marxist groups added their anti-capitalist utopias, which took hold in Urabá from the beginning of banana production in the 1960s. For their part, the seditious projects of the guerrilla groups promised a democratic redistribution of agrarian property. These four elements made up a conflictive social and political atmosphere in the region, to which must be added the authoritarianism of the investors in the area. Supporters of the Communist Party founded the first trade union in 1964 (Sintrabanano) among the workers employed by the Frutera de Sevilla (United Fruit Company). When the company learned about the union, they fired the workers, then convinced the authorities to jail them, and finally the same fate met the Communist leaders in the area. The general guideline was to fire first, and if this was not enough to quell the problems, to then turn to the military authorities or the police (García, 1996: 112-15).

Blacklisting workers, pre-emptive firings, and the promotion of parallel company unions were the employers' responses in the 1970s to the organizing efforts initiated by the workers in the 1960s. The composition of the national political regime did not allow the existence of local authorities that enforced the law and defended rights, so that these remained at the whim of local elites, mostly Liberals in Urabá. Nevertheless, the hope of legal redress was always present. From the first records of worker movements one constant was the petition to central powers. These petitions called for the establishment of offices to resolve labor conflicts according to the law (García, 1996: 109), something that only occurred at the end of the 1980s after widespread and violent strikes supported by guerrilla groups had taken place.

The relationship of social movements and armed actors has persisted in Urabá from the late 1970s to date, although little is known of the character of these links. Furthermore, there has been a tendency to victimize the social organizations without recognizing the opportunities to promote their agendas that the actions of armed groups opened up for them. The use of force by the guerrillas not only attracted the expected state repression, it also gained concrete improvements for the region's inhabitants. To all intents and purposes, the guerrillas imposed trade union organization and collective bargaining on employers in the region (Madarriaga, interview, 11 July 2000), an occurrence that was propitiated by the opportunity for democratization opened up by the Conservative government of Belisario Betancur in 1982. Direct negotiations between the presidency and the guerrillas, without demanding that they first surrender, which had been the position of the preceding Liberal government, represented the first steps to this opening.

This recognition as political actors had significant consequences in the regions influenced by insurgent movements, the case of Urabá. The presidential initiative to offer guerrilla groups negotiating room coincided with a change of strategy on the part of the guerrillas, who, beginning in the early 1980s, decided to seek a larger presence in economically important regions, and also to try to influence the workers who produced this wealth. In Urabá, the EPL began to move beyond their earlier focus on an agrarian agenda in 1980, and to join the struggle for unionization among the banana workers, the urban movements for housing and public services, and the invasions of vacant land in the center of the banana belt (García, 1996: 122-3; M. T. Uribe, 1992: 164–214). Sintagro, a union founded in 1972 by activists close to the Conservative Party but penetrated by the EPL, was the main instrument of labor activism.

In December 1984, four months after the EPL and the government signed the peace agreements in Medellín, the first massive and coordinated strike in the history of Urabá took place. Fifteen hundred workers on 18 banana plantations that covered 2,000 hectares declared an indefinite strike to pressure for the negotiation of collective contracts. Likewise, it was the first time that the banana producers' association Augura initiated a joint campaign to oppose union action (García, 1996: 125). To end the strike, the government, producers and unions signed a tripartite agreement, the first of its type in the history of the region. In this agreement, the Ministry of Labor was appointed to hear complaints on violations of labor law, state-owned social insurance was established in the zone to replace the undependable medical service offered by private producers on the farms, and Sintagro was guaranteed the opportunity to hold an assembly of workers. The workers' petitions were remarkable for their modesty in contrast to the disproportionate means used to achieve them, which demonstrates the degree of labor and union repression.

In 1985, 127 collective agreements were signed that covered 60 per cent of the banana-growing area. Union membership rose abruptly and reached almost 60 per cent of the workers, 43 per cent organized in Sintagro and 14 per cent in Sintrabanano (Villarraga and Plaza, 1994: 205). The truce between the government and the guerrilla groups allowed the unions to act publicly for the first time. The armed forces took a tolerant line and did not get involved in the strikes or movement during the first months. Then, "everything began to break open [...] people came from the farms to tell us that there they had so many to join [...] and we got to know the future leaders that way. It was no longer like at first, when we had to go to the plantations at night to convince our fellow workers. No! Now people began to come to the union office to say to us, look, go to this or that farm where we have organized such and such a number of workers," says Mario Agudelo, a political leader of the EPL (García, 1996: 126–7).

Although the peace talks made room for the guerrilla groups, it was also an opportunity for different social sectors to speak out publicly about their demands and mobilize for their rights, and their only allies in this undertaking were the armed groups. This was the case of the banana workers. Their organizational development found support in the Presidency's democratization policies, which provided political instruments to neutralize the local elites and the security forces for a time, opening possibilities to broaden the elitist local order (Ortíz, 1999).

Nevertheless, with the change of government from the Conservative Betancur to the Liberal Virgilio Barco (1986–90) and the hardening of the presidential position, the peace negotiations stalled and the situation in Urabá became even more polarized. Following a fierce competition for worker support, Sintagro and Sintrabanano agreed to work together. The same thing occurred with the FARC and the EPL, which now jointly used the name Simón Bolívar Guerrilla Coordination (Coordinadora Guerrillera Simón Bolívar) in association with other armed groups.

> The year 1986 passed with threats and assassinations, fires in the packing houses, destruction of cable trolleys, petitions, strikes on the plantations over workplace issues, strikes on 120 farms to 'protect life and on another 130 as a protest over the assassination of a union leader,' suspension of loading and shipping, and work-to-rule campaigns to pressure for the payment of salaries lost during strike days or as a result of sabotage. (Ortíz, 1999: 134–5)

Obviously this was not a situation in the best interests of the business community.

Labor modernization and new directions for social mobilization

All the same, 1987 was an important year for the modernization of labor relations in Urabá. The creation of the United Workers Federation, CUT (Central Unitaria de Trabajadores), in 1986, in which conservatives, liberals, communists and other leftist groups converged after more than forty years of division, contributed to this advance. Sintrabanano and Sintagro presented a joint negotiating package for more than 200 agreements in an equal number of plantations that consisted of a single list of demands for the sector. This put on the table the *de facto* recognition of bargaining by an industrial sector, a situation never before seen in the private sector in Colombia (Villarraga and Plazas, 1994: 205). The banana producers, through Augura, also had a unified front for the negotiations, and they accepted the collective bargaining but complemented it with farm-by-farm bargaining according to farm productivity, in order to "establish a relationship of cause and effect between the work and its payment" (García, 1996: 136).

The presence of Ministry of Labor and CUT delegates revived the tripartite commission of 1984. The outcome was an important advance in the recognition of workers' rights: acceptance of the union as the legitimate representative of the workers at the bargaining table and entitled to speak on their behalf to employers and the government; labor stability; an eight-hour day; union privileges; improved salaries. Also agreed was the beginning of the dismantling of the system of plantation camps and the financing of urban housing. The latter, changing the workers' housing from the plantations to the towns, was key to the future changes of strategy and objectives on the part of the EPL in the 1990s, by then operating under the name of Esperanza, Paz y Libertad. The change tended to stabilize families and to broaden the concerns of the workers to include public services, education, health and recreation, with which the state was directly involved, whether at the national, departmental, or local level. No longer did the workers limit themselves only to labor issues in a confrontation with the business sector (Mario Agudelo, interview, 12 July 2000).

Despite the rapprochement described above, the assassination of labor leaders and negotiators did not stop in 1987. From the beginning of the negotiations in the first week of February until the signing of the first agreement in April, 24 union leaders were murdered by hired assassins, and the headquarters of Sintagro was destroyed by a bomb for the second time. By September the number of unionists who had been assassinated had reached 40, and the focus of the discussions between the workers and the government and business shifted to the subject of human rights and the responsibility of the state for these acts of violence (García, 1996: 136–7). While at the national level the positions of the guerrillas and the government were polarized, in Urabá, the calls to "partial insurrection" or to a "popular uprising" made by the national leadership of the guerrillas were not well received by some of the region's militants and activists. These wanted to consolidate the gains made since 1984 and to contribute to a climate of political guarantees that would encourage respect for life, social welfare, and the stimulation of regional development (Villarraga and Plazas, 1994: 205–6).

The consequences of union participation in the uprisings were the suspension of their legal license to act on behalf of their members and an increased militarization of the region. A new military command was established in Urabá in 1987, and its commander had not only military but also political and civil powers (Botero, 1990: 180–9; M. T. Uribe, 1992: 251–6). Despite this, the union leaders came up with a resourceful legal mechanism to restore their legal standing and their power to represent the workers in the renegotiation of almost 300 collective agreements on an equal number of plantations in 1989. Sintragro and Sintrabanano fused into a new entity called Sintrainagro, following the example of CUT at the national level, which also formalized the alliance of the former regional antagonists represented by the two great tendencies in international communism: Soviet and Chinese-Albanian (Ramírez, 1997: 97).

The outcome of the new round of negotiations consolidated the union role, and collective bargaining by sector was firmly established. Nevertheless, this was not easy and did not mean the absence of mobilization, although there was a change in the use of armed pressure and, with this, of the revolutionary objectives. Mario Agudelo, one of the political leaders of the EPL, states that:

> when the strike of 1989 came, we saw that to combine guerrilla action with the social conflict was not the best strategy. So we worked in reverse: we tried to profile the labor conflict and give space to the social movement. Our interest was to prevent other external factors, such as guerrilla action, from latching onto the movement. We thought this was a good strategy because it avoided tensions; it avoided the acquisition of new enemies or new factors against the movement. (Villarraga and Plazas, 1994: 389–90)

Before the union negotiations of the second semester of 1989, the leadership of the new Sintrainagro wanted to ease tensions. The state, banana producers, and local elites had directed a fierce repression against the region in response to the challenges of the guerrillas, the workers, and the urban and rural land invaders.

> We tried to manage the conflict differently, and we were able to convince some authorities to begin to pressure Augura to come to the table. [...] We knew that there was a clear intention from Augura to resist the union, to strike a blow at it and to attempt claw-backs. [...] Experience was teaching us to change the approach: to smooth ruffled feathers, to open spaces for negotiation and dialogue, to begin a dialogue and the possibility of a unilateral truce. (Villarraga and Plazas, 1994: 389–90)

The possibilities of a regional crisis caused by the flight of capital from the zone and its movement to Central America and other areas of Colombia created a noticeable impact on the regional leadership of the EPL and the workers. Mario Agudelo indicates that "we saw the real danger of the disappearance of the banana belt, the weakening of the workers' power and retaliation against us, should this occur" (Villarraga and Plazas, 1994: 389–90). The idea of "salvation of the region and the defense of banana production" was added to the search for an agreement with authorities and business leaders and the elimination of armed pressure on the labor negotiations. This changed everything, because it implied making common cause with producers and investors, the archenemies of the workers, according to the revolutionary ideas of the EPL. As Agudelo points out,

> we made the proposal of an alliance with banana producers around the themes of economic development, problems of a social nature and threats to human rights [...]. It was our decision [...]. It was not preceded by a decision from the national directorate. (Villarraga and Plazas, 1994: 391)

The dynamic described in the change of strategy and objectives of the EPL revolutionaries in Urabá clarifies many of the questions that later arose about the demobilization of this guerrilla group and the way that the banana workers participated in the regional political restructuring of the 1990s in Urabá. One point worth highlighting is the difference in the positioning of the EPL and the FARC in the region. Despite being an organization with a national presence, the EPL had its main front and its general staff headquarters in Urabá and nearby regions. The FARC, on the other hand, had its Fifth Front in the region, but its leadership and most important forces were located in the southern part of the country (Ortíz, 1999). When making significant decisions, the feelings and opinion of the local population were decisive for the EPL, while for the FARC's Fifth Front the determinations of the national leadership, located outside the region, carried more weight than the opinions of the different regional social sectors. This difference strongly influenced the divergent paths followed by these insurgent organizations.

No to the revolution, yes to citizenship

The demobilization of the EPL in March 1991, their reintegration into civilian life as the movement Esperanza, Paz y Libertad, and the role of the banana workers in this process was the object of a bloody confrontation with the FARC in Urabá. The legalization of the former insurgent group set off reactions from its rivals, both its revolutionary rivals and legal political competitors. The situation became even more complex as a result of the growing influence of counter-insurgent paramilitary groups in the region throughout the 1990s, and the "dirty war" that accompanied it. The lethal consequences of this confrontation are well documented (CINEP, 1995; Comisión Andina de Juristas, 1994; Defensoria del Pueblo, 1992; Fundación Progresar, 1996), as are some reflections on the early years of the reinsertion (Uribe, 1994). However, little is known about the analysis of the members of Esperanza, Paz y Libertad about the way in which this reintegration into civilian life occurred and its results. Nor is there work about their explanations for their relative electoral success in the local elections of October 2000 or about the effects of these alliances on the banana workers' trade union practices.

One of the first doubts or questions that arises concerns the EPL's relationship with different armed forces, especially with the constitutionally mandated Army and with the paramilitary groups. In the case of the army, Mario Agudelo, one of the strategists of the reinsertion, indicates that the demobilization opened the political scene to them "for the democratic struggle and the search for social justice." However, this implied an acceptance of the authority of the national institutions, hence the army, and the monopoly on the use of force by the state. So, when the aggressions (presumably from the FARC against the leaders, activists and workers that supported the EPL) began, "the first thing that was done was to approach the army and design a security plan for the population, in particular for those communities sympathetic to the EPL. To this end we proposed the creation of military posts in the high risk communities" (Mario Agudelo, interview, 12 July 2000).

The most widespread complaint of the reinserted guerrillas was that "the massacres were announced ahead of time and the security forces paid no attention." According to Agudelo, this was the case of the massacres at the Bajo del Oso, Osaka and Las Cunas plantations in 1995. On these farms, unknown persons assassinated close to fifty workers who supported Esperanza, Paz y Libertad. Las Cunas was located ten kilometers from a military base in the municipality of Carepa. For Agudelo, the armed forces "were more interested in taking care of the roads, especially the highway to Medellín, than protecting the population." Agudelo comments that "the relationship between the communities and the army was strengthened" with the arrival of General Rito Alejo del Río as the commander of the army brigade in Urabá in 1995. "The relationship became more spontaneous, while it was more complicated with the DAS (Administrative Department of Security), the Ministry of Defense, the Reinsertion Program, and the Ministry of Internal Affairs" (Mario Agudelo, interview, 12 July 2000). The rapprochement between the organization's supporters and the army was favored by the decision of General del Río to protect the areas where the former guerrilla members were living from attacks by the other armed groups.

As for the paramilitaries, Agudelo says that "when the proposal of a pact was made to the business sector in 1988–89, there were no paramilitaries in the region and the context of the proposal was peace-building, not armed conflict like we have now." Moreover, Agudelo argues that the proposal that they made implicitly acknowledged that labor conflicts would be defined at the bargaining table between labor and management without interference from armed actors:

The social pact with business meant that labor issues were no longer in the hands of the guerrillas, the army, and the paramilitaries, because it was no longer necessary to resort to them. This shows that the construction of democratic opportunities, negotiating spaces, contributes to the reconstruction of the country's institutions. Moreover, when we signed the social pact with Augura in 1991, there were no self-defense groups in Urabá. (Mario Agudelo, interview, 12 July 2000)

Although it is clear that a negotiated agreement between workers and business does not mean a formal agreement with the paramilitaries, it is good to remember that General del Río was withdrawn from command in Urabá in 1998 and discharged in 1999 on suspicion of tolerating paramilitary groups.[6] Guillermo Rivera, president of Sintrainagro, was one of the speakers in a ceremony of redress prepared for General del Río and organized by Augura and Fuerza Colombia, the political organization of the former Army commander General Harold Bedoya.[7] The event was held in the Hotel Tequendama, one of the capital's most prestigious establishments, in May 1999. The slogan of the meeting was "For a Colombia That Doesn't Surrender," suggesting that peace talks with the guerrillas were a capitulation.

All the same, it should be underlined how difficult the agreement with the armed apparatuses actually was. Agudelo maintains that when the paramilitaries arrived in the banana zone around 1997, they wanted to referee labor relations as the guerrilla groups had done before them. "We opposed this and the producers did as well, and we managed to make them respect the agreements to eradicate armed involvement in labor disputes" (Mario Agudelo, interview, 12 July 2000). Likewise, in the collective bargaining in the first semester of 2000 there were threats of a strike from the workers who were accused of attempting to disturb the peace in the region. To this, Sintrainagro responded that there could be no talk of democracy in Urabá if the right to strike was prohibited (Madarriaga, interview, 11 July 2000). Finally, a consensus was reached and there was no necessity to test forces, but the tension made it evident that there were potential cracks in the alliance. And although violence against labor leaders has diminished drastically in Urabá, the same has not occurred in Magdalena, the other banana-growing zone in Colombia. In January 2001, the president of the Sintrainagro affiliate in this department was murdered. Including this case, there have been twenty leaders assassinated in the Magdalena branch since its creation in 1991 (*El Tiempo*, 26 January 2001). In this region, to be a trade unionist still means to walk with death daily.

Nevertheless, for the members of Esperanza, Paz y Libertad and the labor leaders the most significant occurrence has been "the change in the way of thinking about things." For the trade unionists, the former model was polarized and rebellious and led to violence between workers and producers, and between them and administrators. Guillermo Rivera, president of Sintrainagro, says, "this culture of rebellion, of anarchy, leads to failure to follow the rules, to looking for a paycheck without working, attitudes that gained some currency among workers" (Rivera, interview, 12 October 2000). In this context, the social referent of the workers was the guerrillas, because there was no sense of future, and without this there was no sense of social and institutional belonging, explains Agudelo.

Moreover, "the worker was reduced to a salary, to a stable labor supply, without taking into account the human dimension, that is, his or her housing, family, region" (Mario Agudelo, interview, 12 July 2000). A fund for social security was included in the social pact, and in 1993 social security, as a state institution, opened in Urabá. This ended the medical service offered by the plantations and with it the conflicts over diagnoses and the assignment of sick days (time off) and medications. Likewise, a surcharge was levied on each box exported for the financing of urban housing and the elimination of the camps. With this "the worker's dignity was restored, and especially that of the worker's family. This helped the workers to feel that they had rights as persons, as individuals, and not only as a factor of production." In María de Agudelo's view, "what we are building is another standpoint, one that is closer to citizenship. The true revolution in Urabá is the construction of citizenship. We have moved from being subjects to feeling like citizens" (María de Agudelo, interview, 12 July 2000).

Social unionism and labor internationalism

The banana workers have not acted alone for this purpose of improving their living conditions—or of becoming citizens, as one of their leaders put it. In this unfavorable context for collective mobilization, they have received an extraordinary expression of international solidarity from Danish, Finnish and Spanish unions, as well as the advice of the International Union of Food and Allied Workers' Associations (IUF-UITA). This alliance, based in Geneva, Switzerland, seeks to unite the agribusiness workers on plantations and in the food industry into an international federation. In concrete terms, the Federation of Danish Workers, in association with the Danish government, renewed the financing of a training program for union leaders for a further six years. The initial grant ran for three years, until 2000. Finland's Centre for Union Solidarity is doing something similar through the National Trade Union School at Antioquia. Education is one of the most outstanding benefits won by Sintrainagro over the last decade. Every month they have between forty and fifty permits for two-day paid leave for courses in labor capacitation (Ríos, interview, 12 July 2000). For their part, the Spanish Unión Sindical is financing part of the construction costs of a 450-seat school in the La Chinita neighborhood of Apartadó, for children of workers and residents. Some European currents call this approach "social unionism." Traditionally, union organizations have turned their backs on the problems of the communities where they live if these are not directly related to labor issues. "The need is for unions to go beyond labor problems and confront social necessities," says Guillermo Rivera.

Worker-leaders are being encouraged to be political leaders as well. That is how the candidates associated with Sintrainagro or with Esperanza, Paz y Libertad won two of the four mayoralties in the banana belt in the October 2000 elections, and in Apartadó they obtained five of the twelve seats on the municipal council (Ríos, interview, 12 July 2000). International activities are also commonplace for the hardened leaders of Sintrainagro. They led the organizing process of a Latin American coordinator of banana workers' trade unions from its first meeting in Costa Rica in 1993, attended by workers from the host country, Colombia and Honduras. One year later, these countries formally established the coordinating body in a meeting held in Guatemala; the 1994 meeting was also attended by representatives from trade unions in Nicaragua, Guatemala, Panama, Ecuador, and Belize. The objectives that have been defined are respect for human rights, labor rights and the ILO conventions. The experience of the unions is that when a crisis occurs in the banana industry—generally a saturation of the market—national producers tend to violate the conventions in response to the low prices being paid (Rivera, interview, 12 October 2000).

This is the risk of the abolition of the European Union's quota system and the imposition of a first come, first served system. In practice, it favors countries such as Ecuador, where trade union freedoms are virtually nil and labor costs are lower. A worker earns between two and three dollars a day on average in Ecuador, while in Colombia or Costa Rica a worker earns five dollars, according to *El Tiempo* (13 October 2000). Up to now Ecuador has been the only Latin American country to accept the new rules of the game as laid out by the EU, which eliminate country quotas and allow supply and demand to set the price of a box of bananas.

In talks with the three largest banana merchants—Chiquita, Delmonte, and Dole—the coordinating body of the banana workers' unions has tried to get an agreement on respect for labor and union rights in the producing countries. Recently, an agreement was signed with Chiquita to end union persecution in Panama, and another is being negotiated to stimulate unionization and collective bargaining in Ecuador. There is an additional difficulty in implementing the ILO conventions in Ecuador, because parts of their banana plantations are state-owned. State and private sectors see it to be in their interest not to stick to international treaties. If the subject of labor and union rights is examined from a regional perspective, the producers in the countries with the most advanced national legislation—Colombia and Costa Rica—are interested in making standards uniform. Then all the producing countries would have a similar cost structure with respect to labor, and there would be no comparative advantage for the countries with weak unions. This could explain the support of Colombian business for the labor internationalism promoted by Sintrainagro.

Finally, the banana workers' unions are planning to broaden their scope to include the producers of sugar cane and African palm oil and, with the support of the ILO and the IUF, to begin organizing as they did in the banana industry, although this proposal is still in the planning stage. Up to now, the union organizations in Latin American countries exporting agricultural raw materials or produce have usually been grassroots unions. These are small, dispersed, and weak, and what are needed are industry unions, says Rivera. On this point "the Colombian banana workers are the most advanced, and we have paid a very high price for that," the president of Sintrainagro concludes.

These international alliances between Sintrainagro and progressive European unions, and the labor activism of Sintrainagro beyond the regional borders of Urabá, seem to contrast with the local public agendas, focused on order and security. This is the context in which the union has to operate, though it appears contradictory. Knowing the strategic capabilities of the Sintrainagro leadership and their allies, the possibility cannot be dismissed that this international activism is being used to counteract the relative isolation of Sintrainagro on the national union scene, and to construct alliances and supports *vis-à-vis* eventual changes in the national political arena as a result of the peace process with the FARC. Likewise, these international links can give Sintrainagro autonomy in relation to dominant local powers. International solidarity is backing the workers of Urabá. Evaluation reports of Finnish solidarity indicate that these organizations are forewarned of the situation and the political risks (Teivainen, 2000). The violence to which these workers have been subjected, their history of struggle and their project of abandoning armed insurrection, in favor of a more conciliatory strategy, have obtained support, although with a vigilant eye to the evolution of their local alliances.

Conclusion

This study has attempted to present a more complex portrait of a regional reality that has tended to be discredited and portrayed in black and white. The fact that a paramilitary force such as the AUC has gained military and political dominance in the region of Urabá should not inhibit the analysis of the forms of integration or "accommodation" of the different social sectors to these new realities. The argument developed here tries to rescue the historical agency of groups such as the banana workers and the supporters of Esperanza, Paz y Libertad. These actors are not just "victims" of a historical process or a more powerful force, but also builders and beneficiaries of a social order that is still undergoing transformation. What is interesting is to analyze how these radical projects and identities are consorting with groups considered to be foes only twelve years ago, and to examine the dynamic that brought them to this point.

This leads us to reflect on the impossibility of attributing behaviors to specific groups according to *a priori* classifications, without analyzing the relational settings in which they are acting. This is clear in the case of the banana workers of Urabá: in a single decade they moved from being considered as inhabitants of the "red zone" of Latin America and the vanguard of the Colombian insurrection, to participants in the project of restoring "law and order" in the region, a project that has an authoritarian character. Probably, they were not as revolutionary as they were once accused of being by the authorities and today they are not as reactionary as their opponents claim. Rather, they have had to move according to the changes in the relational contexts.

It is still surprising that the revolutionaries of a decade ago have today opted for citizenship, and that this is the way they now understand and narrate their experience. The respect for the law and the social solidarity associated with this concept cannot be separated from the violence and death to which the inhabitants of a region like Urabá have been subjected for the last 25 years. Besides, it must also be remembered that citizen rights make reference to a democratic struggle, and this is what the workers of Urabá appear to be attempting. Recently, their relative electoral success has shown this. How emancipatory their participation and that of their allies in this type of undertaking will be is yet to be seen, as well as the type of leadership that the new mayors and the councilmen elected with their support will exert. For the moment, being part of this coalition has allowed the workers to attain positions that until a decade ago were forbidden to them, at the risk of death.

The possibility that this group of workers, activists, and radical politicians ends up being co-opted by the coalition of power in Urabá is high; nevertheless, it should be kept in mind that they have led one of the most notable mobilizations for rights and recognition of recent decades in Colombia. Its history cannot be discredited with a stroke of the pen. It is true that in a context of armed conflict such as Urabá, the gains of the EPL represented the negation of rights and even life for the UP and groups close to it. However, it cannot be forgotten that the FARC front operating in Urabá has tried to force this region into submission at gunpoint, exposing it to the strategic ploys of a national leadership far away from its immediate needs. The EPL better understood the expectations of the region's inhabitants. It is worth remembering that in a context of war, initiatives that seem liberating can also be converted into forms of oppression and negation. The attempt here is not to endorse the political project underway in Urabá, far from it, but to call attention to the facile way in which an experience of social emancipation has been defamed in an environment where there have been more enemies than friends.

This text has shown the dilemmas confronted by labor and political activists in their struggles for emancipation in an authoritarian and violent environment. The first thing that has to be underlined is the loss of the monopoly over the means of coercion by the Colombian government, and the consequent collapse of the rule of law. In these circumstances, the logic of protection is imposed, and alignments are obligatory under pain of exposure to retaliation. The trajectory followed by the regional conflict was not inevitable in Urabá and could have taken another route. However, the national context of failed peace talks with the strongest guerrilla group, the FARC, the political and military rivalry between the FARC and the EPL, and the more regional character of the latter as opposed to the more national character of the FARC, converged to delineate a direction and an alignment of forces that unfortunately have prolonged the war.

Something that does indeed represent a truly new state of affairs, at least for Colombian unionism, is the new labor internationalism in the banana sector and the protagonism of the workers of Urabá. This new direction also represents a response to the new ways in which the commercial fruit empires function, as well as a result of the advice of and coordination with international organizations concerning the application of the minimum standards of labor legislation at the national level, as outlined by the ILO. Although the results of this new type of collaboration are yet to be seen, it is quite possible that it will bring benefits to the workers of countries with less developed labor and union legislation. However, as the lengthy, conflictive and bloody mobilization of Sintrainagro shows, these gains will not come by themselves.

Notes

1 This work received financial support from COLCIENCIAS, as part of the project "Regional Elites, Security and the Contemporary Crisis of the State in Colombia."

2 The banana belt generates approximately 18,000 direct and 5,000 indirect jobs in a region of about 30,000 hectares, divided among 409 plantations and 310 owners. The annual exports produce approximately 350 million dollars (CINEP, 1995) and place Colombia third among exporting countries, behind Ecuador and Costa Rica. The zone includes the municipalities of Chigorodó, Carepa, Apartadó, and Turbo.

3 Sindicato Nacional de Trabajadores de la Industria Agropecuaria (National Union of Workers of the Farming Industry).

4 Autodefensas Unidas de Colombia (United Self-Defense Groups of Colombia).

5 Autodefensas Campesinas de Córdoba y Urabá (Peasant Self-Defense Groups of Córdoba and Urabá).
6 See the weekly newsmagazine *Cambio*, 311, May 31–7 June 1999.
7 Following public criticism about the peace policies of his government, President Samper forced Bedoya to resign in 1997.

Bibliography

Alvarez, S., E. Dagnino and A. Escobar (1998). "Introduction: The cultural and the political in Latin American social movements," in S. Alvarez, E. Dagnino and A. Escobar (eds), *Culture of politics/politics of cultures. Re-visioning Latin American social movements*. Boulder, CO: Westview.

Botero, F. (1990). *Urabá. Colonización, violencia y crisis del estado*. Medellín: Universidad de Antioquia.

Calhoun, C. (1991). "The problem of identity in collective action," J. Huber (ed.), *Macro-micro linkages in sociology*. London: Sage.

CINEP (1995). *Urabá*. Coleccion Papeles de Paz. Bogotá: CINEP.

Comisión Andina de Juristas (1994). *Urabá*. Bogotá: Editorial Códice.

Dagnino, E. (1998). "Culture, citizenship, and democracy: changing discourses and practices of the Latin American left," S. Alvarez, E. Dagnino and A. Escobar (eds), *Culture of politics/politics of cultures. Re-visioning Latin American social movements*. Boulder, CO: Westview.

Defensoria del Pueblo (1992). *Estudio de caso de homicidio de miembros de la Unión Patriótica y Esperanza, Paz y Libertad*. Bogotá: Ediciones Jurídicas Gustavo Ibañez Ltda.

"Educación y Paz," supplement to *El Tiempo*, 16 August 2000.

Fundación Progresar (1996). "Recuperar el proceso de paz en Urabá. Informe sobre derechos humanos en Urabá con relacion al proceso de paz del EPL." Unpublished manuscript.

García, C. I. (1996). *Urabá: region, actores y conflicto, 1960-1990*. Medellín: INER–CEREC.

Ortíz, C. M. (1999). *Urabá: tras las huellas de los inmigrantes, 1955–1990*. Bogotá: ICFES.

Pécaut, D. (2000). "The loss of rights, the meaning of experience, and social connection: a consideration of the internally displaced in Colombia," *International Journal of Politics, Culture, and Society*, 14(1).

Ramírez, W. (1997). *Urabá: Los inciertos confines de una crisis*. Bogotá: Planeta.

Sandoval, M. (1997). *Gloria Cuartas: Por qué no tiene miedo*. Bogotá: Planeta.

Silva, R. (ed.) (1994). *Territorios, regiones, sociedades*. Cali: Departamento de Ciencias Sociales–CEREC.

Somers, M. (1993). "Citizenship and the Place of the Public Sphere: Law, Community, and Political Culture in the Transition to Democracy," *American Sociological Review* 58(2).

Teivainen, T. (2000). "Reporte evaluatorio de la actividad educativa de Sintrainagro." Unpublished manuscript. Helsinki: SASK (Centre for Union Solidarity of Finland).

Tilly, C. (1998). "Political identities," M. Hanagan *et al.* (eds), *Challenging authority. The historial study of contentious politics.* Minneapolis: U of Minnesota P.

— (1996). "Citizenship, Identity, and Social History," C. Tilly (ed.), *Citizenship, Identity, and Social History.* International Review of Social History Supplement 3. Cambridge: Cambridge UP.

— (1995). "Democracy is a lake," G. R. Andrews and H. Chapman (eds), *The social construction of democracy, 1870–1990.* New York: New York UP.

Uribe, M. T. (1992). *Urabá: region o territorio? Un analisis en el contexto de la politica, la historia y la etnicidad.* Medellín: CORPOURABA-INER.

Uribe, M. V. (1994). *Ni canto de gloria, ni canto fúnebre. El regreso del EPL a la vida civil.* Bogotá: CINEP.

Villarraga, A. and N. Plazas (1994). *Para reconstruir los sueños (una historia del EPL).* Bogotá: Fundacion Progresar-Fundación Cultura Democrática.

Warren, K. (1993). "Introduction," K. B. Warren (ed.), *The Violence Within. Cultural and Political Opposition in Divided Nations.* Boulder, CO: Westview.

Interviews

Agudelo, Mario, former EPL commander in the banana-growing zone, political leader of Esperanza, Paz y Libertad and mayor-elect of Apartadó; Medellín, 12 July 2000.

Agudelo, María, former Communist Party (M-L) militant, married to Mario Agudelo; Medellín, 12 July 2000.

Cuartas, Gloria, former mayor of Apartadó (1995-98), elected by a coalition of twelve political groups; Bogotá, 26 October 2000.

Madarriaga, Antonio, president of the board of directors of the ENS (National Trade Union School), Antioquia, and advisor to Sintrainagro; Medellín, 11 July 2000.

Ríos, Norberto, director of the ENS-Antioquia, which coordinates educational programs at Sintrainagro; Medellín, 12 July 2000 and 8 November 2000.

Rivera, Guillermo, president of Sintrainagro; Medellín, 12 October 2000.

Vásquez, Héctor, in charge of collective conventions, ENS-Antioquia; Medellín, 8 November 2000.

Part IV

PARTICIPATORY DEMOCRACY
IN ACTION

10

Social Emancipation in a Context of Protracted War: The Case of the Community of Peace in San José de Apartadó

María Teresa Uribe de H

INTRODUCTION

The purpose of this chapter is to present the experience of San José de Apartadó, a small village located in Colombia's Urabá region, whose inhabitants reacted to the escalation of armed conflict threatening village life by adopting a strategy of unarmed civil resistance against the war in order to defend their right to remain on their lands and in their homes, signing a public pact of non-collaboration with any armed actors, including the Colombian state.

By declaring itself a community of peace, this heterogeneous group of villagers recovered the autonomy to make its own decisions and to emancipate itself from the vertical and authoritarian powers that hovered over them. The village organized itself and gained public recognition by establishing ties with national institutions, but particularly with NGOs and foreign governments working to protect universal public goods.

This chapter is divided into four sections: the first deals with the relation between sovereignty under threat and social self-determination. The former helps explain the nature of the armed conflict in Colombia and the village in question, and how its escalation shaped the war-torn social backdrop against which the people of San José devised group actions and resistance strategies. The notion of self-determination helps us to interpret and make sense of the actions and strategies adopted by the villagers who, by rebelling against warring authoritarian powers and emancipating themselves from oppressive political orders, discovered news ways in which to produce power through innovative social compacts based on traditional participative democratic formulas.

The second section provides an overview of the social context of war in the Urabá region, discussing the significance of a protracted state of war and its role in creating *de facto* alternative orders that have sought to impose their hegemonic sovereignty over local groups and territories. San José de

Apartadó was only one of many villages faced with this situation, but thanks to its decision to adopt a community strategy for peace, its fate contrasts sharply with those of other villages in similar circumstances that succumbed to the effects of an escalating war by opting for exile.

The third section describes the process of the declaration of the community of peace and the actions and reactions of the different groups confronting each other and/or cooperating in the area, how the peace process evolved, and the advances and setbacks it has undergone during the four years of group effort.

The fourth section presents a reflection on the significance, meaning, and reach of the villagers' emancipatory discourses and protest actions, discussing how these actions and discourses may lead to new political practices and conceptions, or to establishing new connections to the nation, to citizenship, and to international cooperation.

THE RELATION BETWEEN THREATENED SOVEREIGNTY AND SOCIAL SELF-DETERMINATION

The relation between sovereignty under threat and social self-determination can help explain the importance and meaning of the persistent and courageous unarmed struggle being fought by the people of San José de Apartadó. Sovereignty is a canonical philosophical concept with fixed contents and substantive attributes having to do with the exclusivity, indivisibility, permanence, and totality of power. Modern states base their claims of legitimacy and hegemony on these attributes; it is sovereignty that allows state bodies to wield power, to demand the allegiance, submission, and obedience of those inhabiting their national territory, as well as to demand international recognition, their right to represent the nation as a whole and respect for their autonomy in decisions concerning internal matters (Badie, 2000: 43).

However, these substantive attributes may be jeopardized as a result of internal warring disputes, direct foreign intervention or by strategies of resistance and rebellion carried out by various unarmed social groups and actors defying public institutional power in varying degrees.

The specific nature of Colombia's armed conflict, with different types of outbreaks occurring simultaneously in its regions, the mutual involvement of military, paramilitary, delinquent, and social actors, the long duration of the war, and its moments of escalation, make it clear that the Colombian state, while having the substantive attributes of sovereignty (an ultimate, total, indivisible and exclusive power) and being internationally recognized, does not have the power or the ability to establish a nationwide public order, whether achieved by consensus or imposed by violence (Uribe de H, 1998). Furthermore, its ostensible representation of the country at the international level is challenged by processes of cooperation and protection of universal public goods, which establish direct and unmediated relations between parts of the national territory and diverse international actors.

The nature of the Colombian armed conflict reveals the fragility of the sovereignty of the state, raises doubts about its pervasiveness throughout the national territory, and about the indivisibility of the Republic. It further raises reasonable doubts as to whether the state has the power or the ability to put an end to hostilities and violence and to create a peaceful, unarmed society, thus inverting the terms of the equation: sovereignty–declared war (Hobbes, 1980: 22–45). If sovereignty is weak or under threat within many territories and social groups, this means that supreme power is decided in the spaces of war, and it is here that the competencies, domains, prerogatives, obligations and commitments of the citizens are defined. This would be an undeclared war, fought over the sovereign power of the nation; in other words, a war for the building of a nation in an era of globalization (Uribe de H, 1999).

Undeclared war or an almost permanent state of war (Schmitt, 1997: 31) has been one of the historical axes of life in Colombia. If a state's sovereignty is endangered and unevenly present in different national regions for prolonged periods of time, one would expect society to be in a state of chaos. However, this is not the case in Colombia. Amidst the intersecting dynamics of war, new alternative *de facto* orders are constantly taking shape. These are non-institutional authorities that exert power and make sovereign decisions for long periods of time within the territories they hold, since they hold the monopoly on all arms and taxes and control the resident population. These non-institutional authorities define and control territories, claiming an exclusive and permanent power over them. They draw up new geographical borders, changing the divisions of the national territorial layout, provide order and organization for the population, demand obedience, achieve some degree of consensus, and establish embryonic forms of political representation (Alonso and Vélez, 1998).

Thus we have a legally established political order imbued with the formal attributes of national sovereignty that coexists with regional *de facto* political orders, sustained by the force of arms, that likewise claim legitimacy and exclusive power. The result is an increasingly acute and open conflict over nation building. This is an apparently archaic war, already fought in the west during the eighteenth and nineteenth centuries, and one that supposedly has no place in an era of globalization.

Against this backdrop of a dispute waged by armed actors that include counter-institutional (guerrillas), para-institutional (paramilitary) and institutional groups (the army), all claiming sovereign power, civilian populations, pushed to the limit by the avatars of war, are developing peaceful, emancipatory strategies in defiance of all. These populations are devising their own forms of social self-determination while discovering other modes of producing power and gaining national and international visibility as they reinvent participatory democratic practices through socio-economic and political-ethical pacts, thus taking an alternative stance in the fight for sovereignty.

Self-determination has to do with a given social group's ability to emancipate itself from hegemonic, or purportedly hegemonic powers, which they perceive as being oppressive, discriminatory and unjust, limiting the freedom of their collective life, debasing their dignity, violating their rights or endangering their lives, their property or their collective goods (Arendt, 1974: 233-319). From this standpoint, self-determination implies freely taking responsibility for their own future as a people and as a social group, with no outside interference; it means making their own decisions about rules of sociability and political order, according to the general will or the will of the majority; it means devising the administrative and management structures required to put the chosen political order in place, as well as preserving what the group has defined as its cultural and historical heritage.

Self-determination as conceived by the traditional social sciences (Miller, 1997: 149) seemed to lead inevitably to political independence, to the founding of a distinct sovereign state that represented a collectivity in both domestic and international contexts. However, the emergence in the public sphere of new social actors who make specific claims (concerning the recognition of differences in gender, ethnicity, culture, or age) and who denounce, among other things, inequality in social development or social status, has led to a redefinition of the contents of political self-determination within transversal and highly complex domains, where those contents would no longer have the foundation of a modern state as their teleological end. On the contrary, these struggles for individual and group recognition may be bringing about a new political matrix, not state-centered but de-centered, with multiple nodal points providing differentiated meanings and directions to social tensions and conflicts (Cavarozzi, 1993).

For these reasons, struggles for self-determination can develop in multiple social spheres, and be set against differentiated forms of power (Santos, 2000). These struggles can be waged by a wide variety of subjects who, depending on the cultural, economic or social contexts in which they live, devise significant emancipatory and counter-hegemonic actions and discourses that are capable of transforming the referents of a whole society, while not necessarily leading to political independence or the founding of a new sovereign state.

These processes of social self-determination may have a broad scope of action with very different institutional implications. They may include rebellion, autonomy and recognition, demanding institutional and legally binding changes (García and Uprimny, 2000), struggles for inclusion according to differentiated statuses (feminists and ethnic groups), or changes in the political regime that imply some form of federation (Kymlika, 1996). Such

processes might not find any expression on the legal and institutional frameworks, but do find it within the social world, in the ways power is produced
and the forms of action and knowledge put into practice by heterogeneous
groups fighting against situations they deem oppressive, as they demand
recognition, respect, moral restitution or quasi-sovereign autonomy for
matters affecting the conditions of their life in society.

The novel and defiant experience of San José de Apartadó in its transversal approach to self-determination within a turbulent, multifocal, war-torn
social context, in an effort aspiring not to social inclusion, reform or overthrow of the regime in power, but rather to unarmed civilian resistance against
the oppressive situation created by war, requires that a new look be taken at
the possible contents of self-determination, beyond the traditional definition
of political science.

Within the context of war, political self-determination implies self-
knowledge, that is, approaching a situation perceived as oppressive, discriminatory or exclusionary from the perspective of personal or social experience.
Several types of social responses could be expected from people facing such
experiences. One is conformity (Santos, 2000), but there is also a series of
strategies that could be termed "invisible resistance." These do not imply
direct action against hegemonic or authoritarian powers; rather, they are ways
of evading the control being imposed on them, ways of denying their domination or apparent accommodation to such powers while waiting for a better
moment to stand up and act. However, these responses may express hostility, rebellion, non-conformity, and rejection of any type of submission or
acceptance of the dominant powers.

A variety of strategies can be used to express this so-called invisible resistance. These can include accommodation or passive acceptance of the
dominant order or of competing orders, eschewing any participation in them,
using hostile silence and passive rejection; self-imposed invisibility or strategic withdrawal from public life or from areas controlled by the institutional
power can also be used as a means of preserving identity, autonomy and
freedom in the face of established authorities who have sovereign, hegemonic
aspirations and who attempt to civilize, discipline, control, dominate, exploit,
or include the population in a political order it rejects but cannot confront
openly. Finally, there is a dual type of action that implies a partial and selective acceptance of the various competing orders vying for the allegiance of
the war zone populations, while steering clear of direct confrontation with
or public rejection of any of the disputing parties (Uribe de H, 1999).

These different strategies of invisible and oblique resistance employed in
highly conflictive areas submerged in a long-term state of war might simply
be defined as means of social survival for the people in question. But even
though they do not signify alternative forms of producing power, they do
disclose silent and non-visible forms of expression, showing how a culture

has learned to avoid the violent and hegemonic claims of dominant actors. These forms are already part of the stock of common sense shared by the excluded and oppressed people in Colombia.

In order for rebellion to assume emancipatory forms, recognition is required in addition to self-knowledge. This means that the situation perceived as oppressive, discriminatory, or exclusionary must be presented in the public sphere, reasonably discussed, and narrated to other social actors outside the immediate environment. From here, autonomous forms of social organization and alternative ways of producing power can be developed for the purpose of confronting the existing oppressive hegemonic powers.

Emancipatory rebellion can take myriad forms, ranging from disruptive practices—such as mobilizations, peasant marches, occupation of public buildings, or roadblocks—to armed insurgency, and including unarmed civil resistance. Its purpose may be to overthrow an oppressive regime, express rejection of an action considered to be discriminatory or injurious, or to safeguard the right to autonomy and self-determination by setting limits to authoritarian powers.

Emancipatory rebellion is visible, publicly demonstrated, discursive and dialogic, and develops counter-hegemonic practices that may lead to alternative ways of producing power and of organizing the collectivity for a shared, autonomous and self-determining way of life, providing new contents to the traditional formulas of participatory democracy.

SAN JOSÉ DE APARTADÓ WITHIN THE REGIONAL CONTEXT OF URABÁ—A TRADITION OF REFUGE AND RESISTANCE

Urabá, the region where San José de Apartadó is located, is one of the territories where different *de facto* orders and insurgent political actors are established, each claiming sovereign power. A geographical area of great contrasts and marked ethnic diversity, Urabá is home to zones of accelerated and unplanned urbanization mixed with small traditional farmhouses and villages of indigenous and black people. The economy combines banana production for export (based on high technology and an entrepreneurial organization of work) with extensive cattle-raising, large areas of peasant economies, and spontaneous settlements that encroach on the surviving jungles and primeval forests. The region's forms of political and social organization are equally diverse and contrasting. There are farmer's unions (now silenced or co-opted) juxtaposed with community organizations, associations of peasants, indigenous councils (*cabildos*) and different organizations of blacks. Small cooperatives subsist alongside the huge producers' and exporters' guilds. Moreover, every single political party in the country has some type of representation in Urabá, although the historically strong left-wing parties have now been virtually eradicated (Uribe de H, 1992: 63–102).

If to this already complex scenario we add Urabá's strategic geographical location and the domestic and international interests at play, it makes for an even more complicated situation. It could be said that Colombia is personified in Urabá, one of the regions with the best prospects for entering international market networks. Its location between the Atlantic and Pacific Oceans, its proximity to Central America, the Caribbean, Panama, and Venezuela, its tradition in exports, its natural resources and the megaprojects designed to make it a globalized economic zone clearly denote the multiplicity of domestic and international economic interests that are found in a region plagued by major social conflicts and intense armed confrontation (Planea, 1999).

The Urabá territory was the entry point used by the Spanish from the sixteenth century on. But indigenous resistance to the Spanish, disputes between groups of conquistadors and between these and other foreign colonists (French, Scottish, and English), as well as the constant presence of pirates along the coasts, all helped to feed conflicts to such an extent that it was all but impossible to establish permanent settlements. This meant that Urabá was left out of the Spanish process of colonization and population. The beginning of the republic did not change this situation, and for centuries Urabá remained a vast, sparsely inhabited territory in which institutions had a weak hold; its economy was based on scavenging and exploiting the forest, and forms of semi-forced labor and rapacious capitalism predominated (Parsons, n.d.: 43–51).

Vast territory that it was, Urabá gradually became a refuge and stronghold for all those who, for whatever reason, did not fit within the narrow bounds of the desired national identity: runaway negro slaves fleeing the mines and *haciendas*, Indians fleeing the reservations and opposing the authority of whites and creoles, outlaws, smugglers of gold and European contraband, people vanquished during the endemic civil wars, political refugees, and societal outcasts, all gravitated to Urabá to form a highly diverse population, sharing only the stigma of exclusion, the need for refuge, and the desire to become invisible, far from the control of civil and religious authorities (Uribe de H, 1992: 39–52).

This was Urabá until the 1960s, when colonization was finally achieved thanks to two major events: the first being the opening of the 1954 highway that linked the region with central Colombia, which immediately led to a huge influx of peasants from provinces all over the nation fleeing the partisan violence of the 1950s; the second event being a proposal by the United Fruit Company, made through its affiliate Frutera de Sevilla, which offered highly attractive economic incentives to any would-be Colombian national banana entrepreneurs willing to take a business risk in this area. The proposal was very well received, and in only a few years a major portion of the territory was transformed by capitalist agricultural undertakings and rapid urban development (Botero, 1990: 13–41).

But these processes of economic integration were not accompanied by an institutional presence, respect for the rule of law or the recognition of the rights and guarantees of the region's residents and workers. Private interests, left to their own devices, imposed their own laws through the use of force, outright violence and territorial, authoritarian control of the inhabitants, who were violently ousted from flatlands due to the expansion of entrepreneurial agriculture. The same method was used on newcomers, who were subjected to a vertical labor regime, with no institutional mediation or social support. In this context of violent, abrupt and rapid change, San José de Apartadó was founded in the foothills of the Abibe mountain range, very near to the heart of the *bananera* zone and its main urban center, Apartadó.

Its historical role as a zone of refuge, combined with the social upheaval caused by an economic transformation that occurred in the absence of institutional mediation, led to armed confrontation in Urabá. By the late 1960s, the region had become a territory at war, with several armed factions in the area, the most important being the communist-leaning FARC and the Maoist EPL, although the latter became a political movement in 1991 after the conclusion of a peace process with the national government.

For the armed organizations, especially for FARC, the *bananera* zone was a site for military action, serving not only as a source of financial gains made from kidnapping and economic blackmail, but also as a field for political action. Here they exerted their influence over trade unions and social organizations, established negotiations with farm-owners and overseers whom they forced to take on workers, and pressured public administrators to channel social investments into the neighborhoods and rural areas where the armed organizations had political influence. These actions helped them gain favor with some, but also led to harsh reactions from those whose economic interests they harmed or whose lives they threatened (Uribe de H, 1992: 237–41).

However, in the areas of the peasant economy, the settlement zones and small villages such as San José de Apartadó, relations were smoother and tensions lower, because people did not feel threatened by the guerrilla presence, since they were not the direct target of their military actions. In these areas the armed groups maintained a significant influence. They played a role in the processes of settlement and occupation of territories, in the distribution of commons or squatter lands, in the definition of the rights to possession, and of the size and boundaries of peasants' individual plots; they also controlled timber-cutting and water use, monitored the price of supplies and goods distributed in the villages, forced local bosses to adhere to minimum wages and to create adequate living conditions for workers, helped social organizations carry out small-scale public works (some using government funding) and at times exercised pressure to channel public spending to these villages (personal interviews, 1999).[1]

Over a period of more than forty years—and in the case of San José de Apartadó, since its founding—these insurgent powers have become a point of reference for those who have taken refuge in these settlements, people with highly diverse regional and ethnic backgrounds and with cultural practices that have sometimes clashed. However, this situation of domination, control, and management has developed in many instances into the exercise of judicial functions: the insurgent groups have solved family conflicts and disputes between neighbors, they have gotten petty delinquency under control and provided semi-state functions of protection, order and security in exchange for unconditional allegiance and absolute, unquestioning obedience.

The settlers were drawn to the insurgents by a kind of shared morality rather than by political identification or ideological agreement. This was due to their own experiences, with exclusion and seeking refuge, their moral outrage at abuses, inequalities and lack of recognition, and perhaps also because they shared the armed organizations' notions of rebellion and justice—something akin to vengeance—that for them legitimized the armed groups' violent actions as a way of re-establishing a balance destroyed by earlier violence. The insurgent actions were seen by the settlers as "another form of law" capable of imposing sanctions and punishment, a law wielded by a different authority that also aspired to be absolute, total, permanent, and indivisible, but which for the peasants served as an intelligible principle of the social environment, and as a point of reference for their actions and behavior.

The uneven and regionalized development of the state of war in Colombia ended up activating private and illegal counter-insurgent processes, with the eruption of different paramilitary movements. Among these, the communist-leaning Autodefensas Campesinas (Peasant Self-Defenses) in Córdoba and Urabá were the most important. These groups focused their actions mainly on territories in which guerrilla organizations had had a longstanding organizational presence, in an effort to reconquer the territory and dismantle the insurgent control. Their strategy did not differ greatly from that of their enemies: it was a war of movements (Cubides, 1997).

These groups deployed a "full sweep" strategy, starting with the northern area of Urabá and moving southward. They left the reconquered zones bathed in blood, leading to massive, forced displacement; civilian and military authorities were co-opted or overpowered, and social networks and organizations were broken up or reorganized to further their plans for domination. And of course they also left behind armed groups and unarmed sympathizers to control the populations and hold on to the newly conquered military terrain. This paramilitary incursion began in Urabá in the late 1980s, but did not manage to subjugate the town of Apartadó or its jurisdiction, San José, until early 1996 (personal interviews, 1999).

SAN JOSÉ DE APARTADÓ: A STORY OF REBELLION, RESISTANCE AND SOCIAL ORGANIZATION

One of the bloodiest and most violent chapters of the war over Urabá was written in San José de Apartadó. The paramilitary groups were suspicious of its history of resistance and rebellion. From the time the settlers arrived in the mountains in the 1960s, tensions mounted and there was constant conflict with the absentee landlords, who used dubious deeds to claim they owned the land. The newly arrived settlers quickly organized a communal action committee and carried out collective actions that brought them in contact with the Asociación de Usuarios Campesinos (Peasant Land Users' Association). The association taught them the tactics of squatting, how to claim their rights and guarantee their ownership of the land they farmed.

They also used their community organization to get in touch with the Apartadó local authorities and with politicians from the traditional political parties to demand that government funds be allocated to build a road linking San José with Apartadó. At the time there was only a mule path, which was impassable in winter, forcing the peasants to travel for at least twelve hours to get their products to the thriving municipal market. They further demanded state funding to build a school, a community center and money to buy the land for the village from the absentee landowner (Uribe de H, 1992: 116–17).

Since the landowner refused to sell, they began squatting. There were evictions, jail time for the leaders, and wounded and battered participants. But thanks to the effective work of the Asociación de Usuarios Campesinos, they won the lawsuit and began to build their village. They set aside plots for a chapel and a local police station, and reserved space for a town square, from which the main streets fanned out, much as they did in the old villages of the provinces of Antioquia and Caldas, from which most of the early settlers came.

This squatting invasion was followed by another to settle inhabitants who did not have their own plots of land. This second invasion was less traumatic than the first, since the landowner decided to reach an amicable agreement through Incora (the Colombian Institute for Agricultural Reform), which was carrying out a census of landowners in the area. The decision was also helped along by the presence of guerrilla organizations in the area. In this way, Mariano, as the settlement was first called, was founded (Parsons, n.d.: 224). The settlers later changed the name to San José, the patron saint of farmers, since all shared a dedication to life in the country and a love of the land. Thanks to social rebellion and organized resistance, the settlement was founded and the surrounding areas opened up.

From that point on, the settlers developed a dual approach: one with the state and another with the counter-state. The guerrillas set the guidelines for local life, establishing order in the process of settlement within the territory, resolving conflicts and controlling small-time criminals. But at the same time the inhabitants also maintained relations with the municipal authorities through their community action, seeking funds for the settlement's infrastructure and new social improvement programs. Shortly thereafter, they gained the ear of the Corpourabá, the Regional Development Corporation, which started up cooperative programs for cocoa and banana production, supporting them with funding, technical assistance, post-harvest management, and crop sales (Corpourabá, 1990).

For the San José settlers, it was clear that two opposing political orders hovered over them. One was the institutional legal order, from which the settlers demanded economic support, public investment, social improvement programs, and other means for collective consumption, while rejecting any of its attempts to control public life, the use of force or a military presence in their area; judicial authorities and the police were absent from the village.

Juxtaposed with the selectively accepted public institutional order was the military-political order of the guerrillas, who defined authoritatively the rules of social coexistence, including where the residents lived within the territory; they controlled the forest, water sources, the price of supplies, wages, and the establishment of shops and canteens. They further served as a police force, keeping down petty crime, and as judge and jury, alleviating tension in cases of domestic conflicts and disagreements among neighbors.

After the municipal political regime was reformed and mayoral popular elections were held for the first time, the leftist party Unión Patriótica—fruit of the early peace agreements with FARC—managed to take over four municipalities in the Urabá region, including Apartadó, and obtained majority representation on several city councils after 1986. This was a major step forward for San José, because it began to receive a good part of city funding (Comunidad de Paz, 1998: 3).

The settlers, who in the past had barely taken part in elections, now threw all their efforts into supporting this political project, thus turning San José into one of party's major electoral strongholds in the region. Institutional recognition was achieved through the establishment of the jurisdiction of San José, and the population enjoyed a period of significant social and economic expansion. By the early 1990s, San José had slightly over 3,000 inhabitants living within the town limits and in 32 hamlets along the slopes of the Abibe mountain range (Comunidad de Paz, 1998: 2).

Its history of rebellion, social resistance, and organization, and then its status as a political sympathizer of Unión Patriótica, placed the jurisdiction in one of the hotspots of national armed conflict, on the FARC's side. This was reason enough for paramilitary action to focus on this small settlement, but there was an even more important reason that had to do with the geographical strategy of the war. In effect, San José de Apartadó is the main entrance point into the Abibe mountains, which have been a guerrilla sanctuary for many years; it is only 12 km from Apartadó, the most important economy in the region, and a vital center of the banana farming zone. All of the above meant that the guerrillas could carry out their military actions in the zone and quickly hide out in the mountains, in addition to having access to a rich agricultural zone nearby for their supplies and logistical support from the settlers. The main routes used by the guerrillas also run through San José: the route linking Urabá with western Córdoba through the Abibe mountains; the one providing access to the middle and lower Atrato; and another connecting Urabá with the south of Bolivar and with western and northeastern Antioquia through the Paramillo crossroads, now a paramilitary stronghold.

Thus whoever holds control of the San José de Apartadó territory enjoys a comparative military advantage for controlling the entire region as well as a good portion of north-western Colombia. And so San José's destiny became linked to the dynamics of the armed conflict and, furthermore, to the strategic demands of the war for national sovereignty, which meant that the settlers lost their political bargaining power and even their livelihood. Their right to remain on the land was placed once again in question.

San José's tradition of rebellion, resistance and social organization, as well as its strategic location made it into one of the hubs of the war for Urabá. It was in this context that the strategy to declare itself a community of peace was framed.

The tragic trajectory of the Community of Peace

Armed conflict in San José de Apartadó escalated in the early 1990s. Unión Patriótica party members were systematically exterminated, and several of their supporters residing in San José were also killed. Armed confrontation between the army and the guerrillas became increasingly frequent, leading some peasants to flee to Apartadó, and to return gradually only when the attacks were over (Nieto, 1998). But most settlers remember 1996 as the year the paramilitaries came onto the scene and the war took a marked turn for the worse.

On 28 February 1996, several settlers were murdered at a paramilitary checkpoint set up at the only entrance to the village. A march was organized to denounce the crime, but at least ninety families fled the area, fearful and confused at being accused of aiding the guerrillas (Naranjo, 2000).

On 27 March of the same year San José declared its neutrality with respect to all armed groups. Although this was a strategy already adopted by some municipalities and indigenous communities in the region, that same night the paramilitary groups attacked the residents of the municipal seat, and told them that they would maintain the road blockade. At the same time, the guerrillas continued to patrol the surrounding area, clearly unaware of the population's decision (Naranjo, 2000).

Declaring neutrality was a very difficult decision for the jurisdiction's residents to make since it meant emancipating themselves from the guerrillas, an armed contingent with whom the village had maintained complex multilateral relations almost since their arrival in the area. This implied giving up a political order that had been the main referent for the settlement's actions and structuring principles and that had significantly contributed to community cohesion, management and organization. Furthermore, the decision of non-collaboration implied setting limits to the paramilitary advance, as well as denying the sovereign attributes of the state, since neutrality included refusing to allow the security forces access to the territory or to occupy its seat. In short, declaring neutrality was tantamount to "declaring war on the war."

The declaration rapidly received a bloody baptism. In the second week of September 1996, a paramilitary group raided the homes of Gustavo Loaiza, chairman of Community Action, Juan González, chairman of the Cocoa Growers' Cooperative, María Eugenia Usuga, a member of the Women's Committee, and Samuel Arias, a well-known union leader, detained, and then murdered all four. "Strangely enough, the day before the murders, the army had withdrawn from the hamlet (*caserío*) it had been occupying since August" (Comunidad de Paz, 1998: 6). The population's response to the massacre was one of mass exodus, and the few who dared remain behind dispersed to sleep in the foothills "to keep from being killed by the paramilitary groups, who were acting jointly with the army, something we, the inhabitants, have witnessed" (Comunidad de Paz, 1998: 6). Of those killed, some had promoted collective actions defending the right to life, had denounced the paramilitary nine-month road blockade, and in July of that year had signed a letter of reconciliation with the national government in which they promised to stop the peasants' exodus in return for the government's promise to provide minimum guarantees for the return of those who had already fled (*El Colombiano*, 1996: 5).

1997 dawned no brighter for San José. One day in February,

[a] group of 40 paramilitaries, most of whom we recognized as being reinserted EPL members, showed up at six in the morning and forced all the villagers to go to the sports park and, after threatening to kill them if they did not leave the village, started tying up several people who were found dead on the road to Apartadó the next day. From that point on, the paramilitaries totally controlled the road. They controlled the passage of all food, constantly commandeered vehicles of passers-by, checked people's documentation against a list they had, and killed those whose names were on the list. (personal interviews, 2000)

San José was besieged by hunger and terror, while civil and military authorities stood idly by, doing nothing to stop the situation. This unbearable
situation forced most of those living in the urban center to flee. With the
town nearly uninhabited, the peasants attempting to hold out on their own
plots of land were left totally isolated. All of their strategies (the formal complaints, the peasant marches, the declaration of neutrality) appeared to have
failed to keep the war from sweeping through their territory. But the remaining peasants decided to resist the onslaught, stay on their land, and rework
their proposal of neutrality by declaring themselves a Community of Peace
(Naranjo, 2000).

The Community of Peace agreement was signed on 23 March 1997. To
help draft it, the settlers had the aid and support of the Apartadó Diocese,
the Intercongregational Commission for Justice and Peace, and Cinep.
Thanks to the intermediation of these NGOs the settlers began establishing
contact with international human rights' organizations, who helped
denounce the dramatic situation of the San José settlers (Naranjo, 2000).
Although the Community of Peace declaration qualified the former neutrality statement, and went into greater detail as to the commitments to be
undertaken, it elicited no positive response from the armed groups, who continued with their armed actions as before, totally ignoring the wishes of a
group of people who no longer accepted any of them as representatives.

On 28 March 1997, a skirmish between army and guerrilla troops in a
rural area of the jurisdiction reportedly left four guerrillas dead at La Unión.
The veracity of this information was disputed by the peasants, who said the
dead were in fact unarmed peasants out working in their fields. Hostilities
continued for several days, including massive bombings of the area. Shortly
thereafter, paramilitary troops appeared in Arenas, La Unión, Las Nieves, and
El Guineo. After murdering some peasants, they issued strict permanent evac-
uation orders to those remaining, saying their lands had to be vacated within
two to five days (Comunidad de Paz, 1998: 18).

But the peasants refused to give up, and continued to stick to their project.
Since it was nearly impossible to survive in isolation out on their individual
plots, they returned to the nearly abandoned seat of the jurisdiction and
together restarted their movement of resistance. Despite the lack of governmental guarantees, some evacuees returned armed only with the conviction
that the moral strength of a community determined to live under terms of
neutrality and collective work was powerful enough to allow them to remain
on their lands and resist the ravages of war (Naranjo, 2000).

In May 1997, only two months after the Community of Peace agreement
was signed, the settlers of San José, during an event on active neutrality held
among the returned communities of Atrato Medio, reported that Francisco
Turqunico, one of the most fervent and dedicated promoters of the
Community of Peace, had been murdered. They also reported that 32 people

had died at the hands of the armed groups over the previous year. The guerrillas were cited as being responsible for the violent death of a young woman engaged to a soldier in the national army, and that of one male peasant accused of being an informer for the paramilitaries, who in turn were held responsible for the remaining 30 murders (Comunidad de Paz, 1997: 6b).

The guerrillas, now relatively isolated, suffering from supply problems, and missing the logistic support they had counted on in the past, began to place increasing pressure on the San José settlers. As a response to the settlers' persistent refusal to help them, they killed Ramiro Correa, a member of the internal council of the Community of Peace, along with Luis Fernando Espinosa and Fernando Aguirre, members of the community work groups, at Cristalina on October 6, 1997 (*El Tiempo*, 1997: 7a).

1997 was one of Urabá's most tragic and bloodiest years. Virtually the entire region was in flames, one population after another fled *en masse*, and the number of murders and massacres rose dramatically. San José de Apartadó was only one of the numerous settlements and hamlets under siege. The residents of middle and lower Atrato, of Mutatá and Bajirá, as well as the inhabitants of the municipalities of the *bananero* axis were in the same straits (Naranjo, 2000). Nevertheless, this organized social group somehow continued to resist. Hopeless though it seemed, they stubbornly adhered to their decision to remain on their land and rebuild daily life within the framework of the founding agreement of the Community of Peace.

Despite this situation, one year after proclaiming itself a community of peace, those who had sought refuge in the urban area began to return to their lands. In March 1998, a group of 300 peasants returned to their fields in La Unión. This courageous, risky step initiated a kind of second stage in the process: as the year progressed, more and more waves of peasants returned, and the organization became stronger, gained greater visibility with national state bodies and established major ties and links with international non-governmental organizations that decided to directly support the peasants' resistance and quest for autonomy.

The increasing international support led the paramilitaries to issue a declaration saying they would respect the community of peace as long as the guerrillas left the zone. The insurgents made no formal statement, but did adopt a more cautious attitude, and so an entente was reached between the armed groups and the community. This lasted a few months, long enough for the peasants to restart crop production, consolidate their organizational strategy and begin to implement the goals of their community of peace (personal interviews, 2000).

On a national level, the settlers established contacts with the office for displaced persons, the Ombudsman's Office, the Ministry of the Presidency, and the Social Solidarity Network, among others, to request minimum guarantees that they could stay on their lands. They also sought economic aid, since food and basic goods were becoming increasingly scarce, due to the roadblocks, the controls on food supplies, the loss of crops, tools and domestic animals and their months of absence from their lands (GAP, 1998). Neither municipal nor departmental authorities served as their interlocutors; the settlement made its case known nationally, sidestepping intermediate administrative bodies and relying on the constant help of NGOs who had worked with them from the onset. But perhaps the most significant contacts were the strategic alliances with different international non-governmental actors who were also the only reasonably effective guarantee for the continuity of the Community of Peace project (Arenas, 1999).

The NGOs with the longest and most enduring relationship with the Community of Peace are the Intercongregational Committee for Peace and Justice, a national body comprising several Catholic NGOs, and the International Peace Brigades, whose work in Colombia focuses on protecting vulnerable groups and persons placed at risk by the war. Both organizations have been following the process since its inception and have representatives living in the community, assisting it in many different ways. They work with the settlers on their unarmed civil resistance strategy, travel with them to the fields, to the municipal seat at Apartadó, to the capital, Bogotá, or to other regions. They collaborate in organizational and pedagogical tasks and have also helped put the settlers in touch with the representatives of foreign governments and other NGOs working to protect universal public goods.

Moreover, their ongoing presence serves as a reminder to all armed actors, including the state, that this group that has opted for peace and resistance to the war is protected by the Catholic Church and the international community. Therefore, any aggression against these inhabitants will meet with energetic protests from the countries and organizations the NGOs represent. This collaboration, as well as the letters and communiqués of solidarity and support arriving continuously from all over the world (around one thousand per month), is what the inhabitants of San José value most. In their own words,

> international solidarity [...] is what has helped us to maintain the strength of our convictions and to endure all this suffering [...] because it is a way to tell the state that our community is not alone, and because we ourselves realize we have many friends all over the world who are concerned about us. (Arenas, 2000)

Thanks to the intermediation of the International Peace Brigades and Peace and Justice, the settlers have been receiving economic aid in the form of food, seeds and farm tools, as well as the logistic support they need to start producing crops again and so guarantee their survival. The UN Association for Cooperation with Refugees has been in constant communication with the settlers of San José and has accompanied many refugees as they return to the zone. The office of the UN Advisor for the Protection of Human Rights has also sent representatives on several occasions to hear the settlers' accounts of murders and abuses and to launch the corresponding actions. Other international NGOs, such as Pax Christi and Amnesty International, have also helped out at different moments of this process (Naranjo, 2000).

York University in Canada, the University of Wisconsin-Madison in the United States and the cities in which they are located have declared themselves twin cities of San José, providing highly valuable support, and keeping in constant touch. These bodies help disseminate the San José experience of unarmed resistance internationally and coordinate the collection and shipping of different types of aid to the settlers. Colombia Support is a North American NGO that is helping to relaunch cocoa and exotic banana crops, and working to market and eventually export the banana crops (Arenas, 2000).

Through the NGO Echo, the Dutch parliament and the Spanish organization Paz y Tercer Mundo, the European Union has recognized San José's experiment in social reconstruction with aid allocation. In 1998, San José was awarded the Pfeffer Peace Prize by the Fellowship of Reconciliation, international recognition of the example it was setting for a world in search of peace (Naranjo, 2000). A contingent of settlers went to accept the award and had the opportunity to explain their situation to the people of the United States. They toured the USA again in 1999, visiting the Madison, Wisconsin, area among others. That same year, thanks to the support of the European Union, representatives of the Community of Peace visited the Netherlands, Belgium, and Germany. The community of San José also received and met with a delegation of more than ten European ambassadors, who heard them out and later manifested their concern to the Colombian government regarding the ongoing violation of the terms of the peace project (Arenas, 2000).

The people of San José highly value such international solidarity:

> The fact that we are carrying out production processes, that the children are back in school—the schools had first been first closed, then destroyed—that we have minimal health care is the most important thing, because we achieved it by fighting back, and sacrificing the lives of our people! (Arenas, 2000)

These strategic alliances with international non-governmental actors are leading to what might be called the globalization of the local. A tiny settlement of peasants who had probably never traveled outside their own region managed to make their case known to the world. They have been visited by foreign ambassadors and government representatives, they have traveled to other continents, and have received expressions of solidarity and economic aid from many different sources. And more importantly, they have defied their hierarchical subordination to the state itself, bypassing the substantive attributes of sovereignty and establishing direct contact with a wide variety of international actors. It is as if the Euclidean space of national states and of the world organization that is based upon them had been replaced by a quantum space that shapes decentered networks and waves whose purpose, as Badie would say, is to build responsible communities (Badie, 2000: 128), which, although made of fragmentations and interpenetrations, aim at protecting universal public goods such as the right to life, peace, human rights, the environment, and the fight against poverty.

The uneasy balance achieved by the settlement during 1998 started to crumble at the time of the second anniversary of the Community of Peace. In March 1999, a group of Urabá cattlemen, merchants, and industrialists issued a communiqué stating that they felt it was too much of a coincidence that the guerrillas maintained a presence in the localities receiving aid from international and national NGOs (El Colombiano, 1999: 8a). These accusations were refuted by national supervisory bodies, such as the Attorney-General's Office and the Ombudsman's Office. Nevertheless, the allegation sowed seeds of doubt, not only as to the neutrality and autonomy of the different peace communities in the region, but also as to the work of the NGOs that backed them. Using this pretext, direct attacks against the communities of peace were resumed, unleashing another cycle of atrocities and murders in San José that has not yet ended.

In April 1999, the community suffered a new paramilitary attack. According to several eyewitnesses, members of the Self-Defense Brigades of Córdoba and Urabá entered the village and intimidated the population with threats, herding them all into the community center. Once there, they selected six previously identified persons and killed them in front of their neighbors and families (El Colombiano, 1999: 7a). This massacre was followed by bloody guerrilla attacks. By the year 2000, barely three years after the establishment of the community of peace, the village's death toll had risen to 83.[2] After these bloody events the precarious equilibrium attained over the previous year was lost, and the logic of war once again came onto the scene.

In July 2000, a new massacre shook the foundations of the community organization. This time a group of paramilitarists invaded La Unión, one of the most resistant and courageous hamlets. The victimizers once again gathered all the villagers at one site and asked them to identify their leaders. Given the response that the entire village was involved in moving the peace process forward, they selected six people at random and executed them on the spot (telephone interview, 2000).

From that moment, harassment and violence escalated. By December 2000, the Intercongregational Committee for Justice and Peace issued a communiqué to Colombia's highest-ranking public authorities denouncing a new road blockade. They said that, both in the village and in the municipal seat of Apartadó, the residents and the international NGO representatives accompanying them were followed and threatened by paramilitary groups, who seized the aid and money donated from outside sources, as well as what the residents got from the sale of their crops and products, while threatening to occupy the village if the population did not leave within a reasonable period of time. The communiqué ended by denouncing complicity between the army's 17th Brigade and the paramilitaries in the area (Justicia y Paz, 2000).

In March 2001, four years after the establishment of the community of peace, they made good on their threat. A paramilitary commando entered the village, took it over, and partially burned the headquarters out of which the Community of Peace operated, which was where aid materials were stored and also where religious representatives and members of the International Peace Brigades were housed. They burned 15 homes to the ground while repeatedly ordering the population to leave the area; in cases of disobedience, they swore to return and massacre the population, starting "with the women and children" (Justicia y Paz, 2001). The communiqué issued by Justicia y Paz denouncing this situation to national authorities and the international community ended in the following words:

> The recommendations made by the international community through the United Nations or the regional Organization of American States are not enough; the words of accredited diplomats in Colombia are not enough; the resolutions of the European Union are not enough; the recent statements made by two US senators on the situation of San José de Apartadó's Community of Peace are not enough; international solidarity is not enough and the moral support of international observers are not enough; the testimony given by the Community of Peace before the Human Rights Unit of the Nation's Attorney General is not enough to open the paths of truth and justice. Today, given the announced bloodletting, we hope that it is the last time that we manifest our constancy and moral censure, and that, by fulfilling your constitutional duty, you will keep those who have threatened us from carrying out the criminal actions of the state. (Justicia y Paz, 2001)

Even though the people of San José's dreams of peace had been shattered once again, they decided to continue to resist, stay on their lands and rekindle their hopes of a future where dignity, respect, and autonomy would be possible.

THE COMMUNITY OF PEACE: A FOUNDING PACT

The declaration of the Community of Peace was the result of an accelerated process of collective political learning through which the inhabitants of San José discarded, one by one, all the resistance and rebellion strategies they had used to resolve crises in the past: mass demonstrations, the occupation of public buildings, forced exile, hiding in remote, abandoned areas, the alliance with different armed groups for protection and support, and even the declaration of active neutrality. But the shift from a state of war to active war meant a break with traditional practices; they had to invent new strategies and come up with a different socio-political order that would ensure minimum conditions for survival. Upon declaring itself a Community of Peace the group was forced to design new forms of community production, to devise political referents and ethical foundations for action in times of war, to make individual decisions and assume social commitments that gave them visibility and helped open up a dialogue not only with the armed groups, but also with national and international actors. Thus they recovered their autonomy, sovereignty and self-determination, adhering to a new founding pact they called the "Declaration of the Community of Peace."

The collective organization of production

The inhabitants of San José had ample experience in the cooperative marketing and sale of their crops and products, particularly cocoa. Associational experiments for the purpose of improving income and better prices were not unfamiliar to them. In fact, the cocoa growers' cooperative became one of the main community referents by attracting settlers scattered around the jurisdiction who came to understand the meaning of associationism and solidarity from the co-op. Even so, at first, individuals worked alone or with their families in their economic units, but the backdrop of the war and the extreme situation they faced led to a change in production, transforming a traditional peasant economy into a collective unit (Uribe de H, 1992: 293).

After having abandoned their individual plots of land to take refuge in the seat of the jurisdiction, the peasants began venturing out in groups to work the fields, due to the continuing harassment of any peasants who ventured out alone, as well as to the paramilitary blockade whose purpose was to starve them out. Their first crops were merely to help stave off hunger and complement the food rations they received from the international community. But later they renovated the old cocoa plantations from which they are now harvesting crops that they market in Medellín through the National Chocolate Company. They also began developing other crops such as exotic bananas, sowing around 20 hectares with 26,000 individual plants, and hope to export the fruit in the future. According to the settlers, "in the Community of Peace we don't want to exploit others' work, we don't want to sell our products and let others reap the profits; you can't work just for yourself, because strength lies in unity" (Arenas, 1999).

Working jointly implied subverting the idea of individual property and collectivizing the use of the lands, which became the property of the group. It also meant that the crops themselves or proceeds from their sale were equally divided among the settlers: "any crop we raise or sell is for the benefit of all and not only for those who work the land; since we all perform our assigned tasks within the Community of Peace, we all have a right to those products" (personal interviews, 2001). They began a system of planned production, organized by work committees under a coordinator appointed by the community. These committees jointly decide where to sow and which crops will be raised, and make the work assignments, reporting later to the community as a whole.

Although this process of collective organization was initially begun due to the war, the settlers now feel it is a central element of their emancipation and a logical result of the sense of community participation. For them, working together for the benefit of all means opposing vertical forms of power such as those of capitalism (Community of Peace, 1998: 11). According to them, this is a way of establishing an alternative form of power, turning group participation and joint work into a strategy to combat economic exploitation.

The political referents of the declaration of the Community of Peace

In the words of the settlers, the Community of Peace has been an experiment in civil resistance, an effort to recover the dignity of all those people caught in the crossfire of a war of which they were the main victims, even though they were not active participants. Civil resistance for them meant several things: refusing to be forced into exile, staying on their plots of land and continuing to work the land, living alongside their neighbors as before. It also implied demanding the respect of all the armed groups—including those of the state—for their persons and their property, as well as the recognition of their right not to become unwillingly involved in any direct or indirect military actions that benefited any of the armed forces fighting for control over the territory and its populations (Community of Peace, 1998: 11–13). In short, they rejected "exclusionary and discriminatory vertical forms of power," proposing instead to create strategies of pluralistic and autonomic participation different from those "imposed on us through the use of weapons and economic power" (Community of Peace, 1998: 10).

But civil resistance also meant resistance by unarmed citizens: a rational, voluntary and public opposition to a war of which they wanted no part. This included a formal declaration rejecting the way the armed groups were representing their interests, utopias and goals, and informing these groups that the people of San José were prepared to take charge of their own destiny, through self-determination. Thus, for the settlers of San José, the Community of Peace became more than a strategy to avoid the devastating effects of war. It was, they say, a political option

> to respond in an organized way to a war that has victimized the civilian pop-
> ulation and so become an alternative to that very war [...], to become a
> power the armed groups have to reckon with, one that challenges the logic
> that sustains them [...], constructing, on the basis of the communities them-
> selves, different alternatives to those imposed by war and by economic
> oppression and capitalism. (Community of Peace, 1998: 11)

Taking the political option meant proposing an alternative project, entering an agreement among equals to reinvent the rules of social coexistence. It meant instituting a different political order, unlike those that had shaped their lives in the past, and recovering individual sovereignty. Thus it meant opposing politics to war, changing the dynamics of the conflict and opting for peaceful coexistence. The new order proposed would work only within its boundaries, confronting through locally based unarmed resistance the armed actors fighting for sovereignty over all of Colombia. This made the Community of Peace in San José doubly vulnerable: first, in relation to the geo-strategy of internal war, which requires the conquering of territory; and second, in relation to the state, which would be left out and explicitly unrec-ognized by the signers of the new social pact.

The ethical foundations of the pact

The Community of Peace proposal is based on highly significant political and ethical foundations. The first of these is social participation: "we all take part and have the right to make decisions" (Community of Peace, 1998: 19). This means that any member of the political body enjoys equal opportuni-ties to lead the process, but also that individual actions affect the group and therefore that the solidarity and responsibility of its members is extremely important: "that is why every step we take is taken in the knowledge that our actions affect others" (Community of Peace, 1998: 20) and the ethical force of the project rests on the concept of a solidary, fraternal group. The principles of solidarity and responsibility are put into practice in the meetings, training workshops and shared work in the fields so as to strengthen the ties of solidarity and to allow the joint planning of political actions and produc-tion processes.

The second ethical principle is freedom. This is defined by the group as "the capacity that communities and individual members have of making autonomous decisions, without any kind of pressure and without feeling excluded for dissenting with the majority" (Community of Peace, 1998: 19). Thus, it rediscovers a basic principle of democracy: one of accepting difference and even dissent without the threat of exclusion from the body politic.

> Based on respect for the great principle of neutrality, each individual has a right to argue, disagree and propose alternatives, whether that individual is black, indigenous, mestizo, white, liberal, conservative, or communist. All receive equal respect because we are fighting for something much more important: our lives. (Community of Peace, 1998: 10)

The third ethical principle is transparency:

> In order to survive in a war zone, it was necessary to lie to the armed groups. Conversely, the Community of Peace has based its possibilities for survival on truthfulness, telling the armed groups that we cannot cooperate because that would involve us in a war in which we have declared ourselves neutral. (testimony, 2000)

The signatories of the pact realize that their transparency is one of the conditions for the existence, or more precisely the reason for the existence of the Community of Peace. And while this has not guaranteed survival, it has given them the moral strength to protest and be heard by national and international organizations protecting universal public goods.

These modern, democratic and pluralist ethical principles are a contrast to some of the criteria derived from traditional rules and religious morality, which in theory would deny the former. It is extremely striking that the internal by-laws of the Community of Peace strictly prohibit the consumption of alcohol. One of the duties of the Internal Council is to "prevent the consumption of alcohol, which is prohibited in the Community of Peace, and if violated, both the consumer and the seller shall be called in, and section d of this article shall be applied" (Community of Peace, 1998a: 2). The procedure for violators is two warnings, and in case of a third violation, expulsion from the Community.

The Internal Council also appears to be too much involved in other aspects of the private lives of community members, making regular home inspections (Community of Peace, 1998a: 3) and keeping watch over persons entering and leaving the jurisdiction, as well as over those who fail to attend meetings or do not take part in work assignments. The ethical foundations of the San José Community of Peace are a paradoxical mixture of modernity and tradition, of lay ethics and Catholic morality, of public liberties and control of private life by neighbors and family, of collective production and liberal individualism. Such mixtures reveal what an extreme situation can do to traditional groups that rediscover politics in the midst of war.

Rational, voluntary, and public decision-making

The declaration of the Community of Peace meant a step forward in relation to the declaration of territorial neutrality, since it implied an explicit, voluntary and public commitment, made by individuals and communities, to the political and ethical principles of the founding pact, which included the following: no direct or indirect participation in the war; no bearing or keeping of arms, ammunition, or explosives; no provision of support to any parties involved in the conflict; no requests for help from the armed groups to resolve personal or family problems; no handling or delivery of information to any of the parties; a commitment to take part in community work and to reject injustice and impunity (Community of Peace, 1998: 10). In the settlers' own words:

> Each of us, according to our occupation, assumes specific commitments. For example, if I am a shopkeeper who has signed on with the process, I cannot sell to any armed actor [...]. Furthermore, we try to involve those who do not live in the jurisdiction but with whom we are in constant contact, convince them to observe the same principles, and to join the Community of Peace. One example is that of the bus drivers covering the Apartadó route; they have agreed to refuse to transport any armed actor, because they pose a danger for persons using that same form of public transport [...]. Another very touchy subject is the orders and errands the armed actors ask us to perform, like carry messages, give information, hide arms, give them a place to sleep or feed them, because we as peasants end up paying for anything we do. (Personal interviews, 2000)

In order to join the Community of Peace, each individual must voluntarily and individually express his/her desire to join the project, and must take part in four workshops offered over a one-month period by the training committee. Then they must formally apply for admission in a "document signed by each individual over 12 years of age, indicating their acceptance of the process. Parents or responsible adults take responsibility for children under twelve" (Community of Peace, 1998: 1). Once the commitment has been signed or marked by the applicant, the Internal Council will officially issue a membership card, accrediting that person as a member of the Community of Peace.

In addition to the above requirements, before taking possession of the card, the applicant must show that he/she is familiar with the declaration of the Community of Peace; that he/she takes no direct or indirect part in the conflict; accepts the internal rules; will faithfully keep the symbols of the community; is actively committed to the success of the process and will carry out the community tasks assigned (Community of Peace, 1998a: 3). This explicit, informed, voluntary and rational consent serves to reconstruct the group through another path, a political one, thus leaving behind traditional nationalistic notions like territorial belonging, proximity, blood ties or cultural and historical circumscription to a given community. It helps build an incipient body politic, with obligations (neutrality and participation) and rights (protection and voting).

Given the voluntary and individual nature of the Community of Peace, not all inhabitants of the jurisdiction are members. Of the 32 hamlets around San José, only 17 have signed on. Besides the village of San José, the hamlets comprising the Community of Peace are the following: La Unión, Arenas Altas, La Cristalina, Mulatos Medio and Mulatos Alto, La Resbalosa, Las Nieves, El Guineo, La Linda, Alto Bonito, Las Playas, El Porvenir, Buenos Aires and La Esperanza Bellavista (Community of Peace, 1998: 4).

The socio-political organization of the collectivity

The Community of Peace declaration and the concern for neutrality called for a solid organizational model, one vested with authority and recognition that would provide minimum guarantees of compliance with the objectives proposed. The Internal Council is the sole and highest authority within the territory. It is responsible for administrative and disciplinary functions, coordinating all the group's activities and resolving the inhabitants' conflicts through discussion and dialogue. It also keeps a vigilant eye on the population, imposing sanctions on signatories who violate the terms of the agreement (Community of Peace, 1998a: 1–4). But it is a non-institutional authority with no official recognition and no formal or constitutional ties with other regional or national authorities. It is a pluralistic, collectively managed social authority that is elected by the people and that directs the lives of the signatories of the pact, although it exercises an undeniable influence on all inhabitants of the jurisdiction.

The Internal Council also represents the community on different fronts: it speaks with the armed actors, demands that they take responsibility for their actions, defends any member of the community whose actions are questioned by them and clears up ambiguous situations. The Council also represents the Community before national and international social organizations and national state bodies providing humanitarian aid or protecting rights and liberties. Within the Community, the Council is seen as the authority to which they owe obedience and respect.

The Council's disciplinary functions are focused mainly on ensuring neutrality and compliance with the prohibition on the sale and consumption of alcohol. The pact states that "the Council shall call in any violator for the purpose of resolving the problem [...], if there is a second infraction, he/her will be called in again, and upon the third infraction the violator will be expelled from the Community of Peace" (Community of Peace, 1998a: 3). The Council applies no penal sanctions, but it should be noted that expulsion from the Community is practically the equivalent of being exiled from the territory.

The Internal Council is made up of eight members: a general coordinator, an assistant coordinator, a treasurer, an inspector, a secretary and three electors; if the Council so decides, it can be assisted by representatives of the Apartadó Diocese and of one of the NGOs working in San José (Community of Peace, 1998a: 2). The Council is elected by all the members of the Community of Peace, who decide whether it should continue in office every six months; a minimum of two persons from the previous Council are to be kept in office in order to ensure the continuity of the process. It meets once a week, on Saturday, or at any other time if the situation so requires; sessions can take place only when the absolute majority of its members are present. Council members are elected in the following manner:

> We meet in groups and by hamlets to reflect on the desired traits of each council member. Based on this we propose candidates, a list is drawn up, and then we hold elections. The eight candidates receiving the most votes will become the new Council, if each freely chooses to accept the position. (Community of Peace, 1998: 25)

The working groups and committees report to the Council. The first are in charge of food production in order to meet the most basic needs of the members of the Community of Peace. There are 22 groups of men and eleven of women, each with its own coordinator who is in charge of organizing the work and of reporting to the open information assemblies on the advances or setbacks encountered in the group tasks (testimonies, 2000). The committees work on specific thematic aspects central to the organization of collective life, such as health, education, work, sports, culture, women's issues, and the political training of the Community of Peace members. Each committee has a coordinator who, besides his/her specific functions, is in charge of organizing the delivery of received aid to families, working groups or individuals, depending on the case. All the signatories of the peace pact agree to participate in collective tasks, and have to take part in working groups or committees. This is not a choice but a commitment undertaken by anyone signing on with the Community of Peace (personal interviews, 2000).

This program of collective production, with a strong community focus, contrasts sharply with a socio-political organization centered on the individual, on personal autonomy and on a liberal democratic pluralism. It is this that makes San José de Apartadó a hybrid or mixture where one can find traces of several political systems, of different historical periods, of overlapping spaces, openings, and closures that make the apparently simple destiny of this group of peasants so complex.

Thus, this organized community, permanently mobilized, facing adversity, has managed, through collective and solidary work, to fulfill its basic needs, resisting imposed exile. Showing extraordinary dignity and courage, it has attempted to hold in check the forces of war. Perhaps without realizing it, this community is now creating a new political order based on the local.

Notes

1 To ensure the safety of those interviewed, no names or places are given. The interviews were conducted between 1999 and 2001 with settlers, displaced persons, members of the clergy, and NGOs.
2 Data supplied by an eyewitness working with international NGOs in the area and confirmed by the Apartadó Diocese.

Bibliography

Alonso, Manuel Alberto, and Juan Carlos Vélez (1998). "Guerra, soberanía y órdenes alternos," *Estudios Políticos*, 13. Medellín: Universidad de Antioquia, Instituto de Estudios Políticos, 41–75.

Arenas, Juan Carlos (2000). E-mail to the author, 12 December 2000.

Arendt, Hannah (1974). *La Condición Humana*. Barcelona: Seix Barral.

Badie, Bertrand (2000). *Un Mundo sin Soberanía. Estados entre Artificio y Responsabilidad*. Bogotá: Tercer Mundo.

Botero, Fernando (1990). *Urabá Colonización Violencia y Crisis del Estado*. Medellín: Editorial Universidad de Antioquia.

Cavarozzi, Marcelo (1993). "Transformación de la política en la América Latina contemporánea," *Análisis Político*, 19. Bogotá, 25–40.

Comisión Intercongregacional de Justicia y Paz (2000). "Carta al presidente de la República de Colombia," e-mail to the author, 20 December 2000.

— (2001). "Carta al Presidente de la República de Colombia," e-mail to the author, 8 March 2001.

Comunidad de Paz de San José de Apartadó (1998). "Caminos de Resistencia. Alternativas de la población Civil en medio del conflicto." Apartadó (mimeo).

— (1998a). "Reglamento Interno." Apartadó (mimeo).

"Comunidad de Urabá en contra de las ONGs," *El Colombiano*, Medellín, 25 March 1999.

Corpourabá, Corporación Regional de Urabá (1990). "Plan de Desarrollo de Urabá," Medellín (mimeo).

Cubides, Fernando (1997). "Los Paramilitares y su estrategia." Programa de estudios sobre seguridad, justicia, violencia y paz pública. Bogotá (mimeo).

"Exigen respeto a las Comunidades de Paz," *El Tiempo*, Bogotá, 9 October 1997, 8.

GAP: Grupo de apoyo a los desplazados (1998). "Foro sobre desplazamiento interno en Antioquia." Medellín (mimeo).

García, Mauricio, and Rodrigo Uprimny (2000). "Corte Constitucional y emancipación social en Colombia," paper presented to the Symposium *Reinventing Social Emancipation*. Coimbra: Centro de Estudos Sociais/Faculdade de Economia da Universidade de Coimbra, 23–26 November 2000.

Hobbes, Tomás (1980). *Leviatán*. Madrid: Editora Nacional. 2nd edn.

Kymlicka, Will (1996). *Ciudadanía Multicultural*. Barcelona: Paidos, 240–55.

Miller, David (1997). *Sobre la Nacionalidad, Autodeterminación y Pluralismo Cultural*. Barcelona: Paidos.

Naranjo, Gloria (2000). "San José de Apartadó, Primera Comunidad de Paz," Documentos preliminares para la investigación, Desplazamiento forzado en Antioquia. Medellín: Instituto de Estudios Políticos, Universidad de Antioquia (mimeo).

Nieto, Patricia (1998). "Los vencidos. Una historia sobre el desplazamiento forzado en Colombia." Medellín: Instituto de Estudios Políticos, Universidad de Antioquia. Post-graduate dissertation.

"Paras Atacan Comunidad de Paz," *El Colombiano*. Medellín, 4 April 1999, 6A.

Parsons, James (n.d.). *Urabá: Salida de Antioquia al mar*. Medellín: Instituto de Integración Cultural – Corpourabá.

Planea (1999). *Plan Estratégico de Antioquia – Subregión de Urabá. De la visión de futuro hacia la identificación de líneas estratégicas*. Medellín: Gobernación de Antioquia, Departamento Administrativo de Planeación.

"San José Sale en busca del derecho a la vida," *El Colombiano*. Medellín, 12 September 1996, 8A.

"San José una Comunidad de Paz," *El Colombiano*. Medellín, 22 March 1998, 6A.

"San José de Apartadó," *El Colombiano*. Medellín, 23 May 1997, 5A.

Santos, Boaventura de Sousa (2000). "Reinvenção da Emancipação Social. Uma visão geral," Symposium *Reinventing Social Emancipation*. Coimbra: Centro de Estudos Sociais/Faculdade de Economia da Universidade de Coimbra, 23 November 2000.

Schmitt, Carl (1997). *El Leviatán en la doctrina del Estado de Tomás Hobbes*. México: Anagrama.

Uribe de H, Maria Teresa (1992). *Urabá, ¿Región o territorio?* Medellín: Corpourabá-Iner, Universidad de Antioquia.

— (1998). "Las Soberanías en vilo en un contexto de guerra y paz," *Estudios Políticos,* 13. Medellín: Instituto de Estudios Políticos, Universidad de Antioquia, 11–41.

— (1999). "Las Soberanías en disputa: Conflicto de Identidades o de Derechos?", *Estudios políticos*, 15. Medellín: Instituto de Estudios políticos, Universidad de Antioquia, 23–49.

11

Participatory Budgeting in Porto Alegre: Toward a Redistributive Democracy[1]

Boaventura de Sousa Santos

INTRODUCTION

The widespread adoption of representative democracy—its having become one of the pillars of the Washington Consensus since the 1980s—has had a significant impact on democratic theory. In many countries, however, the expectations regarding the new democratic regimes were in part frustrated—namely, expectations related to the distribution of wealth, social security, and the transparency of political power. If in some cases the frustration resulted in political instability, in others the expectations were channeled, particularly at the local level, toward another form of democracy: participatory democracy. The latter was put in place according to different systems of complementarity *vis-à-vis* representative democracy. This is what happened in Porto Alegre. In this Brazilian city, a form of participatory democracy, designated as participatory budgeting, has been in place since 1989, with widely acknowledged success. The UN has pronounced it one of the 40 best practices of urban management in the world. This success had admittedly a lot to do with the choice of Porto Alegre to host the World Social Forum. Under various forms, the participatory budget is now in place in 144 Brazilian cities, in several other cities in Latin America (for instance, Rosario and Córdoba in Argentina, and Montevideo in Uruguay), in Spain (namely in Barcelona and neighboring cities, such as San Feliu de Llobregat), in France (in cities close to Paris, such as Saint-Denis and Bobigny), in Italy (Grottammare), in Canada (Toronto), and in the states of Kerala and West Bengal in India. It can be asserted, therefore, that the aspiration to participatory democracy underlying the different forms of participatory budgeting and planning constitutes today a form of counter-hegemonic globalization.

The participatory budget is an emanation of the theory of participatory democracy, which maintains that citizens must participate directly in political decisions and not merely, as representative democracy would have it, in the choice of political decision makers. It is, therefore, a system of co-governance in which civil society, far from being a haven of survival before an absent or hostile state, is rather a regular and well-organized way of exerting public control over the state by means of institutionalized forms of cooperation and conflict.

In this chapter I present the results of empirical research on the participatory budget of Porto Alegre conducted from 1995 onwards. The most intensive fieldwork was carried out between 1995 and 1997, but I followed the evolution of the participatory budget until January 2002 and have updated the statistical data whenever possible. In the first part, I briefly describe the recent history of Porto Alegre and its government in the context of the Brazilian political system and provide some basic information about the city. In the second part I describe the main features of the institutions and processes of the participatory budget: institutions and processes of participation; criteria and methodology for the distribution of resources. In the third part I analyze the evolution of this institutional innovation from its creation until recently. Finally, in the fourth part, I analyze the participatory budgeting process along the following vectors: redistributive efficiency; accountability and quality of representation in a participatory democracy; autonomy of the participatory budget *vis-à-vis* the executive government of the city; from technobureaucracy to technodemocracy; dual power and competing legitimacies: the relations between the participatory budget and the legislative body vested with the formal legal prerogative of budget approval. In the concluding section and postscript I focus on the lessons to be drawn from this democratic experiment, especially bearing in mind the processes of self-learning and self-transformation that have characterized it since its inception.

URBAN POLITICS: THE CASE OF PORTO ALEGRE

Brazil is a society with a long tradition of authoritarian politics. The predominance of an oligarchic, patrimonialist and bureaucratic model of domination has resulted in a state formation, a political system and culture characterized by the following: political and social marginalization of the popular classes, or their integration by means of populism and clientelism; restriction of the public sphere and its privatization by the patrimonialist elites; "artificiality" of the democratic game and liberal ideology resulting in a huge discrepancy between the "legal country" and the "real country." Brazilian society and politics are, in sum, characterized by the predominance of the state over the civil society and by huge obstacles against the construction of citizenship, the exercise of rights, and popular autonomous participation. Brazil is also a society characterized by outrageous social inequalities, which have in fact increased tremendously in the past 20 years because of the crisis of the developmental state, the deregulation of the economy, and the dismantling of the already utterly deficient welfare state.

The crisis of the developmental state coincided with the democratic tran-sition in the late 1970s. The political debate at the time put the democratization of Brazilian political life and the actual construction of cit-izenship at the very center of the national political agenda. Such concerns in this regard surfaced in the emphasis on rights of citizenship, political decen-tralization, and strengthening of local power in the debates that led to the 1988 Constitution. This new political context created the conditions for political forces on the left to set up innovative experiments in popular par-ticipation in municipal government. This political opportunity was facilitated by the fact that the political forces in question were closely related to the popular movements that in the 1960s and 1970s had struggled locally, both in the cities and in the countryside—and in a doubly hostile context of tech-nobureaucratic military dictatorship and clientelistic patrimonialism—for the establishment and recognition of collective subjects among the subaltern classes.

Amongst such political forces the Partido dos Trabalhadores (Workers' Party, henceforth, PT) is to be singled out. The PT was founded in the early 1980s out of the labor movement, which was particularly strong in the state of São Paulo and one of the most important forces in the struggle against the military dictatorship. The electoral gains of PT have been dazzling. In the early 1990s the PT was already the major opposition party. In 2003 one of its founders—Lula da Silva—became president of the republic. In the late 1980s, the PT, in coalition with other leftist political forces, won the local elections in several important cities—such as São Paulo, Porto Alegre, Santos, Belo Horizonte, Campinas, Vitória, Goiania—and introduced in all of them institutional innovations encouraging popular participation in municipal government.[2] Of all these experiments and innovations, those implemented in Porto Alegre have been by far the most successful, with wide recognition both inside and outside Brazil.[3]

The Porto Alegre democratic experiment is one of the best known world-wide, acclaimed for both the efficient and the highly democratic management of urban resources that it has made possible.[4] The "popular administration" of Porto Alegre was selected by the United Nations as one of the forty urban innovations worldwide to be presented at the Second Conference on Human Settlements (Habitat II), which was held in Istanbul in June 1996. During the last decade, Porto Alegre has staged several international conferences on democratic urban management and, together with Montevideo (where a similar local government innovation has been implemented), is leading a movement toward the introduction of participatory budget institutions in the "Mercocities," the cities integrating the regional economic pact, Mercosul (Brazil, Argentina, Uruguay, and Paraguay).

In Brazil there have been many manifestations of the success of Porto Alegre,[5] the most significant being the electoral gains of the PT in the 1990s and the public acceptance of its municipal government. In the first election, won in 1988 with a coalition of left parties—the Popular Front—the PT carried 34.3 per cent of the vote. In the second election, in 1992, the PT and the Popular Front carried 40.8 per cent, and in 2000 the PT carried 59.6 per cent. Another manifestation of the success of the PT government of Porto Alegre is the fact that *Exame*, an influential business journal, has nominated Porto Alegre several times as the Brazilian city with the best quality of life on the basis of the following indicators: literacy, enrollment in elementary and secondary education, quality of higher and postgraduate education, per capita consumption, employment, child mortality, life expectancy, number of hospital beds, housing, sewage, airports, highways, crime rate, restaurants, and climate.

What is the secret of such a success?

When, in January 1989, the PT took over the administration of Porto Alegre, a new modality of municipal government was installed, known as "popular administration." It was based on an institutional innovation aimed at guaranteeing popular participation in preparing and carrying out the municipal budget, hence, in the distribution of resources and the definition of investment priorities. This new measure, which became known as "participatory budget," is the key to the success of the PT municipal government. In this chapter, I shall begin by describing how the participatory budget works, with special emphasis on its evolution from when it was first put in place to this day. I shall then attempt an evaluation of its impact on the redistribution of municipal resources and on the political culture and system of the city, namely by analyzing both the tensions between representative and participatory democracy, and the reach of participatory budgeting into other areas of urban government. Finally, I shall try to define the contribution of participatory budgeting as institutional mediation for the reinvention of democratic theory, while questioning the potentialities and limits of its universalization as an organizing principle of democratic and redistributive municipal government.

The city of Porto Alegre[6]

With a population of 1.3 million inhabitants and 495.53 km², Porto Alegre is of major economic importance in the state of Rio Grande do Sul, with an estimated GNP of US$6.7 billion (1994).[7] It is the largest industrial city, producing 12.4 per cent of the state's industrial gross product and being responsible for nearly one-third of the income produced in the service sector. Its total population corresponds to 13 per cent of Rio Grande do Sul. In national terms, its influence is mainly political, since many prestigious local politicians have served in the national government in this century. The most significant of them was Getúlio Vargas, who served two mandates as president; the first one as a dictator, between 1930 and 1945, and then as an elected president between 1951 and 1954.

Like other Brazilian capitals, in the last decades of the twentieth century Porto Alegre experienced an accelerated process of urbanization. Its population doubled in 20 years (between 1960 and 1980). In the 1990s, however, the total population grew only 12 per cent, when new industrial centers in the state attracted migrants from the capital. Between 1970 and 1980 the participation of the industry of Porto Alegre in the total industrial production of Rio Grande do Sul declined from 26 per cent to 18 per cent (Oliveira, Pinto and Torres, 1995: 22). Porto Alegre is a city that has been traditionally organized around service and government sectors. In 1949, 73 per cent of the city's income came from the service sector, and in 1980, 78 per cent. The relative de-industrialization in the early 1980s did not affect the centrality and hegemony of Porto Alegre as a regional metropolis.

Rio Grande do Sul presents some of the best social indicators of the country. According to Navarro, citing official statistics (1996: 3), among the fifty best Brazilian cities in educational performance (eradication or lower levels of illiteracy), 32 are in the state. Other social indicators show that life expectancy in the state reaches 68 years for men and 76 years for women,[8] the highest if compared to other Brazilian states. Infant mortality rates fell in the last two decades from 52.6 to 18.4 deaths per one thousand children of less than one year of age. In Porto Alegre, the latter was reduced from 37.2 deaths, in 1980, to 13.3 in 2000, one of best performances among *all* Brazilian capitals.[9] Nevertheless, there are also contrasting negative indicators, such as deep social inequalities (like the rest of Brazil), the housing problem, and unemployment. One-third of its population lives in slums and a recent report indicates that the total population in these areas more than doubled between 1981 and 1990.

Porto Alegre is a city of ample democratic traditions, a strong, highly organized civil society. The military dictatorship met with fierce political resistance in Rio Grande do Sul, especially in Porto Alegre. For example, because of the pressure exerted by the democratic opposition against the repressive institutions of the dictatorship, political prisoners could not be "safely imprisoned" in the city and were often sent outside the city, usually to São Paulo. The opposition was led by intellectuals, labor unions, and the only legalized opposition party, Movimento Democrático Brasileiro (Brazilian Democratic Movement, henceforth MDB). The MDB attracted all the clandestine organizations—whether socialist, communist or revolutionary-Christian—opposed to the military dictatorship. Since the political situation rendered unviable almost all political struggle at the national (macro-political) level, the abovementioned organizations focused their activity on strengthening the unions and on such community movements as neighborhood and street associations, soccer clubs, cooperatives, mother's clubs, cultural groups, and so on. These movements and organizations were either of a general nature or concerned with specific demands, such as the struggle for bus lines, the struggle for sewers or street paving, the struggle for housing or health centers, and so on. A powerful, diversified popular movement thus emerged, one that in the early 1980s became deeply involved in local government.[10]

In the first half of the 1980s the grassroots movements, even though highly heterogeneous both in political and organizational terms, gained new political clout in local politics. In 1983 the UAMPA (Federation of Neighborhood Associations of Porto Alegre) was founded and in 1985 held its first congress. Besides "specific demands" on housing, education, health, nutrition, human rights, and unemployment, the congress called for the "effective democratization of political structures at the federal, state and city level" (Oliveira, Pinto, and Torres, 1995: 31). In the first democratic municipal elections, in 1985, the PDT (Democratic Labor Party), with a long tradition in the state, won easily the elections with 42.7 per cent of the total votes. The PT, still struggling to expand its influence among the popular and labor movements, received 11.3 per cent.[11] Heir to a pro-labor populist tradition, the newly elected mayor decreed the establishment of "popular councils" in the city, but in real terms exercised municipal power in the old clientelistic, paternalistic way, frustrating the democratic expectations and failing most of the electoral promises.

In 1988, the PT began its amazing political success. Without precedent in the city, in 1992 and again in 1996 the party in government managed to elect its successor: Tarso Genro, vice-mayor in the first PT mandate, became mayor in the second, and Raul Pont, vice-mayor in the second mandate, became mayor in the third. In 2000 Tarso Genro was re-elected mayor. The mayoralty was taken over by his vice-mayor in 2002, when Tarso Genro became the PT candidate in state elections. He lost the elections and, in early 2003, became a minister in the first Lula government.

PARTICIPATORY BUDGETING IN PORTO ALEGRE

In the current, New Republic period of the Brazilian political system, municipal power lies in two separately elected bodies: the mayor (Prefeito), the executive body, and the Chamber of Deputies (Câmara de Vereadores), the legislative body. According to the 1988 Constitution, the competence to approve the budget is vested in the Câmara de Vereadores. Since 1989, the Workers' Party and the Popular Front control the Prefeitura but do not have the majority in the Câmara de Vereadores.

One hardly needs to stress the importance of participatory budgeting for the political and administrative relations between the state and the citizens. The budget is the basic tool of the political contract underlying such relations and the interactions among the various state organisms charged with executing such a contract. By defining the use of public funds, participatory budgeting becomes the core mechanism for the public control of the state. Budgetary decisions are thus crucial political decisions. Nevertheless, in a society with a strong patrimonialist and clientelist tradition, as is the case of Brazil, the public budget has been less the expression of the political contract than the expression of its absence. Technocratic and bureaucratic criteria prevail in the definition of the budget, criteria that are vague enough to allow for the clientelist privatization of the public decisions that concern the redistribution of resources. Once the clientelist political game with its mechanism of exchange of favors controls the implementation of the budget, the latter becomes a fiction, a shocking evidence of the discrepancy between the formal institutional framework and the real practices of the state (Fedozzi, 1997: 109).

In Brazil the public budget includes three levels: federal, state, municipal. Municipalities have relative autonomy in determining revenue and expenditure. Revenue is either local (taxes and tariffs of various kinds) or the result of federal or state transferences. Expenditure is classified in three large groups: a) personnel; b) public services; c) investment in works and equipment. The relative autonomy of municipalities occurs mainly in the third type of expenditure. Since the budget does not have to identify the works and services to be carried out—the establishment of expenditure ceiling sufficing—the executive has ample leeway for budgetary implementation. The budget must however be approved by the legislative body.

The participatory budget promoted by the Prefeitura of Porto Alegre is a form of public government that tries to break away from the authoritarian and clientelist tradition of public policies, resorting to the direct participation of the population in the different phases of budget preparation and implementation, with special concern for the definition of priorities for the distribution of investment resources. The participatory budget and its institutional framework have no formal legal recognition.[12] Such legal recognition could only be provided by the Câmara de Vereadores, albeit within the limits of federal and state legislation. As we will see below, the issue of the legalization of the participatory budget is a major topic in an ongoing conflict between the executive and the legislative in Porto Alegre politics. As things stand now, since the definition and approval of the budget is a legal prerogative of the Câmara de Vereadores, the Prefeitura, in strict legal terms, limits itself to submitting to the Câmara a budget proposal that the Câmara is free to approve, to change or to defeat. In political terms, however, because the executive's proposal is sanctioned by the institutions of the participatory budget and thus by the citizens and community organizations and associations that participate in them, the executive's proposal becomes a *fait accompli* for the legislative body in view of the political risks for the deputies in voting against the "will of the citizens and the communities." The majority of the

Chamber thus claims that by institutionalizing the participatory budget without involving the legislative body, the executive has in real terms emptied out the latter's jurisdiction over budgetary matters. Hence the political conflict that will be dealt with in greater detail below.

Institutions of participation[13]

The participatory budget (henceforth PB) is a structure and a process of community participation based on three major principles and on a set of institutions that function as mechanisms or channels of sustained popular participation in the decision-making process of the municipal government. The three principles are:

a) all citizens are entitled to participate, community organizations having no special status or prerogative in this regard;
b) participation is governed by a combination of direct and representative democracy rules, and takes place through regularly functioning institutions whose internal rules are decided upon by the participants; and
c) investment resources are allocated according to an objective method based on a combination of "general criteria"—substantive criteria established by the participatory institutions to define priorities—and "technical criteria" —criteria of technical or economic viability as defined by the executive and federal, state or city legal norms, which it is up to the executive to implement.

The basic institutional set-up of the PB consists of three kinds of institutions (see Figure 11.1).

The first kind of institutions consists of the administrative units of the Municipal Executive charged with managing the budgetary debate with the citizens: Gabinete de Planejamento (Planning Office, henceforth GAPLAN), Coordenação de Relações com as Comunidades (Coordination of Relations with the Communities, henceforth CRC), Fórum das Assessorias de Planejamento (Forum of Advisors for Planning, henceforth ASSEPLAS), Fórum das Assessorias Comunitárias (Forum of Community Advisors, henceforth FASCOM), Coordenadores Regionais do Orçamento Participativo (Regional Coordinators of the Participatory Budgeting, henceforth CROPs), and Coordenadores temáticos (Thematic Coordinators, henceforth CTs). Of this set of institutions the two most important ones are the CRC and the GAPLAN. The CRC, both directly and through its regional or thematic coordinators (CROPs and CTs) is a mediating agency linking the municipal government with the community leaders and their associations. It has also a central role in coordinating the assemblies and the meeting of the COP (participatory budgeting council). The GAPLAN, which shares

Figure 11.1. BASIC INSTITUTIONAL SETUP OF PARTICIPATORY BUDGETING.

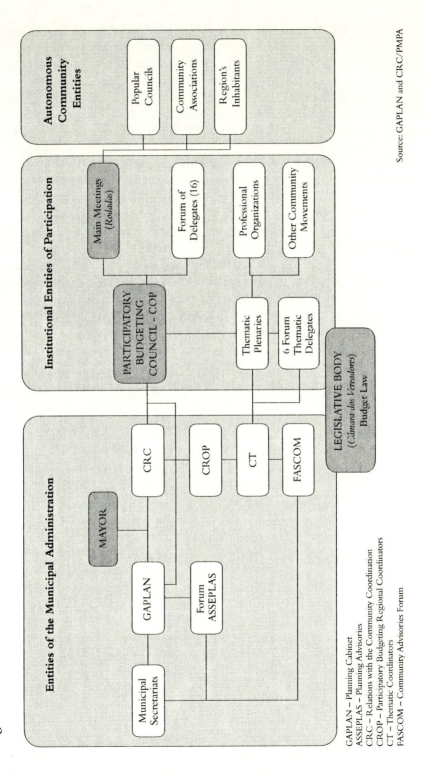

GAPLAN – Planning Cabinet
ASSEPLAS – Planning Advisories
CRC – Relations with the Community Coordination
CROP – Participatory Budgeting Regional Coordinators
CT – Thematic Coordinators
FASCOM – Community Advisories Forum

Source: GAPLAN and CRC/PMPA

with the CRC the coordination functions, is in charge of translating the citizens' demands into technically and economically viable municipal action by submitting them both to the general and the technical criteria.

The second kind of institutions are the community organizations, with autonomy *vis-à-vis* the municipal government, constituted mainly by regionally based organizations, which mediate between citizen participation and the choice of priorities for city regions. Since they are autonomous structures and hence depend on the organizing potential of each region, these popular organizations do not occur in every region concerning the PB. They bear different kinds of organization and participation according to the local traditions of the regions. They are the Conselhos Populares (Popular Councils), Uniões de Vilas (Township Unions) and Articulações Regionais (Region Articulations).

The third kind of institutions is designed to establish a permanent mediation and interaction between the first two kinds. They are regularly functioning institutions of community participation: Conselho do Plano do Governo e Orçamento (Council of the Government Plan and Budget), also known as Conselho do Orçamento Participativo (Participatory Budget Council, COP), Assembleias Plenárias Regionais (Regional Plenary Assemblies), Fórum Regional do Orçamento (Regional Budget Forum), Assembleias Plenárias Temáticas (Thematic Plenary Assemblies) and Fórum Temático do Orçamento (Thematic Budget Forum).

The participatory process

The main goal of the PB is to encourage a dynamics and establish a sustained mechanism for joint management of public resources through shared decisions on the allocation of budgetary funds and for government accountability concerning the effective implementation of such decisions. In a brief summary, the PB centers around the regional and thematic plenary assemblies, the *Fórum de Delegados* (Forum of Delegates)[14] and the COP.[15] The city is divided into 16 regions[16] (see Map 11.1) and six thematic areas. The latter were established in 1994. Today they are: 1) Transportation and Circulation; 2) Education and Leisure; 3) Culture; 4) Health and Social Welfare; 5) Economic Development and Taxation; 6) City Organization, Urban and Environmental Development.

There are two rounds (*rodadas*) of plenary assemblies in each of the regions and on each of the thematic areas.[17] Between the two rounds there are preparatory meetings in the micro-regions and on the thematic areas. The assemblies and the meetings have a triple goal: to define and rank regional or thematic demands and priorities; to elect the delegates to the Fora of Delegates and the councilors of the COP; to evaluate the executive's performance. The delegates function as intermediaries between the COP and the citizens, individually, or as participants in community or thematic

Map 11.1. THE CITY OF PORTO ALEGRE AND THE 16 REGIONS OF
THE PARTICIPATORY BUDGET

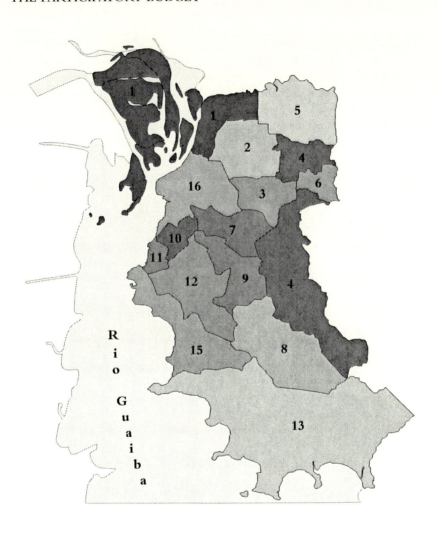

1] Humaitá-Navegantes / Ilhas
2] Noroeste
3] Leste
4] Lomba do Pinheiro
5] Norte
6] Nordeste
7] Partenon
8] Restinga
9] Glória

10] Cruzeiro
11] Cristal
12] Centro Sul
13] Extremo Sul
14] Eixo da Baltazar
15] Sul
16] Centro ("downtown"
    Porto Alegre, in the
    eastern part of the city)

organizations. They also supervise the implementation of the budget. The councilors define the general criteria that preside over the ranking of demands and the allocation of funds and vote on the proposal of the Investment Plan presented by the executive. Next I will describe in greater detail how the PB works (see Figure 11.2).

As I said, two rounds (*rodadas*) of Regional and Thematic Assemblies are held annually. These *rodadas* are open to the individual participation of any inhabitant of the city, as well as to the delegates of civic organizations and associations, even though in the Regional Assemblies only local residents are entitled to vote. They are coordinated by members of the municipal government (CRC, CROP and GAPLAN) as well as by PB delegates and councilors.

Before the annual assemblies, there are preparatory meetings of the citizens that ordinarily take place during the month of March, in total autonomy and without the interference of the municipality. The aim of these preparatory meetings is to collect the demands and claims of individual citizens, grass-roots movements, and community institutions, concerning regional or thematic issues; they also initiate community mobilization to select regional delegates. These meetings are crucial to ventilate community demands and to discuss their relative priority. These meetings are convened and chaired by the popular councils or by the community leaderships and are at times very conflictual, since the different political orientations of the community organizations surface in the identification and formulation of demands, and tend to impregnate the whole debate. Below I shall deal with the issue of the autonomy of these meetings, as well as the autonomy of the intermediate meetings mentioned next.

The first *rodada* of assemblies, held in March and April, has the following objectives: a rendering of accounts, by the executive, of the Investment Plan of the previous year and presentation of the Plan approved for the current budget; the evaluation, by the citizens (by region or themes) and the executive, of the Investment Plan of the previous year; the first partial election of the delegates to the Fora of Delegates (regional and thematic); the remaining regional or thematic delegates will be elected during the next step of the process. The regional assemblies are open to the public but only the registered inhabitants of the region have the right to vote.

The evolution of the criterion to determine the number of delegates to the regional and thematic fora bears witness to the increasing involvement of the citizens in the PB. Initially the criterion was one delegate for every five people attending the assembly; in the early 1990s it changed to one delegate for every ten people and later on to one delegate for every 20 people in force until 1996. After several revisions—in the course of which, for example, the criterion would vary according to the total number of participants at the meeting—in 1999 a fixed number was adopted (one delegate per each group of ten participants), which was implemented in 2000–01.

Figure 11.2. THE CYCLE OF PARTICIPATORY BUDGETING IN PORTO ALEGRE.

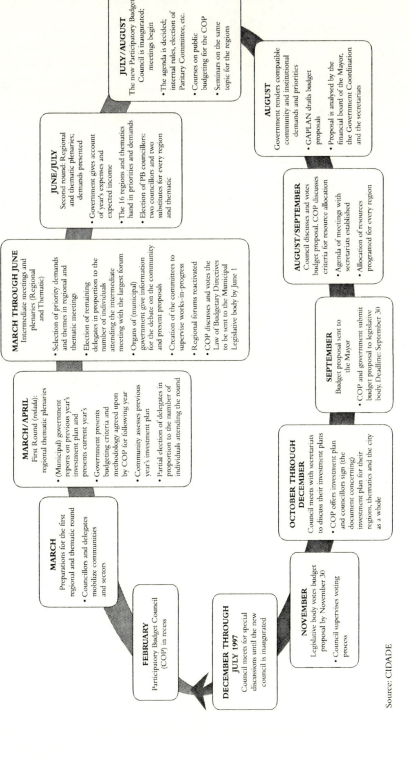

FEBRUARY
Participatory Budget Council (COP) in recess

MARCH
Preparations for the first regional and thematic round

• Councillors and delegates mobilize communities and sectors

MARCH/APRIL
First Round (*rodada*): regional and thematic plenaries

• (Municipal) government reports on previous year's investment plan and presents current year's

• Government presents budgeting criteria and methodology agreed upon by COP for following year

• Community assesses previous year's investment plan

• Partial election of delegates in proportion to the number of individuals attending the round

MARCH THROUGH JUNE
Intermediate meetings and plenaries (Regional and Thematic)

• Selection of priority demands and themes in regional and thematic meetings

• Election of remaining delegates in proportion to the number of individuals attending the intermediate meeting with the largest forum

• Organs of (municipal) government give information for the debate on the community and present proposals

• Creation of the committees to supervise works-in-progress

• Regional forums reactivated

• COP discusses and votes the Law of Budgetary Directives to be sent to the Municipal Legislative body by June 1

JUNE/JULY
Second round: Regional and thematic plenaries; demands presented

• Government gives account of year's expenses and expected income

• The 16 regions and thematics hand in priorities and demands

• Election of PB councillors: two councillors and two substitutes for every region and thematic

JULY/AUGUST
The new Participatory Budget Council is inaugurated; meetings begin

• The agenda is decided; internal rules, election of Paritary Committee, etc.

• Courses on public budgeting for the COP

• Seminars on the same topic for the regions

AUGUST
Government renders compatible community and institutional demands and priorities

• GAPLAN drafts budget proposals

• Proposal is analysed by the financial board of the Mayor, the Government Coordination and the secretariats

AUGUST/SEPTEMBER
Council discusses and votes budget proposal. COP discusses criteria for resource allocation

• Agenda of meetings with secretariats established

• Allocation of resources programed for every region

SEPTEMBER
Budget proposal sent to the Mayor

• COP and government submit budget proposal to legislative body. Deadline: September 30

OCTOBER THROUGH DECEMBER
Council meets with secretariats to discuss their investment plans

• COP offers investment plan and councillors sign (the document concerning) investment plan for their regions, thematics and the city as a whole

NOVEMBER
Legislative body votes budget proposal by November 30

• Council supervises voting process

DECEMBER THROUGH JULY 1997
Council meets for special discussions until the new council is inaugurated

Source: CIDADE

This option reflects the Prefeitura's concern with getting more people involved in the PB.

The delegates elected in the first round of plenary assemblies and then in the "intermediary meetings" are usually indicated by the leaders of the associations present at the meetings. Thus, a citizen not integrated in a collective structure does not have much chance of being elected delegate (more on this below).

Between the first and the second *rodada* of the assemblies, March through June, the so-called intermediate preparatory meetings take place. They are organized by the community or thematic organizations and associations, though now "coached" by the regional or thematic CROP and other representatives of the executive. At such meetings the demands approved by each association or organization (Neighborhood Associations, Mothers Clubs, Sports or Cultural Centers, Housing Cooperatives, Unions, Non-Governmental Organizations, and so on) are ranked by the participants according to priorities and general criteria. The better-organized regions have an internal micro-regionalization for their choice of priorities. Later, the resulting priority lists will be fought for at meetings involving the whole region or at thematic plenaries. In the intermediate meetings there is much discussion and voting but the real negotiations leading to proposals to be voted for tend to take place behind the scenes at informal meetings of the community leaders. The levels of conflictuality depend on the level of community organization and on the level of political polarization among the leaderships.

At these intermediate meetings each region or theme hierarchizes the sectorial priorities. Until 1997, the regions hierarchized four priorities among the following eight sectors or themes: sewerage, housing, paving, education, social assistance, health, transportation and circulation, city organization. In 1997, the COP introduced some changes in this regard. From 1998 onwards, the regions hierarchized four priorities among twelve themes and, starting in 2001, 13 themes: sewerage, housing, paving, public transportation and circulation, health, social work, education, leisure, sports, public lighting, economic development, culture, and environment. As we will see later, these changes reflect the discussions in the COP in recent years in which the majority of councilors had claimed the expansion of themes covered by the PB. Each sector or theme is divided up into sub-themes. For instance, housing includes land legalization (regularization of landed property), land and house registration, urbanization, and social housing projects.

The elected priorities are given grades according to their ranking: 1st priority, grade 4; 4th priority, grade 1. Likewise, the specific works proposed by the citizens in every theme or sector are hierarchized as well (pavement: 1st priority, street A; 2nd priority, street B, and so on). Sectorial priorities and hierarchy of works in every sector are forwarded to the executive.[18] On the basis of these priorities and hierarchies, adding up the grades of the different priorities in all the regions the executive establishes the three first priorities of the budget in preparation. In the course of years, housing, sewerage, paving and land legalization (regularization of landed property) have been the commonest themes of the three main priorities, the order of priority oscillating amongst them. For instance, for the 2001 budget the three priorities were: paving (34 points), housing (32 points), and sewerage (27 points). During the past few years, education and health care have emerged as priorities.

The second *rodada* of Regional and Thematic Assemblies held in June and July is coordinated and chaired by representatives of the executive in conjunction with the popular organizations of the region or theme.

The structure of the meetings is as follows: the executive presents the most important principles of the fiscal and revenue policies and expenditure policies that will have a bearing on the preparation of the budget for the following year; the executive also proposes the general criteria for the distribution of investment resources. The delegates of the communities present to the citizens and the executive the hierarchized demands approved in the intermediate meetings (regional or thematic).

In these assemblies two effective councilors and two substitutes in every region and theme are elected for the COP. The councilors are elected for a one-year mandate and can be re-elected only once. Their mandate can be revoked by the Regional or Thematic Forum of Delegates in a meeting especially called for that purpose and announced with an advance notice of two weeks. Once the quorum established (50 per cent + one of the delegates) the mandate can be revoked by a two-thirds majority vote.

The institutional organs of community participation are then constituted: the Fora of Delegates (16 regional and six thematic ones) and the COP. The Fora of Delegates are collegiate organs with consulting, controlling, and mobilizing functions. The Fora meet once a month and the two major tasks of the delegates are to supervise the works and to act as intermediaries between the COP and the regions or thematic areas. As we will see below, the information flows are not without problems.

The COP is the main participatory institution. It plans, proposes, supervises, and deliberates on the budget's revenue and expenditure (Budgetary Proposal). There the elected citizens get acquainted with the municipal finances, discuss and establish the general criteria for resource allocation, and defend the priorities of regions and themes. At the Council sessions the institutional mediation between citizens and community organizations on one side and municipal government on the other concerning budgetary decisions is conducted at the most concrete and intense level. Once inaugurated in July/August, the Council meets once a week on a set day, usually from 6 to 8 pm.

During the month of August, the detailed preparation of the budget begins. While the executive conciliates the citizens' demands with the so-called "institutional demands" (the proposals of the Municipal Secretariats) and prepares the budgetary proposal on revenue and expenditure, the COP engages in the internal process of training the newly elected councilors to familiarize them with the internal rules (*regimento interno*) and the criteria for resource distribution.[19]

The tasks of the COP are carried out in two phases. In August and September, the COP discusses the budget matrix (*matriz orçamentária*). On the basis of revenue and expenditure forecasts made by the executive during the second *rodada*, the major sets of investment are allocated according to the thematic priorities established in the regional discussions. In this phase, on the basis of the government's proposal, the councilors take a vote, for example, on how many roads will be paved, or how much money will be allocated to health, housing, and so on. Major or structural constructions, whether proposed by the thematic assemblies or by the government itself, are also discussed. Once approved by the COP, this *matrix* is turned into a draft of the Budget Law to be handed out to the Câmara de Vereadores (Chamber of Deputies) by 30 September. From September until December the COP prepares the Investment Plan, which includes a detailed list of the works and activities prioritized by the Council, and thus the specific allocation of resources programmed for every region and thematic area. The debate concerning investments is limited by the estimated general revenue and expenditure with personnel and other expenses estimated by the executive, including fixed expenditures enforced by federal legislation, such as the percentages constitutionally ascribed to education and health.

At the same time, the COP follows the debates on the budget proposal in the Câmara de Vereadores and puts pressure on the legislators by meeting with individual members of the Chamber, mobilizing the communities and thematic areas to attend the debates or to organize rallies outside the building.

During the whole process, the executive participates in the definition of investments through its Planning Office (GAPLAN), and also through the Municipal Secretariats attending the Council meetings, by proposing works and projects of general interest and multiregional ambit, or even works deemed necessary, upon technical evaluation, for a given region of the city. Thus the Investment Plan includes works and activities suggested by the regions and thematic areas as well as works and activities involving several regions or even the whole city. In the last phase of the procedure the Investment Plan approved is published as a booklet and becomes the basic document to refer to by the community delegates in their supervising capacity and by the executive when rendering account before the organs of the Participatory Budget.

Throughout the participatory budgeting process the executive plays a decisive role, and this is particularly evident in the COP meetings. Through the CRC and the GAPLAN the executive coordinates the meetings and sets the agenda. The meetings start with information given both by the government representatives and by the councilors. The themes of the agenda are then introduced by the permanent government representatives or by the representatives of the different municipal secretariats in charge of the theme under discussion. In a disciplined way the councilors, in three-minute interventions, raise issues and ask questions. After a number of interventions, the executive representatives answer the questions and give the information requested. A second set of interventions by the councilors is followed by the representatives' answers, and so on. Both regional and thematic delegates may also intervene, but they cannot vote.[20]

At times there are more direct and intense debates but I have been told that the most conflictual and even tumultuous debates occur in those rare "special" meetings of the COP that are not coordinated by the executive but by the councilors themselves. The political and even personal cleavages surface then more openly. In recent times, the executive's coordination of the meetings has been questioned by some councilors in the name of the autonomy of the COP (more on this below). According to the rules, the coordination belongs to the Parity Commission (Comissão Paritária), so designated because it is composed by an equal number of councilors and government representatives, four each. But in reality the government representatives do most of the coordination, if for no other reason than because of their privileged access to relevant information. In any case, probably to accommodate increasing concerns about the limited autonomy of the COP expressed by the councilors, the most recent version of the rules determines that the government representatives and the councilors of the Parity Commission will alternate in chairing the meetings.

The distribution of investment resources: methodology and criteria of decision-making

The distribution of investment resources follows a method of participatory planning that begins when priorities are indicated at the regional and thematic plenaries and at the intermediate meetings, and reaches its climax when the COP approves the Investment Plan with detailed works and activities discriminated by investment sector, region, and the whole city.

As we saw above, the regions and thematic areas begin by defining the sectorial priorities that are to preside over the drafting of the budget proposal concerning the global distribution of investment resources. The regions also define and hierarchize the specific demands within each priority. Once the priorities of the different regions are established, the distribution of investments is carried out according to the general criteria defined by the COP and the technical criteria defined by the executive. Concerning the regional assemblies, the general criteria are: lack of urban infrastructures and/or services; total population of the region; priority given by the region to specific sector or theme. To each criterion is ascribed a weight in a scale that has varied through the years—from 1 to 4 or from 1 to 5—in direct proportion to the importance attributed to it by the COP. Each region is given a grade concerning each one of the criteria and the type of investment as related to the second and third criterion. The grades are determined in the following way: a) according to the region's total population as provided by the executive's official statistical data;[21] the larger the region's total population, the higher the grade; b) according to the region's need *vis-à-vis* the investment item in question; the higher the need, the higher the grade; c) according to the priority ascribed to the items of investment chosen by the region; the higher the priority of the sectorial demand presented by the regions, the higher their grade in the investment sector in question.

An example may illustrate how the general criteria are translated into a quantified allocation of resources. In 1997 the relative priority given by the 16 regions to street paving determined the inclusion in the Investment Plan of a global expenditure item for street paving corresponding to 20 kilometers of streets to be paved. The distribution of this amount by the different regions was the result of the application of the criteria, their weight and the grade of the region in each one of them. The grade received by each region in each criterion is multiplied by the general criterion's weight. The sum of the partial points (grades x weight) amounts to the total grade of the region in that specific sectorial demand. This total grade determines the percentage of the investment resources that will be allocated to the region in that sector. Let us analyze the case of two contrasting regions: Extremo Sul, a region with 80.21 per cent need of pavement, and Centro with 0.14 per cent. Concerning the need criterion, which at the time carried a general weight of 3, Extremo Sul had the highest grade (4)[22] and accordingly got 12 points (3 x 4), while Centro, with the lowest grade (1), got 3 points (3 x 1). Concerning the criterion of total population, which at the time carried the general weight of 2, Extremo Sul, with a population of 20,647 inhabitants, had the lowest grade (1) and hence got 2 points (2 x 1), while Centro, with a much bigger population (293,193 inhabitants), had the highest grade (4) and hence got 8 points (2 x 4). Finally, concerning the criterion of the priority given by the region, which at the time carried a general weight of 3, Extremo Sul gave the highest priority to paving and, accordingly, had the highest grade (4) and thus got 12 points (3 x 4), while Centro gave a very low priority to paving and thus had the lowest grade (0) and consequently no points (3 x 0). As a result, the total sum of points for Extremo Sul in the item of street paving was 26 points (12 + 2 + 12) while Centro's total sum was 11 points (3 + 8 + 0). Since the global number of points for all regions was 262 points, Extremo Sul received 9.9 per cent of the investment, that is, 1,985 meters of street pavement, while Centro received only 4.2 per cent of the investment, or 840 meters of pavement.

When the first PT executive took office in 1989, the administration's three major objectives were: reversal of priorities; administrative transparency; and popular participation in the city's governance (Genro and Ubiratan, 1997). The first objective—reversal of priorities—was reached in the four (now three) criteria and their respective weights proposed by the executive and accepted by the regions. For several years, the need criterion (services or infrastructure want) was ascribed the highest weight, whereas the population criterion was ascribed a lesser weight. This discrepancy was justified by the need to transfer resources from the region with the most population, the Center, which was also the richest one, to the poorest and less well equipped regions. As a matter of fact, the Center has always been a problematic region for the PB, and there has been a lot of discussion about the need to subdivide it. Moreover, the Center is internally widely differentiated in social and economic terms. Some of the poorest people of Porto Alegre live in sections of this region. When the COP decided to eliminate the criterion of population percentage in situations of extreme want, weight 2 was ascribed to the criterion of population dimension. Thus the other two criteria—need and regional priority—were getting the highest weight (currently weight 4 and 5 respectively).

In the early 1990s, the criterion of the priority established by the region had weight 2. Debates inside the COP resulted in strengthening this criterion, the argument being that this is the criterion that best reflects what the region really wants, given that the regions have so many different needs and resources are scarce. For example, the South, which in 1992 considered sewage to be its most pressing need, while paving was only its third priority, in 1995 went on to take paving as its major priority. The reason may well be that, since sewage was one of the most remarkable successes of the PT administration, it ceased being objectively a real priority.

In the 1998 budget, the weight of the three criteria was changed following debates inside the COP during 1997. The already mentioned concerns, that the Center would always be "ahead" because of its total population, resulted, on the one hand, in widening the gap between this criterion and the other two (from weight 2 vis-à-vis weight 3 it went to weight 2 vis-à-vis weight 4). On the other hand, the thresholds of the different grades were changed: the threshold for the highest grade became 120,000 inhabitants rather than the previous 200,000, and thus regions other than the Center managed to get the highest grade according to this criterion.

In the cycle of 2000–01, the threshold of the highest grade is 90,001 inhabitants, the ratio of the three criteria being the following: total population of the region, weight 2; lack of service or infrastructure, weight 4; thematic priority of the region, weight 5 (see Table 11.1).

Table 11.1. CRITERIA, WEIGHT AND GRADES FOR THE DISTRIBU-
TION OF THE INVESTMENTS IN THE 2001 BUDGET

Lack of services and infrastructure	**WEIGHT 4**
From 0.01% to 14.99%	**grade 1**
From 15% to 50.99%	**grade 2**
From 51% to 75.99%	**grade 3**
76% and higher	**grade 4**
Total population of the region	**WEIGHT 2**
Up to 25,000 inhabitants	**grade 1**
From 25,001 to 45,000 inhabitants	**grade 2**
From 45,001 to 90,000 inhabitants	**grade 3**
Above 90,001 inhabitants	**grade 4**
Priority given by the region	**WEIGHT 5**
Fourth priority	**grade 1**
Third priority	**grade 2**
Second priority	**grade 3**
First priority	**grade 4**

Source: GAPLAN and Mayor's Office, Porto Alegre

THE EVOLUTION OF THE PARTICIPATORY BUDGET:
ON LEARNING PARTICIPATORY DEMOCRACY

The structure and development of the PB has undergone important transformations since it was first initiated in 1989. This evolution illustrates the
internal dynamics of the PB and, above all, the institutional learning by both
state and civil society.

When, in 1989, the PT took over the government of Porto Alegre, the
party leadership was involved in an intense internal debate, which essentially
may be summarized as follows: is the PT government a government for the
workers or is it a leftist government for the whole city, though with a special
commitment to the popular classes? Initially, the position that the PT should
govern for the workers alone prevailed. Such a position was deeply rooted
in the political culture of the PT, closely linked to the political theories of

the popular urban movements in the 1970s centered around the core concepts of dual power and popular councils derived from the Bolshevik Revolution. Under these premises, considering that the state is always particularist and exists only to fulfill the interests of the bourgeoisie, it should likewise be the task of the PT to carry out a particularist government, only now favoring the interests of the workers. Since such government would be exercised in the institutional context of the bourgeois state, its major objective would be to provoke confrontation and bring about crisis so as to unveil the classist nature of the state (Utzig, 1996: 211).

Such a political stance held for the first two years. The aim was to hand over power to the popular councils derived from community organizations so that they could be the ones to take decisions about municipal policy, especially the budget. According to Tarso Genro, who was then the vice-Mayor, by the end of the first year it was already obvious that such a political and administrative strategy reflected a "romantic conception" of popular participation and was destined to fail for three main reasons. First, neither the party leaders heading the executive nor the community leaders had any experience in promoting institutionalized participation. Both had been socialized in a political culture of confrontation and were not ready to go beyond protest and confrontation.[23] Such a context did not allow for the creation of spaces for negotiation capable of articulating and making compatible all the different claims and demands from different regions, let alone establising a political contract and taking part in the institutional mediations necessary to make it effective. Second, it was soon quite evident that the community leaders were not only socialized in a political culture of confrontation but also in a political culture of clientelism, on the basis of which they channeled resources to the communities. Thus careerism in community power went on reproducing careerism in traditional politics.[24] Popular participation of a non–clientelist type was therefore upsetting both for traditional politics and community power structures. And finally, the municipality was bankrupt. During the previous decade the municipal revenue had decreased and the former mayor had approved a dramatic salary raise for the municipal workers just before he left office. As a consequence, in the budget for 1989, expenditure with personnel carried around 96 per cent and only 3.2 per cent of the revenue was left for investment. With such scarce resources it was impossible to meet adequately the demands of the communities.

In the first year, then, the experience of the participatory budget could not but be frustrating.[25] Very few of the works planned were carried out. For example, none of the 42 kilometers of pavement projected for the communities was completed. In the following year, the extent of the frustration was quite visible. Tarso Genro recalls that meeting attendance, which had been relatively large in 1989, dropped in 1990. At a particular meeting in one of the regions, there were more members of the executive (25) than people from the community (16).

The years of 1990 and 1991 were devoted to recuperating the financial and investment capacity of the municipality. Expenditure control combined with municipal fiscal reform and larger federal and state transferences allowed by the 1988 Constitution were the policies that increased investment percentage of the budget to 10 per cent in 1990, 16.3 per cent in 1991, and 17 per cent in 1992. As regards the municipal fiscal reform, progressivity was introduced in the tax on urban property (IPTU, Property Tax on Urban Land and Homeownership), the ISSQN (literally, tax on any kind of service), and several tariffs concerning municipal services were updated (for instance, garbage collection) and indexed to inflation (then skyrocketing), at the same time that the surveillance of tax and tariff payments was made more efficient. The most dramatic change concerned the IPTU and the ISSQN. In the case of the former, in 1990 it amounted to 5.8 per cent of municipal revenue, in 1992 it reached 13.8 per cent, and today it varies between 17 and 18 per cent. The ISSQN represented 20 per cent of the municipal revenue in 1998.

The tax reform, which was crucial to relaunch the popular administration, had to be approved by the Câmara de Vereadores. Because the Popular Front did not have the majority in the Câmara, the PT and the executive promoted a massive mobilization of the popular classes to pressure the legislators to approve the tax reform law. As Tarso Genro recalls, the rightist and centrist legislators, taken by surprise, could not understand why the people would pressure them to raise taxes (Harnecker, 1993: 10).

The executive's response to the initial failure of the participatory budget did not limit itself to overcoming the financial crisis. It also included deep political-administrative changes inside the executive itself and a significant swerve in the political-ideological debate inside the party leadership. Also introduced was a conception of strategic planning influenced by Salvador Allende's experience in Chile (Fedozzi, 1997: 136, 225). The coordination of the PB was taken from the Secretariat for Planning, whose technical body was prey to clientelist policies, and centralized in two organs answering directly to the Mayor's Office: the GAPLAN and the CRC.

On the other hand, institutional mediation between the executive and the community organizations was started so as to combine effective participation with the preparation of an efficient, coherent, and realistic budget. This kind of mediation amounts to the structures and processes of the PB, which have not stopped being improved to this day. Thus new regional division was discussed with the community delegates, and the previous five regions gave way to the actual 16.

In the 1991 budgeting debate a methodology was introduced for the first time for the distribution of resource investments amongst the city regions and choice of budgetary priorities. Always as a result of discussion with community delegates, it was decided to concentrate 70 per cent of the resources for investment in five regions considered priorities. The choice of regions was based on the following criteria: popular mobilization in the region; importance of the region for the urban development of the city; lack of public services and/or infrastructures in the region; number of people living in conditions of extremely deficient public services or infrastructures in the region (Fedozzi, 1997: 137).

At the same time, there was evident progress concerning the creation of community-based representative institutions for the specific discussion of the budget. The Comissão dos Representantes Comunitários (Committee of Community Delegates), which had initiated popular participation in the preparation of the budget, was eventually replaced by two important institutions still existing today: the COP, and the Fórum de Delegados. This model of institutionalized participation and decision-making, based on a strong binding link between the municipal administration and the communities, amounted in practice to putting aside the dual power thesis. This, however, did not mean the marginalization of the popular councils. On the contrary, they continued to be acknowledged as autonomous regional organizations vis-à-vis the state.[26]

From 1992 onwards, popular participation increased significantly as a result of the recuperation of the credibility of the PB, which in turn was due to investment increase, particularly from 1991 on, as well as to the fact that investment was carried out in strict compliance with the decisions taken by the COP. New changes and improvements were then introduced as regards the methodology used to distribute the resources. Thus, the discontent of the eleven regions considered non-priority and, therefore, granted only 30 per cent of the investment, led to the abandonment of the criterion that prescribed concentration of investment in priority areas and the adoption of a systematic selection of priorities within the different investment sectors (paving, sewerage, land legalization, and so on) throughout all the regions of the city.

On the other hand, while the notion of objective criteria for determining priorities and selecting investments was maintained, the criteria underwent many changes. Two criteria were abandoned—"popular mobilization in the region" and "importance of region for the organization of the city"—the former for being considered subjective and allowing for manipulation (for instance, artificial promotion of participation to suggest high levels of mobilization), the latter for being vague and allowing for technicist deviation, since the grades for each region in this criterion were given by the technical staff of the Prefeitura. The remaining criteria were kept and two others added: "priority of investment chosen by the region" and "total population of region." The former reflected the demand of community delegates to have the priorities of the inhabitants of each region better contemplated in the allocation of municipal resources. The latter, claimed by the delegates of some regions and by the executive itself, aimed at making the allocation of resources a more universalizing process (Fedozzi, 1997: 140).

From 1993 onwards, when the second PT term began, the pattern of participation and institutionalization of the PB entered a phase of consolidation, as indicated by the significant increase of participation in assemblies and meetings, as well as the acknowledgement of the COP by both the executive and the community movements, as a crucial institutional mediation for the democratic distribution of budget resources. However, this pattern of participation and institutionalization left intact the conflictive nature of participation and indeed drew its strength from the permanent tension between conflict and negotiation (more on this below).

In the following years, institutional learning and dynamics continued to be the main features of the PB. We might even say that from 1993 onwards the structure and functioning of the PB gained increasing operational complexity, which did not prevent—quite the opposite—the number of participants from rising and their social composition from getting more diversified.[27] One of the criticisms addressed by the opposition and the media at the experiment of the PB was that, all in all, the PB was just a new version of "rice and beans" politics, that is to say, a formula for solving a few of the urgent problems affecting the popular classes, perhaps a less clientelist version than the traditional one, but no less immediatist and electoralist. Also, the fact that participation had a regional basis made impossible any discussion of the city as a whole, any definition of sectorial policies concerning every region, and, above all, any definition of a strategic plan for the city. On the other hand, focusing on the basic needs of the popular classes had resulted in neglecting issues of interest to other social sectors: the middle classes, business groups, and even the trade unions. For this reason, these sectors had been absent from the PB up to then.

Such criticisms coincided in part with the evaluation the PT government itself made of the first years of the PB. To respond to them two important initiatives were taken right at the start of the second term (1993): the Congresso da Cidade (City Congress) began to be held regularly[28] and the plenárias temáticas (thematic plenaries) were created. The first Congress, known as the First Congress of the Constituent City (echoing the large democratic mobilization at the root of the 1988 Constitution) took place in December 1993, its main topic being urban development. Participants were all the PB delegates and councilors, civil society organizations of all kinds (community organizations, trade unions, cultural and business associations, and so on), the university, and organs of municipality from the state of Rio Grande do Sul and the federal government. The conclusions of the Congress defined the "major lines of economic and urban development" that from then on became the guiding principles of the municipal government and the PB. Two years later the Second Congress was held, focusing on the strategic plan of the city, known as *plano director* (master plan).

The meetings known as *plenárias temáticas*, which from 1994 onwards became part of the PB cycle, were the way found to commit the PB to the principles approved by the City Congress. To further the directives of the first City Congress, five themes (*temáticas*) were initially created;[29] currently there are six thematic plenaries. The thematic plenaries are organized in a similar way as the regional assemblies: they include two rounds of general assemblies (*rodadas*) and elect delegates according to the number of participants in the assemblies as well as two representatives for the COP. However, while in the regional plenaries, even though anyone may participate, only the inhabitants of the region have the right to vote, in the thematic assemblies, any citizen, whatever his or her region, may participate and vote in the thematic plenaries. Among the most important decisions of the first few thematic plenaries was the decision to clean up the pollution in the river and on the beaches of Porto Alegre, an issue of general interest for the city as a whole and not just for the region where the beaches are located, and the decision to restore the public market, a public space of great architectural value and with great symbolic value in the social and cultural imaginary of the city.

The thematic plenaries were the means of expanding both the matters for discussion and participatory decision, as well as the social composition of the participants, thereby improving the quality and complexity of the participation. According to municipal data, of a total of 1,011 people attending the second *rodada* of thematic plenaries in 1994, 11.5 per cent belonged to the trade union movement, 14.3 per cent represented business interests, 20 per cent belonged to community movements, 35 per cent to other institutions of the civil society and the state, 14.4 per cent were individuals with no organizational affiliation, and 0.7 per cent were representatives of political parties. Nevertheless, the fact that the participation of community or regionally based associations was still predominant may have resulted in a certain overlapping of spaces of participation and representation in the regional and thematic plenaries. Fedozzi (1997: 144) mentions a survey in 1995 according to which, when asked about what distinguishes regional from thematic plenaries, 60 per cent either answered that they did not know the difference or did not answer at all.

The relationship between regional participation and thematic participation is not merely a question of an overlapping of spaces of participation. It is above all a question of urban politics and has over the years become ever more contentious. In the early 1990s the regions were mainly concerned with the lack of physical infrastructures and this explains why leisure or culture were not even considered as possible topics for prioritization. But the regions had always a tradition of lively leisure and cultural activities. Many of them had cultural and sports clubs, theatre groups, and so on. As the want of physical infrastructures was attenuated as a result of the success of the PB, the demands for "post-materialist" improvements increased and hence the relative overlap with the thematic plenaries. The overlap hides a conflict of conceptions about city culture that may be related to the different social composition of the regional and the thematic plenaries. However, the conflict in this respect is mainly between the regions and the executive itself. The COP, dominated by the regions, has been fighting with increasing aggressiveness for the expansion of the topics of regional interest under PB decision-making. Among such topics, culture is always mentioned.

Through the CRC and the GAPLAN the executive has on several occasions resisted such an expansion with the argument that such topics, rather than being of regional interest, concern the city as a whole. This argument has not convinced the councilors who in 1997 were very critical of the cultural proposals presented by the executive, accusing them of being biased in favor of "high culture" activities. The truth of the matter is that many regions have their own cultural traditions, programs, and facilities, and want above all to improve them. In the COP meeting of 1 March 1997, one thematic councilor, representing the theme Education, Culture and Leisure, challenged the executive representatives: "our concern in the thematic is that in fact the activities in the area of culture end up being chosen by the Mayor's Secretariat for culture and regions, and the people are excluded. Notwithstanding the thematic's attempt it has not received any response from the Secretariat. Our interest is that the popular will is respected in the cultural programs of Porto Alegre. Because the thematic believes that culture is how we live."

During the second term, and also to respond to a demand by the PB councilors that the realm of the PB be expanded to other areas of municipal spending, a Three-Party Commission (Comissão Tripartite) was set up, composed of six PB councilors (three effective and three substitutes), representatives of the SIMPA, and members of the executive. Its purpose is to participate in decisions concerning policies related to personnel and municipal administration.

Two other institutional changes introduced after 1993 must be mentioned. Since the beginning of the 1990s, the Fórum do Orçamento (Budget Forum) was the means of gathering together all the delegates of all the regions. Although its existence was highly justified because of the need for a trans-regional, citywide mediation, the truth is that the Forum did not have clearly defined functions, and its dynamics were deficient. The decision, therefore, was taken to cancel the Budget Forum and create in its stead fora of delegates in every region and in each one of the thematic plenaries. On the other hand, with the objective of refining the methodology of participation and representation, the election of delegates stopped taking place only in the second *rodada* of the regional or thematic assemblies and began to occur in two moments: a part of the delegates was elected in the first *rodada* of the plenary assemblies and the other part in the intermediate meetings that take place between the first and second *rodada* of the regional or thematic assemblies. The other institutional innovation was the approval, in 1994, of the Regimento Interno (internal rules) of the COP summing up the normative framework underlying the PB's operations and procedures.

The PB learning process in the course of the past decade reveals itself not so much in formal institutional innovations but in the internal operation of the existing institutions. As we saw above, some substantial changes in the criteria for resource allocation have been introduced. Moreover, conflicts of interest and political cleavages have been surfacing ever more openly. In recent years the COP has become more assertive, challenging what is sometimes considered tutelage or even manipulation by the executive. In sum, the PB has become more transparent regarding its core character: a democratic political struggle centered on different conceptions of fair distribution of scarce public resources in an extremely unequal society.

By the end of 2000 a new phase in the PB's learning process began, including a wider reflection on the past and future of the PB. This process is reflected in the creation, in 2001, of a Work Group for the Modernization of the Participatory Budget, to which I shall refer in my conclusion to this chapter.

PARTICIPATORY BUDGETING:
TOWARD A REDISTRIBUTIVE DEMOCRACY

In this section some of the most salient political features of the PB will be briefly analyzed. I will also identify the major challenges facing the PB as well as the problems and even dilemmas lying ahead. Figure 11.3 will be helpful to structure the discussion.

Participation, negotiation, and redistribution

The PB is a process of decision-making based upon general rules and criteria of distributive justice discussed and approved by regular, institutional organs of participation in which the popular classes have majority representation. The communities in which they live and organize are recognized as having urban collective rights that legitimate both their claims and demands and their participation in the decisions taken to meet them.

The selection of priorities and works included in the Investment Plan is reached by means of objective criteria, defined through a complex process of negotiation that takes place at the intermediate meetings, regional assemblies, thematic plenaries and COP. It is today generally recognized that the

Figure 11.3. PARTICIPATORY BUDGET POLITICAL CONSTELLATION

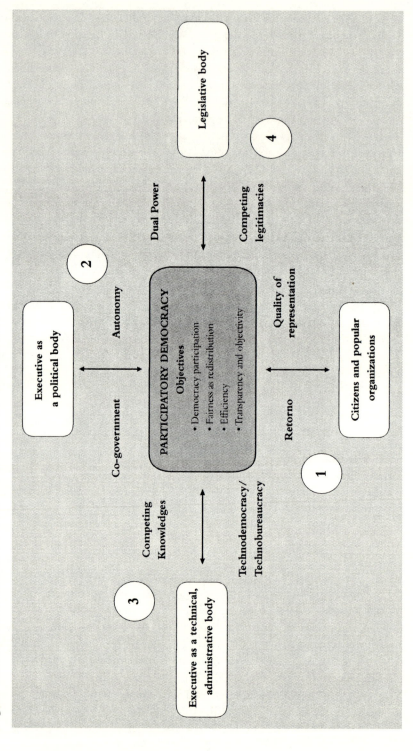

PB changed the political culture of community organizations, from a culture of protest and confrontation to a culture of conflict and negotiation. Indeed, conflict and negotiation occur not among the regions alone but inside each region as well, and it is equally complex and tense at the intra-regional as it is at the inter-regional level.

The objectivity and transparency of the criteria are expressed in the points earned by each region and the percentage of investment resources into which they are converted. The point system was the methodology conceived to hierarchize priorities and to turn them into resource and investment quantities determined by general criteria. For each one of the priorities, the weight of the criterion and the grade given to the region define the points, which in turn decide the percentage of resources to be invested. The point system aims at converting the political decisions reached through complex negotiations in the detailed distribution of resources included in the Investment Plan and make sure that such conversion is as faithful and objective as possible.

The latter concern implied successive refinements of the distributive methodology that endowed the PB with great operational and functional complexity. The increase and diversity of participation, together with the increasing intensity and differentiation of demands, has also contributed decisively to making calculating methodologies even more complex and sophisticated.[30] The complexity of the point system resides in the fact that it seeks to articulate measures of participation, on the one hand, with measures of priority and recognized necessity, on the other. The participation measure guarantees the democratic legitimacy of political decisions, whilst the priority and necessity measure guarantees the fidelity, objectivity, and transparency of the conversion of political decisions into distributed resources.

Once the amount to be invested in the region according to the priorities defined by the region has been decided, that sum has to be distributed inside the region itself. The latter distribution is often extremely difficult, given the internal diversity of the regions and the political struggles concerning community leadership. These difficulties led to the creation of micro-regions, that is to say, social spaces with some identity inside the regions themselves. The aim was to reproduce inside the regions the same decision processes and criteria adopted for resource distribution among regions.

In 1995, the COP approved non-binding directives for resource distribution inside the regions, proposing the adoption of objective criteria for the hierarchization of priorities and choice of investment that were similar to the ones adopted for the interregional hierarchization and distribution: thematic priority of micro-region or neighborhood (Vila); lack of services or infrastructures; population benefiting from the work demanded. According to Fedozzi (1997: 161), in most regions, especially those not divided into micro-regions, decisions did not obey the point system; there was rather political negotiation and the direct vote of the delegates of each neighborhood for the choice of priorities. Regardless of the difficulty in measuring, for example, the lack of services or infrastructures in each micro-region or neighborhood, most community leaders chose the distribution of the resources according to the criterion of the participation of the neighbors in the meetings. Only four of the 16 regions used some kind of system based on the calculation of the choice of priorities.

Because of its major concern with the democratic nature of the distribution, the PB may be considered the embryo of a redistributive democracy. As I have indicated, the democratic nature of the distribution is guaranteed by a calculating methodology that has become increasingly sophisticated. One could say that, when it does not evolve in a Weberian way, that is to say, together with an increase of bureaucracy, democracy evolves together with an increase of decisional complexity. The following working hypothesis could indeed be formulated: in internally differentiated societies, the stronger the bond between democracy and distributive justice, the more complex the methodology that guarantees such a bond tends to be. The decrease of complexity that bureaucracy allows for cannot but bring about the loosening of the bond between democracy and distributive justice.

The redistributive efficiency of the PB has been fully confirmed. Suffice it to mention that in the PB the poorest region of the city, Ilhas (nowadays a micro-region of Humaitá/Navegantes/Ilhas), with a population of about five thousand inhabitants, almost entirely classified as needy people, has the same decisional weight as the wealthiest region, Centro, with 271,294 inhabitants, of whom fewer then 3 per cent are considered needy (see also Larangeira, 1996: 4). When, during the 1992 election campaign, those opposed to the PT candidate argued that the PT government only provided "rice and beans" works, this criticism was actually the great lever for popular mobilization in favor of the PT government. The communities then participating in the PB assumed the "rice and beans" works as being in their favor, for the communities themselves had voted for them in the PB. The pejorative nature of the phrase "rice and beans" works, pointing to the popular classes as socially devalued subjects, was neutralized by the popular classes themselves as citizens of the democratic decisions that led to the works. Thus the unequal and conflictive nature of power relations in the city became visible and a field for political strife itself.

By reversing the priorities that traditionally presided over the resource distribution by the municipal government, the PB reached striking material results. As regards basic sanitation (water and sewerage), in 1989 only 49 per cent of the population was covered. By the end of 1996, 98 per cent of the households had water and 85 per cent were served by the sewerage system. According to the influential newspaper, O Estado de São Paulo, while all the previous municipal governments of Porto Alegre had built some 1,100 kilometers of sewage, the two PT administrations alone built 900 kilometers between 1989 and 1996. As concerns street pavement, 215 kilometers were built at the rate of 30 kilometers per year. Even so, only one-half of the street pavement deficit (approximately 500 kilometers) was eliminated.

The legalization of land ownership, which, as we have seen, is a high priority in many regions where the popular classes live, is an issue where the power relations of the city have eloquent expression, since 25 per cent of the available urban land is owned by fourteen people or entities. Nevertheless, in the past seven years it was possible to urbanize the slums and build many houses for the marginal populations. As regards education, between 1989 and 1999 the number of students enrolled in the elementary and secondary schools doubled.[31]

The investment effort made by the executive was possible because the revenue increased dramatically, due to federal and state transferences and to the tax reform. In the period under analysis, a 48 per cent increase of revenue was made possible. The former mayor, Tarso Genro, believes that the transparency in municipal spending brought about by the PB contributed to the motivation to pay taxes.

The PB and the people

The main issues concerning the relations between the PB and the citizens and popular organizations are the articulation of representation with participation, and the quality of representation.

According to the estimate of the Mayor's Office, if the hundreds of intermediate meetings, both regional and thematic, were to be taken into account, total participation would come close to 100,000 people, that is to say, 8 per cent of the city population. According to a survey conducted in 1998, the majority of participants—a balanced group of men and women with ages up to 41 years—belong to the popular classes: 24.8 per cent have a household income of one to two times the minimum wage and have elementary education, and 54.1 per cent of the participants have an income of up to four times the minimum wage.[32] A significant number of the people surveyed have flexible jobs as regards time and schedule—for example, self-employed, retired, and at-home workers. In comparison with a similar survey done in 1995, an increase in income and education is detected (CIDADE and CRC, 1999: 25–9).

Concerning the participation of women, though rather balanced at the base, it decreases as the decision scale rises. The gender factor is particularly noticeable in the following categories: board of directors of neighborhood association (20 per cent are women); COP (20 per cent); and the Forum of Delegates (16.9 per cent).[33] On the other hand, the participation of women in community associations and basic structures of the PB (assemblies) is higher than is usually reported in similar participatory experiences in Brazil and other countries of Latin America. The data of the research conducted by CIDADE, an NGO that very closely follows the PB, show that the participation of women increased significantly between 1995 and 2000, both at the level of the regional and thematic assemblies, and today is the equivalent of the sexual composition of the population. According to the data of the 1998 survey, the difference between men and women as regards active intervention in meetings is small in the majority of regional or thematic assemblies (14.2 per cent and 17.2 per cent, respectively). There are, nevertheless, some significant differences. For example, in thematic meetings on economic development and taxation, education, culture, and leisure women intervene more than men. With some exceptions, in regional assemblies men intervene more.

The same survey shows that the people participating in thematic assemblies have considerably higher levels of income and schooling. Fulfilling their original purpose, the thematic plenaries are evidently attracting a more varied set of entities and organizations than the regional assemblies (see Baiocchi, 2001a). Nevertheless, most of the participants indicated that they represented neighborhood associations, whether in regional or thematic assemblies. 75.9 per cent declared that they belonged to some entity or association and 50.5 per cent declared that they belonged to neighborhood associations. That is to say, of those belonging to associations, 66 per cent belong to neighborhood associations. Although the thematic assemblies were conceived of as a privileged space for the participation of the labor unions, the average participation of unions in thematic assemblies is the same as their average participation in regional assemblies. As regards "2nd level" autonomous structures[34]—Popular Councils and Regional Articulations—surprisingly they show more participation in the thematic than in the regional assemblies, even though their constitution is based on the region.

As we have seen, the concern has always been there to achieve a fine-tuning between participation and representation, that is, to improve the mechanisms of representation needed to have participatory democracy itself function adequately (see Dias, 2000; Baiocchi, 2001a, 2001b). Indeed, even in such a vibrant participatory environment there is no guarantee that representation may not be thwarted, either because the principles of the mandate are not respected, and the priorities decided by the assemblies are manipulated, or because representation becomes professionalized when a delegate holds the post for too long. In order to neutralize the possibility of such deviations, the term of the PB councilors may be revoked at any time by the assemblies that elected them, and no candidate can be elected to a given position more than twice. Moreover, members of any other municipal council, holders of elected public positions, and people with a contractual relationship with the municipal administration cannot be elected for the COP.

This same concern with binding participation to representation led in the past few years to the addition of a few alterations in the electoral system. Thus, the increase in participation and the need to safeguard minority positions led to the adoption of the proportional method in the election of the PB delegates and councilors.

Finally, since 1994 the incentives to participation stopped being merely materialist and became cultural as well, although these changes were also seen as an attempt to fight the boredom of some meetings. Thus, in order to make the assemblies more attractive and lively, plays and sketches prepared by cultural associations in the region are performed before they begin, and a video is shown displaying the works in progress or works already completed that had been decided the previous year in the Investment Plan, along with tables and charts demonstrating their conformity to the decisions of the COP.

The relations between popular participation and popular representation in the PB are not as smooth as they appear, and the problems center on the following two questions: ratio of represented/representatives; quality of representation (autonomy, accountability and *retorno* or transparency). From the very beginning there was a tension between the executive and the popular movement concerning the criteria to determine the ratio between the number of people attending the meetings and the number of delegates elected. As the attendance increased, the executive proposed that the ratio one delegate for every five people change to one delegate for every ten people. As I mentioned above, the ratio or proportion suffered several changes; it is now again one delegate for every ten people. Some of the leaders of the popular organizations of the PT have always contended that the number of delegates should be as large as possible. Considering that the PB is a learning process and that important information circulates inside its institutions (mainly the COP and the Forum of Delegates), the exposure to such learning and information should be as widespread as possible. The executive has always responded with the argument of deliberative efficiency and the need to make direct democracy and representative democracy compatible.

The question of the quality of representation is discussed in light of the following main issues. The first issue concerns the autonomy of the popular representatives in the PB *vis-à-vis* the government. Leaders of the popular movement not affiliated with the PT claim that the government, through the PB, has co-opted the popular movement, distorting its priorities and subjecting it to the executive's political agenda. As a result, the popular movement has concentrated too much on local politics and neglected the critique of and confrontation with the state and federal government. Moreover, the tensions inside the community movement have been submerged and left unresolved because the new political culture aimed at by the PB has not been filtered down to the popular movement. The new agendas have silenced the old ones instead of incorporating them. The issue of the autonomy of the PB *vis-à-vis* the executive will be dealt with below in greater detail.

Related to this issue is that of how closely the views and positions of the delegates and councilors reflect those of the regions they represent. This issue was not very relevant as long as the institutions of the PB were concerned exclusively with the physical infrastructures of the communities. More recently, however, as the debates and demands expanded into other areas (culture, and so on) and both the delegates and the councilors started participating in numerous events on very different topics, the bond between the population of the region and its representatives has loosened. The positions assumed by the delegates or councilors may reflect their personal preferences more than anything else. It is feared that this "autonomy" of the representatives *vis-à-vis* their constituencies may bring back in a new guise the old populist, clientelist system of resource allocation and vote exchange. CIDADE reports on a certain uneasiness in the communities both because the councilors assume positions without previously consulting with them and because they fail to report back to the communities and inform them about the debates and decisions in the COP and other committees (Pozzobon, Baierle and Amaro, 1996: 2). *Retorno*, literally "return," has become a key word in this debate. It means the demand of transparency, of reporting back, of diffusion of information. *Retorno* has been demanded by the popular organizations *vis-à-vis* delegates and councilors, by delegates *vis-à-vis* councilors, by councilors *vis-à-vis* the councilors that are members of the Parity Commission, and the Three-Party Commission. *Retorno*, the flow of information, is crucial for the effective control over the representatives of popular participation and thus for their accountability.

The *retorno* raises another issue, related to the quality of representation: the issue of specialized knowledge and its impact on training and reelection. To have access to and master relevant information is probably the most basic condition for the effective operation of the PB. Such information is often technical and difficult to grasp by people without a high level of education. As we will see below, the popular administration has made a genuine effort to make accessible much of the information that was previously a monopoly of the technical staff (engineers, lawyers, public administrators, architects, and so on).[35] Still the councilors and delegates claim sometimes that they have been denied important information or that they have had access to it too late or even that it is too cumbersome to get it. In the COP meeting of April 6, 1997, the difficulty in having access to information was raised by one of the most influential councilors. The executive representative, from GAPLAN, answered that the criticism was fair and that the electronic data-processing system of the municipality had suffered some delays. The councilor counter-argued that the firm in charge of installing such a system should be summoned to the COP for a hearing. The GAPLAN representative commented later in the meeting:

> I would like to clarify the following. There is information. It may be incomplete, but it is there and although the councilors keep talking about autonomy the fact of the matter is that they don't use information that is available. For instance, the record (*cadastro*) of the streets. We in the GAPLAN have insisted that the *cadastro* is at your disposal and that you should go through it to detect possible mistakes. How many councilors have checked the *cadastro*? Three!

After the new COP is inaugurated some training seminars are organized to familiarize the new councilors with the complex operation of the PB. Moreover, in recent years, through protocols established between the *Prefeitura*, the University and NGOs, the training of councilors and delegates has intensified. The need to get familiarized with the PB process and to master the relevant information has raised still another issue, the reelection of councilors. According to the rules, the councilors can be re-elected only once. But both inside and outside the COP the question has been raised whether the reelection should be admitted without term limits, the justification being that one year is too short a period to get fully acquainted with the operation of the PB. The CIDADE has even proposed that the councilors be elected for a two-year term or that, as an alternative, the effective councilors in a given year become substitute councilors in the following year thus allowing for the transmission of their knowledge and experience to the newcomers.

In the popular movement this position is often looked at with suspicion, fearing that reelection might lead to a new breed of professionalized elected officials easily prey to the old populist, clientelist system.[36] In the COP meeting of 4 March 1997, in which the internal rules were on the agenda, the issue of reelection was once again raised. Some councilors defended the reelection with two very different arguments. One argument was about the quality of representation: the knowledge and the experience acquired would improve the quality of representation. The other argument was about the autonomy of popular participation. One councilor said:

> To limit the reelection amounts to saying to the communities and the delegates: "look, you don't know how to vote and for that reason you are not allowed to vote on anyone more than twice." If someone is a good councilor why should he not be allowed to stay for four or five years? The Council denies the delegates the option to vote how they like and the assumption of responsibility for the way they voted.

Other councilors counter-argued. One said: "Look, in my region for a long time only X knew about PB. Only one person. The essence of the PB is to form leaders, in the plural, not one leader that knows everything while the rest know nothing." Another said: "Why are new councilors here today? Precisely because of this provision of the rules. Fortunately it privileges the arrival of new councilors every year. Otherwise many of you would not be here today." The representative of the executive expressed the same opinion:

> We had a similar discussion three years ago. In the first years of the PB various councilors stayed for three or four years. The idea was, "let us support the one with greater experience." But then we came to the conclusion that we were perpetuating the same people in the same position. We were preventing the emergence of new leaderships. Today the PB is the vanguard. Neither the bourgeois parliament nor the trade unions or other entities do as we do. They allow for consecutive reelections and thus perpetuate the same leaders. They are lagging behind.

After some more interventions the issue of re-election was voted on. There were two proposals: to maintain the current system; to allow reelection without limits. The first proposal won with 17 votes in favor and eleven votes against.

Concerning the quality of representation there is still another issue to be mentioned: the degree of participation of the councilors at the meetings and other activities of the COP. Throughout the years the COP met regularly once a week but in 1997 met twice a week for several months. The meetings last two hours and sometimes longer and since most councilors live in the peripheral regions the time spent on long bus rides should also be added. It is thus a very intense type of voluntary work and some councilors find it impossible to attend all meetings.[37] Moreover, whenever the meetings take too long some councilors must leave before the meeting ends in order to catch the last bus to his/her region. The more assiduous councilors have been very critical of absenteeism. In the meeting of 6 March 1997, one of them said: "The Councilor does not represent one person. He/she represents thousands of people. They represent the city of Porto Alegre. If a councilor assumes the responsibility of discussing the problems of the city but when the time to vote comes he leaves because he has another engagement I think this behavior amounts to an insult to the COP and to the people."

At this meeting the question of the quorum needed to take a vote was raised and vividly debated. There were three proposals. According to the first proposal the quorum should be a simple majority of the councilors (23, even though the government representatives do not vote) established at the beginning of the meeting. If the quorum was fulfilled at the beginning of the meeting then decisions could be taken even if in the course of the meeting the number of presences fell below the quorum. The second proposal defined the same quorum but required it for all the decisions taken. The third proposal, which had already been adopted in the previous year, proposed two formulas for the quorum: simple majority of the councilors, or, in its absence, the simple majority of the regions and thematic areas, that is, nine and three respectively. The first proposal was defended by some councilors that felt "penalized by the colleagues that abandon the meeting making it impossible to take decisions. These colleagues are the ones that should be penalized. We should be able to decide without them and without regard for their positions." Other councilors and the executive representatives were in favor of the third proposal. Said the GAPLAN representative: "Often the discussion becomes heated, takes more time and many councilors start leaving to catch the bus. It is frustrating because we discuss and discuss, and all of a sudden we don't have a quorum. I am also concerned with the representativeness of the discussion and debate. The third formula is a compromise. At least the majority of the regions and of the thematic areas are present." The proposals were then voted on: first proposal: seven votes; second proposal: four; third proposal: 12 votes.

In my view, the way the different issues involving the quality of representation have been debated inside and outside the PB institutions bear witness to the engagement of the popular sectors of Porto Alegre in preventing the PB from falling into the trappings of the old clientelist, authoritarian system. Indeed the specter of the continuities between the old and new system surfaces occasionally in the debates.

Autonomy and co-government

For its founders and activists, the PB is the manifestation of an emergent, non-state public sphere where citizens and community organizations, on the one hand, and the municipal government, on the other, converge with mutual autonomy. Such convergence occurs by means of a political contract through which this mutual autonomy becomes mutually relative autonomy. The experience of PB configures, therefore, a model of co-government, that is to say, a model for sharing political power by means of a network of democratic institutions geared to reaching decisions by deliberation, consensus, and compromise.

The problems facing a system of power sharing are well expressed in the relationship between the COP and the executive. Such a relationship has been polemical all along. In the beginning, while the community leaders wanted the COP to have unconditional deliberative power, the executive searched for a formula capable of reconciling the decisions of the COP and the political representativity of the mayor inscribed in the Constitution of the Republic. The formula is as follows: the deliberations of the COP are taken by simple majority; the decisions are forwarded to the executive; in the case of veto by the mayor, they return to the Council for a new evaluation; rejecting the mayor's veto requires a qualified majority of two-thirds of the vote; if rejection occurs, the matter goes back to the mayor for evaluation and final decision. Since, according to the Constitution, the power to approve the budget is vested in the legislative body, this formula accommodates the constitutional requisite: formally, the budget proposal submitted to the Câmara de Vereadores is the mayor's proposal.

The mayor's veto must be substantiated and can only be exercised for technical reasons and financial evaluation. To this date, however, the veto was never exercised, since whenever the executive had reservations concerning a work, its position was explained to the community by its technical staff and the community ended up agreeing.[38]

The consensus-building process is complex because the problems under discussion as well as the decisions taken often have, besides the political dimension, a strong technical dimension. Moreover, "technical criteria" constitute one of the limits of participation and are sometimes the object of debate and conflict themselves. The internal rules of the PB include the technical criteria established by the various departments of the executive and justify them as follows: "the presentation and clarification of the technical and legal criteria, utilized by the secretariats and departments, will make the PB procedure more transparent for, having been previously enlightened, the community, when discussing its priorities, will avoid the selection of works that cannot be implemented by the Municipal Mayoralty. The totality of technical criteria was submitted to the Parity Commission for evaluation, debate and deliberation."

As mentioned above, the Parity Commission is another of the institutional creations of the second term of the popular administration. It is now composed of two representatives of the CRC and two representatives of the GAPLAN (Baierle, 1998).[39] The CRC and GAPLAN are the two main institutions of the executive that guarantee institutional mediation between the executive and community organizations and associations. The main function of the Parity Commission has been up until now to legitimate the definition of the technical criteria by submitting it to some kind of participatory decision-making. In real terms, given the technical complexity and knowledge behind the criteria, the commission has always rubber-stamped the executive's proposals. Since 1997, the Parity Commission was endowed with broader tasks of coordination of the COP's activities and meetings but, as I suggested, the real coordination belongs still to the government representatives.

Here are some of the technical criteria currently in force: all community claims and demands found technically nonviable by the Municipality are cancelled; preference is given to works in progress; the pluvial network will not be installed in streets without pavement because the network, being open to allow for the captation of rain water, might be blocked by sand and rubbish; in streets with heavy traffic, a minimum of ten meters width is required: seven meters for the lanes and three meters for the sidewalks.

In such a system of co-government, the executive does have a very active role, if for nothing else than because it controls technical knowledge and also because it either generates the relevant information or has privileged access to it. Its presence in the PB is quite strong by reason of its coordinating functions both in the COP through its two representatives (one from GAPLAN, another from CRC), even though they do not have the right to vote, and in the regional assemblies through the CRC delegate (the CROP) in the region. Furthermore, the executive itself forwards autonomous investment proposals to the COP, the so-called "institutional demands," which have their origin in executive departments and which usually concern the maintenance or improvement of urban infrastructures of the city.

Besides technical limits, there are financial limits not always duly considered by the assemblies. Suffice it to mention that, for financial reasons, only 30 per cent of the demands originally formulated by the community can be taken care of. Sometimes, the way the demands and priorities are formulated does not take into account certain technical conditionalities that increase the cost beyond what the communities themselves consider reasonable. For example, the fact that street pavement must include street lighting increases its cost by a large amount. Nowadays, the percentage of investments included in the budget varies between 15 and 20 per cent, a percentage that, according to Brazilian standards, must be considered high.[40] On the other hand, community councilors in the COP have always questioned the amount of expenses with the personnel and services of the executive and argued that the PB process should contemplate such expenses. To meet this demand to some extent, a representative and a substitute of the SIMPA now take part in the COP; on the other hand, as mentioned above, a Three-Party Commission was created in the COP—composed of councilors, representatives of SIMPA, and representatives of the government—whose objective is to debate and deliberate on the admission of personnel to the municipal government.

The decision-model resulting from power sharing in the PB is quite complex, a complexity that emerges in the way the PB is seen by the participants in regional assemblies and thematic plenaries. According to the 1995 survey already mentioned, to the question on the decision power of the communities, 33 per cent replied that the population decides "always," 27.3 per cent replied that the population decides "almost always," and 23.8 per cent replied that it decides "sometimes." Significantly enough, 15.3 per cent did not or did not know how to reply. These data did not significantly change in the survey carried out in 1998 (CIDADE and CRC, 1999: 12).

The credibility of the political contract that constitutes the PB resides in the effectiveness of the decisions and in the accountability both of the executive and the representatives of the civil society in the COP (see also Abers, 1998, 2000). The fact that only 30 per cent of the demands may be considered is less important than the effective satisfaction of the demands selected for inclusion in the Investment Plan. Several mechanisms guarantee effectiveness and accountability. First, the political will of the executive must be mentioned. The basic principle of the municipal government is to fulfill as rigorously as possible the Investment Plan and justify what is left unfulfilled. Second, there are committees—created within the Fora of Delegates—whose function is to supervise the works. In the case of delays or alterations, the delegates have direct access to the Mayor's Office to ask for explanations. Third, the very structures of the PB strongly encourage accountability themselves. The two institutions of regular functioning—the COP and the Forum of Delegates—are bound to the grassroots institutions: the Regional Assemblies and the Thematic Plenaries. The two latter organs, because they are open to the individual and collective participation of all citizens, exercise a double popular control, upon the performance of the executive and upon community representation itself. As we saw above, in practice, the exercise of control is problematic, as witness the debates about the quality of representation and about *retorno*.

A possible demonstration of the effectiveness of the decisions can be observed in the 1995 survey I have been referring to: 56.6 per cent of participants in regional and thematic assemblies declared themselves to have benefited from works and services of the PB.[41] It is significant that this percentage increases with the number of years of participation in the PB. Thus, amongst those that had participated in the PB for six years, 72.7 per cent claimed to have benefited. The percentage is also higher among leaders of neighborhood associations (67.9 per cent) and those who have already been elected (either as delegates or councilors) to the organs of the PB (74.3 per cent).[42]

As I have indicated, the close linkage of participation to resource distribution and to the effectiveness of decisions is one of the nuclear features of the PB. This alone explains why, for five months, the PB councilors meet at least once a week, often twice or thrice a week, with no remuneration, even without fare expenses (fare expenses are actually a demand that to present has not been attended to). This linking of participation to distribution is, no doubt, one of the virtues of the PB, but perhaps also its limit. According to Tarso Genro, it is common for a region or micro-region to stop participating in the meetings and assemblies after their demands have been met. Later they usually come back, once they have realized that in the year in which they did not participate there was no investment in their region or micro-region.

As far as accountability goes, rendering accounts and providing information are crucial for the intelligibility and transparency of the whole process. As early as 1990, the executive declared the Municipal Day of Accountability, on which, at a public meeting downtown, the executive was to render an account of the works decided upon in the PB. Nowadays, accountability is performed in many ways, often by means of flyers widely distributed throughout the city and at the beginning of the assemblies and plenaries of the *rodada*.[43] On the other hand, the GAPLAN publishes a booklet with the Investment Plan, a list of all the approved works described in detail, a list of the names and addresses of every councilor, as well as the telephone number of the PB Coordinator (CROP) in every region. This document circulates widely and reaches all the regions, giving citizens the opportunity to see if their decisions are being executed.[44] In the 1995 survey, when asked about the degree of satisfaction concerning the accountability of the executive, 47.6 per cent replied that it was satisfactory, while 23.6 per cent said it was "in part" satisfactory.

The close binding articulation of participation, distribution, and the effectiveness of decisions may eventually provoke some additional tension in the already tense field of co-government that constitutes the political contract between the executive and the organized communities, for two main reasons: the limits to investment and the major works. In the past seven years, the Municipality of Porto Alegre managed to increase its investment resources more than any other Brazilian city. According to Navarro (1996: 22), budget resources available for investments accounted for US$54 million in 1992; US$31.5 million in 1993; US$82 million in 1994; US$65.7 million in 1995; and US$70 million in 1996. The global investment figures indicate that municipal investment has probably reached its maximum limit. Since to an increase of participation corresponds an increase of demands, it is to be expected that the struggle for resource sharing will become fiercer in the near future. If, as a consequence, the percentage of demands-attended decreases significantly, we may well witness a lack of interest in participation emerge, as indeed happened in the early years of the PB. This problem becomes more serious in light of the budgeting crisis of 1998. In fact, the level of investment has decreased in the execution of the 1998 budget due to the sudden reduction of federal transferences at the end of 1997. The reduction of federal transferences derived mainly from the Kandir Law (after the name of the then Minister of Planning), which granted generous tax exemptions to the export industrial sector.[45] The sustained growth of municipal revenues could not compensate for the reduction of federal transferences.[46]

By its very genesis, the PB has been the privileged mechanism to decide the works that are directly relevant to the communities. It has been, in a word, closer to "rice and beans" works than to "major works." The 1993 and 1995 Congresses of the Constituent City, as well as the creation, from 1994 onwards, of the thematic plenaries, were an attempt at expanding the reach of the decisions. However, given the predominance of the regions in the COP, it is not easy to keep the political contract when the material results turn out to be more abstract. By way of example, let us consider the case of the loans that the executive was forced to take from international banks, in view of the ceiling of the investment with locally obtained revenue, in order to carry out works deemed important for the city as a whole. Thus, having obtained a loan from the World Bank to build various infrastructures, the executive proposed to the COP the construction of five avenues. There was great resistance on the part of the community councilors, who wanted the money to be invested in street pavement in the regions. Tarso Genro recounts:

> I, myself, and the executive's staff engaged in a dispute right in the middle of the Council and I threatened: "if you want to break it, OK, we'll break it and build a tiny street in every region. But you will be held responsible and shall answer before the city and will give arguments to the Right for whom you have no vision of how the city should be developed. The five avenues are crucial for all the city population, especially for those living in the periphery."

After a long debate, the Council approved the construction of the five avenues with one vote against.

Actually, resorting to international loans to promote urban development immediately poses problems for the PB. Such loans require the previous, detailed indication of the investment to be made, which may collide with the decision-making process of the PB. It so happens, however, that meanwhile, the PB gained some international recognition as a transparent and efficient means of resource distribution. So, recently, the Interamerican Development Bank agreed to grant a loan for the construction of a turnpike (the III Perimetral), approving at the same time a loan for street pavement in areas around the turnpike without requiring the usual specifications. In other words, the money will be released in order to be applied to street paving, but the specific streets and extension (up to 100 kilometers) will be decided later on by the PB instances.

Is the political contract of co-government that sustains the PB a contract among equal partners? This question raises the issue of the autonomy of the institutions and processes of the participatory budget. I said above that this political contract is based on the premise that the autonomy of both the elected mayor and the popular movement becomes a mutually relative autonomy. The question is: whose autonomy is more relativized by entering the contract? The PB is an initiative of the PT popular administration of Porto Alegre and its basic institutional outline has been designed over the years by the executive. It is part of a political program of redistribution of public resources and democratization of the state. This political program is also the meeting ground for a demand with a similar political orientation advanced by the popular movement and sustained over the years by much struggle. The issue is, then, how this convergence of political will has been carried out, on whose terms and timetables and with what outcomes.

As said above, the executive has a prominent role in the PB. The cycle, the agenda, and the timetables are set by the municipal government according to legal requirements but certainly also according to political strategy. But the initiative of the executive only becomes effective if the communities and popular movements participate actively in the process. Without any doubt the popular participation in the PB is very active. Is it also autonomous? What does it mean to be autonomous? Should the issue of autonomy be discussed solely in the context of the relations between the popular movement and the government or rather also in the context of the relations of the popular movement *vis-à-vis* the other parties and political forces integrating the political field of Porto Alegre?

There is a long tradition of party involvement in the popular movements. The PT won the elections in part by creating a political base among the community organizations. Other parties tried to do the same. The PDT, for instance, has had for a long time a presence and an influence in the neighborhood associations movement and is still very strong in the UAMPA. Autonomy cannot therefore be conceived as popular spontaneity, as a native capacity to organize poor people in degraded communities without the support or influence of external, organized political forces. Autonomy must rather be conceived as the popular capacity to channel external support and put it at the service of objectives, demands, and agendas generated in the communities. In the Brazilian context, autonomy is measured by the capacity to develop organizational strength and effectivity by maneuvering among competing external political influences, using such competition to impose demands that, however important for the community, do not represent a priority for any of the political forces in competition.

Since the PB is not a popular movement but an institutional constellation designed to function as a sustained, regularly functioning meeting place for the popular movement and the municipal government, the question of the autonomy of the PB must be formulated as the real capacity of the popular representatives in such institutions to shape agendas, timetables, debates, and decisions. In this sense, autonomy, rather than a stable characteristic of a given political process, is the ever-provisional outcome of an ongoing struggle. Thus conceived, the autonomy of the PB must be discussed at two levels: the operational functioning of the PB institutions, including coordination, agendas, and timetables; and the impact on the PB of changes in the political orientation of the executive.

Concerning the first level, I have mentioned that the coordination of PB institutions is in the hands of the executive's representatives and that the agenda and the timetable is proposed by them. But I have also mentioned that the executive's role in this regard has been increasingly questioned and challenged by the councilors and delegates. The observation of the COP meetings in particular shows that the councilors have become more assertive and aggressive, and that the procedural rules of the meetings have often been disrupted by heated debates. One of the widely violated rules is the prohibition of direct dialogue among the councilors. Such rule states that the interventions have to be previously registered by the coordination and take place in the order in which they have been registered.

Concerning the agenda, the conflict between some councilors and the executive is often quite open. The councilors have been consistently fighting for the expansion of the municipal activities to be submitted to the PB and they have in general been met with the resistance of both the CRC and GAPLAN representatives. The basic argument of the government is that there are topics that engage the city as a whole and which for that reason cannot be submitted to a debate that tends to promote particularistic solutions, be they relative to the regions or to the themes. The councilors counterargue that they represent the whole city and that the real issue is a different one: the opposition of the executive to the further decentralization of municipal services (culture, health, sports, leisure, and so on). The councilors have been more and more openly critical of the executive coordination and agenda setting. In an interview, one councilor, a woman very active in the popular movement, told me: "Sometimes I feel that I am being manipulated, that I am here to legitimate the popular administration and nothing else. The PB is the best thing that could happen in this city but it has to operate according to our way." Probably as a response to the greater assertiveness of the councilors there are indications that the setting of the agenda is now more shared and that whenever there are overarching constraints they are better explained. Besides, the proposals made by the executive representatives are sometimes voted down.

Concerning timetables, deadlines and times for debate, the discussions in the COP have also become more conflictual. On one side, the councilors claim that they need more time to process information, to ask for clarification and to consult with their constituencies. On the other side, the executive representatives claim that the deadlines are not an invention or whim of the executive but rather are established in laws promulgated by the Câmara dos Vereadores. They also claim that to debate is fine but that it is very frustrating to verify that after heated, long discussions there is no quorum to vote because in the meantime some less interested or more pressed councilors have left the meeting. One good instance of this conflict occurred in the COP meeting of 8 August 1996, when the municipal secretariat for housing submitted a vast housing program (PRO-MORADIA) to the COP and asked for a decision in two days in order to be able to comply with legal deadlines. Some councilors considered that request outrageous in light of the extension and complexity of the document. As a result, the housing question has become a contentious issue in the PB. In interviews, the councilors have recurrently voiced the concern that the discussions are rushed, there not being enough time to clarify doubts and vote with full knowledge of what is at stake. Sometimes the vote is decided on the basis of a trust relationship with another, more knowledgeable councilor or with the executive representative.

The other dimension of the relative autonomy of the PB concerns the impact of changes in political orientation of the executive upon the PB institutions. Between the leadership of the municipal government and the leadership of the popular movement there have always been some elective political affinities. Leftist political orientations have dominated both leaderships, and the conflicts among them, sometimes very sectarian, cannot be understood without contextualizing them in the historical conflicts within the left.

The now four terms of popular administration have been dominated by different political tendencies inside the PT. These differences have expressed themselves both as different political languages and different political initiatives. In the third term, under a mayor of the Socialist Democracy tendency with a Trotskyite leaning—Raul Pont—and, just to pick one language example, the plenary assemblies were renamed "popular general assemblies" (Pont, 2000; Dias, 2000).[47] It remains to be seen whether such name changes correspond to real changes in the operations of these institutions. So far, no radical change has been detected.

But changes in political orientation have repercussions above all in policy changes. One of such changes concerns the Pluriannual Investment Plan, the plan for the whole term, in this case, 1998-2000. While Tarso Genro discussed and formulated the Pluriannual Plan inside the executive and did not submit it in any meaningful way to the COP, Raul Pont, in a highly politicized statement, decided to submit the Pluriannual Plan to the COP in very much the same way as the annual budget. The objective was precisely to expand the ambit of the COP attributes, a demand frequently voiced by the councilors themselves, as we saw above. Another objective was probably to call the attention of the popular leadership to the changing macro-political context: the cuts on social policies at the federal level and the consequent impact on the financial transferences to the cities and on employment and the standard of living; the struggles by the city governments around the country, some of them bankrupt, others forced to embark on aggressive and unpopular measures to attract foreign investment to the city.[48] Contextualized by this macro-political environment, the political decisions of the executive would stand out in a brighter light and the difficulties ahead could be better understood.

The initial expectations about the debate on the Pluriannual Investment Plan somehow got frustrated. The debate on the Pluriannual Plan was added up to the debate on the annual budget, thus forcing the COP to an extra effort, as the need for two meetings per week well illustrates. Moreover, this effort was not well understood by all councilors. More familiarized with the annual budget, some of them could not see a clear distinction between the Pluriannual Investment Plan and the annual budget. Accordingly, they made suggestions and demands that could fit the annual budget but not the Pluriannual Plan. This forced the government representative to endless explanations about the differences between the two documents and the criteria for their respective items. In the COP meeting of 22 April 1997, the GAPLAN representative said: "We cannot include a public toilette in the region X in the Pluriannual Plan. The Pluriannual is a plan; it is not a budget. It is reference planning to guide us in the elaboration of the annual budget." The frustration of the councilors increased when they became aware that their demands, no matter how just or justified, would be met only if the necessary funds became available in the next coming years.

Irrespective of changes in political leadership, a gradual but consistent movement toward the greater autonomy of the COP and the PB in general *vis-à-vis* the executive can be detected. The autonomy of the PB has become an ever more cherished value for the councilors and delegates. At the end of 1996, when the Investment Plan for 1997 was presented in a public ceremony attended by the mayor and the councilors of the COP, there were some derogative comments against the councilors in the local press, which has been in general hostile to the PB. The councilors interpreted those comments as an insult against their autonomy and, at the meeting of 7 January 1997, discussed ways of responding to the insults. A committee was nominated and in the following month of April the COP decided to create a Media Commission in charge of following the media reporting on the COP and PB and to respond whenever necessary.[49]

From techno-bureaucracy to techno-democracy

Conflict and mediation between technical and political issues, between knowledge and power, is one of the main features of the PB. If it is true that technical criteria limit the field of participation and deliberation, it is likewise true that the PB process has radically changed the professional culture of the technical staff of the executive. The technical staff has been increasingly submitted to a profound learning process concerning communication and argumentation with lay populations. Their technical recommendations must be conveyed in accessible language to people who do not master technical knowledge; their reasonability must be demonstrated in a persuasive way, rather than imposed in an authoritarian fashion; no alternative hypothesis or solution may be excluded without showing its unviability. Where earlier a technobureaucratic culture prevailed, gradually a techno-democratic culture has emerged.

This transformation has not been easy. According to Tarso Genro, during the period between 1992 and 1996, there was more progress in changing the language and discourse of the engineers when addressing the people in the communities than in changing their dismissive attitudes *vis-à-vis* what people had to say. In other words, the capacity to make him or herself understood has improved more than the capacity to listen. When Raul Pont initiated his mandate (1996–2000), he became particularly sensitive to the fact that the structure and process of the PB were very little known among the municipal workers and staff. In view of this, in 1997 the mayor launched a program targeted at the municipal personnel, which he called "Program for Internalization of Participatory Budgeting." This was announced as part of a much broader program of an overall internal democratization of the state. In an interview the official in charge of coordinating this program told me that, "in order to be fully consolidated the PB must be part of the everyday work of a municipal worker." A working group was set up to organize workshops with the workers and staff about the cycle, rules, criteria, and methodology of the PB. The targets of the workshops were to be addressed sequentially: personnel that deal directly with the PB; personnel that mediate between the executive and the community (such as the community advisors of the FASCOM); and finally the supervisors and directors.

Once we analyze in detail the functioning of the PB it will not be difficult to detect, among the multiple interactions between the participants of the PB and the personnel, situations that, no matter how apparently trivial, may be a source of tension, even when the personnel support the PB. As an example of such a situation, I may mention the accreditation procedure. This is the process by which the people, the delegates, and the councilors identify themselves as they enter the room where the meeting is to be held. They must show their ID card and fill out a form. The accreditation is entrusted to a group of municipal personnel designated by the mayor. Even if we only take into account the regional and thematic plenaries, the staff must verify the credentials of hundreds of people in 22 meetings per month (16 regional and six thematic). Because it resulted from a personal nomination by the mayor, the verification of credentials was understood for a while as a political job to be performed as militant work. As time went by, however, some of the people refused to go on performing the job, invoking the many evenings they could not spend with their families. As a result, the coordinator of the Internalization Program told me that the executive was considering paying extra hours to the credentials personnel, and that she was in favor.[50] As a consequence, the COP has now an executive secretary paid for by the Municipal Administration through the CRC.

The road from techno-bureaucracy to techno-democracy is a bumpy one. In the course of time, as the delegates and councilors have become more assertive, disputing more openly the technical criteria and solutions presented by the professional staff, the latter have become more defensive, yet the conflict between competing knowledges has all but faded away. In my field observations I witnessed many lively debates between residents and engineers about pavement, location of sewerage pipes, etc., etc., and was impressed by the argumentative capacity of the community leaders.

Competing legitimacies: the PB and the Câmara de Vereadores

In theoretical debates on the relationship between representative and participatory democracy it is often forgotten that one does not exist without the other. Participatory democracy, in particular, in complex political processes always presupposes the creation of instances of delegation and representation. The PB experience is eloquent in this respect. As we saw, the basic structures of the PB aim at an institutional articulation not only with the institutions of representative democracy at the urban level (the mayor and his/her executive) but also with the representative institutions derived from participatory democracy at the community level. This articulation between participation/representation at the community level calls for careful reflection that cannot be undertaken here.

I mentioned above that the PB decision model tries to reconcile the principle of the democratic representativeness of the mayor and his/her executive with the principle of participatory democracy of the citizens organized in grassroots associations and assemblies. However, the government is not limited to the executive; rather, it includes also the Câmara dos Vereadores, the municipal legislative body.

The political contract that exists between the executive and the communities has thus far not been extended to the Legislative. On the contrary, the relation between the PB and the Legislative has been one of constant conflict (sometimes involving physical confrontation).[51] The reason for the conflict is quite obvious. According to the Constitution, it behooves the Legislative to approve the municipal budget. Now, the PB has totally preempted this incumbency. To be sure, as we have seen, according to the PB cycle the proposal of the budget law, after having been prepared in the COP, is forwarded to the Legislative for debate and approval. Theoretically, the Legislative could reject the proposal but the fact that it has already been legitimated by the large participation of citizens mobilized by the PB compels the Legislative to always approve the budget presented. It ends up, therefore, being a formality.

According to some, however, given the budgeting technique traditionally adopted in Brazil, the Legislative has never actually deliberated substantially on the budget. The truth is that, given the fact that the indication in the budget of the concrete works to be carried out is not required, the executive has always had ample leeway in budget execution. But the fact of the matter is that such a system also created the opportunity for the Legislative to influence the execution by the traditional populist and clientelist methods.

The legislators had their electoral folds in the different regions and the votes they gathered from them were directly entailed to the works they managed to include in the budget. Now, this was precisely the clientelist system that the PB intended to put an end to, and herein for the most part resides the hostility or distance with which the legislators not linked to the PT regard the PB. While the duality of power between the PB and the executive—notwithstanding the problems and tensions identified here—has been dominated by a logic of complementarity and cooperation, the duality of power between the PB and the Legislative Chamber has been dominated by a logic of open or latent conflict. It is both a duality of power and a duality of legitimacy. As one legislator told me in an interview: "The PT has co-opted and demoralized the popular movement. The PB is a diabolic invention of the PT to stay in power forever. Look, how many people participated in the PB last year? A little more than 10,000 people. Well, I was elected by a larger number. Why am I less representative than the councilors of the COP?" Another legislator less hostile to the PB said in the interview: "I think the PB is an excellent idea but I don't see—except for political reasons of the PT—why the Câmara de Vereadores is not involved. We don't want to absorb the PB. We would like to have a part in it. For instance, a percentage of the investment fund should be left to the Chamber to allocate." As another legislator put it: "The budget arrives at the Chamber in a cast (*engessado*). We're tied up. It is not fair because after all we are the legislators."

One of the angles of the tension between representative and participatory democracy has been the debate of the last few years on the official legal institutionalization of the PB. As it stands today, the PB is based on a political contract with the executive and is ruled only by its internal rules and the organic law of the Prefeitura. The crucial question is whether the future safeguard of the PB should not include its juridical consolidation. The positions diverge, even inside the PT and the executive themselves. While some believe that the legal consignation of the PB will help to defend its existence if in the future an executive hostile to citizen participation is elected, others argue that such legalization would be a submission of participatory democracy to representative democracy, do away with the political autonomy of the PB, and subject it in the future to legislative manipulation according to the majorities obtainable in the Legislative Chamber. Said one of the PT legislators in an interview: "I participate in the plenaries of the PB and I even have a vote as a legislator. The legislators should integrate themselves in the PB and not seek separate and privileged participation and decision-making." Other PT legislators and leaders think that the tension between the PB and the Chamber is not a "healthy one" and may be risky in the future. According to them it is not in the interest of the PT to demoralize the legislative body and contribute to empty out its prerogatives. Some of them have even presented law proposals concerning the legalization of the PB. One of them said in an interview: "I am in favor of a type of legalization that does not plaster the PB, and that contributes to consolidate it as an official component of our political system, a mark of our specificity."

The issue of legalization is one among many dimensions of the conflict between the executive and the Câmara de Vereadores, where the PT does not hold the majority.[52] The COP councilors have a clear understanding of this and the divisions inside the COP on this issue reflect broader cleavages in the city politics and community movement. In spite of the political restrictions on the budgetary prerogatives of the Câmara de Vereadores, the latter makes many amendments every year, not so much to the budget proposal submitted by the executive before 30 September, but to the proposal of budgetary directives submitted before 15 July of every year. These amendments are discussed in the COP. In the meeting of 7 August 1997, the GAPLAN representative read the most important amendments. One of them, coming from a rightist legislator and former mayor, consisted in restricting the mayor's expenses on publicity—a major weapon of the mayor to reach out to the communities and maximize the flow of information about the PB between the executive and the communities. The GAPLAN representative intervened then to draw attention to the negative impact of this and other amendments, emphasizing that through them the legislators are trying to limit the autonomy of the PB. He exhorted the councilors and delegates to mobilize quickly and strongly in order to try to defeat these amendments in the Câmara. He concluded: "They want to embarrass the PB. This is war and when you are at war you don't stop the war to prepare and debate." Some councilors were displeased by this comment and asked for more time to analyze the amendments, because after all it is in the interest of the PB to cut some of the executive expenditures. One of them said: "I don't agree with X [the GAPLAN representative]. This is not a war. We are democratically debating and discussing with the Câmara de Vereadores [...]. I don't disagree with the proposal of the coordinators, but the proposal is also a way of appropriating the issue. If we are going to discuss what the autonomy of the COP is, then there is much more to be discussed." Implied in this comment is, of course, the fact that the issue of the autonomy of the COP must be raised not only *vis-à-vis* the Câmara but also *vis-à-vis* the executive.

On and off, the issue of legalization of the PB has been discussed in the COP. Some councilors have favored some kind of legalization. Others have opposed it in the name of the autonomy of the PB. In this debate the international recognition and praise of the PB is often mentioned. One of the councilors commented in the COP meeting of 3 March 1997: "The way the PB has been operating in the last eight years without any regulation by the government is what makes it possible for us to go ahead and be internationally recognized."

The issue of legalization will probably remain as an unresolved tension in the PB of Porto Alegre for some time. The PB has, indeed, destabilized the old ways of doing politics in Porto Alegre, and the Câmara de Vereadores is trying to reconstitute its political space in the new political conditions created by the PB. This reconstitution may, nevertheless, reveal some unexpected continuities with the "old ways."

CONCLUSION: BETWEEN THE PAST AND THE FUTURE

Since participatory budgeting is a very dynamic social and political process, it is difficult to draw from it many conclusions or projections. Up until now, the PB has been a remarkable means of promoting citizen participation in decisions concerning distributive justice, the effectiveness of decisions, and the accountability of the executive and of the delegates elected by the communities to the COP and the Forum of Delegates. The success of the PB has been widely recognized, not only in the city of Porto Alegre and in Brazil, but also internationally. Many Brazilian cities have been adopting the PB system, under various forms, at the same time that different international organizations have come to regard it with increasing appreciation, although they are more interested in its technical virtues (efficiency and effectiveness in resource distribution and utilization) than in its democratic virtues (the sustainability of a complex system of participation and distributive justice).

To my mind, the future of the PB depends, to a large extent, on how its principles and practices of democratic participation are strengthened and extended to areas or issues that have not yet been included in the PB.[53] It also depends on how its autonomy is improved and consolidated so that the break with the old clientelist politics becomes irreversible.

The assessment of the PB shows that these are very demanding conditions and may even involve some dilemmas. For instance, the consolidation of the PB makes political sense only if it breaks with the old patrimonialist-clientelist system. But is such consolidation possible without some form of continuity with the old system? As an emergent political reality, the PB tends to have a destabilizing effect, not only in political terms, but also in ideological and cultural terms. However, a destabilizing idea that succeeds in becoming a sustainable practice is always in danger of losing its destabilizing potential as its success increases. The routine of mobilization leads to routine mobilization. Participation remains high but common citizens are gradually replaced by specialized participatory citizens. The dilemma here rests in the fact that, although the radicalization of the experiment is the only weapon against routinization, there is an undeterminable threshold beyond which radicalization will irreversibly compromise the success of the experiment. There is no way out of this dilemma. Yet the tension it creates may itself be sustainable—thus contributing to the continuing, if always problematic, success of the experiment —provided that the participants engage in a reflective self-subversion: by this I mean the constant radicalization of political consciousness centered on the limits of the radicalization of political practice.

Haunting the PB is another dilemma that, however, has less to do with the experiment itself than with the interpretations and evaluations made of it by both academic and political observers and analysts. In a historical period of structural pessimism, there is a tendency to be too complacent toward what exists and is familiar, and excessively reticent or suspicious about what is merely emerging and, therefore, unusual. This suspicion consists in interpreting all the characteristics and developments of a destabilizing emergent reality as steps or movements toward a final and inevitable failure. This interpretation of an announced death, which can come from the left as well as from the right, works as an intellectual trap. Once the trap is set, the exquisite bird of realistic utopia will sooner or later fall into it.

This kind of interpretation tends to be articulated with the interpretation of abridgement. This consists in interpreting the institutional innovation in isolation from its historical and sociological embeddedness and specificity, thereby reducing it to a handful of abstract traits that compose a model to be applied anywhere and everywhere by expert knowledge. Caught between the interpretation of suspicion and the interpretation of abridgement, popular initiatives like the PB are placed in a cruel dilemma: they either fail in a concrete situation and are declared to be bound to fail and therefore dismissed as foolish utopias of participation, or they succeed in a concrete situation and are turned into a general recipe for participatory institutionality, to be adopted by the World Bank (increasingly interested in participation), being ground up, pasteurized, and converted into new items of conditionality for the concession of subsidies or loans.[54]

What is most remarkable in the case of Porto Alegre is the acute awareness of these problems and dilemmas shown by the political staff of the city and their political courage to face these obstacles openly and without prejudice. The best illustration of this was the constitution, in the beginning of 2001, of the Work Group for the Modernization of Participatory Budgeting (Grupo de Trabalho de Modernização do Orçamento Participativo), with the purpose of reflecting on the PB experiment in the last twelve years and of presenting proposals for its revision and reformulation. The proposal drafted by this group, which will be analyzed in the final section of this chapter, was presented in December of 2001 and put to a vote on 16 January 2002. The first document drafted by the work group, significantly entitled "Breaking our limits: a first assessment of the points of strangulation in the participatory budgeting process in Porto Alegre" (2001), presents a vast and bold list of the problems and challenges faced by the PB, many of which converge with those already reported in this study, as a result of my research and observation of the PB in the last eight years. The setting up of this work group and the depth of the reflection on the PB, carried out both within the PB and among the political class, and even among the international community of social scientists who have been studying the process, bear witness to the political determination to bring about its renovation. This process of reflection did not derive from the need to remedy the failure of an initiative of participatory democracy, but rather from the need to solve the problems created by its success. In this sense, it was a unique exercise, given that the experiments of participatory democracy almost never reach a level of consolidation capable of raising these sorts of problems.

I will now describe the main problems and challenges identified in the document "Breaking our limits," relating them both to my own research and to the research of the social scientists who were invited by the work group to present documents of reflection on the PB. The order of presentation does not imply any hierarchization. It follows, up to a certain point, the sequence adopted in the document mentioned above.

1. *The densification of participatory organs and the conflicts of responsibilities.* The strengthening of participatory culture in Porto Alegre throughout the decade brought about two important institutional developments: the complexification of the PB and the creation of participatory institutions, to a certain degree external to the PB, but vested with complementary functions, either parallel to or intersecting those of the PB. In this chapter I have analyzed how the internal rules of the PB have gradually become denser and how the fulfillment of sectorial demands, not strictly regionalizable, led to the creation of thematic plenaries. The institution of thematic plenaries significantly expanded the horizon of expectations regarding participation but, at the same time, made more complex the participation in the PB. Indeed, although in the abstract it is easy to distinguish between regional and thematic demands, in actual terms, especially when the debate centers on a given cultural, educational or health facility that has to be installed in a given region, there may exist (and has existed) a degree of overlapping and, consequently, a potential conflict between regional participation and thematic participation. This potential conflict increased as infrastructural demands (of street paving, of basic sanitation) were met and as the regions engaged in other types of demands, demands of a "more thematic" nature.

Moreover, the strengthening of participatory culture has led to the institution of other forms of participation, namely the sectorial Municipal Councils (there are at present 35 such councils) whose purpose is to debate sectorial policies and, in some cases, the budgetary proposals of the executive's secretariats to which they are connected. The articulation of the Municipal Councils with the thematic plenaries and with the central institution of the PB, the COP, is problematic and sometimes raises conflicts of responsibilities. One of the most intense debates that I have witnessed within the COP opposed the councilors and the representatives of the Municipal Council for the Rights of Children and Adolescents. This debate centered precisely on budgetary priorities—the basic needs of the population versus the rights of children.[55] To my mind, the articulation between different organs of participation must be built on the basis of a clear political premise: the centrality of the COP in the process of budgetary decision.[56]

The fact that Olívio Dutra—from the PT—was elected governor of the state of Rio Grande do Sul (1998–2002) meant the institutionalization the Participatory Budget of the state, the opening of a new space of participatory articulation between the PB of the city and the PB of the state. Even though this was an essential articulation, the practice has shown it to be more difficult to achieve than it had initially appeared, particularly if we have in mind the different levels of consolidation of the two PBs and the different expectations they create. According to a survey conducted in 2002, the majority of the interviewees (78.3 per cent) do not participate in the PB of the state (PMPA-CIDADE, 2002: 45). In the gubernatorial elections of 2002 the PT candidate—Tarso Genro—lost the elections and the new governor announced shortly thereafter his intention to replace the PB by other forms of public consultation.

2. *Representativeness and the quality of participation.* I have already mentioned the problem of representativeness, especially with reference to the tension between the PB and the Chamber of Deputies. This problem echoes the much broader one of the relation between participatory democracy and representative democracy. The tension between these two forms of democracy seems to be constitutive of modern democracies, since neither political practice nor democratic political theory have been able to formulate a new relation between them, other than that of a zero sum: the expansion of the one can only be obtained at the expense of the contraction of the other. This tension is not expected to be fully resolved in Porto Alegre, in spite of the existence of a hybrid public sphere—the result of the joint management of civil society and the municipal executive—symbolized by the PB, which represents outstanding progress toward overcoming the zero-sum relation.[57]

It is not surprising that the numbers of participation and their interpretation should be the cause of political dispute. Nor is it surprising that the political and social forces that support the PB should look for solutions to increase participation, on the basis of the assumption that more participation is always better than less participation. The fact is that this self-evident assumption hides a dilemma: since different social groups mobilize for participation with different objectives, it is only possible to increase participation beyond a certain limit if the scope of competing objectives, now more numerous, is restricted. One possible solution to minimize this dilemma—given the impossibility of resolving it—consists in establishing differentiated costs of participation through the multiplication of the forms of participation, some more intense than others. For example, the introduction of referenda and the use of electronic democracy (via the Internet) may become solutions, provided that the objectives of these more individualistic and less intense forms of participation are clearly established. In this way, the ranking of objectives, to be established by the more intense forms of participation, can open space for the less intense forms, which, in their turn, do not aggravate the abovementioned problem of the conflict of responsibilities.

A further question concerning the quantity of participation has to do with the accessibility and, therefore, with the existence of obstacles to the admission to the PB. We are now aware that the most deprived and least organized sectors of the population have increased difficulties in participating. Democratic participation is a form of political investment for which the minimum political capital—that of being formally a citizen—is not enough. There is thus the need to think of forms of affirmative action capable of facilitating the participation of those in dire need of it but who are too deprived to even have access to it without external support.

In addition to this, the most deprived very often have demands that are not easily formatable by the institutions of the PB. We know, for instance, that without the regularization of landed property it is not possible to make adequate investments in services and infrastructures, although it is precisely in the irregular squatter settlements (where an estimated 25 per cent of the population still live) that those investments are most needed. For decades the popular sectors repeatedly defined the regularization of landed property as one of their chief priorities but, to their disappointment, what has been accomplished in this domain does not come close to meeting the allotted priority. Sérgio Baierle accurately points out this discrepancy, noting that of the one hundred areas for regularization "imposed" on the executive by the communities about ten years ago, only ten have in fact been regularized one decade later (2001: 16). While there may be other factors contributing to this situation—such as, for example, the slowness of the courts—it is possible that, through slowness and inertia, the administrative and legal structure of the municipality "boycotts" the satisfaction of such a basic demand.

The accessibility of the PB is also related to two other questions: the access to information and the expansion of the PB process. The first question concerns not only the diffusion of information but also the source and content of the information. The Prefeitura has invested enormously in the diffusion of information, to the point that the opposition parties frequently question the expenditure of the executive in what they consider political propaganda. Although the Internet is not yet broadly accessible in the city, the fact that it is a source of information and interaction with the PB is yet one more sign of the municipal investment in the diffusion of information.

However, the accessibility of information depends on the intelligibility of the information—that is to say, on the content of the information. As I have pointed out, one of the tensions of the PB has been precisely the clash between rival forms of knowledge—between the technical knowledge of the professionals working for the Prefeitura and the practical knowledge of the citizens and their associations. This clash is also one between different languages, and to the extent that the technical language prevails, the availability of the information does not necessarily mean the accessibility of the information. This is one area in which the pedagogy of the PB must take up a more central role in the future, becoming a two-way pedagogy: directed to the citizens and their organizations and directed to the administrative and technical staff of the municipality.

In addition to considering the quantity and quality of the information, it is also necessary to examine the source of the information. In fact, there has been a recurrent complaint that the municipal executive has practically been the sole source of information about the PB. It is probably inevitable that it should be that way, even though something can be done in order to increase the flow of information from the bottom up, especially the information that is produced by the entities of the community movement. However, the Prefeitura's near-monopoly of the information raises yet another question: that of the independence of the information, especially concerning the indicators of the efficiency of the PB in effecting the inversion of priorities in favor of the most deprived classes. Although, according to my evaluation, the popular administration has never fallen into gross manipulation of data, it would be reasonable to expect that the institutions of the PB, namely the COP, be invested with the necessary resources to obtain and diffuse independent information and evaluation. The PB is an important hybrid political project, whose self-reflexivity has been a permanent stimulus to learning. The evaluation of the project is part of this self-reflexivity and cannot be exclusively left to just one of the components of the political hybridization.

Finally, the intensity of participation is related to the constitutional design and the rules for the running of the participatory organs. As I have pointed out in this chapter, as the PB became more solid, its operating procedures became more complex. With the broadening of the PB's scope of decision and the expansion of its public, the process of debate and political negotiation became more intense and demanding. It is a known fact that participatory democracy demands a greater degree of transparency between political action and its results than that which is typical of representative democracy. This transparency depends on three major factors: the efficient management of participatory actions; the direct relationship between the latter and concrete results; and the "return" capacity of the structures of delegation and representation that emerge within participatory democracy whenever it expands beyond micro-societies.

The efficient management of participatory actions is complex, involving various factors: the frequency, organization, and length of the meetings; the accessibility of the meeting places; the positive relationship between the investment in these actions and their results. There is still work to be done at all these levels. Concerning the third factor, an example of the sort of work required is given by the work group, whose insistent questioning of the utility of the second *rodada* led to its being suppressed in the new PB program.

The direct relationship between participation and results is a crucial factor in the sustainability of participatory democracy. As we have seen, this relationship was initially vague and this vagueness was immediately felt in the following PB cycle. In this respect, the main question today is that of guaranteeing that the distribution of resources in the remote areas of a given region has a participatory character similar to that of interregional distribution. Many regions have been divided into micro-regions, some better organized than others. In addition, many of these regions have significant internal differences, both in terms of the scarcity of services and in terms of the social profile of the populations. As I have pointed out, in the remote areas of the regions, people have been reluctant to resort to mechanisms of distribution that ensure the same degree of transparency as that of interregional distribution; but it is also true that in regions that are quite uneven internally, it is difficult to make priority criteria work equitably. One of the possible ways of dealing with this problem is to redesign the regions and increase their number in order to make the basic participation units more homogeneous. This is a very complex solution, since the PB, like any political contract, includes, but also excludes. The included cannot be expected to accept without resistance the deterioration of their inclusion as a requirement for the inclusion of the excluded. The solution to this problem will be the ultimate test to the quality of the participation prompted by the PB. To overcome that resistance it will be necessary to neutralize the two mechanisms employed by societies to trivialize social exclusion: minimizing its extension and blaming the excluded for their own exclusion.

However, as I have suggested, the high degree of transparency required by participatory democracy depends also on the capacity of the structures of delegation and representation (i.e., the Fora of Delegates and the COP councilors) to "return to the base" and on the quality of that "return." No doubt, this is one of the dimensions of the quality of participation that deserves more careful attention. What is at stake is knowing if and to what extent the political culture of participation prompted by the PB has been internalized by its public—both by the citizens and their associations and by the delegates and councilors.[58]

The political culture of participation and solidarity is a countercurrent culture in societies dominated by the possessive and mercantile individualism that neoliberalism has taken to the point of paroxysm. This political culture cannot therefore be satisfied with its practical reiteration through the institutions of participation, since the latter, in the context of neoliberalism, are always threatened with perversion and decharacterization. In order to maintain and strengthen itself, the culture of participation and solidarity has to be served by an ambitious pedagogical project involving the educational system as a whole, the public services, and above all the third sector that, notwithstanding the increasingly important role it has been playing in the provision of public policies, has used its private nature as a means of defending itself from public control and of refusing the establishment of internal mechanisms of participation.

3. *Particularism, the city as a whole, and strategic planning.* As I have already mentioned, the PB has always been criticized by its opponents for focusing exclusively on local and immediate demands and for not allowing an adequate analysis of the problems of the city as a whole in the long and the medium term. This criticism is also heard today within the PB, which means that, paradoxically, today the city as a whole and its strategic planning have come closer than ever to being part of the political agenda of the PB. This development needs to be intensified, especially in the context of the extreme competition fomented by neoliberalism, not only between states but also between regions and between cities. The City Congresses, the thematic plenaries, and later the regional planning fora constituted important measures to give back Porto Alegre, as a whole body, to the citizens.

There is still a lot to be done in this respect, especially because the city is not a monolithic whole: it is a very differentiated whole internally, and many of the differences have escaped the notice of the PB. From among these we can highlight gender differences (the discrepancy between women's capacity of participation and women's capacity of representation), ethnic differences (black and indigenous issues), age differences (seniors and adolescents), functional differences (the physically and mentally disabled).

4. *Autonomy versus dependence.* As I have already devoted considerable attention to this problem, it will not be detailed here. It is a central question, which is, to some extent, inherent to the political form of the PB—a hybrid public sphere composed of the relative and reciprocal autonomies of society and of the municipal state. It is the contractualized relativity of autonomy that creates the equally contractualized relativity of dependence, and vice-versa. The tension between the autonomy and the dependence of the PB in relation to the municipal government is therefore constitutive of the PB, and thus cannot be decided in favor of one of the sides of the tension. It becomes a real question only when there is a discrepancy between the contractualized tension in the regulated structure of the PB and the tension in the practical life of

the PB. That is to say, this tension, as a political question, exists only if civil society, the citizens and community movements yield more of their autonomy than they obtain in government dependence on them. In the last decade there were many signs suggesting that this might be happening. I will name only three: the fact that the regularization of land property, although a structural question—in the sense of being an issue whose resolution affects significantly the pattern of social redistribution—has been incorporated in the PB too slowly and deficiently; the deceleration of the autonomous community movement (popular councils, neighborhood associations, township unions, the UAMPA) and the decline of their legitimacy in so far as they lose the monopoly of the political construction of popular demands; the decisive role the government has always played in the functional management of the PB, in setting the agenda and the political calendar, in creating and diffusing relevant information, in formulating technical criteria and "institutional demands."

As I have remarked above, these problems have all been identified and their resolution depends on political will. In my opinion, however, the current formulation given to the question of autonomy/dependence does not allow the perception that what is truly at stake in Porto Alegre is not so much the issue of autonomy/dependence but rather the pluralism of political orientations, the freedom with which this pluralism is being manifested, and the way it is either encouraged or repressed. The community movements have never been autonomous in the sense of being a spontaneous generation of society outside the context of the political forces organized at the level of political society and the political system. The hegemony of the PT today, clearly evident in the party sympathies of the public of the PB, represents a new political responsibility for the PT: to guarantee and promote pluralism and tolerance, without which participatory democracy will wither away. In the specific context of Porto Alegre, pluralism and tolerance have to be guaranteed and stimulated within the PT, a political party historically inclined to fractionalism, which the Brazilian right has not yet been able to take advantage of.

5. *The PB and the democratization of the state.* This is perhaps the most complex challenge posed to participatory democracy in Porto Alegre, and I have also referred to it in this chapter. If we ask what has changed in Porto Alegre's civil society in the past twelve years, we cannot but recognize that a lot has changed, both at the material level and at the institutional and cultural level. If, on the other hand, we ask what has changed in the administrative and legal structure of the municipal government, we are forced to acknowledge that there have been few changes, both at the organizational and the cultural level. Consequently, we are forced to conclude that the PB democratized the political state but failed to democratize the administrative state. This

discrepancy will necessarily cause confrontation, especially insofar as the democratic deficit of the administrative state becomes translated—as a result of the strengthening of the PB—into increasing inefficiency, slowness, and insensitivity toward expectations that have been intensified by the democratization of participation. It is not surprising, therefore, that the most recent City Congresses should have identified the democratization of the municipal government as a priority.

The democratization of the administrative state is in itself a political good, and it is especially important for repoliticizing the PB itself. By facing the limits of the democratization of public administration, the PB confronts itself not only with bureaucratic cultures but also with increasingly uneven articulations between the municipal administration and the state administration and between either of these and the federal administration.

This comprehensive political perspective, not only of the city and of the state government as a whole, but also of the country as a whole, will be fundamental to strengthening and focusing the PB as a political project. In the process, the PB will simultaneously gain a greater awareness of its potentialities and limits. In the words of Sérgio Baierle, one of the most lucid experts on the PB, "Porto Alegre is not an oasis in the neoliberal desert" (2001: 3); it suffers the consequences of the macro-policies of structural adjustment imposed at the federal level and it cannot defend itself thoroughly from the new neoliberal common sense, especially from the individualistic, market-oriented, managerial logic by which it is characterized. According to Baierle, it is therefore necessary to examine three sets of questions, all of which are aimed at repoliticizing the PB:

> (1) the need to politicize the experiments of direct community management which rely on the transfer of municipal resources (both financial and material); (2) the need to articulate the public budget with city planning, opening space for a more profound discussion of the municipal finances and public policies; and (3) the need to open space for debating the political perspectives of the PB experiment, both through the critique of "localist boasting" (democratic radicalization in a single city) and the critique of the method of recruiting staff from among the community leaderships and the increasing massification of the experiment (the hiatus between a specialized leadership body and grassroots participants). (Baierle, 2001: 2)

To my mind, the dynamics revealed by participatory democracy in Porto Alegre in the last 13 years gives us no reason to believe that it will not be capable of meeting these challenges.

POSTSCRIPT

On 16 January 2002, the COP approved the alterations to the PB recommended by the Work Group for the Modernization of Participatory Budgeting, the latter thus ceasing its activities. Given the expectations created around the Work Group, the process of reformulating the PB did not have as much participation or depth as had been expected. As I have mentioned above, some of the councilors and delegates contended that a greater amount of time should have been given to debate the proposals of the Work Group conveyed by the GAPLAN. The scanty two-week period given to the councilors to examine the proposals was justified by the executive with the need to initiate the 2002 PB cycle according to the new rules.

The central ideas of the proposals can be summed up in two words: simplification and capacitation. As I have remarked in the conclusion, during a period of twelve years the organs for and the scope of participation have multiplied. If, on the one hand, the densification of participation contributed to differentiating and intensifying the mobilization of the city for the PB, on the other hand, it posed the danger of participatory saturation and of the overlapping between different participatory organs. This saturation was intensified in 1998 with the adoption of the PB at the state level in Rio Grande do Sul, which has come to rival the PB of Porto Alegre in terms of the appeal to participation. Given the strong implantation of the latter, it is not surprising that initially the city of Porto Alegre had a modest participation in the state PB.

To provide an answer to this question, the main change introduced in the beginning of 2002 was the substitution of the two rounds of regional and thematic assemblies by one single round. In fact, participation in the second round had been decreasing, since all the work of prioritizing demands was being done beforehand, mostly in the intermediate meetings, and participation was significant only when there was a particularly conflictive question.

The substitution of the two rounds by a single round has altered the PB cycle.[59] In the single round, to be held now between April and May, regional and thematic assemblies elect thematic priorities and councilors, and at the same time they define the number of delegates to the Forum of Delegates who will analyze and rank the specific investment demands and follow the execution of the Investment Plan.

It is also in the single round that the executive renders accounts of the execution of the Investment Plan of the previous year. The intermediate meetings that used to be held between the two rounds have now been replaced by preparatory meetings to take place between March and April. Regional and thematic meetings will be held between May and July to elect the delegates (whose number per region and per theme has been established in the single round) and to rank the specific demands, works, and services in accord with the thematic priorities also established in the single round.

Yet another alteration was the reinstitution of the Municipal Assembly, which had existed in the beginning of the 1990s, under the name of Budgeting Forum (Fórum do Orçamento). The Municipal Assembly is a public act, a "great meeting of the population" whose aim is, according to the Prefeitura, to "install in office the new councilors of the PB and deliver to the government the ranking of works and services." This assembly is held in the first two weeks of July. From here onwards, the new PB cycle is similar to the former one, with one exception. Whereas up until now the Investment Plan was approved only by the COP, according to the new rules it will also have to be approved in the fora of regional and thematic delegates meeting for that purpose in October and November. According to Sérgio Baierle (personal communication, 3 May 2002), the purpose of this alteration is to stimulate continuity in the participation of delegates who up until now tended to demobilize after handing over the priorities in July. This alteration left the COP with no room for maneuver in negotiating the transfer of some resources to specific programs (such as housing and income-generating cooperatives) considered by the regions to be secondary. It remains to be seen whether this negotiation will be able to take place in the regional and thematic fora.

The second leading idea that presided over the changes more recently introduced in the PB is the capacitation of the councilors and delegates. The increasing complexity of the PB and the need to maintain great proximity between the citizens and their representatives has made it imperative to improve the technical and political quality of representation through actions of capacitation. Such capacitation will also be crucial in the creation of an institutional culture capable of overcoming the conflicts and the overlapping of responsibilities between the COP and the other municipal councils, an issue that has not yet been contemplated in the alterations already approved.

In general, we can conclude that there have not been major alterations in the PB, only a few adjustments, with the purpose of simplifying and improving it.

Notes

1 During the field research, I interviewed and held meetings with political leaders, both in government and in the opposition, with the leaders of the grassroots movements, and with the participants in the participatory budgeting institutions. The councilors and the delegates of the participatory budgeting kindly allowed me to attend their meetings. Mayors Tarso Genro and Raul Pont generously opened the doors of the Mayoralty for me. I had enlightening

discussions with colleagues at the Federal University of Rio Grande do Sul, in particular, with José Vicente Tavares dos Santos, Sonia Larangeira, Luciano Fedozzi and Zander Navarro. A very special word of thanks to Consuelo Gonçalves and Regina Maria Pozzobon, Sérgio Gregório Baierle and Vera Regina Amaro of CIDADE for their research assistance, and to Maria Paula Meneses for her help in preparing and updating the manuscript. My thanks also to Erik O. Wright for engaging discussions on the topic of participatory democracy. I am grateful to Luciano Brunet for providing precious and detailed information on the latest developments of participatory budgeting. I would also like to thank my Portuguese research assistants at the Center for Social Studies (CES): Lassalete Simões, Nuno Serra, Ana Cristina Santos, and Sílvia Ferreira. The editorial help of Maria Irene Ramalho has, as always, been invaluable.

2 See Villas-Bôas, 1999, Carvalho and Felgueiras, 2000, Avritzer, 2002, Carvalho *et al.*, 2002.

3 For a comparison with the application of the participatory budget in Barcelona, see Moura (1997). Echevarría (1999) offers a comparative study of Porto Alegre and Córdoba (Argentina). The book edited by Becker (2000) includes several examples of the application of the principles of participatory democracy, both in the American continent and in Europe.

4 More concerned with efficiency than with democracy, as early as 1993 the World Bank drew attention to the "early success" of Porto Alegre in light of the three criteria established by the Bank's Urban Management Program: the mobilization of resources to finance the delivery of urban services; the improvement of the financial management of those resources; the organization of municipal institutions to promote greater efficiency and responsiveness in urban service delivery (see Davey, 1993). Since then the World Bank has on several occasions publicized and promoted the Porto Alegre model of urban management and has rewarded the municipality with loan grants.

5 Porto Alegre, the capital of the state of Rio Grande do Sul, is frequently visited by local government and grassroots movement leaders from other Brazilian cities to analyze *in loco* the workings of participatory budgeting. The cities where "popular administration" candidates have won the elections have asked Porto Alegre for advice and consultancy. In a few cases, the municipality has assigned one of its cadres to help the implementation of participatory budgeting in neighboring cities.

6 Based on Navarro, 1996, and on Oliveira, Pinto, and Torres, 1995.

7 Data obtained from IBGE—Instituto Brasileiro de Geografia e Estatística—Census 2000 (http://www.ibge.gov.br/ibge/estatistica/populacao/censo2000/default.shtm)

8 Data from IBGE and the Health Secretariat of the state of Rio Grande do Sul, corresponding to 1997.

9 Data from IBGE (2000 Census).

10 According to Tarso Genro, when, by the end of 1988, the PT won the

mayoralty of Porto Alegre for the first time, around one thousand community organizations were identified in the city.

11 In the 1982 elections for state governor, won by the conservative party, the PDT received 31.7 per cent of the votes in the city of Porto Alegre and the PT only 3.9 percent. The Rio Grande do Sul elections of 1998 were won by the PT with 50.88 percent of the votes. In 2002, the PT lost the state elections.

12 The Organic Law of Porto Alegre states that the budget must be discussed with the population. Recently the Mayoralty won a suit of unconstitutionality put against the PB (Sérgio Baierle, personnal communication).

13 In this section I follow Luciano Fedozzi (1997), who presents the best description of the way the PB works. The Mayoralty of Porto Alegre also has a web page describing the way the PB works (http://www.portoalegre.rs.gov.br/Op/default.htm).

14 The Forum is composed of delegates elected according to a criterion based on the number of participants in each of the Regional and Thematic Assemblies (more on this below).

15 The COP is composed of councilors elected in Regional and Thematic Assemblies. It also includes one representative of UAMPA and another of SIMPA (Union of Municipal Workers), as well as two representatives of the Mayoralty who have no right of vote.

16 In 1989, the first executive of PT started out by dividing the city into five regions. The leaders of community organizations argued that those regions were too large, raised transportation problems regarding meeting attendance, and had no relation whatsoever to any political tradition. In collaboration with those leaders, the decision was then made to have 16 regions. With some small changes, such is today the regional division of Porto Alegre.

17 As I shall stress below, in the course of years there have been many changes in the way the PB functions, a fact that highlights the dynamism of the democratic learning process embodied by the PB. At the end of this chapter, I shall give an account of the most recent changes. The most significant one was the substitution of one single *rodada* for two *rodadas* of assemblies.

18 For more details on resource allocation criteria see the following section.

19 The discussion, revision, and approval, of the Regimento Interno to be in force in the next cycle occur between the months of December and January. The revision of rules is included in the PB's agenda of activities.

20 In one of the meetings I attended, the councilors expressed opposition against too many delegates' interventions since they reduced the intervention time of the councilors and because, after all, the "delegates' place is in the regional or thematic fora."

21 Occasionally, the delegates, councilors, and community leaders question the figures, arguing that they are outdated, and provide more accurate figures.

22 In the 1998 budget, the grades in this criterion ranged from 1 to 5.

23 See also Fedozzi (1997: 134) and Utzig (1996: 211–12). The relations between

the party and the executive were then very tense. While the mayor, Olívio Dutra, belonged to the Articulation tendency and the vice-mayor to the New Left tendency, the PT municipal organization was dominated by a more leftist tendency, the Socialist Democracy. The tensions centered on the role of the party in the supervision of the executive and in the nomination of political appointees to the mayor's office, namely the municipal secretaries. While the mayor and the vice-mayor defended the autonomy of the executive against party interference on the basis that, in contrast with the party, they were confronted not only by political issues but also by technical ones for which technically qualified personnel was required, the party defended a decisive intervention of the party in the government since the latter's failures or mistakes would have repercussions on the party as a whole in the following elections. The mayor—a founder of the party and a charismatic leader—and the vice-mayor—a brilliant lawyer, persecuted by the military dictatorship and who had been for a long time a militant of the communist movement—somehow managed to prevail.

24 On this subject, see Abers, 1998, 2000.

25 The institutional base of the PB was then very embryonic. It consisted of public consultations conducted by the executive in five regions during the month of August (see also Fedozzi, 1997: 134).

26 The truth is, however, that as the PB was being consolidated, the Popular Councils gradually yielded to the Regional Fora. Research carried out in 1998 (CIDADE and CRC, 1999) shows a decrease of more than 50 per cent regarding the participation in Popular Councils between 1995 and 1998. As a matter of fact, as we shall see below, the importance given by the communities to participation in the PB ended up affecting participation in other forms of community organization. This is the case of UAMPA, which, although still active, suffered a certain emptying out of its structures. The same could be said of the Popular Councils or Unions of Townships. Increase in participation in religious or cultural groups is, however, noteworthy.

27 According to the data of the Prefeitura, citizen participation in the preparation of the PB went from 1,000 participants in 1998 to reach 19,025 in 2000. The first *rodada* of assemblies has always had more participation than the second one. The lesser participation in the second *rodada* may account for the reason that led to the elimination of one of the *rodadas* in 2002. On this subject, see the postscript. On the evolution of the social composition of the PB public, see CIDADE and CRC, 1999: 15–41, and Baiocchi, 2001a.

28 The last congress took place on 17–19 October 2003.

29 For some of the more leftist tendencies in the PT, the creation of the thematic plenaries was mainly justified by the need to integrate the labor movement in the PB. The choice of themes was supposed to correspond in some way to the different profession-based labor unions. In reality, the interest of the labor unions in the thematic areas has been very moderate.

30 The set of rules and criteria that regulate the way the PB works—the Regimento Interno, including general criteria for the distribution of resources as well as technical criteria—amounts today to a volume of 60 pages.

31 It went from 24,232 enrolled students in 1989 to a total of 51,476 students in 1999. This also implied a significant increase of the number of schools. (Data obtained from SMED [Secretaria Municipal da Educação (Municipal Secretary of Education)].)

32 According to the data of IBGE (2000), the average family income in Porto Alegre is the equivalent of six minimum wages.

33 In the COP elected in 2000, 30 per cent were women; the percentage would be lower if we were to consider only the effective councilors.

34 They are considered "2nd-level" organizations because they are constituted by the grassroots movements, neighborhood associations, and so on, that are considered to be base organizations or 1st-level organizations.

35 As I have already said, participation in the PB via Internet has recently become possible (gathering information and submitting suggestions and demands). The Internet also gives you access to the PB's investment plan every year and allows you to check all the works completed since 1990. At any rate, according to the information gathered by the survey of 1998, 70 per cent of those elected to the PB (delegates and councilors) think that the available information is adequate (CIDADE and CRC, 1999: 12, 65).

36 This concern is still in place, since, although the 1998 data show that 74 per cent of the elected acknowledge the openness of the choice of delegates, about 21 per cent of the elected councilors and 14 per cent of the elected delegates think that the choice depends on nomination (CIDADE and CRC, 1999: 91).

37 According to the 1998 data (CIDADE and CRC, 1999: 12), in 1998 56.4 per cent of the elected councilors and 40.9 per cent of the elected delegates usually enroll themselves to speak "always" or "almost always" at these meetings.

38 On the government's initiative, in the Regimento Interno voted on in 1999 and to be implemented in 2000, the paragraph mentioning the government's veto was suppressed. The government's argument was that such a paragraph was useless, since the decision process constructed during all those years had rendered it obsolete. Thus, not only did the veto become a remote possibility, but its being contemplated by the Regimento Interno became a mere excuse for the attacks of those opposed to the PB. I owe this piece of information to Luciano Brunet. It is, however, significant that the new municipal executive, elected in 2000, again included the possibility of the veto in the PB's Internal Rules (article 13, paragraphs 2, 3, and 4).

39 Four members are elected as effective, and four as substitutes.

40 For 2002, the government foresaw that this would fall to 8 per cent given the increase in current (non-investment) expenditures.

41 In the 1998 survey, this is 58.5 per cent (CIDADE and CRC, 1999: 63). This tendency continued in the 2000 survey, where the percentage of the people

interviewed who claimed to have benefited from the PB's works or services was 60.1 per cent (PMPA-CIDADE, 2002: 57).

42 Effectiveness of decisions has increased in the past few years. According to the *Correio do Povo*, of April 29, 1996, of all the public works planned for 1995, 95 per cent were in progress or completed by April 1996. There were, however, delays in some works planned for in the 1995 Investment Plan and throughout the first quarter of 1997 the councilors of the COP criticized the executive for the delays. The same happened in the first quarter of 1998.

43 At the end of the year, a statement of account rendering is published and distributed among the fora of delegates and the general population. For the past years, account rendering has become more sophisticated, including a photographic show in a public space, organized according to thematic axes. It is customary for the mayor and several teams of secretaries to go to places where people gather more frequently, and distribute the publication of account rendering. This publication is available as well on the Internet.

44 This information is also available through the Internet.

45 According to the PB's statements of account rendering, in 1997 Porto Alegre may have lost 16.69 million *Reais* because of the Kandir Law.

46 In the words of one of the councilors interviewed about the PB's reformulation in 2001: "the PB must be reformulated first as regards the increase of the amount of expenditures to be distributed according to it. The amount we deal with is very small and the problems are many" (*De Olho no Orçamento*, 11 October 2001, 3).

47 About the same time, but by initiative of the cooperative movement itself, housing cooperatives were designated as self-managed housing cooperatives. The objective of the semantic politics was to distinguish low-income popular cooperatives from corporation cooperatives.

48 At the time, a nearby city, Gravataí, also governed by the PT, had made "excessive" and highly polemical concessions (tax incentives, infrastructure, and so on) to General Motors, interested in installing a plant in the city.

49 On the tense relations between the PB experiment and the mass media in Porto Alegre, see Genro and Souza, 1997: 36–41.

50 The adopted system ended up avoiding the payment of extra hours. The work of PB officers gathers points for future promotions.

51 The conflict has been ignited by the parties that oppose the Popular Front, that is, by the majoritarian parties in the Chamber of Deputies. But among the non-PT forces we can identify different stances, some parties being totally opposed to the PB and others assuming a more conciliatory position (trying to co-opt rather than eliminate the PB). More on this below.

52 In the 2000 elections for the Câmara de Vereadores of Porto Alegre, the Popular Front won twelve of the 33 seats. Of these, ten belong to the PT.

53 In fact, the political staff of the Prefeitura is well aware of this and has lately experimented with combining participation with contractualization in various

areas, both in the social and the economic fields. In the social field, we should highlight community kindergartens, which result from partnerships between the executive and non-profit local organizations. In the economic field, I would emphasize the creation of the Community Credit Institution (Instituição Comunitária de Crédito), designed to encourage micro-credit.

54 In an interview given in 2001 to the Brazilian newspaper *O Estado de São Paulo*, one expert of the World Bank Institute recognized the merits of the PB, pointing out that it is "one of the most positive and innovative administrative experiments in Latin America [...] because it demystifies the model of government and the management of public resources. It is a modern form because it transforms representative democracies into participatory democracies" (5 March 2001: A7). In the same interview the information was given that the World Bank had translated Tarso Genro's book on participatory budgeting into Spanish, there being a great demand for it in Latin America. When asked if the PB is a program of parties of the Left, the interviewee answered, significantly, that "There is no ideological origin. Participatory budgeting is only a good model of government, of decision and consensus. It is not a political form of government, it is a technique of decision-making."

55 The councils have varying degrees of activity and intervention. Some of the most active are the Municipal Council for the Rights of Children and Adolescents, the Municipal Council of Health (the oldest one, predating the establishment of the PB), the Municipal Council of Social Welfare, the Municipal Council of Education, the Municipal Council of Science and Technology, the Municipal Council of Urban and Environmental Development, and the Municipal Council of Historical and Cultural Heritage.

56 I agree with Luciano Brunet when he states that the PB is the "carro-chefe" ("lead car") of the participatory system set up in Porto Alegre (personal communication, November 2001).

57 This question has been debated throughout this text and has earned the attention of various authors in recent times. See, for example, Abers 2000; Dias 2000; and Baiocchi 2001a.

58 The survey conducted by PMPA and CIDADE indicates that 77.4 per cent of the people who participate in the entities of the PB have been doing so for more than ten years, suggesting that the expectations brought into the mobilization for the PB have not been frustrated. This survey also points to a strong correlation between the participation in the entities of the PB and nomination as councilors and delegates (2002: 50, 53).

59 For more information, consult the PB web page, at http://www.portoalegre.rs. gov.br/Op/default.htm.

Bibliography

Abers, Rebecca (1998). "From clientelism to cooperation: local government, participatory policy, and civic organizing in Porto Alegre, Brazil," *Politics and Society*, 26(4), 511–37.

— (2000). *Inventing Local Democracy: grassroots politics in Brazil*. Boulder: Lynne Rienner.

Avritzer, Leonardo (2002). "Modelos de Deliberação Democrática: uma análise do orçamento participativo no Brasil," in Boaventura de Sousa Santos (ed.), *Democratizar a Democracia: os caminhos da democracia participativa*. Rio de Janeiro: Record, 561–97.

Baierle, Sérgio (1998). "Experiência do Orçamento Participativo: um oásis no deserto neoliberal?" At http://www.portoweb.com.br/ong/cidade/texto3.htm, accessed on November 16, 2001.

— (2001). "OP ao Termidor?" Paper presented at the workshop *O Orçamento Participativo visto pelos seus investigadores*, 31 May–2 June 2001. Porto Alegre: Prefeitura de Porto Alegre.

Baiocchi, Gianpaolo (2001a). From Militance to Citizenship; The Workers' Party, Civil Society, and the Politics of Participatory Governance in Porto Alegre, Brazil. Madison: University of Wisconsin, Department of Sociology, Ph.D. dissertation.

— (2001b). "Subsídios, hegemonia, e diferença: o lugar da sociedade civil dentro do OP de Porto Alegre." Paper presented at the workshop *O Orçamento Participativo visto pelos seus investigadores*, 31 May–2 June 2001. Porto Alegre: Prefeitura de Porto Alegre.

Becker, A. J. (ed.) (2000). *A cidade reinventa a democracia: as contribuições do Seminário Internacional sobre democracia participativa*. Porto Alegre: Prefeitura de Porto Alegre.

Carvalho, Maria do Carmo, and Débora Felgueiras (2000). *Orçamento Participativo no ABC: Mauá, RibeirãoPires e Santo André*. São Paulo: Polis.

Carvalho, Maria do Carmo Albuquerque, Ana Cláudia C. Teixeira, Luciana Antonini, and Inês Magalhães (2002). *Orçamento participativo nos municípios paulistas: gestão 1997–2000*. São Paulo: Pólis.

CIDADE, and CRC (1999). *Quem é o público do Orçamento Participativo: seu perfil, por que participa e o que pensa do Processo*. Porto Alegre: CIDADE and CRC.

Davey, Kenneth (1993). "Elements of Urban Management," *Urban Management Programme Discussion Paper*, 11, 1–55.

Dias, Márcia Ribeiro (2000). Na encruzilhada da teoria democrática: efeitos do Orçamento Participativo sobre a Câmara Municipal de Porto Alegre. Rio de Janeiro: IUPRJ, Ph.D. dissertation.

Echevarría, Corina (1999). Democratización del espacio público municipal mediante la implementación de instituciones de géstion participativa: estudio comparado de los caos de la Municipalidad de la ciudad de Córdoba (Argentina) y la prefectura de Porto Alegre (Brasil). Córdoba: Universidad Nacional de Córdoba, Master's thesis.

Fedozzi, Luciano (1997). *Orçamento Participativo. Reflexões sobre a Experiência de Porto Alegre*. Porto Alegre: Tomo.

Genro, Tarso, and Ubiratan de Souza (1997). *Orçamento Participativo: A Experiência de Porto Alegre*. Porto Alegre: Fundação Perseu Abramo.

Grupo de Trabalho de Modernização do Orçamento Participativo (2001). "Rompendo nosso limites: Uma primeira avaliação dos pontos de estrangulamento que vivemos no processo do Orçamento Participativo de Porto Alegre." Paper presented at the workshop *O Orçamento Participativo visto pelos seus investigadores*, 31 May 31–2 June 2001. Porto Alegre: Prefeitura de Porto Alegre.

Harnecker, Marta (1993). "Alcaldia de Porto Alegre: Aprendiendo a Gobernar," *Haciendo Camino al Andar*, 2.

Larangeira, Sónia (1996). "Gestão Pública e Participação: A Experiência do Orçamento Participativo em Porto Alegre (1989-1995)." Paper presented at the *48° Encontro Anual da Sociedade Brasileira Para o Progresso da Ciência*, July 1996. São Paulo.

Moura, Maria Suzana (1997). Cidades Empreendedoras, Cidades Democráticas e Redes Públicas: Tendências à Renovação na Gestão Local. Salvador: Universidade Federal da Bahia, Ph.D. dissertation.

Navarro, Zander (1996). "'Participatory Budgeting'—The Case of Porto Alegre (Brazil)." Paper presented at the workshop *Regional Workshop: Decentralization in Latin America—Innovations and Policy Implications*. 23–24 May 1996. Caracas.

Oliveira, Carlos, João Pinto, and Ciro Torres (1995). *Democracia Nas Grandes Cidades: A Gestão Democrática da Prefeitura de Porto Alegre*. Rio de Janeiro: IBASE, 20–44.

Orçamento Participativo (1999). *Regimento Interno: critérios gerais, técnicos e regionais para a gestão de 1999/2000*. Porto Alegre.

Pont, Raul (2000). *Democracia, Participação, Cidadania: uma visão de esquerda*. Porto Alegre: Palmarinca.

Pozzobon, Regina Maria (2000). "Uma experiência de Gestão Pública: O Orçamento Participativo de Porto Alegre, RS." Paper presented at the *III Fórum CONTAG de Cooperação Técnica*. June 2000. Porto Alegre. At http://www.portoweb.com.br/ong/cidade/texto8, accessed on 27 November 2001.

Pozzobon, Regina, Sérgio Baierle, and Véra Amaro (1996). "Refletindo sobre o Exercício da Cidadania (1ª Parte)," *De Olho no Orçamento*, 2.

PMPM (Prefeitura Municipal de Porto Alegre), and CIDADE (Centro de Assessoria e Estudos Urbanos) (2002). *Quem é o público do Orçamento Participativo – 2000*. Porto Alegre: CIDADE.

Santos, Boaventura de Sousa (1998). "Participatory Budgeting in Porto Alegre: Toward a Redistributive Democracy," *Politics & Society*, 26(4), 461–510.

Utzig, Luis Eduardo (1996). "Notas sobre o Governo do Orçamento Participativo em Porto Alegre," *Novos Estudos CEBRAP*, 45, 209–22.

Villas-Boâs, Renata (ed.) (1999). *Balanço das experiências de orçamento participativo nos governos locais*. São Paulo: Instituto Pólis.

12

Modes of Democratic Deliberation: Participatory Budgeting in Brazil

Leonardo Avritzer

In the last one hundred years, democracy has become the standard form of organization of political rule within Western modernity. At the beginning of modernity, in the seventeenth century, Leibniz summarized the skepticism about democracy that dominated the previous historical period in the following sentence: "[T]oday there is no prince so bad that it would not be better to live under him than in a democracy" (Dunn, 1979: 4). Leibniz's remark reveals a critical assessment of democracy as a form of political organization that rapidly changed in the following two hundred years. In the middle of the nineteenth century, Alexis de Tocqueville summarized the new mood in relation to democracy:

> [A] gradual development of the democratic principle must follow from the irresistible march of events. Daily some further privilege of the aristocracy comes under attack; it is a slow war waged about details, but infallibly in time it will bring the whole edifice down (Tocqueville, 1958: 67–8).

At that point, democracy was about to become the hegemonic form of organization of political rule in the United States and in some parts of Europe. Yet the whole world was still struggling over whether or not to adopt democratic forms of political organization. In 1897, Liang Ch'i Cha'o, a Chinese Mandarin, published an article in a Shanghai newspaper that shows the growing influence of democracy outside the West. For this author, the expansion of democracy was inevitable:

> [W]hen the cycles of the world are about to move [...] this is not something restricted to the West, nor something that China can avoid. I know that in less than a hundred years all five continents will be under the rule of the people, and our China will not be able to continue unchanged (Dunn, 1979: 11).

Liang Ch'i Cha'o was right. By the end of the twentieth century democracy had become the hegemonic form of organization of political rule.

The belief that democracy has become a hegemonic form of organization of political rule is quite widespread. However, an assessment of what has been gained and what has been lost in this process is yet to be made. In the one hundred years that mediate between Liang Ch'i Cha'o's prediction and the realization of democratic hegemony, the meanings and practices of democracy have undergone important changes. These include the significant restriction of the concept of sovereignty, the growing consensus about the desirability of non-participatory forms of administration, and the rejection of participatory political models due to their non-institutional impact. All of these new consensual positions are connected to the inter-war events in Europe and to the consolidation of democracy on the European continent at the end of the so-called "second wave of democratization."[1]

Still, at the end of the eighteenth century, the democratic idea was associated with a strong conception of sovereignty. Jean Jacques Rousseau clearly expressed this association in a remark on the organization of the British parliament. For Rousseau,

> sovereignty cannot be represented for the same reason that it cannot be alienated. [...] The people's deputies are not and could not be their representatives; they are merely their agents. [...] Any law which the people have not ratified in person is void; it is not a law at all. The English people believe themselves to be free. [...] In fact, they are seriously mistaken; they are only free on the day of the election of their representatives (Rousseau, 1968: 141).

Rousseau's analysis of the nature of sovereignty has not become the hegemonic conception of sovereignty within Western modernity. His conception did not prevail due to the emergence of complex forms of state administration that have led to the consolidation of specialized bureaucracies in most of the arenas of the modern state. The modern individual has lost control over the political, administrative, military, and scientific spheres, as well as many others, as Max Weber had already observed at the beginning of the twentieth century. In each of these spheres of activity, the modern individual came under the control of a hierarchical and specialized bureaucracy, no longer wielding the means of producing material goods, political decisions, scientific knowledge, and legal justice.

The reason for this process of "disappropriation" of the control of the individuals over their own lives is to be found in the enormous expansion of the arenas in which decisions are made, in the issues that were made political (among others, health, education, and social welfare). According to the Weberian perspective, which is part of the hegemonic conception of democracy, a specialized bureaucracy is more prepared than the common individual to be in charge of these decisions. Complex decisions require the capacity of actors to have a

previous knowledge of the issues dealt with and to pursue aims in a systematic manner (Kronman, 1983: 131). For Weber, only a specialized bureaucracy
could handle this dimension of the modern polity.[2] This constituted the first
source of the restriction of the concept of sovereignty in modern democracies.

A second source of this restriction is related to the debates on rationality
and mobilization that took place in the inter-war period in Europe.
Democratic theory emerged in association with the idea of the rationality
of the *homo politicus*. Since the Enlightenment (Kant, 1781 [1959]; Rousseau,
1968), the prevalence of rationality at the political level has been associated
with the rejection of illegitimate forms of government, a view based on the
perception that rationality is the basis of individuals' primary act of authorizing government.

At the beginning of the twentieth century, however, and particularly in
the inter-war period, the link between democracy and rationality was undermined by what has been called "the emergence of particularistic interests."
Eighteenth- and nineteenth-century democratic theory understood free
public debate as an intrinsic part of the formation of the general will. Yet it
failed to perceive that the path that leads from Rousseau to Marx admits the
entrance of particular interests into public debate, and thus to the triumph
of particular interests and manipulation over political rationality. Authors
such as Ortega y Gasset, Karl Mannheim, Erich Fromm, and Max
Horkheimer argued against the possibility of rational participation in politics.
For them, non-differentiation within the polity caused by the end of the
insulation of elites (Ortega y Gasset, 1930; Kornhauser, 1959), as well as by
the rise of forms of cultural domination at the private level (Horkheimer,
1947; Arendt, 1951) transformed the nature of politics at the beginning of
the twentieth century. This diagnosis led to a critique of democracy according to which the preservation of values critical to democratic politics requires
the insulation of those social groups that best embody such values
(Kornhauser, 1959: 22)—that is, the insulation of the elites from the masses.
The mass society argument breaks the association between democracy and
political participation because it sees broader political participation leading
not to the enlargement of actors and issues in the political sphere, but rather
to the irrational pressure of the masses on the political system. The consequence of this argument is rule by elites, since this is the only guarantee that
cultural values not shared by the masses will be preserved. The mass society
critique of popular sovereignty also involved the effects of mass society on
political institutions, in particular the risk that mass mobilization would
bypass the institutions in charge of the formation of the general will. Thus,
the preservation of the values of democracy was made dependent on the
insulation of elites from the political pressure of the masses.

Weber's positions on the loss of sovereignty and mass society theorists'
positions on the irrationality of mass participation in politics were integrated

into a common framework for the understanding of democracy at the end of the Second World War, by Joseph Schumpeter, the author who proposed a reconstruction of democracy in Europe based on a restricted conception of popular sovereignty. Schumpeter took the transformations in democratic practice such as it had been conceived in the eighteenth and nineteenth centuries as his point of departure. The central idea of the section of his magnum opus, *Capitalism, Socialism and Democracy*, that is devoted to the discussion of democracy is therefore the validity of the concept of popular sovereignty. Schumpeter picked up an issue already raised by Weber: how is it possible for the people to govern? His answer to this question is that if we understand sovereignty in a broad sense as the formation and determination of the general will, it is impossible for the people to govern. For Schumpeter, in order to make the concept of democracy useful it is necessary to separate it from the pursuit of a substantive notion of the common good, and to transform it into a process of choice of governing bodies: "Democracy is a political *method*, that is to say, a certain type of institutional arrangement for arriving at political—legislative and administrative—decisions and hence incapable of being an end in itself" (Schumpeter, 1942: 242).

Reducing the scope of sovereignty allows Schumpeter to limit the role of the people to producing governments, that is to say, to choosing the particular group among the elites that seems most qualified to govern. Through this operation the people remain the ultimate arbiter of democratic politics in only one capacity, as the arbiter of competing elites. This reduction of the scope of the concept of sovereignty simultaneously implies a change in how the relationship between democracy and rationality is conceived. For Schumpeter, as political elites join a competitive system of representation, the access of the most qualified to positions of political leadership is guaranteed (Schumpeter, 1942: 280).

Democracy was consolidated in Europe in the aftermath of the Second World War through the application of a restricted conception of sovereignty. To be sure, the second wave of democratization, which covers the period between 1943 and 1962, was highly successful in regard to the implantation and consolidation of democracy within Europe, in a form very similar to the prescriptions of Schumpeter. In the most important cases of newly consolidated democracies in this period, particularly Germany, Italy, and Japan—countries that had broken with democratic practices as a consequence of the conflicts of the inter-war period—a restricted conception of sovereignty followed the reintroduction of democracy after 1945. On the other hand, if we look elsewhere, we immediately perceive a different phenomenon: the attempt to extend democracy to Latin America, Asia, and Africa in the same period was a complete failure. By the mid-1970s, one-third of the world's 32 previously active democracies had reverted to some form of authoritarianism. In 1973, only two Latin American countries had democratically elected presidents.

An analysis of the sources of the breakdown of democracy in Latin America reveals two facts, each equally problematic for the theory of democratic elitism: either the most important democratic elitist assumptions, such as the analysis of mass society and the rationality of elites, were clearly contradicted, or they were at least unable to explain the so-called "second reverse wave of democratization." What seems to be at the root of the failure of the establishment of democracy in Latin America between 1964 and 1973 are the contradictions intrinsic to the model of inter-elite competition, a model that led to a broadened exercise of sovereignty by the elites themselves (Avritzer, 2001). Thus, two characteristics of democratic elitist theory seem from the very beginning not to have operated in Latin America.

First, the elites' presumed adherence to democratic values, an *ad hoc* assumption derived from the conservative version of mass society theory (Kornhauser, 1959), was unable to explain the instability caused by inter-elite disputes in Latin American democracies. Elite attempts to reverse the results of democratic elections were responsible for the breakdown of democracy in Argentina in 1966, Brazil in 1964, and Chile in 1973, among other cases. Second, the role of mass mobilization in this period must also be re-addressed. Mass mobilizations sought in most cases to secure the rules of the game for inter-elite competition. No democratic breakdown in Latin America was coordinated with large-scale mass mobilizations. On the contrary, most of them were coordinated with some form of elite support triggered by the attempt to reverse political elections *ex-post*. Thus, there seem to be two gaps in democratic elitism's approach to democracy: first, its failure to differentiate between democratic and non-democratic elites, a gap bridged in a structural and quite problematic form in the work of Almond and Verba at the end of this period, and, second, its inability to understand mass mobilization. There are two different types of mass mobilization: the first type, studied in depth within the democratic elitist tradition, is an anti-institutional mobilization that can eventually disrupt the political process. The second type, however, consists in forms of collective action within voluntary associations, social movements, and other forums of participation. In this latter case, collective action draws on pre-existing networks of association and is fully compatible with democratic life. Much of the political activity in Latin America fits into the second category, anticipating an approach developed later by social movement theorists about the possibility of democratic collective action (Tilly, 1986; Cohen, 1985; Melucci and Avritzer, 1995). By assuming *a priori* a direct relationship between mass mobilization and democratic breakdown, democratic elitism missed the possibility of collective action in favor of the maintenance of democracy.

This chapter will seek to challenge three assumptions of the hegemonic conception of democracy, which will be called the democratic elitist conception: first, the widespread conception that, in order to be consolidated, democracy should restrict the forms of participation; second, the idea that rational, hierarchical forms of administration can only be pursued by an insulated bureaucracy; and third, that all forms of collective action are alike and that they generate a contradiction between mobilization and institutionalization. In opposition to this, it will be shown, for the case of Brazil, that most forms of collective action are democratic and that they are able to produce new institutional designs that are participatory and incorporate new cultural elements into the polity. I will discuss these three elements with reference to one case of participatory democracy in Brazil: the case of the participatory budgeting process.

Democratization in Brazil and the emergence of innovation at the societal level

Brazil's political system throughout the twentieth century has been highly unstable due to inter-elite political disputes. Between 1930 and 1945, the dominant political system was corporatist authoritarianism. In its first phase, this regime sought to introduce regular elections. However, after 1937, the conflict between agrarian and modernizing elites led to a shift from democratic to authoritarian corporatism, with the suspension of both elections and individual liberties. Between 1945 and 1964, the dominant regime was an unstable form of democratic populism, where all presidential mandates were subject to some kind of anti-democratic challenge. Vargas (1950–54) faced a rebellion and did not complete his mandate; Kubitschek (1956–60) needed the support of the army to seize office; Jânio Quadros resigned the presidency after the failure of an anti-congressional coup he had sponsored; and finally, João Goulart (1960–64) was overthrown by a military coup. Between 1964 and 1985 the country suffered its worst authoritarian experience. Congress was closed twice by the regime, once in 1968 and again in 1977. Presidential elections were suspended, and, after 1968, most individual guarantees, such as habeas corpus, were suspended as well. Thus, in contrast to the assumption of the hegemonic conception of democracy, the Brazilian political process shows, above all, that elites are not necessarily the guarantors of democratic political values. In the Brazilian case, most of the anti-democratic attempts between the 1930s and the 1980s involved inter-elite conflicts over the role of the state.

Redemocratization in Brazil took place through a restricted pact between the opposition party, the PMDB, and a faction within the party that had supported the regime, the PDS, in 1985. A new constitution has been in place since 1988 and regular presidential elections have been held since 1989.

Throughout the twentieth century, Brazilian elites had one principal political project: modernization. They led a modernizing project that transformed a predominantly rural country into the world's tenth largest industrialized nation. The share of the population working in the industrial sector increased from 10.4 per cent in 1940 to 24.3 per cent in 1980, while that working in agriculture decreased from 65.8 per cent to 29.9 per cent (Santos, 1987: 137). Far from being simply a success story of economic modernization, this process has revealed a number of social drawbacks: in the twentieth century Brazil became one of the world's most socially unequal countries. In 1984, the last year of authoritarianism in Brazil, more than 35 per cent of Brazilians were poor or very poor; in the northeast, this was true for more than half the population. Brazil's economic modernization created sharp political and economic inequalities at the local level. The largest Brazilian cities grew at an unbelievable rate between 1950 and 1980: the population of São Paulo increased from 2,198 million to 8,493 million; Belo Horizonte grew from 352,000 to 1,780 million; and Porto Alegre, from 394,000 to 1,125 million (IBGE, 1983). The increase of the urban population and the creation and expansion of a rationalized public administration were not followed by a proportional increase in urban services. On the contrary, most of the services required by an urban population were very poorly provided in the 1980s. In 1984, only 80.2 per cent of city-dwellers in the southeast—Brazil's wealthiest region—and only 59.6 per cent in the south had access to treated water. Access to sewerage was even lower: only 55 per cent of the urban population in the southeast and 11.8 per cent in the south had access to it in 1984 (Santos, 1987: 161–2). Thus, Brazil's process of modernization, which implied the creation of a specialized bureaucracy according to Weberian prescriptions, was not able to address the country's most pressing social needs.

Two factors might explain the low level of public infrastructure and services in most Brazilian cities in this period: the limited organization of the urban population and the country's strong tradition of clientelism. The level of organization of the Brazilian population was traditionally very low. Some Brazilian cities had some very limited forms of neighborhood associations during the democratic populist period (1946–64): only 124 neighborhood associations were created in Rio de Janeiro during the whole period (Boschi, 1987), and only 71 were created in Belo Horizonte between the 1920s and the 1970s (Avritzer, 2000a). Thus, in general, it is possible to say that the Brazilian population was relatively unorganized when the democratic regime collapsed in 1964. In addition, state violence prevented organization throughout the authoritarian period. Afonso and Azevedo (1988) found fear to be the main reason the urban poor did not resist urban relocation in Belo Horizonte in the early 1970s; Gay (1994) found the same to be true for the Vidigal population in Rio de Janeiro during this period.

The second reason for the poor provision of urban services is the reliance on clientelism, the main political tradition at the local level in Brazil (Nunes Leal, 1946; Cammach, 1990; Mainwaring, 1990; Avritzer, 1998). Brazilian political life, since the nineteenth century, has been characterized by the presence of political mediators in charge of delivering public goods (Graham, 1990). Only in the late 1970s, as part of the reaction against authoritarianism and the break between Church and state, did this process begin to change with the formation of independent neighborhood associations. These associations blossomed as part of a general associative movement in reaction to authoritarianism. In Rio de Janeiro, 166 neighborhood associations were formed between 1979 and 1981 (Boschi, 1987). In Belo Horizonte, 80 per cent of the existing neighborhood associations date from after 1980. In all cases these associations were an expression of a change in patterns of association. They claimed organizational autonomy from the state; they challenged the presence of political mediators; and they challenged the tradition of considering urban services as a favor to be delivered by the state (Avritzer, 2000a). Thus an analysis of the Brazilian process of societal reorganization shows a second important departure from the hegemonic conception of democracy. New forms of collective action emerged during the Brazilian process of democratization. At the urban level, new associations emerged, challenging the existing pattern of relations between the State and society, and introducing new cultural elements such as democratic forms of organization at the local level. Hence cultural innovation introduced by social actors, an element not tackled by the hegemonic conception of democracy, was a central aspect of the Brazilian process of democratization.

Social innovation and the emergence of participatory budgeting

Brazilian redemocratization involved large doses of political continuity mixed with smaller doses of social innovation. At the political level, in spite of early signs of forms of social organization, the hegemonic forces of the modernization process retained control of the political system. The first civilian president, José Sarney (1985–90), had led the party that supported the authoritarian regime during its final period. Within the Constituent Assembly, there were more MPs who had belonged to the authoritarian regime's party (Arena) than to the opposition (PMDB) (Rodrigues, 1987). There was continuity not only in the political actors but also in their policies. One of the most important institutional leftovers of authoritarianism was the clientelist system built in the nineteenth and early twentieth centuries and strengthened by the authoritarian regime. Clientelism increased after 1986 through the creation of what can be called a "patrimonial budget." The Ministry of Planning—the institution in charge of elaborating the federal budget—was transformed into a mechanism for organizing patrimonial exchanges. Every year when Congress votes on the federal budget, MPs present amendments involving public works in the regions where their electorate is concentrated. The total amount of the patrimonial budget—the portion of the budget to be allocated to local public works—is, however, preset by the federal government, resulting in a tendency to divide the resources. Thus two elements of authoritarian Brazil continue to show their presence in democratic Brazil: first, the lack of prerogatives of a disempowered Congress that votes on legislation on a non-political basis; and second, clientelism, which is still strong and constitutes the dominant currency inside the Brazilian Congress, disempowering local forms of organization and leading to widespread administrative inefficiency.[3]

However, the Brazilian democratization process was not informed solely by processes of political continuity. Inside the Constituent Assembly, proposals for the empowerment of social actors showed their strength. Article 14 of the new Constitution guaranteed "popular initiative" in the process of the exercise of peoples' sovereignty. Article 29, on the organization of cities, required the participation of association representatives in the process of city planning. Other articles establish the participation of civic associations in the implementation of health and social welfare policies. Thus, the Constitution incorporated the new cultural changes that occurred in the eighties into the emerging institutional framework. The acknowledgement of the importance of the participation of voluntary associations in the process of city planning, as well as in the decision-making process on social policies, was one of the long-term legacies of the 1988 Constitution. It led to new forms of organization at the local level such as councils with the participation of social actors in the areas of health care, education, social welfare, and the environment (Raichellis, 1999; Tabagiba, 2000). In the case of the city of Porto Alegre, the first article of the city's master plan asserts the need for a "democratic, participatory, and decentralized" management. Yet participatory budgeting does not have an exclusively institutional origin. On the contrary, it was a proposal made by neighborhood associations in the 1980s and incorporated by a left-wing party, which then led to the creation of a new form of participatory institution.

The idea of participatory budgeting emerged for the first time in the response of neighborhood associations in the city of Porto Alegre—the capital of Rio Grande do Sul, a city with 1.3 million inhabitants—to a proposal of participation made by the Alceu Collares administration in March 1986. Collares, the first democratically elected mayor of the city after the authoritarian period, belonged to a populist party (PDT) and proposed the participation of the population in his administration through neighborhood monitors (Baierle, 1998). In a meeting in March 1986, UAMPA, the umbrella organization for neighborhood associations, made a counterproposal that contained the first elements of the idea of participatory budgeting: "The most important element in city politics is the definition of where the resources will be applied. [...] That is the reason why neighborhood associations should seek to directly influence the elaboration of the city's budget" (UAMPA, 1986). The document also stated that "UAMPA's aim is to find out the investment priorities of each neighborhood, each area, and the city in general." This is the first available document in which the concept of the centrality of the budget in the democratization of local politics emerges.

The Workers' Party (PT), which won the mayoral elections in Porto Alegre in 1988, was part of the movement for the organizational autonomy of labor unions from the state and, at the same time, advocated an idea of participatory democracy inspired more by the Marxian conception of labor councils than by the trajectory of social movements in Brazil. Its program upheld the idea of local councils, which would generate city councils and furnish a worker-based form of parallel administration (Abers, 1996: 38).[4] The party had its first important victories in the local elections of 1988, when it elected the mayors of São Paulo and Porto Alegre, among other cities; in some cases, like that of São Paulo, it decided to practice something very similar to its workers' councils proposal. Even in Porto Alegre, the conception that prevailed during the first year of the Workers' Party administration was deeply influenced by the idea that politics always involves the representation of particular interests; the Workers' Party would only change *those* particular interests that prevailed within the local administration (Utzig, 1996: 211). Thus, the Workers' Party did not have at that point in its program the idea of participatory budgeting, but only a general idea of participatory government.

The political decisions on participatory budgeting were taken in an overlapping way during the first two years of the Workers' Party rule in Porto Alegre. From its inauguration, the Olívio Dutra administration tried to increase participation at large. In the first year, most of the secretaries introduced some participatory elements into their health, education, and planning proposals. At the same time, in its first thirty days the Olívio Dutra administration took the crucial decision of making the CRC (Coordenação de Relações com a Comunidade / Coordinating Committee of Relations with the Community) responsible for centralizing all of the community's claims. The CRC thus became central to the PB process. Although it had existed prior to 1989 (Lima, 1999), the CRC's role had been to provide city associations with tax exemption certificates (*atestado de utilidade pública*). Thus, four steps toward participatory budgeting overlapped in the beginning of the Dutra administration: the concern of urban social movements with budgetary control and with direct participation at the local level; the emphasis the Workers' Party placed on participation and councils; the decentralized initiative of several secretaries, including the planning secretary, to encourage popular participation; and the idea, which emerged in the first 30 days, to centralize participation in the CRC.

The process of creation of participatory budgeting, as a form of decision-making on the budget, is linked to the action of multiple actors and the overlapping of two factors: the presence of new cultural elements at the neighborhood level and the formation and development of neighborhood movements in the city of Porto Alegre.[5] It was not by chance that these movements were able to identify, for the first time, the budget issue as a contentious issue. On the other hand, we should also highlight the fact that civil society in Brazil was able to recover the idea of citizenship and to incorporate it into the Constitution in the form of hybrid institutions with the participation of social actors.

Thus, it is important to point out that the Brazilian process of democratization and the emergence of participatory budgeting are processes that contradict important elements of the hegemonic conception of democracy: first of all, the political forms that are characteristic of a democratic elitist conception, and which resemble the institutions created in Europe during the second wave of democratization show, in the Brazilian case, surprising continuities with the practices that were dominant during the authoritarian period. They were taken over by clientelism, they were unable to produce administrative efficiency, and, last but not least, they are unable to produce democratic legitimacy. Second, the forms of collective action that emerged during the democratization process, in spite of an initial anti-institutional stand, found institutionalization in articles 14, 29, 204, and 227 of the 1988 Constitution, as well as in the charters of several cities, including Porto Alegre and Belo Horizonte. In this sense, the opposition between collective action and institutionalization postulated by the hegemonic theory of democracy does not apply to the Brazilian case. Third, the format of the new Brazilian democracy was not simply the reproduction of the format produced by the second wave of democratization; there were innovations introduced by the cultural debates of the democratization process that produced new institutions in which participation was broadened rather than restricted. Allow me to describe the participatory budgeting process in order to show how it innovates *vis-à-vis* the institutional format proposed by the hegemonic conception of democracy.

Participatory budgeting in Porto Alegre and Belo Horizonte

Participatory budgeting (PB) is a local participatory policy that responds to the plight of the poor in major Brazilian cities. It includes social actors, neighborhood association members, and common citizens in a process of negotiation and deliberation that takes place in two stages: a participatory stage, in which participation is direct, and a representative stage, in which participation takes place through the election of delegates and/or councilors. Since the process is different in Porto Alegre and Belo Horizonte, I shall describe its operation in these two cities.

The PB in Porto Alegre

The PB in Porto Alegre involves two rounds of regional assemblies, one round of intermediary meetings, and the yearlong operation of a councilors body called the PB Council. The process begins every year in April when the first round of district assemblies takes place. In this first stage, the population attends an assembly in each of the regions. Every first-round regional assembly is attended by the mayor, and a short account-settling process begins with a description of the administrative implementation of the decisions taken in the previous year. The floor is open for about an hour, during which citizens voice possible points of disagreement with the administration, and express their opinions about what has been taking place and what should be done in the region in the coming year. Participation in these meetings is crucial because they constitute the basis for participating in the remaining parts of the process. Although participation is on an individual basis, throughout the registration process individuals are required to demonstrate membership in voluntary associations. In 1999, about two-thirds of the participants were involved in regional associations. At the end of the first round of regional assemblies, delegates are elected from the total number of people attending the assembly. The formula to determine the number of delegates in Porto Alegre is as follows: for "up to 100 people attending, 1 delegate for every 10 people; from 101 to 250, 1 for every 20; from 251 to 400, 1 for every 30; over 401, 1 for every 40" (Poa, 1999: 6). For instance, in 1999, the first-round regional assemblies in the center of Porto Alegre were attended by 520 people; thus, the region elected 26 delegates (ten for the first 100, eight for the next 150, five for the next 150, and three for the remaining 126 people who attended the meeting).

The second stage of the PB involves the so-called intermediary meetings. They have two responsibilities: ranking priorities and deliberating about which public works the region will claim. Ranking is a process through which five out of twelve types of public goods (paving of streets, sewerage, legalization of urban property, organization of the city, housing, education, health and social welfare, transportation and circulation, leisure, sports, economic development, and culture) are selected as priorities. It involves two processes carried out earlier by the public administration: the evaluation of the population's previous access to public goods and the classification of each of the city's regions according to its population. Thus three criteria are used in the ranking: the first is previous access (and therefore present need). Priorities are graded in inverse relation to the region's previous access to a particular public good. According to the 1999 criteria, up to 80 per cent of previous access to a public good leads to grade 1, up to 60 per cent of previous access, grade 2, and up to 20 per cent, grade 5. The second criterion is the population of the region and the third the community's own ranking of its priorities, again on a scale of 5 to 1. At the end of this process, a region can attain up to 15 points if it previously had less than 20 per cent of access to a public good, if it chooses this good as a top priority, and if it has more than 120,000 inhabitants.

In the second round of regional assemblies, the region elects delegates to the PB council. This process, which takes place annually in June, leads to the formation of a council composed as follows: two councilors from each of the 16 regions (32), two from each of the five thematic assemblies (ten), one from the UAMPA—the umbrella organization of neighborhood communities—and one from the municipal workers' trade union (two). The PB council thus has 44 members.

Thematic meetings. The second Workers' Party administration (1993–96) introduced so-called "thematic oriented meetings." They grew out of a process called "the constituent city," which aimed to incorporate into the PB social sectors that still stood outside of the process (Navarro, 1998). The result was the introduction of five thematic assemblies on the following issues: city organization and development, health and social welfare, economic development and tax systems, transport and circulation, and education, culture and leisure (Navarro, 1998). The cycle of the thematic meetings is parallel to that of regional meetings, and they are entitled to elect ten delegates to the PB Council.

The PB Council. The PB council is inaugurated each July. It creates a budget proposal based on the rankings and decisions that took place in the intermediary meetings. The Council then revises the final budget proposal elaborated by the GAPLAN (City Planner's Office) and the mayor's cabinet. By September, a final budget proposal is in place. The Council also monitors the implementation of its decisions by the city's administrative agencies during the year.

The PB in Belo Horizonte

The PB has been in practice in Belo Horizonte since 1993. It involves a process of regional assemblies leading to the definition of investment priorities in a similar fashion to the Porto Alegre process. Budget decisions take place in the so-called "regional forum of priorities."

The first round of regional assemblies is similar to its counterpart in Porto Alegre, although it is more an argumentative process than a decision-making one. The administration opens each assembly with a statement on what was decided in the previous year and the current state of implementation of previous decisions. Still in the first round of regional assemblies, the administration points out the resources available for public works in the areas of street pavement, sewage, and housing. The decision-making process is also different from that used in Porto Alegre. The administration announces the resources available for each region using a formula that assigns resources in direct proportion to population and inverse proportion to average income:

$$PVR = \frac{popR}{e(1/Y)^*}$$

50 per cent of the PB's resources are evenly divided among the regions and 50 per cent are allocated according to this formula. Also in the second round, the main proposals for public works in each sub-region (37 in Belo Horizonte) are presented, initiating a process of negotiation among the communities.

The second round of regional assemblies involves the election of delegates who will vote on the public works to be included in the city budget. Delegates were elected in 1998 according to the following criteria: from one to 200 participants, one delegate for every ten people attending the assembly; from 201 to 410 participants, one for every 15; above 410, one for every 20. In addition, each region is entitled to one delegate per legally constituted voluntary association within its boundaries. Once the delegates are elected for the forum on regional priorities, negotiation begins.

Priorities caravans. "Priorities caravans" are a stage within the region in which members of the sub-regions negotiate their different proposals among themselves. Each community that has proposed a public work to be included in the city budget visits other communities in order to evaluate their level of need. At the same time, different communities start to support one another's claims, forming coalitions that will be decisive in the decison-making process.

The Forum of Regional Priorities. At this stage, the delegates from each sub-region, having already visited other sub-regions, negotiate on the final format of the budget. Unlike the situation in Porto Alegre, the final decision in Belo Horizonte takes place through the formation of coalitions that present platforms that include proposals from various sub-regions. Also in contrast to Porto Alegre, the decisions of the regional forums are final. The public works approved by the delegates will be integrated into the budget proposal. Twenty per cent of the delegates present at the regional forums become members of the Comforça, a monitoring body that follows the process of bidding for public works and can negotiate substitutions in cases of technical problems. One element of the PB in its relation to the democratization discussion should be singled out: the fact that the regional assemblies, the common element of the PB in Porto Alegre and Belo Horizonte, draw on pre-existing practices introduced by neighborhood movements in the 1970s and the 1980s. Community actors know how the process of organization works at the local level. They

---

* PVR is the virtual population, popR is the regional population, Y is the regional average revenue, and e is a constant with the value of 2,7182818.

are also well practiced in discussing the needs of their communities. In this sense, if the PB is an institutional invention, it is an institutional invention based on pre-existing practices. It should also be pointed out that the new forms of collective action that emerged at the local level during the democratization process in Brazil have found a form of institutionalization within a specific institutional framework. Thus the PB shows that the broadened forms of participation that are characteristic of the Brazilian process of democratization have not vanished, as many authors have argued (Stepan, 1988; Azevedo and Prates, 1991; Santos, 1993). On the contrary, these new practices have generated forms of participatory democracy that, as I show in the rest of this chapter, have produced more legitimacy and more administrative efficiency, dealing with the problem of complexity in a more democratic manner.

The PB and the amplification of sovereignty at the local level

Participatory budgeting connects in a singular way the amplification of participation to the establishment of criteria of justice. Participation in the PB in Porto Alegre and Belo Horizonte takes place, mainly, at the regional level in the local or intermediary assemblies. An evaluation of the participatory characteristics of the PB shows that, in both Belo Horizonte and Porto Alegre, participation is directly linked to the credibility of the process and the existence of public rules for action. Participation in the PB plays the role of assuring a form of deliberation that is public and that makes information about the access to public goods available. Table 12.1 below shows the levels of participation in Porto Alegre.

Some characteristics of participation in the PB should be stressed. First of all, initial participation in Porto Alegre's PB was low; in the first year, it was low in most regions and very low in those without any previous tradition of social organization, such as Restinga, Glória, Ilhas, and Humaitá (where, respectively, only 36, 20, 80, and ten people participated in the second round of regional assemblies). The low level of participation in almost all regions was probably linked to doubts about the capacity of the process to deliver public goods. Beginning in the second year, however, there was a huge change in the pattern of participation. On the one hand, the effectiveness of the first year's deliberations was a strong incentive in those regions that already had a tradition of community organization, such as the Leste (eastern region), where 705 attended the second regional assembly, or Parthenon, where 264 people attended the second regional assembly. On the other hand, participation remained very low in regions without a tradition of participation or community organization. These regions, which are among the poorest, had low levels of political participation for some years. Thus, we can again note the importance of pre-existing practices at the societal level pre-determining the effectiveness of the

Table 12.1. PARTICIPATION IN THE PB IN PORTO ALEGRE

Region/Year	1990		1991		1992		1993		1994		1995		1996		1997		1998	
Ilhas	14	80	33	90	32	132	148	129	58	77	195	103	131	72	246	104	271	113
Navegantes	5	10	15	32	37	128	68	337	112	227	273	136	215	75	476	91	498	126
Leste	52	100	90	705	125	385	235	467	166	409	243	229	214	409	204	195	591	119
Lomba	24	40	44	119	55	514	207	419	124	551	823	827	679	294	792	362	129	509
Norte	34	50	47	97	90	511	208	224	209	141	240	380	175	317	339	489	538	386
Nordeste	5	28	NA	363	55	221	604	668	323	388	485	283	396	286	530	184	696	210
Partenon	22	53	74	264	174	922	210	569	270	826	595	205	638	171	500	216	465	340
Restinga	NA	36	NA	181	66	303	144	206	196	768	404	480	589	174	834	311	922	426
Glória	10	20	55	142	104	206	127	226	164	350	299	70	321	151	251	133	234	120
Cruzeiro	91	90	101	128	62	235	293	345	59	423	283	283	426	223	430	132	399	205
Cristal	6	10	NA	81	80	388	107	252	157	215	195	74	240	98	278	290	251	81
Centro-Sul	49	52	44	458	89	502	320	1268	156	1051	108	293	1159	354	1571	239	1162	299
Extremo Sul	16	25	64	80	118	569	485	397	238	484	380	420	403	251	542	247	749	257
Eixo da Baltazar	0	28	23	152	97	455	304	405	127	517	376	563	352	391	287	189	528	332
Sul	14	0	NA	29	85	378	119	501	219	390	654	449	492	155	553	424	282	306
Centro	6	6	18	165	173	319	181	562	60	183	329	171	147	153	350	119	669	305
Total	976		3694		7610		10735		9638		11821		10148		11908		13687	

Source: CRC—Coordenação de Relações com a Comunidade/Prefeitura de Porto Alegre (Coordinating Committee of Relations with the Community/Porto Alegre Mayor's Office)

process. In the first years of the PB in Porto Alegre, the feasibility of a form of broadened participation depended on those actors who already shared a tradition of local assemblies at the regional level. It was only after such a tradition became an acknowledged form of claiming public goods that it generalized itself to the city as a whole.

A second element worth noting is how participation is directly linked to deliberation. If we look into the pattern of participation during the first five years, participation in the second regional assembly was larger than in the first (in 1992, for instance, 1,442 people participated in the first round of regional assemblies and 6,168 in the second round). Throughout this period, the most relevant deliberative moment was the second round of regional assemblies in which the election of the councilors took place. Beginning in 1996, delegates were elected in the first round of regional assemblies, which made them more deliberative. Since then, attendance in the first round has become higher than in the second (in 1996, 6,855 people attended the first round of regional assemblies and 4,966 people attended the second round). This tendency of greater participation in the first round persists to this day, showing the ability of the population to identify the deliberative moment and to participate in a rational way.

The most important aspect of the participatory process in Porto Alegre is the continuous increase in participation in spite of the fact that the forums of participation have changed. Participation increased from year to year with very few exceptions (1994 and 1996). This increase can be attributed to the confidence that the deliberative process would continue, due to the political hegemony of the Workers' Party in the city. In this sense, the pattern of participation in Porto Alegre can be contrasted with that in Belo Horizonte, where city politics has been more contentious. Table 12.2 below shows the variations in participation in Belo Horizonte.

Participation in Belo Horizonte shows more variation due to stronger doubts about the continuation of the process. In the first year, participation in Belo Horizonte was already high due to the precedent of the Porto Alegre experience—the population had good reason to assume that it was participating in an effective process. Participation increased still more once the effectiveness of the process at the city level became clear. In its second year of the PB, participation grew more than 50 per cent compared to the previous year, but then decreased in 1996 with the emergence of doubts regarding the PB's future. In that year's city elections, there were serious doubts about whether the Workers' Party candidate would win and, thus, whether the PB's decisions would be implemented. Participation decreased again in 1997 because, despite the fact that the new Brazilian Socialist Party administration promised to continue the PB process, social actors doubted that it would implement the decisions. However, once it became clear that it would keep its promise, participation grew again. Therefore, one can argue that participation

Table 12.2. PARTICIPATION IN THE PB IN BELO HORIZONTE

Year	First round	Second round	Third round	Regional Forum	Total
93/94	3.671	4.215	6.202	1.128	15.216
94/95	5.796	5.323	14.461	1.243	26.823
95/96	5.801	11.796	17.597	1.314	36.508
96/97	2.938	9.586	17.937	1.334	31.795
97/98	3.416	3.081	11.871	1.050	19.418
99/2000	stage suppressed	2.905	16.323	1.947	21.175

Source: Planning Secretary

in the PB varies according to two factors: the existence of an associative tradition and the perceived effectiveness of the process. Thus participation shows rational characteristics, particularly in relation to the willingness of social actors to participate in collective and public forms of deliberation.

A second important element to be discussed is that both in Belo Horizonte and Porto Alegre the participatory process is connected to the existence of criteria of justice. In the case of Porto Alegre, the criteria of justice are determined by the table of previous access to public goods, which has to be made compatible with the participatory process. In the case of Belo Horizonte, the criteria of justice are determined by the formula that distributes resources to the regions (see discussion above). In Porto Alegre, in each of the twelve areas in which decisions are going to be taken in the intermediary meetings, a table of previous access to public goods by the population of the city pre-determines the deliberative process. Table 12.3, below, shows how this process works in what concerns the paving of streets in Porto Alegre.

Table 12.3 allows us to see why the participatory process involved in the PB does not become a particularistic process, as some of the literature on democratic theory argues (Arendt, 1959; Schumpeter, 1942; Sartori, 1987). Participation in the PB is connected with the establishment of rules for the access to public goods. In the case of Porto Alegre, the 16 regions of the city are differentiated according to previous access to the goods in question. For example, some regions have had a high level of previous access to paving— such as the Central region, with more than 99 per cent of paved streets. In other regions of Porto Alegre, such as Extremo-Sul or Lomba do Pinheiro, almost 80 per cent or 55 per cent of the streets, respectively, are not paved. In contrast to the forms of decision-making by a bureaucracy pressured by particular interests, the PB incorporates criteria of justice in the process through a combination of three factors: previous access to a public good, the population of the region, and deliberation by the population in the

Table 12.3. PAVING NEEDS (ELABORATED FOR THE 1999 PB)

Regions	Street total	Paved	Unpaved	Need/ lack (in %)
Humaíta/Navegantes/Ilhas	117.704	100.808	16.896	14.35
Noroeste	147.375	146.345	1.030	0.70
Leste	154.545	136.402	18.143	11.74
Lomba do Pinheiro	90.310	39.818	50.492	55.91
Norte	130.910	110.819	20.091	15.35
Nordeste	56.470	37.233	19.237	34.07
Partenon	122.080	98.969	23.111	18.93
Restinga	73.109	65.110	7.999	10.94
Glória	77.665	47.517	30.148	38.82
Cruzeiro	71.658	62.325	9.333	13.02
Cristal	28.590	27.420	1.170	4.09
Centro-Sul	178.710	128.710	50.000	27.98
Extremo-Sul	183.290	40.148	143.142	78.10
Eixo da Baltazar	83.145	81.555	1.590	1.91
Sul	147.015	130.446	16.569	11.27
Centro	346.155	345.015	1.140	0.33
Total	2.008.731	1.598.640	410.091	

Source: Prefeitura de Porto Alegre (Porto Alegre Mayor's Office)

intermediary assemblies. In each of these factors, a region is evaluated and is given a grade from 1 to 5. Thus a region that has 80 per cent of need for one public good, whose population is more than 120,000, and has chosen that particular public good may attain the total number of points (15). On the other hand, a region that has had more access to this good, or a region with a small population, is not going to make as many points according to the same criteria.

Participatory budgeting is, thus, capable of integrating forms of broadening popular sovereignty with forms of dealing with issues of justice. This combination, again, poses problems for the hegemonic conception of democracy. The hegemonic conception of democracy works within a narrow and individualistic conception of representation of interests, which is used to justify the reduction of the scope of sovereignty. According to authors such as Schumpeter (1942), Downs (1957), and Elster (1988), among others, the problem with forms of broadened participation is that they are supposed to operate in individualistic settings in which it is very difficult to define the common good. As an alternative to such a problem, the hegemonic conception of democracy proposes decentralized forms of representation of interests within a competitive political supply in which it is up to the electorate to choose which will be the dominant articulation of interests. Though the literature in general argues that this form of representation reinforces particular interests (Lowi, 1969), it does not point out participatory democracy as an alternative.

The case of the PB is quite useful for seeing how broadened forms of sovereignty are able to shed new light on this problem. In spite of being a broadened form of sovereignty, the PB does not leave to the participatory institutions the whole decision-making process on the allocation of public goods. It introduces rules that pre-determine the decision-making process. By doing this, it innovates in terms of democratic practices in two ways: first, it establishes limits for particularism—limits that have been historically lacking in the practice of both representative and participatory democracy, thus changing the terms of the democratic debate. Second, interests that are considered legitimate in the PB process are required to be justified, and have to overlap with the criteria of justice outlined above. Thus, the connection established by the PB between participation and rules introduces new elements into the discussion of the role of broadened forms of participation within democratic theory. It shows that the Weberian solution for increasing levels of participation—which implies an increase in bureaucratic control—is not the only possible solution. Another possibility might be available: a solution according to which "in internally differentiated societies, the stronger the bond between democracy and distributive justice, the more complex the methodology which guarantees such bonds" (Santos, 1998: 484). In this sense, the PB represents a new way of making participation and institutionalization compatible, a way in which democratic practices and social complexity—which are the result of new forms of collective action within a differentiated society—are connected with rules for participatory decision-making, thus offsetting the enhancement of the power of the administrative personnel.

Participation, complexity, and monitoring in the PB

A second area in which the PB innovates is in the control the population has over the implementation of the deliberations on city investments. The PB has produced very significant results in terms of the control of the administrative personnel through the establishment of monitoring institutions. Two different forms of monitoring are used: in Porto Alegre, the PB Council is responsible for monitoring budget implementation. This is accomplished through the tension established between the PB Council and two administrative bodies—GAPLAN and CRC. Thus administrative officials are in charge of implementation, but their access to decision-making is not exclusive: they are required to explain choices to a body of representative delegates. In Belo Horizonte, there is a special monitoring body, the COMFORÇAS. According to Faria (1996), its aims are the following: 1) to check and supervise the budget's execution and the schedule of works (timetable, expenses, and accountability); 2) to supervise substitutions or re-dimensionings in cases where choices made by the community face technical problems 3) to present the community's point of view before a technical decision is made; 4) to demand explanations on controversial issues in the implementation of the PB; 5) to organize meetings with the community to explain the administration's point of view on certain issues; 6) to appoint two representatives to follow the bidding of PB public works; 7) to participate in the organization of the regional forum; and 8) to investigate abuses of power and the appearance of special interests in the deliberative process (Faria, 1996: 103-104). Thus, in the establishment of a system of monitoring at the local level, the PB incorporates forms of an autonomous organization of the population, which allows it to control the internal operation of the administration. In this way, there is a connection between the decisions taken by the popular assemblies and the way in which these decisions are translated into administrative orders.

The PB also introduces a new conception of administrative accountability by transforming monitoring into a permanent feature of its administrative process. Forms of monitoring instituted by the PB Council in Porto Alegre or by the COMFORÇAS in Belo Horizonte represent the integration of structures of participation at the local level with the administrative structures. Thus the PB presents a participatory solution to a central problem in Latin American democracies—the lack of control by the population over an autonomous bureaucracy unused to public forms of accountability. This reduces the level of irregularities in public bidding—an endemic problem in Brazil—and at the same time forces administrative organs to adapt to the participation of the population on technical questions.

The monitoring institutions introduced by the PB show how deliberation can be separated from implementation without giving technical bodies exclusive access to administrative arenas, a feature of the hegemonic conception of democracy presented above. The PB has instituted a public body in charge of presenting and representing the community's point of view within the administration. This solution overcomes the disadvantages of elitist models by giving a more democratic, less particularistic solution to the link between technical knowledge and exclusive access to administrative arenas. Monitoring bodies generate groups of active participants who acquire a considerable understanding of technical issues. These groups can convey technical details to the general population and also debate technical issues with administrative bodies. In seven years of the PB in Belo Horizonte, 1,428 people have participated in the PB monitoring body. Asked if participating in COMFORÇAS had led them to a better understanding of the problems of their sub-regions, 88.5 per cent of COMFORÇAS members in the South Central region of the city and 76.9 per cent in the Barreiros region answered affirmatively (Faria, 1996: 126). Thus, an attractive aspect of monitoring institutions is that they differentiate between deliberation and implementation and at the same time make technical bodies more accountable to the population.

The experience of monitoring bodies also suggests that administrative decision-making becomes more efficient under the pressure of participatory bodies. In an interview, the president of Sudecap (the state company in charge of public works in Belo Horizonte) acknowledged that the presence of monitoring bodies with the ability to pose questions about timetables and implementation details increased the need for both accountability and efficiency within the company. The more the population knows about technical details, the less the usual explanations for inefficiency and delays are accepted.

The operation of monitoring bodies challenges a second aspect of the hegemonic conception of democracy, namely, that the central aspect of complex decisions is expert knowledge on the issues involved and the ability of a specialized body to deal with such issues in a systematic and routine way (Weber, 1919). The PB challenges the universal application of these rules in two different ways: first of all, it shows that the role of experts in decision-making bodies should not lead to exclusive prerogatives in the decision-making process (Melucci and Avritzer, 2000). In the Brazilian case, the access of the population to decision-making bodies reduces corruption in bidding processes and speeds up the implementation process. Second, the PB also shows that the problem of knowledge can be addressed in a more democratic form. Though in Porto Alegre and Belo Horizonte the population knew very little about the administrative process of their cities, at the end of a period of one or two years of monitoring bodies their knowledge was significantly enhanced. This shows that the possibility of transferring complex knowledge from technical experts to bodies of representatives of the population is not a closed path, as the hegemonic conception of democracy has argued. In addition, the presence of a monitoring body makes it easier to address conflictual issues between experts and the population. Thus the PB opens up space for the defense of an intermediary conception between the Weberian position on the exclusive access of experts to decision-making bodies and the participatory conceptions of democracy that defend the increase of participation in the administrative process itself. It proposes an intermediary position in which a sphere of control of administrative decision-making and a process of tension between experts and monitoring bodies leads to the control of processes previously considered off limits. In this case, the extension of sovereignty is made compatible with rational administration.

Social innovation and counter-hegemonic forms of participatory democracy

The example of the PB in Porto Alegre and Belo Horizonte indicates that the institutional forms of democracy are not fixed and that new experiments are needed in order to deal adequately with contentious issues. It also shows that the issues with which democracy is concerned change according to different political settings. In the Brazilian case, clientelism, disempowerment of the population, and the unequal distribution of public goods at the local level have been some of the issues that the fixed forms of the democracy generated by the second wave of democratization could not solve. The elitist conception of democracy, which evaluates the success or failure of democracy according to elite practices (O'Donnell, 1996; 1998), is quite pessimistic about the future of Brazil. In the Brazilian case, old practices have, in fact, only led to clientelism, administrative inefficiency, and intra-elite rivalry.

Yet there is a second way of evaluating democracy, a way that requires our departing from the hegemonic conception of democracy outlined above and our taking into account the emergence of new societal practices. The PB in the cases of Porto Alegre and Belo Horizonte indicates the virtue of broadened forms of sovereignty at the local level. It shows that some of the drawbacks of recent democracies are based on their inability to incorporate social innovation. In the case of the PB, innovation, understood as a societal practice of openly negotiating the access to public goods, becomes incorporated into a deliberative model. Such a model substitutes elite practices and their drawbacks for broadened forms of discussion and decision-making. In addition to this, the PB gives a different response to the issue of justice and particularism. Instead of being seduced by the siren song of the inevitability of particularism, the PB introduces rules for its limitation. And, last but not least, the PB also provides a different answer to the issue of control over decision-making bodies by technical experts, a problem not yet resolved by the hegemonic conception of democracy.

The different answers provided by the PB to the issues enumerated above all point in one direction, namely, that the contradiction between collective action, broadened forms of political participation, and de-institutionalization, such as it has been addressed by the hegemonic theory of democracy based on the European experience in the inter-war period, cannot be generalized. Democracy in the countries of the so-called third wave of democratization has not been threatened by undifferentiated forms of political mobilization, as it was in Europe during the inter-war period. The major problem faced by democracy in these countries is a limited stock of democratic practices. Thus, in these cases, institutionalization ceases to be the opposite of mobilization, which becomes a form of collective action in the public space. Under such conditions, institutionalization also assumes a different meaning, namely the connection between new societal practices and new institutional designs. As a broadened form of political participation, the PB shows precisely this fact.

Liang Ch'i Cha'o and Alexis de Tocqueville were both right when they pointed out the inevitability of democracy as a hegemonic form of political rule. Yet they did not perceive that the forms of democracy outside the West are not fixed and do not necessarily reproduce the hegemonic forms. A difference seems to be crucial between Western and non-Western forms of democracy: the availability of a stock of democratic practices and the role of social actors in the process of broadening this stock through the integration of different experiences (Santos, 2000). The Brazilian case, which has been approached in this chapter, is a good example of the limited stock of democratic practices on the part of elites, a drawback only recently offset by the emergence of new societal practices. Thus, the fact that both Tocqueville and Liang Ch'i Cha'o were right should not lead us to think that in the extension of democracy the same cultural forms dominant in the West will prevail. In the case of Brazil, the integration of the country into a democratic tide has been slow and contradictory, involving moves in contrary directions. As a matter of fact, Liang Ch'i Cha'o's definition of the expansion of democracy as a cycle, or Tocqueville's image of a democratic tide, both ignore the fact that those who are losing new privileges every day might adhere to democratic values in an incomplete way. In contrast, the Brazilian experience shows that the democratic tide might be connected to the stocks of practices of those who are not losing privileges, but, on the contrary, have something to gain from the expansion of democracy. These are the social actors whose innovations are creating counter-hegemonic forms of democracy.

Notes

1 I am drawing on Huntington's definition of "wave of democratization": "[A] group of transitions from non-democratic to democratic regimes that occur within a specified period of time and that significantly outnumber transitions in the opposite direction during that period of time" (Huntington, 1991: 15).

2 Within contemporary political science Norberto Bobbio is the author who has best defended the Weberian perspective. In his essay 'The Future of Democracy', he comments: "As societies gradually change from a family economy to a market economy and from a market economy to an economy

which is protected, regulated and planned, there is an increase in the number of political problems whose solutions require technical expertise. Technical problems require experts, an expanding team of specialized personnel. [...] Technocracy and democracy are antithetical: if the expert plays a leading role in industrial society he cannot be considered as just any citizen" (Bobbio, 1987: 37).

3 A good example of administrative inefficiency involves the distribution of resources through MP's amendments. In 1996, a year in which there were local elections, 600 million reais were set aside for the patrimonial budget, reaching an average of about 1.0 to 1.5 million in amendments per MP. Most MPs opted in 1996 to pulverize the resources under their control. Thus, for a public work that is budgeted at 2 or 3 million *reais*, an MP could present an amendment allocating 200,000 *reais*, which means that the forecast for its conclusion could be 15 years or more. In June 1996, 2,214 public works involving resources above 15 billion were paralyzed because the resources needed for their completion had not been budgeted. See Faria, 1996.

4 It is beyond the aims of this chapter to analyze the emergence and consolidation of the Workers' Party in Brazil. Yet it is important to point out that neighborhood associations, which were linked to the activities of the Catholic Church in Brazil in the seventies and eighties, were akin to labor's claim for social autonomy. For an analysis of the movements that demanded labor autonomy in Brazil during democratization, see Sader, 1988; Doimo, 1995; and Avritzer, 1988. For an analysis of the formation of the Workers' Party, see Keck, 1992.

5 Although the early formation of neighborhood associations in Porto Alegre is well known, one author (Baiocc, 1999) insists on the lack of an associative tradition in the city. Using an incomplete list of associations created in the city, the author commits two mistakes: he argues for a very low density of associations in the city before the creation of participatory budgeting, and later he defends an exponential growth of associations after its creation. For a critique, see Avritzer, 2000b.

Bibliography

Abers, R. (1996). "From Ideas to Practice: the P.T. and Participatory Governance in Brazil." *Latin American Perspectives* 23(4): 35–53.

Afonso, Marisa and Sérgio Azevedo (1988). "Cidade, poder público e movimento de favelados," in Malori Pompermayer (ed.), *Movimentos Sociais em Minas Gerais*. Belo Horizonte: Editora da UFMG.

Almond, Gabriel and Sidney Verba (1963). "The Civic Culture: Political Attitudes and Democracy," in *Five Nations*. Boston, MD: Little Brown.

Arendt, H. (1951). *The Origins of Totalitarianism*. Cleveland: World Pub. Co.

— (1959). *The Human Condition*. Chicago: U of Chicago P.

Avritzer, L. (1998). "The conflict between civil and political societies in post-authoritarian Brazil: an analysis of the impeachment of Collor de Mello," in K. Rosenn and R. Downs (eds), *Corruption and Political Reform in Brazil*. Miami: North South Center, 119–40.

— (2000a). "Changes in the Pattern of Association in Brazil." *Journal of Interamerican Studies and World Affairs*, Fall.

— (2000b). "Sociedade Civil, Espaço Público e Poder Local." Research report. Ford Foundation/Campinas.

— (2001). "Sociedade civil, espaço público e poder local: uma análise do orçamento participativo em Belo Horizonte e Porto Alegre" (mimeo).

Azevedo, S. D. and A. A. Prates (1991). *Planejamento Particpativo, Movimentos Sociais e Ação Coletiva*. Anpocs, Caxambu: Ciências Sociais Hoje.

Baierle, S. (1998). "The explosion of experience: the emergence of a new ethical-political principle in popular movements." in S. Alvarez, in E. Dagnino and A. Escobar (eds), *Cultures of Politics/Politics of Culture*. Boulder, CO: Westview Press, 118–40.

Baiocc, G. (1999). *Participation, Activism and Politics*. Experiments in Deliberative Democracy, Madison.

Bobbio, N. (1987). *The Future of Democracy*. Cambridge: Polity/Blackwell.

Boschi, R. (1987). *A Arte da Associação*. Rio de Janeiro: Vértice.

Cammach, P. (1990). "Brazil: the long march to the new republic." *New Left Review*, 190: 21–58.

Cohen, J. (1985). "Strategy or Identity: new theoretical paradigms and contemporary social movements." *Social Research* 52(4): 663–716.

Doimo, A. M. (1995). *A Vez e a Voz do Popular*. Rio de Janeiro: Relume Dumara.

Downs, A. (1957). *An Economic Theory of Democracy*. New York: Harper.

Dunn, J. (1979). *Western Political Thought in the Face of the Future*. Cambridge: Cambridge UP.

Elster, J., R. Slagstad, *et al.* (1988). *Constitutionalism and Democracy*. Cambridge: Cambridge UP.

Faria, C. F. (1996). *Democratizando a Relação entre o Poder Público Municipal e a Sociedade Civil: o orçamento participativo em Belo Horizonte*. Belo Horizonte: UFMG.

Gay, R. (1994). *Popular Organization and Democracy in Rio de Janeiro*. Philadelphia: Temple UP.

Graham, R. (1990). *Patronage and Politics in Nineteenth-century Brazil*. Stanford, CA: Stanford UP.

Horkheimer, M. (1947). *Eclipse of Reason*. New York: Oxford UP.

Huntington, S. P. (1991). *The Third Wave: Democratization in the Late Twentieth Century*. Norman: U of Oklahoma P.

IBGE—Instituto Brasileiro de Geografia Estatística (1993). *Anuário Estatístico*. Rio de Janeiro.

Kant, I. (1959). *Foundations of the Metaphysics of Morals, and What is Enlightenment?* New York: Liberal Arts Press.

Keck, M. E. (1992). *The Workers' Party and Democratization in Brazil*. New Haven, CT: Yale UP.

Kornhauser, W. (1959). *The Politics of Mass Society*. Glencoe: Free Press.

Kronman, A. T. (1983). *Max Weber*. Stanford, CA: Stanford UP.

Lima, Gildo (1999). Interview with Leonardo Avritzer.

Lowi, T. J. (1969). *The End of Liberalism: Ideology, Policy, and the Crisis of Public Authority*. New York: Norton.

Mainwaring, S. (1990). *Clientelism, Patrimonialism and Economic Crisis: Brazil since 1979*. Washington: LASA.

Melucci, A. and L. Avritzer (1995). "Complexity, cultural pluralism and democracy: collective action in the public space." *Social Science Information*, 39(4): 507–27.

Navarro, Zander (1998). "Affirmative democracy and redistributive development: the case of participatory budgeting in Porto Alegre, Brazil." *Programas sociales, pobreza e particpacion ciudadana*. Cartagena: World Bank.

Nunes Leal, José Olympio (1946). *Coronelismo, Enxada e Voto*. Rio de Janeiro: Forense.

O'Donnell, G. A.; Helen Kellogg Institute for International Studies (1996). *Another Institutionalization: Latin America and Elsewhere*. Notre Dame: Helen Kellogg Institute for International Studies.

— (1998). "Horizontal Accountability in New Democracies," *Journal of Democracy*, 112–25

Ortega y Gasset, J. (1930). *La Rebelión de las Massas*. Madrid: Revista de Occidente.

Poa (1999). *Regimento do orçamento participativo*. Prefeitura de Porto Alegre.

Raichellis, R. (1999). *Esfera Pública e Conselhos de Assistência social: caminhos da construção democrática*. São Paulo: Cortez.

Rodrigues, L. M. (1987). *Quem é Quem na Constituinte: uma Análise Sócio-Política dos Partidos e Deputados*. São Paulo, OESP: Maltese.

Rousseau, J.-J. (1968). *The Social Contract*. Baltimore, MD: Penguin.

Santos, Boaventura de Sousa (1998). "Participatory Budgeting in Porto Alegre: Toward a Redistributive Democracy." *Politics and Society*, 26(4): 461–510.

— (2000). *Crítica da Razão Indolente: contra o desperdício da experiência*. São Paulo: Cortez.

Santos, W. G. (1987). *Crise e Castigo: Partidos e Generais na Política Brasileira*. São Paulo, Rio de Janeiro: Vértice; Instituto Universitário de Pesquisas do Rio de Janeiro.

— (1993). *Razões da Desordem*. Rio de Janeiro: Rocco.

Sartori, G. (1987). *The Theory of Democracy Revisited*. Chatham: Chatham House.

Schumpeter, J. A. (1942). *Capitalism, Socialism, and Democracy*. New York: Harper.

Stepan, A. (1988). *Rethinking Military Politics*. Princeton, NJ: Princeton UP.

Tabagiba, L. (2000). "Análise da Literatura Sobre Experiências Recentes da Sociedade Civil." Research report. Campinas.

Tilly, C. (1986). *The Contentious French*. Cambridge: Belknap Press.

Tocqueville, A. de (1958). *Journeys to England and Ireland*. London: Lawrence and Mayer.

UAMPA (1986). *A Participação Popular na Administração Municipal*. Porto Alegre.

Utzig, L. E. (1996). "Notas sobre o governo do PT em Porto Alegre." *Novos Estudos*, 45: 209–222

Weber, Max [1919] (1991). *Economia e Sociedade*. Brasília: Editora da UnB.

13

The Politics and Institutional Design of Participatory Democracy: Lessons from Kerala, India

Patrick Heller and T. M. Thomas Isaac

INTRODUCTION

In evaluating democracy in the developing world, scholars have generally focused on the nature of the regime in power, and have directed much of their attention to the role of political parties and other organized political actors in the electoral arena. Scholars have also of course directed their attention to examining how state structures shape patterns of engagement, and to detailed investigations of patterns and modes of representation. Much of this work has focused on the nation-state as the critical unit of analysis. What has been missing however is a deeper understanding of day-to-day democratic practices, and in particular the nature of the sub-national institutional field(s) on which both formal and informal political agents engage each other and the state. In the absence of such analyses it becomes very difficult to understand why so many developing world democracies have been so ineffective not only in securing social rights but even in providing for basic political and civic rights. The state has certainly been transformed, but has it, in the language that now dominates the post-transition discourses on development, become closer to the people? Why, in particular, has political participation, beyond the periodic exercise of the vote, remained so circumscribed? To what extent have transitions to electoral rule made bureaucratic institutions inherited from authoritarian or colonial pasts more open to involvement by ordinary citizens? Is the reach and robustness of public legality sufficient to guarantee the uniform application of rights of citizenship? Have developing states really changed their modes of governance, the social partners they engage with and the developmental goals they prioritize?

If making a democratic state has been difficult, making a responsive state has been even more difficult. Nowhere is this more the case than in India. The general picture of Indian democracy stands as a reminder that there is no linear progression to democracy. Much as the robustness of India's democratic institutions have been rightfully celebrated, the effectiveness of those institutions is increasingly in doubt. Fifty-four years of almost uninterrupted democratic rule have done little to reduce the multiple exclusions of India's subalterns. Digging below the surface, moreover, one finds that within the unitary institutional domain marked by the boundaries of the Indian nation-state, there are marked degrees of democracy, or, as Guillermo O'Donnell (1993) has put it, differences in the intensity of citizenship. India's post-transition history has produced multiple trajectories of democratization. If at one end it is possible to identify redoubts of quasi-feudal authoritarian-ism (the state of Bihar, for example), at the other it is possible to find cases of ongoing democratic deepening. This most notably is the case of the south-western state of Kerala, which stands out not only because of its storied history of popular movements led by the Communist Party of India—Marxist CPI(M) or CPM[1]—and of an activist state that has achieved some of the most dramatic social and redistributive gains in the developing world (Heller, 1999), but also because since 1996 it has been the site of one of the boldest, most self-conscious and most extensive experiments in empowered partici-patory governance.[2]

In 1996 the Left Democratic Front (LDF) coalition returned to power in Kerala and the CPM-led government immediately fulfilled one of its most important campaign pledges by launching the "People's Campaign for Decentralized Planning." Although the People's Campaign (Campaign here-after) is only in its fifth year, it has already achieved a far greater degree of devolution of decision-making powers than any other Indian state. All 1,214 local governments in Kerala—municipalities and the three rural tiers of dis-tricts, blocks and *grama panchayats* (the all-India term for village councils)—have been given new functions and powers of decision-making, and have been granted discretionary budgeting authority over 40 per cent of the state's developmental expenditures. However, the Campaign repre-sents far more than a simple decentralization of governance powers to lower-level elected bodies. In both its political and institutional design it has the socially transformative ambition—much as in the case of Porto Alegre—of compensating for the deficits of formal representative structures and bureaucratic decision-making by building and capacitating participatory institutions. On a number of counts it quite clearly stands out as a bold experiment in building participatory democracy. The first is its sheer scope and scale. The decentralization of a wide range of developmental responsi-bilities to 1,214 elected local governments represents a profound reconfiguration of the state and its relationship to society and has the poten-tial of dramatically transforming the everyday practice of democracy for Kerala's 31 million inhabitants. Second, the institutional design of the campaign's core institutions—*grama sabha*s (ward-level assemblies), develop-ment seminars, task forces and local governments—has self-consciously attempted to nurture and empower a model of democratic and participatory development planning. On the one hand, by having devolved planning and implementation functions to local arenas, the Campaign has for the first time in India meaningfully empowered local governments and communities to address practical problems. The entire planning cycle—which begins with the collection of local data and ends with the formulation of a comprehensive local plan that consists of hundreds of projects—is basically an extended exercise in practical problem-solving. On the other hand, both the institutional and political character of the Campaign has been centrally concerned with promoting bottom-up participation. The devolution of authority and resources to local governments has significantly reduced the transaction costs of participation, and the knowledge and capacity gap that has traditionally excluded ordinary citizens from playing an effective role in governance has been considerably narrowed by mass training programs, the active mobilization of civil society expertise, and concerted efforts to empower historically marginalized groups—women, *adivasis* ("tribals"), and *dalits* ("untouchables"). Moreover, the participatory institutions of the Campaign are self-consciously deliberative—based on inclusionary and reason-based decision-making—and directly empowered because they tie project choice and formulation to actual implementation. In all these respects the Campaign marks a critical juncture in Kerala's democratization trajectory: it is nothing less than an explicit political project aimed at dismantling entrenched forms of bureaucratic domination and patronage politics by reinvigorating Kerala's tradition of direct, movement-based political engagement and fundamentally democratizing the institutional character of the state.

DISAGGREGATING DEMOCRACY[3]

The debate on democratic transitions has understandably focused on the installation of electoral, constitutional and procedural institutions. The unit of analysis has invariably been the nation-state. While useful for typologizing regimes and differentiating democracy from authoritarianism, focusing on formal national-level institutions provides limited analytical leverage for conceptualizing democratic deepening. Because institutions and politics are relational and configurational, their attributes are never perfectly isomorphic either horizontally across different policy arenas, or vertically from one level of the state to another. As the state radiates out from its geographic and functional core its authority and its effectiveness fluctuates dramatically. Much as state-society theorists have called for disaggregating the state (Migdal *et al.*, 1994), we need to disaggregate democracy.

As conventionally defined, formal democracy is marked by universal suffrage, regular and competitive elections, accountability of state apparatuses to elected representatives and legally codified and enforced rights of association (Huber *et al.*, 1999: 168). An *effective* democracy is one in which democratic practices have spread throughout society, governing not only relations between states and citizens, but also public relations between citizens. Functionally and geographically the degree of public legality in many formal democracies remains severely constrained. In such democracies, notes O'Donnell, "the component of democratic legality and, hence, of publicness and citizenship, fade away at the frontiers of various regions and class, gender and ethnic relations" (1993: 1361). Public spaces disappear to be replaced by areas of privatized power. Local institutions and officials are colonized by bosses, chiefs, dons, or caciques. Patrimonialism, clientelism, and coercion eat away at democratic authority. Thus we must look beyond the macro-institutional level of parliaments, constitutions and elections and investigate the intermediate and local-level institutions and, consultative arenas located in the interstices of state and society where "everyday" forms of democracy either flourish or flounder. We need, in other words, a political sociology of democracy, one that specifically recognizes that a working democracy must be an effective democracy.

An effective democracy has two interrelated characteristics: a robust civil society and a capable state. A free and lively civil society makes the state and its agents more accountable by guaranteeing that consultation takes place not just through electoral representation (periodic mandates) but also through constant feedback and negotiation. Civil society is critical to democratic performance because it extends the scope and style of claim-making beyond the formal interest representation that defines political society. Social movements, associations, and unions raise new issues and mobilize new actors. In doing so they not only provide a counterbalance to more bureaucratic and aggregated forms of interest representation, but they also create new solidarities, which in many instances specifically challenge existing inequalities and hence help democratize society itself. The key point here is that the health of a democracy is measured as much in the qualitative nature of its social patterns of association as in the formal character of its institutions, and that while these two variables condition each other—associational patterns are conditioned by institutional environments, and institutional responsiveness is conditioned by associational vitality—the pattern can be positively reinforcing just as it can be impairing.

The capacity of the state is also central to the effectiveness of democracy. Procedural guarantees of civic and political rights, including rights of association and free speech, do not automatically translate into the effective exercise of democratic rights. Citizenship is not a right, it is a relation. Where inequalities between social categories are so pronounced as to create extra-constitutional forms of binding authority (clientelism, patriarchy, caste subordination), the exercise of citizenship is subverted. As theorists of civil society have long argued, its associational qualities emerge only when it is doubly differentiated from the state and from primary social groupings (families, kinship groups, lineages). A precondition for the effective exercise of civic and political rights requires a state capable of securing the even, uniform and rational-legal enforcement of public authority. Individuals and groups must be protected from arbitrary state action, but also from forms of social authority that might constrain or impinge upon their civic and political liberties. And creating public spaces that are protected from non-democratic forms of authority requires far more than writing constitutions and holding officials accountable. It marks a fundamental shift in the distribution and locus of what Weber called "legitimate domination" from society to state. Given the contested and unfinished process of state-formation in much of the developing world, and most notably the institutional weakness (or vulnerability to elite capture) of local government, the writ of legally enforced public authority remains limited, producing a low-density form of citizenship. This problem is tied to both the infrastructural and authoritative limits of state power. Infrastructurally, the apparatuses of the state—the police, the judiciary, the educational system—are simply cast too thinly and too unevenly to enforce and provide for citizen's rights. Authoritatively, the state's legitimate realm of domination (constitutionally prescribed arenas in which its authority is binding and backed by coercion) is contested and weakened by countervailing sources of authority. And even when central level institutions are robust and fairly well insulated from particular interests (relative autonomy), the meso- and local-level institutions of the state—which are equally critical to securing effective rights of citizenship, including participation—can nevertheless be extremely weak.

THE LIMITS OF EFFECTIVE DEMOCRACY IN INDIA

India's democratic institutions have withstood the test of time and the test of a fissiparous society. The basic procedural infrastructure of democracy—specifically, the constitution and guarantees of the rights of association, the separation of powers, and regular and open elections at both the national and state levels—has become firmly entrenched.[4] At a minimum, despite infamous recent episodes of communal and caste violence, democratic institutions have not only helped forge a nation from multiple nationalities but have also institutionalized acceptance of the uncertainty of rule that comes with competitive elections. The authoritarian episode of 1975–77 notwithstanding, the prospects of a democratic reversal in India are remote. India's dominant class factions, proprietary and professional, support democracy, if for no other reason than because they have benefited so handsomely from the largess of India's democratic politics of patronage (Bardhan, 1984).

The effectiveness of India's democratic institutions is an altogether different matter. Throughout vast regions of India the exercise of citizenship rights, even in the limited political sense of the term, is circumscribed by the persistence of traditional forms of social control. With more than half of India's rural households depending on landlords for access to land or labor, clientelistic ties remain key to the survival strategies of subordinate groups. With its ritualized exclusions and deeply ingrained hierarchical relations, the caste system has inscribed these material inequalities with a degree of social and cultural control that has few parallels. Low levels of literacy and discriminatory treatment by upper-caste-controlled state institutions have further limited the associational autonomy of lower castes and classes. The corollary of this picture is the predominance of fragmented sovereignty. The reach and authority of the juridical and democratic state end, or more accurately are transfigured, where the writ and power of local strongmen and their caste-based followings begin. In a pattern that closely resembles both the Brazilian and African cases, extra-democratic sources of authority not only resist, but also colonize and privatize state power (Weyland, 1996; Mamdani, 1996). Local notables routinely dominate local institutions, including village governments, schools, cooperative societies and the development bureaucracy. The permeability of state authority is most dramatically exposed by the existence of private caste armies (especially in Bihar) and elite control over local police forces.

This is not to say that democratic institutions in India have been altogether lifeless. The past two decades have witnessed an erosion of traditional clientelist politics. Formal and competitive democracy in India has undermined the legitimacy of traditional social authority, spawned a whole new generation of political entrepreneurs and created spaces in which new groups have been successfully mobilized. But the political forces that have emerged are more rooted in social cleavages than ever. The basis for mobilization has shifted from patronage to identity populism. As elections have become more competitive and more groups have been brought into the political arena on their own terms, patronage has become increasingly tied to identity politics. The demand for government quotas and special privileges, whether of majority or minority communities, now dominates claim-making. This explosion of narrow demands has triggered a frantic and zero-sum scramble for preferential treatment that Bardhan has aptly described as "equal-opportunity plundering by all interest groups" (1997: 16).

In this political climate of populism and organizational fragmentation, encompassing political formations have been the exception to the rule. Labor unions have rarely extended beyond the protective confines of the organized sector (large factories and public employees) and in many instances have become little more than vehicles for the political ambitions of local bosses. Farmers' associations have been dominated by the interests of large farmers. With the reach of public legality circumscribed by the power of local elites, lower-class and lower-caste efforts to organize around economic issues (outside of Kerala and West Bengal) have invariably been defeated (Brass,

1994: 334). Against this backdrop of political fragmentation, the capacity of democratic institutions to aggregate interests and in particular address pressing distributional dilemmas is more in doubt than ever. The politics of social citizenship, as Mehta (1997: 64) has remarked, are conspicuous by their absence. Thus, much as in the case of Brazil, political fragmentation has frustrated the equity-enhancing potential (and promise) of democracy (Weyland, 1996).

If the absence of encompassing political formations has left little room for programmatic expressions of lower-class interests, the virtual absence of local democratic institutions has only compounded the problem of democratic ineffectiveness. Until very recently local government in India was not even formally democratic. The leading theorist of the CPM, E. M. S. Namboodiripad, once noted that, "if at the level of center-state relations the constitution gave us democracy, at the level of state–*panchayat* relations the constitution gave us bureaucracy." Indeed, it was not until the passage of the 73rd and 74th amendments to the Constitution of India in 1993 that state governments were mandated to hold regular local government elections. And even when local governments have been electorally accountable, they have enjoyed few if any substantive decision-making powers. Most local governments, and in particular village governments, have acted as little more than administrative conduits for state and center-level programs.

Despite the fact that the idea of empowered local governments has long been a staple of India's Gandhian heritage, from Nehru's Community Development Program to national and sub-national efforts to empower India's *panchayats*, the history of decentralization, much like that of land reform, has been one of broken promises, slow political deaths, bureaucratic obfuscation, and hollow legislation. Where local governments have been given some measure of power they have more often than not been captured by local elites and transformed into instruments of patronage. Regional variations notwithstanding, the balance sheet is clear: with the possible exception of West Bengal the process of shaping and implementing developmental initiatives, including the most basic of day-to-day public services, has remained a top-down affair dominated by the bureaucratic and political elites of state capitals and their intermediaries, brokers and fixers.

DEMOCRACY AND SOCIAL MOVEMENTS IN KERALA

There are probably few examples in the world where the causal link between organized social movements and significant redistributive and social gains is as strong as in Kerala. Briefly put, a long history of social mobilization that began with caste reform movements and sporadic peasant uprisings in the 1920s and 1940s crystallized into a lower-class movement under the organizational umbrella of the Communist Party, which captured power in 1957.

Repeated spells in power by the communists, combined with an almost continuous process of militant mass mobilization, exerted unrelenting pressure on the state to expand social programs, regulate labor markets, and implement land reforms. Despite a two-decade period of virtual economic stagnation (1970–90), social indicators have continued to climb, poverty rates have fallen dramatically, and wages for unskilled workers (agricultural laborers, construction, *beedi* (local cigarettes) and cashew nut processing workers) remain the highest in India. The incidence of class-based mass mobilization did drop significantly beginning in the 1980s, but no government has ever rescinded or cut back a major social program (and this despite increasing fiscal constraints), and in many sectors the state in Kerala (regardless of the party in power) continues to pioneer pro-poor reforms (Heller, 1999). There is little doubt that no other state has been more consistently pro-poor or successfully redistributive in all of India, and possibly anywhere in the democratic world.[5]

All this makes the launching in 1996 by a CPM-led government of the "People's Campaign for Decentralized Planning" rather intriguing. Widely regarded as the most far-reaching and radical experiment in decentralization ever undertaken in India, the campaign's political project has been nothing less than a frontal assault on the bureaucratic fiefdoms of the state and the patronage networks of the political system. The paradox here, as Thomas Isaac has previously noted, is that "a state government launched a movement to force its own hand to radically restructure the mode of governance. Why should any state embark upon such a mission?" (2000: 316). To answer this question requires a brief review of Kerala's political and developmental history.

The trajectory of Kerala's anti-caste, nationalist and radical agrarian movements reached a watershed when the Communist Party won Kerala's first elections in 1957. The Communist Party has never, however, achieved a stable electoral majority and has consequently been in and out of power. This inability to build a sustainable majority support has been the subject of continuous debate in the Party. Its failure to extend its influence among Kerala's large Muslim and Christian minorities in the state has been an important factor. Moreover, the success of the Communist Party itself in the area of the implementation of land reforms, the spread of education and the development of the cooperative sector has brought about significant social and economic changes with which the party has not yet fully come to terms. This, coupled with the fact that the party has always harbored reservations about the scope of "parliamentary democracy"—having in fact been twice evicted from power by the central government—more than anything else explains why the party has continually had to reinvent itself and build its mobilizational capacity. As Thomas Isaac has commented elsewhere, "[t]he Left does not have faith in the autonomous transformative power of the state government, which is only part of the overall bourgeois-landlord Indian state. Therefore, while in power or outside, they continue to mobilize the masses in support of the demands. The constant pressure from below is important in understanding the responsiveness of the state machinery" (2000: 141–2). In the 1940s the communists seized the leadership of the Independence movement. In the 1950s and 1960s the party championed the rights of poor tenants. In the 1970s, having lost the support among many who had bene-fited from land reform, the Party took up the cause of landless laborers. And it also moved aggressively to unionize workers in the informal sector (Heller, 1999).

A critical effect of this sustained history of mobilization was to draw the state in and to extend the reach of public legality. As the state responded to demands from below to redistribute land, to enforce labor legislation, and to provide social services, it enmeshed itself in society. At the meso and local levels, this has produced a rich fabric of democratic institutions and author-ities. In contrast to the modal Indian picture in which district- and village-level institutions are deeply enmeshed in local power configurations and are often in the hands of landed elites or dominant castes, in Kerala a wide range of institutions, including district councils, *panchayats*, student councils, cooperative societies, and quasi-corporatist bodies, have given multi-level representation to lower-class interests.

Because Kerala's popular sectors have been successfully mobilized and effectively represented by a programmatic political party, that state has had a pronounced lower-class bias and has orchestrated significant social and redis-tributive reforms. But if the *political* character of the state has departed significantly from the Indian norm, its *institutional* character—and in partic-ular its highly centralized and bureaucratic character—has not. Despite the strength of grassroots movements and institutions, state power has remained highly centralized and, until the Campaign in 1996, local government in Kerala was little more than an administrative extension of the state govern-ment. Given Kerala's sub-national status, this is hardly surprising. The Indian state—and Kerala as part of it—was born at the intersection of an imperial bureaucracy and Soviet-inspired visions of planned transformation, and deeply imbued with Nehruvian high modernism. In the hubris that marked the nationalist celebration of the state as designated agent of modernization and emancipation, top-down planning became the instrument of develop-ment of choice. As Kaviraj notes:

> By the mid-1950s such an over-rationalistic doctrine became a settled part of the ideology of planning and therefore of the Indian state. 'The state', or whoever could usurp this title for the time being, rather than the people themselves, was to be the initiator and, more dangerously, the evaluator of the development process. (1998: 62)

Without falling into the asocial and reductionist logic of public choice theory that sees a voracious, self-seeking predator in every bureaucrat and politician, the accumulation of such powers, exercised with little accountability from below, has inevitably produced interests and networks of privilege that have nothing to gain and everything to lose from a decentralization of power. The political solidity of this configuration finds its distributive logic in the rental havens that the dominant proprietary classes—including bureaucrats and politicians—have all carved out for themselves (Bardhan, 1984 and 1997).

In its demonstrated capacity to deliver social programs and its much higher degree of public accountability, the state in Kerala is a far cry from the proto-predatory states of northern India. But, as we have seen, the difference is more in the demand-side of the equation—pressure from social movements and a vocal civil society for state action—than the supply side, as the state in Kerala has not been spared the entrenchment and ossification of rent-seeking interests. The size and power of such interests, moreover, is in no small part a product of Kerala's redistributive project, and specifically the exponential growth of the service bureaucracy and the proliferation of (mostly unprofitable) public sector enterprises. The CPM, moreover, has always embraced "democratic centralism" and, with it, a fairly orthodox state-led and top-down vision of development.

To understand the CPM's present emphasis on decentralization, three developments have to be singled out. First, the party has come to recognize the limits of its electoral appeal, and in a context of competitive party politics has identified democratic decentralization—with its attendant principles of non-partisanship, de-bureaucratized government and sustainable development—as the key to appealing to new constituencies. Second, the embrace of decentralization marks a tacit recognition that the redistributive capacities of the developmental state have exhausted themselves. The broad-based social movements that saw the expansion of social citizenship have been weakened and increasingly replaced by more narrow and sectoral interests. The latter vested interests have become rent-seeking and a stumbling block for democratic reforms of the state structure. If a strong, centralized and interventionist state did secure many of the benefits associated with the Kerala model (high levels of social development, extensive public infrastructure, basic institutional reforms), the second-generation social development challenges Kerala faces (the quality, rather than the quantity of public services) call for a fundamentally different mode of governance. Third, despite a recent growth spurt, Kerala's continued economic problems—in particular the lack of dynamism in commodity-producing sectors—has underscored the failures of the dirigiste state, and has prompted the recognition for the need to develop more flexible and decentralized forms of state intervention, designed to nurture, rather than regulate and control economic activity. Finally, the most palpable and devastating blow to top-down development has come from the widely perceived deterioration of public services. In comparative terms, the quality of Kerala's public health and educational services remains decades ahead of any other Indian state. But by local standards, and specifically those of a literate and increasingly middle-class society, what is probably at worst only a marginal decline in the quality of provision has produced widespread public disaffection. Though blamed in large part on a non-performing bureaucracy, the deterioration of the public sector has also been explicitly tied to the commodifying logic of globalization (and specifically the explosion of private clinics and schools in Kerala) and the cost-cutting imperatives of neoliberalism. Faced with significant challenges to the sustainability of Kerala's social gains and the legitimacy crisis of an overly bureaucratized state beleaguered by vested interests, the CPM leadership embraced democratic decentralization in 1996 as a strategy for reinventing and reinvigorating the role of the public sector.

THE PEOPLE'S CAMPAIGN FOR DECENTRALIZED PLANNING

If the CPM's return to power in 1996 provided the critical opening for the transformation of the state, it is the State Planning Board that has formulated, designed and driven the Campaign. In doing so, it is important to highlight that the SPB has relied closely on a stock of practical knowledge, ideas and experiences drawn from twenty-five years of local-level experiments conducted by NGOs, most notably the Kerala Sastra Sahitya Parishad (KSSP)—the People's Science Movement. The KSSP, moreover, has played an active role at the grassroots level in implementing the Campaign. The focus of the rest of this chapter is on describing and evaluating the key institutions and processes of the Campaign and is informed primarily by the direct involvement of one of the authors—T. M. Thomas Isaac—who was a member of the SPB during the first five years of the Campaign and a long time activist in the KSSP, and research conducted by both authors.[6]

As an institutional reform program the Campaign was specifically designed to nurture and facilitate greater direct participation by citizens in decision-making and was predicated on two guiding principles. The first was that local government institutions should be transformed from simple delivery instruments for national and state schemes into fully fledged *governing institutions* with functional, financial, and administrative autonomy, and that devolution of functions and resources should be based on the principle of subsidiarity (what can best be done at the local level must be done there).[7]

The second principle was that traditional representative structures need to be complemented by more direct forms of democracy. Popular participation, it was argued, would make elected representatives *continuously*, rather than just periodically, accountable to citizens and would introduce more transparency into the functioning of the bureaucracy. Increasing levels of direct and informed participation required both mobilizing citizens and designing institutions that enable ordinary citizens to play an active role in the selection, design, and implementation of local development plans.

The campaign's designers also realized from the outset that the instrumentalities of the state would not be equal, either politically or practically, to the task of pushing through the necessary reforms. Given the inertia of existing institutions and the power of vested interests, legislation could never sustain such profound changes. The success of Kerala's land reforms in the 1970s—widely recognized as having been the most far-reaching and equity-enhancing in the sub-continent—was made possible by the backing of a powerful peasant movement. A highly successful mass literacy campaign in 1991 (in which the KSSP was actively involved) also pointed to the importance of mobilizing popular initiative. Building on these lessons, and the recognition that Kerala has an impressive reservoir of mobilizational capacity, the strategic emphasis from the outset was to conduct the reforms as a campaign.

In the next section we present a detailed discussion of the campaign's institutional design and how it has sought to reconcile the democratic objectives of extensive participation and effective deliberation with the need for technical competency and inter-level coordination in the formulation and implementation of development plans. The effectiveness of these mechanisms in achieving the objectives of democratic decentralization is critically evaluated in the last section.

Reversing the sequence of decentralization reforms

Democratic decentralization requires changes in administrative structures, in the allocation of functions and powers, and in the control of resources. All three are interrelated and to an extent need to be introduced simultaneously. In the technocratic model advocated by multilateral development agencies, decentralization is seen as an exercise in incremental institution-building informed primarily by public administration and managerial sciences.[8] Typically it is argued that certain sequenced preconditions, defined by a clear demarcation of functions among the various levels, must be met before genuine authoritative decision-making power can be successfully devolved: administrative support structures have to be created, new organizational procedures have to be put into place, government staff have to be redeployed, a new information base has to be developed, and new personnel—both voluntary and official—have to be trained. Most significantly, the devolution of financial resources has to be carefully calibrated to the absorptive capacity of the nascent institutions.

What is most problematic about this linear model of decentralization is the assumption that the task of transforming the very mode in which government works can be achieved through a prescribed process of introducing a discrete set of technically and managerially rational solutions. A largely frictionless and apolitical world is more or less taken for granted. But successful and sustainable democratic decentralization has been the exception to the rule, frustrated more often than not by bureaucratic inertia—most notably the resistance of powerful line departments—and vested political interests. Kerala certainly has its share of entrenched bureaucratic fiefdoms and political formations with a stake in the status quo. Yet, in the short history of the Campaign, devolution has already gone far beyond the issuance of laws and executive orders.

The most dramatic step has been the devolution since 1997–98 of between 35 and 40 per cent of the annual developmental budget to LSGIs—local self-governing institutions (*grama*, block and district *panchayats*, and municipalities).[9] During 1997–98 the total resources devolved (the "grant-in-aid") amounted to Rs.10,250 million and in 1998–99 Rs. 11,780 million, sums that do not include funds from centrally sponsored schemes and institutional loans to local governments.[10] Before 1996–97, LSGIs received on average a measly Rs 200 million in untied funds per year. There is little doubt that the administrative capacity and the management experience of the newly elected local government representatives was hardly up to the task of accommodating such a large-scale transfer. But devolving fiscal resources and control—even while the immense task of building a new regulatory environment and administrative capacity was only getting under way—has had two critical strategic effects. First, because local governments now enjoy significant budgetary discretion, local planning exercises have a tangible and immediate character. This, as we shall see, has invited high levels of participation. Second, shifting budgetary authority to lower levels has limited the ability of patronage politicians and top-down line departments to derail the process.

Planning as an instrument of social mobilization

The second distinctive feature of the decentralization experiment in Kerala is the central role accorded to the planning function of the LSGIs. As a statutory precondition for receiving the grant-in-aid from the government, LSGIs must prepare a comprehensive area plan. The planning process, as prescribed by the SPB, includes holding *grama sabhas* (ward-level assemblies), and convening sectoral task forces in which non-official experts and volunteers directly prepare reports, formulate projects, and draft sectoral plans. The various stages of plan preparation in effect represent new participatory spaces in which citizens, elected representatives and officials deliberate and prioritize developmental goals and projects.

In order to ensure transparency and participation without compromising the technical requirements of planning, the planning process is divided into discrete phases with distinct objectives, key activities, and associated training programs. Though modifications to the sequence have been made every year, the basic model that was inaugurated in 1997 (Table 13.1) remains the same.

A critical component of the Campaign has been an elaborate training program that has developed into one of the largest non-formal education programs ever undertaken in India. In the first year, in seven rounds of training at state, district and local level, some 15,000 elected representatives, 25,000 officials and 75,000 volunteers were given training. About 600 state level trainees—called Key Resource Persons (KRP)—received nearly 20 days of training. Some 12,000 district-level trainees—District Resource Persons (DRP)—received ten days of training and at the local level more than 100,000 persons received at least five days of training. All the elected representatives were expected to participate in the training program at one level or another. Each round of training focused on specific planning activities. Separate handbooks and guides, amounting to nearly 4,000 pages of documentation, were prepared and distributed for each round.

Building civic engagement

Following the seminal analysis of Putnam (1993) it is now widely accepted that a robust civil society—defined in terms of its "norms of reciprocity and networks of civic engagement" and embodied in different types of civic institutions—is critical to securing the effectiveness of democratic institutions. Putnam's understanding of the contribution that associational life can make to deepening democracy is however informed by an essentialist interpretation that construes civic-minded behavior as deeply engraved in culture and history. It is, as Skocpol and Fiorina (1999) have argued, a social-psychological view that leaves little room for the role of conflict in building democratic capacities. Critics have moreover pointed out that the forms of civic life that contribute to securing developmental goods (that is, social capital) are in fact politically constructed (Evans, 1996), and that associational life is in large part artifactual, the product of institutional environments, shifting social relations, and state interventions (Cohen and Rogers, 1995).

This mutability of civil society is fully illustrated in Kerala's contemporary history. If Kerala's long history of social mobilization has directly contributed to the vibrancy of its civil society, it has also indirectly contributed to developments that have eroded the capacity for civic action. Class-based redistributive conflicts had two notable effects. First, they polarized Kerala's political landscape between two highly mobilized left- and right-wing formations that systematically penetrated civil society organizations. Thus schools, cooperatives, shop floors, and local institutions have all

Table 13.1. DIFFERENT PHASES OF THE PEOPLE'S CAMPAIGN IN ITS INAUGURAL YEAR – 1997–98

Phase	Period	Objective	Activities	Mass participation
1. *Grama sabha*	August–October (1997)	Identify the "felt needs" of the people	*Grama sabha* in rural areas and ward conventions in urban areas	2 million persons attending *Grama sabhas*
2. Development Seminar	October–December (1997)	Assessment of the resources and problems of the area and formulation of a local development strategy	Participatory studies: Preparation of development reports, organization of development	300,000 delegates attending seminars
3. Task forces	November 1997–March 1998	Preparation of projects	Meetings of task forces	100,000 volunteers in task forces
4. Plans of grassroots tiers – municipalities and *panchayats*	March–June (1998)	Formulation of plan of grassroots tiers	Plan formulation and meetings of elected representatives	25,000 volunteers in formulation of plan document
5. Plans of higher tiers – blocks and districts	April–July (1998)	Formulation of plans of higher tiers	Plan formulation meeting of elected representatives	5,000 volunteers in formulation of plan documents
6. Volunteer technical Corps	May–October (1998)	Appraisal and approval of plans	Meetings of Expert Committee	5,000 volunteer technical experts working in the Appraisal Committees

become the object of fierce political competition. With this systematic politicization of civil society it has become increasingly difficult to separate the provision of public services and goods from narrow political-organizational imperatives. Second, redistributive demands saw the expansion of the size and role of the state, and the growth of bureaucratic structures. Although large-scale interventions in education, health, and social protection directly contributed to Kerala's social development, the growth of the bureaucracy has severely circumscribed the scope for civil society initiative. Because the bureaucratic development process is top-heavy and more responsive to highly organized rent-seeking interests than popular forces, ordinary citizens retain an interest in government programs only inasmuch as narrow, individual returns are concerned. The politics of pork have increasingly replaced the politics of community improvement, and Kerala's strong traditions of popular grassroots development action have eroded over time.

The impetus behind the launching of the Campaign stems directly from a critique of the corrosive effects of these developments. On the one hand there is a recognition that a centralized, command-and-control state is no longer capable of driving Kerala's development and that new forms of state and public action are called for. Thus the supporters of the Campaign have been very vocal in arguing that the existing political climate of sectarian and partisan division has become an obstacle to development and that a key objective of the Campaign—much as in the case of popular budgeting in Porto Alegre—is to break the hold of clientelistic politics. On the other hand there is the recognition that civil society initiatives must be afforded more avenues and opportunities for effective engagement with public authorities.

In conceptualizing planning as an instrument of social mobilization, the Campaign has sought to deepen democracy along three different axes. First, devolving planning and authoritative decision-making to local arenas allows for a more integrated approach to development that directly challenges the hold of hierarchical line departments and their extensive powers of control. Second, by providing visible and substantive incentives for participation, and by emphasizing deliberative processes, local development planning holds the possibility of reinvigorating civic action and loosening the grip of patronage and partisan politics. Third, by fundamentally transforming the mode and channels of decision-making, the Campaign has created new political configurations and public policy networks. Thus elected local representatives whose functions were previously mostly ceremonial have now been brought directly into positions of authoritative decision-making, including authority over local officials. Similarly, NGOs and community-based organizations (CBOs) have been offered new opportunities for engaging directly in development and there has been a concerted effort to create new linkages between professionals and academic institutions and communities in order to bring expertise (especially during a transitional phase in which the bureaucracy has been less than cooperative) to the grassroots. This later development in many respects parallels the dynamic blurring of state–society relations marked by the emergence of new associational networks that Chalmers *et al.* (1997) have identified as the defining characteristic of revitalized civil societies in Latin America.

In short, the objective of the People's Campaign for Decentralized Planning has not been simply to draw up a plan from below. The very process of planning has been conceived as a means to fundamentally transform the character and scope of participation and the nature of interest mediation. Such a transformation cannot be secured through government directives alone. It requires the creativity and the social logic of a movement (Isaac, 1999a).

Institutionalization

One of the greatest challenges of promoting participatory democracy is to develop institutional forms that are sufficiently robust as to withstand efforts by traditional interest groups to either subvert or circumvent deliberative processes. In Kerala's highly volatile political climate, in which the two political fronts have historically more or less alternated in power, this problem is particularly acute. Governments formed by the Congress Party have a track record of reversing decentralization reforms, most notably by packing newly created local institutions with political appointees.

The Campaign addressed the challenge of institutionalization by generating as much popular involvement as possible. High levels of participation wielded significant payoffs as some Congress-aligned parties—and most interestingly the conservative Muslim League—expressed their support for the Campaign. The campaign's localized planning structures have moreover created spaces in which new political alliances and commitments have been forged. By replacing the conventional systems of vertical accountability to political parties and bureaucracies with more horizontal forms of cooperation and autonomous sources of authority, the campaign's locally integrated planning structures have provided local politicians and officials with a direct stake in the new system. Political uncertainty has also underscored the need to institutionalize the Campaign in formal terms, that is, through the passage of appropriate legislation. Thus the LDF government comprehensively amended the existing Kerala Panchayathi Raj Act of 1994 and the Kerala Municipality Act of 1994 with the effect of securing the autonomy of LSGIs and mandating the presentation of local plans and budgets to Grama Sabhas. New laws concerning the transparency of administration and access to information have also been passed. Moreover, hundreds of government orders creating new accounting systems, devolving authority to local officials and establishing new procedures for reporting have engraved many of the campaigns design features into the everyday workings of government.

In May 2001, in keeping with a pattern of defeat of incumbent parties that has long been the norm in Kerala, the LDF was ousted from power by a Congress Party-led coalition. Most observers concur that the CPM's defeat was not a judgment about the Campaign.[11] When this article was written (November 2001), it was still too early to evaluate what impact the change in government would have on the Campaign. In contrast to 1991, when the UDF returned to power and immediately scuttled a much less ambitious experiment in decentralization (one that had focused on the district level) the new government has declared its commitment to the Campaign and to redressing its weaknesses. Two factors have pre-empted a frontal assault on the Campaign. One is the popularity of the Campaign at the grassroots level, which cuts across the political divide. The Campaign had succeeded in building a bi-partisan coalition at the grassroots level in favor of decentralization, and any efforts to erode the autonomy and authority of LSGIs will be difficult, not only because it would require significant legislative efforts, but also because such efforts would alienate the Congress party's own rank and file, who in coalition with other parties control roughly half the LSGIs in the state. The second is the prestige that the Campaign had gained in the national and international circles. In addition to significant media attention, the Campaign has attracted the attention of officials from other Indian states and even figured in the remarks made by the president of India in his last independence-day national address.

PARTICIPATORY PLAN FORMULATION AND IMPLEMENTATION

Planning in India has historically been a highly insulated and top-down affair. The official literature on decentralized planning in India has generally been skeptical of direct mass participation in the planning process (Government of India, 1969, 1978 and 1984). District-level plans generally have been formulated by designated experts after what have been at best perfunctory consultations with selected stakeholders. By the early 1980s, some form of district planning machinery existed in most of the states, and the planning process was described by the Report of the Working Group on District Planning (Government of India, 1984) as follows:

> Usually, after the state budget is voted in the assembly, the different heads of departments are requested to make a district-wise break up of the outlays provided in the plan budget. This is then communicated to the districts, either by sectoral departments or by the planning department of the state. This usually takes four-five months after the commencement of the financial year. After this communication is received, the district attempts to incorporate a write up for the district-wise outlay and a document called

'district plan' emerges in this manner, which is *purely an aggregation of departmental schemes.* (our emphasis)

Under the Campaign, the planning process begins at the lowest level of democratic representation, the *grama panchayats* and municipalities. It is only once these local governments have prepared their plans that block- and district-level *panchayats* come into play, and then only to ensure regional coordination. There are 990 *grama panchayats,* 58 municipalities,[12] 152 blocks and 14 districts in Kerala. The councils for each of these levels of local government are directly elected on a first-past-the-post constituency system. At the block and district levels, the democratic character of planning is ensured through the involvement of elected officials and a range of citizen committees. At the municipal and *grama panchayat* level, the planning process is driven by direct mass participation.

Autonomous decision-making power was granted to local governments by providing untied funds ("grants-in-aid"). The heavy hand of bureaucratic traditions has been blunted by ensuring continuous, mass, non-official participation in every phase of plan preparation and implementation. In building continuous deliberative structures, the Campaign has had to tackle two micro-level design challenges. The first has been to create institutional forms that can correct for the asymmetries of power among local agents. The second has been to make local participation *effective* by allowing space for grassroots intervention and deliberation without compromising the technical and economic requirements of planning.

The *Grama Sabhas*

Grama sabhas, the assemblies of ward- or *panchayat*-based residents, represent the key deliberative moment in the planning process. By law they had to be held at least two times during the initial years of the Campaign, and in later years, after amendments to the law, four times a year. The first *grama sabha* serves as an open forum in which residents identify local development problems, generate priorities and form sub-sector development seminars in which specific proposals first take shape. In the second *grama sabha,* the plans approved by the elected *panchayat* council are presented to the public and departures from the original *grama sabha* proposals are explained. Beneficiaries for projects are also selected at the *grama sabhas.*

Rousseau notwithstanding, there is nothing spontaneously democratic about a general assembly, especially in a society as inflected with complex and durable inequalities as India's. The commitment of the campaign's architects and activists to building deliberative institutions is reflected in the time and energy that has been devoted to finding practical solutions to the problems of large meetings. An obvious innovation, but one that nevertheless required significant organizational effort, was to adopt a small group approach. In each *grama sabha*, after an introductory general body meeting (usually of several hundred people), participants are divided into smaller groups, each dealing with a particular development sector, to discuss issues and problems in depth. This small-group arrangement made it possible for ordinary people, particularly women, to be able to participate in the discussions. A second innovation was to provide a semi-formal discussion format and a trained facilitator for each group. Working with a basic template of questions and useful planning concepts, the role of the locally recruited facilitator is to encourage participants to list and analyze local problems based upon their real-life experiences.

Local information gathering

Asymmetries of information are a key source of domination in nominally deliberative institutions. Even in Kerala's social climate of highly politicized and highly literate citizens,[13] durable social and status inequalities and the hoarding of official expertise by state institutions has severely skewed access to useful information. Moreover, though available planning data are a source of significant power, they are anything but accurate or properly adapted to the requirements of local development. Taking much of its inspiration from the KSSP—which since its founding in 1962 has been dedicated to "bringing science to the people"—the Campaign has taken local information gathering as a first critical step in the planning process.

After a first round of *grama sabhas*, *panchayats* in the first year of the Campaign were required to make a formal assessment of the natural and human resources of the locality. The idea was to promote effective integration of planning and resource optimization by actually comparing expressed needs with local assets. With assistance from specially trained resource persons and using techniques developed by the Campaign, a series of participatory studies were undertaken in every *grama panchayat* and municipality. These included the collection and organization of data available in various local-level offices, the identification and mapping of local eco-zones using a rapid appraisal technique, a review of ongoing schemes to be prepared by each local department, a social audit, and a review of local history. By and large, departments refused to cooperate, and this had serious consequences for integrating existing schemes into the new plans. The quality of the data of course varied dramatically from one locality to the other, but the exercise itself had the important effect of helping individuals develop useful skills and of tapping into, and formally incorporating, local knowledge.

Development reports and seminars

The outcome of the data collection exercises was a "development report" prepared according to guidelines set down by the SPB. With a five-year strategic outlook, the reports serve as the basis of the annual planning exercise. Running on average to 75–100 pages, the reports provide a comprehensive overview of local development and include a chapter on local social history intended to underscore the role that social mobilization can play in meeting contemporary development challenges. The body of the reports consists of twelve chapters assessing the current status of each sector, a review of ongoing schemes and problems and a list of recommendations.

Because the recommendations of the development report can differ from the demands raised in the *grama sabhas* and because demands from different wards had to be integrated into an area-wide perspective, the reports were submitted to development seminars. The majority of delegates to the seminars were elected from the subject groups of the *grama sabhas* with, in principle, equal representation for men and women. Local-level government officials from the relevant departments were asked to participate, as were any experts invited by the *panchayat* executive committee. On average, development seminars had 231 delegates, with officials accounting for 13.8 per cent, SC/STs (scheduled castes and scheduled tribes—the official designation for erstwhile "untouchables" and tribal groups) for 10.5 per cent and women for only 22.1 per cent.[14] Extensive preparation went into the organization of the seminars, including the distribution of the development report to all delegates and widespread publicity in the form of leaflets, festivals, *jathas* (marches) and exhibitions. The seminars were given a very high profile, with a member of the legislative assembly or a state minister inaugurating 50 per cent of the seminars. A major proportion of the seminar time was devoted to sector-wise group discussions in order to facilitate in-depth analysis of the development reports and propose amendments. The recommendations of the different groups were then presented to a plenary session and adopted.

Task forces and preparation of projects

At the conclusion of the development seminars in the first year of the Campaign, task forces of around ten persons each were constituted to prepare the project proposals on the basis of the recommendations of the seminar (in subsequent years, task forces became the starting point of the planning process with development seminars being convened at a later stage to review the work of task forces). A key challenge in building participatory institutions is to ensure that experts, rather than simply deliberating amongst themselves, must engage in direct deliberation with citizens (Fung and

Wright, 2002). The work of task forces in fact goes beyond simply leveling the playing field by in fact guaranteeing that the process of project design is informed by experts, but led by citizens. Development seminars form a total of twelve task forces, one for each development sector. The delegates selected from the development seminars are ordinary citizens, though many have undergone specialized training through the Campaign. The chairperson of the task force is an elected ward councilor. This ensures that the work of the task force will be directly linked and supported in subsequent deliberations of the *panchayat* or municipal council. In order to secure the relevant expertise as well as coordination with state structures, the convenor of the task force is an officer from the concerned line department.

The sustainability of a participatory institution is in large part determined by its demonstrated capacity for effective problem-solving. In order to ensure a degree of quality control and effective monitoring, task forces are required to prepare detailed project proposals in accordance with a set of criteria and standards established by the SPB. Thus all project proposals must include a definition of objectives (as far as possible in quantitative/measurable terms), criteria for beneficiaries or areas, a time frame, an organizational overview of the role of implementing agencies, a financial analysis including identification of funding sources, a social and environmental impact review and details of the proposed monitoring mechanisms.

Plan documents and coordination

The fourth and final stage of the local planning process is marked by the prioritization and integration of the projects prepared by the various task into a single *panchayat* or plan document. The final form of the local plan is the legal prerogative of the elected council that must formally vote on the plan. There are, however, a number of formal and informal mechanisms that ensure that elected representatives abide by the recommendations and projects generated by the various participatory processes. Formally, the approved plan must conform to a detailed reporting format that lays out the general strategy and objectives of the plan as well as sectoral and redistributive criteria. Authorized projects must be specifically linked to the strategic statement and the full text of the proposed project must be listed in a separate appendix. This process not only guarantees accountability, but its sheer complexity ensures that the council—which has limited administrative support—has no practical alternative to building on the work of the task forces. The fact that ward councilors participate actively at every level of the participatory process, from attendance at *grama sabhas* and training seminars to chairing the task forces, also ensures integration between the participatory processes and the council's final deliberations. Finally, the entire process of beneficiary selection, which is of course especially vulnerable to political abuse, is, as we shall see, the subject of an entirely separate process of regulated transparency and participation.

Since the beginning of the Campaign, plan allocations have been separately indicated in the state budget, with broad guidelines regarding sectoral allocations to be made by the local body. These guidelines are both of a functional (sectoral) and redistributive character and are designed to coordinate and integrate local allocations with statewide objectives. In order, for example, to shift public investments away from Kerala's traditional strengths in social services and infrastructure, the SPB mandates that 40–50 per cent of plan allocations must be directed to the productive sector. On the redistributive front, local governments are required to spend not less than 10 per cent on projects targeted to women, and in proportion to their local population for Scheduled Castes and Scheduled Tribes.

Block and district *panchayats* start the preparation of their annual plans only after *grama panchayats* have drafted their plans. The sequential ordering is intended to ensure that the plans of the various tiers are integrated and the plans of the higher tiers complement, rather than duplicate, those of the lower tiers. A matrix-based analytical tool has been developed to assist blocks and districts in integrating the analysis and programs of the *grama panchayats* into their own plans. Blocks have also been tasked with integrating into their plans the different centrally sponsored poverty alleviation schemes that have traditionally been implemented at the block level. There has been strong resistance to this move from both bureaucrats and elected representatives. In part this is due to genuine problems arising from the existence of separate guidelines for centrally sponsored programs, but it is mostly a reaction to the prospect of losing significant decision-making powers.

In the first year of the Campaign, a sample review of the projects prepared by the local bodies revealed that a significant proportion of them had to be modified to ensure their technical soundness and viability before they could be approved for implementation.

In all, more than a hundred thousand projects had to be evaluated. The evaluation was not for selection or rejection of the projects, but to rectify the technical and financial weaknesses in the project proposals. This monumental task had to be undertaken within a span of three to four months. The official machinery was neither capable nor willing to cope with the task.

The SPB responded to this problem by launching the Voluntary Technical Corps (VTC). Retired technical experts and professionals were encouraged to volunteer their skills for appraising the projects and plans of the local bodies. A professional or postgraduate degree or officer-level experience in a development sector was specified as the minimum qualification for membership in the VTC. A volunteer expert committed herself/himself to spending at least one day a week giving technical assistance to the *panchayats*. District-level conventions were arranged for the experts who formally offered to join the VTC. More than four thousand technical experts enrolled in the VTC. Expert committees that included a government official were then formed at the various local government levels.

The expert committees act both as advisory arms of the District Planning Committees, helping the latter to appraise the plans and projects, and as advisory committees to local planners. The committees are not empowered to modify priorities set by the local bodies. Their tasks are carefully limited to providing technical and financial advice and appraisal of projects, and to suggesting modifications where necessary. The District Planning Committees approve plans on the recommendations of the expert committees. The formation of expert committees in the course of the campaign's first year was an important organizational innovation that helped to de-bureaucratize the project appraisal and technical sanction procedures. Without this mobilization of extra-bureaucratic expertise these tasks would have bogged down in the line departments through inertia and outright resistance. Not surprisingly, these committees have been the subject of much public debate fuelled in particular by claims that the committees are a partisan attempt to create parallel structures to elected bodies.

Financial procedures

In Kerala's traditional system of development planning the decision-making process was the arbitrary and patronage-driven domain of elected representatives and implementation was the prerogative of the bureaucracy. A key rationale for making the decision-making process more participatory is to ensure the involvement of the beneficiaries and the public at large in the implementation phase. As Fung and Wright note, "direct participation of grassroots operators increases accountability and reduces the length of the chain of agency that accompanies political parties and their bureaucratic apparatus" (2002). Popular involvement increases problem-solving efficiency through better and more rapid feedback and increases accountability by multiplying the points of scrutiny. The Campaign has evolved a wide range of new *fora* and rules to maximize participation and transparency.

The Campaign's financial procedures for regulating the flow of grant-in-aid funds to local bodies and to specific projects has been designed to maximize effective monitoring. To begin with, because the various officers transferred to *grama panchayats* are now directly responsible to the elected council, they can be held more directly responsible for financial flows. Financial allotments to local bodies are released in four installments. All funds must be specifically tied to an approved *panchayat* project or state scheme, and held in special accounts that are managed by the implementing officer. Actual disbursement of funds requires co-authorization from the head of the elected body.

The creation of democratically accountable beneficiary committees has also been an important innovation. Instead of implementing public works through contractors, local bodies are encouraged to form committees of project beneficiaries to undertake the task. The idea here is to break the ties of collusion between contractors, politicians, and government engineers that have historically been the most important sources of corruption. Doing so, however, requires creating beneficiaries committees that are sufficiently autonomous and empowered to resist capture by rent-seeking interests. A key step was to shift effective authority for the technical sanction of projects from department officials to block/municipal- and district-level expert committees. Department officials are the convenors of the subject committees and continue to formally grant technical sanction. However, they now make decisions in their capacity as members of a committee of peers rather than as officials in a departmental hierarchy. A second procedural innovation has been to shift responsibility for examining finished work and authorizing payment from official to non-official engineering experts from the Voluntary Technical Corps.

Beneficiary selection

A major change introduced by the Campaign was in the procedure for selecting beneficiaries for development projects. In the past, beneficiary selection has been little more than a concerted exercise in patronage that has more or less enjoyed the tacit collusion of all political parties. Campaign rules call for *grama panchayats* to extensively publicize the criteria for beneficiary eligibility and prioritization. Notices listing the projects and the criteria have to be prominently displayed in public places as well as printed and circulated. Applications must be printed in the Malayalam language and made freely available. The rules also provide for a system for verifying statements made in the applications. Verification can be conducted by designated officers or by a committee appointed by the *panchayat*. Finally, the list of applicants must be presented to the *grama sabha* with sector subject groups tasked with processing applications. *Grama sabhas*, moreover, are authorized to include sub-criteria for prioritization.

The responsibility for consolidating and finalizing the priority list of beneficiaries received from each *grama sabha* rests with the *panchayat*. The final priority list has to be created on the basis of clearly stated norms. In no case can the relative priorities from each ward be overturned during the process of consolidation. Members of the public and the local press can attend the proceedings of this final selection. The draft list must be exhibited prominently. All public objections must be given consideration and reasons for rejection stated.

CRITICALLY ASSESSING THE CAMPAIGN

So far we have discussed the procedural and institutional design of the Campaign in its ideal type. But how have these new structures actually worked on the ground? Most critically, how deliberative has the planning process been, and to what degree have the activities of decentralized units been effectively coordinated with technical inputs and integrated with higher levels of planning? Given the sheer complexity and scale of the project, the inevitable teething problems, and the absence of cumulative data, it is still too early to pass a definitive judgment. The institutional learning that has already taken place does however hold some important lessons for our understanding of participatory democracy, and the emergence of some fairly transparent and robust trends does allow for some tentative assessments.

Financial resources

As we noted in the introductory section, it was the decision in 1996 to earmark 35 to 40 per cent of the plan funds for the local self-governments that kick-started the Campaign. The most important achievement of the Campaign to date has been sustaining the political will to maintain and even increase the scale of devolution in subsequent years, and this despite very severe financial constraints faced by the state government. Local governments, in other words, have enjoyed a continuous and substantial flow of financial resources.

If the scale of resource devolution has been maintained, its redistributive character has improved significantly. In the first year financial devolution was based on a straight per capita formula that did not take levels of inter-regional poverty and development into account. What was lost in policy was, however, gained in politics. This bland formula had the advantage of being beyond political manipulation and as such was not open to criticism by the opposition of partisanship. Moreover, the formula did effectively correct for the highly skewed patterns of patronage-driven allocation of the past (in which underdeveloped northern Kerala was inevitably short-changed) and as such did have a *de facto* redistributive effect. In subsequent years, the devolution formula has progressively incorporated new indices of poverty and underdevelopment.

Plan formulation

That for the first time in India *grama panchayats* and municipalities throughout an entire state have prepared local area plans is a milestone in and of itself. Given the sheer enormity of the task and the lack of local experience and capacity, plan preparation in the first year ran six months over schedule.

The dramatic returns of learning-by-doing are, however, reflected in the steady reduction in the time overruns that have marked each subsequent planning year.

A major objective of decentralized planning has been to match local needs and potential to actual public expenditure patterns. A rationalization of resource allocation based on more direct, informed and deliberated inputs into the decision-making process represents one of two critical efficiency gains associated with decentralized planning (the other being the increase in accountability). Because of the empirical difficulties of comparing pre- and post-Campaign expenditures patterns (there are no sub-district figures available for the pre-campaign period) a definitive assessment will have to await more intensive research efforts. Three important general trends can however already be highlighted. First, the investment priorities in the plans prepared by the local bodies differ significantly from the investment priorities in the district plans that were formulated from above before decentralization. Much greater priority is now accorded for basic needs such as housing, drinking water and sanitation by the local bodies. In the productive sectors there has been a discernible shift toward animal husbandry, garden crops, and minor irrigation. Both these shifts have significant redistributive implications. Second, in contrast to past patterns, the investment priorities in the special plans prepared for Scheduled Castes and Tribals differed significantly from the overall investment patterns. This points to an effort to take the weak income, asset and skill position of these marginalized communities into account. Third, in contrast to the one-size-fits-all logic of the past, there are significant inter-regional differences in the investment priorities of the local bodies.

The most glaring weakness of the plan preparation in the first year was the quality of the proposed projects. Many of the projects proved to be little more than modified versions of standardized department schemes. There was often little consideration of forward and backward linkages and fully integrated plans were actually rare. The reflex to mechanically allocate funds on a ward basis proved tenacious, particularly among the higher tiers (blocks and districts). Beginning with the second year, measures were adopted to improve the quality of projects and programs. The most important measure has been to introduce subject-specific training programs for task-force members. In the second year the training program consisted of a series of locally organized stopgap measures that produced limited results. In the third year the training program was upgraded and formalized into a state-wide program that is linked to specialized institutions such as the Kerala Agricultural University, the Institute of Management in Government, the KSSP's Integrated Rural Technology Centre, COSTFORD (a low-cost housing NGO training institute), and a few other NGOs involved in watershed management. These specialized training programs, coupled with the greater involvement of VTC members in the task forces, should help improve the quality of project design.

In addition to technical deficiencies, the planning process also suffered from inter-level coordination problems. Effective decentralized planning must by definition be integrated. This is critical not only to optimizing resource allocation, reducing duplication and ensuring sustainability, but also for capturing and diffusing the innovations generated in decentralized units. The comparative advantage of "decentralized coordination" lies in increasing the "learning capacity of the system as a whole by combining decentralized empowered deliberation and centralized coordination and feedback" (Fung and Wright, 2002). This has been one of the most daunting challenges faced by the Campaign.

In the first year a number of factors contributed to weak coordination between the plans of the different tiers of local bodies and that of the state government. Though planning procedures prescribed by the SPB called for higher tiers to take the priorities and programs of lower tiers into account, in actual practice there was little coordination in the first year (in no small part because of a shortage of time). More detailed guidelines were issued in the second year, but problems persisted. In the third year the format and logic of district-level planning was significantly overhauled. More emphasis was given to the district's role in 1) providing a macro perspective for sustainable development of the district, 2) improving integration by consolidating lower level plans and identifying gaps and duplications, and 3) providing a long-term strategic vision for future annual plans.

Physical achievements

A major criticism of the Campaign is that all the attention to process and participation has come at the expense of actual delivery as measured by physical achievements (the process–product trade-off). The logic of this criticism is misplaced inasmuch as it fails to recognize that the quality of participation is an important objective in its own right. To focus on financial targets and expenditures, as many of the campaign's critics have done, reflects a narrow technocratic understanding of development. But even if the building of participatory institutions can be justified on the grounds of extending citizenship alone, their long-term viability, especially under the circumstances of the liberalization of the national economy, will rely on the capacity to provide tangible developmental goods.

At this stage an accurate appraisal of physical achievements is complicated by practical problems of monitoring and aggregating existing data. Physical results, particularly in productive sectors such as industry and agriculture, will take time to materialize. And even in the case of social and infrastructural sectors, the task of actually measuring the quality of project implementation is virtually impossible given the absence of a local data gath-ering system.[15]

The most readily measured physical achievements of the first two years of decentralized planning are, however, impressive. In the two years from 1997 to 1999, 98,494 houses have been built, 240,307 sanitary latrines con-structed, 50,162 wells dug, 17,489 public taps provided, and 16,563 ponds cleaned. A total of 2,800,179 individual beneficiaries received support from the plan for seedlings and fertilizers. And the 8,000 km of roads that were built far surpassed past achievements.[16]

Because the pace of delivery has in fact surpassed expectations, the state government has taken steps to encourage institutional financial loans to the local bodies to provide further resources. And for the first time in Kerala (or for any state in India), the government has actually set a target date (2003) for delivering shelter, sanitary latrines and drinking water (within 200 meters) to all households in the state. The universalization of pre-primary education, improvement in the quality of education and health care centers, and completion of rural electrification are also on the mid-term strategic agenda. Tangible achievements in the above sectors in the imme-diate future could play a critical role in sustaining and stabilizing the process of democratic decentralization.

Quality of deliberation

The Campaign has created numerous opportunities for ordinary citizens to actively participate in the different phases of plan formulation and imple-mentation. But how many citizens have made use of these opportunities? Were the discussions manipulated by locally dominant groups? Were the dif-ferent forums merely a means to legitimize decisions made by the elites?

Every ordinary citizen irrespective of his/her membership in political or non-political social formations has the right and opportunity to intervene in the planning process by participating in the *grama sabhas*. One of the greatest achievements of the Campaign has been to demonstrate that popular assemblies can function effectively. In the year before the Campaign, *grama sabhas* were called after the formation of the new local bodies, but a majority failed to actually convene. In the first *grama sabhas* of the Campaign in August–September 1996, over 2 million people participated, with an average of 180 persons per *grama sabha*, representing 11.4 per cent of the voting pop-ulation and roughly one of every four households. Though participation rates have dropped slightly in subsequent years (possibly because the number of annual *grama sabhas* was increased from two to four), these popular assem-blies have become an essential feature of Kerala's political landscape.

There are, however, significant limitations to the deliberative character of *grama sabhas*. To begin with, they are obviously still too large and unwieldy for meaningful deliberation, the small group approach notwithstanding. Because of Kerala's dispersed settlement pattern, *grama sabhas* participants must travel significant distances and meetings cannot run more than two to three hours. This does not allow for serious discussion of the large number of complex issues that are normally included in the agenda of the *grama sabha*.[17] Participation across socio-economic groups has been uneven. By all accounts middle-class participation has been low, and most participants have been from lower classes that are the targeted beneficiaries of most development projects. In the first year the participation of Scheduled Castes and Scheduled Tribes was below their population share, and women constituted a disappointing 25 per cent. In subsequent years the percentages have increased, but participation remains uneven.

The formation of Neighborhood Groups (NHGs), consisting of 40 to 50 families, has been a response from below—often initiated by KSSP activists— to the limitations of the *grama sabhas*. Though not formally required, NHGs have been formed in around 200 *panchayats*. A study found that in 100 *panchayats* (Isaac, 1999c) NHGs function as mini-*grama sabhas*, discussing local issues and priorities, reviewing plan implementation and selecting beneficiaries. NHG representatives often constitute a ward committee that in many cases becomes the *de facto* executive committee of the *grama sabhas*. NHGs have also taken up other activities such as conflict resolution, after-school educational programs, health clinics, cultural activities, savings schemes, and project implementation. There is currently a campaign being led by the KSSP to extend NHGs to the entire state and to institutionalize what is in effect a new layer of grassroots democracy. The crowding-in effect that the Campaign appears to be having on associational life in Kerala is also evidenced in the proliferation of a variety of self-help groups, particularly women's micro-credit schemes (Seema and Mukherjee, 2000; Manjula, 2000).

Corruption and nepotism

One of the most important criticisms of decentralization is that it often does little more than devolve corruption. Indeed, funneling substantial funds without proper safeguards to localities will inevitably fuel rent-seeking behavior, and possibly even community conflict. The media and opposition parties in Kerala have raised serious allegations of nepotism in beneficiary selection and corruption in the implementation of projects. Of the nearly 30,000 beneficiary committees it has been alleged that a substantial number are led by nominees of contractors (so-called *benami* committees). State investigating agencies have also pointed to widespread irregularities in the first year's plan implementation (Isaac, 1999d).

In its own evaluation the State Planning Board concluded that irregularities during the first annual plan resulted more from inexperience and haste than corruption. For example, when the local bodies in the first year found it difficult to absorb and properly distribute funds, many transferred the funds to non-plan accounts or deposited the money with government or quasi-Government agencies such as electricity boards or the Kerala Water Authority in order to claim full utilization before the spending deadline. Even though regulations were bent and even broken, there was little leakage as such. Irregular expenditures that were identified by the government were disallowed and with the new rules put in place in subsequent years, such improprieties have declined sharply.

There is little doubt that many beneficiary committees have fallen prey to vested interests. But there is also little doubt that the traditional corruption nexus between contractor, engineer, and politician has been decisively broken in a large number of local bodies. For example, in the district of Kannur—a CPM stronghold—an investigation revealed that beneficiary committees have been carefully constituted and run according to the campaign's criteria of transparency and democratic accountability. Strengthening the capacity and accountability of beneficiary committees remains one of the most important priorities of the Campaign, and a number of important reforms have already been introduced.[18] But even if there has been and continues to be some leakage of funds due to the capture or manipulation of beneficiary committees by vested interests, most observers agree that the multiplication of checks and balances and the increased scrutiny associated with citizen participation represents a dramatic improvement of the systematic and routinized plunder that characterized the traditional system.

With respect to the process of selecting beneficiaries, the returns on institutional fine-tuning and increased community experience have been visible. During the first year complaints about the selection process were registered in a majority of local bodies. The volume of registered complaints is in itself indicative of the increased transparency of the system. The traditional system was entirely based on patronage. Complaints were rare simply because the information was accessible only to the patrons and their clients. The rules for beneficiary selection have been modified in every year of the Campaign and by the third year less than a fifth of *panchayats* were registering complaints.

Promoting equity

As much as the Campaign has been concerned with the efficacy of deliberative institutions, it has also, in keeping with Kerala's long history of redistributive struggles, promoted the strategic goal of building equitable forms of participation and reducing substantive inequality. Gender justice in particular has been declared to be one of the major objectives of the

Campaign. We have already noted efforts to increase participation of women in *grama sabhas*, and the extension of Neighborhood Groups and Self-Help organizations are clearly strengthening the associational capacities of women. Two other important strategies have been efforts to build on the constitutional provision for one-third reserved representation of women in LSGIs and the introduction of a special Women Component Plan amounting to 10 per cent of the plan outlay. What has been the experience so far?

The Kerala experience to date certainly bears out the importance of affirmative action ("reservations" in the Indian context) in representative structures and indeed suggests that the principle should be extended to higher levels of government. But affirmative action alone is insufficient. An in-depth study of elected representatives in Kerala revealed that while elected women representatives are better educated than their male counterparts (a social fact that is unique to Kerala in the Indian context), the women were on average younger, much less politically experienced, and inadequately equipped with a basic knowledge of rules, regulations, and administrative issues. Moreover, women representatives have had to bear a triple burden of public office, income-earning activities, and domestic duties. From its outset, the Campaign has run an in-depth and continuous capacity-building program targeted to women representatives. The training program, which has evolved significantly to adapt to new challenges, has yielded impressive results. A self-assessment survey of elected women representatives shows that their administrative knowledge and management skills, as well as their ability to officiate at public functions and interact effectively with their constituencies have improved very significantly over the last three years (Isaac *et al.*, 1999).

The Women Component Plan (WCP) for the first year did not meet campaign targets, in terms of both overall allocation and the relevance of projects. An obvious factor here was the insufficient representation of women among trained resource persons. This problem has been directly addressed in subsequent rounds of training. As women activists and representatives have started to play a more proactive and informed role in the Campaign, the effectiveness, content and scope of the WCP has improved. First, more than the statutory minimum requirement of 10 per cent of the plan's grant-in-aid was earmarked for WCP in all districts. Second, an undue emphasis on credit and beneficiary contribution in women development projects was reduced and more realistic patterns of project financing were adopted during the second year. Third, the quality of projects improved. The tendency to include the general sector projects in WCP on the basis of notional (indirect) benefits to women has declined and the number of projects that specifically address the gender status of women has significantly increased.

The fear that the interests of Scheduled Castes and Scheduled Tribes are more readily subverted at the local level, where severe caste inequality persists, has often been raised by SC/ST leaders. How have SC/STs fared under decentralized planning in Kerala so far?

The Special Component Plan (SCP) and Tribal Sub Plan (TSP) in Kerala have been formulated and implemented in a decentralized manner since the mid-1980s. But this decentralization has been purely bureaucratic and has lacked real participation by any elected representatives, let alone members of the community. Under the Campaign, 75 to 80 per cent of the SCP and TSP funds were devolved to LSGIs—that is, almost entirely taken out of the hands of the state bureaucracy.

The first visible impact of decentralized planning has been a significant increase in the funds actually earmarked and spent for Scheduled Castes and Scheduled Tribes. Careful disaggregation shows that a substantial part of SCP and TSP have always been calculated on the basis of notional flows, that is, by including general schemes that encompass, rather than target, SC and ST communities. The Campaign entirely abolished this system of calculation. As a result, the SPB estimates that real resources for the weaker sections have increased by 30 to 40 per cent as compared to the pre-Campaign period. The SPB plan appraisal also revealed that fears that local bodies would divert funds were misplaced: except in rare instances, local bodies have fully accounted for grant-in-aid from SCP and TSP. And even though it was permissible to allocate up to 30 per cent of the grant-in-aid from SCP and TSP for infrastructure projects such as roads and bridges, actual expenditure under this heading was less than 20 per cent. The emphasis was on projects that could be specifically targeted for individual beneficiaries from SC and ST communities such as housing, latrines, and income-producing animals. It was also later made mandatory that special assemblies of tribal populations had to be convened to discuss and approve the tribal sub-plan. An educated local youth from every tribal hamlet was selected, trained and paid an honorarium to ensure more effective tribal participation in the planning process.

CONCLUSION

The Campaign represents a watershed in the post-independence history of Kerala in that it has made the very nature and institutional character of the state an object of contestation, with the goal of attempting to deepen and widen democracy. With every local plan that is formulated and every local project that is implemented, the new institutions and procedures of decentralized participation take root. Because this in turn strengthens civil society, and brings previously excluded or marginalized actors into the political arena, it may well be that democratic deepening becomes self-sustaining. But because the mobilizational mode that the Campaign has taken will become increasingly difficult to sustain as local planning becomes routinized, sustaining the integrity and efficacy of deliberative institutions will require institutionalizing the authority and resource base of local governments. With respect to passing necessary legislation and new regulations much has already been done. But these gains can be quickly unraveled or hollowed out if the new institutions fail to deliver. And sustainable delivery rests on first maintaining adequate levels of financial devolution, and second on successfully reforming the bureaucracy. Both factors in turn rest on permutations in the political equation.

The return to power of a Congress-led government means that the Campaign will no longer benefit from political leadership and will lose significant state support. Already, despite its public declarations of support for the Campaign, the government has weakened the institutional moorings of the Campaign by promoting parallel structures. Thus it has split the *Panchayat* department into two separate entities, introduced new regulatory authorities that are outside of the Campaign's integrated structures, and has pledged to provide Members of the Legislative Assembly with funds for local development that in effect bypass *panchayats*. The government has also undermined the Campaign's formal and informal support structures by demobilizing trained resource persons, providing only minimal training programs, and putting the redeployment of department officials to the local level in cold storage.

But even if the Campaign now finds itself settling into a lower-level equilibrium, it nevertheless still represents a dramatic advance on the pre-campaign period with local government playing a far greater role in development than anywhere else in India. Moreover, five years of experimentation with decentralized planning in Kerala have created new sources of democratic authority and generated lessons that are certain to have a lasting impact. Politically, the most important lesson has been that decentralization and people's participation can and does work. Even if only a small proportion of *panchayats* have even approximated the ideal of local planning, the demonstration effect of what is possible has had profound reverberations. Very concretely these hundreds of points of experimentation have brought countless innovations to project design and implementation, and these have been energetically diffused through innovative training programs in which *panchayats* teach each other. A once impervious and all-powerful bureaucracy has, in hundreds of local communities, been displaced by the collective efforts of ordinary citizens. Ordinary citizens who have never been afforded an opportunity to effectively engage the state outside of campaign-oriented social movements now routinely deliberate and cooperate with elected representatives and local officials in deciding how to spend large sums of money. And a generalized discontent and even cynical despair about politics has in part been replaced by an open, articulate and relentless attack on patronage politics and the beginnings, through everyday participatory practices, of a new kind of transformative politics. At a very minimum, this is reflected in the new-found respect that political parties have for civil society.

The second broad lesson is that there are no blueprints, and that any successful reform effort of this scope and depth will of necessity be one of learning-by-doing. Being confident about the normative desirability of participatory institutions thus also implies being comfortable with the notion that making such institutions work is a process of trial and error that requires continuous feedback and institutional fine-tuning. What can be asserted is that the required flexibility calls for institutional designs that strike a balance between local autonomy and initiative with enforced procedural and redistributive standards and higher-level strategic integration. What Kerala's experience suggests, however, is that such institutions themselves are most likely to emerge from a programmatic political project that consciously reaches out to civil society and builds on the creative and even mischievous logic of social movements.

Notes

1 The Communist Party of India was unified until 1965, when it split into the CPI and the CPM. The CPM has emerged as the much larger of the two Communist Parties, and is the dominant partner of the Left Democratic Fronts that have come to power in Kerala and West Bengal.

2 For a theoretical view of this concept see Fung and Wright (2001 and 2002). For a detailed examination of the Kerala case as an experiment in empowered participatory governance, see Isaac and Heller (2002).

3 The discussion in the next two sections is taken from Heller (2000).

4 There are a total of 25 states in India, 15 of which have populations surpassing 15 million. Indian states have their own legislatures and executives and under India's federal constitution enjoy a wide range of powers and responsibilities, including independent sources of revenue collection (primarily sales taxes) and a wide range of development functions.

5 On all the key social indicators Kerala has dramatically outperformed all other Indian states and even compares favorably with developed countries. Literacy is over 90 per cent and life expectancy has reached 72. Over the past 30 years the percentage of households under the poverty line has fallen faster than in any other part of India, going from 54.2 per cent in 1973–74 to 24.4 per cent in 1987–88.

6 Much of what follows draws directly on Thomas Isaac and Heller (2002). For the most comprehensive examination of the campaign see Thomas Isaac and Franke (2000).

7 The basic principles of local self-government—autonomy, subsidiarity, role clarity, complementarity, uniformity, people's participation, accountability and transparency—were first formulated by the Committee on Decentralisation of Power (popularly known as Sen Committee, after its late chairperson Dr

Satyabrata Sen) appointed by the Government of Kerala.

8 For a critique of the technocratic paradigm see Bardhan (1999) and Heller (2001).

9 The *grama*, block and district levels under the Indian constitution represent a continuous set of structures and are all referred to as *panchayats*. Municipalities stand alone.

10 In 1998 the exchange rate was $1 to Rs. 42.

11 A variety of factors contributed to CPM's defeat despite the People's Campaign. There was a consolidation of all casteist and communal groups and parties around the Congress Party-led opposition. The organizational problems within the Left-front, including splits in some of its minor constituents, also contributed to the electoral setback. The second set of factors is related to the omissions and commissions of the state government, including a near-paralyzing fiscal crisis of the government on the eve of the elections, a botched reform initiative in education, and a series of high-profile corruption scandals and embarrassing controversies. A third factor was the severe economic crisis that the state economy has been plunged into due to a sharp decline in prices of rubber, coconut and other commercial crops that are the basis of Kerala's agricultural economy. The collapse of commodity prices was a direct result of trade liberalization and the national government's WTO agreement. The incumbent party in power in Kerala was, however, made to pay the price.

12 Village *panchayats* have an average population of 10–15 thousand and are broken down into 10–12 wards, each represented by a single councilor. In Kerala's highly competitive party system, most *panchayats* have multiple-party representation.

13 At 93 per cent, Kerala's literacy rate is almost twice the national average. The information returns of Kerala's high literacy is reflected in the fact that it boasts more daily newspapers (27 at last count) than any other Indian state, despite being amongst the smallest.

14 Tabulated from evaluation forms collected from development seminars, 1996.

15 The Kerala Information Mission has been set up to rectify this situation. The mission's goal is to network the local bodies, train the personnel and generate software for effective plan monitoring and service provisioning by the local bodies. By mid-2001 the Mission plans to have installed a computer in all *panchayats* with links to all other *panchayats* and to the State Planning Board.

16 All figures are from the SPB.

17 A number of steps have been initiated to strengthen the *grama sabhas*. The minimum number of legally required *grama sabhas* meetings in a year has been raised from two to four. The quorum has also been raised from 50 to 100, or 10 per cent of the voters. An official coordinator for each *grama sabha* is now appointed and made responsible for keeping records.

18 The reforms include new standards of transparency, a new training program and the creation of a Technical Audit Team.

Bibliography

Bardhan, Pranab (1984). *The Political Economy of Development in India*. New York: Basil Blackwell.

— (1997). "Sharing the Spoils: Group Equity, Development, and Democracy." (Unpublished paper). University of California, Berkeley.

— (1999). "The State Against Society: the Great Divide in Indian Social Science Discourse," in Sugata Bose and Ayesha Jalal (eds). *Nationalism, Democracy and Development*. New York: Oxford UP, 184–95.

Brass, Paul R. (1994). *The Politics of India Since Independence*. Cambridge: Cambridge UP.

Chalmers, Doug, Scott Martin and Kerianne Piester (1997). "The Associative Network: Emerging Patterns of Popular Representation," in Doug Chalmers *et al.* (eds). *The New Politics of Inequality in Latin America*. New York: Oxford UP.

Cohen, Joshua and Joel Rogers (1995). "Secondary Associations and Democratic Governance," in Erik O. Wright (ed.). *Association and Democracy*. London: Verso.

Evans, Peter (1996). "Government Action, Social Capital and Development: Reviewing the Evidence on Synergy," *World Development*, 24(6), 1119–32.

Fung, Archon and E. O. Wright (2001). "Deepening Democracy: Innovations in Empowered Participatory Governance," *Politics and Society* 29(1), 4–42.

— (2002). "Thinking About Empowered Participatory Governance," in Archon Fung and E. O. Wright (eds), *Deepening Democracy: Institutional Innovations in Empowered Participatory Democracy*. London: Verso.

Government of India (1969). *Guidelines for the Formulation of District Plans*, Planning Commission, New Delhi.

— (1978). *Report of the Working Group on Block Level Planning*, Planning Commission, New Delhi.

— (1984). *Report of the Working Group on District Planning*, Planning Commission, New Delhi.

Government of Kerala (1997). *Budget 1997–98*. Thiruvananthapuram: Ministry of Finance.

Heller, Patrick (1999). *The Labor of Development: Workers in the Transformation of Capitalism in Kerala, India*. Ithaca, NY: Cornell UP.

— (2000). "Degrees of Democracy: Some Comparative Lessons From India," *World Politics*, 52 (July), 484–519.

— (2001). "Moving the State: The Politics of Decentralization in Kerala, South Africa and Porto Alegre," *Politics and Society* 29(1), 131–63.

Huber, Evelyne, Dietrich Rueschemeyer and J. Stephens (1999). "The Paradoxes of Contemporary Democracy: Formal, Participatory, and Social Dimensions," in Lisa Anderson (ed.), *Transitions to Democracy*. New York: Columbia UP.

Kaviraj, Sudipta (1998). "Critique of the Passive Revolution," in Partha Chaterjee (ed.), *State and Politics in India.* Delhi: Oxford UP.

Mamdani, Mahmood (1996). *Citizen and Subject: Contemporary Africa and the Legacy of Late Colonialism.* Princeton, NJ: Princeton UP.

Manjula, B. (2000). "Voices From the Spiral of Silence: A Case Study of Samatha Self Help Groups of Ulloor." Paper presented at the International Conference on Democratic Decentralisation, Thiruvananthapuram, 23–27 May.

Mehta, Pratap (1997). "India: Fragmentation Amid Consensus," *Journal of Democracy*, 8(1), 56–69.

Migdal, Joel, Atul Kohli and Vivienne Shue (1994). *State Power and Social Forces: Domination and Transformation the Third World.* Cambridge: Cambridge UP.

O'Donnell, Guillermo (1993). "On the State, Democratization and Some Conceptual Problems: A Latin American View with Glances at Some Postcommunist Countries," *World Development* 21(8), 1355–9.

Putnam, Robert (1993). *Making Democracy Work, Civic Traditions in Modern Italy.* Princeton, NJ: Princeton UP.

Seema, T. N. and Vanitha Mukherjee (2000). "Gender Governance and Citizenship in Decentralised Planning." Paper presented at the International Conference on Democratic Decentralisation, Thiruvananthapuram, 23–27 May.

Skocpol, Theda and M. Fiorina (1999). *Civic Engagement in American Democracy.* Washington, DC: the Brookings Institution.

Thomas Isaac, T. M. and R. Franke (2000). *Local Democracy and Development: People's Campaign for Decentralised Planning in Kerala.* New Delhi: Leftword.

Thomas Isaac, T. M. (1999a). "The Socio-Economic and Political Context of People's Planning Campaign." National Workshop on Decentralised Governance, organized by Kerala Institute of Local Administration and Swiss Agency for Development and Cooperation, Thrissur.

— (1999b). "People's Planning—Toward a Handbook." Presented at the Workshop organized by the State Planning Board, Tripura, Agarthala, 3 and 4 May.

— (1999c). "Janakeeyasoothranavum Ayalkoottangalum—Anubhavangalum Padangalum" [People's Planning and Neighbourhood Groups–Lessons from Experience], in *Ayalkootta Sangamam* [Neighborhood Groups] Vol. I, Kerala State Planning Board, Thiruvananthapuram.

— (1999d). "Gunabhokthra Samithikalude Anubhava Padangal" [People's Planning and Beneficiary Committees–Lessons from Experience], in *Gunabhokthra Samithikalum Janakeeyasoothranavum* [People's Planning and Beneficiary Committees]. Kerala State Planning Board, Thiruvananthapuram.

Thomas Isaac, T. M. *et al.* (1999). "Gender and Decentralised Planning—The Experience of People's Campaign," (unpublished Working Paper), Center for Development Studies, Thiruvananthapuram.

Thomas Isaac, T. M. and P. Heller (2002). "Decentralisation, Democracy and Development: People's Campaign for Decentralized Planning in Kerala," in A. Fung and E. O. Wright (eds), *Deepening Democracy: Institutional Innovations in Empowered Participatory Democracy.* London: Verso.

Weyland, Kurt (1996). *Democracy Without Equity: Failures of Reform in Brazil.* Pittsburgh: U of Pittsburgh P.

COMMENTARY

14

Toward New Democracies

Emir Sader

LIBERAL DEMOCRACY: ITS TRIUMPH AND CRISIS

One of the most significant political aspects of contemporary history is the contrast between the spreading of liberal democratic regimes and the crisis of liberal democracy. It would appear that the extreme expansion of liberal democracy is necessary to its realization and, at the same time, the cause of its crisis and historical exhaustion.

The liberal form of state organization emerged in opposition to the absolutist state and its constraints upon capital's free expansion. Legitimized by the French Revolution and the Universal Declaration of Human Rights, liberalism gained solidity with the gradual establishment of republican and parliamentary forms of political organization and the expansion of the process of capitalist mercantilization.

Solidarity on the one hand, and on the other the contradictions between political and economic liberalism produced many ambiguities, but this did not prevent either of them from being affected by the consequences of the 1929 crisis. From the hegemonic crisis brought about by the events of 1929, three alternative models emerged, fighting for the space left vacant by liberalism, each of them anti-liberal in different degrees and shapes: "Soviet socialism," Fascism, and Keynesianism.

The failure of each of these alternatives, throughout the following decades, opened the way for the joint emergence of political and economic liberalism as a new hegemonic project that interconnected a minimal state with an unparalleled expansion of mercantile relations under the aegis of liberalism. The world seemed to have been created anew in the image of liberal utopia.

Traditional Western European democracies have been joined in the last two decades by similar regimes in Eastern Europe (replacing what were then called "popular democracies"), Latin America (in countries formerly ruled by military dictatorships), and also in Africa (of which South Africa is the best example, although others, as well, have started to meet the general criteria of liberal democratic systems). The overall picture appears as an overwhelming progress, *still* resisted by a few countries—some characterized as anti-democratic, because anti-liberal, some as "socialist" (such as China, Cuba, or North Korea), because non-"pluralist," and others as Arab fundamentalist (such as Iran, Iraq, and Libya), failing to separate politics from religion.

Also fitting into this trend is the political reconversion of countries like Indonesia and the Philippines, in the wake of dictatorial regimes, or of countries such as Guatemala, El Salvador and Nicaragua, which had experienced political-military conflicts, while in Mexico the Institutional Revolutionary Party suffered its first national defeat, thus making way for a possible shift toward a liberal democratic regime. In the process, projects that advocated alternative political models were either defeated (as was the case of Eastern European regimes and the Sandinista regime) or reconverted (as was the case in Guatemala and El Salvador, where guerrilla movements were incorporated into the institutional political system).

Liberal euphoria celebrated, in the case of Latin America for example, a continent pervaded with democracies, where Cuba featured as the oddity, a remote red dot in a map otherwise converted to democracy. So much so that, on his way back from a visit to Cuba, the then minister of foreign affairs of Brazil (the most unjust, and therefore socially the least democratic country in the world, according to UN reports) stated that Cuba was not prepared to return to the fold of the Latin American community, that is, the OAS, because it was not a democratic country.

This new historical map has provided the basis for the establishment of the ideology of liberal democracy as the most advanced historical horizon in the contemporary world, either in the terms of Fukuyama or Huntington, or even Dahrendorf, democracy thus being identified with liberal democracy. This reductionism has donned the cloak of universality and gained the status of consecrated canonization, having been disseminated at all levels with almost no form of opposition.

Liberal democracy has been gradually naturalized through its North American form—with media-hyped election campaigns, with increasingly look-alike political parties, with exorbitant financing, with the substitution of public gatherings by the privacy of the home. The ideology of liberal democracy seeks to identify the citizen with the consumer and the electoral process with the market, which, in the words of George Soros, is more democratic than elections. Public opinion is increasingly shaped by the mass media, which, in turn, is increasingly subject to commercial criteria—the chase for audiences and advertising. At the same time, the capitalist market economy has been naturalized as *the* form of economic organization. Liberal democracy and the capitalist economy constitute the core of contemporary liberal hegemony.

After a period of euphoria, however, the 1990s witnessed the gradual deterioration of political systems, with the loss of legitimacy of governments, legislatures and Justice, the weakening of social organizations, the demoralization of ideologies and political parties, the lack of interest in elections and politics in general, and the almost total lack of relevant political debate. What is significant is that this deterioration has occurred within liberal political systems without their having collapsed.

The cases, for example, of Fujimori's and Carlos Menem's regimes in Latin America typify such deterioration (in the former it meant the dissolution of the judiciary, the closing down of parliament and the imposition of a new Constitution, with all new judges being appointed by the "president" of Peru) and demonstrate the elasticity that the concept of liberal democracy has acquired, while at the same time revealing its exhaustion. Within Western Europe itself, electoral abstention rose significantly and, surprisingly, reached its peak in the 2000 election for the European Parliament—the political expression of a successful European unification.

But the phenomenon is widespread, since the economic ground on which political systems of liberal democracy stand—the unprecedented expansion of mercantilization—has become universal as a consequence of worldwide neoliberal hegemony. The demoralization of politics, the lack of interest in anything public, the increasing privatization of social relations and of the state itself, all contribute to a crisis in politics, induced by the corrosion of the social structure and of culture, brought about by mercantile relations that lack the countervailing force once provided by the state's regulatory action.

In Latin America (a continent that has suffered its most profound regressive transformations in the course of two decades), neoliberalism has become the official ideology of the "new democracies," which began to be judged according to the degree of state intervention in the economy, the extent of labor market regulation, the degree of economic openness. Mercantile relations have invaded social spaces to such an extent that the very issue of state reform has acquired strictly economic connotations. State reform ceased being synonymous with democratization, and began to be confused with the reduction of its regulating functions, with its effort to meet the supposedly higher purpose of achieving fiscal adjustment. The latter became the sieve through which all policies were filtered, judged as either positive or negative according to whether they contribute to the balance of public accounts and to monetary stability. Any project of political reform presented by governments before parliament can be assessed according to how much one wishes to save in state expenses and how many rights will be suppressed to reach that purpose.

The two sides of liberalism have come into collision: economic liberalism undermines the bases of the rule of law, one of the components of political liberalism. In promoting mercantile relations, economic liberalism by definition disregards *rights*. In addition, labor reforms lead to social fragmentation, weakening individuals' capacity to organize themselves, while neoliberal governments fiercely oppose trade unions and social movements—these being some of their more important adversaries. The result is that the latter's power to make demands is diminished, leading to attempts to find individual solutions—an expression of which is the proliferation of religious affiliations and self-help literature. As a correlate, prominent businessmen have become the model of "success" in their individualistic quest to solve their own problems. Two decades of these hegemonic values and this hegemonic model of society significantly dismantled the productive structure of countries in the South, debilitated their economies with the hegemony of financial capital and the dependence on speculative capital, reduced the state's capacity to guarantee rights and to conduct democratization processes, promoted the fast commodification of culture, and weakened all those elements that politics is made of—the state, governments, political parties, parliaments, electoral campaigns, political debates, political culture, a concern for the fate of societies.

The corrosion produced by neoliberal policies at the very basis of social relations was such that perhaps today one cannot truly say that the political regimes that suffered those transformations correspond to liberal models, so great has been the extent to which governments have concentrated power in their hands (often governing by decree), parliaments have been emptied, political parties have lost their ideological identity, elections have stopped representing a confrontation of alternatives, and the power of money has corrupted electoral processes and government itself. A distorted version of liberal models has been gradually imposed, debilitating politics and the state, in favor of the latter's financialization and of the economy's priority over the whole of social life.

FROM RESISTANCE TO ALTERNATIVES

For peripheral or semiperipheral countries in the capitalist world system, the 1980s represented, not *one* lost decade, but the entrance into *lost decades*, in the sense of a break with economic development projects that, although unevenly, had represented forms of social advancement for significant layers of the population. It was precisely in this period that, against the spirit of the times, social movements developed, as well as forms of organization, local and regional policies, and the struggle for rights that, while tapping into the repressed needs of the population, pointed toward the rejection and the overcoming of the above-described scenario. In the context of these activities, anything that falls under the name of *participatory democracy* has a special meaning, because it overtly represents a counterpoint to some of the essential assumptions of liberal democracy, as advertised by ideological credos and practiced by neoliberal governments.

The forms of imposition of neoliberal hegemony had such an overwhelming character that, for a while, its offensive was basically met only by union movements, community movements, and political resistance movements. It was as if this attack had been successful not only in weakening the social and political bases of alternative movements, but also in undermining them with the idea that "there is no alternative" to its policies, so much so that they even divided their types of reaction into merely defensive actions and those that they considered capable of giving different answers to the problems posed by neoliberalism—such as, for example, fiscal adjustment policies. On the theoretical level there was an almost complete absence of comprehensive historical analyses, as if "grand narratives" were no longer believed to be possible. This period had its climax in the first half of the 1990s, as a direct consequence of the collapse of the Berlin Wall and the end of the USSR, ostensibly "confirmed" by the defeat of the Sandinista regime and the course taken by China.

The first forms of resistance took on *local* shapes. These protests found, in the territories particularly affected by neoliberal restructuring, the privileged ground for bringing together a population victimized in various ways: by the loss of formal jobs, the deterioration of public services, overdue wages, police violence, and so on. Feelings of "social exclusion" (originating from the loss of rights) tended to promote new forms of organization, of protest and of group awareness.

In addition, the fiscal adjustment policies imposed by the state were met with greater resistance in local environments (frequently in municipal governments), in which the impact of these policies was delayed. Moreover, municipal governments are usually responsible, to a considerable degree, for social policies, the kind specifically targeted for attack by fiscal adjustment policies, and therefore a key element in popular resistance and mobilization.

The defense of the *local* thus became disseminated as an ideology (expressed in its most common phrase "Think globally, act locally"), converting limitation into virtue (it abandoned global spaces, in which neoliberalism was being consolidated) and seeking to tap into all the energy those local references provided. Therefore, while neoliberal globalization advanced at the international level and at the level of national states in the course of internationalization, local experiments were being developed by governments, social movements and sectoral policies, renewing social and political praxis where traditional forms of struggle (parliamentary, electoral, unionist) had proved ineffective.

Significantly, the World Social Forum found its headquarters in Porto Alegre, creating the opportunity for the meeting between one of the most advanced experiments in participatory democracy at the local level and the broad and diversified movement that has been questioning liberal globalization. Here, so to speak, they could compare notes, check trends, confront claims, and set the foundations for the construction of an alternative proposal to liberal globalization.

PARTICIPATORY DEMOCRACY AND THE SEMIPERIPHERY

Entitled *Participatory Democracy*, the first volume of the collection *Reinventing Social Emancipation: Toward Other Manifestos* covers various experiences of social movements, institutions, and actors, as well as concrete experiments in participatory democracy in six countries from three different continents, within the so-called semiperiphery of capitalism—with the exception, for purposes of contrast, of Mozambique, located in the poor periphery.

First of all, it is necessary to clarify the meaning of two references central to these choices: the meaning of *participatory democracy* and the meaning of *semiperiphery*.

The political experiences that have become known as participatory democracy generally oppose or seek to complement forms of representative democracy. The experiences considered here deal with policies for establishing the rule of law, with territorial planning, the "social responsibility" of companies, women's participation in political struggle, participatory democracy both in its classical form and as participatory budgeting, and the assertion of social rights. These experiences emerge either in reaction to situations in which formal rights are usually denied, or as attempts to deepen the relations between citizens and political decision-making, or attempts to empower gender or ethnic "minorities."

The greatest novelty, as will be seen, comes from proposals that point toward democratic state reform, dealing with topics essential to liberal models, which postulate a strict separation between the governing and the governed, the former keeping a monopoly on decision-making while systems of political delegation erode the voters' ability to control and influence their representatives. This is the case, for example, with participatory budgeting initiatives that point toward the socialization of politics and power, taking in a positive sense the alternative posed by Gramsci, for whom there are two types of politicians: those who struggle to reduce the separation between the governing and the governed and those who strive to overcome it.

One of the questions raised when discussing proposals for participatory democracy is the definition of the term *participation*. According to the liberal individualistic conception of the world and politics, voting is the central form of participation, the act itself being charged with a sacred, symbolic character. But this tenuous bond hides a delegation similar to a blank check, for that bond is renewed only periodically, according to the electoral calendar. The autonomization of the political—one of capitalism's characteristic structural elements because of the appearance imprinted on the relation between capital and labor as an "exchange among equals," freeing the political to be part of a universe of "equals before the law"—is sharpened in the relation between the voters' passivity and the governing political elite's intense activity. Liberalism would term this *participation*, and we know how some contemporary political theories consider the electorate's apathy (abstention, blank vote) to be a symptom of a society's political "maturity."

Politics have become a private activity, performed by professionals who belong to a political elite responsible for society's "management" through the state, increasingly understood as a "business company." Theories of the elites are thus renovated, reifying politics and separating it from social relations.

The demoralization of politics favors the economy's unconstrained empire, promoting the financialization of the state, the destruction of rights as well as the destruction of forms of state regulation. The general press sets "the market" against "politics," and claims to be the bearer of "rationality" in opposition to the "corporativism," "intolerance," and "incompetence" of politicians.

The polarization between demoralized politicians wrangling over state sinecures and members of ideologically mutating parties, on the one hand, and economists who personify the cold rationality of huge corporations, financial capital, and fiscal adjustment, on the other, disqualifies the political debate, promotes indifference toward politics and favors apathy and demobilization, which, in turn, leaves even more room for private capital, and its logic of incessant profit maximizing, to take over the state.

Initiatives of participatory democracy seek to escape this vicious circle by recovering the public and civic dimension of politics. These initiatives tend to follow different directions: one of these is the mobilization of social sectors interested in establishing public policies in the areas of health, basic sanitation, education, and public security, presenting their demands to governments and parliaments and seeking ways of achieving them by pressuring, controlling, striving to maintain a mobilization level capable of establishing a new bond between citizenship and politics.

A different form of initiative not only seeks to invigorate a debilitated liberal democracy, but also suggests alternative forms for organizing the political system. Nicos Poulantzas's formulations (1981) on the combination of representative democracy and direct democracy had no concrete formula until the project of participatory budgeting pointed precisely in that direction. It introduced strong tensions within the representative system, questioned its forms and at the same time sowed the seeds for a radical democratic reform of the state, thus presenting one of the most advanced and fertile proposals for participatory democracy in the last decades.

Four of the countries chosen in this project—India, South Africa, Brazil and Colombia—belong precisely to what can be called the semiperiphery. Mozambique provides a contrast as a strictly peripheral country. The first four countries were the protagonists of one of the most important phenomena of the twentieth century: the process of industrialization on the periphery of capitalism. Until then, the dichotomy center/periphery had corresponded to the dichotomies industrialized/agricultural countries and urban/agrarian countries. Throughout the twentieth century, countries like India, South Africa, Brazil and Colombia developed different degrees of industrialization, assuming distinctive features and taking up positions that can be described as semiperipheral.

Coincidentally or not, none of these countries (including Mozambique) has a strong democratic tradition. Formally, both India and Colombia have a degree of institutional continuity that is only a few decades old. However, the quality of the democracies that actually exist in these countries does not imply the existence of a consistent democratic system. In Colombia, for example, the existence of the rule of law can be questioned, since two strong guerrilla movements and paramilitary groups control extensive areas of the country over which the Colombian state has no power. South Africa has only recently emerged from a protracted apartheid regime. Mozambique has been an independent regime for a few decades and part of that period has been marked by serious military confrontations. Brazil enjoyed few periods of institutional continuity in the midst of several dictatorial regimes, and has only re-established a democratic regime in the last 15 years.

Located on the periphery of capitalism, five of these six countries have been the privileged victims of liberal globalization, which has undermined their social structures and debilitated their political systems. When four of these countries succeeded in overcoming the limitations intrinsic to agrarian and agricultural countries, even if only to a modest extent, they started to be considered as "emerging intermediary powers"; they developed a certain degree of industrialization and went through rapid urbanization processes, establishing national projects that allowed the economic and social integration of increasing numbers of the population.

The experiences and experiments reported here point toward two distinct directions in the struggle for political emancipation. The first takes shape in the context of guerrilla warfare, that is, through an insurrectional strategy, within which forms of democratic struggle seek to establish space for action and recognition, and of which Colombia is the most significant case. The second is part of a strategy for the radical democratic reform of the state, represented by the experiments of participatory budgeting, particularly those initiated in Porto Alegre, in the south of Brazil. There are also a number of experiments in sectoral struggle, such as that of women in Mozambique, whose strategic boundaries have not yet been clearly defined.

COLOMBIA: BETWEEN TWO WORLDS

Colombia is the subject of three studies that can be discussed as a whole, since they concern the specific situation lived in the country. This specificity arises, on the one hand, from the extreme tensions to which the rule of law is subjected, caught as it is between a formal system of representative democracy and an actual state of war—not only are legal statutes only precariously complied with, but also the state's control over its territory is formally threatened by the existence of an area under the rule of one of the guerrilla movements, while other areas are actually controlled by either the other guerrilla movement or paramilitary forces. On the other hand, the co-existence of governments elected by popular vote (even though in the context of traditionally high abstention levels) with competing powers (open military confrontation between the US-supported army and the guerrilla movements, the overt action of paramilitary forces) generates ambiguous, contradictory, illusory and unheard-of situations.

The term of comparison, or at least the ideal scenario imagined by the US government, is Central America, Guatemala and El Salvador in particular, where guerrilla movements were induced to reconstruct themselves in order to enter the institutional political process after the end of the armed struggle. They began to participate in electoral processes and even, particularly in the case of El Salvador, secured governments (as was the case of that country's capital) and won their first majority in Parliament. On the whole, insurrectional movements have been assimilated into institutional processes at the end of armed struggles that lasted for decades (four, in the case of Guatemala).

Peace negotiations in El Salvador and Guatemala, however similar, have significant differences. In El Salvador they originated in the relations between two parties: the government and guerrilla movements grouped in the Farabundo Martí National Liberation Front; in Guatemala peace negotiations sprang from a tripartite relationship between the government, a guerrilla movement built around Guatemala's National Revolutionary Union and indigenous communities. The latter represented autonomous social movements, with their own platform, resulting in a series of achievements specifically benefiting those communities.

Colombian guerrilla movements, unlike their Central American counterparts, do not seem inclined toward reconversion or toward establishing peace negotiation terms that could lead to the country's pacification, since they have set a series of conditions almost impossible to meet. Furthermore, the conditions under which negotiations have developed in Colombia are not those of stagnation in the expansion capacity of the guerrilla groups (who, at least, do not see it as such), and this strongly hinders institutional recycling, inviting comparisons (also on the side of guerrilla movements) with the terms in which the Vietnamese negotiated with the USA, that is, as one more step in a long process of a revolutionary war that they have not abandoned.

Also specific to the Colombian situation is the challenge of either combining or changing forms of struggle, from the insurrectional strategy to the radical reform of the institutional system. Joan Garces has demonstrated, in her dramatic account of the experience of Salvador Allende's socialist institutional government (Garces, 1996), how the choice of one line of action almost automatically eliminates the other. In other words, once the option has been made toward legal struggle, it becomes impossible, however numerous the arguments in favor of change, to return to the insurrectional route.

This challenge appears in the Colombian case as the product of the political schizophrenia the country has been suffering from since the beginning of the civil war in the late 1940s, which led to open military confrontation in the countryside (first between conservatives and liberals and later between the army and guerrilla movements) and institutional coexistence in the cities. At present this division takes the form of peace-seeking movements in the cities and martial solutions in the countryside—either open confrontations or compromises that define areas of military control.

The relations between the social movements analyzed in the book—the *cocaleros'* struggle in Putumayo and in the Baja Bota Caucana and the case of San José de Apartadó—and guerrilla movements are distinct and have changed over time. When they are victimized by the state (through repression, exclusion, stigmatization) they draw nearer to guerrilla movements, but if they struggle for inclusion, for recognition, for space of action, they implicitly seek for means of incorporation, expanding the state's capacity to include them. The general impression is that the participation demanded by these groups might be able to materialize in a different type of state. From an awareness of a common enemy, some movements establish a sort of "moral union" with guerrilla groups but, at the same time, as they define themselves as members of a Peace Community, and as the guerrillas find their meaning in the exercise of war, they are aware of their different goals.

The fundamental issue is the extent to which a guerrilla warfare process tolerates an analogous process of popular emancipation, either autonomous or guerrilla-promoted. The degrees of strategic centralization required by military strategy, the weight of logistics and of large operations, secrecy, etc., require centralized forms of action and organization, of military discipline, where the logic of war (even when that war claims to have a popular character) encroaches upon that of mass political action and thus subordinates democratic forms of consultation and action to the imperatives of military conflict.

The strategic logic of guerrilla action derives from Mao-Tse-Tung's conceptions of popular warfare, reproduced in Vietnam and adapted to the Cuban guerrilla movement, namely through the construction of liberated zones where dual power organs are set up as the insurrectional armed force gains control over gradually more extensive areas of the disputed territory. All of these cases refer to countries whose popular classes were mainly concentrated in the countryside and where an agrarian economy prevailed. Territorial seizure coincided with the erosion of the social and economic bases of the established power and with the construction of the newly emergent power.

Since the beginning of the Colombian guerrilla movement, the relative weight of urban and rural sectors has changed, as well as the distribution of the population. At present, the country's economy is significantly more diversified than it was in the 1940s and 1950s, having relatively extensive industrial and service sectors in the cities, where the majority of the population is concentrated. Under these circumstances, guerrilla movements face the challenge posed by the divide between the countryside, as the privileged space for armed action and for the construction of liberated zones, and the urban areas, where the majority of the popular classes and the basic centers of power are concentrated.

The phenomena analyzed in the texts included in this book are at the center of these dilemmas: how can popular movements struggle for their interests in the face of a situation of political–military polarization between guerrilla and state forces, further aggravated by the presence of paramilitary forces? One possible route is to fight beside guerrilla movements as allies. Another is to seek autonomy in relation to the conflicting forces. Both imply an awareness that the general solution for conflicts depends on the contest of forces between political–military opponents and, above all, on its outcome.

The alliance with guerrilla movements leads to a defined social and political alignment, in opposition to the state and the paramilitary, allowing the demands of popular movements to be included in a more general platform for structural transformation of both society and the state. However, in these circumstances, movements fall under the full weight of state repression and paramilitary action, and have no means of self-defence. In addition, they are subject to discrediting campaigns by the government, as well as by the pro-government press, which accuse them of being no more than the civil arm of the guerrillas, thus justifying repressive measures. The reduction of these movements to the status of guerrilla-supporting social bases, while not corresponding to effective adherence or to any formal bond, does not allow these movements to openly discuss common strategies with guerrilla forces, and they are therefore trapped in an awkward and, to a certain degree, powerless situation.

Conversely, the possibility of autonomous action would require an equidistance from the two overtly conflicting political–military forces— which is difficult, not to say impossible, in the context of the state's appeal to counterinsurgency methods, with the increasing overt participation of the US government—and the creation of their own space for action and for a build-up of strength capable of dislocating the terms of the conflict. The attempts analyzed here take place in the countryside, the privileged ground for military confrontations, a territory, on the one hand, urgently in need of this sort of action but, on the other hand, where the least room exists for it. The most fruitful attempts (at least as a mirror of feelings shared by significant sectors of the population) take place in the city, in the form of peace demonstrations, especially following terrorist attacks of great impact (for instance, the assassination of people known for their anti-violence action, either journalists or personalities with a strong presence in the media), and attempts to constitute intermediation committees that seek either to strengthen the developing peace process, or to advance new terms for its fulfillment.

The greatest test to the country's future comes from the Colombia Plan. To carry it out will constitute a challenge to the existing institutions and, above all, to the possibilities of creating civic spaces and of asserting citizenship in a context of predictably intensifying and expanding armed conflicts and the consequently greater militarization of the whole country. The struggle to prevent the Plan's full implementation can itself become a stimulus for movements striving to create room for the construction of popular emancipation projects, beyond the terms imposed until now by political-military confrontations that have constrained Colombia in the last decades.

The experience of the struggle to assert the rule of law reflects, significantly, the sort of phenomena taking place in Colombia. The paradox lies in the juxtaposition of a nearly five-decade-long democratic institutional regime (according to liberal standards) with a situation of overt war, in which the rules of military confrontation prevail. Under these circumstances (with deaths, assassinations, kidnappings, threats, extortion), the questions are: What room is left for the action of justice? What degree of legitimacy and effectiveness can justice have, when the state itself engages in overtly illegal actions, either through its army or through state-endorsed paramilitary groups?

It is precisely when the political system loses legitimacy that new possibilities are open for justice to recover the legitimacy of the rule of law, in a struggle to assert fundamental rights. In the context of the state's institutional fragmentation and lack of hegemony, space is open for action by the Constitutional Court—a singular, unique experience in situations similar to that of Colombia's.

The cases considered here reveal unprotected social sectors, caught in the crossfire of the conflicting parties: indigenous groups, unionized workers, gays, mortgagers—all helpless to different degrees, and all without space in which to assert their rights. The struggle toward an awareness that one can be a subject of rights, that is, a citizen, is the central purpose of the court's work, but the unfolding of that awareness also reveals the contradictions and limits of citizenship under the constraints of a wartime situation.

The awareness of one's rights leads to the demand for their fulfillment by those institutions that are supposed to guarantee them, namely justice.

Demands then begin to multiply before a judiciary incapable of turning decisions into actions. Justice thus runs the risk of becoming demoralized, but
there is always a tension between the awareness of rights and the constraints
imposed on those rights. At the same time, this situation fosters the struggle
for the establishment of the rule of law. The thin line between the assertion
of rights and the difficulty in fulfilling them is crucial for those who rightly
see the court as a possible agent of a solution capable of overcoming the conflicts that have led to and have kept Colombia in a situation of war and impasse.

MOZAMBIQUE: WOMEN, INSURRECTIONAL
STRUGGLE AND BEYOND

The experience recorded in this volume on the situation of women militants in post-independence Mozambique (marked by protracted military
confrontations against extreme right-wing forces for some years) represents
a unique case, different from any other, not only because it introduces the
gender issue, but also because it has taken place within the context of a guerrilla movement that did gain access to power, with all the implications of
such a transition.

The dilemmas are difficult and dramatic. In one way or another they have
been reproduced in all similar historical processes: in Cuba, Nicaragua and
Angola, for example. The Nicaraguan Revolution brought innovation when
compared to the Cuban, 20 years earlier. Among the novelties was the
demand for religious militancy (inspired in the theology of liberation) and
women's participation—as militants, as well as leaders, and even as soldiers.
In Cuba women were at best couriers, and the image of the revolutionary
was directly identified with the full-bearded guerrilla.

However, in either case, the most significant transition is usually the one
from the political-military stage (that of "guerrilla warfare") to one characterized by the exercise of power and the construction of a new society. It
can be said that, for women, the alternatives in the Mozambican case are not
substantially different: the continuation of a subordinate position, typical of
insurrectional struggle; the attempt to find room inside the movement or
party; or the search for affirmation outside, through overtly feminist or
feminist-related social movements. All of these have positive and negative
aspects, oscillating between the focus on "politics" in the classical sense of
the traditional left—power relations, discipline, an emphasis (if not an exclusive focus) on class contradictions—and the assumption that it is impossible
to make gender claims compatible with party practices.

The first alternative represents the resignation of women, and of feminist
claims, in favor of the great political confrontations faced by party leaderships, usually composed of men. From this point of view, it does not mean
that militants have no sex, but rather that they are male, and women who

wish to participate in party political activity need to reproduce the practices of traditional politics.

The second alternative poses the greater challenge, that of making women's claims and their recognition as women compatible with party political practice in a context of permanent tensions. This would require the effective realization of the proposition emphasized by Boaventura de Sousa Santos, according to which the claim for equality must be made compatible with the claim of difference. This would mean acknowledging the right women have to hold positions and participate in political life and, at the same time, devising specific means to bring this about, while respecting women's particular situations.

In order to achieve these goals, the conditions of political practice need first to be changed—beginning with long meetings and other time-consuming activities, which suppose a male "exempt" from private functions, performed by wives and other women, and available for prolonged activities. Second, a quota system for party and government positions should be adopted (if only temporarily), similar to that already adopted in various social and political structures, as a means of overcoming historically produced constraints and recovering the conditions that women need in order to acquire the necessary capacities to take up (in their own terms and tempos) positions of greater responsibility inside organizations.

As illustrated in the text about the Mozambican case, difficulties become greater because of the political and ideological weakening of political forces once they reach power. This situation was more pronounced in the context of the identity crisis experienced by left-wing parties after the collapse of the USSR and of the ideological references it represented. Bureaucratization and corruption (as was the case of the Sandinistas in Nicaragua) further weaken the inclination of movements' leaderships toward processes of democratization, an area in which women have demonstrated greater sensitivity—in what concerns both grassroots demands and ethical and transparent forms of administration—due to their status of outsiders to traditional politics.

The implementation of policies centered on the adjustment of public accounts further reduces the supporting social background required by women in order to make their private family roles compatible with public activities. This situation is even more critical in countries with lower degrees of social and economic development, such as Mozambique and Nicaragua.

Following a period of social improvement, the situation of women in society as a whole, as well as women militating in political organizations and governments, stagnated or even backslid. There was an increase, especially among the popular classes, in the number of women having sole responsibility for the care of their children and who have great difficulty combining their private functions with those they struggle to occupy in the public sphere.

The fate of neoliberalism and of its social and economic policies—which exercise an influence over parties and movements originating in the left, including those responsible, in the past, for radical political processes in countries such as Mozambique, South Africa, and Nicaragua, for example—will define the space for women's struggle to assert their rights and their ability to be the protagonists of a renovated politics, or otherwise to remain trapped in the present patterns of discrimination and segregation.

BRAZIL: TOWARD THE SOCIALIZATION OF POLITICS AND POWER

Among the experiments in participatory democracy, the most advanced are those known as "participatory budgeting." Having as their central reference the governments of the Workers' Party (Partido dos Trabalhadores – PT) in Porto Alegre, Brazil, over a period of thirteen years, these experiments have spread to other Brazilian cities and even states, in addition to other forms adopted in other countries.

The most significant feature of these experiments is the attempt to accomplish a radical democratic reform of the state, regarding participation not only as a means of enhancing state transparency but also as a lever to the construction of a different type of state, predicated on a different relationship between the governing and the governed and, therefore, a different form of citizenship and democracy.

Since its transition to democracy, Brazil has attempted to create governments containing forms of participatory democracy, encouraged by the vigorous popular mobilizations that led to the crisis of the dictatorship and its replacement, especially in the first half of the 1980s. Taking advantage of the governments' lesser dimensions, various projects were brought about in inland Brazilian cities, on the whole without great success or continuity. However, they disclosed a problem that soon became very real: the incapacity of democracies of liberal inspiration to include the impulse from below, from popular mobilizations, thus freezing institutionalized political regimes that become trapped in their own administrative shell.

To a greater or lesser extent, social policies became the only possibility left for governments to register the traces of their popular option, without reflection at the political level. The original administrative project of the Workers' Party itself (more directly translated in the formula "the PT style of government" ["O modo petista de governar"], the title of a book edited by Francisco Wefort in 1986) was not centered on the idea of participatory budgeting, which was still incipient at that moment among sectors of the party, but rather on an "inversion of priorities" that privileged the social— as would happen, for example, with Luiza Erindina's mayorship in São Paulo (1988–92).

Twelve years of participatory budgeting policies, continued by the PT's fourth consecutive mandate in Porto Alegre, led not only to the recognition of their role in those governments' success, but also to their extension to hundreds of Brazilian municipalities, to the extent that the government of São Paulo (a city traditionally considered ungovernable, partly because of its scarce resources and its enormous mass of repressed demands) was filled with enthusiasm and resolved to embark on the "adventure" of participatory budgeting. This was an innovative step, since participatory budgeting was, up to a certain time, considered to be a sectoral policy but not as the core of radical democratic state reform. This potential has not yet been included in the PT's national government programs, betraying the uneasiness and disturbance it brings to those determined to govern without altering society's general power structures.

Challenging dominant tendencies, participatory budgeting policies foster the strengthening of the rights of citizenship and the recovering of the importance of political space, as well as of the significance of public interests. Moreover, they initiate a process of radical state reform centered on a renewed public sphere—neither state nor private, but public. These policies point toward a parallel process of socialization of power and politics and the reduction of the separation between the governing and the governed. The strength with which a local experiment gained prominence at the national and international levels derives from the radically differentiating element that is part of this alternative (public, civic, democratic) policy, in opposition to both economic and political liberalism.

Instead of only demanding from neoliberalism coherence with the doctrinal assumptions of liberal democracy, the latter is criticized, not just from the point of view of direct democracy, but of the combination of direct democracy with participatory democracy, following the direction already suggested by Nicos Poulantzas in his recent work. However, this combination is not equated with the formal exercises of so-called "institutional engineering" (which are empty speculations, in concrete social and political terms), but based on the real crisis experienced in an average metropolis on the capitalist semiperiphery. It can thus be generalized to a greater extent than if it were situated in either of the system's extreme poles.

The studies presented in this book systematically note the merits and the working mechanisms of participatory budgeting, which have been much celebrated in prose and verse, but are still little known and have not been duly assessed in their proper political and historical dimension. As made evident in these texts, this is not a social democratic project of institutional re-engineering aiming to invigorate a liberal democracy corroded by social crisis and neoliberal policies. The project is of greater import, although it has been put into practice only at the municipal level. The point is to reformulate the relation between governments and citizenship, to place governmental structures under the direct control of the population, to achieve the permanent mobilization of citizens, pointing toward a different form of state that is in practice incompatible not only with liberal political models (the tensions between municipal governments and the organs of participatory budgeting exemplify, though not exclusively, those contradictions), but also with the very dynamic of capitalism, more sharply so in its neoliberal stage, characterized by the primacy of market mechanisms and private property privilege.

Participatory budgeting policies go beyond the liberal model's separation between the social and the political, constituting citizenship on the basis of social needs, but inscribing them on the political level in order to avoid neutralizing citizenship on the social level—a situation that was typical of Latin American populist governments and their corporative conception of the state. Addressing that sensitive issue gives way to a new, open and creative form of relationship between the economic/social and the political, one of the fertile and subversive issues potentially present in participatory budgeting.

Nor do participatory budgeting policies retake the proposal of the "peaceful route toward socialism" of Salvador Allende's government in Chile. Allende's proposal enclosed an anti-capitalist project within existing state structures, seeking to introduce dual powers within the state and attempting to bring this duality to a positive resolution in time. It accommodated a "social area" that would basically include nationalized properties, with "workers' participation," but without delineating a new form of power in society as a whole to be wielded by organized citizens. Workers would participate corporatively, as unions and labor federations, while political leadership was delegated to the government, with the participation of left-wing political parties.

This prospect meant inheriting the proposal for the transition from "monopolistic state capitalism"—originally formulated by French Communist Party theorists, on the basis of interpretations of Lenin's ambiguous sentence, according to which state capitalism (Lenin was referring to its German form) is the antechamber to socialism—to socialism, founded on a basically economic perception of both systems. The project of participatory budgeting does not slide into that economicist interpretation of both the present hegemonic power and the proposal for overcoming it, but instead seeks to articulate social, economic, political, and cultural demands with an emancipatory project of citizenship, which implies a new form of state and a new relationship between the governing and the governed.

Nor do these policies consist of a new version of the classic historical proposals for "dual powers" in the sense of an insurrectional route. The aim is not to "assault the state" from an outside structure containing an alternative power. The strategy is one of radical state reform, emerging from a sort of transition project inspired in Gramsci's emphasis on the construction of a hegemonic alternative, prior even to the access to power by anti-systemic forces.

The assessment of the first twelve years reveals the undeniable initial success of the experiment, which was recognized and legitimized even by its opponents as evidence of its hegemonic victory. The opposition press, a majority of which was completely aligned against the government of Porto Alegre, failed, for eight years, to mention the phrase "participatory budgeting," only to see this issue being seized upon by opposition candidates themselves from the third election onwards.

To a greater or lesser extent, the assessments of the political success of the Workers' Party governments in Porto Alegre attribute to participatory budgeting policies the central responsibility for its successive re-election and also for the spread of those policies to hundreds of Brazilian municipalities.

However, those directly responsible for these policies consider—as stated in a seminar in Porto Alegre, organized by the municipal government of Tarso Genro in April 2001—that the first stage of participatory budgeting has come to an end; its limits have been made apparent and new prospects are being debated. From these different assessments it is possible to highlight a few issues, chosen by some of the authors of this book as strangulation points, which, at the same time, reveal the perspectives opened by participatory budgeting (PB) policies. Among these it is worthwhile to highlight at least two issues that have repeatedly emerged in the implementation of those policies: the representativeness of PB organs and their corporative risks. However significant the statistics about the number of participants might be, it is possible to question their representativeness not only in terms of the percentage of the total population, but also in terms of the number of voters. The number of participants in participatory budgeting rose from 1,300 in the first year of its implementation in 1989, to 19,025 twelve years later, in 2000, after having reached a peak of 20,724 the previous year, registering a 15-fold increase.

The initially low level of participation is evidence of the absence of a pre-existing political culture that participatory budgeting could appeal to, but its dynamic ended up mobilizing increasingly large sectors of the population, especially the poorer ones, whose demands were most repressed. Research shows that the accomplishment of their decisions was the most important reason that led people to participate in participatory budgeting meetings. In other words, it was this form of direct democracy that was responsible for the fulfillment of popular demands and for the enhancement of governments' legitimacy. A significantly smaller percentage (15 per cent) explain their participation in terms of a political value that must be cultivated, thus revealing their awareness of citizenship, regardless of the results attained.

While one of the reasons for popular involvement could jeopardize the legitimacy of budget-related decisions, the other runs the risk of making particularistic motives prevail in the dispute for public resources. Although different, both point to the same question: that of the congruence between representation and political participation. In other words, to what extent can the mechanisms of participatory budgeting claim to represent popular sovereignty, which, according to the theory of liberal democracy, is vested in the vote? The quality of democracy, in this perspective, would be judged in terms of the level of political participation, while the degree of a government's legitimacy would be measured by its capacity to satisfy popular demands. When citizens' demands are turned into public policies, political participation can be said to have found the channels for its realization.

Taking a different direction, in view of the state's failure to meet social needs, sectors of the so-called "civil society"—either in the shape of non-governmental organizations, business enterprises, or simply civic entities—seek to develop policies capable of satisfying those needs. They act as a counterbalancing power in response to the state's downsizing—preached by some as a virtue, while others seek to minimize the vacuum left by it. Either way, those initiatives appear in the space left by the theories and practices of the so-called "minimal state."

These initiatives coincide with the greater projection of the concept of civil society (capable of including all of them, however diverse) in opposition to anything that is state-related and consensually considered inefficient, either by definition or as a result of the assessment of concrete practices. The most prominent enthusiast for these initiatives was the late Brazilian sociologist Betinho (Herbert José de Souza), known for his Citizen Action against Poverty and for Life and his campaigns against hunger in Brazil. He launched, for the first time in the country, the idea of a "social assessment of companies," enjoining private entrepreneurs to take up social responsibilities left either unanswered or inadequately answered by the state. Such initiatives emerge as piecemeal, localized, compensatory policies, because they hold "civil society" as their reference and not the state as a subject. They thus miss the possibility of becoming universalizing policies, reducing themselves to necessarily local and usually intermittent initiatives. By definition, the action of "civil society" will always have this character and seek to derive its strength from it. However, as a result, private initiatives end up being subsumed under those of the World Bank and of the so-called "solidarity" policies.

The problem is therefore one of access to goods and services that, not being provided by the state, are made available by private entities. Without addressing the capital accumulation processes, this type of initiative can only aspire to mitigate the effects of what is, in fact, an exclusion-producing machine. This is a long way from the assertion of universal rights, the initiatives promoted being intended more as a means to legitimize the image of private entities (usually business companies) than as policies capable of counteracting social problems efficiently and permanently.

Moreover, in the case of countries like Brazil (which has the most unfair income distribution in the world) these initiatives become lost in the magnitude of the countries' accumulated social problems, losing any possible effectiveness. The extent of the decades-long misery cannot be solved (not even partially) without changing social reproduction paradigms, beginning with capital accumulation patterns. This is the sort of action business entities, for instance, can only be insensitive to, precisely because they benefit from those models of capital accumulation.

If "civil society," in the sense of citizenship-congregating entities, defines itself as outside and in opposition to the state, it can hardly overcome those limits. Instead of fighting for universal rights and for the constitution of individuals as citizens, those entities end up contributing to the isolation of the individual inside "civil society" (in the liberal sense of the term); instead of counteracting the mercantile logic, "civil society" ends up being functional to it.

INDIA: TOWARD A LOCAL DEMOCRACY?

The strong centralization of power brought about by fiscal adjustment policies and the transfer of strategic decisions to international finance centers have led to the valorization of local initiatives. Assumed by municipalities, when they manage to become public policies, local initiatives either occupy the space left open by central states, or are explicitly transferred to local governments, as is usually the case with social policies. These initiatives have been subject to some positive theorization, based on the fact that local governments are closer to the population, have greater sensitivity to popular demands and can more easily be controlled by citizens. The motto "Think globally, act locally" has given an even greater prominence to those policies.

Besides the case of the participatory budget in Brazilian cities, this volume records other experiences from India. These experiences have to confront a double movement: the dislocation of strategic centers of decision-making on the issues of government revenue, collected from the population for national states (closely bound to international finance centers); and the greater legitimacy of local governments as a result of their capacity to answer the population's actual needs and of their greater degree of democratization. But if, on the one hand, national governments suffer a rapid loss of legitimacy, on the other, local governments are depleted of the resources necessary to perform the tasks that increase their legitimacy. The strengthening of local democracy, then, collides with the scarcity of financial resources, leading to an overload of unanswered demands that, in turn, may weaken the legitimacy already achieved by those governments.

The strengthening of local democracy—as illustrated by the Indian experiences—requires means for controlling the conditions of people's lives (the environment, and political, economic, and cultural relations), which, in turn, requires resources and the population's political integration. In their struggle to create the conditions necessary to achieve their ends, these experiences collide with central power, instead of finding support and motivation therein. There is thus a tense dialectic between local legitimacy and the material conditions of its existence, which can only be solved through a qualitatively distinct structuring of power relations, in which participatory democracy (in any of its forms) is established as the central criterion of a new political system. Otherwise, these new experiences will tend to retrogress, become sterile, and lose any innovative content.

The experience reported from India is confronted with these dilemmas: new forms of local government, the search for legitimacy in "civil society," the development of policies centered on territorial planning. The tension lies between emancipation and social control, inasmuch as modes of participation involve regulations that can function as modes of integration, and thus of recuperation and co-optation.

As long as the situation remains as it is described by Francisco de Oliveira, according to whom "the complex thread involving the global dimension, the speed of transformations, the depoliticization of the economy and the denationalization of politics have been turning territoriality as the basis of politics into a completely inadequate form of asserting the citizens' will" (2001), the political system will be inaccessible to citizenship. The efforts for emancipation have allowed the reopening of space for the assertion of rights, although under the pressure of new forms of control, mostly originating in fiscal adjustment policies—as is the case of the fiscal responsibility law in force in Brazil, which is tending to spread as a fundamental part of IMF policies.

The perspective of this sort of initiative is not different from that of participatory budgeting, as both seek to promote citizenship as a means to counteract neoliberal policies. The boundary may lie in the role played by budgets. The space for addressing demands will clash with resource constraints, whose elasticity will decide the potential for realizing postulated citizenship rights.

Under the conditions of inequality and exclusion created by prevailing neoliberal policies, the dimensions of equity and social justice would be the guiding elements of an emerging power. A resource distribution based on these criteria would help pave the way to emancipation. There would still be the need to define the extent to which lower-class subjects might be able to become agents in the construction of alternative forms of power, without which any degree of equity and social justice could not be sustained, because of the absence of a supporting political power balance.

Participatory budgeting policies thus appear, as yet, to be the most advanced form of participatory democracy, combining institutional embeddedness and constant processes of popular mobilization. Although they may be subject to attempts of co-optation and social control, these policies maintain the capacity for popular mobilization that can thwart those intents.

The Kerala experiment in India is worthy of notice because of its originality and depth, taking place, significantly, under conditions similar to those of participatory budgeting in Brazil, in a state characterized by its relative level of development in comparison with the rest of the country. In the case of Kerala, development was stimulated by two distinct achievements in the periphery of capitalism, agrarian reform, and literacy campaigns, which were decisive means of recovering from backwardness, as well as basic conditions for asserting citizenship.

Similar to the Brazilian experiment, although with different aspects, the Kerala experiment in participatory democracy meant changing public relations between citizens, mediated by new spaces of intervention and creation of rights. This is a clear example of the authors' observations—that citizenship is not a right, but a relationship, the assertion of which is possible only if there is a transformation in the complex of relations among individuals and if this transformation is mediated by the public space.

It is equally meaningful that the experiment should have been conducted by a communist party, which had to effect a critique, both in theory and practice, of traditional communist conceptions about political democracy, therefore incorporating the critique concerning bureaucratization and development, including its economicist bias. In order to move to an experiment in participatory democracy it was necessary to understand that the classical forms of both state and political democracy had become exhausted. And, unlike the example of other parties coming from the same direction, that critique did not result in the substitution of social democratic concepts for Leninism, as has been the rule, but in the search for the social emancipation of citizenship through the amplification of the public sphere.

Bibliography

Garces, Joan E. (1996). *As armas da política*. São Paulo: Scritta.

Oliveira, Francisco de (2001). "Projeto de pesquisa sobre o orçamento participativo em São Paulo." (Mimeo).

Poulantzas, Nicos (1981). *O Estado, o poder, o socialismo*. Rio de Janeiro: Graal.

Wefort, Francisco, org. (1986). *O modo petista de governar*. São Paulo: Brasiliense.

CONTRIBUTORS

Maria José Arthur, University Eduardo Mondlane (Mozambique)

Leonardo Avritzer, Federal University of Minas Gerais (Brazil)

Sakhela Buhlungu, University of Witwatersrand (South Africa)

Mauricio García Villegas, National University of Bogotá (Colombia)

Patrick Heller, Brown University (USA)

T. M. Thomas Isaac, Centre for Development Studies (India)

Ana María Jaramillo, University of Antioquia (Colombia)

Shamim Meer, University of Witwatersrand (South Africa)

Conceição Osório, University Eduardo Mondlane (Mozambique)

María Clemencia Ramírez, Colombian Institute of Anthropology and
    History (Colombia)

Mauricio Romero, National University of Colombia (Colombia)

Emir Sader, State University of Rio de Janeiro (Brazil)

Francisco Gutiérrez Sanin, National University of Bogotá (Colombia)

Boaventura de Sousa Santos, University of Coimbra (Portugal)

D. L. Sheth, Director of the Centre for the Study of Developing Societies
    (India)

Rodrigo Uprimny, National University of Bogotá (Colombia)

María Teresa Uribe de H, University of Antioquia (Colombia)

INDEX

Miller, C. 121–2, 124

MKSS (*Mazdoor Kisan Shakti Sangathan*; Union for Empowerment of Peasants and Workers, India) 28–9

Molano, Alfredo 238–9

Moore, Barrington *xxxiv–xxxv, xliii*

Mouffe, Chantal 246

Moyser, G. 39

Mozambique 452, 453–4, 459–61

Mtintso, Tenjiwe 122–3, 124

Naidoo, Jay 106

Namboodiripad, E.M.S. 411

Narayan, Jayaprakash 4, 23–4 *see also* J.P. movement

National Alliance for People's Movements (NAPM) 19

Ndinisa, Nelson 50–1

Ndlovu, Moses 54

Nehru, Jawaharlal 411

neoliberalism *xvii*, 128, 449, 451
    feminism and 121–2

New Social Movements (NSMs) 89–91

NHGs (Neighborhood Groups, India) 434

Nicaragua 459, 460

O'Donnell, Guillermo 406, 408

Ocampo, Myriam 200–1, 208–213

Oliveira, Francisco de 467

OMM (*Organização da Mulher Moçambican*; Mozambican Women's Organization) 137–9, 144, 162–3, 167, 169, 174, 179

OTM (*Organização da Trabajador Moçambican*; Mozambican Workers Organization) 160–3, 165, 173–5, 177, 179

Owen, Robert 46

Parlache 196

Parry, G. 39

participatory budget (PB) 384–7, 395–400, 454, 461–8
    in Belo Horizonte 387, 389–91, 394, 397–8
    in Porto Alegre 307–68, 385–9, 390–8

Partido dos Trabalhadores see PT

Pateman, C. 54, 56

Pax Christi 295

PB *see* participatory budget

PDT (Democratic Labor Party, Brazil) 312, 385

People's Campaign for Decentralized Planning (India) 406–7, 413, 415, 420, 421–39

Pérez, Pedro 213

Pinochet, Augusto 86–7

Planning Office, Porto Alegre *see* GAPLAN

PLANTE (*Plan Nacional de Desarrollo Alternativo*; National Plan for Alternative Development, Colombia) 222, 234, 235

Pont, Raul 312, 351, 353

Popular Liberation Army, Colombia *see* EPL

Porto Alegre 307–68, 383, 385
    history of 310–1
    participatory budget in 309–10, 312, 325–8, 330. 339, 355, 360, 365, 386, 390–8
    World Social Forum and 451–2

Poulantzas, Nicos 453, 462

proceduralism *xxxviii–xxxix*
    Habermas on *xliv*

PT (*Partido dos Trabalhadores*; Workers' Party, Brazil) 389, 394, 461–2, 464

Putnam, Robert 418

Quadros, Jânio 382

Rangel, Carlos 200–1, 208–213

rationality 379

A NOTE ON THE TYPE

The text of this book is set in Bembo. This type was first used in 1495 by the Venetian printer Aldus Manutius for Cardinal Bembo's *De Aetna*, and was cut for Manutius by Francesco Griffo. It was one of the types used by Claude Garamond (1480–1561) as a model for his Romain de L'Université, and so it was the forerunner of what became standard European type for the following two centuries. Its modern form follows the original types and was designed for Monotype in 1929.

ALSO FROM VERSO

AVAILABLE IN THE RADICAL THINKERS SERIES

Minima Moralia:
Reflections on a Damaged Life
THEODOR ADORNO

Paperback 1 84467 051 1
$12/£6/$14CAN
256 pages • 5 x 7.75 inches

For Marx
LOUIS ALTHUSSER

Paperback 1 84467 052 X
$12/£6/$14CAN
272 pages • 5 x 7.75 inches

The System of Objects
JEAN BAUDRILLARD

Paperback 1 84467 053 8
$12/£6/$14CAN
224 pages • 5 x 7.75 inches

Liberalism and Democracy
NORBERTO BOBBIO

Paperback 1 84467 062 7
$12/£6/$14CAN
112 pages • 5 x 7.75 inches

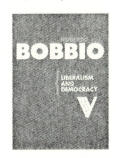